PEARSON

Geosciences 105

Diversity Amid Globalization
Geography of the Non-Western World

Second Custom Edition for Oregon State University

Taken from:
Diversity Amid Globalization: World Regions, Environment, Development,
Fifth Edition
by Les Rowntree, Martin Lewis, Marie Price, William Wyckoff

Cover Art: Color Costume, Iquitos, Java Market, Morocco, Nepal

Taken from:

Diversity Amid Globalization: World Regions, Environment, Development, Fifth Edition
by Les Rowntree, Martin Lewis, Marie Price, William Wyckoff
Copyright © 2012, 2009, 2006, 2003 by Pearson Education, Inc.
Published by Prentice Hall
Upper Saddle River, New Jersey 07458

This special edition published in cooperation with Pearson Learning Solutions.

Pearson Learning Solutions, 501 Boylston Street, Suite 900, Boston, MA 02116
A Pearson Education Company
www.pearsoned.com

Printed in the United States of America

4 5 6 7 8 9 10 V3NL 17 16 15 14 13

000200010270759771

MT

ISBN 10: 1-256-27989-7
ISBN 13: 978-1-256-27989-1

BRIEF CONTENTS

CONTENTS

7   Southwest Asia and North Africa   286

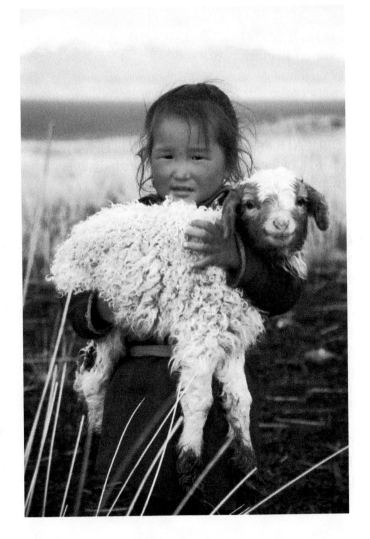

12 South Asia 536

ENVIRONMENTAL GEOGRAPHY: Diverse
Landscapes, from Tropical Islands to Mountain
Rim 539

POPULATION AND SETTLEMENT: Continuing
Growth in a Crowded Land 547

CULTURAL COHERENCE AND DIVERSITY:
A Common Heritage Undermined by Religious
Rivalries 556

GEOPOLITICAL FRAMEWORK: A Deeply
Divided Region 567

ECONOMIC AND SOCIAL DEVELOPMENT:
Burdened by Poverty 575

13 Southeast Asia 586

ENVIRONMENTAL GEOGRAPHY: A Once-
Forested Region 590

POPULATION AND SETTLEMENT: Densely
Settled Lowlands amid Sparsely Settled
Uplands 598

CULTURAL COHERENCE AND DIVERSITY: A
Meeting Ground of World Cultures 607

GEOPOLITICAL FRAMEWORK: War, Ethnic
Strife, and Regional Cooperation 613

ECONOMIC AND SOCIAL DEVELOPMENT:
The Roller-Coaster Ride of Globalized
Development 623

PREFACE

Diversity Amid Globalization is an issues-oriented textbook for college and university world regional geography classes that explicitly recognizes the geographic changes accompanying globalization. With this focus we join the many who argue that globalization is the most fundamental reorganization of the planet's socioeconomic, cultural, and geopolitical structure since the Industrial Revolution; this premise provides the point of departure for this book. As geographers we think it essential for students to understand two interactive tensions. First, they need to appreciate and critique the consequences of converging environmental, cultural, political, and economic systems through globalization. Second, they need to also deepen their understanding of the creation and persistence of geographic diversity and difference. Consequently, the interaction and tension between these opposing forces of homogenization and diversification forms a current running throughout the book's chapters and is reflected in our title, *Diversity Amid Globalization*.

NEW TO THE FIFTH EDITION

Numerous updates and changes have been made to the fifth edition of *Diversity Amid Globalization* to increase and enhance its efficacy as a world regional geography textbook.

- **Expanded, Integrated Treatment of Globalization,** including a revised introductory discussion in chapter 1, and new introductory paragraphs within the regional chapter-opening spreads that briefly frame how the forces of globalization are affecting the region.
- *Exploring Global Connections* are new sidebar essays in each regional chapter that discuss globalization in terms of transregional links—about how different regions are connected.
- *Environment and Politics* are new sidebar essays in each regional chapter that explore the complicated interaction in a globalized world between some aspect of the environment (global warming, rainforest destruction, sustainability, infrastructural construction, historic preservation, etc) and the politics and policies enabling or inhibiting pertinent social action.
- New *Development Issues* maps in each regional chapter highlight some measure of economic and social development, encouraging students to appreciate the many ways to define and measure development in different regional settings.
- Updated *Population* maps now contain more effective density and urban size categories that better represent the reality of the contemporary world.
- **The most current information on global warming** is integrated, including the policies and programs enacted by different countries and regions to address climate change, emission reduction, and energy usage. Updated material is introduced initially in chapter 2, and subsequently integrated through the different regional chapters in dedicated climate change sections.
- **Current data and information** are integrated into all text, tables, and maps.
- **MasteringGeography™** Used by over one million science students, the Mastering platform is the most effective and widely used online tutorial, homework, and assessment system for the sciences. Now available with *Diversity Amid Globalization*, **MasteringGeography™** offers:
  - Assignable activities that include: MapMaster™ interactive maps, geography videos from Television for the Environment's global *Life* and *Earth Report* series, *Encounter World Regional Geography* Google Earth multimedia, Thinking Spatially and Data Analysis.
  - Additional end-of-chapter questions
  - Test Bank questions and Reading Quizzes
  - A student Study Area with MapMaster interactive maps, geography videos, *In the News* RSS feeds, web links, flashcard glossary, quizzes, and more.
  - An eText version of *Diversity Amid Globalization*.

CHAPTER ORGANIZATION

As is true of most other regional geography textbooks, *Diversity Amid Globalization* is organized to describe and explain the major world regions of Asia, Europe, Africa, the Americas, and so on. Our 12 regional chapters, however, depart somewhat from traditional world regional textbooks. Instead of filling these regional chapters with descriptions of individual countries, we place most of that material on the MasteringGeography™ Study Area. This leaves us free to develop five important themes as the structure for each regional chapter. We begin with Environmental Geography by discussing the physical geography of each region, as well as current environmental issues. Next, we assess the region's Population and Settlement geography, in which demography, land use, and settlement (including cities) are discussed. Third is a section on Cultural Coherence and Diversity that examines the geography of language and religion and also explores current cultural tensions resulting from the interplay of globalization and diversity. Following that is a thematic section on each region's Geopolitical Framework that examines the political geography of the region, including micro-regionalism, separatism, ethnic conflicts, global terrorism, and supranational organizations. We then conclude each regional chapter with a section on Economic and Social Development in which we analyze each region's economic framework; this section also examines social development issues, a topic that includes regional and global gender issues.

The regional framework follows two substantive introductory chapters that provide the conceptual and theoretical framework of human and physical geography necessary to understand the contemporary globalized world. In the first chapter students are introduced to the notion of globalization and are asked to ponder the costs and benefits of the globalization process, a critical perspective that is becoming increasingly necessary in the contentious global arena. Following this the geographical foundation for each of the five thematic sections is examined. This discussion draws heavily on the major concepts fundamental to an introductory university geography course. The second chapter, "The Changing Global Environment," as mentioned, presents the themes and concepts of global physical geography, including landforms and geology, climate, global warming, hydrology, biogeography, and food production.

CHAPTER FEATURES

Within each regional chapter several unique features complement the thematic pedagogy of our approach:

- **Comparable Maps** Of the many maps in each regional chapter, 8 are constructed on the same theme and with similar data so that readers can easily draw comparisons between different regions. Thus, in every regional chapter readers will find maps of physical geography, climate, environmental issues, population density, language, religion, development issues, and geopolitical issues of the region.
- **Other Maps** In addition, each regional chapter also has a double handful of other maps illustrating such major themes as urban growth, ethnic tensions, social development, regional development, and linkages to the global economy. As well, the fifth edition presents 30 maps of specific subregions. These maps are linked to a specific theme (or themes) within each chapter and are explicitly discussed in the text. These new subregion maps help the text provide a stronger emphasis on the local scale and how global processes affect places
- **Comparable Regional Data Sets** Again, to facilitate comparison between regions, as well as to provide important insight into the characteristics of each region, each chapter contains two tables. The first provides population data of all sorts, including population density, level of urbanization, total fertility rates, proportion of the population under 15 and over 65 years of age, and net migration rates for each country within the region. The

second table presents economic and social development data for each country including GNI per capita, GDP growth, life expectancy, percent of the population living on less than $2 per day, infant mortality rates, and the UN gender equity index.

- **Sidebar Essays** Within each chapter there is an array of sidebar essays that complement text material.
  - **Cityscapes** These sidebars combine text, maps, and photos to convey a sense of place for a major city within each regional chapter and speak to the fact that our globalized world is now an urban one.
  - **People on the Move** sidebars capture the human geography behind contemporary migration as people migrate—legally and not so legally—responding to the varied currents of globalization.
  - **Global to Local** sidebars highlight how global trends affect local areas and local people. The sidebars foreground the fact that people often respond to homogenizing global forces very differently, and this variation in responses gives unique character to local people and places.
  - **Geographic Tools** sidebars discuss the various tools used by geographers to understand the world. Examples are GIS, aerial photography, field surveys, repeat photography, and so on. This content also links these tools and skills to employment possibilities in geography and allied fields.
  - **Environment and Politics** sidebars reflect that politics and policy shape the global landscape in many different ways, and these new sidebars focus on those relationships with case studies from the region.
  - **Exploring Global Connections** sidebars explore how activities in different world regions are linked so that students understand that in a globalized world regions are neither isolated nor discrete entitiies.
- **Review and Research Questions** There are two sets of review and research questions at the end of each regional chapter. The first set helps readers review basic terminology and concepts. The second set, "Thinking Geographically," asks readers to draw together more abstract themes and problems by doing further research on an issue. Resources for answering these critical thinking exercises are found in the chapter bibliographies, in the *Instructor Resource Manual*, and on MasteringGeography.
- **Regional Novels and Films** Students can learn much about a world region through novels and films with strong local content, thus we include a list of selected works at the end of each regional chapter that we believe complements the understanding of a region's people and places.

ACKNOWLEDGMENTS

We have many people to thank for their help in the conceptualization, writing, rewriting, and production of *Diversity Amid Globalization*. First, we'd like to thank the thousands of students in our world regional geography classes who have inspired us with their energy, engagement, and curiosity; challenged us with their critical insights; and demanded a textbook that better meets their need to understand the diverse people and places of our dynamic world.

Next, we are deeply indebted to many professional geographers and educators for their assistance, advice, inspiration, encouragement, and constructive criticism as we labored through the different stages of this book. Among the many who provided invaluable comments on various drafts and editions of *Diversity Amid Globalization* are:

Gilian Acheson, *Southern Illinois University–Edwardsville*
Joy Adams, *Humboldt State University*
Dan Arreola, *Arizona State University*
Bernard BakamaNume, *Texas A&M University*
Brad Baltensperger, *Michigan Technological University*
Laurence Becker, *Oregon State University*
Max Beavers, *Samford University*
James Bell, *University of Colorado*
William H. Berentsen, *University of Connecticut*
Kevin Blake, *Kansas State University*
Karl Byrand, *University of Wisconsin–Sheboygan County*
Michelle Calvarese, *California State University, Fresno*
Craig Campbell, *Youngstown State University*
Elizabeth Chacko, *George Washington University*
Philip Chaney, *Auburn University*
David B. Cole, *University of Northern Colorado*
Malcolm Comeaux, *Arizona State University*
Jonathan C. Comer, *Oklahoma State University*
Catherine Cooper, *George Washington University*
Jeremy Crampton, *George Mason University*
Kevin Curtin, *University of Texas at Dallas*
James Curtis, *California State University–Long Beach*
Dydia DeLyser, *Louisiana State University*
Francis H. Dillon, *George Mason University*
Jason Dittmer, *Georgia Southern University*
Jerome Dobson, *University of Kansas*
Caroline Doherty, *Northern Arizona University*
Vernon Domingo, *Bridgewater State College*
Roy Doyon, *Ball State University*
Jane Ehemann, *Shippensburg University*
Dean Fairbanks, *California State University–Chico*
Chuck Fahrer, *Georgia College and State University*
Caitie Finlayson, *Florida State University*
Doug Fuller, *George Washington University*
Gary Gaile, *University of Colorado*
Sherry Goddicksen, *California State University–Fullerton*
Sarah Goggin, *Cypress College*

Reuel Hanks, *Oklahoma State University*
Steven Hoelscher, *University of Texas, Austin*
Erick Howenstine, *Northeastern Illinois University*
Peter J. Hugil, *Texas A&M University*
Eva Humbeck, *Arizona State University*
Ryan S. Kelly, *University of Kentucky*
Richard H. Kesel, *Louisiana State University*
Rob Kremer, *Front Range Community College*
Robert C. Larson, *Indiana State University*
Alan A. Lew, *Northern Arizona University*
Catherine Lockwood, *Chadron State College*
Max Lu, *Kansas State University*
Luke Marzen, *Auburn University*
Kent Matthewson, *Louisiana State University*
James Miller, *Clemson University*
Bob Mings, *Arizona State University*
Wendy Mitteager, *SUNY Oneonta*
Sherry D. Morea-Oakes, *University of Colorado, Denver*
Anne E. Mosher, *Syracuse University*
Tim Oakes, *University of Colorado*
Nancy Obermeyer, *Indiana State University*
Karl Offen, *University of Oklahoma*
Thomas Orf, *Las Positas College*
Kefa Otiso, *Bowling Green State University*
Joseph Palis, *University of North Carolina*
Jean Palmer-Moloney, *Hartwick College*
Bimal K. Paul, *Kansas State University*
Michael P. Peterson, *University of Nebraska–Omaha*
Richard Pillsbury, *Georgia State University*
Brandon Plewe, *Brigham Young University*
Jess Porter, *University of Arkansas at Little Rock*
Patricia Price, *Florida International University*
Erik Prout, *Texas A&M University*
David Rain, *United States Census Bureau*
Rhonda Reagan, *Blinn College*
Craig S. Revels, *Portland State University*
Scott M. Robeson, *Indiana State University*
Pamela Riddick, *University of Memphis*
Paul A. Rollinson, *Southwest Missouri State University*
Yda Schreuder, *University of Delaware*
Kathy Schroeder, *Appalachian State University*
Kay L. Scott, *University of Central Florida*
Duncan Shaeffer, *Arizona State University*
Dimitrii Sidorov, *California State University–Long Beach*
Susan C. Slowey, *Blinn College*
Andrew Sluyter, *Louisiana State University*
Christa Smith, *Clemson University*
Joseph Spinelli, *Bowling Green State University*
William Strong, *University of Northern Alabama*
Philip W. Suckling, *University of Northern Iowa*
Curtis Thomson, *University of Idaho*
Suzanne Traub-Metlay, *Front Range Community College*
James Tyner, *Kent State University*
Nina Veregge, *University of Colorado*
Gerald R. Webster, *University of Alabama*
Keith Yearman, *College of DuPage*

Emily Young, *University of Arizona*
Bin Zhon, *Southern Illinois University–Edwardsville*
Henry J. Zintambia, *Illinois State University*

In addition, we wish to thank the many publishing professionals who have been involved with this project, for it is a privilege working with you. We thank Paul F. Corey, President of Pearson's Science division, for his early and continued support for this book project; Geography editor and good friend Christian Botting, for his professional guidance, enduring patience, and high standards; Project Manager Anton Yakovlev, for his daily attention to production matters and his diplomatic interaction with four demanding (and sometimes cranky) authors; Editorial Assistant Christina Ferraro for gracefully taking care of the many, many incidental tasks connected to this project; Marketing Manager Maureen McLaughlin for her sales and promotion work; Production Project Manager Maureen Pancza, *Element* Production Editor Suganya Karrupasamy and *Element* VP of Production Cindy Miller for somehow turning thousands of pages of manuscript into a finished book; *Spatial Graphics* Production Manager and Cartographer Kevin Lear for his outstanding work on our maps, and, finally, photo researchers Kristin Piljay and Caroline Commins for their fine work finding photographs for this new edition of *Diversity Amid Globalization*.

Last, the authors want to thank that special group of friends and family who were there when we needed you most—early in the morning and late at night; in foreign countries and familiar places; when we were on the verge of crying yet needing to laugh; for your love, patience, companionship, inspiration, solace, understanding, and enthusiasm: Eugene Adogia, Elizabeth Chacko, Meg Conkey, Rob Crandall, Karen Wigen, and Linda, Tom, and Katie Wyckoff. Words cannot thank you enough.

Les Rowntree
Martin Lewis
Marie Price
William Wyckoff

THE TEACHING AND LEARNING PACKAGE

In addition to the text itself, the authors and publisher have worked with a number of talented people to produce an excellent instructional package. This package includes traditional supplements as well as new online multimedia and assessment.

MasteringGeography™ with Pearson eText

Used by over one million science students, the Mastering platform is the most effective and widely used online tutorial, homework, and assessment system for the sciences. MasteringGeography™ offers:

- Assignable activities that include: MapMaster interactive maps, geography videos, *Encounter World Regional Geography* Google Earth multimedia, Thinking Spatially and Data Analysis.
- Additional end-of-chapter questions
- Test Bank questons and Reading Quizzes
- Student study area with MapMaster interactive maps, videos, *In the News* RSS feeds, web links, glossary flash cards, quizzes, and more.
- Pearson eText for *Diversity Amid Globalization*, Fifth Edition, which gives students access to the text whenever and wherever they can access the Internet, and includes powerful interactive and customization functions. www.masteringgeography.com

Instructor

- ***Instructor Resource Manual* (online download only)** Includes Learning Objectives, detailed Chapter Outlines, Key Terms, For Thought and Discussion topics to generate classroom motivation, and Exercise Activities that link to features in the students' *Mapping Workbook* and the MapMaster Interactive Maps. www.pearsonhighered.com/irc
- **TestGen® Computerized Test Bank (online download only)** TestGen® is a computerized test generator that lets instructors view and edit *Test Bank* questions, transfer questions to tests, and print the test in a variety of customized formats. This *Test Bank* includes approximately 1000 multiple choice, true/false, and short answer/essay questions. New to this edition are questions that focus on figures and maps from the text. Questions are correlated against the revised National Geography Standards and Bloom's Taxonomy to help instructors better map the assessments against both broad and specific teaching and learning objectives. The *Test Bank* is also available in Microsoft Word®, and is importable into Blackboard and WebCT. www.pearsonhighered.com/irc

- **Blackboard Test Bank (download only)** The Blackboard Test Bank provides *Test Bank* questions for import into Blackboard Learning System. www.pearsonhighered.com/irc
- **Instructor Resource Center on DVD (0-321-72310-4)** Everything instructors need where they want it. The Pearson Prentice Hall *Instructor Resource Center on DVD* helps make instructors more effective by saving them time and effort. All digital resources can be found in one well-organized, easy-to-access place. The IRC on DVD includes:
  - All textbook images as JPEGs, PDFs, and PowerPoint® presentations
  - Pre-authored Lecture Outline PowerPoint presentations, which outline the concepts of each chapter with embedded art and can be customized to fit instructors' lecture requirements
  - CRS "Clicker" Questions in PowerPoint format, correlated against the National Geography Standards and Bloom's Taxonomy
  - The TestGen software, Test Bank questions, and answers for both Macs and PCs, correlated against the National Geography Standards and Bloom's Taxonomy
  - Electronic files of the *Instructor Resource Manual* and *Test Bank*
  - Approximately 100 Geography Video Clips

  This Instructor Resource content is also available completely online via the Instructor Resources section of www.mygeoscienceplace.com and www.pearsonhighered.com/irc.
- **Television for the Environment *Earth Report* Geography Videos on DVD (0-32-166298-9)** This three-DVD set is designed to help students visualize how human decisions and behavior have affected the environment, and how individuals are taking steps toward recovery. With topics ranging from the poor land management promoting the devastation of river systems in Central America to the struggles for electricity in China and Africa, these 13 videos from Television for the Environment's global *Earth Report* series recognize the efforts of individuals around the world to unite and protect the planet.
- **Television for the Environment *Life* World Regional Geography Videos on DVD (0-13-159348-X)** From the Television for the Environment's global *Life* series this two-DVD set brings globalization and the developing world to the attention of any world regional geography course. These 10 full-length video programs highlight matters such as the growing number of homeless children in Russia, the lives of immigrants living in the United States trying to aid family still living in their native countries, and the European conflict between commercial interests and environmental concerns.

- **Television for the Environment *Life* Human Geography Videos on DVD (0-13-241656-5)** This three-DVD set is designed to enhance any human geography course. These DVDs include 14 full-length video programs from Television for the Environment's global *Life* series, covering a wide array of issues affecting people and places in the contemporary world, including the serious health risks of pregnant women in Bangladesh, the social inequalities of the "untouchables" in the Hindu caste system, and Ghana's struggle to compete in a global market.

- **Aspiring Academics: A Resource Book for Graduate Students and Early Career Faculty (0-13-604891-9)** Drawing on several years of research, this set of essays is designed to help graduate students and early career faculty begin their careers in geography and related social and environmental sciences. This teaching aid stresses the interdependence of teaching, research, and service—and the importance of achieving a healthy balance in professional and personal life—in faculty work, and does not view it as a collection of unrelated tasks. Each chapter provides accessible, forward-looking advice on topics that often cause the most stress in the first years of a college or university appointment.

- **Teaching College Geography: A Practical Guide for Graduate Students and Early Career Faculty (0-13-605447-1)** Provides a starting point for becoming an effective geography teacher from the very first day of class. Divided in two parts, the first set of chapters addresses "nuts-and-bolts" teaching issues in the context of the new technologies, student demographics, and institutional expectations that are the hallmarks of higher education in the 21st century. The second part explores other important issues: effective teaching in the field; supporting critical thinking with GIS and mapping technologies; engaging learners in large geography classes; and promoting awareness of international perspectives and geographic issues.

- **AAG Community Portal for Aspiring Academics & Teaching College Geography** This website is intended to support community-based professional development in geography and related disciplines. Here you will find activities providing extended treatment of the topics covered in both books. The activities can be used in workshops, graduate seminars, brown bags, and mentoring programs offered on campus or within an academic department. You can also use the discussion boards and contributions tool to share advice and materials with others. www.pearsonhighered.com/aag/

Student

- **MasteringGeography™ Student Access Code Card (0-321-72052-0)** This is the student access code card for MasteringGeography™.

- **Mapping Workbook (0-321-72312-0)** This workbook, which can be used in conjunction with either the main text or an atlas, features political and physical outline maps of every global region, printed in black and white. These maps, along with the names of the regional key locations and physical features, are the basis for identification exercises. Conceptual exercises are included to further exam students' comprehension of the Key Points presented in the main text chapters. These exercises review both the physical and human environment of the regions. An answer key for the mapping workbook exercises is also available.

- **Study Guide (0-321-75091-8)** The *Study Guide* includes additional learning objectives, a complete chapter outline, critical thinking exercises, problems and short essay work using actual figures from the text, and a self-test with an answer key in the back.

- **Encounter World Regional Geography Workbook & Website (0-321-68175-4)** *Encounter World Regional Geography* provides rich, interactive explorations of world regional geography concepts through Google Earth™ explorations. Students explore the globe through the themes of Environment, Population, Culture, Geopolitics, and Economy and Development, answering multiple choice and short answer questions. All chapter explorations are available in print format as well as online quizzes, accommodating different classroom needs. All worksheets are accompanied with corresponding Google Earth™ media files, available for download from www.mygeoscienceplace.com.

- **Encounter Earth: Interactive Geoscience Explorations Workbook & Website (0-321-58129-6)** *Encounter Earth* gives students a way to visualize key topics in their introductory geoscience courses. Each exploration consists of a worksheet, available in the workbook and as a PDF file, and a Google Earth™ KMZ file, containing placemarks, overlays, and annotations referred to in the worksheets. All chapter explorations are available in print format as well as online quizzes, accommodating different classroom needs. All worksheets are accompanied with corresponding Google Earth™ media files, available for download from www.mygeoscienceplace.com.

- **Goode's World Atlas 22nd Edition (0-321-65200-2)** Goode's World Atlas has been the world's premiere educational atlas since 1923, and for good reason. It features over 250 pages of maps, from definitive physical and political maps to important thematic maps that illustrate the spatial aspects of many important topics. The 22nd edition includes 160 pages of new, digitally produced reference maps, as well as new thematic maps on global climate change, sea level rise, CO^2 emissions, polar ice fluctuations, deforestation, extreme weather events, infectious diseases, water resources, and energy production.

- **Dire Predictions (0-13-604435-2)** Periodic reports from the Intergovernmental Panel on Climate Change (IPCC) evaluate the risk of climate change brought on by humans. But the sheer volume of scientific data remains inscrutable to the general public, particularly to those who may still question the validity of climate change. In just over 200 pages, this practical text presents and expands upon the essential findings of the 4th Assessment Report in a visually stunning and undeniably powerful way to the lay reader. Scientific findings that provide validity to the implications of climate change are presented in clear-cut graphic elements, striking images, and understandable analogies.

ABOUT THE AUTHORS

Les Rowntree is a Visiting Scholar at the University of California, Berkeley, where he researches and writes about environmental issues. This career change comes after three decades of teaching both Geography and Environmental Studies at San Jose State University in California. As an environmental geographer, Dr. Rowntree's interests focus on international environmental issues, biodiversity conservation, and human-caused global change. He sees world regional geography as a way to engage and inform students by giving them the conceptual tools needed to critically assess global issues. Dr. Rowntree has done research in Iceland, Alaska, Morocco, Mexico, Australia, and Europe, as well as in his native California. Current writing projects include a book on the natural history of California's coast, as well as textbooks in geography and environmental science.

Martin Lewis is a Senior Lecturer in History at Stanford University. He has conducted extensive research on environmental geography in the Philippines and on the intellectual history of global geography. His publications include *Wagering the Land: Ritual, Capital, and Environmental Degradation in the Cordillera of Northern Luzon, 1900–1986* (1992), and, with Karen Wigen, *The Myth of Continents: A Critique of Metageography* (1997). Dr. Lewis has traveled extensively in East, South, and Southeast Asia. His current research focuses on the geographical dimensions of globalization. In April 2009 Dr. Lewis was recognized by *Time* magazine, as a favorite lecturer.

Marie Price is a Professor of Geography and International Affairs at George Washington University. A Latin American specialist, Marie has conducted research in Belize, Mexico, Venezuela, Cuba, and Bolivia. She has also traveled widely throughout Latin America and Sub-Saharan Africa. Her studies have explored human migration, natural resource use, environmental conservation, and regional development. She is a non-resident fellow of the Migration Policy Institute, a non-partisan think tank that focuses on immigration. Dr. Price brings to *Diversity Amid Globalization* a special interest in regions as dynamic spatial constructs that are shaped over time through both global and local forces. Her publications include the co-edited book, *Migrants to the Metropolis: The Rise of Immigrant Gateway Cities* (2008, Syracuse University Press) and numerous academic articles and book chapters.

William Wyckoff is a geographer in the Department of Earth Sciences at Montana State University specializing in the cultural and historical geography of North America. He has written and co-edited several books on North American settlement geography, including *The Developer's Frontier: The Making of the Western New York Landscape* (1988), *The Mountainous West: Explorations in Historical Geography* (1995) (with Lary M. Dilsaver), *Creating Colorado: The Making of a Western American Landscape 1860–1940* (1999), and *On the Road Again: Montana's Changing Landscape* (2006). In 2003 he received Montana State's Cox Family Fund for Excellence Faculty Award for Teaching and Scholarship. A World Regional Geography instructor for 26 years, Dr. Wyckoff emphasizes in the classroom the connections between the everyday lives of his students and the larger global geographies that surround them and increasingly shape their future.

Linking people and places through globalization

From population to environment, economic development to cultural diversity, the process of globalization is dramatically changing our world. Using a consistent thematic structure to examine world regions, ***Diversity Amid Globalization: World Regions, Environment, Development,* Fifth Edition** explores the diverse geography of the world, and the dynamic causes and effects of globalization.

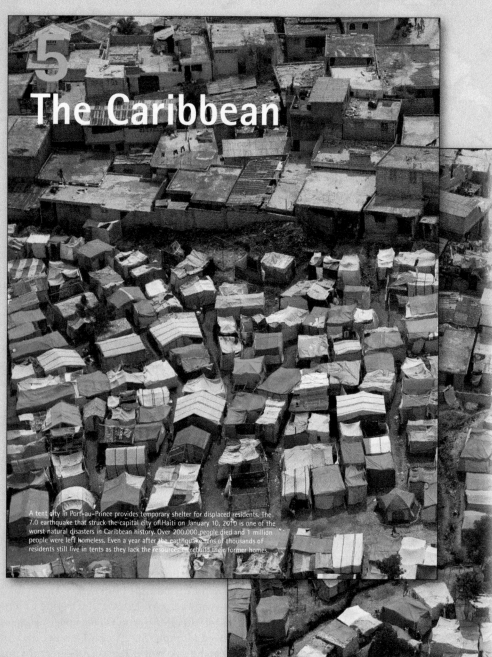

5 The Caribbean

A tent city in Port-au-Prince provides temporary shelter for displaced residents. The 7.0 earthquake that struck the capital city of Haiti on January 10, 2010 is one of the worst natural disasters in Caribbean history. Over 200,000 people died and 1 million people were left homeless. Even a year after the earthquake, tens of thousands of residents still live in tents as they lack the resources to rebuild their former homes.

DIVERSITY AMID GLOBALIZATION

Named for some of its former inhabitants—the Carib Indians—the modern Caribbean is a culturally complex and economically peripheral world region. Settled by various colonial powers, the residents of this region are mostly a mix of African, European, and South Asian peoples. Greatly impacted by the global economy but with relatively little influence on it, the livelihoods of Caribbean peoples are filled with uncertainty.

ENVIRONMENTAL GEOGRAPHY
Climate change threatens the Caribbean, with the potential for stronger and more frequent hurricanes, loss of territory due to sea level rising, and destruction of coral reefs.

POPULATION AND SETTLEMENT
The earthquake that leveled Port-au-Prince, Haiti, in 2010 showed the vulnerability of this large but very poor Caribbean city. Throughout the region, large numbers of people have emigrated in search of economic opportunity and are sending back millions of dollars in remittances.

CULTURAL COHERENCE AND DIVERSITY
Creolization, the blending of African, European, and even Amerindian elements, has resulted in many unique Caribbean expressions of culture, such as *rara, reggae,* and steel drum bands.

GEOPOLITICAL FRAMEWORK
The first area of the Americas to be extensively explored and colonized by Europeans, the region has seen many rival European claims and, since the early 20th century, has experienced strong U.S. influence.

ECONOMIC AND SOCIAL DEVELOPMENT
Environmental, locational, and economic factors make tourism a vital component of this region's economy, particularly in Puerto Rico, Cuba, the Dominican Republic, and the Bahamas.

The changing face of globalization

Today, the world is experiencing the most fundamental reorganization of its socioeconomic, cultural, and geopolitical structure since the Industrial Revolution. ***Diversity Amid Globalization*** focuses on these changes by examining both the homogenizing and diversifying forces inherent to the globalization processes.

NEW! Environment and Politics
These new sidebar essays examine the complicated interaction between the environment, politics, and policies that enable (or inhibit) social action in a globalizing world.

Figure 2.15 **Methane Emissions from Arctic Wetlands** About 10 percent of global methane emissions are released from the Arctic tundra. Although a natural process, these methane emissions have increased with global warming. Some scientists are concerned that the tundra may reach a tipping point where the amount of methane emissions increases dramatically, resulting in a sudden change to the global climate.

Figure 8.11 **Glacial Retreat in the Austrian Alps** The blue sign in the foreground marks where the snout of the Pasterze glacier was in 1985, and illustrates how far the glacier has retreated in the last 25 years, shrinkage that is probably a result of global warming. This glacier is the largest in Austria and has its origin on Austria's highest mountain, the Grossglockner.

Integrated Coverage of Global Warming and Climate Change
Each regional chapter has a section on the projected effects of global warming, as well as actions being taken (or not) for mitigating climate change.

Consistent, Compelling Thematic Cartography
Eight thematic maps in each regional chapter empower readers to make critical inter-regional comparisons of physical geography, environmental issues, population and settlement, language, religion, geopolitics, and development issues. The **new Development Issues maps** highlight a specific measure of economic and social development, encouraging students to appreciate the many ways to define development in different regions.

NEW! Exploring Global Connections
These new informative sidebar essays discuss globalization in terms of transregional links, illustrating how different regions are interconnected.

www.masteringgeography.com

Immerse your students in the study of world regions and globalization with MasteringGeography. Used by over one million students, the Mastering platform is the most effective and widely used online tutorial, homework, and assessment system in the sciences.

Assignable Content:

- MapMaster™ Place Name Interactive Map activities
- MapMaster Layered Thematic Interactive Map activities
- Geography videos with multiple-choice quizzes
- *Encounter World Regional Geography* Google Earth™ activities
- End-of-chapter questions
- Reading Quizzes
- Thinking Spatially & Data Analysis activities
- Test Bank Questions

For Student Self Study:

- Pearson eText
- Geography Videos
- MapMaster Place Name and Layered Thematic Interactive Maps
- Outline maps
- Quizzes
- Country Profiles
- *In the News* RSS feeds
- Web links
- Key Terms Study Tools (Glossary, Key Terms, and Flash Cards)
- Authors' Blog at www.geocurrents.info

MapMaster is a powerful tool that helps students practice, improve, and master map reading, spatial reasoning, geographic literacy, and critical-thinking skills. All of the interactive map activities are designed to be modular and flexible. When combined with associated quizzes correlated against the U.S. National Geography Standards, MapMaster can be used for assigned homework, pre- and post-testing, and formal assessment by instructors, as well as for self-study by students.

◄ *MapMaster* Place Name Interactive Map Activities have students identify place names of political and physical features at regional and global scales, as well as explore select country data from the CIA World Factbook. Multiple-choice quizzes for the place name labeling activities and country data sets offer instructors flexible opportunities for summative assessment and pre- and post-testing.

MapMaster Layered Thematic Interactive Map Activities act as a mini-GIS tool, allowing students to layer various thematic maps to analyze spatial patterns and data at regional and global scales. Multiple-choice and short-answer quizzes are organized around themes of Physical Environment, Population, Culture, Geopolitics, and Economy, giving instructors flexible, modular options for assessing student learning.

world regions and globalization

Encounter World Regional Geography with Google Earth™
Students use the dynamic features of Google Earth to visualize and explore world regions and answer questions related to the themes of Environment, Population, Culture, Geopolitics, and Economy & Development. All Explorations include corresponding Google Earth KMZ media files, and questions include hints and specific wrong-answer feedback to help coach students towards mastery of the concepts.

Geography Videos

Short videos from Television for the Environment's *Life* and *Earth Report* global series explore a range of topics related to world regions, globalization, physical geography, and climate change. Examples of topics include the growing number of homeless children in Russia, the serious health risks of pregnant women in Bangladesh, and the struggles for electricity in China and Africa. Accompanying video quizzes include multiple choice and short-answer questions with hints and specific wrong-answer feedback for each of the episodes.

Thinking Spatially & Data Analysis

These activities help students develop spatial reasoning and critical thinking skills by identifying and labeling features from maps, illustrations, photos, graphs, and charts. Students then examine related data sets, answering multiple-choice questions and increasingly higher order conceptual short-answer questions, both of which include hints and specific wrong-answer feedback.

Motivating students to learn and explore

www.masteringgeography.com

With easy-to-customize, easy-to-assign, and automatically graded assessments, instructors can maximize class time and motivate students to learn outside of class and arrive prepared for lecture.

MasteringGeography offers:

- Assignable activities, including MapMaster™ interactive maps, geography videos, *Encounter World Regional Geography* Google Earth™ multimedia, Thinking Spatially & Data Analysis
- End-of-chapter questions
- Test Bank questions
- Student study area with MapMaster interactive maps, videos, RSS feeds, web links, quizzes, flashcard glossary, and more
- Optional Pearson eText

MasteringGeography Gradebook

Provides instructors with quick results and easy-to-interpret insights into student performance. Every assignment is automatically graded, with shades of red highlighting struggling students and challenging assignments.

geography beyond the classroom

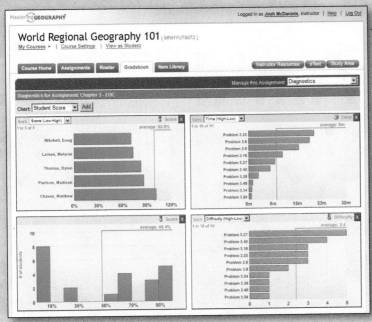

Gradebook Diagnostics
Enables an instructor to see class performance as a whole to fine-tune lectures before class.

Continuously Improving Content

MasteringGeography offers a dynamic pool of assignable content that improves with student usage. Detailed analysis of student performance statistics—including time spent, answers submitted, solutions requested, and hints used—ensures the highest quality content.

1. **We conduct a thorough analysis** of each problem by reviewing student performance data that has been generated by real students.

2. **We make enhancements** to improve the clarity and accuracy of content, answer choices, and instructions for each problem.

3. **We repeat the process.** This ongoing, **two-way learning process** helps students learn as students help the system improve.

Pearson eText
Search, annotate, zoom, highlight, and more—all electronically with Pearson eText.

Pearson eText gives students access to the text whenever and wherever they can access the Internet. The eText pages look exactly like the printed text, and include powerful interactive and customization functions.

1
Diversity Amid Globalization

In many ways Singapore and its harbor are icons of globalization. Not only is the city itself a focal point of international finance, but the Port of Singapore is the world's busiest transshipment harbor.

Some of the most important challenges facing the world in the 21st century are associated with **globalization**, the increasing interconnectedness of people and places through converging economic, political, and cultural activities. Once-distant regions and cultures are now increasingly linked through commerce, communications, and travel. Although earlier forms of globalization existed, especially during Europe's colonial period, the current degree of planetary integration is stronger than ever. In fact, many observers argue that contemporary globalization is the most fundamental reorganization of the world's socioeconomic structure since the Industrial Revolution. While few dispute the widespread changes brought about by globalization, the topic is controversial because not everyone agrees on whether the benefits outweigh the costs.

Although economic activities may be the main force behind globalization, the consequences affect all aspects of land and life: Cultural patterns, political arrangements, and social development are all undergoing profound change. Because natural resources are now global commodities, the planet's physical environment is also affected by globalization. Financial decisions made thousands of miles away alter local ecosystems, and the cumulative effects of these far-ranging activities often have negative consequences for the world's climates, oceans, waterways, and forests.

These immense, widespread global changes make understanding our contemporary world a challenging yet necessary task. Although globalization cuts across many academic disciplines, world regional geography is a fundamental starting point because of its focus on regions, environment, geopolitics, culture, and economic and social development. This book seeks to impart knowledge of globalization by carefully outlining the basic patterns of world geography and showing how they are being reorganized by global interconnections (Figure 1.1).

CONVERGING CURRENTS OF GLOBALIZATION

Most scholars agree that the major component of globalization is the economic reorganization of the world. Although different forms of a world economy have existed for centuries, a well-integrated and truly global economy is primarily the product of the past several decades. The attributes of this system, while familiar, bear repeating:

- Global communication systems that link all regions and most people on the planet instantaneously (Figure 1.2)
- Transportation systems capable of moving goods quickly by air, sea, and land
- Transnational business strategies that have created global corporations more powerful than many sovereign nations
- New and more flexible forms of capital accumulation and international financial institutions that make 24-hour trading possible
- Global agreements that promote free trade
- Market economies and private enterprises that have replaced state-controlled economies and services
- An abundance of planetary goods and services that have arisen to fulfill consumer demand, real or imagined (Figure 1.3)
- Economic disparities between rich and poor regions and countries that drive people to migrate, both legally and illegally, in search of a better life
- An army of international workers, managers, and executives who give this powerful economic force a human dimension

As a result of this global reorganization, economic growth in some areas of the world has been unprecedented

Figure 1.1 Global Communications
The effects of globalization are everywhere, even in remote villages in developing countries. Here, in a small village in southwestern India, a rural family earns a few dollars a week by renting out viewing time on its globally linked television set.

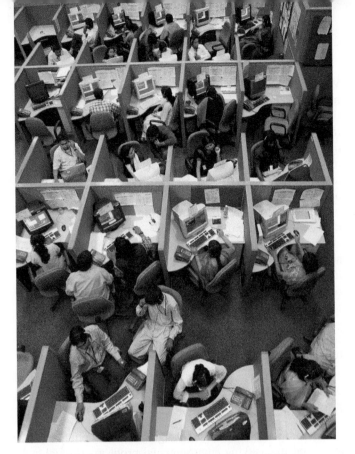

Figure 1.2 Global-to-Local Connections A controversial aspect of globalization is the outsourcing of jobs from developed to developing countries. One example is the relocation of customer call centers away from Europe and North America to India where educated English-speaking employees work for relatively low wages. This photo shows a call center in Bangalore, India.

Fast-food franchises are changing—some would say corrupting—traditional diets, with the explosive growth of McDonald's, Burger King, and KFC outlets in the world's cities. While these changes may seem harmless to North Americans because of their familiarity, they are not just expressions of the deep cultural changes the world is experiencing through globalization but also generally unhealthy and environmentally destructive. The expansion of the cattle industry, for example, a result of the new global demand for beef, is doing serious environmental damage to tropical rain forests.

Although the media give much attention to the rapid spread of Western consumer culture, nonmaterial culture is also becoming more dispersed and homogenized through globalization. Language is an obvious example. Many a Western tourist in Russia or Thailand has been startled by locals speaking an English made up largely of Hollywood movie phrases. But far more than speech is involved as social values also are dispersed globally. Changing expectations about human rights, the role of women in society, and the intervention of nongovernmental organizations are also expressions of globalization that may have far-reaching effects on cultural change.

It would be a mistake, however, to view cultural globalization as a one-way flow that spreads from the United States

Figure 1.3 Global Shopping Malls Once a fixture only of suburban North America, the shopping mall is now found throughout the world. This mall is in downtown Kunming, the capital city of Yunnan province, China.

during recent decades. International corporations, along with their managers and executives, have amassed vast amounts of wealth, profiting from the new opportunities unleashed by globalization. Not everyone, however, has gained from economic globalization, nor have all world regions shared equally in the benefits. While globalization is often touted as benefiting everyone through trickle-down economics, there is mounting evidence that this trickling process is neither happening in all places nor for all peoples. Additionally, as was demonstrated in the global recession of 2008–2010, economic interconnectivity can also increase economic vulnerability; this is illustrated by the precipitous decline in Hawaii's tourist trade as the economies of both Japan and the United States went flat at the same time.

Globalization and Cultural Change

Economic changes also trigger cultural changes. The spread of a global consumer culture that masks local diversity often accompanies globalization, frequently creating deep and serious social tensions between traditional cultures and new, external globalizing currents. Global TV, movies, Facebook, Twitter, and videos promote Western values and culture that are imitated by millions throughout the world. But reactions to westernization, can take sometimes violent forms, such as that from radical Islamism.

and Europe into the corners of the world. In actuality, when forms of U.S. popular culture spread abroad, they are typically melded with local cultural traditions in a process known as *hybridization*. The resulting cultural "hybridities," such as hip hop and rap music or Asian food, can themselves resonate across the planet, adding yet another layer to globalization.

In addition, ideas and forms from the rest of the world are also having a great impact on U.S. culture. The growing internationalization of American food, the multiple languages spoken in the United States, and the spread of Japanese comic book culture among U.S. children are all examples of globalization's effects within the United States (Figure 1.4).

Globalization and Geopolitics

Globalization also has important geopolitical components. To many, an essential dimension of globalization is that it is not restricted by territorial or national boundaries. For example, the creation of the United Nations following World War II was a step toward creating an international governmental structure in which all nations could find representation. The simultaneous emergence of the Soviet Union as a military and political superpower at that time led to a rigid division into Cold War blocs that slowed further geopolitical integration. But with the peaceful end of the Cold War in the late 1980s and early 1990s, the former communist countries of eastern Europe and the Soviet Union were opened almost immediately to global trade and cultural exchange that has changed those countries immensely.

Further, there is a strong argument that globalization—almost by definition—has weakened the political power of individual states by strengthening the power of regional economic and political organizations such as the European Union or the World Trade Organization. In some world regions, a weakening of traditional state power has resulted in stronger local and separatist movements as illustrated by the turmoil on Russia's southern borders or the plethora of separatist organizations in Europe.

Environmental Concerns

As mentioned, the expansion of a globalized economy is creating and intensifying environmental problems throughout the world. **Transnational firms**, which do global business through international subsidiaries, disrupt local ecosystems with their incessant search for natural resources and manufacturing sites. Landscapes and resources previously used by only small groups of local peoples are now thought of as global commodities to be exploited and traded on the world marketplace. As a result, native peoples are often deprived of their traditional resource base and displaced into marginal environments. On a larger scale, economic globalization is aggravating worldwide environmental problems such as global warming, air pollution, water pollution, and deforestation. And yet it is only through global cooperation, such as the UN treaties on biodiversity protection or global warming, that these problems can be addressed. These topics are discussed further in Chapter 2.

Social Dimensions

Globalization has a clear demographic dimension. Although international migration is not new, increasing numbers of people from all parts of the world are crossing national boundaries, legally and illegally, temporarily and permanently (Figure 1.5). Migration from Latin America and Asia has drastically changed the demographic configuration of the United States, and migration from Africa and Asia has transformed western Europe. Countries such as Japan and South Korea that have long been perceived as ethnically homogeneous now have substantial immigrant populations. Even a number of relatively poor countries, such as Nigeria and the Ivory Coast, encounter large numbers of immigrants coming from even poorer countries, such as Burkina Faso. Although international migration is still curtailed by the laws of every country—much more so, in fact, than the

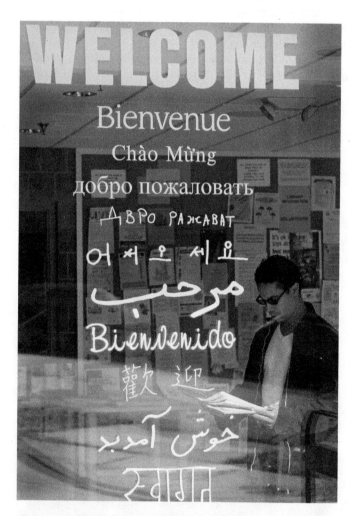

Figure 1.4 Global Culture in the United States The multilingual welcome offered by a public library in Montgomery County, Maryland, not only illustrates the many different languages spoken by people in the suburbs of Washington, DC, but also reminds us that expressions of globalization are found throughout North America.

Figure 1.5 International Migration Workers from southern India dig a hole to install a street sign in Dubai, United Arab Emirates. This Persian Gulf emirate is experiencing a massive construction boom as it shifts from an oil-based economy to an economy based on real estate, tourism, and international finance. As a result, temporary migrant workers from India and Pakistan constitute much of the labor force.

movement of goods or capital—it is still rapidly mounting, propelled by the uneven economic development associated with globalization.

Finally, there also is a significant criminal element to contemporary globalization, including terrorism (discussed later in this chapter), drugs, pornography, slavery, and pros-

titution. Illegal narcotics, for example, are definitely a global commodity (Figure 1.6). Some of the most remote parts of the world, such as the mountains of northern Burma, are thoroughly integrated into the circuits of global exchange through the production of opium and, therefore, into the world heroin trade. Even many areas that do not directly

Figure 1.6 The Global Drug Trade The cultivation, processing, and transshipment of coca (cocaine), opium (heroin), and cannabis (marijuana) are global issues. The most important cultivation centers are Colombia, Mexico, Afghanistan, and northern Southeast Asia, and the major drug financing centers are located mostly in the Caribbean, the United States, and Europe. In addition, Nigeria and Russia also play significant roles in the global transshipment of illegal drugs.

produce drugs are involved in their global sale and transshipment. Nigerians often occupy prominent positions in the international drug trade, as do members of the Russian mafia. Many Caribbean countries have seen their economies become reoriented to drug transshipments and the laundering of drug money. Prostitution, pornography, and gambling have also emerged as highly profitable global businesses. Over the past decades, for example, parts of eastern Europe have become major sources of both pornography and prostitution, finding a lucrative but morally questionable niche in the new global economy.

ADVOCATES AND CRITICS OF GLOBALIZATION

Globalization, especially in its economic form, is one of today's most contentious issues (Figure 1.7). Supporters believe that it results in a greater economic efficiency that will

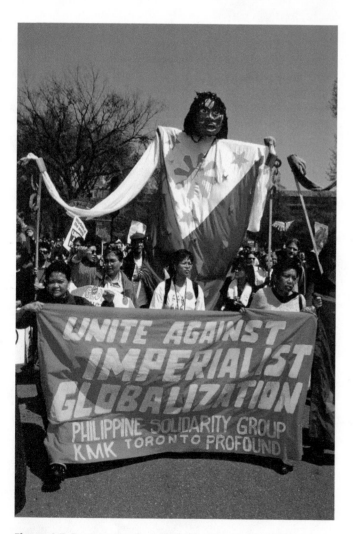

Figure 1.7 Protests Against Globalization Meetings of international groups such as the World Trade Organization, World Bank, and International Monetary Fund (IMF) commonly draw large numbers of protesters against globalization. This demonstration took place at a Washington, DC, meeting of the World Bank and IMF.

eventually result in rising prosperity for the entire world. In contrast, critics think that globalization will largely benefit those who are already prosperous, leaving most of the world poorer than before as the rich and powerful exploit the less fortunate.

Economic globalization is generally applauded by corporate leaders and economists, and it has substantial support among the leaders of both major political parties in the United States. Beyond North America, moderate and conservative politicians in most countries generally support free trade and other aspects of economic globalization. Opposition to economic globalization is widespread in the labor and environmental movements, as well as among many student groups worldwide. Hostility toward globalization is sometimes deeply felt, as massive protests at World Bank and World Trade Organization meetings have made obvious.

The Pro-globalization Stance

Advocates of globalization argue that globalization is a logical and inevitable expression of contemporary international capitalism that will benefit all nations and all peoples. Economic globalization can work wonders, they contend, by enhancing competition, allowing the flow of capital to poor areas, and encouraging the spread of beneficial new technologies and ideas. As countries reduce their barriers to trade, inefficient local industries will be forced to become more efficient in order to compete with the new flood of imports, thereby enhancing overall national productivity. Those that cannot adjust will most likely go out of business, making the global market place more efficient.

Every country and region of the world, moreover, ought to be able to concentrate on those activities for which it is best suited in the global economy. Enhancing such geographic specialization, the pro-globalizers argue, creates a more efficient world economy. Such economic restructuring is made increasingly possible by the free flow of capital to those areas that have the greatest opportunities. By making access to capital more readily available throughout the world, economists contend, globalization should eventually result in a certain global **economic convergence**, implying that the world's poorer countries will gradually catch up with the more advanced economies.

Thomas Friedman, one of the most influential advocates of economic globalization, argues that the world has not only shrunk but has also become economically "flat" so that financial capital, goods, and services can flow freely from place to place. For example, the need to attract capital from abroad forces countries to adopt new economic policies. Friedman describes the great power of the global "electronic herd" of bond traders, currency speculators, and fund managers who either direct money to or withhold it from developing economies, resulting in economic winners and losers (Figure 1.8).

To the committed pro-globalizer, even the global spread of **sweatshops**—crude factories in which workers sew clothing, assemble sneakers, and perform other labor-intensive

Figure 1.8 The "Electronic Herd" One facet of economic globalization is the rapid movement of capital as bond traders, currency speculators, and fund managers direct money in or out of the economies of developing countries. In this picture, traders and clerks work on the Eurodollar Futures floor of the Chicago Mercantile Exchange.

tasks for extremely low wages—is to be applauded (Figure 1.9). People go to work in sweatshops because the alternatives in the local economy are even worse. Once countries achieve full employment through sweatshops, the argument goes, they can gradually improve conditions and move into more sophisticated, better-paying industries. Proponents of economic globalization also commonly argue that multinational firms based in North America or Europe often offer better pay and safer working conditions than do local firms and thus contribute to worker well-being. Extreme pro-globalizers go so far as to assert that poor countries ought to take advantage of their generally lax environmental laws to attract highly polluting industries from the wealthy countries because acquiring such industries would enhance their overall economic positions.

The pro-globalizers also strongly support the large multinational organizations that facilitate the flow of goods and capital across international boundaries. Three such organizations are particularly important: the World Bank, the International Monetary Fund (IMF), and the World Trade Organization (WTO). The primary function of the World Bank is to make loans to poor countries so that they can invest in infrastructure and build more modern economic foundations. The IMF is concerned with making short-term loans to countries that are in financial difficulty—those having trouble, for example, making interest payments on the loans that they had previously taken. The WTO, a much smaller organization than the other two, works to reduce trade barriers between countries to enhance economic globalization. It also tries to mediate between countries and trading blocs that are engaged in trade disputes (Figure 1.10).

To support their claims, pro-globalizers argue that countries that have been highly open to the global economy have generally had much more economic success than those that have isolated themselves by seeking self-sufficiency. The world's most isolated countries, Burma (Myanmar) and North Korea, have become economic disasters, with little growth and rampant poverty, whereas those that have opened themselves to global forces, such as Singapore and Thailand, in the same period have seen rapid growth and substantial reductions in poverty.

Critics of Globalization

Virtually all of the claims of the pro-globalizers are strongly contradicted by the anti-globalizers. Opponents often begin by arguing that globalization is not a "natural" process. Instead, it is the product of an explicit economic policy promoted by free-trade advocates, capitalist countries (mainly the United States, but also Japan and the countries of Europe), financial interests, international investors, and multinational firms. Opponents also point out that the processes of globalization today are more pervasive than those of the historical past, even during the period of European colonialism. Thus, while global economic and political linkages have been around for centuries, their contemporary expression is unprecedented.

Because the globalization of the world economy appears to be creating greater inequity between rich and poor, the "trickle-down" model of developmental benefits for all people in all regions has yet to be validated. On a global scale, the richest 20 percent of the world's people consume 86 percent of the world's resources, whereas the poorest 80 percent use only 14 percent. The growing inequality of this age of globalization is apparent on both global and national scales.

Figure 1.9 Global Sweatshops One of the most debated aspects of economic globalization is the crude factories, or sweatshops, in which workers sew clothing, assemble sneakers, stitch together soccer balls, and perform other labor-intensive work for low wages. This is a Chinese-owned factory in Nicaragua.

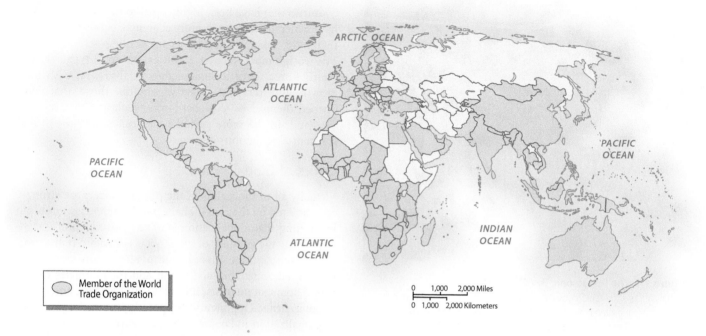

Figure 1.10 World Trade Organization One of the most powerful institutions of economic globalization is the World Trade Organization (WTO), which was created in 1995 to oversee trade agreements, encourage open markets, enforce trade rules, and settle disputes. The WTO currently consists of 153 member countries. In addition to these member countries, more than 30 states have "observer status," including Russia, Iran, and Iraq.

Globally, the wealthiest countries have grown much richer over the past two decades, while the poorest have become more impoverished. Nationally, even in developed countries such as the United States, the wealthiest 10 percent of the population have reaped almost all of the gains that globalization has offered; the poorest 10 percent have either seen their income decline in recent decades as wages have remained static or they have actually lost their jobs to outsourcing.

Opponents also contend that globalization promotes free-market, export-oriented economies at the expense of localized, sustainable activities. World forests, for example, are increasingly cut for export timber rather than serving local needs. As part of their economic structural adjustment package, the World Bank and the IMF encourage developing countries to expand their resource exports so they will have more hard currency to make payments on their foreign debts. This strategy, however, usually leads to overexploitation of local resources. Opponents also note that the IMF often requires developing countries to adopt programs of fiscal austerity that often entail substantial reductions in public spending for education, health, and food subsidies. By adopting such policies, critics warn, poor countries will end up with even more impoverished populations than before.

Anti-globalizers also dispute the evidence on national development offered by the pro-globalizers. Highly successful developing countries such as South Korea, Taiwan, and Malaysia, they argue, have indeed been engaged with the world market, but they have generally done so on their own terms rather than those of the IMF and other advocates of full-fledged economic globalization. These countries have actually protected many of their domestic industries from foreign competition and have, at various times, controlled the flow of capital.

Furthermore, anti-globalizers contend that the "free-market" economic model commonly promoted for developing countries is not the one that Western industrial countries used for their own economic development. In Germany, France, and even to some extent the United States, governments historically have played a strong role in directing investment, managing trade, and subsidizing chosen sectors of the economy.

Those who challenge globalization also worry that the entire system—with its instantaneous transfers of vast sums of money over nearly the entire world on a daily basis—is inherently unstable. The noted critic John Gray, for example, argues that the same "electronic herd" that Thomas Friedman applauds is a dangerous force because it is susceptible to "stampedes." International managers of capital tend to panic when they think their funds are at risk; when they do so, the entire intricately linked global financial system can quickly become destabilized, leading to a crisis of global proportions. The rapid downturn of the global economy in late 2008 seems to support that assertion (Figure 1.11).

Even when the "herd" spots opportunity, trouble may still ensue. As vast sums of money flow into a developing country,

Figure 1.11 Global Economic Recession
Unused shipping containers pile up on parking lots and vacant space near a residential area in northwest Hong Kong because of the downturn in China's export economy during the global recession of 2009. During the height of the economic downturn, about 25 percent of the world's container ships were idled.

they may create a speculatively inflated **bubble economy** that cannot be sustained. Such a bubble economy emerged in Thailand and many other parts of Southeast Asia in the mid-1990s. Analysts have also used the concept of bubble economy to explain the tragic collapse of the Icelandic and Irish economies in 2009 (Figure 1.12).

A Middle Position

A number of experts, not surprisingly, argue that both the anti-globalization and the pro-globalization stances are exaggerated. Those in the middle ground tend to argue that economic globalization is indeed unavoidable; even the anti-globalization movement, they point out, is made possible by the globalizing power of the Internet and is, therefore, itself an expression of globalization. They further contend that while globalization holds both promises and pitfalls, it can be managed, at both the national and international levels, to reduce economic inequalities and protect the natural environment. These experts stress the need for strong yet efficient national governments, supported by international institutions (such as the UN, World Bank, and IMF) and globalized networks of environmental, labor, and human rights groups.

Unquestionably, globalization is one of the most important issues of the day—and certainly one of the most complicated. While this book does not pretend to resolve the controversy, it does encourage readers to reflect on these critical points as they apply to different world regions.

Figure 1.12 Economic Turmoil in Iceland Protesters burn an effigy of Iceland's prime minister during a demonstration against the government's handling of the 2009 economic crisis. Given the relatively small size of Iceland's economy, the collapse of its bubble economy was the largest downturn in percentage terms suffered by any country in history.

DIVERSITY IN A GLOBALIZING WORLD

As globalization increases, many observers foresee a world far more uniform and homogeneous than today's. The optimists among them imagine a universal global culture uniting all humankind into a single community untroubled by war, ethnic strife, or resource shortage—a global utopia of sorts.

A more common view, however, is that the world is becoming blandly homogeneous as different places, peoples, and environments lose their distinctive character and become indistinguishable from their neighbors. While diversity may be difficult for a society to live with, it also may be dangerous to live without. Nationality, ethnicity, cultural distinctiveness—all are the legitimate legacy of humanity. If this diversity is blurred, denied, or repressed through global homogenization, humanity loses one of its defining traits.

But even if globalization is generating a certain degree of homogenization, the world is still a highly diverse place (Figure 1.13). One still finds marked differences in culture (language, religion, architecture, foods, and many other at-

Figure 1.14 Tribal Warfare Rebels from the Sudan Liberation Movement (SLM) declared war against the Sudanese government in the province of Darfur. The two groups that originated the rebellion have now morphed into dozens of warring factions, complicating the search for peace amid a profound humanitarian crisis.

Figure 1.13 Local Cultures This family in Ghana reminds us that although few places are beyond the reach of globalization, many unique local landscapes, economies, and cultures still exist. For example, most of the belongings of the family in this photograph are local in origin and come from long-standing cultural tradition.

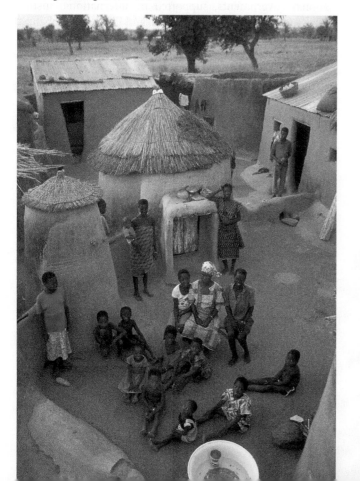

tributes of daily life), economy, and politics—as well as in the physical environment. Such diversity is so vast that it cannot readily be extinguished, even by the most powerful forces of globalization. In fact, globalization often provokes a strong reaction on the part of local people, making them all the more determined to maintain what is distinctive about their way of life. Thus, globalization is understandable only if one also examines the diversity that continues to characterize the world and, perhaps most importantly, the tension between these two forces—the homogenization of globalization and the reaction against it in terms of protecting cultural and political diversity. Unfortunately, this tension sometimes takes negative and violent forms, as illustrated today by radical Islam and tribal warfare in Nigeria and Sudan (Figure 1.14).

The politics of diversity also demands increasing attention as we try to understand worldwide tensions over terrorism, ethnic separateness, regional autonomy, and political independence. Groups of people throughout the world seek self-rule of territory they can call their own. Today, most wars are fought *within* countries, not *between* them. As a result, our interest in geographic diversity takes many forms and goes far beyond simply celebrating traditional cultures and unique places. People have many ways of making a living throughout the world, and it is important to recognize this fact as the globalized economy becomes increasingly focused on mass-produced retail goods. Furthermore, a stark reality of today's economic landscape is unevenness: While some people and places prosper, others suffer from unrelenting poverty. This, unfortunately, also is a form of diversity amid globalization.

In summary, globalization can be defined as the increasing interconnectedness of people and places through converging processes of economic, political, and cultural change. Globalization is pervasive and unrelenting and is a dominant feature of the contemporary world. Furthermore, its benefits are uneven. Although economic restructuring is a prime cause, globalization is not simply the growth and expansion of international trade. It is also represented by converging and homogenizing forces that many people resist. Thus, an equally important theme is how geographic diversity comes in conflict with globalization—how globalization in different places and at different times is suppressed, renegotiated, hybridized, protected, preserved, or extinguished. Because of the importance of this theme, globalization and diversity should be examined as inseparable—often in conflict but at other times complementary.

GEOGRAPHY MATTERS: Environments, Regions, Landscapes

Geography is one of the most fundamental sciences, a discipline awakened and informed by a long-standing human curiosity about our surroundings and the world environment. The term *geography* has its roots in the Greek words for "describing the Earth," and this discipline has been advanced since classical times by all cultures and civilizations. Along with the inherent satisfaction of knowing about different environments also come practical benefits through exploration, resource use, world commerce, and travel. In some ways, geography can be compared to history: While historians describe and explain what has happened over time, geographers describe and explain Earth's spatial dimensions, and how the world differs from place to place (see "Geographic Tools: From Satellites to Shovels").

Given the broad scope of geography, it is no surprise that geographers have many different conceptual approaches to investigating the world. At the most basic level, geography can be broken into two complementary pursuits, *physical and human geography*. Physical geography examines climate, landforms, soils, vegetation, and hydrology, while human geography concentrates on the spatial analysis of economic, social, and cultural systems.

A physical geographer, for example, studying the Amazon Basin of Brazil might be interested primarily in the ecological diversity of the tropical rain forest or the ways the destruction of that dense vegetation changes the local climate and hydrology. The human geographer, in turn, would focus on the social and economic factors explaining the migration of settlers into the rain forest, or the tensions and conflicts over land and resources between these migrants and indigenous peoples.

Another basic division is that between focusing on a specific topic or theme contrasted with analyzing a place or a region. The former approach is referred to as *thematic* or *systematic geography*, while the latter is called *regional geography*. These two perspectives are complementary and by no means mutually exclusive. This textbook, for example, draws upon a regional scheme for its overall architecture, dividing the globe into 12 separate world regions, yet it organizes each chapter thematically, examining the topics of environment, population and settlement, cultural differentiation, geopolitics, and economic development in a systematic way. In doing so, each chapter combines four kinds of geography: physical, human, thematic, and regional geography.

A fundamental component of geographic inquiry is the examination of the basic yet highly complex relationship between humans and their environment. Though this analysis may take many different forms, three overarching questions form the foundation:

- Where and under what conditions does nature control, constrain, or disrupt human activities, and what kinds of societies are most vulnerable to these environmental influences (Figure 1.15)?
- How have human activities affected natural systems such as the world's climate, vegetation, rivers, and oceans, and what are the consequences of these actions?
- Is there any evidence that humans can live in balance with nature so that human use of natural resources might be sustainable over a longer period of time, or is environmental damage an inevitable consequence of human settlement?

While there are no simple answers to these three questions, the study of world regional geography offers valuable insights from different cultural and regional perspectives.

Areal Differentiation and Integration

Geography is considered the spatial science, charged with the study of Earth's space (or surface area), and the uniqueness of places as well as the similarities between them. One component of that responsibility is describing and explaining the differences that distinguish one piece of the world from another. The geographical term for this is **areal differentiation** (*areal* means "pertaining to area"). Why is one

GEOGRAPHIC TOOLS From Satellites to Shovels

Geographers use a wide array of tools—from satellites to shovels—to explain the world and solve environmental problems (Figure 1.1.1). While some geographers get their information from aerial photos and satellite images, others work at ground level, digging holes to sample soils, mapping trees and plants, or even interviewing people in their homes and at the mall. While geographers' toolboxes and methods may differ, the goals are the same: a better understanding of global environments and the people who inhabit them.

Many of our tools are commonplace, like maps, compasses, handheld GPS (global positioning system) devices, or computers.

Figure 1.1.1 Satellites to Shovels A graduate student gathers a soil sample for her master's thesis on the ecology of native plants in coastal California.

Other tools, though, are highly specialized, such as multi-spectral satellite images of vegetation, computer models of refugee migration, or soil-boring tools to capture prehistoric pollen samples. As readers of this book about the world, you might be interested in how geographers collect and analyze information about different places and different issues. Toward that goal, each chapter includes a sidebar called *Geographic Tools* that illustrates how specific tools and methods are used to expand our understanding of the world. The complete chapter list follows:

Chapter 2: Reconstructing Climates of the Past
Chapter 3: Counting North Americans: The Censuses of 2010 and 2011
Chapter 4: Participatory Mapping in the Slums of Rio de Janeiro
Chapter 5: Tracking Hurricanes
Chapter 6: Monitoring Land Cover and Conservation Changes in Niger
Chapter 7: Measuring the Urban Impact of Islamic Banking
Chapter 8: Landscape Restoration in England
Chapter 9: Mapping Russian Forests
Chapter 10: Remote Sensing, GIS, and the Tragedy of the Aral Sea
Chapter 11: The East Asian Gazetteer and the Reconstruction of Historical Geography
Chapter 12: Survey Work on Contraceptive Use in West Bengal
Chapter 13: Statistical Comparisons and the Assessment of Philippine Deforestation
Chapter 14: Fire Ecology and Management in Australia

Many colleges and universities offer courses in the use of these tools, particularly GIS (geographic information systems), remote sensing (interpreting aerial photographs and satellite imagery), and computer-aided cartography (mapmaking). Such tools can provide students with technical skills that are much sought after in today's job market. If you are interested, ask your world regional geography professor about those kinds of opportunities at your college.

Figure 1.15 Natural Hazards and Globalization The eruption of Iceland's Eyjafjallajokull volcano in April 2010 brought chaos to world commerce by closing down air traffic in Europe and the North Atlantic. Along with its disruption to air passengers, the effects rippled through the world economy in thousands of ways. Farmers in Kenya, for example, could not get their fresh fruits and vegetables to European markets.

Figure 1.16 Areal Differentiation In this satellite photo the California–Mexico border is apparent because of the different sizes of agricultural fields. The larger red pattern in the upper left is the irrigated fields of the United States, while in the bottom right the much smaller and less irrigated fields of Mexico have a different landscape signature when seen from space. Explaining such differences is a central focus of geography.

part of Earth humid and lush while another just a few hundred kilometers away is an arid desert (Figure 1.16)?

Geographers also are interested in the connections between different places and how they are linked. This concern is one of **areal integration**, which is the study of how places interact with each other. An example is the analysis of how and why the economies of Singapore and the United States are closely intertwined even though the two countries are situated in entirely different physical, cultural, and political environments. The questions of areal integration, obviously, are becoming increasingly important because of the varied global linkages that are inherent to globalization.

Regions: Formal and Functional

The human intellect seems driven to make sense of the universe by lumping phenomena together into categories of similarity. Biology has its taxa of living objects, history its eras and periods of time, geology its epochs of Earth history. Geography, too, organizes information about the world by compressing it into units of similarity, which are called **regions**.

Sometimes the unifying threads of a region are physical, such as climate and vegetation, resulting in a regional designation like the *Sahara Desert* or the *Amazonian rain forest*. Other times the threads are more complex, combining economic and cultural traits, as in the use of the term *Corn Belt* for parts of the central United States. Human beings commonly compress large amounts of information into stereotypes; in a way, a geographic region is just that—a spatial stereotype for a portion of Earth that has some special signature or characteristic that sets it apart from other places (Figure 1.17).

Some caution is advised, however. First, no region is homogeneous throughout its area; thus even though there may be a single characteristic that unites an area, there will also be diversity and differences within it. Second, regional borders are fuzzy. Except for political borders that separate countries, states, or provinces, regional boundaries are rarely as abrupt as they appear on a map. Just as mountain ranges usually rise gradually from lowland areas or deserts transition gradually into grasslands, so do manufacturing regions thin out toward the periphery, or linguistic regions blend gradually with each other. Put differently, while those traits used to define a geographic region are most explicit and clear in the core area, the defining traits usually weaken and grow less apparent moving away from the core to the boundary.

The Cultural Landscape: Space into Place

Human beings transform space into distinct places that are unique and heavily loaded with meaning and symbolism. This diverse fabric of *placefulness* is of great interest to geographers because it tells us much about the human condition as it varies throughout the world. Places can tell us how humans interact with nature and among themselves; where there are tensions and where there is peace; where people are rich and where they are poor.

A common tool for the analysis of place is the concept of the **cultural landscape**, which is, simply stated, the visible, material expression of human settlement, past and present. Thus the cultural landscape is the tangible expression of the human habitat. It visually reflects the most basic human needs—shelter, food, work. Additionally, the cultural landscape acts to bring people together (or keep them apart), because it is a marker of cultural values, attitudes, and symbols. As cultures vary greatly around the world, so do cultural landscapes (Figure 1.18).

Most of the French countryside, for example, with its modestly sized agricultural fields enclosed by hedgerows and small stone houses clustered together in villages, looks very different from a typical farm landscape of the Midwestern United States, where fields cover several square miles and people are separated from each other by large distances. From the contrasting look of these two landscapes, we can learn much about the social and economic systems underlying the two different societies.

Increasingly, however, we see the uniqueness of places being eroded by the homogeneous landscapes of globalization—shopping malls, fast-food outlets, business towers, theme parks, industrial complexes. Understanding the forces behind the spread of these landscapes is important because they tell us much about the expansion of global economies and cultures. While a modern shopping mall in Hanoi, Vietnam, may seem familiar to someone from North America, this new landscape represents yet another component of globalized world culture that has been implanted into a once remote and distinctive city.

Scales: Global to Local

There is a sense of scale to all systematic inquiry, whatever the discipline. In biology some scientists study the smaller units of cells, genes, or molecules, while others take a larger

Figure 1.17 Geographic Regions This map illustrates three different kinds of geographic regions: vernacular, formal, and functional. A vernacular region is an abstraction that has indistinct cognitive borders, as shown by the general outline of what the public considers to be Silicon Valley. Other vernacular regions would be "The Midwest," "The Deep South," "The Pacific Northwest," and so on. In contrast, formal regions have distinct boundaries, such as that for the Santa Clara Valley, defined as the lowland between two bordering mountain ranges. Last, a functional region is based on a certain activity or organizational structure, such as the civic government of San Jose, delimited by its legal city limits.

Figure 1.18 The Cultural Landscape Despite globalization the world's landscapes still show great diversity, as shown by this village and its surrounding rice terraces on the island of Luzon, Philippines. Geographers use the cultural landscape concept to better understand how people interact with their environment.

view, analyzing plants, animals, or ecosystems. Similarly, some historians may focus on a specific individual at a specific point in time, while others take a broader view of international events over many centuries.

Geographers also work at different scales. While one may concentrate on analysis of a local landscape—perhaps a single village in southern China—another will focus on the broader regional picture, examining all of southern China (Figure 1.19). Others do research on a still larger global scale, perhaps studying emerging trade networks between southern India's center of information technology in Bangalore and North America's Silicon Valley, or investigating how India's monsoon might be connected to and affected by the Pacific Ocean's El Niño. But even though geographers may be working at different scales, they never lose sight of the interactivity and connectivity between local, regional, and global scales, of the ways that the village in southern India might be linked to world trade patterns, or how the late arrival of the monsoon (delayed, perhaps, by El Niño in the Pacific Ocean) could affect agriculture and food supplies in different parts of India (see "Global to Local: How the World Is Connected").

GLOBAL TO LOCAL   How the World Is Connected

As noted in the text, the ability to move between different scales—global, regional, local—is critical for understanding contemporary world regional geography because of the way globalization links all peoples and places. Few villages today, however remote, are unconnected to the modern world. Global economies draw upon local crops and resources, and, conversely, fluctuations in world commodity prices affect the well-being of local people (Figure 1.2.1). Global TV and videos introduce foreign styles, ideas, mannerisms, and expectations into small towns and remote settlements in formerly isolated parts of the world, and global tourism brings strangers (some welcome, some not) to far-flung places, often corrupting and compromising the very uniqueness the tourists had sought.

In this book, we use the phrase *global to local* to capture the range of scales necessary for placing regions, places, landscapes, and people in their globalized context. Because our premise is that no place in today's world is completely isolated from the larger currents of a globalizing society, we need this perspective to examine the complicated linkages connecting people and places with the larger, dynamic world. These points are elaborated upon in the *Global to Local* sidebars in each regional chapter.

Chapter 2: The Globalization of Bushmeat and Animal Poaching
Chapter 3: Alaska's Climate Refugees
Chapter 4: Can Eco-Friendly Fair Trade Coffee Promote Biodiversity and Rural Development?
Chapter 5: Caribbean Carnival Around the World
Chapter 6: Roses to Europe, Thanks to Kenya
Chapter 7: How Morocco Went Hollywood in Ouarzazate
Chapter 8: European Hip Hop and Hyperlocality
Chapter 9: The Tale of Two Siberias
Chapter 10: The Mongolian Cashmere Industry Readjusts
Chapter 11: The Korean Wave
Chapter 12: The Sialkot Industrial Complex
Chapter 13: Poipet and Southeast Asia's Other "Sin Cities"
Chapter 14: Nauru and the Mixed Benefits of Globalization

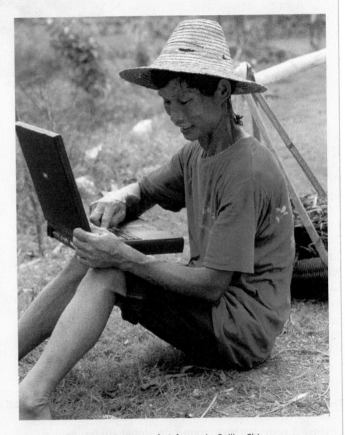

Figure 1.2.1 Global to Local A farmer in Guilin, China, uses a laptop to check local and global grain prices before taking his crop to market.

Figure 1.19 Geographic Scales Geographers work at many different scales, from large regional or even global analyses, to micro-studies of one specific environment or landscape. This photo is of Zhujiajiao village in China's Shanghai province.

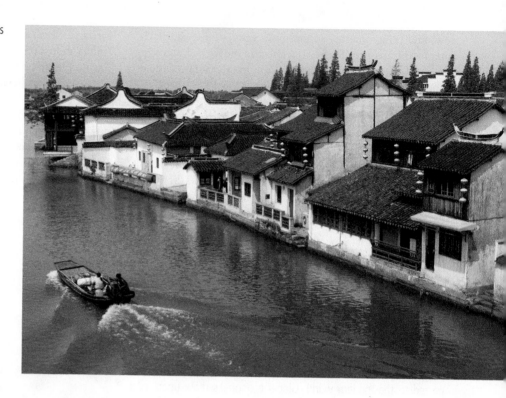

THEMES AND ISSUES IN WORLD REGIONAL GEOGRAPHY

Following two introductory chapters, this book adopts a regional perspective, grouping all of Earth's countries into a framework of 12 world regions (Figure 1.20). We begin with a region familiar to most of our readers, North America, and then move to Latin America, the Caribbean, Africa, the Middle East, Europe, Russia, and the different regions of Asia, before concluding with Australia and Oceania. Each of the 12 regional chapters employs the same five-part thematic structure—environmental geography, population and settlement, cultural coherence and diversity, geopolitical framework, and economic and social development. The concepts and data central to each theme are discussed in the following sections.

Environmental Geography

Chapter 2 provides background on global environmental geography, outlining the global environmental elements fundamental to human settlement—climate, geology, hydrology, and vegetation, along with a discussion of the linkages between environment, globalization, and world food problems.

As well, in the regional chapters, the Environmental Geography section discusses the environmental issues relevant to each world region, topics such as global warming, sea level rise, acid rain, tropical rainforest destruction, and wildlife conservation. These environmental issues sections are not simply a list of problems but also discuss plans and policies developed to resolve those issues.

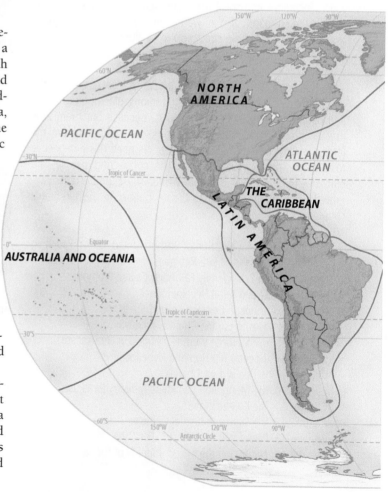

Population and Settlement: People on the Land

The human population is far larger than it has ever been, and there is considerable debate about whether continued growth will benefit or harm the human condition. This concern is not only about the total population of the world but also about the geographic patterns of human settlement. As the world map shows, while some parts of the world are densely populated, other places remain almost empty (Figure 1.21).

With nearly 7 billion humans on Earth, we currently add about 131 million people each year, at a rate of 15,000 births per hour. About 90 percent of this population growth takes place in the world regions of Africa, South and East Asia, and Latin America. Because of rapid growth in developing countries and emerging economies, perplexing questions dominate discussions of many global issues. Can these countries absorb the rapidly increasing population and still achieve the necessary economic and social development to ensure some level of well-being and stability for their populations? What role, if any, should the developed countries of North America, Europe, and East Asia play in helping developing countries with their population problems? While population is a complex and contentious topic, several points help focus the issues:

- Very different rates of population growth are found in different regions of the world. While some countries are growing rapidly, others have no natural growth at all. Instead, any population growth comes from in-migration. India is an example of the former; Italy of the latter.
- Population planning takes many forms, from the fairly rigid one- or two-child policies of China and other Asian countries to the "more children, please" programs of no-growth western European countries (Figure 1.22).
- Not all attention should be focused on natural growth because migration is increasingly the root cause of population change in the globalized world. Most international migration is driven by a desire for a better life in the richer regions of the developed world. But there are also millions of migrants who are refugees from civil strife, persecution, and environmental disasters.
- The greatest migration in human history is now going on as people move from rural to urban environments. In 2009 a landmark was reached when population experts estimated that more than half the world's population now lived in towns and cities. As with natural population growth, the developing countries of Africa, Latin America, and Asia are experiencing the most rapid changes in urbanization.

Figure 1.20 World Regions These regions are the basis for the 12 regional chapters in this book. Countries or areas within countries that are treated in more than one chapter are designated on the map with a striped pattern. For example, western China is discussed in both Chapter 10, on Central Asia, and Chapter 11, on East Asia. Also, three countries on the South American continent are discussed as part of the Caribbean region because of their close cultural similarities to the island region.

Figure 1.21 World Population This map shows differing population densities in the areas of the world. East Asia stands out as the most populated region, with high densities in Japan, Korea, and eastern China. The second-most populated region is South Asia, dominated by India, which is second only to China in population. In North Africa and Southwest Asia, population clusters are often linked to the availability of water for irrigated agriculture, as is apparent with the population cluster along the Nile River. Higher population densities in Europe, North America, and other countries are usually associated with large cities, their extensive suburbs, and nearby economic activities.

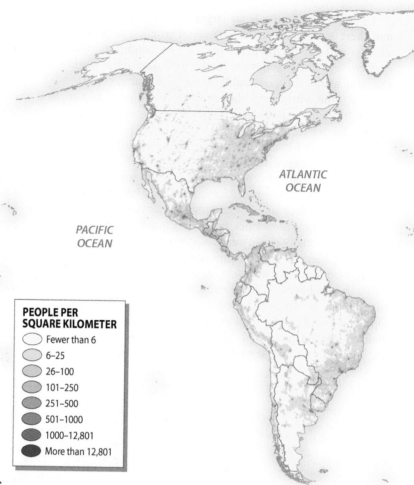

PEOPLE PER SQUARE KILOMETER
- Fewer than 6
- 6–25
- 26–100
- 101–250
- 251–500
- 501–1000
- 1000–12,801
- More than 12,801

Population Growth and Change

Because of the centrality of population growth, each regional chapter in this book includes a table of population data for the countries within that region (Table 1.1). Although at first glance the statistics in these tables might seem daunting, this information is crucial to understanding the population geography of the regions.

Natural Population Increase

A common starting point for measuring demographic change is the **rate of natural increase (RNI)**, which depicts as a percentage the annual growth rate for a country or region. This statistic is produced by subtracting the number of deaths in a given year from the births. Important to remember is that gains or losses through migration are not considered in the RNI.

Further, instead of using raw numbers for a large population, demographers divide the gross numbers of births or deaths by the total population, thereby producing a figure per 1,000 of the population. This is referred to as the *crude birthrate* or the *crude death rate*. For example, in 2010 the crude birthrate for the whole world was 20 per 1,000, with a crude death rate of 8 per 1,000. Thus, the natural growth rate was 12 per 1,000. Converting that figure to a percentage al-

lows us to express it as the RNI; therefore the rate of natural increase for the world in 2010 was 1.2 percent per year.

Because birthrates vary greatly amongst peoples and cultures (and between countries and regions of the world), rates of natural increase also vary greatly. In Africa, for example, several countries have crude rates of more than 40 births per 1,000 people. Because their death rates are generally less than 20 per 1,000, RNIs are greater than 3 percent per year, which are among the highest population growth numbers found anywhere in the world.

Total Fertility Rate

While the crude birthrate gives some insight into current conditions in a country, demographers place more emphasis on the **total fertility rate (TFR)** to predict future growth. The TFR is a synthetic and hypothetical number that measures the fertility of a statistically fictitious, yet average group of women moving through their childbearing years. If women marry early and have many children over a long span of years, the TFR will be a relatively high number. Conversely, if data show that women marry late and have few children, the number will be correspondingly small. Important to note is that any number less than 2.1 implies that a population has no natural growth since it takes a

Figure 1.22 Family Planning Policies Many countries in the developing world have concluded that unrestrained population growth may keep them from realizing their development goals, and therefore have put family planning policies in place that promote birth control. This poster in Vietnam urges smaller families.

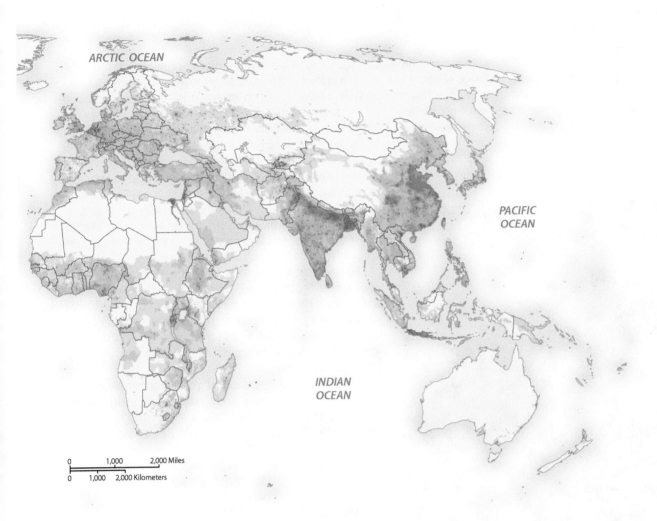

TABLE 1.1 Population Indicators of the World's Ten Largest Countries

Country	Population (millions) 2010	Population Density (per square kilometer)	Rate of Natural Increase (RNI)	Total Fertility Rate	Percent Urban	Percent <15	Percent >65	Net Migration (Rate per 1000) 2005–10[a]
China	1,338.1	140	0.5	1.5	47	18	8	−0.3
India	1,188.8	362	1.5	2.6	29	32	5	−0.2
United States	309.6	32	0.6	2.0	79	20	13	3.3
Indonesia	235.5	124	1.4	2.4	43	28	6	−0.6
Brazil	193.3	23	1.0	2.0	84	27	7	−0.2
Pakistan	184.8	232	2.3	4.0	35	38	4	−1.6
Bangladesh	164.4	1,142	1.5	2.4	25	32	4	−0.7
Nigeria	158.3	171	2.4	5.7	47	43	3	−0.4
Russia	141.9	8	−0.2	1.5	73	15	13	0.4
Japan	127.4	337	−0.0	1.4	86	13	23	0.2

[a]Net Migration Rate from the United Nations, Population Division, World Population Prospects: The 2008 Revision Population Database.
Source: Population Reference Bureau, World Population Data Sheet, 2010.

PEOPLE ON THE MOVE   The Geographies of Global Migration

Globalization has led to one of the largest migrations in human history as people leave their homes to take advantage of booming economies and better living conditions in other countries (Figure 1.3.1). Either desperate conditions at home—what geographers call "push forces"—or the lure of promising pastures elsewhere—the "pull forces"—can lead to migration. Often, though, it's a combination of the two that make people move.

While accurate data on migration is notoriously difficult to gather because people often migrate without documentation, the United Nations says that currently at least 190 million people are legally living in a country different than where they were born. Although most of those people have moved to cities in the developed western world, there is also considerable migration to magnet cities in the developing world, places such as Delhi, Dubai, Rio, and Mexico City. Furthermore, that UN statistic does not include those people who stay within their own country, yet leave home, like the highland peasants of Bolivia moving to La Paz or a farmer from Iowa cashing in to take a job in Atlanta.

Nor does that statistic count the estimated 35 million people who are classified as refugees, those who have fled violence or natural disasters. Or the untold number who are not in established refugee camps but, instead, making do somehow on their own. Although the push and pull forces for refugees may not have been caused directly by globalization, often, if one digs deep enough, a connection can be found.

Because the human geography of global migration wears many different faces and tells many different stories, each of our chapters sheds light on this complicated process of migration through our *People on the Move* sidebars. More specifically, they are:

Chapter 3: Skilled Immigrants Fuel Big City Growth
Chapter 4: National Identity and Japanese Brazilians
Chapter 5: The Diaspora Drifts Back
Chapter 6: The New African Americans
Chapter 7: Jordanian Bedouins and the Badia Project
Chapter 8: Smuggling Illegal Immigrants into Europe
Chapter 9: Chinese Immigrants in Russia's Far East
Chapter 10: Migration In and Out of Kazakhstan
Chapter 11: Rural Migrants Flock to China's Cities
Chapter 12: Punjabis Leaving Agriculture and Leaving India
Chapter 13: The Rohingyas Seek Sanctuary
Chapter 14: Does Australia Have a Population Problem?

Figure 1.3.1 People on the Move A boat carrying 179 illegal immigrants who had hoped to reach Europe is stopped by the Spanish Coast Guard before it reached Spain's Canary Islands.

minimum of two children to replace their parents. From population data collected in the past decade, the current TFR for the world is 2.5. While that is the average for the whole world, the variability between regions is striking. To illustrate, the current TFR for Africa is 4.7, whereas in no-growth Europe it is only 1.6 (Figure 1.23).

Young and Old Populations One of the best indicators of the momentum (or lack of) for continued population growth is the youthfulness of a population because these data show the proportion of a population about to enter their prime reproductive years. The common statistic for this measure is the *percentage of a population under age 15*. As a global average, 27 percent of the population is younger than age 15, but in fast-growing Africa, that figure is 41 percent, with several African countries approaching 50 percent. This suggests strongly that rapid population growth in Africa will continue for at least another generation, despite the tragedy of the HIV/AIDS epidemic. In contrast, Europe has only 16 percent of its population under 15, and North America 20 percent.

The other end of the age spectrum is also important, and it is measured by the *percentage of a population over age 65*. That figure is useful for inferring the needs of a society to provide social services for its senior citizens and pensioners. Japan and most European countries, for example, have a relatively high proportion of people over age 65. As a result, concerns are raised about whether there will be enough wage earners to support the social security needs of a large elderly population.

Figure 1.23 Fertility and Mortality Birthrates and death rates vary widely around the world. Fertility rates result from an array of variables, including state family-planning programs and the level of a woman's education. This family is in Bangladesh, a country that is working hard to reduce its birthrate through education programs.

The structure of a population, which includes the percentage of young and old, is presented graphically as a **population pyramid**. This graph plots the percentage of all different age groups along a vertical axis that divides the population into male and female (Figure 1.24). The large percentage of young people in a fast-growing population provides a wide base and the small percentage of elderly a narrow tip, thereby giving the graph its pyramidal shape. Older populations, in contrast, with fewer young people and an aging population, give the graph a very different shape, with a narrow base and broader upper segment.

Life Expectancy Another demographic indicator that contains information about health and well-being in a society is *life expectancy*, which is the average length of a life expected at the birth of a typical male or female in a specific country. Because a large number of social factors such as health services, nutrition, and sanitation influence life expectancy, these data are often used as an indicator of the level of social development in a country. Because this book uses life expectancy as a social indicator, life expectancy data are found in the economic and social development tables, not with other population statistics.

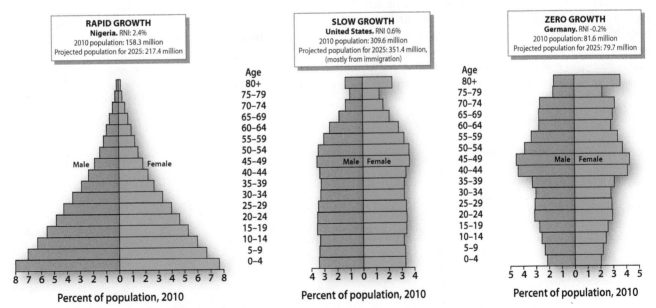

Figure 1.24 Population Pyramids The term *population pyramid* comes from the form assumed by a rapidly growing country such as Nigeria, when data for age and sex are plotted graphically as a percentage of the total population. The broad base illustrates the high percentage of young people in the country's population, which indicates that rapid growth will probably continue for at least another generation. This pyramidal shape contrasts with the narrow bases of the slow- and negative-growth countries, the United States and Germany, which have fewer people in the childbearing years.

Not surprisingly because social conditions vary widely around the world, so do life expectancy figures. In general, though, life expectancy has been increasing over the decades, implying that the conditions supporting life and longevity are improving. To illustrate, in 1975, the average life expectancy figure for the world was 58 years, whereas today it is 69. In Sub-Saharan Africa, however, life expectancy has changed very little over the last 30 years because of the HIV/AIDS epidemic. As a result, the life expectancy for the region is the same (52) as it was in 1975. In Russia, life expectancy has fallen in the past two decades, probably because of the deterioration of social services accompanying economic restructuring in the post-Soviet era.

The Demographic Transition The historical record shows that population growth rates commonly change over time. More specifically, in Europe, North America, and Japan, growth declined as countries became increasingly industrialized and urbanized. From this historical data, demographers generated the **demographic transition model**, a four-stage conceptualization that tracks changes in birthrates and death rates through time as a population urbanizes (Figure 1.25).

In the demographic transition model, Stage 1 is characterized by both high birthrates and death rates, leading to a very slow rate of natural increase. Historically, this stage is associated with Europe's preindustrial period, a period that also predated common public health measures such as sewage treatment, the scientific understanding of disease transmission, and the most fundamental aspects of modern medicine. Not surprisingly, death rates were high and life expectancy was short. Tragically, these conditions are still found today in some parts of the world.

In Stage 2, death rates fall dramatically while birthrates remain high, producing a rapid rise in the RNI. Again, in both historical and modern times, this decrease in death rates is usually associated with the development of public health measures and modern medicine. One of the assumptions of the demographic transition model is that these services become increasingly available only after some degree of economic development and urbanization takes place.

However, even as death rates fall, it takes time for people to respond with lower birthrates, which begin in Stage 3. This, then, is the transitional stage in which people apparently become aware of the advantages of smaller families in an urban and industrial setting.

In Stage 4, a very low RNI results from a combination of low birthrates and very low death rates. As a result, there is very little—if any—natural population increase. Today, the United States, Japan, and most European countries are clearly in Stage 4 of the demographic transition model.

Migration Patterns Never before in human history have so many people been on the move. Today, more than 190 million people live outside the country of their birth and thus are officially designated as migrants by international agencies. Much of this international migration is directly linked to the new globalized economy because half of the migrants live either in the developed world or in developing countries with vibrant industrial, mining, or petroleum extraction economies. In the oil-rich countries of Kuwait and Saudi Arabia, for example, the labor force is composed primarily of foreign migrants. In total numbers, fully one-third of the world's migrants live in seven industrial countries: Japan, Germany, France, Canada, the United States, Italy, and the United Kingdom. Moreover, most of these migrants have moved to cities; in fact, 20 percent of migrants live in just 20 world cities. Further, because industrial countries usually have very low birthrates, immigration accounts for a large proportion of their population growth. For example, about one-third of the annual growth in the United States is due to in-migration.

But not all migrants move for economic reasons. War, persecution, famine, and environmental destruction cause people to flee to safe havens elsewhere. Accurate data on refugees are often difficult to obtain for a number of reasons (such as individuals not legally crossing international boundaries or countries deliberately obscuring the number for po-

Figure 1.25 Demographic Transition
As a country goes through industrialization, its population moves through the four stages in this diagram, referred to as the *demographic transition*. In Stage 1, population growth is low because high birthrates are offset by high death rates. Rapid growth takes place in Stage 2, as death rates decline. Stage 3 is characterized by a decline in birthrates. The transition ends with low growth once again in Stage 4, resulting from a relative balance between low birthrates and death rates. With a large number of developed countries now showing no natural growth, demographers talk of adding a 5th stage to the traditional demographic transition model, one where there is negative natural growth.

Figure 1.26 **Refugees** About 35 million people are refugees from ethnic warfare and civil strife. Most of these refugees are in Africa and western Asia. These women wait in line for water at a refugee camp in southern Sudan.

litical reasons), but UN officials estimate that some 35 million people should be considered refugees. More than half of these are in Africa and western Asia (Figure 1.26).

Push and Pull Forces While its causes may be complicated, the migration process can be understood through three interactive concepts. First, *push* forces, such as civil strife, environmental degradation, or unemployment, drive people from their homelands. Second, *pull* forces, such as better economic opportunity or health services, attract migrants to certain locations, within or beyond their national boundaries. Connecting the two are the *informational networks* of families, friends, and sometimes labor contractors who provide information on the mechanics of migration, transportation details, and housing and job opportunities.

Net Migration Rates The amount of immigration (in-migration) and emigration (out-migration) is measured by the **net migration rate,** a statistic that depicts whether more people are entering or leaving a country. A positive figure means the population is growing because of in-migration, whereas a negative number means more people are leaving than arriving. As with other demographic indicators, the net migration rate is provided for the number of migrants per 1,000 of a base population. To illustrate, the net migration rate for the United States is 3 per 1,000 people, whereas Canada, which receives even more immigrants than the United States, has a net migration rate of 8. In contrast, Mexico, the source of many migrants to North America, has a net migration rate of −3.

Some of the highest net migration rates are found in countries that depend heavily on migrants for their labor force, such as the United Arab Emirates, with a net migration rate of 16, and Kuwait at 8. Countries with the highest negative migration rates are Marshall Islands −23, Federated Micronesia −15, and a number of the Caribbean island states, with net migration rates around −5.

Settlement Geography Data on **population density,** which is the average number of people per area unit (square mile or square kilometer), conveys important information about settlement in a specific country. In Table 1.1 one sees the striking difference between the high population density of India contrasted to the much lower figure for the United States. Flying over these two countries and looking down at the settlement patterns would explain this contrast (Figure 1.27). While much of the United States is covered by farms covering hundreds of acres, with houses and barns several miles from their neighbors, the landscape of India is made up of small villages, distanced from each other by only a mile or so. This results in a population density three times higher in India than in the United States. Japan has a similar settlement pattern to India, even though it is primarily an urban, industrial country. Bangladesh, one of the most densely settled countries in the world, must squeeze its large and rapidly growing population into a limited amount of dry land built by the delta of two large rivers, the Ganges and the Brahmaputra.

Because population densities differ considerably between rural and urban areas, the national figure can be a bit misleading. Many of the world's cities, for example, have densities of more than 30,000 people per square mile (10,344 per square kilometer), with the central areas of Mumbai (Bombay) and Shanghai easily twice as dense because of the prevalence of high-rise apartment buildings. In contrast, most North American cities have densities of fewer than 10,000 people per square mile (3,861 per square kilometer)

Figure 1.27 **Contrasting Settlement Density: U.S. and India** In the U.S. the population density is 32 per square kilometer, contrasted with 356 per square kilometer in India. Besides the difference in the size of each country's population, another factor in the contrasting densities is the difference in settlement patterns. In the United States people commonly settle on dispersed farms on large acreage, as illustrated by the landscape in Iowa, whereas as in India there is dense settlement in both towns and rural landscapes.

Figure 1.28 Growth of World Cities This map shows the 20 largest cities in the world, along with their projected growth by the year 2020. Note that the greatest city growth in the next decade will be in the developing world. In contrast, there is little growth forecast for large cities like Tokyo or New York in the developed world.

because of the cultural preference for single-family dwellings on individual urban lots.

An Urban World Cities are the focal points of the contemporary, globalizing world, the fast-paced centers of deep and widespread economic, political, and cultural change. Because of this vitality and the options cities offer to impoverished and uprooted rural peoples, they are also magnets for migration. The scale and rate of growth of some world cities is absolutely staggering. Estimates are that between natural growth and in-migration, Mumbai (Bombay), India, will add over 7 million people by the year 2020, which, assuming growth is constant throughout the period (which is questionable), would mean the urban area adds over 10,000 new people each week. The same projections would have Lagos, Nigeria, which has the highest annual growth, adding almost 15,000 per week (Figure 1.28).

Based upon data on the **urbanized population**, which is the percentage of a country's population living in cities, as mentioned, at least half the world's population now lives in cities. Further, demographers predict that the world will be 60 percent urbanized by the year 2025.

Tables in this book's regional chapters include data on the urbanization rate for each country. To illustrate, more than 80 percent of the populations of Europe, Japan, Australia, and the United States live in cities. Generally speaking, most countries with such high rates of urbanization are also highly industrialized because manufacturing tends to cluster around urban centers. In contrast, the urbanized rate for developing countries is usually less than 50 percent, with figures closer to 40 percent not uncommon. Urbanization

figures also show where there is high potential for urban migration. If the urbanized population is relatively small, as in Zimbabwe (Africa), where only some 37 percent of the population lives in cities, the probability of high rates of urban migration in the next decades is great.

Conceptualizing the City Given the important role of cities in world regional geography, it seems appropriate to offer a brief conceptual framework for examining urban settlements.

- Cities are interdependent with other cities and towns, both regionally and globally, and are linked in an urban system of interactive settlements. As some cities expand or come to specialize in a specific function, such as banking or manufacturing, the relationships and interactions within that urban system may change. The largest city within the city system may have **urban primacy**, a term used to describe a city that is disproportionately large and dominates economic, political, and cultural activities within the country. In many countries, one large primate city usually stands out in that country's urban system. Examples include Bangkok, Mexico City, Cairo, Paris, and Buenos Aires.
- Although cities are highly complicated settlements, they often share traits of **urban structure**, a term that refers to the distribution and patterning of land use within the city. Land use is linked to specific functions, such as finance, governmental activities, housing, retailing, and industry. Almost all large cities, for example, contain a *central business district* (CBD) in which banks and business headquarters are located. Because these functions

Figure 1.29 Urban Form This photo of downtown Caracas, Venezuela, shows that city form expresses both local and global influences. In the foreground are low-income "ranchitos" where recent migrants to the city live, whereas in the background are the high-rise buildings of the financial center that are linked to global trade.

Figure 1.30 Squatter Settlements Because of the massive migration of people to world cities, adequate housing for the rapidly growing population becomes a daunting problem. Often, migrant housing needs are filled with illegal squatter settlements, such as this one in New Delhi, India.

are not randomly distributed, but instead follow well-understood location principles, it is possible to generate models of urban structure that convey the commonalties between cities within a specific region. An example is the model of Latin American cities discussed in Chapter 4.

- Closely related to urban structure is the landscape of the city, the **urban form** or physical arrangement of buildings, streets, parks, and architecture that gives each city its unique sense of place. For example, Cairo, Egypt, clearly looks and feels very different from New Delhi, India, or Caracas, Venezuela (Figure 1.29). The reasons for the range of urban landscapes include differences in histories, economies, planning policies, and cultural values (see "Cityscapes: Exploring the World's Urban Places").

- Because urban migration has taken place so rapidly in developing countries, many cities have reached a state of **overurbanization**, in which the urban population grows more quickly than the provision of necessary support services such as housing, transportation, waste disposal, and water supply. Unfortunately, this is a fairly common situation in the developing world. The hundreds of thousands of "street people" of Kolkata (Calcutta), India, are legendary, although the phenomenon of mass homelessness is by no means restricted to South Asia.

- Overurbanization often results in **squatter settlements**, illegal developments of makeshift housing on land neither owned nor rented by their inhabitants. Such settlements often are built on steep hillsides or on river floodplains that expose the occupants to the dangers of landslide and floods. Squatter settlements also are often found in the open space of public parks or along roadways, where they are regularly destroyed by government authorities, usually to be quickly rebuilt by migrants who have no other alternatives (Figure 1.30). Even for those who have found more permanent housing, water and sewer connections are often rudimentary at best. Water service can be sporadic and restricted to a few hours a day, and open sewers are a disturbingly com-

CITYSCAPES Exploring the World's Urban Places

More than half of the people in the world live in cities. From North America to Asia, Africa to Australia, we have become an urban species, clustering in cities that continue to expand upward and outward at unprecedented rates of growth. Although many countries have long been urbanized, until this decade most of the world's population still lived in the countryside. But all that is changing rapidly, with profound implications for the new urban dwellers, as well as for the larger global environment.

What are these cities like and what do people do there? How are they changing as globalization aggravates tensions between the traditional and modern worlds (Figure 1.4.1)?

Although the broad currents of urbanization are discussed throughout this book, we focus on a specific town or city within each regional chapter to convey a particular sense of that place, of what it looks and feels like, and what issues the people of that city face. These *Cityscapes* sidebars describe an array of cities, large and

small, rich and poor (but usually a combination of both), and offer a series of regional snapshots that illustrate how these special localities are growing and changing. More specifically, they are:

Chapter 3: Miami
Chapter 4: Panama City—Latin America's Aspiring Crossroads
Chapter 5: The Caribbean Metropolis of Santo Domingo
Chapter 6: Africa's Golden and Global City
Chapter 7: Dubai's Rocky Road to Urbanization
Chapter 8: Berlin Reinvents Itself
Chapter 9: St. Petersburg
Chapter 10: The Storied City of Samarkand
Chapter 11: The Varied Neighborhoods of Tokyo
Chapter 12: Life on the Streets of Mumbai (Bombay)
Chapter 13: Metro Manila, Primate City of the Philippines
Chapter 14: Apia, Capital of Samoa

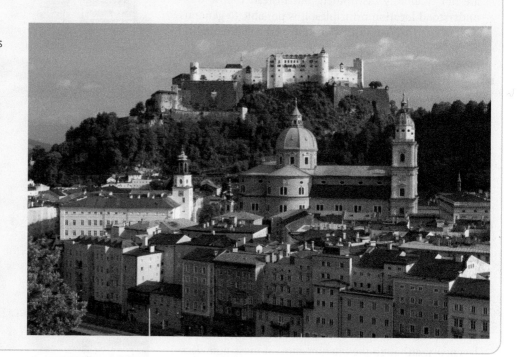

Figure 1.4.1 Cityscapes The appearance and form of a city tells us much about its past history and its present-day activities. A picturesque example is Salzburg, Austria, with its medieval fortress in the background, and the 17th century cathedral rising above the traditional city center.

mon feature of many cities. The World Bank estimated recently that 60 percent of the people in less-developed cities lived in homes that are not connected to sewers.

Cultural Coherence and Diversity: The Geography of Tradition and Change

Social scientists like to say that culture is the weaving binding together the world's diverse social fabric. If true, one glance at the daily news suggests this complex global tapestry is unraveling with widespread cultural tension and conflict. As noted earlier, with the recent rise of global communication systems (satellite TV, films, videos, etc.), stereotypical

Western culture is spreading at a rapid pace, and while some cultures accept these new cultural influences willingly, others resist this new form of cultural imperialism through protests, censorship, even terrorism.

The geography of cultural cohesion and diversity, then, entails an examination of tradition and change, of language and religion, of group belonging and identity, and of the complex and varied currents that underlie 21st-century ethnic factionalism and separatism (Figure 1.31).

Culture in a Globalizing World Given the diversity of cultures around the world, coupled with the dynamic changes associated with globalization, traditional definitions of cul-

Figure 1.31 Ethnic Tensions Unfortunately, much contemporary cultural change is characterized by violence among different ethnic groups. In this photo, a commuter in the Indian state of Gujarat passes by a car burned during rioting between Muslims and Hindus.

ture must be stretched somewhat to provide a viable conceptual framework. A basic definition provides a starting point. **Culture** is learned, not innate, and is shared behavior held in common by a group of people, empowering them with what could be called a "way of life."

In addition, culture has both abstract and material dimensions: speech, religion, ideology, livelihood, and value systems, but also technology, housing, foods, and music. These varied expressions of culture are relevant to the study of world regional geography because they tell us much about the way people interact with their environment, each other, and the larger world. Finally, especially given the widespread influences of globalization, it is best to think of culture as dynamic rather than static. That is, culture is a process, not a condition, something that is constantly adapting to new circumstances. As a result, there are always tensions between the conservative, traditional elements of a culture and the newer forces promoting change (Figure 1.32).

(a)

(b)

Figure 1.32 Folk, Ethnic, Popular, and Global Culture A broad spectrum of cultural groups characterizes the world's contemporary cultural geography. Representing global culture (a) is a Korean woman in downtown Washington, DC, with a mobile phone and laptop computer. In Amsterdam, the Netherlands, two visitors (b) wear the universal clothes of popular culture, while at the opposite end of the spectrum are the ethnic cultures of (c) Garifuna women in Honduras and (d) men in Peru performing the Chonguinada dance.

(c)

(d)

ENVIRONMENT AND POLITICS   Controversies and Complexities

Because the environment is fundamental to our existence and humans have many different opinions and values about its usage, environmental issues are almost always controversial, whether the topic is territorial rights, resource usage, or simply preserving and protecting nature (Figure 1.5.1). Who gets to use water, cut trees, till the land, or control the territory? And with controversy comes politics, at all scales and in all forms, as stakeholders air their differences and local, national, or international governmental representatives mediate and seek solutions.

Because of the extended reach of international commerce, economic globalization has aggravated many environmental issues. What were once local environmental controversies have often been expanded and recast in the global arena. In the regional chapters of this book we have taken a closer look at the interactions between *Environment and Politics* in sidebars that examined a variety of issues.

Chapter 3: Deconstructing a Landscape: Dam Removal in the United States
Chapter 4: The Political Ecology of Extraction
Chapter 5: Los Vieques: From Naval Testing Ground to Upscale Resort and Superfund Site
Chapter 6: Africa's Conflict Diamonds
Chapter 7: Water and the Palestinians in the Middle East
Chapter 8: The Iron Curtain Green Zone
Chapter 9: Sochi 2014: Russia's Struggle for a Green Winter Olympics
Chapter 10: Tajikistan and Uzbekistan's Environmental Cold War
Chapter 11: China Embraces Green Energy
Chapter 12: Insurgency and National Parks in Northeastern India
Chapter 13: Dam Building on the Mekong River
Chapter 14: Land, Native Rights, and Sovereignty in Hawaii

Figure 1.5.1 Environment and Politics
Local, regional, national, and international politics reshape the global environment in many different ways. Here, in Nogales, Mexico, is the other side of the border fence built by the United States to restrict illegal entry into the United States from Mexico

When Cultures Collide Cultural change often takes place within the context of international tensions. Sometimes one cultural system will replace another; at other times, resistance will stave off change. More commonly, however, a newer, hybrid form of culture results in an amalgamation of two cultural traditions. Historically, colonialism was the most important perpetuator of these cultural collisions; today, globalization in its varied forms can be thought of as the major vehicle of cultural tensions and change.

Cultural imperialism is the active promotion of one cultural system at the expense of another. Although there are still many expressions of cultural imperialism today, the most severe examples occurred in the colonial period when European cultures spread worldwide, often overwhelming, eroding, and even replacing indigenous cultures. During this period, Spanish culture spread widely in Latin America; French culture diffused into parts of Africa and Southeast Asia; and British culture overwhelmed South and Southwest Asia. New languages were mandated, new education systems were implanted, and new administrative institutions replaced the old. Foreign dress styles, diets, gestures, and organizations were added to existing cultural systems. Many vestiges of colonial culture are still evident today. In India, the makeover was so complete that many are fond of saying, with only slight exaggeration, that "the last true Englishman will be an Indian."

Today's cultural imperialism is seldom linked to an explicit colonizing force but more often comes as a fellow traveler with economic globalization. Though many expressions of cultural imperialism carry a Western (even U.S.) tone—

such as McDonald's, MTV, Marlboro cigarettes, and the use of English as the dominant language of the Internet—these facets result more from a search for new consumer markets than from deliberate efforts to spread modern U.S. culture throughout the world.

The reaction against cultural imperialism is **cultural nationalism,** which is the process of protecting and defending a cultural system against diluting or offensive cultural expressions, while at the same time actively promoting national and local cultural values. Often cultural nationalism takes the form of explicit legislation or official censorship that simply outlaws unwanted cultural traits. Examples of legislated cultural nationalism are common. France has long fought the Anglicization of its language by banning "Franglais," the use of English words such as "Le weekend," in official French. More recently, France has sought to protect its national music and film industries by legislating that radio DJs play a certain percentage of French songs and artists each broadcast day (40 percent currently). In addition, many Muslim countries censor Western cultural influences by restricting and censoring international TV, an element they consider the source of many undesirable cultural influences. Most Asian countries as well are increasingly protective of their cultural values, and many are demanding changes to tone down the sexual content of MTV and other international TV networks.

As noted, the most common product of cultural collision is the blending of forces to form a new, synergistic form of culture, called **cultural syncretism or hybridization** (Figure 1.33). To characterize India's culture as British, for example, would be to grossly oversimplify and exaggerate England's colonial influence. Instead, Indians have adapted many British traits to their own circumstances, infusing them with their own meanings. India's use of English, for example, has produced a unique form of "Indlish" that often befuddles visitors to South Asia. Nor should we forget that India has added many words to our English vocabulary—*khaki, pajamas, veranda,* and *bungalow,* among others. Clearly, both the Anglo and Indian cultures have been changed by the British colonial presence in South Asia.

Language and Culture in Global Context Language and culture are so intertwined that in the minds of many language is the characteristic that best differentiates and defines cultural groups (Figure 1.34). Furthermore, because language is the primary means for communication, it obviously folds together many other aspects of cultural identity such as politics, religion, commerce, and customs. In addition, language is fundamental to cultural cohesiveness. It not only brings people together but also sets them apart; it can be an important component of national or ethnic identity and a means for creating and maintaining boundaries of regional identity.

Because most languages have common historical (and even prehistorical) roots, linguists have grouped the thousands of languages found throughout the world into a handful of language families. This is simply a first-order grouping of languages into large units, based on common ancestral speech. For example, about half of the world's people speak languages of the Indo-European family, a large group that includes not only European languages such as English and Spanish but also Hindi and Bengali, dominant languages of South Asia.

Within language families are smaller units that also give clues to the common history and geography of peoples and cultures. *Language branches and groups* (also called *subfamilies*) are closely related subsets within a language family in which there are usually shared and similar sounds, words, and grammar. Well known are the similarities between German and English and between French and Spanish. Because of their similarities, these languages are placed into the same linguistic groupings.

Additionally, individual languages often have very distinctive forms associated with specific regions, which are called *dialects*. Although dialects of the same language have their own unique pronunciation and grammar (think of the distinctive differences, for example, between British, North American, and Australian English), they are—sometimes with considerable effort—mutually intelligible.

When people from different cultural groups cannot communicate directly in their native languages, they often agree on a third language to serve as a common tongue, a **lingua franca.** Swahili has long served that purpose between the many tribal languages of eastern Africa, and French was historically the lingua franca of international politics and diplomacy. Today, English is increasingly the

Figure 1.33 Cultural Hybridity The hybridization of culture is clearly visible in this photo of South Asians (India vs. Pakistan) playing cricket, which was, before the colonial period, a uniquely English sport. Note, too, that this traditional sport now carries the logos and advertisements of global culture.

Figure 1.34 World Languages Most languages of the world belong to a handful of major language families. About 50 percent of the world's population speaks a language belonging to the Indo-European language family, which includes languages common to Europe, but also major languages in South Asia, such as Hindi. They are in the same family because of their linguistic similarities. The next largest family is the Sino-Tibetan family, which includes languages spoken in China, the world's most populous country.

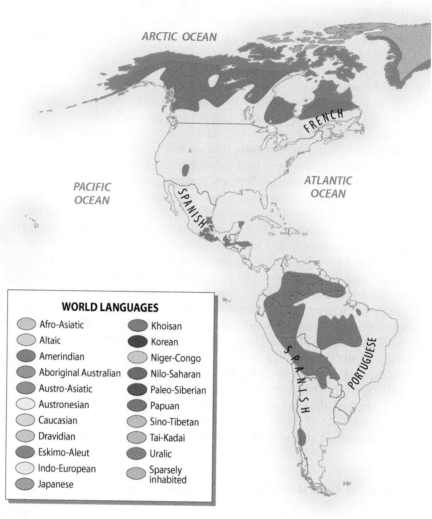

WORLD LANGUAGES

Afro-Asiatic	Khoisan
Altaic	Korean
Amerindian	Niger-Congo
Aboriginal Australian	Nilo-Saharan
Austro-Asiatic	Paleo-Siberian
Austronesian	Papuan
Caucasian	Sino-Tibetan
Dravidian	Tai-Kadai
Eskimo-Aleut	Uralic
Indo-European	Sparsely inhabited
Japanese	

common language of international communications (Figure 1.35).

A Geography of World Religions Another extremely important defining trait of cultural groups is religion (Figure 1.36). Indeed, in this era of a totalizing global culture, religion is becoming increasingly important in defining cultural identity. Recent ethnic violence and unrest in far-flung places such as the Balkans, Iraq, and Indonesia illustrate the point.

Universalizing religions, such as Christianity, Islam, and Buddhism, attempt to appeal to all peoples, regardless of location or culture; these religions usually have a proselytizing or missionary program that actively seeks new converts. In contrast are the **ethnic religions,** which remain identified closely with a specific ethnic, tribal, or national group. Judaism and Hinduism, for example, are usually regarded as ethnic religions because they normally do not actively seek new converts. Instead, people are born into ethnic religions.

Christianity, a universalizing religion, is the world's largest religion in both areal extent and number of adherents. Although fragmented into separate branches and churches, Christianity as a whole has 2.1 billion adherents, or about one-third of the world's population. The largest number of Christians can be found in Europe, Africa, Latin America, and North America. Islam, which has spread from its origins on the Arabian Peninsula as far east as Indonesia and the Philippines, has about 1.3 billion members.

While not as severely fragmented as Christianity, Islam should not be thought of as a homogeneous religion because it is also split into separate groups. The two major branches are Shiite Islam, which constitutes about 11 percent of the total Islamic population and represents a majority in Iran and southern Iraq, and the more dominant Sunni Islam that is found from the Arab-speaking lands of North Africa to Indonesia. Both of these forms of Islam are experiencing fundamentalist revivals in which proponents are interested in maintaining purity of faith distanced from Western influences.

Judaism, the parent religion of Christianity, is also closely related to Islam. Although tensions are often high between Jews and Muslims, these two religions, along with Christianity, actually share historical and theological roots in the Hebrew prophets and leaders. Judaism now numbers about 14 million adherents, having lost perhaps one-third of its total population due to the systematic extermination of Jews by the Nazis during World War II.

Hinduism, which is closely linked to India, has about 900 million adherents. Outsiders often regard Hinduism as polytheistic because Hindus worship many deities. Most Hindus argue, however, that all of their faith's gods are merely representations of different aspects of a single divine, cosmic unity. Historically, Hinduism is linked to the caste system, with its segregation of peoples based on ancestry and occupation. Today, however, because India's democratic government is committed to reducing the social distinctions between castes, the connections between religion and caste are now much less explicit than in the past.

Buddhism, which originated as a reform movement within Hinduism 2,500 years ago, is widespread in Asia, extending from Sri Lanka to Japan and from Mongolia to Vietnam (Figure 1.37). In its spread, Buddhism came to coexist with other faiths in certain areas making it difficult to accurately estimate the number of its adherents. Estimates of the total Buddhist population range from 350 million to 900 million people.

Finally, in some parts of the world, religious practice has declined significantly, giving way to **secularization,** in which people consider themselves either nonreligious or outright atheistic. Though secularization is difficult to measure, social scientists estimate that about 1.1 billion people fit into this category worldwide. Perhaps the best example of secularization comes from the former communist lands of Russia and eastern Europe, where, historically, there was overt hostility between government and church. Since the demise of Soviet communism in the 1990s, however, many of these countries have experienced modest religious revivals.

Figure 1.35 English as Global Language A bilingual traffic sign in Dubai, United Arab Emirates, is a reminder that English has become a universal form of communication for transportation, business, and science.

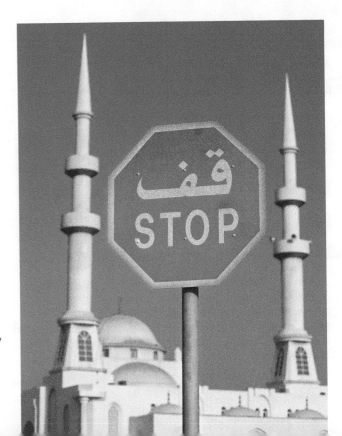

Figure 1.36 Major Religious Traditions This map shows the major religions throughout the world. For most people, religious tradition is a major component of cultural and ethnic identity. While Christians of different sorts account for about 34 percent of the world's population, this religious tradition is highly fragmented. Within Christianity, there are about twice as many Roman Catholics as Protestants. Islam accounts for about 20 percent of the world's population; Hindus make up about 14 percent.

DOMINANT RELIGIOUS TRADITIONS
- Sunni Islam
- Shiite Islam
- Judaism
- Eastern Orthodox
- Coptic Christian
- Roman Catholic
- Protestant Christian
- Mixed Christianity
- Buddhism
- Buddhism mixed with Taoism and Confucianism
- Buddhism mixed with Shinto
- Hinduism
- Sikhism
- Complex mixture of Christianity, Islam, and indigenous African religions
- Indigenous religion (Animism)
- Syncretic Catholicism mixed with Amerindian religious traditions
- Syncretic Catholicism mixed with African religious traditions
- Uninhabited

Figure 1.37 Religious Landscapes The varied expressions of a culture's religion commonly appear in the landscape—the mosques and minarets of Islam, the churches and cathedrals of Christianity, the synagogues of Judaism, the shrines of Hinduism, or the temples and statues of Buddhism. An example is this statue of the sea deity *Kwun Yum* at the Tin Hau Temple in Repulse Bay, Hong Kong.

Secularization has also grown more pronounced recently in western Europe. Although historically and to some extent still culturally a Roman Catholic country, France possibly has more people (mostly migrants) attending Muslim mosques on Fridays than it has attending Christian churches on Sundays. Japan and the other countries of East Asia are also noted for their high degree of secularization.

Geopolitical Framework: Unity and Fragmentation

The term *geopolitics* is used to describe and explain the close link between geography and politics. More specifically, geopolitics focuses on the interactivity between power, territory, and space at all scales, from the local to the global. Un-

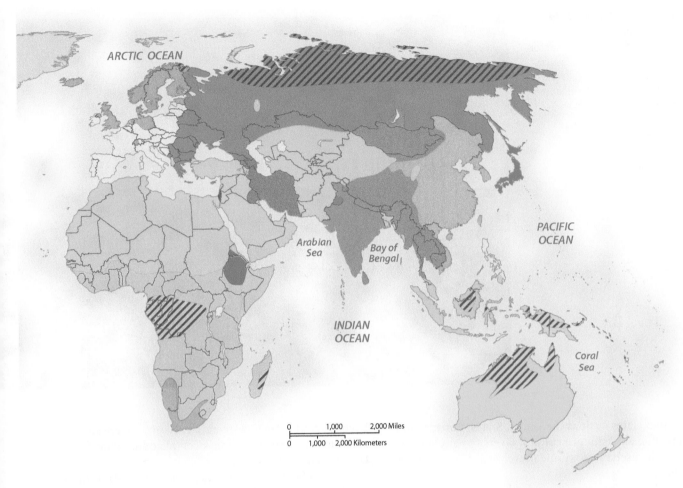

questionably, one of the world's characteristics of the last several decades has been the speed, scope, and character of political change in various regions of the world, thus discussions of geopolitics are central to world regional geography.

With the demise of the Soviet Union in 1991 came opportunities for self-determination and independence in eastern Europe and Central Asia, resulting in fundamental changes to economic, political, and even cultural alignments (Figure 1.38). Religious freedom helped drive national identities in some new Central Asian republics, while eastern Europe was primarily concerned with new economic and political links to western Europe. Russia itself still wavers perilously between different geopolitical pathways. All of these topics are discussed further in chapters 8, 9, and 10.

While international conflicts remain a nagging concern of diplomats and governments, more common are strife and tension within—rather than between—nation-states. Civil unrest, tribal tensions, terrorism, and religious factionalism have created a new fabric and scale of political tension.

Nation-States and Beyond A traditional reference point for examining geopolitics is the concept of the nation-state. The term *state* refers to a political entity with territorial boundaries recognized by other countries and internally governed by an organizational structure, whereas *nation* refers to a large group of people who share numerous socio-cultural elements such as language, religion, tradition, and identity. A **nation-state**, then, is a relatively homogeneous cultural group occupying its own fully independent political territory. Historical France and England are often used as the type examples of nation-states, while contemporary countries such as Albania, Egypt, Bangladesh, Japan, and the two Koreas qualify as areas where there is close overlap between nation and state.

Overall, however, globalization has weakened the concept of the nation-state. Today, in fact, most of the world's 200 or so political entities are questionable fits with the traditional definition. International migration, for example, has led to large populations of immigrants within countries, people who do not necessarily share the national culture of the majority. In England, large numbers of South Asians form their own communities, speak their own languages, have their own religions, and dress to their own standards. Similarly, France is home to a mosaic of peoples from its former colonial lands in Africa and Asia. In North America Canada and the United States also have large immigrant populations who are legal citizens of the political state, yet who have either changed the very nature of the national culture by their presence or live on its margins.

Figure 1.38 The End of the Cold War With the fall of Soviet communism, many nations rushed to remove the symbols of their former governments, to forget the past and make room for a new future. In this photo taken in 1990, a monument to Lenin is toppled in Bucharest, Romania.

The fact that states such as the United States, Canada, and Germany officially embrace cultural diversity with policies declaring themselves as multicultural states underscores these changes.

As well, there are many states that have groups of people who seek autonomy from the central government with the right to govern themselves. This is the case with the French-speaking people of Quebec province in Canada, as well as the Catalonians and Basques of Spain, to name just a few separatist groups (Figure 1.39). A closer look at France, Italy, and the United Kingdom would reveal more separatist groups.

Even in North America there are Native American groups and Native Hawaiians who seek complete autonomy from the U.S. or Canadian governments.

Not to be overlooked is how the rise of giant multinational firms and regional organizations have eclipsed the power of political units. This is certainly the case for the 27 member states of the European Union, a topic discussed in more detail in Chapter 8.

Finally, there are cultural groups who lack political voice and representation due to the way political borders have been drawn. In Slovakia, to illustrate, a group who trace their cul-

Figure 1.39 Ethnic Separatism A major aspect of contemporary geopolitics is the way ethnic groups are demanding recognition, autonomy, and often independence from larger political units. These Basque women in southwestern France are protesting the outlawing of a Basque youth group French and Spanish authorities suspect of aiding Basque terrorists.

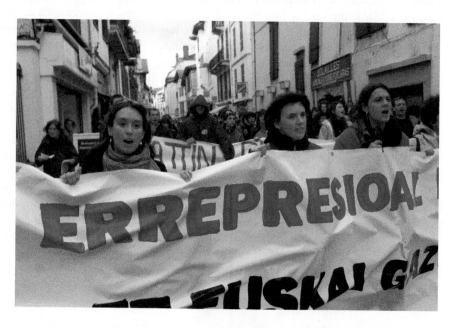

tural heritage to adjacent Hungary agitate for re-drawing the political border between the two states. In Southwest Asia, the Kurdish people have long been considered a nation without a state because they are divided by the political borders of Turkey, Syria, Iraq, and Iran (Figure 1.40).

Colonialism and Decolonialization One of the overarching themes in world geopolitics is the waxing and waning of European colonial power over much of the world. **Colonialism** refers to the formal establishment of rule over a foreign population. A colony has no independent standing in the world community but instead is seen only as an appendage of the colonial power. Generally speaking, the main period of colonialization by European states was from 1500 through the mid-1900s. (Figure 1.41).

Decolonialization refers to the process of a colony's gaining (or regaining) control over its own territory and establishing a separate, independent government. As was the case with the Revolutionary War in the United States, this process often begins as a violent struggle. As wars of independence became increasingly common in the mid-20th century, some colonial powers recognized the inevitable and began working toward peaceful disengagement from their colonies. In the late 1950s and early 1960s, for example, Britain and France granted independence to most of their former African colonies, often after periods of warfare or civil unrest. This process was nearly completed in 1997, when Hong Kong was peacefully restored to China by the United Kingdom.

But decades and even centuries of colonial rule are not easily erased; thus, the influence of colonialism is still commonly found in the new nations' governments, education, agriculture, and economies. While some countries may enjoy special status with, and receive continued aid from, their former colonial masters, others remain disadvantaged because of a reduced resource base exploited by colonial powers. In fact some scholars regard the continuing economic ties between certain imperial powers and their former colonies as a form of exploitative neocolonialism. On the other hand, some remaining colonies such as the Dutch Antilles in the Caribbean have made it clear that they have no wish for independence, finding both economic and political advantages in continued dependency. Because the consequences of colonialism differ greatly from place to place, the final accounting of its effects is far from complete (Figure 1.42).

Global Terrorism and Insurgency As mentioned earlier, challenges to a centralized political state or authority have long been part of global geopolitics as rebellious and sepa-

Figure 1.40 A Nation Without a State Not all nations or large cultural groups control their own political territories and thus are without a state. As this map shows, the Kurdish people of Southwest Asia occupy a larger cultural territory that is in four different political states—Turkey, Iraq, Syria, and Iran. As a result of this political fragmentation, the Kurds are considered a minority in each of these four countries.

ratist groups seek independence, autonomy, and territorial control. Armed conflict in the form of insurgency has also been part of this process as illustrated by the American and Mexican Revolutions that successfully fought against European colonial powers. Terrorism, which can be defined as violence directed at nonmilitary targets, has also been common, albeit to a far lesser degree than today.

Further, until the September 2001 terrorist attacks on the United States by Al Qaeda, terrorism was usually directed at specific local targets and committed by insurgents with focused goals. The Irish Republican Army (IRA) bombings in Great Britain and Basque terrorism in Spain are illustrations. The attacks on the World Trade Center and the Pentagon (as well as the thwarted attack on the Capitol), however, went well beyond conventional geopolitics as a small group of religious extremists attacked the symbols of Western culture, finance, and power. Experts assume the goal of the Al Qaeda terrorists was less to disrupt world commerce and politics and more to make a statement about the strength of their own convictions and power. Regardless of

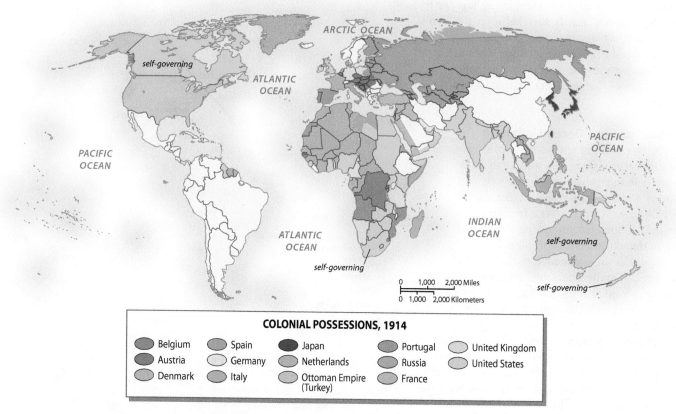

Figure 1.41 The Colonial World, 1914 This world map shows the extent of colonial power and territory just prior to World War I. At that time, most of Africa was under colonial control, as were Southwest Asia, South Asia, and Southeast Asia. Australia and Canada were very closely aligned with England. Also note that in Asia, Japan controlled colonial territory in Korea and northeastern China, which was known as Manchuria at that time.

motives, those acts of terrorism underscore the need to expand our conceptualization of the linkages between globalization and geopolitics (Figure 1.43).

More to the point, many experts argue that global terrorism is both a product of and a reaction to globalization. Unlike earlier geopolitical conflicts, the geography of global terrorism is not defined by a war between well-established political states. Instead, the Al Qaeda terrorists appear to belong to a web of small, well-organized cells located in many different countries. These cells are linked in a decentralized network that provides guidance, financing, and political autonomy and that has used the tools and means of globalization to its advantage. Members communicate instantaneously via mobile phones and the Internet. Transnational members travel between countries quickly and frequently. The network's activities are financed through a complicated array of holding companies and subsidiaries that traffic in a range of goods, including honey, diamonds, and opium. To recruit members and political support, the network feeds on the unrest and inequities (real and imagined) resulting from economic globalization. The network's terrorist acts then target symbols of those modern global values and activities it opposes. Even though the 9/11 attacks focused terror on the United States, the casualties and resultant damage were inter-

national, as citizens from more than 80 countries were killed in the World Trade Center tragedy.

Although Al Qaeda is the most visible and possibly the most threatening of contemporary global terrorist groups, the U.S. State Department names 45 groups on its list of foreign terrorist organizations. While most of these are clustered in North Africa and Southwest and Central Asia, this list also includes insurgent groups in South America, Africa, and Asia.

The military responses to global terrorism and insurgency involve several components ranging from neutralizing terrorist activities, known as counterterrorism, to counterinsurgency, a more complicated, multifaceted strategy that combines military warfare with social and political service activities designed to win over the local population and deprive insurgents of a political base. These counterinsurgency activities include, first, clearing and then holding territory held by insurgents, followed by building schools, medical clinics, and a viable (and legal) economy. Often these nonmilitary activities are referred to as nation-building since the goal is to replace the separatist insurgency with a viable social, economic, and political fabric more complementary to the larger geopolitical state. This, of course, is the current strategy employed by the United States in Iraq and Afghanistan.

Economic and Social Development: The Geography of Wealth and Poverty

The pace of global economic change and development has accelerated dramatically in the past several decades, first ascending rapidly, then, in late 2008, dropping precipitously as the world fell into an economic recession (Figure 1.44). While the linkages between these economic fluctuations and globalization are complex, the overarching question remains: Do the positive changes of economic globalization outweigh the negative? Answers vary and are often elusive and incomplete; however, a starting point in world regional geography is to link economic change to social development.

Economic development is commonly accepted as desirable because it generally brings increased prosperity to people, regions, and nations. By conventional thinking, at least, this usually translates into social improvements such as better health care, improved education systems, and more progressive labor practices. However, one of the most troubling expressions of recent economic growth has been the geographic unevenness of prosperity and social improvement. While some regions prosper, others languish and, in fact, fall farther behind more developed countries. As a result, the gap between rich and poor regions has increased over the past several decades, and this economic and social unevenness has, unfortunately, become one signature of globalization. Today, according to the World Bank, about half the people in the world live on less than $2 a day, which is the commonly accepted definition of poverty (Figure 1.45).

These inequities are problematic because of their inseparable interaction with political, environmental, and social issues. For example, political instability and civil strife within a nation are often driven by the economic disparity between a poor periphery and an affluent, industrial core, between the haves and have-nots, causing instability throughout the country, and influencing international economic interac-

Figure 1.42 Colonial Vestiges in Vietnam The red star flag of communist Vietnam flies in front of the Hotel de Ville in Ho Chi Minh City (formerly Saigon). This juxtaposition of the contemporary government's symbol and an artifact of the French colonial period captures the process of decolonialization and independence.

Figure 1.43 Global Terrorism The September 11, 2001 attacks by Al Qaeda terrorists on the World Trade Center, the Pentagon, and the thwarted plan to destroy the U.S. Capitol building resulted in more than 3000 deaths.

Figure 1.44 The 2009 Global Recession Two indicators of the global economic activity, the price of crude oil and the Baltic Dry Index (BDI), which is linked to world shipping activity, reflect the expansion and, more recently, the sudden contraction of the global economy in 2009. The last data points show a slow recovery as of mid-2010.

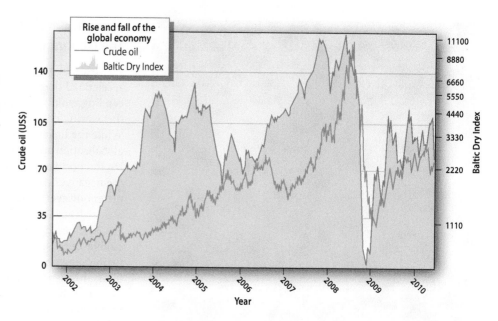

tions. The concept of a developed and affluent economic core and a less-well off periphery has also been applied at a larger global scale in development studies.

More- and Less-Developed Countries Until the 20th century, economic development was centered in North America, Japan, and Europe while most of the rest of the world remained gripped in poverty. This uneven distribution of economic power led scholars to devise a **core–periphery model** of the world. According to this scheme, the United States, Canada, western Europe, and Japan constituted the global economic core of the north, whereas most of the areas to the south made up a less-developed periphery. Although oversimplified, this core–periphery dichotomy does contain some

Figure 1.45 Living on Less than $2 a Day More than half the world's people live on less than $2 a day, which is the UN's definition of poverty. In South Asia, where these workers are making bricks, about three-quarters of the population is considered impoverished.

truth. All the G8 countries—the exclusive club of the world's major industrial nations, made up of the United States, Canada, France, England, Germany, Italy, Japan, and Russia—are located in the Northern Hemisphere. In addition, many critics postulate that the developed countries achieved their wealth primarily by exploiting the poorer countries of the southern periphery, historically through colonial relationships and today with economic imperialism.

As a result, much is made today of "north–south tensions," a phrase implying that the rich and powerful countries of the Northern Hemisphere are still at odds with the poor and less, powerful countries of the south. Over the past several decades, however, the global economy has grown much more complicated. A few former colonies of the south, most notably Singapore, have become very wealthy. In addition, a few northern countries, namely Russia, have experienced economic decline in recent decades. Further, the developed countries of Australia and New Zealand never fit into the north–south division because of their Southern Hemisphere location. For these reasons, many global experts conclude that the designation *north–south* is now outdated and, thus, should be avoided.

The *third world* is another term often used erroneously as a synonym for the developing world. This phrase implies a low level of economic development, unstable political organizations, and a rudimentary social infrastructure. Historically, however, the term came from the Cold War vocabulary used to describe countries that were independent and neither allied with the capitalist and democratic first world or the communist second world superpowers of the Soviet Union and China, thus had little to do with levels of economic development. Today, because the Soviet Union no longer exists and China has changed its economic orientation, the term *third world* has lost its original political meaning. In this book, therefore, we avoid that term and instead use relational terms that capture the complex spec-

EXPLORING GLOBAL CONNECTIONS   A Closer Look at Globalization

Globalization comes in many shapes and forms as it connects far-flung people and places. While many of these interactions are expected and common knowledge, such as the global reach of multinational corporations, other global connections are more surprising (Figure 1.6.1). Who would expect to find Australian firefighters dowsing California wildfires, or Russians investing in Thailand's coastal resorts, or Bronx hip hop music becoming the favored voice of Europe's youth?

Indeed, global connections are complex and ubiquitous—so much so that an understanding of the many different shapes, forms, and scales of these interactions is a key component of the study of global geography. To complement that study, each chapter contains an *Exploring Global Connections* sidebar that examines a wide variety of topics. More specifically they are:

Figure 1.6.1 Exploring Global Connections By definition globalization means there are new and different interactions between far-flung places around the world, and examining those relationships is an important part of world regional geography.

If there's one symbol of modern globalization that is understood by all, it is the shipping container, an invention of the 1970s that changed the way goods are transported on both land and sea.

---

trum of economic and social development—*more-developed country (MDC)* and *less-developed country (LDC)*. The global pattern of more- and less-developed countries can be inferred from a map of gross national income (Figure 1.46), one of several indicators used to assess development and economic wealth.

Indicators of Economic Development   The terms *development* and *growth* are often used interchangeably when referring to international economic activities. There is, however, value in keeping them separate. *Development* has both qualitative and quantitative dimensions. Common dictionary definitions use phrases such as "expanding or realizing potential" and "bringing gradually to a fuller or better state." When we talk about economic development, then, we usu-

ally imply structural changes, such as a shift from agricultural to manufacturing activity that also involves changes in the allocation of labor, capital, and technology. Along with these changes are assumed improvements in standard of living, education, and political organization. The structural changes experienced by Southeast Asian countries such as Thailand and Malaysia in the past several decades illustrate this process.

Growth, in contrast, is simply the increase in the size of a system. The agricultural or industrial output of a country may grow, as it has for India in the past decade, and this growth may—or may not—have positive implications for development. Many growing economies, in fact, have actually experienced increased poverty with economic expansion. When something grows, it gets bigger; when it develops, it

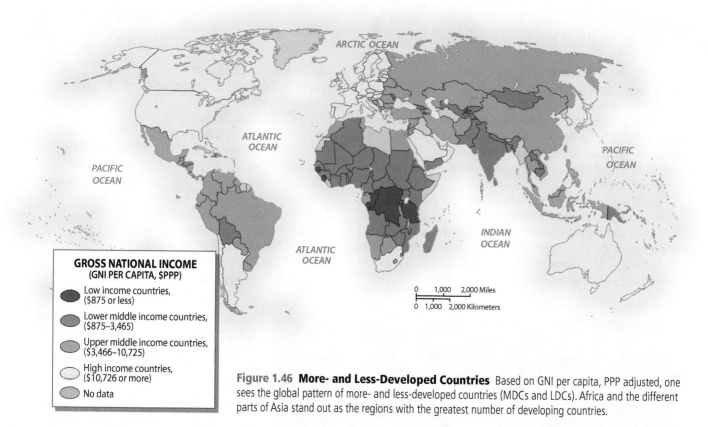

Figure 1.46 More- and Less-Developed Countries Based on GNI per capita, PPP adjusted, one sees the global pattern of more- and less-developed countries (MDCs and LDCs). Africa and the different parts of Asia stand out as the regions with the greatest number of developing countries.

improves. Critics of the world economy are often heard to say that we need less growth and more development.

In this book, each of the regional chapters includes a table of both economic and development indicators (Table 1.2). A few introductory comments are necessary to explain these data.

Gross Domestic Product and Income The traditional measure of the size of a country's economy is the value of all final goods and services produced within its borders, called the **gross domestic product (GDP)**. When combined with net income from abroad, this domestic income constitutes a country's **gross national income (GNI)** (formerly referred to

TABLE 1.2 Development Indicators for the World's Ten Largest Countries

Country	GNI per capita, PPP 2008	GDP Average Annual % Growth 2000–08	Human Development Index (2007)[a]	Percent Population Living Below $2 a Day	Life Expectancy (2010)[b]	Under Age 5 Mortality Rate (1990)	Under Age 5 Mortality Rate (2008)	Gender Equity (2008)[c]
China	6,010	10.4	0.772	36.3	74	46	21	103
India	2,930	7.9	0.612	75.6	64	116	69	92
United States	48,430	2.4	0.956		78	11	8	100
Indonesia	3,590	5.2	0.734	60.0	71	86	41	98
Brazil	10,070	3.6	0.813	12.7	73	56	22	102
Pakistan	2,590	5.4	0.572	60.3	66	130	89	80
Bangladesh	1,450	5.8	0.543	81.3	66	149	54	106
Nigeria	1,980	2.5	0.511	83.9	47	230	186	85
Russia	15,440	6.7	0.817	<2	68	27	13	98
Japan	35,190	1.1	0.960		83	6	4	100

[a]United Nations, Human Development Report, 2009.

[b]Population Reference Bureau, World Population Data Sheet, 2010.

[c]Gender Equity—Ratio of female to male enrollments in primary and secondary school. Numbers below 100 have more males in primary/secondary school, numbers above 100 have more females in primary/secondary schools.

Source: World Bank, World Development Indicators, 2010.

Figure 1.47 PPP and Local Currencies The concept of purchasing power parity (PPP) is used to generate a sense of the true cost of living for different countries so that economic data can be adjusted for local conditions based upon a common market basket of goods. This outdoor produce market is in Chichicastenango, Guatemala.

as gross national product [GNP]). Although the term is commonly used, GNI is an incomplete and sometimes misleading economic indicator because it ignores nonmarket economic activity such as bartering or household work, and also because it does not take into account ecological degradation or depletion of natural resources. For example, if a country were to clear-cut its forest, an activity that could severely limit future growth if forest resources were in short supply, this cutting would nevertheless increase the GNI for that particular year. Further, diverting educational funds to purchase military weapons might also increase a country's GNI in the short run, but the economy would likely suffer in the future because of its less-well-educated population. In other words, GNI is a snapshot of a country's economy for a specific period, not an infallible indicator of continued vitality or social well-being.

Because GNI data vary widely between countries and are commonly expressed in mind-boggling numbers such as billions and trillions of dollars, a better comparison is to divide GNI by the country's population, thereby generating a **gross national income (GNI) per capita** figure. This way, one can compare large and small economies in terms of how they may (or may not) be benefiting the population. For example, the annual GNI for the United States is over $9 trillion. Dividing that figure by the population of 309 million results in a GNI per capita of around $48,000. Japan has a GNI about half the size of the United States; however, because that country has a much smaller population of 127 million, its unadjusted GNI per capita is about $39,000; thus, one could conclude that the two economies are almost comparable.

An important qualification to these GNI per capita data is the concept of adjustment through **purchasing power parity (PPP)**, an adjustment that takes into account the strength or weakness of local currencies (Figure 1.47). When not adjusted by PPP, GNI data are based on the market exchange rate for a country's national currency as compared to the U.S. dollar. As a result, the GNI data might be inflated or un-

dervalued, depending on the strength or weakness of that currency. If the Japanese yen were to fall overnight against the dollar as a result of currency speculation, Japan's GNI would correspondingly drop, despite the fact that Japan had experienced no real decline in economic output. Because of these possible distortions, the PPP adjustment provides a more accurate sense of the local cost of living. To illustrate, when Japan's GNI per capita is adjusted for PPP, which takes out the inflationary factor, the figure is $35,000, which is lower than the unadjusted GNI per capita figure.

Economic Growth Rates A country's rate of economic growth is measured by the average annual growth of its GDP over a 5-year period, a statistic called *GDP average annual percent growth*. The average growth rate for developing countries such as China, India, and Nigeria is considerably higher than those of the developed countries of the United States and Japan (see Table 1.2). This difference in economic growth rates is expected, given that developing countries are just that—developing; thus one would expect a higher annual growth rate than from a mature, developed economy like that of the United States.

Indicators of Social Development Although economic growth is a major component of development, equally important are the conditions and quality of human life. As noted earlier, the standard assumption is that economic development and growth will spill over into the social infrastructure, leading to improvements in public health, gender equity, and education. Unfortunately, even the briefest glance at the world reveals that poverty, disease, illiteracy, and gender inequity are still widespread, despite a growing global economy. Even in China, which has experienced unprecedented economic growth in recent decades, half the population is still impoverished; in Pakistan, two-thirds live below the poverty line of $2 per day, and in some African countries, that figure approaches 90 percent.

However, there are hints of improvement in some developing countries. For example, the percentage of those living in deep poverty, which the UN defines as living on less $1 per day, has fallen from 28 percent in 1990 to just under 20 percent today. Life expectancy, too, has increased in those countries, rising from 60 in 1990 to 65.

The Human Development Index For the past three decades, the United Nations has tracked social development in the world's countries through the **Human Development Index (HDI)**, which combines data on life expectancy, literacy, educational attainment, gender equity, and income (Figure 1.48). In a December 2009 analysis, the 182 countries that provided data to the UN are ranked from high to low, with Norway achieving the highest score, Australia in second place, and Iceland third (despite, somehow, its economic meltdown of 2008) At the lowest end of the HDI are a handful of African countries, including Central African Republic, Sierra Leone, with Niger in last place. Noteworthy is that second to last place is occupied by Afghanistan, a

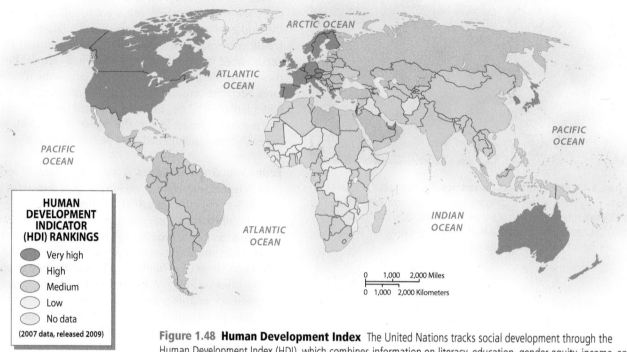

Figure 1.48 Human Development Index The United Nations tracks social development through the Human Development Index (HDI), which combines information on literacy, education, gender equity, income, and life expectancy. This map depicts the most recent rankings assigned to four categories. In the numerical tabulation, Norway, Australia, and Iceland have the highest rankings, while several African countries are lowest in the scale.

country where U.S. economic and military investment is considerable.

Although the HDI can be criticized for using national data that overlook the diversity of development within a country, overall, the HDI conveys a reasonably accurate sense of a country's human and social development; thus, we include country-by-country data in social development tables throughout this book.

Poverty and Infant Mortality The international definition of *poverty* is living on less than $2 per day. *Deep poverty* is defined as existing on less than $1 per day. Granted, the cost of living varies greatly around the world, nevertheless the United Nations has found these definitions work well for measuring poverty and its associated social conditions. While poverty data are usually presented at the national level, the UN and other agencies are attempting to compile data at a local scale in order to better understand—and, hopefully, improve—the economic landscape within a country. The patterns of poverty in the African country of Madagascar provide an instructive example (Figure 1.49).

PERCENT OF POPULATION LIVING BELOW POVERTY LINE

- Less than 58
- 58–71
- 72–79
- 80–86
- 87–97

Figure 1.49 The Landscape of Poverty As is true of most other countries, the distribution of poverty within Madagascar is uneven, with clusters of abject poverty contrasting with regions that are less poor. This map shows that the highest rates of poverty are in the central highlands, where the country's population is concentrated and the density is highest. In contrast, the northern and eastern lowlands are less poor. (*Map adapted from* Where the Poor Are: An Atlas of Poverty, *Center for International Earth Science Information Network, 2006*)

Figure 1.50 Child Mortality The mortality rate of children under the age of 5 is an important indicator of social conditions such as health services, food availability, and public sanitation. In this photo kindergarten children in Jakarta, Indonesia, receive an oral polio vaccine.

Under age five mortality depicts the number of children who die per 1,000 humans within that age bracket, and is another widely used indicator of social conditions. Aside from the tragedy of infant death, child mortality also reflects the wider conditions of a society, namely, the availability of food, health services, and public sanitation. If those factors are lacking, children under age five suffer most, therefore their death rate is taken as an indication of whether a country has the necessary social infrastructure to sustain life

(Figure 1.50). In the social development tables throughout this book, child mortality data are given for two points in time, 1990 and 2008, to indicate whether the social structure improved over that period. Although most countries have seen improvement over the past decades, disturbing differences in child mortality rates still exist on a global level.

Gender Equity The ratio of male to female students enrolled in primary and secondary schools is a measurement of *gender equity*. If the gender equity ratio is below 100, then more males are enrolled in schools than females. Conversely, a ratio over 100 means more females are enrolled than males in primary and secondary schools. Used by the UN as a measure of equality in education, this statistic is linked closely to literacy rates, which in turn are linked to social development. The assumption is that if females are not enrolled in school, a high rate of female illiteracy results in negative social development.

Although sex discrimination takes other forms, such as the preference for male children in India and China or the barriers erected against women in business and politics, the United Nations is currently focusing on correcting the gender inequity in education (Figure 1.51). Specifically, the UN has made neutralizing educational disparity one of its Millennium Development Goals. Gender equity now has higher priority because increasing women's literacy has positive outcomes that complement social development. For example, some studies indicate a strong correlation between lower birthrates and female literacy, probably because literate women are more open to family planning measures.

Besides gender equity, there are many other linkages between economic and social development. This introductory chapter has discussed only a few and on a general scale; the regional chapters of this book examine other issues in more detail.

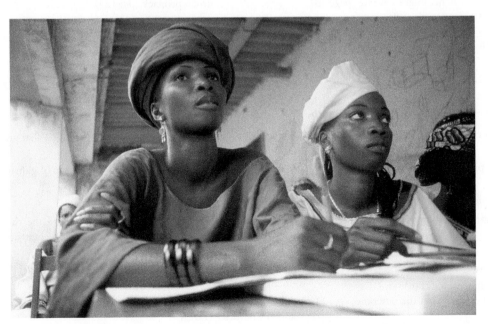

Figure 1.51 Women and Literacy Gender inequities in education lead to higher rates of illiteracy for women. However, when there is gender equity in education, female literacy has a number of positive outcomes in a society. For example, educated women have a higher participation rate in family planning, which usually results in lower birthrates.

Summary

- As the world becomes increasingly interdependent, globalization is driving a fundamental reorganization of cultures and economies through instantaneous global communication, the growth of transnational firms, and the spread of Western consumer habits.

- Because globalization involves both positive and negative changes, it is a controversial and contentious topic. While proponents argue that economic globalization will benefit everyone as regional activities become more efficient in the face of global competition, opponents counter this argument with evidence that only the rich are benefiting and that poorer countries are falling farther behind. The truth, however, is more complicated, as is globalization itself, thus unwise to generalize it as either positive or negative.

- In most regions of the developing world, population and settlement issues revolve around four issues: rapid population growth, family planning (or its absence), migration to new centers of economic activity (both within and outside the region), and rapid urbanization.

- A major theme in cultural geography is the tension between the forces of global cultural homogenization and the countercurrents of local cultural and ethnic identity. Throughout the world, small groups are setting themselves apart from larger national cultures with renewed interest in ethnic traits, languages, religion, territory, and shared histories. Not merely a matter of colorful folklore and local customs, this cultural diversity is translated into geopolitics and linked to agendas of regional autonomy or separatism.

- One issue—terrorism—tops the list of global geopolitical issues and can be triggered by local groups with limited agendas (such as Basque autonomy), as well as larger, more complex terrorist networks (namely Al Qaeda) with wider, more abstract goals. Besides terrorism, there are many other kinds of geopolitical tensions, including ethnic strife, border disputes, and movements for regional autonomy and independence.

- The theme of economic and social development is dominated by one issue—the increasing disparity between rich and poor, between countries and regions that already have wealth and are getting even richer through globalization and those that remain impoverished. Often, blatant inequities in social development, education, health care, and working conditions accompany these disparities in wealth.

Key Terms

areal differentiation (*page 11*)
areal integration (*page 13*)
bubble economy (*page 9*)
colonialism (*page 35*)
core-periphery model (*page 38*)
cultural imperialism (*page 28*)
cultural landscape (*page 13*)
cultural nationalism (*page 29*)
cultural syncretism or hybridization (*page 29*)
culture (*page 27*)
decolonialization (*page 35*)
demographic transition model (*page 22*)

economic convergence (*page 6*)
ethnic religion (*page 30*)
globalization (*page 2*)
gross domestic product (GDP) (*page 40*)
gross national income (GNI) (*page 40*)
gross national income (GNI) per capita (*page 41*)
lingua franca (*page 29*)
nation-state (*page 33*)
net migration rate (*page 23*)
overurbanization (*page 25*)
population pyramid (*page 21*)
purchasing power parity (PPP) (*page 41*)

rate of natural increase (RNI) (*page 18*)
region (*page 13*)
secularization (*page 31*)
squatter settlement (*page 25*)
sweatshops (*page 6*)
total fertility rate (TFR) (*page 18*)
transnational firm (*page 4*)
universalizing religion (*page 30*)
urban form (*page 25*)
urban primacy (*page 24*)
urban structure (*page 24*)
urbanized population (*page 24*)

Review Questions

1. What is globalization? What are the different components or attributes? Give examples of each.

2. Summarize the arguments used by proponents and opponents of globalization.

3. Why is scale important to geographic analysis?

4. Define three different kinds of geographic regions. Give examples of each.

5. How do you calculate the RNI for a country? How and why does RNI vary amongst different countries?

5. What are the four stages of the demographic transition? Explain how they differ from each other, and what the outcome is in terms of RNI.

6. What is *overurbanization* and why is it happening? What are the consequences?

7. What is a workable definition of *culture* in this age of globalization?

8. Define and give examples of *culture hybridity*.

9. What is the global distribution of Islam? What are the two major divisions within Islam? Give examples of countries where each group is dominant.

10. Define GNI. What are its shortcomings as a measure of development?

11. What are the best indicators of social development in Less Developed Countries (LDCs)?

Thinking Geographically

1. Select an economic, political, or cultural activity in your city and discuss how it has been influenced by globalization.

2. Choose a specific country or region of the world and examine the benefits and liabilities that globalization has posed for that country or region. Remember to look at different facets of globalization, such as the environment and cultural cohesion and conflict, as well as the economic effects on different segments of the population.

3. Drawing on information in current newspapers and magazines and on TV and the Internet, apply the concepts of cultural imperialism, nationalism, and syncretism to a region or place experiencing cultural tensions.

4. Select an African country with a colonial past and, first, trace out its pathway of decolonization, and then, second, describe and analyze its contemporary relations with its former colonial master.

5. Using the tables of social indicators in the regional chapters of this book, identify traits shared by countries in which there is a high percentage of female illiteracy. What general conclusions do you reach based on your inquiry?

Bibliography

Boo, Katherine. 2004. "Letter from India. The Best Job in Town: The Americanization of Chennai." *The New Yorker,* July 5, 2004, 54–69.

Friedman, Thomas L. 2009 *Hot, Flat, and Crowded 2.0: Why We Need a Green Revolution—And How It Can Renew America.* New York: Farrar, Straus and Giroux.

Friedman, Thomas L. 2006. *The World is Flat: A Brief History of the Twenty-first Century.* New York: Farrar, Straus and Giroux.

Gilpin, Robert. 2000. *The Challenge of Global Capitalism: The World Economy in the 21st Century.* Princeton, NJ: Princeton University Press.

Lemann, Nicholas. 2010. "Terrorism Studies: Social Scientists Do Counterinsurgency." *The New Yorker,* April 26, 2010, 73–77.

McFalls, Joseph, Jr. 2007. *Population: A Lively Introduction.* 5th ed. Washington, DC: Population Reference Bureau.

Schaeffer, Robert K. 2009. *Understanding Globalization: The Social Consequences of Political, Economic, and Environmental Change.* 4th ed. Lanham, MD: Rowman & Littlefield.

Stiglitz, Joseph E. 2006. *Making Globalization Work.* New York: W.W. Norton.

The World Bank. 2007. *The World Bank Atlas.* Washington, DC: International Bank for Reconstruction and Development/The World Bank.

 Mastering Geography

 MapMaster™

Log in to www.masteringgeography.com for MapMaster™ interactive maps, geography videos, RSS feeds, flashcards, web links, an eText version of *Diversity Amid Globalization,* and self-study quizzes to enhance your study of Diversity Amid Globalization.

MapMaster™ presents 13 Place Name and 13 Layered Thematic interactive maps to help students practice and master their geographic literacy, spatial reasoning, and critical thinking skills.

2
The Changing Global Environment

The Athabasca Glacier in Canada's Jasper National Park has retreated about a mile over the last century because of global warming, and is currently receding at between 70 and 100 feet (20–30 meters) per year.

The human imprint is everywhere on Earth, from the highest mountains to the deepest ocean depths; from dry deserts to lush tropical forests; from frozen Arctic ice caps to the atmospheric layers we breathe. Hundreds of spent oxygen canisters clutter the heights of Mt. Everest, for example, and castoff plastic water bottles litter coastlines and oceans worldwide (Figure 2.1). As deserts bloom in North America with irrigated cotton fields, tropical forests in Brazil are laid waste by logging to create pastures for cattle.

Although many changes to the global environment are intentional and have improved the quality of human life, other changes are inadvertent and have proven harmful to both humans and the environment. Because of the importance of these issues, a study of the changing global environment is central to the study of world regional geography since environmental issues are deeply intertwined with globalization and diversity. The destruction of tropical rain

forests, for example, is a response to international demand for wood products, beef, soybeans, and biofuels. Similarly, global warming is closely linked to world industry, commerce, and consumption.

GEOLOGY AND HUMAN SETTLEMENT: A Restless Earth

Geology shapes the fundamental form of Earth's surface by giving a distinctive character to world landscapes through the physical fabric of mountains, hills, valleys, and plains. The geologic environment is also critical to a wide spectrum of human activities and concerns; the relationship between soil fertility and agriculture or the distribution of mineral resources are examples. Additionally, the geologic environment presents humans with challenges and hazards in the form of devastating earthquakes, unstable landscapes, and explosive volcanoes. Clearly, a basic understanding of the physical processes that shape Earth's surface is crucial to comprehending human settlement in different parts of the world.

Plate Tectonics

The starting point for understanding the dynamic geology of Earth is **plate tectonics**, a geophysical theory that postulates that Earth is made up of a large number of geologic plates that move very slowly across its surface. This theory explains and describes both the inner workings of our planet as well as many surface landscape features. Additionally, plate tectonic theory also explains the world distribution of hazardous earthquakes and volcanoes.

Earth's interior is separated into three major zones with very different physical characteristics. Those three parts are the core, the mantle, and the outer crust. Tectonic plate theory is built on the assumption that a significant heat exchange takes place deep within Earth due to the cooling of the inner core. As a result, molten material is circulated through the mantle area (Figure 2.2).

This exchange of heat occurs in numerous **convection cells**, large areas of very slow-moving molten rock within Earth. Much like a stove provides heat for boiling water in a pan, radioactive decay deep within Earth's core drives these convection cells. As the molten material reaches Earth's surface, it cools and becomes denser, causing the material to sink back into the mantle. Although geophysicists assume that convection cells circulate molten material at different rates, generally speaking that movement is only a few inches or centimeters per year, a rate roughly similar to the growth of human fingernails.

In turn, these interior convection cells drag **tectonic plates**, which are huge, continent-size blocks of rock, in different directions across Earth's surface. On top of the tectonic plates sit assemblages of continents and the ocean

Figure 2.1 The Human Imprint Trash dumped at sea litters an isolated beach in the Outer Hebrides islands of the Atlantic, attesting to the fact that there's probably not an environment on Earth untouched and unaffected by human activities.

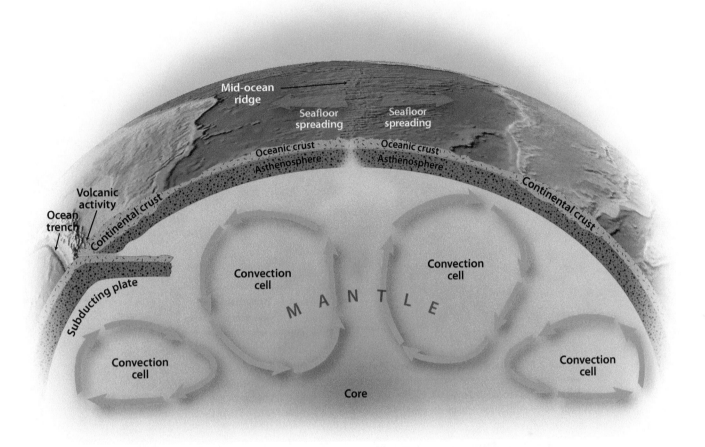

Figure 2.2 Plate Tectonics According to plate tectonics theory, large convection cells circulate molten rock in different directions within Earth's mantle. Near the crust the slow movement of the cells drags tectonic plates away from the mid-oceanic ridges, resulting in the collision of plates in convergent plate boundaries. While the rate of movement differs between convection cells, in general it is only a few inches (or centimeters) per year.

basins. The map of world tectonic plates (Figure 2.3) shows that these plates vary significantly in size. It is important to note that the continents are not identical to the tectonic plates; in fact, rarely is there a close match between the two. More often continents straddle several tectonic plates. For example in western North America, California lies atop two different tectonic plates, the Pacific Plate and the North American Plate, on what is called a **convergent plate boundary**. This means that the two plates are converging, or being forced together by convection cells deep within Earth. The notorious San Andreas Fault, which runs north and south through coastal California, is the actual plate boundary, and this explains why the large cities of Los Angeles and San Francisco are vulnerable to destructive earthquakes (Figure 2.4).

As well, major mountain ranges have resulted from the tectonic convergence or collision of these two plates. The volcanic Cascade Range of Oregon and Washington and the massive Sierra Nevada of California are two examples. Similarly, in Latin America, the Andes Mountains are also prod-

ucts of two colliding plates, the eastward-moving Nazca Plate and the westward-moving South American Plate.

Often in these collision zones one tectonic plate dives below another, creating a **subduction zone** characterized by deep trenches where the ocean floor has been pulled downward by tectonic movement. Subduction zones exist off the western coast of South America, the northwest coast of Oregon, Washington, and Alaska, and also near the Philippines, where the Mariana Trench forms the world's deepest ocean depths at 35,000 feet (10,700 meters). These subduction zones are also the location for Earth's most powerful earthquakes, as illustrated by the 8.8 magnitude Chile quake of 2009 and the 9.2 magnitude Alaska quake of 1964.

In other parts of the world, tectonic plates move in opposite directions, forming a **divergent plate boundary**. As plates diverge, magma usually flows from Earth's interior, creating mountain ranges with active volcanoes. In the North Atlantic, Iceland is formed on a divergent plate boundary that bisects the Atlantic Ocean. In other places,

Figure 2.3 Global Pattern of Tectonic Plates Similar to the fractures of a jigsaw puzzle, Earth's tectonic plates vary in size and shape. Where plates collide, earthquakes and volcanoes are common, as are folded and faulted mountain ranges. In other areas, where one plate dives below another, deep oceanic trenches result, as is the case off the coast of South America and in the western Pacific Ocean.

divergent boundaries form deep depressions, or **rift valleys,** such as that occupied by the Red Sea between northern Africa and Saudi Arabia. To the west, in Africa, a splinter of this boundary has created the extensive African rift, a part of which is the famous Olduvai Gorge, where tectonic activity has preserved the earliest traces of our human ancestors in volcanic soils.

Geologic evidence suggests that some 250 million years ago all the world's plates were tightly consolidated into a supercontinent centered on present-day Africa. Through time, this large area, called *Pangaea,* was broken up as convection cells moved the tectonic plates apart. A hint of this former continent can be seen in the jigsaw puzzle fit of South America to Africa, and of North America to Europe.

Although tectonic plate theory explains many of the world's large mountain ranges, it does not account for all highlands. Although both the Himalaya and Alpine mountain ranges were created by the colliding forces of tectonic plates, there are also many mountain ranges far removed from tectonic boundaries. In North America, the Rocky Mountains serve as an illustration, as do the Ural Mountains

Figure 2.4 The San Andreas Fault Zone in California A string of lakes and reservoirs traces the notorious San Andreas Fault in coastal California. This view is looking north, with San Francisco and the Golden Gate visible in the upper right. When combined with other faults in the area, the Bay area has 63% chance of suffering a major earthquake in the next 30 years.

Figure 2.5 The World's Mountains Many, but not all, of the mountainous areas of the world are created by the collision of tectonic plates, examples being the Alps of Europe, the Andes of South America, and the Himalayas of South Asia. However, some significant mountains, such as the Rockies of North America, are relatively far from current tectonic boundaries, illustrating that tectonic stresses and strains are transmitted long distances in Earth's crust.

in the center of Russia (Figure 2.5). This reminds us that local geologic forces also play an important role in shaping the landscape.

Geologic Hazards: Earthquakes and Volcanoes

Although floods and hurricanes usually take a higher human toll than geologic hazards, nonetheless earthquakes and volcanoes can have a major impact on human settlement and activities. In January 2010, for example, over 230,000 people died from a magnitude 7.0 earthquake in Haiti, and although deaths were much lower from a stronger quake (8.8 magnitude) in Chile several weeks later, millions became homeless and the country's economy was in shambles (Figure 2.6). The vastly different effects of those two quakes underscore the

fact that vulnerability to geologic hazards differs considerably around the world.

The most vulnerable societies are those where urbanization has taken place rapidly and recently, creating situations where much of the population dwells in substandard housing. Tragically, even if reasonable building codes and construction standards exist, enforcement is often lax, leading to shoddy, hazardous buildings. Another variable is the ability of a society to respond immediately after an earthquake with medical care, search and rescue operations, and the provision of food and shelter for its population. Since these activity resources are often a function of the relative wealth of a country, poorer countries are generally more susceptible to disaster than richer ones. At a global scale, this means that billions of people in the fast growing cities of the Caribbean, Southwest, South, Southeast, and East Asia—all of whom live in active seismic zones—are vulnerable to a geologic disaster (Figure 2.7).

However, this does not mean that North Americans are immune to geologic disaster. Mentioned earlier is the vulnerability of San Francisco and Los Angeles to a large earthquake. Even with high building standards and rigorous code enforcement, estimates are that 10 to 30 thousand deaths will result when one of those cities experiences a major earthquake. A similarly high toll can be expected from a major quake in other vulnerable cities, namely Portland, Seattle, and Salt Lake City. Even Midwestern and East Coast cities are vulnerable, although earthquakes are rare, yet the regional geology of those areas is capable of producing a catastrophic quake.

In addition to earthquakes, volcanic eruptions are also found along most tectonic plate boundaries and can also cause major destruction. In 1985, for example, a volcanic eruption resulted in 23,000 deaths in Colombia, South America. In some cases eruptions can be predicted days in advance, which usually provides enough time for evacuation. During the 1991 eruption of Mt. Pinatubo in the Philippines, 60,000 people were evacuated, although 800 did die in the disaster (Figure 2.8). Because of their

Figure 2.6 Earthquake Damage in Haiti In January 2010 Haiti was devastated by a magnitude 7.0 earthquake that killed an estimated 230,000 people, injured a similar amount, and left a million Haitians homeless.

Figure 2.7 Global Earthquakes and Volcanoes The distribution of earthquakes and volcanoes is closely associated with tectonic plate boundaries. The circum-Pacific zones of activity, from the western Americas (both North and South) to East Asia is particularly active and is often referred to as the Pacific Rim of Fire. Another dangerous zone runs east-west, from northern South Asia to Mediterranean Europe. Between these two active earthquakes, billions of the world's population are at risk from destructive earthquakes.

predictability, the loss of life from volcanoes is generally a fraction of that from earthquakes. In the 20th century, an estimated 75,000 people were killed by volcanic eruptions while approximately 1.5 million died in earthquakes.

Unlike earthquakes, volcanoes also provide some benefits to people. In Iceland, New Zealand, and Italy, geothermal activity produces energy to heat houses and power factories. In other parts of the world, such as the islands of Indonesia, volcanic ash has enriched soil fertility for food crops. Additionally, local economies benefit from tourists attracted by scenic volcanoes in such places as Hawaii, Japan, and the Pacific Northwest.

Figure 2.8 Volcanic Eruptions Active volcanoes are also associated with plate tectonic borders throughout the world. Unlike earthquakes, there are usually a string of precursors before volcanic eruptions, allowing time for humans to evacuate the danger zone. This dramatic photo is from the 1991 eruption of Mt. Pinatubo in the Philippines.

GLOBAL CLIMATES: A Troublesome Forecast

Human settlement and food production are closely linked to patterns of local weather and climate. Where it is dry, such as in the arid parts of Southwest Asia, life and landscape differ considerably from the wet tropical areas of Southeast Asia. This is because people in different parts of the world adapt to weather and climate in widely varying ways, depending on their culture, economy, and technology. Although some desert areas of California are covered with high-value irrigated agriculture that produces vegetables for the global marketplace year around, most of the world's arid regions support very little agriculture and barely participate in global commerce. Moreover, when drought hits one portion of the world, such as Russia's grain belt or Africa's Sahel, the socioeconomic repercussions are felt throughout the world. As a result, climate links us together in our globalized economy, providing opportunities for some, hardships for others, yet challenges for all in the struggle to supply food and shelter.

Additionally, one of the most pressing problems facing the world today is that human activities are changing Earth's climate through global warming. Just what the future will bring is not entirely clear. However, even if the forecast is uncertain, there is little question that many forms of life—including humans—will face difficulties adjusting to the changes brought about by global warming (Figure 2.9).

Climatic Controls

Although weather and climate differ tremendously around the world, an accepted set of atmospheric processes control and influence meteorological conditions. More specifically, there are five main factors that explain differences in global weather and climate—solar energy, latitude, interaction between land and water, world pressure systems, and global wind patterns.

Solar Energy Both the surface of Earth and the atmosphere immediately above it are heated by energy from the Sun as our planet revolves around that large star. Solar energy is one of the most important variables producing different world climates; it explains, for example, the great differences between tropical climates near the equator and the cold climates closer to the poles.

Most incoming solar energy, or **insolation**, is absorbed by Earth's land and water surfaces. These surfaces, in turn, heat the lower atmosphere through the process of reradiation. This reradiated energy is trapped by clouds and water moisture in the air adjacent to Earth, providing a warm envelope that makes life possible on our planet. Because there is some similarity between this process and the way a garden greenhouse traps sunlight to make that structure's interior warmer than the outside, this natural process of atmospheric heating is known as the **greenhouse effect** (Figure 2.10). Were it not for this process, Earth would be far too cold for human habitation. More specifically, with-

Figure 2.9 Polar Bears Threatened by Global Warming Ice floes are an important part of the polar bear's habitat. Because Arctic ice is melting more rapidly now due to global warming, the 20,000 bears living in the wild face an uncertain future. Recently, polar bears have been reported drowning trying to swim long distances between ice sheets.

out the greenhouse effect our climate would be much like that on Mars.

Latitude Because of the curvature of Earth, the highest amounts of insolation are received in the equatorial region, the area between the equator and 23.5° north and south latitude. Poleward of this equatorial region, Earth receives less insolation. As a result, not only are the tropics much warmer than the middle or high latitudes, but there is also a buildup of heat energy that must be redistributed through other processes, namely global wind systems, ocean currents, and even massive tropical storms, typhoons and hurricanes (Figure 2.11).

Interaction between Land and Water Because land and water differ in their abilities to absorb and reradiate insolation, the global arrangement of oceans and continents is a major influence on world climates. Land areas heat and cool faster than bodies of water, which explains why temperature extremes such as hot summers and cold winters are always found away from coasts. Conversely, because water bodies retain solar heat longer than land areas, oceanic or maritime climates usually have moderate temperatures without the seasonal extremes found inland. The climatic characteristics of land and water differ so much that geographers use the term **continentality** to describe inland climates with hot summers and cold, snowy winters such as those found in interior North America and Russia. In contrast, **maritime climates,** or those close to the ocean, generally have cool, cloudy summers (Oregon, Washington, and British Columbia are good examples), with winters that are cold but lack the extreme subfreezing temperatures of interior locations.

Figure 2.10 Solar Energy and the Greenhouse Effect The greenhouse effect is the trapping of solar radiation in the lower atmosphere, resulting in a warm envelope surrounding Earth.

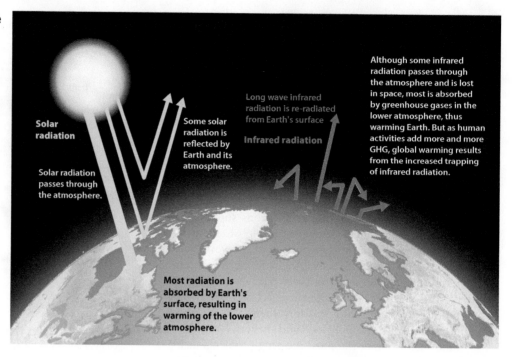

Solar radiation

Solar radiation passes through the atmosphere.

Some solar radiation is reflected by Earth and its atmosphere.

Long wave infrared radiation is re-radiated from Earth's surface

Infrared radiation

Although some infrared radiation passes through the atmosphere and is lost in space, most is absorbed by greenhouse gases in the lower atmosphere, thus warming Earth. But as human activities add more and more GHG, global warming results from the increased trapping of infrared radiation.

Most radiation is absorbed by Earth's surface, resulting in warming of the lower atmosphere.

Global Pressure Systems The uneven heating of Earth due to latitudinal differences and the arrangement of oceans and continents produces a regular pattern of high- and low-pressure cells that, in turn, drive the world's wind and storm systems (Figure 2.12). To illustrate, the interaction between high- and low-pressure systems in the North Pacific produces the storms that are driven onto the North American continent in both winter and summer. Similar processes in the North Atlantic produce winter and summer weather for Europe.

Farther south in the subtropical zones, large oceanic cells of high pressure cause different conditions. These high-pressure cells expand during the warm summer months because of the subsidence of warm air from the equatorial regions. As they enlarge, the cells produce the warm, rain-less summers of the Mediterranean area of Europe and California. In the equatorial zone itself, summer weather spawns the strong tropical storms known as typhoons in Asia and hurricanes in North America and the Caribbean. The map of global pressure systems shows that this same

Figure 2.11 Hurricanes and Typhoons Strong tropical storms result from the differential heating of Earth's surface and, while often damaging to human settlement, are a natural process of atmospheric physics. This photo was taken in Baja, Mexico during Hurricane Jimena in September 2009.

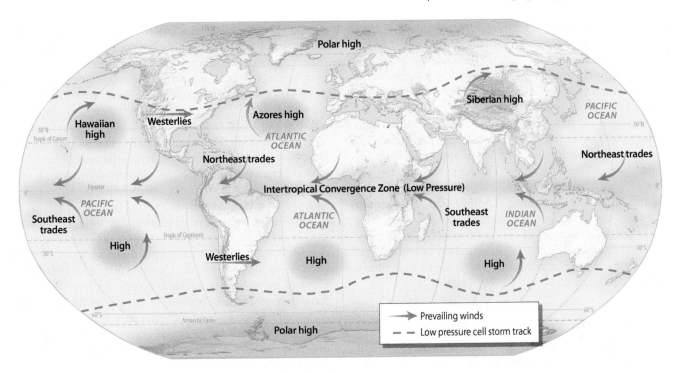

Figure 2.12 Global Pressure Systems The global pattern of high- and low- pressure systems results from the unequal heating of Earth's surface. The Intertropical Convergence Zone (ITCZ) is where the pressure systems and winds of the Northern and Southern hemispheres meet; poleward of the ITCZ, westerly winds move storm systems through the middle latitudes.

alternating pattern of high- and low-pressure systems is also found in the Southern Hemisphere.

Global Wind Patterns The pressure systems also produce global wind systems. It is important to remember that air flows from high pressure to low (just as water flows from high elevations to low), thus, winds flow away from high-pressure and into low-pressure cells. This explains the monsoon in India, for example, which arrives in June as moisture-laden air masses flow from the warm Indian Ocean over land into the low-pressure area above northern India and Tibet. In the winter the opposite is true: As high pressure builds over these same areas, winds flow outward from cold Tibet and the snowy Himalayas toward the low pressure over the warm Indian Ocean.

World Climate Regions

The interaction of the meteorological processes just discussed produces the world's weather and climate. Before going further, though, it is important to note the difference between these two terms. *Weather* is the short-term, day-to-day expression of atmospheric processes: Our weather can be rainy, cloudy, sunny, hot, windy, calm, or stormy all within a short time period. This ever-changing weather is measured at regular intervals each day, often hourly. Data are

then compiled on temperature, pressure, precipitation, humidity, and so on; and, over a period of time, statistical averages from these daily observations provide a quantitative picture of what are statistically common conditions. From these data, a sense of a regional *climate* is generated. Usually at least 30 years of daily weather data are required before climatologists and geographers construct a picture of an area's climate. In summary, weather is the short-term expression of highly variable meteorological processes, whereas climate is the long-term, average conditions. Or as weather pundits like to say, "climate is what you expect; weather is what you get" (see "Geographic Tools: Reconstructing Climates of the Past").

Where similar conditions prevail over a larger area, boundaries are drawn cartographically around that area, which is then called a **climate region**. Knowing the climate type for a specific part of the world not only conveys a clear sense of average rainfall and temperatures, but also allows larger inferences about human activities and settlement. If an area is categorized as desert, then we infer that rainfall is so limited that any agricultural activities require irrigation. In contrast, if we see an area characterized by the climatic designation for tropical monsoon, we know there are warm temperatures and adequate amounts of rainfall for agriculture.

A standard scheme of climate types is used throughout this book, and each regional chapter contains a map showing the different climate regions in some detail. Figure 2.13 shows these climatic regions for the world. The regional climate maps also contain **climographs**, graphs of average high and low temperatures and precipitation for an entire year at a specific location. In Figure 2.13 the climate of Cape Town, South Africa, is presented as an example. Two lines for temperature data are presented on each climograph: The upper one plots average high temperatures for each month, while the lower shows average low temperatures. These monthly averages convey a good sense of what typical days might be like during different seasons. Besides temperatures, climographs also contain bar graphs depicting average monthly precipitation. Not only is the total amount of rain and snowfall important, but also the seasonality of this precipitation provides valuable information for making inferences about agriculture and food production.

Global Warming

Human activities connected with economic development and industrialization are changing the world's climate in ways that will have significant consequences for all living organisms, be they plants, animals, or human. More specifically, **anthropogenic**, or human-caused, pollution of the lower atmosphere is increasing the natural greenhouse effect so that worldwide **global warming**—an increase in the temperature of Earth's atmosphere—is taking place. This warming, in turn, may change rainfall patterns so that some marginal agricultural areas become increasingly arid; melt polar ice caps, causing a rise in sea levels that will threaten coastal settlement; increase the number of heat waves that strike urban areas, causing death from heat stroke; and possibly lead to a greater intensity in tropical storms. In addition, plants and animals, both terrestrial and oceanic, will also experience changes to their environment. While some will probably become extinct, others will have to migrate to find more familiar conditions.

Moreover, because of climate change from global warming, the world may experience a dramatic change in food production regions. Whereas some prime agricultural areas, such as the lower Midwest of North America, may suffer because of increased dryness, other areas, such as the Russian steppes, may actually become better suited for agriculture. Although it is too early to tell when these changes may occur, there is little question that these climate changes will have a dramatic effect on human settlement, world trade, and global food supplies.

Figure 2.13 World Climate Regions A standard scheme, called the *Köppen system*, after the Austrian geographer who devised it in the early 20th century, is used to describe the world's diverse climates. Combinations of letters refer to the general climate types, and precipitation and temperature characteristics are given for each type. Specifically, the *A* climates are tropical, the *B* climates are dry, the *C* climates are generally moderate and are found in the middle latitudes, and the *D* climates are associated with continental and high-latitude locations.

A WET CLIMATES

- **Af-Am** Tropical rainy and Tropical monsoon
- **Aw** Tropical wet and dry and savanna

B DRY CLIMATES

- **BS** Steppe
- **BW** Desert

C MILD MIDLATITUDE CLIMATES

- **Ca** Humid subtropical
- **Cb** Marine west coast
- **Cs** Mediterranean

D CONTINENTAL MIDLATITUDE CLIMATES

- **Da** Humid continental, with dry season, warm summer
- **Db** Humid continental, with dry season, cool summer
- **Dc** Subarctic

E POLAR CLIMATES

- **ET** Tundra
- **EF** Ice cap

F HIGHLAND

- **H** Complex mountain climates

Causes of Global Warming As noted, the natural greenhouse effect provides us with a warm atmospheric envelope that supports human life. This warmth comes from the trapping of incoming and outgoing (or re-radiated) solar radiation by an array of natural greenhouse gases in the atmospheric layer closest to Earth. Although natural greenhouse gases have varied somewhat over long periods of geologic time, they were relatively stable until recently. However, within the past 130 years, coincidental with the Industrial Revolution in Europe and North America, the composition and amount of those greenhouse gases have changed dramatically, primarily from the burning of fossil fuels. As a result, the average temperature for Earth has increased markedly over the past century (Figure 2.14).

Four major greenhouse gases account for the bulk of this change:

1. *Carbon dioxide (CO$_2$)* accounts for more than half of the human-generated greenhouse gases. The increase in atmospheric CO$_2$ is primarily a result of burning fossil fuels such as coal and petroleum. To illustrate, in 1860 atmospheric CO$_2$ was measured at 280 parts per million (ppm). Today it is around 390 ppm, and it is projected to exceed 450 ppm by 2050, assuming that fossil fuels remain a major source for the world's energy needs.

2. *Chlorofluorocarbons (CFCs)* make up nearly 25 percent of the human-generated greenhouse gases and come mainly from widespread use of aerosol sprays and refrigeration (including air conditioning). Although CFCs have been banned in North America and most of Europe, they are still increasing in the atmosphere at the rate of 4 percent each year. These gases are highly stable and reside in the atmosphere for a long time, perhaps as long as 100 years. As a result, their role in global warming is highly significant. Recent research has shown that a molecule of CFC absorbs 1,000 times more infrared radiation from Earth than a molecule of CO$_2$.

3. *Methane (CH$_4$)* has increased 151 percent since 1750 as a result of vegetation burning associated with rainforest clearing, anaerobic activity in flooded rice fields, cattle and sheep effluent, and leakage from pipelines and refineries connected with natural gas production

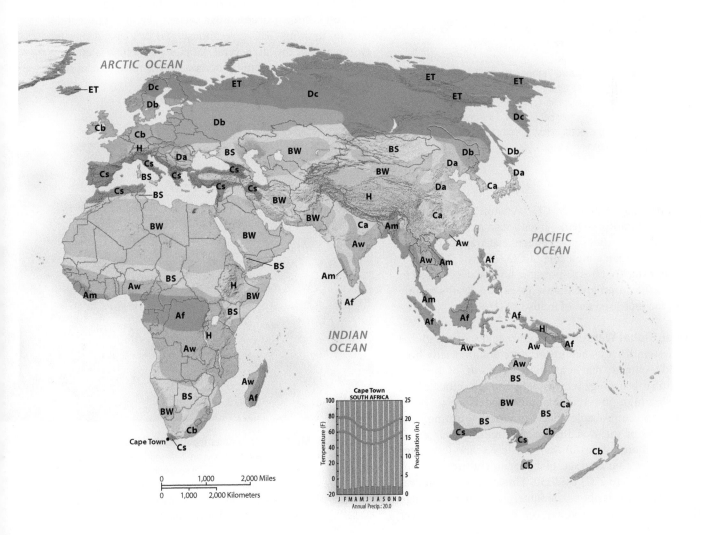

1000 Years of Changes in Carbon Emissions, CO₂ Concentrations and Temperature

Figure 2.14 Increase in CO₂ and Temperature These two graphs show the relationship between the rapid increase of CO_2 in the atmosphere and the associated rise in average annual temperature for the world. The graphs go back 1,000 years and show both CO_2 and temperature to have been relatively stable until the recent industrial period, when the burning of fossil fuels (coal and oil) began on a large scale.

(Figure 2.15). Currently, CH_4 accounts for about 16 percent of anthropogenic greenhouse gases, and each molecule is 23 times more effective at trapping atmospheric heat than a molecule of CO_2 (Figure 2.15).

4. *Nitrous oxide* (N_2O) is responsible for just over 5 percent of human-caused greenhouse gases and results mainly from the increased use of industrial fertilizers.

Effects of Global Warming The complexity of the global climate system leaves some uncertainty about exactly how the world's climate may change as a result of human-caused global warming. Increasingly, though, climate scientists using high-powered computer models are reaching consensus on the probable effects of global warming. Unless countries of the world drastically reduce their emission of greenhouse gases in the next few years, computer models predict that average global temperatures will increase 2 to 4°F (1 to 2°C) by 2030. This may not seem dramatic at first but it is about the same magnitude of change as the cooling that caused the ice age glaciers to cover

much of Europe and North America 30,000 years ago. More problematic is that this temperature increase is projected to double by 2100.

As mentioned, this climate change could cause a shift in major agricultural areas. For example, the Wheat Belt in the United States might receive less rainfall and become warmer and drier, endangering grain production as we know it today. While more northern countries, such as Canada and Russia, might experience a longer growing season because of global warming, the soils in these two areas are not nearly as fertile as in the United States. As a result, food experts are predicting a decrease in the world's grain production by 2030. In addition, the southern areas of the United States and the Mediterranean region of Europe can expect a warmer and drier climate that will demand even more irrigation for crops.

Warmer global temperatures will also cause sea levels to rise as oceans warm and polar ice sheets and mountain glaciers melt. Currently, projections are for an increase of at least 3.3 feet (1 meter) by 2100. Although this may not seem like much, even the smallest increase will endanger low-lying island nations throughout the world as well as coastal areas in Europe, Asia, and North America (Figure 2.16).

Globalization and Global Warming: The International Debate on Limiting Greenhouse Gases The international debate on limiting GHG (greenhouse gas) has passed through two phases in the last several decades and is now is entering a third, a stage that many experts say is the most crucial since

Figure 2.15 Methane Emissions from Arctic Wetlands About 10 percent of global methane emissions are released from the Arctic tundra. Although a natural process, these methane emissions have increased with global warming. Some scientists are concerned that the tundra may reach a tipping point where the amount of methane emissions increases dramatically, resulting in a sudden change to the global climate.

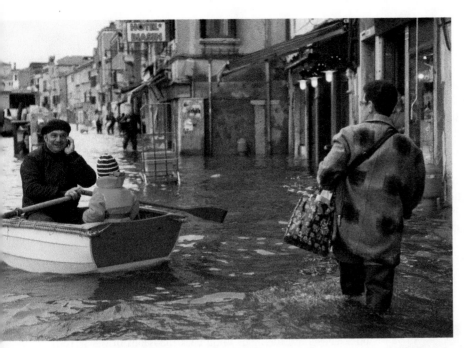

Figure 2.16 Sea Level Rise from Global Warming
Predictions are that global warming will cause Earth's oceans to rise by at least 39 inches (1 meter) by the end of the 21st century because of the melting of ice caps and glaciers, coupled with the thermal expansion of warming ocean waters. Some settlements, such as Venice, Italy, will suffer greatly from sea level rise. Currently, Venice is flooded about four times a year from natural high tides. but with the predicted sea level rise, this flooding may take place at least 30 times a year.

emission reduction actions taken in the next 10 years will determine the extent of global warming for the rest of the century.

The first phase began at the UN-sponsored 1992 Earth Summit in Rio de Janeiro when 167 countries signed an agreement to voluntarily limit their greenhouse gas emissions. However, because none of the signatories reached their emission reduction target, a more formal second phase began with the 1997 meeting in Kyoto, Japan. At that meeting the 30 western industrialized countries that were responsible for most GHG emissions agreed to reduce their emissions back to 1990 levels by the year 2012. Unlike the Rio agreement, which was voluntary, the Kyoto Protocol had the force of international law once it was ratified. But ratification came neither quickly nor easily. One reason was that the United States, which at that time was the largest emitter of greenhouse gas pollution, never ratified the agreement because of political resistance based on concerns that emission regulation would harm the U.S. economy. Additionally, Congress

was uncomfortable with the fact that India and China, as developing countries, were not subject to any kind of emissions restrictions even though they had substantial and increasing emissions (Table 2.1).

Despite resistance from the U.S. government, the Kyoto Protocol became international law in early 2005 when Russia ratified the agreement. But even with the political change from presidential administrations that opposed Kyoto (Bush) to one supporting it (Obama), U.S. congressional opposition remained strong. There were also problems with Kyoto at a global scale, namely because most signatories were not on track to meet their 2012 emission reduction targets. As well, when China, which, to repeat, was not bound by Kyoto, surpassed the United States as the largest GHG emitter in 2008, it became increasingly clear that the 1997 agreement had to be fundamentally revised.

Thus, the third phase of international emission reduction negotiations has begun with a series of meetings to con-

TABLE 2.1 The World's Major CO_2 Polluters				
Country	Total CO_2 Emissions in MMT[a] (2008)[b]	Percent Change (1998–2008)	Percent of World Total, CO_2 Emissions	Per Capita Emissions of CO_2, Metric Tons
China	6,533	65	21	4.9
United States	5,832	4	19	19.1
Russia	1,729	18	6	12.3
India	1,494	64	5	1.3
Japan	1,214	9	4	9.5
Germany	828	−5	3	10.0
World	30,377	32	58% of world total	4.5

[a]Million metric tons.
[b]The most current and compatible international data from the Energy Information Administration (EIA) are for 2008.

GEOGRAPHIC TOOLS   **Reconstructing Climates of the Past**

Geographers, along with scientists from many other fields, are deeply involved in studying global warming. This research involves not only analyzing modern-day weather records for signs of climate change but also reconstructing the climates of past centuries to provide a longer term view of Earth's weather and climate fluctuations. Because accurate weather instruments have been used only for the last 200 years, a number of tools are necessary to probe into the climate of past centuries, using what are called *climate proxy tools*. These methods have now become refined to the point where they provide a fairly accurate record of global climates going back at least 15,000 years.

Scientists use three main tools to reconstruct past climates: tree-ring analysis, or *dendrochronology*; pollen analysis, or *palynology*;

Figure 2.1.1 Tree Rings and Past Climates Annual growth rings in trees give clues to past climates by showing years when growth was greater or lesser than normal as indicated by the width of the annual tree ring. In this photo there are several years where narrow tree rings may indicate a drought that inhibited tree growth.

and ice-core isotope analysis from the world's glaciers and ice caps. The first two are discussed here.

The annual growth rings of a tree give clues about the growing conditions in a given year. Because trees are sensitive to moisture, a wider growth ring suggests a wetter year, whereas narrower rings imply drier years. Additionally, yearly growth rings also give clues about temperature, with wider growth rings resulting from more moderate temperatures and narrow rings suggesting a harsher (usually colder) year. Rather than cutting down trees to examine the rings, scientists instead extract from the trunk thin cores that contain growth rings showing the complete history of the tree's growth. After these rings are measured precisely under a microscope, they are subjected to a number of statistical tests to assure validity in replicating past climatic conditions.

One obstacle to the use of tree rings for constructing past climates is that most trees live only for several hundred years. So how do scientists use tree rings to go back thousands of years? Logs found in prehistoric dwellings, or dead trees found in bogs or underwater in lakes, can be cored and tree ring chronologies constructed for the period when the tree was living. When cobbled together from various sources, tree-ring chronologies can provide a good sense of the climate back 5,000 years.

The pollen given off by plants, shrubs, and trees is also useful to reconstruct growing conditions hundreds and thousands of years ago. Plants, shrubs, and trees produce pollen as part of their reproductive process, and commonly the fine-grained pollen material is carried by the wind to other plants. Pollen also collects on lake surfaces, and eventually it sinks to the lake bottom where it collects in the mud and is preserved for thousands of years.

Palynologists, then, seek out these prehistoric lakes, many of which are now bogs, and take samples from the lake bottom to retrieve the ancient pollen. Using high-powered microscopes, they then can identify the pollen and link it to specific plant, shrub, and tree species, thus reconstructing the vegetation that covered the landscape thousands of years ago and, by inference, the climate of that period.

Given the need to decipher past climates to better understand global warming, geography students who become acquainted with the methods and tools of climate reconstruction can find rewarding careers with research labs and government agencies doing this kind of work.

struct a new international agreement. While the content of a new agreement is far from clear, many believe (at least in late 2010) it will build on the structure of the Copenhagen Accord, a working document signed by 188 countries at the UN-sponsored Copenhagen meeting in December 2009. The major points of this document are:

- An agreement by the signatories that global warming is an urgent problem, and that they commit themselves to

action based upon ". . . common but differentiated responsibilities and respective capabilities . . . and on the basis of equity." This wording sets the scene for a more flexible document than the Kyoto Protocol, and one more sensitive to achieving equity between traditional western industrial powers and emerging economies such as China and India.

- Further, the Copenhagen signatories agreed action is urgently needed for adapting to the effects of global warming, particularly in the least developed countries, small island states, and Africa. Unlike Kyoto, which was primarily concerned with reducing emissions, Copenhagen recognizes that global warming is already causing hardships for many countries because of more frequent drought, sea level rise, and forest degradation, and that action must be taken soon to help those countries. Equally important is an agreement that western developed countries will provide financial resources to support adaptation.

- In what is referred to as the "portfolio approach," instead of imposing emission regulations from the top down by a UN agency, the Copenhagen Accord recognizes the importance of local, regional, and national policies for emission reduction. In the absence of a national program in the United States, state programs, such as California's emission reduction plan, have become increasingly important

- A very significant component of the Copenhagen Accord is the emphasis placed on reducing GHG emissions from deforestation and forest degradation, particularly from tropical areas where large amounts of CO_2 are emitted during rain-forest cutting. Additionally, developed countries commit themselves to financial resources to help reduce deforestation in emerging economies, a measure that could have profound implications for preserving tropical rain forests.

Despite the progress made with the Copenhagen Accord (and many environmental groups were profoundly disappointed that not more was achieved), significant stumbling blocks remain. Three stand out:

First, China and India have now become significant contributors to global GHG pollution, and yet currently both those countries emphatically reject the notion that they must adhere to an international emission reduction plan because of fear it will injure their growing economies (Figure 2.17). Here the question of equity becomes central, for both China and India still consider themselves developing countries, different in structure, character, and history than the developed economies of the United States, Europe, Russia, and Japan, and therefore think they should be treated differently than those western countries who created the global warming problem by their unrestricted GHG emissions during the 19th and 20th centuries.

Second, the issue of just how much financial aid developed countries will contribute to less developed countries as aid for adaptation to global warming is highly controversial, not simply because of the dollar and cents cost, but also because some developed countries see this foreign aid as a form of scapegoating by developing countries—accusing them of using global warming as an excuse to extort money from richer countries when the causes of their problems are failures within their own governments.

Last, questions are raised as to whether the United Nations is the appropriate agency through which to forge a global warming agreement. Why not, ask some, form a working group of the major polluters (China, United States, Russia, India, Europe) and discuss solutions at that smaller scale instead of involving over 200 UN members? The counterargument, of course, is that global warming affects all countries, large and small, polluter or not, and therefore a global solution is necessary.

WATER:
A Scarce Global Resource

Water is central to human life and our supporting activities, agriculture, industry, transportation, even recreation. And yet water is unevenly distributed around the world, being plentiful in some areas and distressingly scarce in others.

The Global Water Budget

A world map shows that more than 70 percent of the surface area of the world is covered by oceans. As a result, 97 percent of the total global water supply is saltwater and only 3 percent is freshwater. Of the minuscule amount of freshwater on Earth, almost 70 percent is locked up in polar ice caps and mountain

Figure 2.17 China's Energy Needs and Global Warming Emissions Several years ago China surpassed the United States as the largest emitter of greenhouse gases. A major component of this global warming pollution is that China is also the world's largest consumer of coal, most of which fuels the country's growing network of power plants that are needed to supply electricity for the country. Although China has some so-called "clean" coal-fired power plants that reduce emissions, most power generating plants are not. In fact, many lack even the most basic pollution control devices. As a result some experts predict China's greenhouse gas emissions will actually double in the next two decades, a worrisome prospect that could have significant effects on the global climate.

glaciers. Furthermore, groundwater supplies account for almost 30 percent of the world's freshwater, which leaves less than 1 percent accessible from surface rivers and lakes.

Another way to conceptualize this limited amount of freshwater is to think of the total global water supply as 100 liters, or 26 gallons. Of that amount, only 3 liters (0.8 gallon) would be freshwater; and of that small supply, only a mere 0.003 liters, or about half a teaspoon, would be available to humans.

Water planners use the concept of **water stress** to map where water problems exist and, as well, to predict where future problems will occur (Figure 2.18). Water stress data are generated by calculating the amount of freshwater available in relation to current and future population amounts. Africa stands out as a region of high water stress, a region where hydrologists predict that three-quarters of Africa's population will experience water shortages by the year 2025. Other problem areas will be northern China, India, much of Southwest Asia, Mexico, the western U.S., and even parts of Russia. Although global warming may actually increase rainfall in some parts of the world, scientists forecast that in general climate change will aggravate global water problems. Four areas of concern occupy water planners: scarcity, sanitation, access, and management.

Water scarcity Currently, about half the world's population lives in areas where water shortages are common, and, as the population in these areas increases, these water problems will become more acute. Additionally, since 70 percent of the world's freshwater usage is for agriculture, food production will probably decline as water becomes increasingly scarce.

Water sanitation Where clean water is not available, people use polluted water for their needs, resulting in a high rate of sickness and death. As a general statement, polluted water sources are the greatest source of illness and death worldwide. Not surprisingly, the largest source of water pollution is lack of sewage treatment facilities.

Water access By definition, when a resource is scarce, access is problematic, and these hardships take many forms. Women and children, for example, often bear the burden of providing water for family use, and when this means walking long distances to pumps and wells, and then waiting in long lines to draw water, their daily time budget is severely curtailed for other activities such as school or work (Figure 2.19). Given the amount of human labor involved in providing water for crops, it is not surprising that some studies have shown that in certain areas people expend as many calories of energy irrigating their crops as they gain from the food itself.

Ironically, some recent international efforts to increase people's access to clean water have gone astray and, instead, have actually aggravated access problems. Historically, domestic water supplies have been public resources organized and regulated, either informally by common consent, or more formally as public utilities, resulting in free or low

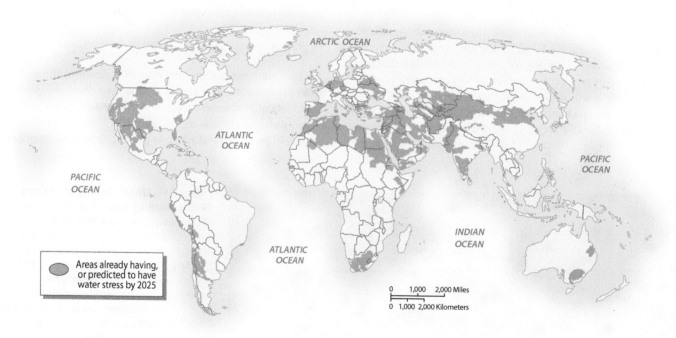

Figure 2.18 Global Water Stress This map shows those parts of the world forecast by the UN to have serious water shortages by the year 2025. In many of the areas, water stress is already evident, namely in northern Africa and Southeast Asia. Global warming will aggravate the water situation as temperatures increase. Africa, in particular, will suffer greatly; projections are that fully 75 percent of its population will face water shortages by 2025.

Figure 2.19 Women and Water In many parts of the world women and young girls spend much of their day providing water for their homes and villages. For young girls this task often interferes with their schooling. These women and girls are fetching water in the Punjab region of India.

cost water. In the recent decades, however, the World Bank and the International Monetary Fund have promoted the privatization of water systems as a condition for providing loans and economic aid to developing countries. While the agency's goals have been laudable, the means have been controversial because, commonly, the international engineering firms that have upgraded rudimentary water systems by installing modern water treatment and delivery technology usually have increased the costs of water delivery to recoup their investment. Although the people may now have access to cleaner and more reliable water, in many cases the price is higher than they can afford, forcing them to either do without or go to other unreliable and polluted sources.

In Cochabamba, Bolivia, the privatization of the water system resulted in a 35 percent increase in water costs. In response, the people rebelled and rioted with demonstrations that became tragically violent. Eventually the water system was returned to public control. Reportedly, however, still today half the city's population is without reliable water.

Water resource management The governmental regulation and allocation of water is usually rife with conflict, often resulting in inefficient uses of this scarce resource as political bodies vie with each to monopolize water supplies. In the western United States, the conflict between or within states is legendary as demonstrated by California internal water politics, or between California and Arizona. In other parts of the arid and semiarid world, where rivers start and end in different independent entities, such as the Nile or the Tigris Rivers, water and war, unfortunately, come close to being synonymous.

HUMAN IMPACTS ON PLANTS AND ANIMALS: The Globalization of Nature

One aspect of Earth's uniqueness compared to other planets is the rich diversity of plants and animals covering its continents. Geographers and biologists think of the cloak of vegetation as the "green glue" that binds together life, land, and atmosphere. Humans are very much a part of this interaction. Not only are we evolutionary products of a specific **bioregion**, an assemblage of local plants and animals (most probably the tropical savanna of Africa), but our human prehistory also included the domestication of certain plants and animals. From this process has come agriculture. Further, humans have changed the natural pattern of plants and animals dramatically by plowing grasslands, burning woodlands, cutting forests, and hunting animals.

However, the pace and magnitude of these changes have accelerated in recent decades, and have led to a crisis in the biological world as ecosystems are devastated and entire species exterminated. Many of these problems can be explained by the globalization of nature and of local ecologies. Until the last half century, tropical forests were primarily homes for small populations of indigenous peoples who made modest demands on local environments for their sustenance and subsistence. But today these same tropical forests are capital for multinational corporations that clear-cut forests for international trade in wood products or search out plants and animals to meet the needs of far-removed populations. For example, Japanese lumber companies cut South American rain forests; German pharmaceutical corporations harvest medicinal plants in Africa; poachers kill North American bears and then sell their gallbladders on the Asian black market as elixirs and sexual stimulants. Unfortunately, the list of destructive human interactions with nature is a long one (see "Global to Local: The Globalization of Bushmeat and Animal Poaching").

Biomes and Bioregions Biome is the biogeographic term used to describe a grouping of the world's flora and fauna into a large ecological province or region; in this book we use the terms **biome** and bioregion interchangeably. These terms are closely connected with climate regions because the major characteristics of a climate region—temperature, precipitation, and seasonality—are also the major factors influencing the distribution of natural vegetation and animals. A brief overview of the most important bioregions follows (Figure 2.20).

Tropical Forests and Savannas

Tropical forests are found in the equatorial climate zones of high average annual temperatures, long days of sunlight throughout the year, and heavy amounts of rainfall. This bioregion covers about 7 percent of the world's land area (roughly the size of the contiguous United States) in Central

Figure 2.20 World Bioregions Although global vegetation has been greatly modified by clearing land for agriculture, settlements, and cutting forests for lumber and paper pulp, there is still a recognizable pattern to the world's bioregions, ranging from tropical forests to Arctic tundra. Each bioregion has its own array of ecosystems, containing plants, animals, and insects.

and South America, Sub-Saharan Africa, Southeast Asia, Australia, and on many tropical Pacific islands. More than half of the known plant and animal species live in the tropical forest bioregion, making it the most diverse of all biomes.

The dense tropical forest vegetation is usually arrayed in three distinct levels that are adapted to decreasing amounts of sunlight from the canopy to the forest floor (Figure 2.21). The tallest trees, around 200 feet (61 meters) high, receive open sunlight; the middle level (around 100 feet, or 31 meters) gets filtered sunlight; the third level is the forest floor, where plants can survive with very little direct sunlight. Even though much organic material accumulates on the forest floor in the form of falling leaves, tropical forest soils tend to be very low in stored nutrients. The nutrients are stored instead in the living plants. As a result, tropical forest soils are not well suited for intensive agriculture.

Figure 2.21 Tropical Rain Forest As fragile as they are diverse, tropical rain-forest environments feature a complex, multilayered canopy of vegetation. Plants on the forest floor are well adapted to receiving very little direct sunlight.

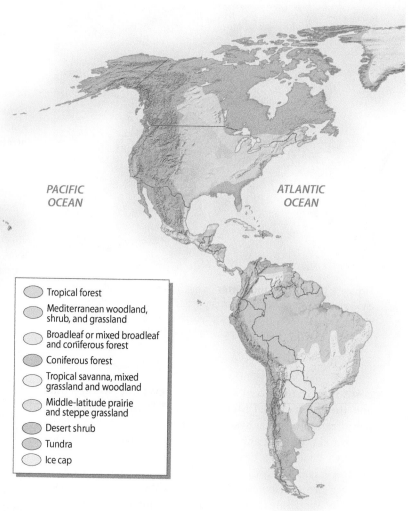

PACIFIC OCEAN

ATLANTIC OCEAN

- Tropical forest
- Mediterranean woodland, shrub, and grassland
- Broadleaf or mixed broadleaf and coniferous forest
- Coniferous forest
- Tropical savanna, mixed grassland and woodland
- Middle-latitude prairie and steppe grassland
- Desert shrub
- Tundra
- Ice cap

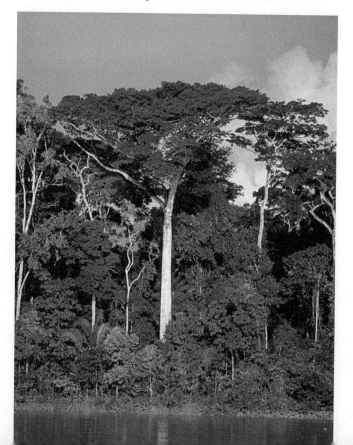

Deforestation in the Tropics

Tropical forests are being devastated at an unprecedented rate, creating a crisis that tests our political, economic, and ethical systems as the world searches for solutions to this pressing problem. Although deforestation rates differ from region to region, each year an area of tropical forest about the size of Wisconsin or Pennsylvania is denuded. Spatially, almost half of this activity is in the Amazon Basin of South America. However, deforestation appears to be occurring faster in Southeast Asia, where some estimates suggest that logging is occurring three times faster than in the Amazon. If these estimates are accurate, Southeast Asia might be completely stripped of forests within 15 years (Figure 2.22).

An important side effect of tropical deforestation is the release of CO_2 into the atmosphere. Current estimates suggest that fully 20 percent of all human-caused greenhouse gas emissions result from cutting and burning tropical forests.

Behind this widespread cutting of tropical forests lies the recent globalization of commerce in international wood products. Reportedly, Japan was the first to globalize its timber business by reaching far beyond its national boundaries to purchase timber in North and South America and South-

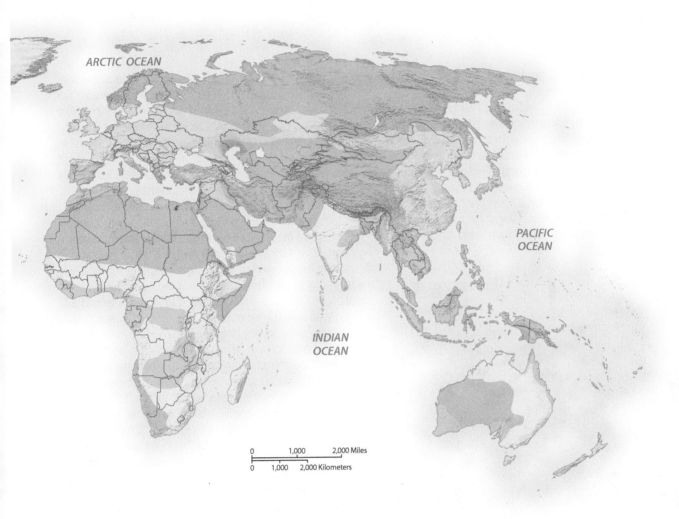

east Asia. This was a two pronged strategy for meeting the increased demand for wood products in Japan while at the same time protecting its own rather limited forests for recreational use. Currently, about one-half of all tropical forest timber is destined for Japan. Unfortunately, much of it is used for throwaway items such as chopsticks and newspapers.

Another factor contributing to the rapid destruction of tropical rain forests is the world's seemingly insatiable appetite for beef. Cattle species originally bred to survive the hot weather of India are now raised on grassland pastures created by cutting tropical forests throughout the tropical world. Unfortunately, because tropical forest soils are poor in nutrients, cattle ranching is not a sustainable activity in these new grassland areas. After a few years, soil nutrients become exhausted, making it necessary to move ranching activities into newly cleared forestland. As a result, more forest is cut, more pasture is created, more soil is destroyed, and the process goes on at the expense of forestlands.

Figure 2.22 Tropical Forest Destruction There are many ill effects resulting from tropical rain-forest destruction including loss of plants and animals, the loss of homeland for native peoples, and the release of large amounts of global warming greenhouse gases. This photo is of a new cacao plantation on Borneo Island, East Malaysia.

A third factor behind tropical forest destruction is that these forest areas are often the last settlement frontiers for the rapidly growing population of the developing world. Brazil has used much of its interior Amazon rain forest for settlement to ease population pressure along its densely settled eastern coast, where rural lands are controlled by powerful landowners. Brazil had a choice: Either address the troublesome issue of land reform and break up the coastal estates or open up the interior rain forests. It chose the path of least resistance, allowing settlers to clear and homestead

GLOBAL TO LOCAL   The Globalization of Bushmeat and Animal Poaching

Today, as a result of globalization, plants and animals in one part of the world are commonly threatened by the desires and decisions of people thousands of miles away. A middle-aged Beijing gentleman's sex life, for example, may determine whether an endangered African rhino lives or dies; Europe's ravenous appetite for fish endangers Africa's treasured lions, leopards, and great apes; and Internet Websites and chat rooms facilitate the poaching of endangered species.

In Africa, the market for wild animal meat—"bushmeat" in local parlance—is a major conservation issue. Justin Brashares, a University of California, Berkeley conservation biologist, has revealed a close connection between international fishing fleets along Africa's west-

Figure 2.2.1 Bushmeat in Africa This bushmeat market in Gabon displays a collection of bush pigs, duikers (small antelope) and monkeys. Wildlife conservation agencies have found the illegal killing and marketing of bushmeat has increased recently as the local population looks for alternatives to seafood resources depleted by European fishing fleets.

ern coast and the increased killing of bushmeat on land. The relationship is simple: When West Africans cannot find affordable fish in local markets, they turn to bushmeat for their protein supply. And this problem has worsened with the recent appearance of European fishing fleets off Africa's coastline. More specifically, the European fish catch off West Africa has increased 20-fold in the past several decades, resulting in fewer fish for local fishermen, thus leading to a higher kill rate of terrestrial bushmeat as great apes, lions, leopards, elephants, and hippos are poached from national parks and game reserves to fulfill the food needs of West Africa's growing population.

Also taking a heavy toll on the world's wildlife are global poaching networks that constitute a black-market activity comparable to the trade in illegal narcotics and weapons. Much of the activity in the trafficking of poached animal parts is thought to be run by international drug cartels and is estimated to be worth around $20 billion a year. In Brazil, for example, more than 20 million animals are taken out of the country illegally each year, making that country one of the top sources for smuggled fauna. According to government officials, poaching has brought 208 species to the brink of extinction. A blue macaw, one of Brazil's most threatened species, with only 200 left in South America, will sell for over $50,000 in Europe. Further, a toucan is worth $7,000 in the United States, and a collection of rain-forest butterflies sells for $3,000 in China.

As well, the Internet poses "one of the biggest challenges facing CITES (the Convention on International Trade in Endangered Species)," said Paul Todd of the International Fund for Animal Welfare (IFAW) in March 2010. The IFAW found that thousands of endangered species are sold on auction sites, classified ads, and chat rooms, mostly in the United States and Europe, but also in China, Russia, and Australia. Much of what is traded is illegal African elephant ivory, but the group also found exotic birds, pelts from polar bears and leopards, and tiger bones and bear bladders that are used as sexual stimulants.

the tropical forestlands of the interior. Many other countries are doing the same, looking at the vast tracts of tropical rain forest as a safety valve of sorts, a landscape that can be used to temporarily deflect the pressures of land hunger by opening up land for migration and settlement.

Deserts and Grasslands

Large areas of arid and semiarid climate lie poleward of the tropics, and here are found the world's extensive deserts and grasslands. Fully one-third of Earth's land area qualifies as true desert, with annual rainfall of less than 10 inches (25 centimeters). In areas receiving more rainfall, grassy plants appear, often forming a lush cover during the wet season. In North America, the midsection of both Canada and the United States is covered by grassland known as **prairie**, which is characterized by thick, long grasses. In other parts

of the world, such as Central Asia, Russia, and Southwest Asia, shorter, less dense grasslands form the **steppe**.

The boundary between desert and grassland has always fluctuated naturally because of changes in climate. During wet periods, grasslands might expand, only to contract once again during drier decades. The transition zone between the two is a precarious environment for humans, as the United States learned during the 1930s, when the semiarid grasslands of the western prairie lands turned into the notorious "Dust Bowl." At that time, thousands of farmers watched their fields devastated by wind erosion and drought—a disaster that led to an exodus from these once-productive lands.

Farming marginal lands may actually worsen the situation, leading to **desertification**, or the spread of desertlike conditions into semiarid areas (Figure 2.23). This has happened on a large scale throughout the world—in Africa, Australia, and South Asia, to name just a few regions. In fact, in the past several decades, an area estimated to be about the size of Brazil has become desertified through poor cropping practices, overgrazing, and the buildup of salt in soils from irrigation. In northern China, an area the size of Denmark became desertified between 1950 and 1980, with the expansion of farming into marginal lands. Historically this region averaged 3 sandstorms a year; today 25 such storms are common each year, with the choking sand and dust traveling eastward into China's large cities.

Temperate Forests

The large tracts of forests found in middle and high latitudes are called *temperate forests*. Their vegetation is different from the low-latitude forests found in the equatorial regions. In temperate forests, two major tree types dominate. One type is softwood coniferous evergreen trees, such as pine, spruce, and fir, which are found in higher elevations and higher latitudes. The second category comprises deciduous trees, which drop their leaves during the winter. Examples are elm, maple, and beech. Because these trees are hardwood, hence harder to mill, they are generally less favored by the timber industry than softwood species.

In North America, conifers dominate the mountainous West, Alaska, and Canada's western mountains, while deciduous trees are found on the Eastern Seaboard of the United States north to New England. There the two tree types intermix before giving way to the softwood forests of Maine and the Maritime provinces of eastern Canada.

In the coniferous forests of western North America, the struggle between timber harvesting and environmental concerns remains controversial. Whereas timber interests argue that increased cutting is the only way to meet high demand for lumber and other wood products, environmental concerns over the protection of habitat for endangered species (the northern spotted owl, for example) have caused the government to make large tracts of forest off-limits to commercial logging (Figure 2.24). Further complicating the future of western forests are global market forces. Many Japanese and Chinese timber firms pay premium prices for logs cut from U.S. and Canadian forests, outbidding domestic firms for these scarce resources. Because these trees are often cut from public lands, this facet of globalization raises an interesting question about the appropriate use of public forests that are maintained by tax money.

In Europe, hardwoods were the natural tree cover in western countries such as France and Great Britain before these once-extensive forests were cleared away for agriculture. In the higher latitudes of Norway and Sweden, coniferous species prevail in the remaining forests. These conifers also populate extensive forests across Germany and Eastern Europe, as well as through Russia into Siberia, creating an almost unbroken landscape of dense forests.

The Siberian forest is a resource that could become a major source of income for financially strapped Russia. Some argue that if the Siberian forests are put on the market for global trade, it will reduce logging pressure on North America's western forests, which, in turn, could make it easier to enact and enforce comprehensive environmental protection in the United States. On the other hand, cutting this large forest would release huge amounts of CO_2 and methane into the atmosphere, aggravating global warming. This example illustrates once again how the multifaceted forces of globalization are intertwined with the fate of local ecosystems.

FOOD RESOURCES: Environment, Diversity, and Globalization

If the human population continues to grow at expected rates, food production must double by 2025 just to provide each person in the world with a basic subsistence diet. Every minute of

Figure 2.23 Desertification Climatic fluctuations and human misuse combine to produce desertification in certain localities, where marginal lands are overcropped or grazed heavily, resulting in expansion of nearby deserts. Globally, many rangelands remain threatened by desertification.

Figure 2.24 Clear-Cut Forest Commercial logging in Washington's Olympic Peninsula has dramatically reshaped this landscape. Throughout the Pacific Northwest, environmental lobbies have successfully restricted logging to protect habitat for endangered species and recreation.

each day, 258 people are born who need food; during that same minute, about 10 acres of cropland are lost because of environmental problems such as soil erosion and desertification. Furthermore, many scientists argue that the interaction between global warming, water problems, and food scarcity will be the defining issues of the next decade (Figure 2.25).

The Green Revolutions

The world's population doubled during the last 40 years of the 20th century and, remarkably, during that same period, global food production also doubled to keep pace with this population explosion. This increase in food production came primarily from the expansion of intensive industrial agriculture into those areas that historically produced only subsistence crops.

More specifically, since 1950, the increases in global food production have come from changes associated with the **Green Revolution**, innovations that involved new agricultural techniques using genetically altered seeds coupled with

high inputs of chemical fertilizers and pesticides. The first stage of the Green Revolution combined three processes: first, the change from traditional mixed crops to monocrops, or single fields, of genetically altered, high-yield rice, wheat, and corn seeds; second, intensive applications of water, fertilizers, and pesticides; and, third, additional increases in the intensity of agriculture by reduction in the fallow, or field-resting time, between seasonal crops.

Since the 1970s, a second stage of the Green Revolution has evolved. This phase emphasizes new strains of fast-growing wheat and rice specifically bred for tropical and subtropical climates (Figure 2.26). When combined with irrigation, fertilizers, and pesticides, these new varieties allow farmers to grow two or even three crops a year on a parcel that previously supported only one. Using these methods, India actually doubled its food production between 1970 and 1992.

However, some argue that the practices associated with the Green Revolution carry high environmental and social costs. Because these crops draw heavily on fossil fuels, there has been a 400 percent increase in the agricultural use of fossil fuels during the past several decades. As a result, Green Revolution agriculture now consumes almost 10 percent of the world's annual oil output. Earlier, cheap oil prices facilitated much of this increased agricultural usage of fossil fuel; but today, higher oil prices raise questions about the sustainability of these revolutionary methods. More to the point, the question is whether these higher energy costs will raise the price of food beyond what people in developing countries can afford.

The environmental costs of the Green Revolution have also been significant, resulting in damage to habitat and wildlife from diversion of natural rivers and streams for irrigation, pollution of rivers and water sources by pesticides and chemical fertilizers applied in heavy amounts to fields, and increased regional air pollution from factories and chemical plants that produce these agricultural chemicals.

There is also evidence that the Green Revolution can bring high social costs and disruption to some areas. Because the financial costs to farmers participating in the Green Revo-

Figure 2.25 Food Supplies and Global Warming This farmer in southwest China gathers water to irrigate his crops during one of the worst droughts in China's history. Most predictions are that droughts like this will become increasingly common as global warming worsens, impacting global food supplies to the point of causing considerable hardship for large populations in Africa and Asia.

Figure 2.26 The Green Revolution in India Because of its large and expanding population, India is a region where food supplies may be a problem in the near future. The country doubled its food production between 1970 and 1992, primarily due to the expansion of rice and wheat yields. Nonetheless, the future of food security in this large country is uncertain. In this photo, a woman is planting rice seedlings in the Rishi Valley of Andhra Pradesh state.

lution are higher than with traditional farming, successful farmers must have access to capital and bank loans to purchase hybrid seeds, fertilizers, pesticides, and even new machinery. For those with high social standing, a family support system, or good credit, the rewards can be great; but for those without access to loans or family support, the toll can be heavy, for traditional farmers cannot compete against those raising Green Revolution crops in the regional marketplace.

In some wheat-growing areas of India, the social and economic distance between the well-off Green Revolution farmers and poor traditional farmers has become a major source of economic, social, and political tension. An area where once all shared a common plight has now become a highly stratified society of rich and poor. These social costs can be condoned only because of the pressing need for food in this rapidly growing country.

Problems and Projections

Even though agriculture has been able to keep up with population growth in the past decades, few experts are confident that this pace will continue. Although the regional chapters of this book include fuller discussion of food and agriculture issues, four general points offer a framework for understanding the world's food security issues:

■ While overall food production remains an important global issue, it is in fact local and regional problems that often keep people from obtaining needed food supplies. To many experts, the issue is not so much global food production as the widespread poverty and civil unrest at local levels that keep people from growing, buying, or receiving adequate food.

■ Political problems are more commonly responsible for food shortages and famines than are natural events such as drought and flooding. Distribution of world food supplies is often highly politicized, starting at the global level and continuing down to the local. Usually food aid goes to political friends and allies, while those allied with enemies go without.

■ Globalization is causing dietary preferences to change worldwide, and the implications of these changes could be profound. Currently two-thirds of the world population is primarily vegetarian, eating only small portions of meat since it is usually beyond their means. However, because of recent economic booms in some developing countries, an increasing number of people in these countries are now regularly eating meat, having moved up the food chain from a subsistence diet based on local resources to a global diet containing a greater amount of meat (Figure 2.27). In many cases this change in diet comes not just from new economic prowess but also from changing cultural tastes and values, as people are exposed to new products through economic and cultural globalization.

There are, however, constraints on the world's ability to supply these new tastes because of the agricultural and environmental support system needed to produce and market meat. According to food experts, the global food production system could sustain only half the current world population if everyone ate the same meat-rich diet of North America, Europe, and Japan because this diet contains three or four times as much meat as the traditional diet of people in developing countries.

■ Most food supply experts agree that the two world regions of greatest concern are Africa and South Asia. Until 1970, Africa was self-sufficient in food, but since that time there have been serious disruptions and even breakdowns in the food supply system. These problems stem from rapid population increase and civil disruption from

Figure 2.27 Cattle Ranching in Brazil Growing global demands for meat are reshaping the world's agricultural landscapes. Cattle ranching in western Brazil's rain forest reflects these changing market conditions, and the practice is also introducing new environmental problems.

tribal warfare. As a result, one of every four people faces food shortages in Sub-Saharan Africa. (Chapter 6 contains more detail on these issues). South Asia's future is also problematic. The United Nations predicts that currently almost 200 million people in South Asia suffer from chronic undernourishment. (Further discussion of these problems is found in Chapter 12.)

There is some good news in this otherwise bleak picture. Because population growth rates are generally declining in the industrializing areas of East Asia and food production there is still increasing, the United Nations predicts that the percentage of undernourished people in that region will actually drop by 5 percent in the next 10 years. Similar gains were made in Latin America because of lower population growth and higher agricultural production. World food experts report that in 2010 the proportion of chronically hungry in South America fell to about 6 percent, half the 1990 rate.

Summary

- Global environmental change is driven by human activities. While some changes are intentional and are beneficial for humankind, such as the irrigation of arid lands to increase the world's food supplies, other environmental changes have resulted in unintentional negative consequences. Global warming from fossil fuel consumption is an example.

- Globalization is both a help and a hindrance to world environmental problems. As a positive force, globalization is central to sharing information and increasing public awareness of environmental issues. In addition, many would argue that globalization facilitates a new willingness of countries to work together under the umbrella of international agreements to resolve environmental problems. Such cooperation has led to international treaties on ocean pollution, global warming, and protection of wildlife species.

- The arrangement of tectonic plates on Earth is not only responsible for diverse global landscapes, but also for earthquake and volcanic hazards that threaten the well-being of billions of humans, particularly in the large cities of developing countries in Asia and South America.

- Climate change and global warming resulting from pollution of the atmosphere by greenhouse gases is a by-product of industrialization, both past and present. A major facet of this problem is the burning of fossil fuels—petroleum and coal—that releases CO_2 into the atmosphere. Historically, the developed countries of Europe and North America were the major greenhouse gas producers; today, however, the developing economies of China and India have become major polluters as well.

- Plants and animals throughout the world face an extinction crisis because of habitat destruction from human activities, economic exploitation, and blatantly illegal poaching activities. Tropical forests are a focus of these problems since they contain the most plant and animal species of any bioregion, yet are threatened by numerous forces including the world's demands for wood products, cattle ranching for global meat-eaters, and resettlement of a country's own people.

- Even though the world's population is growing more slowly than in the past, and food supplies are increasing, there are still serious issues of food security for at least half the world's population. A raft of causes lie behind these problems, including governmental policies emphasizing export crops at the expense of crops fulfilling local food needs; international free trade policies and local protectionism that manipulates food markets; and political turmoil and favoritism that hinders effective food distribution within countries.

Key Terms

anthropogenic (*page 56*)
biome (*page 63*)
bioregion (*page 63*)
climate region (*page 55*)
climograph (*page 56*)
continentality (*page 53*)
convection cells (*page 48*)
convergent plate boundary (*page 49*)

desertification (*page 66*)
divergent plate boundary (*page 49*)
global warming (*page 56*)
greenhouse effect (*page 53*)
Green Revolution (*page 68*)
insolation (*page 53*)
maritime climate (*page 53*)
plate tectonics (*page 48*)

prairie (*page 66*)
rift valley (*page 50*)
steppe (*page 66*)
subduction zone (*page 49*)
tectonic plates (*page 48*)
water stress (*page 62*)

Review Questions

1. Explain the role of convection cells in tectonic plate theory.
2. Describe several kinds of tectonic plate boundaries, along with the landforms and landscapes usually associated with these boundaries.
3. Describe the natural greenhouse effect.

4. How do continental and maritime climates differ? What causes this difference?
5. Which major human activities cause global climate change and warming? More specifically, how have greenhouse gases changed because of these activities?

6. Describe the ecological characteristics of a tropical rain forest.

7. What are the different causes of tropical forest deforestation? How are they linked to globalization?

8. What is *desertification*? Why, and where, is it a problem?

9. Describe the characteristics of the Green Revolution.

10. What are the reasons behind food shortages in most parts of the world?

Thinking Geographically

1. What are the most threatening natural hazards in your region—earthquakes, tornadoes, hurricanes, floods, drought? Do research through local agencies or the public library to learn about disaster preparedness plans for your community.

2. Which climate region do you live in? What are the major weather problems faced by people in your area? How do they adjust to these problems?

3. Visit some of the many Internet websites that relate to global warming. Once you have an overview of the different positions, concentrate on one or two of the most contentious issues, such as the debate within the United States between environmentalists and business interests, or the difference in opinion between developed and developing countries. Discuss the different stakeholders and vested interests holding contrasting views.

4. How has the vegetation in your area been changed by human activities in the past 100 years? Have these changes led to the extinction of any plants or animals or placed them on the endangered list? If so, what is being done to protect them or restore their habitat?

5. Study the globalization of wood products by acquainting yourself with the source areas for different items, such as building lumber, paper, furniture, or other items found in a local import store. More specifically, does the lumber used in construction in your area come from Canada or the United States? Which items in local stores come from tropical forests?

6. Conduct a detailed analysis of the food issues in a foreign country of your choice and answer the following questions. In general, has food supply kept up with population growth? Has the country suffered recently from food shortages or famine? If so, were these shortages the result of natural causes, such as drought or floods, or distribution problems resulting from civil disruption? Which segments of the population have food security, and which segments have recurring problems obtaining adequate food? How is this inequity best explained? Finally, have food preferences or diets changed recently? If so, how and why?

Bibliography

Ecological Society of America. 2007. *Frontiers in Ecology and the Environment*. Special Issue: Ecology in an Era of Globalization. May, 5(4).

Gleick, Peter, et al. 2008 *The World's Water: The Biennial Report on Freshwater Resources, 2008–2009*. Washington, DC: Island Press.

IPCC. 2007. *Climate Change 2007: The Scientific Basis. A Report of Working Group 1 of the Intergovernmental Panel on Climate Change*. New York: United Nations Environmental Programme (UNEP).

IPCC. 2007. *Climate Change 2007: Synthesis Report. Summary for Policymakers. A Report of Working Group 1 of the Intergovernmental Panel on Climate Change*. New York: United Nations Environmental Programme (UNEP).

Mann, Michael, and Lee Krump. 2009. *Dire Predictions: Understanding Global Warming*. Upper Saddle River, N.J.: Prentice Hall.

Paarlberg, Robert. 2010. *Food Politics: What Everyone Needs to Know*. New York: Oxford University Press.

Rosegrant, Mark, et al. 2003. "Will the World Run Dry? Global Water and Food Security." *Environment* 45(7), 24–36.

Shiva, Vandana. 2000. *Stolen Harvest: The Hijacking of the Global Food Supply*. Cambridge, MA: South End Press.

Williams, Michael. 2003. *Deforesting the Earth: From Prehistory to Global Crisis*. Chicago: University of Chicago Press.

Mastering Geography

MapMaster™

Log in to www.masteringgeography.com for MapMaster™ interactive maps, geography videos, RSS feeds, flashcards, web links, an eText version of *Diversity Amid Globalization*, and self-study quizzes to enhance your study of The Changing Global Environment.

MapMaster™ presents 13 Place Name and 13 Layered Thematic interactive maps to help students practice and master their geographic literacy, spatial reasoning, and critical thinking skills.

6
Sub-Saharan Africa

Young boys play soccer on a field overlooking Mazeppa Bay
in Eastern Cape Province, South Africa. Sub-Saharan Africa
is a youthful region, with 43 percent of the population
under 15 years old.

DIVERSITY AMID GLOBALIZATION

Struggling with extreme poverty, Sub-Saharan Africans have experienced few of the benefits of globalization. Yet over the past decade, foreign assistance to the region grew substantially, access to mobile phone technology enhanced communication, and many in the region expressed pride in the fact that Africa hosted its first World Cup in the summer of 2010.

ENVIRONMENTAL GEOGRAPHY

Wood is a main source of energy for this region. Kenyan Professor Wangari Maathai won the Noble Peace Prize for her Greenbelt Movement, which led to the planting of millions of trees by rural women. In areas such as the Sahel, policies that provided ownership or incentives for the protection of trees have resulted in an increase in tree cover.

POPULATION AND SETTLEMENT

Sub-Saharan Africa has the highest infection rates of HIV/AIDS. As a result of this disease, many countries have seen life expectancy rates plummet into the 40s. Yet the population continues to grow at a 2.5 percent rate of natural increase, which is the highest rate for any world region.

CULTURAL COHERENCE AND DIVERSITY

This is a region with large and growing numbers of Muslims, Christians, and animists. With a few exceptions, religious diversity and tolerance has been a distinctive feature of the region.

GEOPOLITICAL FRAMEWORK

Most countries gained their independence in the 1960s. Since then, many ethnic conflicts have resulted as governments struggle for a sense of national unity within the boundaries drawn by European colonialists.

ECONOMIC AND SOCIAL DEVELOPMENT

The Millennium Development Goals created by the United Nations to reduce extreme poverty by 2015 will not be met by most of the states of this region. Yet as global demand for natural resources grows, investors from China, Europe, and North America are eager to extract the region's metals and fossil fuels.

225

Figure 6.1 Sub-Saharan Africa Africa south of the Sahara includes 48 states and one territory. This vast region of rain forest, tropical savanna, and desert is home to 865 million people. Much of the region consists of broad plateaus ranging from 1,600 to 6,500 feet (500 to 2,000 meters) in elevation. Although the population is growing rapidly, the overall population density of Sub-Saharan Africa is low. Considered one of the least developed regions of the world, it remains an area rich in natural resources.

Compared with Latin America and the Caribbean, Africa south of the Sahara is poorer and more rural, and its population is very young. Nearly 865 million people reside in this region, which includes 48 states and one territory. Demographically, this is the world's fastest-growing region (2.5 percent rate of natural increase); in most countries, nearly half the population (43 percent) is younger than 15 years old. Income levels are extremely low: 74 percent of the population lives on less than $2 per day. Life expectancy is only 52 years. This part of the world is known for poverty, disease, violence, and refugees. Overlooked in the all-too-frequent negative headlines are initiatives by private, local, and state groups to improve the region's quality of life. Many states have reduced infant mortality, expanded basic education, and increased food production in the past two decades, yet many economic and political crises still hinder the region's development.

Sub-Saharan Africa—that portion of the African continent lying south of the Sahara Desert—is a commonly accepted world region (Figure 6.1). The unity of this region has to do with similar livelihood systems and a shared colonial experience. No common religion, language, philosophy, or political system ever united the area. Instead, loose cultural bonds developed from a variety of lifestyles and idea systems that evolved here. The impact of outsiders also helped to determine the region's identity. Slave traders from Europe, North Africa, and Southwest Asia treated Africans as chattel; up until the mid-1800s millions of Africans were taken from the region and sold into slavery. In the late 1800s, the entire African continent was divided by European colonial powers, imposing political boundaries that remain to this day. In the postcolonial period, which began in the 1960s, Sub-Saharan African countries faced many of the same economic and political challenges.

When setting this particular regional division, the major question is how to treat North Africa. Some scholars argue for treating the African continent as one world region because the Sahara has never formed a complete barrier between the Mediterranean north and the rest of the African landmass. Regional organizations such as the African Union are modern expressions of this continental unity. Yet North Africa is generally considered more closely linked, both culturally and physically, to Southwest Asia. Arabic is the dominant language and Islam the dominant religion of North Africa. Consequently, North Africans feel more closely connected to the Arab hearth in Southwest Asia than to the Sub-Saharan world.

In this chapter we focus on the states south of the Sahara. We preserve political boundaries when delimiting the region so that the Mediterranean states of North Africa are discussed with Southwest Asia. Sudan—Africa's largest state in terms of area—will be discussed in both Chapters 6 and 7 because it shares characteristics common to both regions. In the more populous and powerful north, Muslim leaders have crafted an Islamic state that is culturally and politically oriented toward North Africa and Southwest Asia. Southern Sudan, however, has more in common with the animist and Christian groups in Sub-Saharan Africa.

The example of Sudan underscores the cultural complexity of the states in this region. In one large state it is not usual for 20 or more languages to be spoken. Consequently, most Africans understand and speak several languages. Ethnic identities do not conform to the political divisions of Africa, sometimes resulting in bloody ethnic warfare, as witnessed in Rwanda in the mid-1990s and in Sudan today. Nevertheless, throughout the region peaceful coexistence among distinct ethnic groups is the norm. The cultural significance of European colonizers cannot be ignored: European languages, religions, educational systems, and political ideas, were adopted and modified. Yet the daily rhythms of African life are often far removed from the industrial or postindustrial world. Most Africans engage in subsistence and cash-crop agriculture. Women in particular are charged with tending crops and procuring household necessities (Figure 6.2). Male roles revolve around tending livestock and the public life of the village and market.

The influence of African peoples outside the region is great especially when one considers that human origins are traceable to this part of the world. In historic times, the legacy of the slave trade resulted in the transfer of African peoples, religious systems and even musical traditions throughout the Western Hemisphere. Even today, African-based religious systems are widely practiced in the Caribbean and Latin America, especially in Brazil. American jazz, Brazilian samba, and Cuban rumba would not exist but for the influence of Africans. The popularity of "world music" has created a large international audience for performers such as Senegal's Youssou N'Dour or South Africa's Ladysmith Black Mambazo. Through music and the arts,

Figure 6.2 Women Farmers in Senegal Senegalese women grow manioc, a drought-resistant staple introduced from the Americas. Throughout Sub-Saharan Africa, subsistence agriculture is still widely practiced, and women are often responsible for tending these crops.

Sub-Saharan Africa has exerted a significant influence on global culture.

The African economy, however, is marginal when compared with the rest of the world. According to the World Bank, Sub-Saharan Africa's economic output in 2008 amounted to less than 2 percent of global output, even though the region contains 12 percent of the world's population. Moreover, the gross national product of just one country, South Africa, accounts for one-third of the region's total economic output. It is the region's grinding poverty and the unnecessary vulnerability of its people that draws the concern of the global community.

Many scholars feel that Sub-Saharan Africa has benefited little from its integration (both forced and voluntary) into the global economy. Slavery, colonialism, and export-oriented mining and agriculture served the needs of consumers outside the region but undermined domestic production for those within. Foreign assistance in the post-independence years initially improved agricultural and industrial output, but also led to mounting foreign debt and corruption, which over time undercut the region's economic gains. Ironically, many of these same scholars and politicians worry that negative global attitudes about the region have produced a pattern of neglect. Private capital investment in Sub-Saharan Africa lags far behind other developing regions. The idea of debt forgiveness for Africa's poorest states is steadily being applied as a strategy to reduce human suffering in the region.

The past few years have witnessed a surge in philanthropic outreach to the region. Rock star Bono of U2 and the Bill and Melinda Gates Foundation have led the One Campaign, directing millions of dollars to support health care, disease prevention, education, and poverty reduction in Sub-Saharan Africa and other developing areas. Through a combination of internal reforms, better governance, foreign assistance, and foreign investment in infrastructure and technology, many believe that social and economic gains are possible for the region.

ENVIRONMENTAL GEOGRAPHY: The Plateau Continent

The largest landmass straddling the equator, Sub-Saharan Africa is vast in scale and its physical environment is remarkably beautiful. Called the *plateau continent,* the African interior is dominated by extensive uplifted areas that resulted from the breakup of **Gondwanaland**, an ancient mega-continent that included Africa, South America, Antarctica, Australia, Madagascar, and Saudi Arabia. Some 250 million years ago, it began to split apart through the forces of continental drift. As this process unfolded, the African landmass experienced a series of continental uplifts that left much of the area with vast elevated plateaus. The highest areas are found on the eastern edge of the continent, where the Great Rift Valley forms a complex upland area of lakes, volcanoes, and deep valleys. In contrast, lowlands prevail in West Africa (see Figure 6.1).

The landscape of Sub-Saharan Africa offers a palette of intense colors: deep red soils studded with bright green food crops; the blue tropical sky; golden savannas that ripple with the movement of animal herds; dark rivers meandering through towering rain forests; and sun-drenched deserts. Amid this beauty, however, one finds relatively poor soils, persistent tropical diseases, and frequent droughts. Large areas exist with greater potential for agricultural development, especially in southern Africa; and throughout the continent significant water resources, biodiversity, and mineral wealth abound.

Plateaus and Basins

A series of plateaus and elevated basins dominate the African interior and explain much of the region's unique physical geography. Generally, elevations increase toward the south and east of the continent. Most of southern and eastern Africa lies well above 2,000 feet (600 meters), and sizable areas sit above 5,000 feet (1,500 meters). These areas are typically referred to as High Africa; Low Africa includes West Africa and much of Central Africa. The high plateaus in countries such as Kenya, Zimbabwe, and Angola are noted for their cooler climates and relatively abundant moisture. Steep escarpments form where plateaus abruptly end, as illustrated by the majestic Victoria Falls on the Zambezi River (Figure 6.3). Much of southern Africa is rimmed by a landform called the **Great Escarpment** (a steep cliff separating the coastal lowlands from the plateau uplands), which begins in southwestern Angola and ends in northeastern South Africa, creating a natural barrier to coastal settlement. South Africa's Drakensberg Mountains (with elevations

Figure 6.3 Victoria Falls The Zambezi River descends over Victoria Falls. A fault zone in the African plateau explains the existence of a 360-foot (110-meter) drop. The Zambezi has never been important for navigation, but it is a vital supply of hydroelectricity for Zimbabwe, Zambia, and Mozambique.

Figure 6.4 The Rift Valley Tucked into a fertile area of the Rift Valley in Kenya, this Kikuyu village of small landholders produces subsistence and market crops. Parts of the Rift Valley have East Africa's highest population densities.

reaching 10,000 feet, or 3,100 meters) rise up from the Great Escarpment. Because of this landform, coastal plains tend to be narrow, with few natural harbors, and river navigation is impeded by a series of falls.

Though Sub-Saharan Africa is an elevated landmass, it has few significant mountain ranges. The one extensive area of mountainous topography is in Ethiopia, which lies in the northern portion of the Rift Valley zone. Yet even there the dominant features are high plateaus intercut with deep valleys rather than actual mountain ranges. Receiving heavy rains in the wet season, the Ethiopian Plateau is densely settled and forms the headwaters of several important rivers, most notably the Blue Nile, which joins the White Nile at Khartoum, Sudan.

A discontinuous series of volcanic mountains, some of them quite tall, are associated with the southern half of the Rift Valley. Kilimanjaro at 19,000 feet (5,900 meters) is the continent's tallest mountain, and nearby Mount Kenya (17,000 feet, or 5,200 meters) is the second tallest. The Rift Valley itself reveals the slow but inexorable progress of geological forces. Eastern Africa is slowly being torn away from the rest of the continent, and within some tens of millions of years it will form a separate landmass. Such motion has already produced a great gash across the uplands of eastern Africa, much of which is occupied by elongated and extremely deep lakes (most notably Nyasa, Malawi, and Tanganyika). In central East Africa this rift zone splits into two separate valleys, each of which is flanked by volcanic uplands. Between the eastern and western rifts lies a bowl-shaped depression, the center of which is filled by Lake Victoria—Africa's largest body of water. Not surprisingly, some of the densest areas of settlement are found amid the fertile and well-watered soils that border the Rift Valley (Figure 6.4).

Watersheds Africa south of the Sahara conspicuously lacks the broad, alluvial lowlands that influence patterns of settlement throughout other regions. The four major river systems are the Congo, Nile, Niger, and Zambezi. Smaller rivers—such as the Orange in South Africa; the Senegal, which divides Mauritania and Senegal; and the Limpopo in Mozambique—are locally important but drain much smaller areas. Ironically, most people think of Africa south of the Sahara as suffering from water scarcity and tend to discount the size and importance of the watersheds (or catchment areas) that these river systems drain.

The Congo River (or Zaire) is the largest watershed in the region in terms of drainage and volume of flow. It is second only to South America's Amazon River in terms of annual flow. The Congo flows across a relatively flat basin that lies more than 1,000 feet (300 meters) above sea level, meandering through Africa's largest tropical forest, the Ituri (Figure 6.5). Entry from the Atlantic into the Congo Basin is prevented by a series of rapids and falls, making the Congo River only partially navigable. Despite these limitations, the Congo River has been the major corridor for travel within the Republic of the Congo and the Democratic Republic of the Congo (formerly Zaire); the capitals of both countries, Brazzaville and Kinshasa, rest on opposite sides of the river.

The Nile River, the world's longest, is the lifeblood of Egypt and Sudan. Yet this river originates in the highlands of the Rift Valley zone, and is an important link between North and Sub-Saharan Africa. The Nile begins in the lakes of the rift zone (Victoria and Edward) before descending into a vast wetland in southern Sudan known as the Sudd. Agricultural development projects in the 1970s greatly increased the agricultural potential of the Sudd, especially its peanut crop. Unfortunately, the past three decades of civil war in Sudan ravaged this area, turning farmers and herders into refugees and undermining the productive capacity of this important ecosystem. A more extensive discussion of the Nile River is in Chapter 7.

Like the Nile, the Niger River is the critical source of water for two otherwise arid countries: Mali and Niger. Originating in the humid Guinea highlands, the Niger flows first to the northeast and then spreads out to form a huge inland delta in Mali before making a great bend southward at the margins of the Sahara near Gao. On the banks of the Niger River are the capitals of Mali (Bamako) and Niger (Niamey), as well as the historic city of Tombouctou (Timbuktu). After flowing through the desert, the Niger River returns to the humid lowlands of Nigeria, where the Kainji Reservoir temporarily blocks its flow to produce electricity for Africa's most populous state.

The considerably smaller Zambezi River originates in Angola and flows east, spilling over an escarpment at Victoria Falls, and finally reaching Mozambique and the Indian Ocean. More than other rivers in the region, the Zambezi is a major supplier of commercial energy. Sub-Saharan Africa's two largest hydroelectric installations, the Kariba on the border of Zambia and Zimbabwe and the Cabora Bassa in Mozambique, are on this river.

Figure 6.5 Congo River A small fishing village on the banks of the Congo River. The Congo River is an important transportation corridor and source of fish. Behind the village lies the immense Ituri rain forest.

Soils With a few major exceptions, Sub-Saharan Africa's soils are relatively infertile. Generally speaking, fertile soils are young soils, those deposited in recent geological time by rivers, volcanoes, glaciers, or windstorms. In older soils—especially those located in moist tropical environments—natural processes tend to wash out most plant nutrients over time. Over most of Sub-Saharan Africa, the agents of soil renewal have largely been absent; the region has few alluvial lowlands where rivers periodically deposit fertile silt, and it did not experience significant glaciation in the last ice age, as did North America.

Portions of Sub-Saharan Africa are, however, noted for their natural soil fertility, and not surprisingly these areas support denser settlement. Some of the most fertile soils are in the Rift Valley, enhanced by the volcanic activity associated with the area. The population densities of rural Rwanda and Burundi, for example, are partially explained by the highly productive volcanic soils. The same can be said for highland Ethiopia, which supports the region's second largest population, with more than 80 million people. The Lake Victoria lowlands and central highlands of Kenya also are noted for their sizable populations and productive agricultural bases.

In the drier grasslands and semi-desert areas one finds a soil type called *alfisols*. High in aluminum and iron, these red soils have greater fertility than comparable soils found in wetter zones. This helps to explain the tendency of farmers to plant in drier areas, such as the Sahel, even though they risk exposure to drought. With irrigation, many agronomists suggest that the southern African countries of Zambia and Zimbabwe could greatly increase commercial grain production on these soils.

Climate and Vegetation

Sub-Saharan Africa lies in the tropical latitudes. Beginning just north of the Tropic of Cancer, crossing the equator, and extending past the Tropic of Capricorn in the south, it is the largest tropical landmass on the planet. Only the far south of the continent extends into the subtropical and temperate belts. Much of the region averages high temperatures from 70°F to 80°F (22° to 28°C) year-round. The seasonality and amount of rainfall, more than temperature, determine the different vegetation belts that characterize the region. As Figure 6.6 shows, Addis Ababa, Ethiopia, and Walvis Bay, Namibia, have similar average temperatures, but the former is in the moist highlands and receives nearly 50 inches (127 centimeters) of rainfall annually, while Walvis Bay rests on the Namibian Desert and receives less than 1 inch (2.5 centimeters).

To understand the relationship between climate and vegetation in Sub-Saharan Africa (see Figure 6.6), imagine a series of concentric vegetation belts that begin in the western equatorial zone as forest (Am and Af), followed by woodlands and grasslands (Aw), semidesert (BSh), and finally desert (BWh). The montane zones of East Africa, Cameroon, Guinea, and South Africa (especially along the Drakensberg Range) exhibit the forces of altitudinal zonation discussed in Chapter 4. Capturing more rainfall than the surrounding lowlands, these mountains often support unique flora with large numbers of native species. The only midlatitude climates of the region are found in South Africa. The southwestern corner of South Africa contains a small zone of Mediterranean climate that is comparable to that of California and noted for its production of fine wine (Csb). The eastern coast of South Africa has a moist subtropical climate, not unlike that of Florida (Cfa).

Tropical Forests The core of Sub-Saharan Africa is remarkably moist. The world's second-largest expanse of humid equatorial rain forest, the Ituri, lies in the Congo Basin, extending from the Atlantic Coast of Gabon two-thirds of the way across the continent, including the Republic of the Congo and northern portions of the Democratic Republic of the Congo (Zaire). The conditions here are constantly warm to hot, and precipitation falls year-round (see the graph for Kisangani in Figure 6.6).

Commercial logging and agricultural clearing have degraded the western and southern fringes of this vast forest, but much of the northeastern section of the forest is still intact. Considering the high rates of tropical deforestation in Southeast Asia and Latin America, the Central African case is a pleasant exception. Major national parks such as Okapi and Virunga have been created in the Democratic Republic of the Congo. Virunga National Park—one of the oldest in Africa—is on the eastern fringe of the Ituri forest. It is home to the endangered mountain gorillas. Poor infrastructure and political chaos in the Democratic Republic of the Congo over the past 15 years has made large-scale logging impossible but it has

Figure 6.6 Climate map of Sub-Saharan Africa Much of the region lies within the tropical humid and tropical dry climatic zones; thus, the seasonal temperature changes are not great. Precipitation, however, varies significantly. Compare the distinct rainy seasons in Lusaka and Lagos: Lagos is wettest in June and Lusaka receives most of its rain in January. Although there are important tropical forests in West and Central Africa, much the territory is tropical savanna. (Temperature and precipitation data from *The World Weather Guide* [1984] by E. A. Pearce and C. G. Smith. London: Hutchinson)

also made conservation difficult. Due to regional conflict, parks such as Virunga have been repeatedly taken over by rebel groups and park rangers have been killed; poaching has become a means of survival for people in the region. In the future, it seems likely that Central Africa's rain forests could suffer the same kind of degradation experienced in other equatorial areas. As deforestation proceeds elsewhere in the world, the trees of equatorial Africa become increasingly valuable and, hence, more vulnerable.

Savannas Wrapped around the Central African rain forest belt in a great arc lie Africa's vast tropical wet and dry savannas. Savannas are dominated by a mixture of trees and tall grasses in the wetter zones immediately adjacent to the forest belt and shorter grasses with fewer trees in the drier zones. North of the equatorial belt, rain generally falls only from May to October. The farther north one travels, the less the total rainfall and the longer the dry season. Climatic conditions south of the equator are similar, only reversed, with the wet season occurring between October and May and precipitation generally decreasing toward the south (see

the graph for Lusaka in Figure 6.6). A larger area of wet savanna exists south of the equator, with substantial woodlands in southern portions of the Democratic Republic of the Congo, Zambia, northern Zimbabwe and eastern Angola. These savannas also are a critical habitat for the region's large fauna (Figure 6.7).

Deserts The vast extent of tropical Africa is bracketed by several deserts. The Sahara, the world's largest desert and one of its driest, spans the landmass from the Atlantic coast of Mauritania all the way to the Red Sea coast of Sudan. A narrow belt of desert extends to the south and east of the Sahara, wrapping around the **Horn of Africa** (the northeastern corner that includes Somalia, Ethiopia, Djibouti, and Eritrea) and pushing as far as eastern and northern Kenya. An even drier zone is found in southwestern Africa. In the Namib Desert of coastal Namibia, rainfall is a rare event, although temperatures are usually mild (see the graph for Walvis Bay in Figure 6.6). Inland from the Namib lies the Kalahari Desert. Most of the Kalahari is not dry enough to be classified as a true desert, because it receives slightly more than 10 inches (25 centimeters) of rain a year (Figure 6.8). Its rainy season, however, is brief. Most of the precipitation is immediately absorbed by the underlying sands. Surface

Figure 6.7 African Savannas Buffalo gather at a watering hole in Zambezi National Park in Zimbabwe. The savannas of southern Africa are a noted habitat for the region's larger mammals such as buffalo, elephant, zebra, and lions.

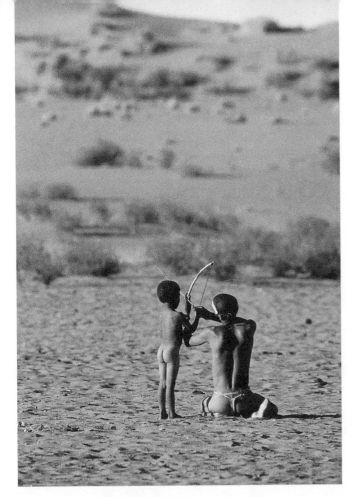

Figure 6.8 Kalahari Desert A San man teaches his four-year-old son to hunt with a bow and arrow. The Kalahari, though not a true desert, does not get enough rain to support agriculture. Yet this ecosystem is home to abundant wildlife and hunter-gatherers, such as the San (formerly known as the Bushmen).

water is thus scarce, giving the Kalahari a desertlike aspect for most of the year.

Africa's Environmental Issues

The prevailing perception of Africa south of the Sahara is one of environmental scarcity and degradation, no doubt fostered by televised images of drought-ravaged regions and starving children. Single explanations such as rapid population growth or colonial exploitation cannot fully capture the complexity of Africa's environmental issues or the ingenious ways that people have adapted to living in stressed ecosystems. Because much of Sub-Saharan Africa's population is rural and poor, earning its livelihood directly from the land, sudden environmental changes are keenly felt and can cause mass migrations, famine, and even death. As Figure 6.9 illustrates, **desertification**, the expansion of desertlike conditions as a result of human-induced degradation, and deforestation are commonplace. Sub-Saharan Africa is also vulnerable to drought, most notably in the Horn of Africa, parts of southern Africa, and the Sahel. Many scientists fear that droughts will come more often and be prolonged with global warming.

As Sub-Saharan cities grow in size and importance, urban environments increasingly face problems of air and water pollution as well as sewage and waste disposal. At the same time, wildlife tourism is an increasingly important source of foreign exchange for many African states. Throughout the region, national parks have been created in an effort to strike a balance between humans' and animals' competing demands for land.

The Sahel and Desertification In the 1970s, the **Sahel** became an emblem for the dangers of unchecked population growth and human-induced environmental degradation when a relatively wet period came to an abrupt end and 6 years of drought (1968–74) ravaged the land. The Sahel is a zone of ecological transition between the Sahara to the north and wetter savannas and forest in the south. Life depends on a delicate balance of limited rain, drought-resistant plants, and a pattern of animal **transhumance**, the movement of animals between wet-season and dry-season pasture. Parts of the Sahel were important areas of settlement long before European colonization. What appears to be desert wasteland in April or May is transformed into a lush garden of millet, sorghum, and peanuts after the drenching rains of June. Relatively free of the tropical diseases found in the wetter zones to the south, Sahelian soils also are quite fertile, which helps to explain why people continue to live there despite the unreliable rainfall patterns (Figure 6.10). During the drought of the early 1970s, rivers in the area diminished and desertlike conditions began to move south. Unfortunately, tens of millions of people lived in the areas, and farmers and pastoralists whose livelihoods had come to depend on the more abundant precipitation of the relatively wet period were temporarily forced out.

Considerable disagreement continues over the basic causes of desertification and drought in the Sahel. Was it a matter of too many humans degrading their environment, unsound settlement schemes encouraged by European colonizers, or a failure to understand global atmospheric cycles? Agricultural practices certainly contributed to desertification. Throughout most of the Sahel, French colonial authorities forced villagers to grow peanuts as an export crop, a policy continued by the newly independent states of the region. However, peanuts tend to deplete several key soil nutrients, which means that peanut farms are often abandoned after a few years as cultivators move on to fresh sites. Since peanuts grow underground, moreover, the soil must be overturned at harvest time. This typically occurs at the onset of the dry season, when dry winds from the Sahara can carry away the fine dirt of the newly harvested field. With the loss of topsoil, the ground no longer absorbs the precipitation that does fall—often in drenching torrents—during the brief rainy season. The end result of this grim process is the spread of desertification regardless of actual changes in precipitation.

Overgrazing also has been implicated in Sahelian desertification, as is true in other regions of the world. Livestock is a traditional product of the region, and animal production dramatically expanded after World War II as the population

Reforestation efforts. *Wanagri Maathai's Green Belt Movement organized 50,000 women to plant more than one million trees to reduce soil erosion and satisfy demand for household biofuels.*

The troubled Sahel. *Drought and desertification have contributed to a greater risk of famine for the farmers and pastoralists in these lands. In the early 1970s several million people and their livestock were at risk due to drought and crop failures in the Sahel. In 2002 and 2003 Ethiopians faced a similar situation.*

Ituri Rain Forest. *Africa's largest tropical rain forest is found in the watershed of the Congo River. While large areas of untouched forest remain, the seven states that contain portions of the Ituri export its valuable and rare tropical hardwoods.*

Legend:
- Areas prone to drought
- National parks
- Tropical forest
- Forest destroyed
- Desert
- Desertification
- Coastal pollution
- Polluted rivers

0   400   800 Miles
0   400   800 Kilometers

ATLANTIC OCEAN

INDIAN OCEAN

Red Sea

Figure 6.9 Environmental Issues in Sub-Saharan Africa Given the immense size of Sub-Saharan Africa, it is difficult to generalize about environmental problems. Dependence on trees for fuel places strains on forests and wooded savannas throughout the region. In semiarid regions, such as the Sahel and Horn of Africa, population pressures, climate change, and land-use practices seem to have exacerbated desertification. Yet Sub-Saharan Africa also supports the most impressive array of wildlife, especially large mammals, on Earth.

(Adapted from *DK World Atlas*, 1997, 75. London: DK Publishing)

swelled and the need for export earnings grew. In many areas, natural pasture was greatly reduced by intensified grazing pressure, leading to increased wind erosion. National and international developmental agencies, hoping to increase production further, began to dig deep wells in areas that previously had been unused by herders through most of the year. The new supplies of water, in turn, allowed year-round grazing in places that, over time, could not withstand it. Large barren circles around each new well began to appear even on satellite images.

Expansion of agriculture and overgrazing are often cited as major factors leading to the loss of natural vegetation and declines in soil fertility in the Sahel. Yet in the case of the Sahelian portion of Niger, local agronomists have documented

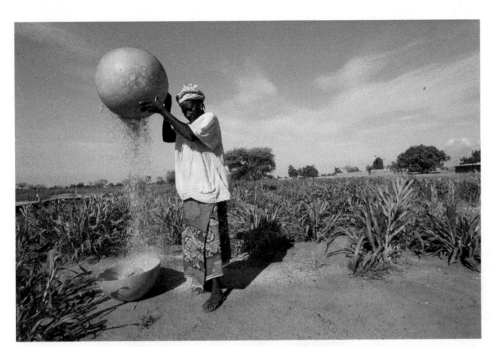

Figure 6.10 Sahel in Bloom A woman prepares millet grains grown near the city of Maradi, Niger. The soils of the Sahel are fertile and peasant farmers can produce a surplus when adequate rain falls. Yet in times of drought, crop failures can lead to famine in this region.

an unanticipated increase in tree cover the past 30 years. More interesting still, increases in tree cover have occurred in some of the most densely populated rural areas. The relative greening of this area is attributed to simple actions taken by farmers, a change in government policy and better rainfall (see "Geographic Tools: Monitoring Land Cover and Conservation Changes in Niger"). Regardless of the causes given or action taken, many of the areas experiencing desertification are the same ones most vulnerable to drought and famine. These conditions may become more frequent with global climate change.

Deforestation Although Sub-Saharan Africa still contains extensive forests in some areas, much of the region has relatively little tree cover. Unlike tropical America, forest clearance in the wet and dry savanna is of greater local concern than the limited commercial logging of the rain forest. North of the equator, for example, only a few wooded areas remain in a landscape dominated by grasslands, savanna (grassland with scattered trees and shrubs), and cropland. Highland Ethiopia once was covered with lush forests, but these have long since been reduced to a few remnant patches. Loss of woody vegetation has resulted in extensive hardship, especially for women and children who must spend many hours a day scrounging for wood for home consumption or to sell in local markets (Figure 6.11). Deforestation, especially in the woodlands of the savannas, aggravates problems of increased runoff, soil erosion, and shortages of **biofuels** (wood and charcoal used for household energy needs, especially cooking).

In the southern tropical savanna, where human population has historically been lighter, extensive tracts of dry woodland remain intact. The trees of the dry forest have little commercial value compared to some of the species found in the rain forest, but they provide vital subsistence resources for local people as well as wildlife habitat. Even in

these more abundant areas, biofuel scarcity is common around the larger towns and villages.

In some countries, village women have organized into community-based nongovernmental organizations (NGOs) to plant trees and create greenbelts to meet future fuel needs. One of the most successful efforts is in Kenya under the leadership of Wangari Maathai. Maathai's Green Belt Movement has more than 50,000 members, mostly women, organized into 2,000 local community groups. Since the movement's inception in 1977, these local groups have successfully planted millions of trees. In those areas, village women now spend less time collecting fuel, and local environments have im-

Figure 6.11 Wood Fuel in Ethiopia A women walks to Addis Ababa with a large bundle of firewood to sell in the city market. Collecting firewood is the work of women, both for household subsistence needs and for sale in local markets.

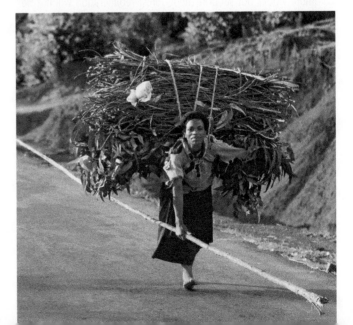

GEOGRAPHIC TOOLS Monitoring Land Cover and Conservation Changes in Niger

Much to everyone's surprise, Niger is becoming greener. Through satellite imagery and field inventories at the village level, local agronomists have documented that tree-covered areas have increased by 7 million acres (Figure 6.1.1). These basic geographic tools were used to reveal unexpected improvements in tree cover. It appears that better local conservation practices and improved rainfall have led to a dramatic increase in vegetation over the past 30 years. More interesting still, increases in tree cover have occurred in some of the most densely populated rural areas. Given that the Sahel is an area noted for drought, famine, and desertification, documenting land cover change and explaining how such changes happen offers valuable lessons for other drought-prone areas.

The greening of Niger was not the result of a large-scale government effort or a foreign assistance program. The impetus for change came from farmers themselves who realized after the drought of 1984 that maintaining tree cover was important for the long-term sustainability of farming practices. Farmers began actively protecting saplings instead of clearing them from their fields, including the nitrogen-fixing goa tree which had disappeared from many villages. During the rainy season, the goa tree loses its leaves, so it does not compete with crops for water or sun. The leaves themselves are added fertilizer to the soil. In general, trees and shrubs reduce wind erosion, and their presence also reduces runoff and erosion when the rains do come. Sahelian farmers also use branches, pods, and leaves from trees for fuel and animal fodder. Any excess can be sold at market.

Given the utility of native trees, why were farmers removing them? Much vegetation disappeared in the 1970s when the region suffered prolonged drought. Until the 1990s, all trees were considered property of the state of Niger, thus giving farmers little incentive to protect them. Since then, the government has recognized the value of allowing individuals to own trees. Not only can farmers sell branches, pods, fruit, and bark, they also conserve them to insure their agricultural livelihood.

For forest regeneration to work it requires the effort of the whole community. If farmers do not take action themselves and the community does not support them, forest regeneration will not be successful. Consequently, some villages in Niger are much greener than others. In the village of Moussa Bara, where regeneration has been a success, not one child died of malnutrition in the famine of 2005, largely because farmers were able to earn income from selling firewood when their crops failed.

The Sahel is a poor region that has always been vulnerable to drought. It is uncertain how global climate changes will impact this region; some years may be wetter than average but there is the possibility of more prolonged droughts. For now, at least, Niger offers a provocative example of how small and relatively simple conservation practices can have a positive impact.

(a)

(b)

Figure 6.1.1 More Trees in Southern Niger These satellite images demonstrate an increase in tree cover in Niger. In 1975 (a), there were relatively few trees in this part of the Sahel. By 2003 (b), tree cover had increased substantially.

Source: Adapted from Lydia Polgreen, "In Niger, Trees and Crops Turn Back the Desert," *New York Times,* Feb, 11, 2007.

Figure 6.12 Deforestation in Madagascar A man fills a bag with charcoal made from burning tropical forest. Much of the island has been deforested, due to a reliance on slash-and-burn agriculture and biofuels. Loss of forest cover has led to serious problems with soil erosion and species extinction for the island nation. About 3 percent of the national territory is in protected areas.

proved. As a result of these efforts, the total forest area of Kenya remained about the same between 1990 and 2007 even though the population greatly increased. Maathai's success has drawn interest from other African countries, spurring a Pan-African Green Belt Movement largely organized through nongovernmental organizations interested in biofuel generation, protection of the environment, and the empowerment of women. In 2004 Professor Maathai was awarded a Nobel Peace Prize for her contribution to sustainable development, democracy, and peace.

Destruction of rain forest for logging is most evident in the southern fringes of Central Africa's Ituri forest (see Figure 6.9). Given the vastness of this forest and the relatively small number of people living there, however, it is less threatened than other forest areas. Two smaller rain forests, one along the Atlantic coast from Sierra Leone to western Ghana and the other along the eastern coast of the island of Madagascar, have nearly disappeared. These rain forests have been severely degraded by commercial logging and agricultural clearance. At present rates, several countries in West Africa will be completely deforested early in this century. For example, according to World Bank estimates, only 5 percent of the West African nation of Togo is forested. Off the coast of southern Africa, Madagascar's forests have suffered serious degradation in the past four decades (Figure 6.12). Deforestation in Madagascar is especially worrisome because the island forms a unique environment with a large number of native species. Many species of fauna (including birds, reptiles, and lemurs) now are endangered, and several face imminent extinction. Thankfully, over the past decade deforestation rates have slowed, which is a good sign, but less than a quarter of the island remains forested.

Wildlife Conservation Sub-Saharan Africa is justly famous for its wildlife. In no other region of the world can one find such abundance and diversity, especially of large mammals.

The survival of wildlife here reflects, to some extent, the historically low human population density and the fact that sleeping sickness (transferred by the tsetse fly) and other diseases have kept people and their livestock out of many areas. In addition, many African peoples have developed various means of successfully coexisting with wildlife and about 12 percent of the region is under nationally protected lands.

But as is true elsewhere in the world, wildlife is quickly declining in much of Sub-Saharan Africa. West Africa now has few areas of prime habitat, and what remains is rapidly shrinking. The most noted wildlife reserves are in East Africa; in Kenya and Tanzania these reserves are economically important major tourist attractions. Even there, however, population pressure, political instability, and poverty make the maintenance of large wildlife reserves difficult. Poaching is a major problem, particularly for rhinoceroses and elephants; the price of a single horn or tusk in distant markets represents several years' wages for most Africans. Ivory is avidly sought in East Asia, especially in Japan. In China, powdered rhino horn is used as a traditional medicine, whereas in Yemen rhino horn is prized for dagger handles. During the 1980s, the region's elephant population fell by more than half, to 600,000, in part due to the ivory trade.

The most secure wildlife reserves now are located in southern Africa. Zoologists and park guides have employed handheld global positioning systems, called *CyberTrackers*, to record wildlife observations and map their findings. In Botswana, the San (a tribal group) have been given these devices to record the animal movements that only these expert hunters usually observe. In fact, elephant populations are considered to be too large in countries such as Botswana and South Africa. Some wildlife experts here contend that herds should be culled to prevent overgrazing and that the ivory should be legally sold in the international market in order to generate revenue for further conservation. Only such a market-oriented approach, they argue, will give African countries a long-term incentive to preserve habitat. Many environmentalists, not surprisingly, disagree strongly.

In 1989, a worldwide ban on the legal ivory trade was imposed as part of the Convention on International Trade in Endangered Species (CITES). While several African states, such as Kenya, lobbied hard for the ban, others, such as Zimbabwe, Namibia, and Botswana, complained that their herds were growing and the sale of ivory had helped to pay for conservation efforts. Conservationists feared that lifting the ban would bring on a new wave of poaching and illegal trade. In the late 1990s, the ban was lifted so that some southern African states could sell down their substantial inventories of ivory and continue with limited sales. The long-term repercussions for elephant survival are not yet known, although political leaders from Kenya and India have voiced strong opposition to all ivory sales. In 2000 elephant population estimates ranged from 400,000 to 600,000, with the majority of these animals found in protected areas. Rhino populations are far smaller at 10,000 to 15,000. The black rhino is a critically endangered species and the white rhino is more numerous but endangered as well (Figure 6.13).

Both are protected under CITES and rhino horn trade is illegal. The ivory controversy, however, shows how global markets and international conservation policies impact elephant survival in Sub-Saharan Africa.

Global Warming and Vulnerability in Sub-Saharan Africa

Global climate change poses extreme risks for this region due to its widespread poverty, recurrent droughts, and overdependence upon rain-fed agriculture. Sub-Saharan Africa is the lowest emitter of greenhouse gases in the world, but it is likely to experience greater human vulnerability to global warming because of the region's limited resources to both respond and adapt to environmental change. The areas most vulnerable are arid and semiarid regions such as the Sahel and Horn of Africa, some grassland areas, and the coastal lowlands of West Africa and Angola.

Climate change models suggest that parts of highland East Africa and equatorial Central Africa may receive more rainfall. Thus some lands that are currently marginal for farming might be made more productive. These effects are likely to be negated by the decline in agricultural productivity in the Sahelian belt as well as the grasslands of southern Africa, especially in Zambia and Zimbabwe. Drier grassland areas could deplete wildlife populations, which are a major source behind the growing tourist economy. As in Latin America, higher temperatures in the tropics may also result in the expansion of vector-born diseases such as malaria and dengue fever into the highlands where they were once relatively rare. Given the relatively high elevations in the region, the negative consequences of sea-level rising would be mostly felt on the West African coast (Senegal, Gambia, Sierra Leone, Nigeria, Cameroon, and Gabon).

The World Food Program estimates that millions of Africans struggle against starvation each year. Famine occurs when there is a surge in hunger-related mortality. Most

Figure 6.14 Map of Food Insecurity in Eastern Africa Anticipating areas of food insecurity based upon the timing and amount of rainfall and changes in vegetation/crop cover is the mission of FEWS network. FEWS has existed since the late 1980s to map areas of potential famine, especially in Sub Saharan Africa. (Source: Famine Early Warning System (FEWS) Network, April to September 2010 Report, U.S. Agency for International Development)

Figure 6.13 South African Wildlife A white rhinoceros grazes the savannas of Kruger National Park in South Africa, one of the region's oldest wildlife parks. A protected and endangered species, white rhinos are found in South Africa, Zimbabwe, Botswana, Angola and Kenya.

global warming scenarios show that prolonged drought will become more common in parts of the region over time. As critical resources such as water and food become scarce, resource-driven conflicts and human displacement become more likely. Some scholars argue that the ethnic conflict in Sudan's Darfur region is driven, in part, by resource competition between pastoralists and agriculturalists in an ecosystem that is experiencing water scarcity.

Even without the threat of global warming, famine stalks many areas of Africa. The Famine Early Warning Systems (FEWS) network is in place to monitor food insecurity throughout the developing world, but especially in Sub-Saharan Africa. By tracking rainfall, vegetation cover, food production, food prices, and conflict, the network maps food security along a continuum from food secure to famine. In 2005, crops in Niger failed due to drought and an estimated 2.5 million people were vulnerable to famine but early warning systems were taken seriously and relief efforts resulted in relatively low mortality rates. Figure 6.14 shows the status of food security in eastern Africa during a relatively wet year in 2010 when food insecurity conditions were expected to remain stable or improve slightly and there were no areas under famine status. Still, even in a good year, the FEWS report estimated that 19 million people faced food insecurity in eastern Africa, especially in Somalia and eastern Ethiopia.

POPULATION AND SETTLEMENT: Young and Restless

Sub-Saharan Africa's population is growing quickly. While the global population is projected to increase by nearly 40 percent by 2050, the projected population growth for Africa south of the Sahara is over 100 percent over the same time period. It is also a very young population with 43 percent of the people younger than age 15, compared to just 17 percent for more-developed countries. Only 3 percent of the region's population is over 65 years of age, whereas in Europe 16 percent is over 65. Families tend to be large, with a woman having an average of five or six children (Table 6.1). Yet child and maternal mortality rates are high, reflecting disturbingly low access to basic health services. The most troubling indicator for the region is its stubbornly low life expectancy of 52 years. Life expectancy in other developing nations is much better; India's is 64 years and China's 74 years. The growth of cities also is a major trend. In 1980 it was estimated that 23 percent of the population lived in cities; now the figure is 35 percent.

Behind these demographic facts lie complex differences in settlement patterns, livelihoods, belief systems, and access to health care. Although the region is experiencing rapid population growth, Sub-Saharan Africa is not densely populated. The entire region holds 865 million persons—roughly half the population that is crowded into the much smaller land area of South Asia. In fact, the overall population density of the region (36 people per square kilometer) is similar to that of the United States (32 people per square kilometer). Just six states account for over half of the region's population: Nigeria, Ethiopia, the Democratic Republic of Congo, South Africa, Tanzania, and Sudan (see Table 6.1). Some states have very high population densities (such as Rwanda or Mauritius) while others are sparsely settled. Namibia and Mauritania have just 3 people per square kilometer.

Crude population density is an imperfect indicator of whether a country is overpopulated. Geographers are often more interested in **physiological density**, the number of people per unit of arable land. The physiological density in Chad, where only 3 percent of the land is arable, is much higher than its crude population density of 9 people per square kilometer. Perhaps a more telling indicator of population pressure and potential food shortages is **agricultural density**, the number of farmers per unit of arable land. Because the majority of people in Sub-Saharan Africa earn their livings from agriculture, agricultural density indicates the number of people who directly depend on each arable

square kilometer. The agricultural density of many Sub-Saharan countries is 10 times greater than their crude population density.

Population Trends and Demographic Debates

The growth in particular areas of Sub-Saharan Africa with high agricultural densities and rates of natural increase has combined with reversals in some economic and social indicators to make demographers concerned about the region's overall well-being. The Horn of Africa, for example, is not crowded by European or Asian standards, but it may already contain too many people for the land to support given the unpredictability of its limited rainfall.

This assertion remains controversial, however—as does the entire field of African demography. Some believe that the region could support many more people than it presently does and, as a whole, it is still underpopulated. Others argue that the region is a demographic time bomb and that unless fertility is quickly reduced, Sub-Saharan Africa will face continued food insecurity and suffering. The majority of African states officially support lowering rates of natural increase and are steadily promoting modern contraception practices both to reduce family size and to protect people from sexually transmitted diseases. One thing is certain: the region is, demographically, the fastest growing world region.

Family Size A preference for large families is the basis for the region's demographic growth where most women have 5 to 6 live births in a lifetime. In the 1960s many areas in the developing world had total fertility rates (TFR) of 5.0 or higher. Today Sub-Saharan Africa is the only region with such a high TFR at 5.2. A combination of cultural practices, rural lifestyles, high child mortality, and economic realities encourages large families (Figure 6.15).

Throughout the region, large families guarantee a family's lineage and status. Even now, most women marry young, typically when they are teenagers, which increases

Figure 6.15 Large Families This family in Senegal includes five children. Large families are still common in Sub-Saharan Africa. The average total fertility rate for the region is 5.2 children per woman.

TABLE 6.1　Population Indicators

Country	Population (millions) 2010	Population Density (per square kilometer)	Rate of Natural Increase (RNI)	Total Fertility Rate	Percent Urban	Percent <15	Percent >65	Net Migration (Rate per 1000) 2005–10[a]
Angola	19.0	15	2.5	5.8	57	45	2	0.9
Benin	9.8	87	3.0	5.6	41	45	3	1.2
Botswana	1.8	3	1.9	3.2	60	33	5	1.6
Burkina Faso	16.2	59	3.4	6.0	23	46	3	−0.9
Burundi	8.5	306	2.1	5.4	10	41	3	8.1
Cameroon	20.0	42	2.3	4.7	53	41	4	−0.2
Cape Verde	0.5	128	2.0	2.9	61	35	5	−5.1
Central African Republic	4.8	8	2.2	4.8	38	41	4	0.2
Chad	11.5	9	2.9	6.2	27	46	3	−1.4
Comoros	0.7	309	2.6	4.1	28	38	3	−3.1
Congo	3.9	12	2.5	5.0	60	42	4	−2.8
Dem. Rep. of Congo	67.8	29	2.9	6.4	33	48	3	−0.3
Djibouti	0.9	38	1.8	4.0	76	37	3	0.0
Equatorial Guinea	0.7	25	2.3	5.5	39	42	3	3.1
Eritrea	5.2	44	2.9	4.7	21	42	2	2.3
Ethiopia	85.0	77	2.7	5.4	16	44	3	-0.8
Gabon	1.5	6	1.9	3.6	84	39	4	0.7
Gambia	1.8	155	2.7	5.3	54	43	3	1.8
Ghana	24.0	101	2.2	4.0	48	39	4	−0.4
Guinea	10.8	44	3.0	5.7	28	43	3	−6.1
Guinea-Bissau	1.6	46	2.4	5.8	30	43	3	−1.6
Ivory Coast	22.0	68	2.4	4.9	61	40	2	−1.4
Kenya	40.0	69	2.7	4.6	18	42	3	−1.0
Lesotho	1.9	63	0.9	3.2	23	34	6	−3.5
Liberia	4.1	37	3.3	5.9	58	44	3	13.3
Madagascar	20.1	34	2.7	4.8	31	43	3	−0.1
Malawi	15.4	130	2.9	6.0	14	46	3	−0.3
Mali	15.2	12	3.1	6.6	33	48	3	−3.2
Mauritania	3.4	3	2.3	4.5	40	40	3	0.6
Mauritius	1.3	628	0.5	1.5	42	22	7	0.0
Mozambique	23.4	29	2.3	5.1	31	44	3	−0.2
Namibia	2.2	3	1.9	3.4	35	38	4	−0.1
Niger	15.9	13	3.5	7.4	20	49	2	−0.4
Nigeria	158.3	171	2.4	5.7	47	43	3	−0.4
Reunion	0.8	333	1.3	2.4	92	26	8	0.0
Rwanda	10.4	395	2.9	5.4	17	42	2	0.3
São Tomé and Principe	0.2	170	2.9	4.9	58	44	4	−8.8
Senegal	12.5	64	2.8	4.9	41	44	2	−1.7
Seychelles	0.1	193	1.0	2.3	53	22	10	
Sierra Leone	5.8	81	2.4	5.1	36	43	2	2.2
Somalia	9.4	15	3.0	6.5	34	45	3	−5.6
South Africa	49.9	41	0.9	2.4	52	31	5	2.8
Sudan	43.2	17	2.2	4.5	38	41	3	0.7
Swaziland	1.2	69	1.5	3.7	22	40	3	−1.0
Tanzania	45.0	48	3.0	5.6	25	45	3	−1.4
Togo	6.8	119	2.5	4.8	40	41	3	−0.2
Uganda	33.8	140	3.4	6.5	13	49	3	−0.9
Zambia	13.3	18	2.5	6.2	37	46	3	−1.4
Zimbabwe	12.6	32	1.3	3.7	37	42	4	−11.1

[a]Net Migration Rate from the United Nations, Population Division, World Population Prospects: The 2008 Revision Population Database.

Source: Population Reference Bureau, World Population Data Sheet, 2010 their opportunities to have more children. Demographers often point to the limited formal education available to women as another factor contributing to high fertility. Stubbornly high child mortality rates may encourage women to have more children. In most states one in ten children die before their fifth birthday; in the poorest and war-torn countries, such as Chad and Somalia, one in five children perish. Interestingly, religious affiliation seems to have little bearing on the region's fertility rates; Muslim, Christian, and animist communities all have similarly high birthrates.

The everyday realities of rural life make large families an asset. Children are an important source of labor; from tending crops and livestock to gathering fuel, they add more to the household economy than they take. Also, for the poorest places in the developing world, such as Sub-Saharan Africa, children are seen as social security. When parents' health falters, they expect their grown children to care for them.

Government policies toward family size have shifted dramatically in the past four decades. During the 1970s, population growth was not perceived as a problem by many African governments; in fact, many equated limiting population size with a neocolonial attempt to slow regional development. By the 1980s, a shift in national policies occurred. Following the United Nations International Conference on Population and Development in Cairo, Egypt, African governments announced their intent to bring natural increase rates down to 2.0 and to increase the rate of contraceptive use to 40 percent by 2020. They may reach their goal: As of 2010, the regional rate of natural increase was 2.5 percent, and nearly one-quarter of married women used some method of contraception.

Migration patterns within the region and out of it are also influencing growth rates. Africans are mobile people and movement across borders within the region has long been a part of livelihood systems and survival strategies during times of conflict. As Table 6.1 shows, some African states such as Burundi and Liberia have very high rates of net migration either due to receiving refugees or former refugees returning home. Similarly, the states with some of the highest negative net migration rates are places experiencing conflict such as Zimbabwe, or are states extremely dependent upon foreign labor migration such as Cape Verde. In general, many of the international flows in Africa are from one poor country to another and most are not recorded. Sub-Saharan Africans are also leaving the region in small but substantial numbers, especially to Europe and North America.

Other factors are converging to slow the growth rate. As African states slowly become more urban, there is a corresponding decline in family size—a pattern seen throughout the world. Tragically, declines in natural increase also are occurring as a result of AIDS.

The Impact of AIDS on Africa Now entering its fourth decade, HIV/AIDS may become one of the deadliest epidemics in modern human history. As of 2008, two-thirds of the HIV/AIDS cases in the world were found in Sub-Saharan Africa, where 22.4 million adults and children are living with HIV/AIDS. In 2008 there were 1.9 million new HIV infections, down from 2.3 million in 2001. This is the world region most heavily affected by HIV. Yet there are some hopeful signs as the number of newly infected people and the number of deaths due to AIDS have started to decline slowly.

The virus is thought to have originated in the forests of the Congo, possibly crossing over from chimpanzees to humans sometime in the 1950s. Yet it was not until the 1980s that the impact of the disease was widely felt. In Sub-Saharan Africa, as in much of the developing world, the disease is transmitted by unprotected heterosexual transmission. Mother-to-child transmission through the birthing process or breast feeding also contributes to the number of new cases, although strides have been made reduce these numbers. Women bear a disproportionate burden of the HIV/AIDS epidemic. They account for approximately 60 percent of the HIV infections and they are usually the caregivers for those who are infected. Until the late 1990s, many African governments were unwilling to acknowledge publicly the severity of the situation or to discuss frankly the measures necessary for prevention. The consequences of this inaction were deadly.

Southern Africa is ground zero for the AIDS epidemic that is ravaging the region (Figure 6.16). The nine countries with the highest HIV prevalence are all located there. In South Africa, the most populous state in southern Africa, 5.7 million people (nearly one in five people aged 15–49) are infected with HIV/AIDS. The rate of infection in neighboring Botswana is 24 percent (down from a staggering 36 percent in 2001) for the same age group. Although the rate of infection is highest in southern Africa, East Africa and West Africa are seeing increases. In Ivory Coast, it is estimated that 4 percent of the 15–49 age group has HIV or AIDS. For Kenya the figure is 6 percent. By comparison, only 0.6 percent of the same age group in North America is infected.

Sadly, the social and economic implications of this epidemic are profound. Life expectancy rates have tumbled in the last decade, in a few places dropping to the early 40s. AIDS typically hits the portion of the population that is most active economically. Time lost to care for sick family members and the outlay of workers' compensation benefits has reduced economic productivity and overwhelmed public services in hard-hit areas. The disease makes no class distinctions, so that countries are losing peasant farmers and educated professionals (doctors, engineers, and teachers). Infection rates among newborns are high but several countries have been successful at using antiviral medicines to block the transmission of HIV from mothers to children at birth. Many countries are struggling to care for nearly 12 million children orphaned by AIDS.

There was a scaling-up of access to antiretroviral therapies and AIDS prevention education in the past decade. For some countries, such as Botswana, Kenya, and Uganda, this has resulted in significantly lower death rates due to the disease (Figure 6.17). Prevention education has resulted in a significant decline in HIV incidence in Tanzania. HIV testing, counseling, and prevention services in prenatal settings

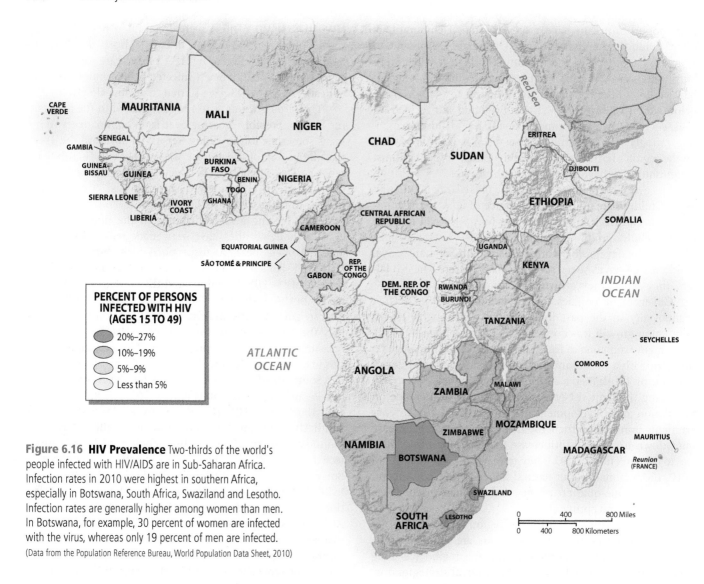

Figure 6.16 HIV Prevalence Two-thirds of the world's people infected with HIV/AIDS are in Sub-Saharan Africa. Infection rates in 2010 were highest in southern Africa, especially in Botswana, South Africa, Swaziland and Lesotho. Infection rates are generally higher among women than men. In Botswana, for example, 30 percent of women are infected with the virus, whereas only 19 percent of men are infected.

(Data from the Population Reference Bureau, World Population Data Sheet, 2010)

have proven to be important in preventing newborns from being infected and increasing the life expectancy of HIV-infected women in the region.

For now, the surest way to stem the epidemic is through prevention, mostly through educating people about how the virus is spread and persuading them to change their sexual behavior. In Uganda, state agencies, along with NGOs, began a national no-nonsense campaign for AIDS awareness in the 1980s that focused on the schools. President Museveni of Uganda pioneered the catchy phrase "Abstain-Be faithful-use a Condom" (ABC). As a result of explicit materials, role-playing games, and frank discussion, the prevalence of HIV among women in prenatal clinics had declined by the late 1990s.

Patterns of Settlement and Land Use

Because of the dominance of rural settlements in Sub-Saharan Africa, people are widely scattered throughout the region (Figure 6.18). Population concentrations are the highest in West Africa, highland East Africa, and the eastern half of South Africa. The first two areas have some of the region's best soils, and indigenous systems of permanent agriculture developed there. In South Africa, the more densely settled east results from an urbanized economy based on mining, as well as the forced concentration of black South Africans into eastern homelands.

West Africa is more heavily populated than most of Sub-Saharan Africa, although the actual distribution pattern is patchy. Density in the far west, from Senegal to Liberia, is moderate; this area is characterized by broad lowlands with decent soils, and in many areas the cultivation of wet rice has enhanced agricultural productivity. Greater concentrations of people are found along the Gulf of Guinea, from southern Ghana through southern Nigeria, and again in northern Nigeria along the southern fringe of the Sahel. Nigeria is moderately to densely settled through most of its extensive territory; with nearly 160 million inhabitants, it stands as the demographic core of Sub-Saharan Africa. The next largest country, Ethiopia, has a population of 85 million.

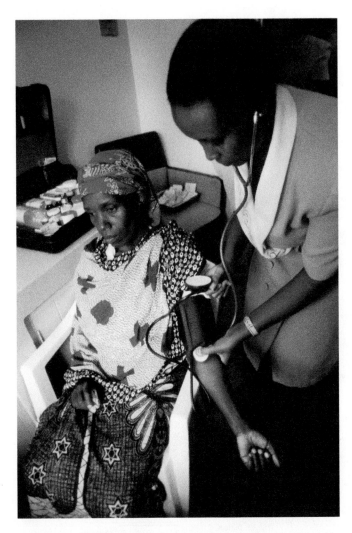

Figure 6.17 HIV/AIDS Clinic in Tanzania A woman with AIDS receives a check-up in a Tanzanian clinic. Greater availability of antiretroviral medication in the region has improved the life expectancy of people living with HIV/AIDS. Still the infection rates are high, especially among women.

As more Africans move to cities, patterns of settlement are evolving into clusters of higher concentration. Towns that were once small administrative centers for colonial elites grew into major cities. The region even has its own megacity, Lagos, which recently topped 10 million residents. Throughout the continent, African cities are growing faster than rural areas. But before examining the Sub-Saharan urban scene, a more detailed discussion of rural subsistence is needed.

Agricultural Subsistence The staple crops over most of Sub-Saharan Africa are millet, sorghum, rice, and corn (maize), as well as a variety of tubers and root crops such as yams. Irrigated rice is widely grown in West Africa and Madagascar. Geographer Judith Carney in her book *Black Rice* documents how African slaves introduced rice cultivation to the Americas. Corn, in contrast, was introduced to

Africa from the Americas by the slave trade and quickly grew to become a basic food. In higher elevations of Ethiopia and South Africa, wheat and barley are grown. Intermixed with subsistence foods are a variety of export crops—coffee, tea, rubber, bananas, cocoa, cotton, and peanuts—that are grown in distinct ecological zones and often in some of the best soils.

In areas that support annual cropping, population densities are greater. In parts of humid West Africa, for example, the yam became the king of subsistence crops. The Ibos' mastery of yam production allowed them to procure more food and live in denser permanent settlements in the southeastern corner of present-day Nigeria. Much of traditional Ibo culture is tied to the arduous tasks of clearing the fields, tending the delicate plants, and celebrating the harvest.

Over much of the continent, African agriculture remains relatively unproductive, and rural population densities tend to be low. Amid the poorer tropical soils, cropping usually entails shifting cultivation, or **swidden**. This process involves burning the natural vegetation to release fertilizing ash and planting crops such as maize, beans, sweet potatoes, banana, papaya, manioc, yams, melon, and squash. Each plot is temporarily abandoned once its source of nutrients has been exhausted. Swidden cultivation often is a very finely tuned adaptation to local environmental conditions, but it is unable to support high population densities.

Women are the subsistence farmers of the region, producing for their household needs as well as for local and foreign markets. In the densely settled country of Rwanda, most farms are small but the mountainous volcanic soil is ideal for growing coffee. In an effort to rebuild the country after the ethnic genocide in the 1990s, the government targeted improving the quality of the country's coffee through the formation of cooperatives that would bring ethnic groups together and improve farmers' incomes. The cooperatives have taken off and farmers, many of them war widows, have seen their incomes improve. For decades the country's coffee production languished, and farmers earned very little for their low-quality beans. Yet across Rwanda's hillsides were older varieties of coffee plants with high value in today's premium coffee market. Farmers just needed a better way to prepare the beans and market them. Through community-run cooperatives the quality of their washed and sorted beans improved. So too did their ability to bargain with major buyers such as Starbucks or Green Mountain, leaving out the middleman. For many small farmers in Rwanda, their premium coffee is now a source of pride (Figure 6.19).

Plantation Agriculture Designed to produce crops on a large scale for export, plantation agriculture is also critical to the economies of many states. If African countries are to import the modern goods they require, they must sell their own products on the world market. Because the region has few competitive industries, the bulk of its exports are primary products derived from farming, mining, and forestry.

A number of African countries rely heavily on one or two export crops. Coffee, for example, is vital for Ethiopia,

Figure 6.18 Population Distribution The majority of people in Sub-Saharan Africa live in rural areas. Some of these rural zones, however, are densely settled, such as West Africa and the East African highlands. Major urban centers, especially in South Africa and Nigeria, support millions. There is only one megacity in the region with more than 10 million (Lagos, Nigeria), but over two dozen cities have more than 1 million residents.

Kenya, Ivory Coast, and Rwanda. Tea is significant in the East African countries of Kenya, Uganda, and Tanzania. Peanuts have long been the primary foreign exchange earner in the Sahel, while cotton is tremendously important for Mali, Benin, Sudan, Zimbabwe, Ivory Coast, and Cameroon. Ghana and the Ivory Coast have long been the world's main suppliers of cacao (the source of chocolate); Liberia produces plantation rubber; and many farmers in Nigeria specialize in palm oil. The export of such products can bring good money when commodity prices are high as they are now, but when prices periodically collapse, economic devastation may follow.

Nontraditional agricultural exports have emerged in the last two decades that depend upon significant capital inputs

and refrigerated air transportation. One industry is floriculture for the plant and cut flower industry. Here the highland tropical climate of Kenya, Ethiopia, and South Africa is advantageous. Each of these states has experienced growth in floriculture. Similarly, the European market for fresh vegetables and fruits in the winter is being met by some African producers in both West and East Africa.

Pastoralism Animal husbandry (the care of livestock) is extremely important in Sub-Saharan Africa, particularly in the semiarid zones. Camels and goats are the principal animals in the Sahel and the Horn of Africa, but farther south cattle are king (Figure 6.20). Many African peoples have traditionally specialized in cattle raising and are often tied into

Figure 6.19 Rwandan Coffee Farmer A farmer picks coffee berries at her farm outside of Kigali, Rwanda. Coffee was first domesticated in Ethiopia. Today, several African states, such as Rwanda, depend upon coffee as an important export crop.

mutually beneficial relationships with neighboring farmers. Such **pastoralists** typically graze their stock on the stubble of harvested fields during the dry season and then move them to drier uncultivated areas during the wet season when the pastures turn green. Farmers thus have their fields fertilized by the manure of the pastoralists' stock, while the pastoralists find good dry-season grazing. At the same time, the nomads can trade their animal products for grain and other goods of the sedentary world. Several pastoral peoples of East Africa, however, are noted for their extreme reliance on cattle and general (but never complete) independence from

agriculture. The Masai of the Tanzanian–Kenyan borderlands traditionally derive a large percentage of their nutrition from drinking a mixture of milk and blood. The blood is obtained by periodically tapping the animal's jugular vein, a procedure that evidently causes little harm.

Large expanses of Sub-Saharan Africa have been off-limits to cattle because of infestations of **tsetse flies**, which spread sleeping sickness to cattle, humans, and some wildlife. Where wild animals, which harbor the disease but are immune to it, were present in large numbers, especially in environments containing brush or woodland (which are necessary for tsetse fly survival), cattle simply could not be raised. Some evidence suggests that tsetse fly infestations dramatically increased in the late 1800s, greatly harming African societies dependent on livestock but benefiting wildlife populations. At present, tsetse fly eradication programs are reducing the threat, and cattle are spreading into areas that were previously unsuitable. When people and their livestock move into new areas in sizable numbers, wildlife almost inevitably declines.

Sub-Saharan Africa thus presents a difficult environment for raising livestock because of the virulence of its animal diseases. In the tropical rain forests of Central Africa, cattle have never survived well and the only domestic animal that thrives is the goat. Raising horses, moreover, has historically been feasible only in the Sahel and in South Africa. As we shall see later, the disease environment of tropical Africa has presented a variety of problems for humans as well.

Figure 6.20 Pastoralists in the Horn of Africa Two Ethiopian girls walk along a herd of camels. Camels are well suited for the arid conditions of eastern Ethiopia and Somalia. Pastoralists rely on their camels for milk, transport and trade.

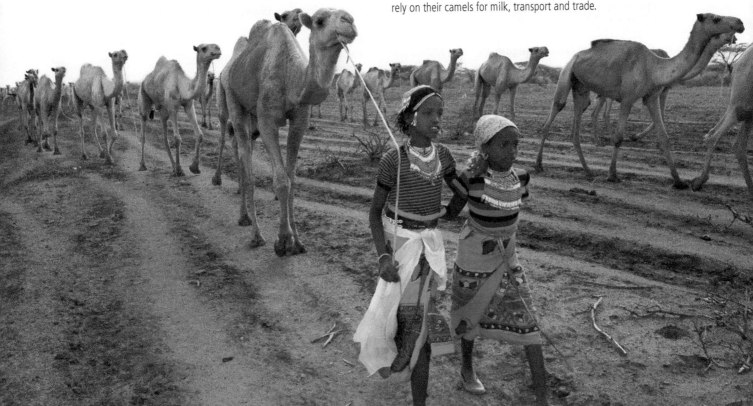

Urban Life

Although Sub-Saharan Africa is considered the least urbanized region in the developing world, most Sub-Saharan cities are growing at twice the national growth rates. If present trends continue, half of the region's population may well be living in cities by 2030. One of the consequences of this surge in city living is urban sprawl. Rural-to-urban migration, industrialization, and refugee flows are forcing the cities of the region to absorb more people and use more resources. As in Latin America, the tendency is toward urban primacy, the condition in which one major city is dominant and at least three times larger than the next largest city. Luanda, the capital of Angola, was built for half a million people but now has at least 4 million residents (many of them were displaced during the country's long years of war). Most of the city's inhabitants live in the growing slums that surround the colonial core (Figure 6.21). In such rapidly growing places, city officials struggle to build enough roads and provide electricity, water, trash collection, and employment for all these people.

European colonialism greatly influenced urban form and development in the region. Africans, however, had an urban tradition prior to the colonial era, although a very small percentage of the population lived in cities. Ancient cities, such as Axum in Ethiopia, thrived 2,000 years ago. Similarly, in the Sahel, prominent trans-Saharan trade centers, such as Timbuktu (Tombouctou) and Gao, have existed for more than a millennium. In East Africa, an urban mercantile culture emerged that was rooted in Islam and the Swahili language. The prominent cities of Zanzibar, Tanzania, and Mombasa, Kenya, flourished by supporting a trade network that linked the East African highlands with the Persian Gulf. The stone ruins of Great Zimbabwe in southern Africa are testimony to the achievements of stone working, metallurgy, and religion achieved by Bantu groups in the 14th century. West Africa, however, had the most developed precolonial urban network, reflecting both indigenous and Islamic traditions. Today it supports some of the region's largest cities.

West African Urban Traditions The West African coastline is dotted with cities, from Dakar, Senegal, in the far north to Lagos, Nigeria, in the east. Half of Nigerians live in cities, and seven of Nigeria's metropolitan areas have populations of more than 1 million. Historically, the Yoruba cities in southwestern Nigeria are the best documented. Developed in the 12th century, cities such as Ibadan were walled and gated, with a palace encircled by large rectangular courtyards at the city center. An important center of trade for an extensive hinterland, Ibadan also was a religious and political center. Lagos was another Yoruba settlement. Founded on a coastal island on the Bight of Benin, most of the modern city has spread onto the nearby mainland. Its coastal setting and natural harbor made this relatively small, indigenous city attractive to colonial powers. When the British took control in the mid-19th century, the city's size and importance grew.

Whereas in 1960, Lagos was a city of only 1 million, today it is well over 10 million residents, making it the largest city in the region. Unable to keep up with the surge of rural migrants, Lagos's streets are clogged with traffic; for those living on the city's periphery, three- and four-hour commutes (one way) are common. For many, the informal sector (unregulated services and trade) provides employment. Crime is another major problem. The chances of being attacked on the streets or robbed in one's home are quite high, even though most windows are barred and houses are fenced. To deal with

Figure 6.21 Urban slums of Luanda, Angola The Roche Santiero market on the outskirts of Luanda serves the city's growing urban poor. Like many Sub-Saharan African cities, Luanda is growing much faster than rural areas in the country.

Figure 6.22 Downtown Lagos, Nigeria A sea of shoppers, vendors and buses fill the streets of the Oshodi Market, the commercial hub of Lagos. Lagos is the largest city in Sub-Saharan Africa with over 10 million inhabitants.

this problem, Lagos has the highest density of police in Nigeria, but the weak social bonds between urban migrants, widespread poverty, and the gap between rich and poor seem to encourage lawlessness (Figure 6.22).

Most West African cities are hybrids, combining Islamic, European, and national elements such as mosques, Victorian architecture, and streets named after independence leaders. Accra is the capital city of Ghana and home to nearly 2 million people. Originally settled by the Ga people in the 16th century, it became a British colonial administrative center by the late 1800s. Here again, the modern city is being transformed through neoliberal policies introduced in the 1980s that attracted international corporations. A growth in foreign investment in financial and producer services led to the creation of a "Global CBD" on the east side of the city away from the "National CBD" (Figure 6.23). Here foreign companies clustered in areas with secure land title, new modern roads, parking, and access to the airport. Upper-income gated communities have also formed near the Global CBD. Accra, like other cities in the region, is rapidly changing due to an influx of foreign capital. The result is highly segregated urban spaces that reflect a global phase in urban development in which world market forces, rather than colonial or national ones, are driving the change.

Urban Industrial South Africa The major cities of southern Africa, unlike those of West Africa, are colonial in origin. Cities such as Lusaka, Zambia, and Harare, Zimbabwe, grew as administrative or mining centers. South Africa is one of the most urbanized states in the entire region, and it is cer-

Figure 6.23 Contemporay Accra, Ghana This model represents the global phase of Accra's development with three distinct CBDs. The national CBD developed from the former European Town. The local CBD is nearby and formed from the Native Town. The Global CBD, fostered by international investment, is removed from the other two and close to the international airport. (From Grant and Nijman, 2002, "Globalization and the Corporate Geography of Cities in the Less-Developed World," *Annals of the Association of American Geographers* 92(2): 320–40.)

CITYSCAPES   Africa's Golden and Global City

Johannesburg is a city of contradictions, where business executives and peasants, artists and refugees, blacks and whites, converge on a sprawling chaotic plateau 5700 ft (1750 m) above sea level in South Africa's *highveld*. Part of Gauteng Province, South Africa's smallest and most urbanized province, over 10 million people reside here in three major metropolitan areas. At the core is the City of Johannesburg (3.6 million), then there is Ekurhuleni (a recently consolidated metropolitan area of former townships to the east with 3.2 million), and Pretoria in the north (1.3 million and one of South Africa's three capitals). Gauteng is a Sesotho word meaning "place of gold," which is how the world came to know Johannesburg when immense gold deposits were discovered there in 1886 (Figure 6.2.1).

Figure 6.2.1 Gauteng Province, South Africa One of nine provinces in post-Apartheid South Africa, it is the smallest by size but the largest in population. The economic engine of the country, Guateng means 'place of gold' and gold production has long been important in this region.

During apartheid, Johannesburg was reworked and segregation intensified. Blacks were forcibly removed from the city center and into all-black townships (segregated neighborhoods on the outskirts of cities) to the east and southwest of the downtown. To the north, wealthier white suburbs formed. In between the commercial center and the townships were the gold mines, where black laborers worked. In fact, Soccer City, the premier stadium site during South Africa's World Cup, is located on a former mine, near the township of Soweto.

Like other townships, Soweto was linked to the mines and the city proper by trains—today's metrorail. A rail for the black masses, this old and over-crowded system was created so that townships would be far from white areas but black and coloured laborers could get to their places of employment. Through in-migration Soweto became one of the biggest townships in the country, and a center for political resistance. Both Nelson Mandela and Bishop Desmond Tutu, leaders against apartheid, had their homes in Soweto. In the post-apartheid era, Soweto is a mixture of lean-tos and middle class housing that attracts mostly black migrants from the former homelands and immigrants from neighboring countries such as Zimbabwe and Mozambique. Soweto was formally incorporated into the City of Johannesburg in the 1990s. And times are changing for Soweto; neat townhouses are replacing squatter homes and Maponya Mall, one of the largest in South Africa, opened in 2007 (Figure 6.2.2).

As apartheid ended, Johannesburg became infamous for its high crime rate. Many white-owned businesses fled the central business district for the northern suburb of Sandton. By the late 1990s, Sandton emerged as the new financial and business center of the City of Johannesburg. When Gauteng province invested $3 billion dollars in a new high-speed commuter rail called Gautrain, it was no accident that the first functioning line linked Sandton with Tambo International Airport. Eventually these luxurious trains will link other parts of Johannesburg as well as the city of Pretoria (Figure 6.2.3).

Whatever your image of Johannesburg may be—be it city of gold, sprawling slums, violent gangsters or cosmopolitan playground—this is the African metropolitan area that aspires to global city status. By successfully hosting the World Cup in 2010—the most watched international sporting event—South Africa, and especially Johannesburg, showed the world the economic vibrancy of this golden city.

tainly the most industrialized. The foundations of South Africa's urban economy rest largely on its incredibly rich mineral resources (diamonds, gold, chromium, platinum, tin, uranium, coal, iron ore, and manganese). Seven of its metropolitan areas have more than 1 million people; the largest of them are Johannesburg, Durban, and Cape Town.

The form of South African cities continues to be imprinted by the legacy of **apartheid**, an official policy of racial segregation that shaped social relations in South

Africa for nearly 50 years. Even though apartheid was abolished in 1994, it is still evident in the landscape. Under apartheid rules, all cities were divided into residential areas according to racial categories: white, **coloured** (a South African term describing people of mixed African and European ancestry), Indian (South Asian), and African (black). In Cape Town, whites occupied the largest and most desirable portions of the city, especially the scenic areas below Table Mountain (Figure 6.24). Blacks were crowded into

Figure 6.2.2 Maponya Mall, Soweto Soweto residents leaving Maponya Mall after shopping. This shopping center, which opened in 2007, is emblematic of the new Soweto where first-world comforts meet the gritty reality of former township life. Soweto is home to some of South Africa's most important landmarks in the struggle over white-minority rule. There is still tremendous poverty here but increasingly shopping centers, middle class housing and landscaped parks are also part of the landscape.

Figure 6.2.3 Sandton, Johannesburg. Just north of Johannesburg's Central Business District, Sandton has emerged as the financial and business center of the New South Africa. Many businesses relocated here, fleeing high crime rates in the old CBD. With world-class shopping, hotels, a convention center, and even Nelson Mandela Square, Sandton has become the part of Johannesburg that most tourists and business people experience.

the least desired areas, forming squatter settlements called **townships** in places such as Gugulethu. Today blacks, coloureds, and Indians are legally allowed to live anywhere they want. Yet the economic differences between racial groups, as well as deep-rooted animosity, hinder residential integration. Post-apartheid settlements, such as Cape Town's Delpht South, promote residential integration of black and coloured households, something that was forbidden during the apartheid years.

Post-Apartheid South African cities, such as Cape Town and Johannesburg, are consciously being developed to reflect a multi-racial and globalized reality (see Cityscapes: Africa's Golden and Global City). As evidenced by the many construction projects completed to host the 2010 World Cup, the country sought to project a modern and progressive image. The relative economic strength of South Africa also means that thousands of immigrants from other African states have settled there in the last decade in search of eco-

Figure 6.24 Elite Cape Town Landscape Europeans settled in this prize farmland to the east and south of Table Mountain. Today this area is home to South Africa's best vineyards.

nomic opportunities not available in their countries of origin. This has produced tensions, as many black South Africans fear that African immigrants are competing with them for jobs and scare resources. Yet the economic clout and ethnic diversity of Johannesburg—along with its sister metropolitan area Ekurhuleni—make this urban space extremely significant in shaping cultural and urban trends for the rest of Sub-Saharan Africa.

CULTURAL COHERENCE AND DIVERSITY: Unity through Adversity

No world region is culturally homogeneous, but most have been partially unified in the past by widespread systems of belief and communication. Traditional African religions, however, were largely limited to local areas, and the religions that did become widespread, Islam and Christianity, are primarily associated with other world regions. A handful of African trade languages have long been understood over vast territories (Swahili in East Africa, Mandingo and Hausa in West Africa), but none spans the entire Sub-Saharan region. Sub-Saharan Africa also lacks a history of widespread political union or even of an indigenous system of political relations. The powerful African kingdoms and empires of past centuries all were limited to distinct subregions of the landmass.

The lack of traditional cultural and political coherence across Sub-Saharan Africa is not surprising if one considers the region's huge size. Sub-Saharan Africa is more than four times larger than Europe or South Asia. Had foreign imperialism not impinged on the region, it is quite possible that

West Africa and southern Africa would have developed into their own distinct world regions.

An African identity south of the Sahara was forged through a common history of slavery and colonialism as well as struggles for independence and development. More telling, the people of the region often define themselves as African, especially to the outside world. That Sub-Saharan Africa is poor by most economic measures, no one will argue. And yet the cultural expressions of its people—its music, dance, and art—are joyous. Africans share an extraordinary resilience and optimism that visitors to the region often comment on. The cultural diversity of the region is obvious, yet there is unity among the people drawn from surviving many adversities.

Language Patterns

In most Sub-Saharan countries, as in other former colonies, multiple languages are used that reflect tribal, ethnic, colonial, and national affiliations. Indigenous languages, many from the Bantu subfamily, often are localized to relatively small rural areas. More widely spoken African trade languages, such as Swahili or Hausa, serve as a lingua franca over broader areas. Overlaying native languages are Indo-European (French and English) and Afro-Asiatic ones (Arabic). Figure 6.25 illustrates the complex pattern of language families and major languages found in Africa today. Contrast the larger map with the inset that shows current "official" languages. A comparison of the two shows that most African countries are multilingual, which can be a source of tension within states. In Nigeria, for example, the official language is English, yet there are millions of Hausa, Yoruba, Igbo (or Ibo), Ful (or Fulani), and Efik speakers, as well as speakers of dozens of other languages.

African Language Groups Three of the six language groups mapped in Figure 6.25 are unique to the region (Niger-Congo, Nilo-Saharan, and Khoisan), while the other three (Afro-Asiatic, Austronesian, and Indo-European) are more closely associated with other parts of the world. Afro-Asiatic languages, especially Arabic, dominate North Africa and are understood in Islamic areas of Sub-Saharan Africa as well. Amharic in Ethiopia and Somali of Somalia are also Afro-Asiatic languages. The Malayo-Polynesian language family is limited to the island of Madagascar, which many believe was first settled by seafarers from Indonesia some 1,500 years ago. Indo-European languages, especially French, English, Portuguese, and Afrikaans, are a legacy of colonialism and widely used today.

Of the three language groups found exclusively in the region, the Niger-Congo language group is by far the most influential. This linguistic group originated in West Africa and includes Mandingo, Yoruba, Ful (ani), and Igbo, among others. Around 3,000 years ago a people of the Niger-Congo stock began to expand out of western Africa into the equatorial zone. This group, called the Bantu, commenced one of

Figure 6.25 African Language Groups and Official Languages Mapping language is a complex task for Sub-Saharan Africa. There are languages with millions of speakers, such as Swahili, and there are languages spoken by a few hundred people living in isolated areas. Six language families are represented in the region. Among these families are scores of individual languages (see the labels on the map). Because most modern states have many indigenous languages, the colonial language often became the "official" language because it was less controversial than picking from among several indigenous languages. English and French are the most common official languages in the region (see inset).

the most far-ranging migrations in human history, which introduced agriculture into large areas of central and southern Africa. One Bantu group migrated east across the fringes of the rain forest to settle in the Lake Victoria basin in East Africa, where they formed an eastern Bantu core that later pushed south all the way to South Africa (Figure 6.26). Another group moved south, into the rain forest proper. The equatorial rain-forest belt immediately adjacent to the original Bantu homeland had been very sparsely settled by the ancestors of the modern pygmies (a distinct people noted for

their short stature and hunting skills). Pygmy groups, having entered into close trading relations with the Bantu newcomers, eventually came to speak Bantu languages as well. While several pygmy populations have persisted to the present, their original languages disappeared long ago.

Once the Bantu migrants had advanced beyond the rain forest into the savannas and woodlands, their agricultural techniques proved highly successful and their influence expanded (see Figure 6.26). Around 650 CE, Bantu-speaking peoples reached South Africa. Over the centuries, the various

Figure 6.26 Bantu Migrations Bantu languages, a subfamily of the Niger-Congo language family, are widely spoken throughout Sub-Saharan Africa. The out-migration of Bantu tribes from an original core in West Africa and a secondary core in East Africa helps to explain the diffusion of Bantu languages, which include Zulu, Swahili, Bemba, Shona, Lingala, and Kikuyu, among others. (From Newman, 1995, *The Peopling of Africa*, New Haven: Yale University Press, 141)

languages and dialects of the many Bantu-speaking groups, which often were separated from each other by considerable distances, gradually diverged from each other. Today there are several hundred distinct languages in the Bantu subfamily of the great Niger-Congo group. All Bantu languages, however, remain closely related to each other, and a speaker of one can generally learn any other without undue difficulty.

Most individual Sub-Saharan languages are limited to relatively small areas and are significant only at the local scale. One language in the Bantu subfamily, Swahili, eventually became the most widely spoken Sub-Saharan language. Swahili originated as a trade language on the East African coast, where a number of merchant colonies from Arabia were established around 1100 CE. A hybrid society grew up in a narrow coastal band of modern Kenya and Tanzania, one speaking a language of Bantu structure enriched with many Arabic words. While Swahili became the primary language only in the narrow coastal belt, it spread far into the interior as the language of trade. After independence, both Kenya and Tanzania adopted Swahili as an official language. Swahili, with an estimated 60–90 million speakers, is the lingua franca of East Africa. It has generated a fairly extensive literature and is often studied in other regions of the world.

Language and Identity Ethnic identity as well as linguistic affiliation have historically been highly unstable over much of Sub-Saharan Africa. The tendency was for new groups to form when people threatened by war fled to less-settled areas, where they often mixed with peoples from other places. In such circumstances, new languages arise quickly, and divisions between groups are blurred. Nevertheless, distinct **tribes** formed that consisted of a group of families or clans with a common kinship, language, and definable territory. The impetus to formalize tribal boundaries came from

European colonial administrators who were eager to establish a fixed indigenous social order to better control native peoples. In this process, a flawed cultural map of Sub-Saharan Africa evolved. Some tribes were artificially divided, meaningless names were applied, and territorial boundaries were often misinterpreted.

Social boundaries between different ethnic and linguistic groups have become more stable in recent years, and a number of individual languages have become particularly important for communication on a national scale. Wolof in Senegal; Mandingo in Mali; Mossi in Burkina Faso; Yoruba, Hausa, and Igbo in Nigeria; Kikuyu in central Kenya; and Zulu, Xhosa, and Sesotho in South Africa all are nationally significant languages spoken by millions of people (Figure 6.27). None, however, has the status of being the official language of any country. With the end of apartheid in South Africa, the country officially recognized 11 languages, although English is still the lingua franca of business and government. Indeed, a single language has a clear majority status in only a handful of Sub-Saharan countries. The more linguistically homogeneous states include Somalia (where virtually everyone speaks Somali) and the very small states of Rwanda, Burundi, Swaziland, and Lesotho.

Figure 6.27 Multilingual South Africa A South African sign warns pedestrians not to cross a highway in three languages: English, Afrikaans, and Zulu. Throughout Sub-Saharan Africa, many people are multilingual because of the diversity of languages that exist in each state.

European Languages In the colonial period, European countries used their own languages for administrative purposes in their African empires. Education in the colonial period also stressed literacy in the language of the imperial power. In the postindependence period, most Sub-Saharan African countries have continued to use the languages of their former colonizers for government and higher education. Few of these new states had a clear majority language that they could employ, and picking any minority tongue would have aroused the opposition of other peoples. The one exception is Ethiopia, which maintained its independence during the colonial era. The official language is Amharic, although other indigenous languages are also spoken.

Two vast blocks of European languages exist in Africa today: Francophone Africa, encompassing the former colonies of France and Belgium, where French serves as the main language of administration; and Anglophone Africa, where the use of English prevails (see inset, Figure 6.25). Early Dutch settlement in South Africa resulted in the use of Afrikaans (a Dutch-based language) by several million South Africans. Portuguese is spoken in Angola and Mozambique, former colonies of Portugal. In Mauritania and Sudan, Arabic serves as the main language.

Religion

Indigenous African religions generally are classified as *animist*, a somewhat misleading catchall term used to classify all local faiths that do not fit into one of the handful of "world religions." Most animist religions are centered on the worship of nature and ancestral spirits, but the internal diversity within the animist tradition is vast. Classifying a religion as animist says more about what it is not than what it actually is.

Both Christianity and Islam actually entered the region early in their histories, but they advanced slowly for many

centuries. There are even ancient Jewish populations in the region–especially in Ethiopia–but many Ethiopian Jews resettled in Israel in the 1980s. Since the beginning of the 20th century, both Christianity and Islam have spread rapidly—more rapidly, in fact, than in any other part of the world. But tens of millions of Africans still hold animist beliefs, and many others combine animist practices and ideas with their observances of Christianity and Islam.

The Introduction and Spread of Christianity Christianity came first to northeast Africa. Kingdoms in both Ethiopia and central Sudan were converted by 300 CE—the earliest conversions outside of the Roman Empire. The peoples of Ethiopia adopted the Coptic form of Christianity and have thus historically looked to Egypt's Christian minority for their religious leadership (Figure 6.28). Today, roughly half of the population of both Ethiopia and Eritrea follow Coptic Christianity; most of the rest are Muslim, but there are still some animist communities.

European settlers and missionaries introduced Christianity to other parts of Sub-Saharan Africa beginning in the 1600s. The Dutch, who began to colonize South Africa

Figure 6.28 Eritrean Christians at Prayer Coptic Christians gather in front of St. Mary's Church in Asmara, Eritrea, on Good Friday, a holy day for Christians. Half of the populations in Eritrea and Ethiopia belong to the Coptic Church, which has ties to the Christian minority in Egypt.

at this time, brought their Calvinist Protestant faith. Later European immigrants to South Africa brought Anglicanism and other Protestant creeds, as well as Catholicism. A substantial Jewish community also emerged, concentrated in the Johannesburg area. Most black South Africans eventually converted to one or another form of Christianity as well. In fact, churches in South Africa were instrumental in the long fight against white racial supremacy. Religious leaders such as Bishop Desmond Tutu were outspoken critics of the injustices of apartheid and worked to bring down the system.

Elsewhere in Africa, Christianity came with European missionaries, most of whom arrived after the mid-1800s. As was true in the rest of the world, missionaries had little success where Islam had preceded them, but they eventually made numerous conversions in animist areas. As a general rule, Protestant Christianity prevails in areas of former British colonization, while Catholicism is important where France, Belgium, and Portugal had staked their empires. In the postcolonial era, African Christianity has diversified, at times taking on a life of its own independent from foreign missionary efforts. Increasingly active in the region are various Pentecostal, Evangelical, and Mormon missionary

groups, mostly from the United States. Yet many areas also have seen the emergence of syncretic faiths, in which Christianity is complexly intertwined with traditional belief systems. It is difficult to map the distribution of Christianity in Africa, however, because it has spread irregularly across the entire non-Islamic portion of the region.

The Introduction and Spread of Islam Islam began to advance into Sub-Saharan Africa 1,000 years ago (Figure 6.29). Berber traders from North Africa and the Sahara introduced the religion to the Sahel, and by 1050 the Kingdom of Tokolor in modern Senegal emerged as the first Sub-Saharan Muslim state. Somewhat later, the ruling class of the powerful Mande-speaking mercantile empires of Ghana and Mali converted as well. In the 14th century, the emperor of Mali astounded the Muslim world when he and his huge entourage made the pilgrimage to Mecca, bringing with them so much gold that they set off an inflationary spiral throughout Southwest Asia.

Mande-speaking traders, whose networks spanned the area from the Sahel to the Gulf of Guinea, gradually introduced the religion to other areas of West Africa. There, however, many peoples remained committed to animism, and

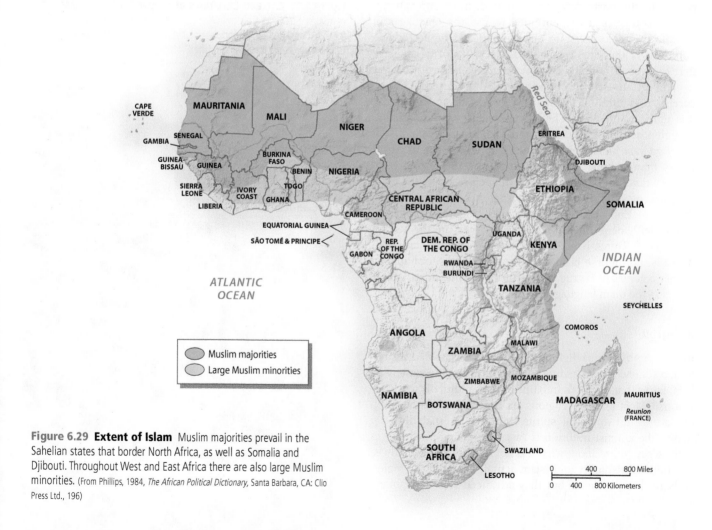

Figure 6.29 Extent of Islam Muslim majorities prevail in the Sahelian states that border North Africa, as well as Somalia and Djibouti. Throughout West and East Africa there are also large Muslim minorities. (From Phillips, 1984, *The African Political Dictionary*, Santa Barbara, CA: Clio Press Ltd., 196)

Figure 6.30 West African Muslims Villagers leave the Larabanga mosque after Friday prayers. The Muslim village of Larabanga in northern Ghana is home to one of the oldest mosques in West Africa and was recently declared a UN World Heritage Site.

Islam made slow and fitful progress. Even in the Sahel, syncretic forms of Islam prevailed through the 1700s. In the early 1800s, however, the pastoral Fulani people launched a series of successful holy wars designed to shear away animist practices and to establish pure Islam. Today orthodox Islam prevails through most of the Sahel. Farther south Muslims are mixed with Christians and animists, but their numbers continue to grow and their practices tend to be orthodox as well (Figure 6.30).

Interaction Between Religious Traditions The southward spread of Islam from the Sahel, coupled with the northward dissemination of Christianity from the port cities, has generated a complex religious frontier across much of West Africa. In Nigeria, the Hausa are firmly Muslim, while the southeastern Igbo are largely Christians. The Yoruba of the southwest are divided between Christians and Muslims. In the more remote parts of Nigeria, moreover, animist traditions remain vital. But despite this religious diversity, religious conflict in Nigeria has been relatively rare until recently. In 2000, seven Nigerian states imposed Muslim sharia laws, which triggered intermittent violence ever since, especially in the northern cities of Kano and Kaduna. More recently in 2010 near the central city of Jos, hundreds of Christian and Muslim villagers were slaughtered in violent clashes and retaliatory killings. Many of the victims were women and children. Still, most of West Africa's regional conflicts continue to be framed more along ethnic terms, rather than religious ones.

Religious conflict historically has been far more acute in northeastern Africa, where Muslims and Christians have struggled against each other for centuries. Islam came early

to the coastal areas of the Horn, and soon it had virtually isolated the Ethiopian highlands from the rest of the Christian world. In recent years, religious conflict in the Horn has remained muted and has been largely replaced by ethnic and ideological struggles. The new country of Eritrea, which is roughly half Christian and half Muslim, has in the past few years emerged as something of a model of peaceful coexistence between members of different faiths.

Sudan, on the other hand, is currently the scene of an intense conflict that is both religious and ethnic in origin. Islam was introduced to Sudan in the 1300s by an invasion of Arabic-speaking pastoralists who destroyed the indigenous Coptic Christian kingdoms of the areas. Within a few hundred years, central and northern Sudan became completely Islamic. The southern equatorial provinces of Sudan, however, where tropical diseases and extensive wetlands stalled Arab advances, remained animist or converted to Christianity under British colonial rule. In the 1970s, the Arabic-speaking Muslims of north and central Sudan emerged as the country's dominant group and began to build an Islamic state. Experiencing both religious discrimination and economic exploitation, the Christian and animist peoples of the south subsequently launched a massive rebellion. Fighting began in the 1980s and was intense until 2003 when an agreement was reached between Sudan People's Liberation Army (SPLA) and the government of Khartoum. During the conflict the government generally controlled the main towns and roads and the rebels maintained power in the countryside. Southern Sudan has excellent soils and oil reserves, which have been only partially exploited because of the years of conflict. As part of the peace agreement southern Sudan was also promised an opportunity to vote on secession from the north in 2011 (although many doubt that the north will allow the vote to happen). Just as peace was finally brokered in southern Sudan, a brutal ethnic conflict broke out in the western province of Darfur, which will be discussed in detail later in the chapter.

With the exception of Sudan, a pattern of peaceful coexistence among different faiths is a distinguishing feature of Sub-Saharan Africa that deserves further study. Sub-Saharan Africa is a land of religious vitality. Both Christianity and Islam are spreading rapidly, but animism continues to hold widespread appeal. Many new syncretic (blended) forms of religious expression are also emerging. With such diversity of faiths, it is fortunate that religion is not typically the cause of overt conflict.

Globalization and African Culture

The slave triangle that linked Africa to the Americas and Europe set in process patterns of cultural diffusion that transferred African peoples and practices across the Atlantic. Tragically, slavery damaged the demographic and political strength of African societies, especially in West Africa, from where the most slaves were taken. An estimated 12 million Africans were shipped to the Americas as slaves from the 1500s until 1870 (Figure 6.31). Slavery impacted the entire

Figure 6.31 African Slave Trade The slave trade had a devastating impact on Sub-Saharan societies. From ship logs, it is estimated that 12 million Africans were shipped to the Americas to work as slaves on sugar, cotton, and rice plantations; the majority went to Brazil and the Caribbean. Yet other slave routes existed, although the data are less reliable. Africans from south of the Sahara were used as slaves in North Africa. Others were traded across the Indian Ocean into Southwest Asia and South Asia.

region, sending Africans not just to the Americas, but to Europe, North Africa, and Southwest Asia. The vast majority, however, worked on plantations across the Americas.

Out of this tragic diaspora came a blending of African cultures with Amerindian and European ones. African rhythms are at the core of various musical styles from rumba to jazz, the blues, and rock and roll. Brazil, the largest county in Latin America, is claimed to be the second largest "African state" (after Nigeria) because of the huge Afro-Brazilian population. Thus the forced migration of Africans as slaves had a huge cultural influence on many areas of the world.

Cultural exchanges are never one-way. Foreign language, religion, and dress were absorbed by Africans who remained in the region. With independence in the 1960s and 1970s, several states sought to rediscover their ancestral roots by openly rejecting European cultural elements. Ironically, the search for traditional religions found African scholars traveling to the Caribbean and Brazil to consult with Afro-religious practitioners about ceremonial elements lost to West Africa.

Africans are also emigrating from the region in record numbers, and in the process they are influencing cultures of many world regions. Whether it is the selection of

African soccer stars for prestige European clubs, to the election in 2007 of Nigerian-native, Rotimi Adebari, as mayor of Porlaoise, Ireland, to the settlement of Somali refugees in Minneapolis, Minnesota, contemporary African migration is creating new transnational connections and reshaping the ethnic composition of localities around the world. Perhaps one of the most celebrated persons of African decent is President Barack Obama, the son of a Kenyan man and a woman from Kansas. Obama's heritage and upbringing embody the forces of globalization. In Kenya, he is hailed as part of the modern African diaspora—young professionals and their offspring who leave the continent and make their mark somewhere else. As an indicator of our global age, Kenyan President Mwai Kibaki declared a Kenyan national holiday after Obama won the U.S. election in November 2008 (People on the Move: The New African Americans).

Popular culture in Africa, like everywhere else in the world, is a dynamic mixture of global and local influences. Kwaito, the latest musical craze in South Africa, sounds a lot like rap from the United States. A closer listen, however, reveals an incorporation of local rhythms, lyrics in Zulu and Xhosa, and themes about life in the post-apartheid town-

PEOPLE ON THE MOVE The New African Americans

Since the 1990s tens of thousands of African immigrants have settled in the US, making Africa one of the fastest growing source regions for new immigrants. Like other immigrants, they come for economic opportunity, family reunification and as resettled refugees. There are about 1.5 million African-born immigrants in the U.S., the majority (75 percent) settled here since 1990. Nigeria and Ethiopia are the biggest sending countries, which is not terribly surprising since they are also the biggest countries in terms of population.

The latest arrivals from Africa are a mix of highly educated college graduates and refugees seeking asylum. Over 40 percent of African immigrants have college degrees, a figure that is much higher than the U.S. population as a whole. In particular, many women come as health care professionals, especially nurses. While Africans are found throughout the country, one-third of them are concentrated in three metropolitan areas: New York, Washington DC, and Atlanta. For example, Metropolitan Washington hosts the largest concentration of Ethiopians in the United States. They have established scores of restaurants and businesses in the Shaw Neighborhood, a historic African American section of the District of Columbia that is now often referred to as "Little Ethiopia" (Figure 6.3.1). Similarly in New York and Atlanta, African foods, music, and cultural events have been incorporated into the urban-cultural landscape.

Refugees are also an important part of the immigrant flow. Through resettlement programs, concentrations of Africans have emerged in Minneapolis–St. Paul, Boston, and Columbus. In Minneapolis–St. Paul, where many Somali refugees were resettled, Africans account for 20 percent of all immigrants in the Twin Cities. In general, refugees are a more needy population, arriving with less social capital and economic resources. Unlike economic migrants, refugees are assisted in their settlement and job placement as part of the federally funded Refugee Act of 1980. The major African refugee populations in the U.S. include Ethiopians, Eritreans, Somalis, Liberians, and Sudanese.

People of African ancestry have lived in the United States for nearly as long as people of European ancestry, and account for 12 percent of the total U.S. population. The percentage of African Americans in the US population was significantly higher in 1800. The percentage declined, in part, due to the abolition of slavery. Yet in the late 19th century restrictive measures were also put into place that made it virtually impossible for Africans to emigrate to America until 1965, when the Immigration and Nationality Act opened up immigration to peoples from Africa and Asia.

In the United States, African immigrants often find the term African American confusing. As newcomers from Africa, some have proposed the term *Neo* African Americans because their cultural and social history is so different from native-born African Americans. African immigrants have also maintained important ties with their countries of origin through remittances and transnational businesses. In fact, several African governments actively court this modern diaspora in the hope that some will return and invest in their home countries.

Figure 6.3.1 Ethiopian businessman in Washington, DC
An Ethiopian entrepreneur stands in front of his shop in the Shaw Neigborhood of Washington DC. Metropolitan Washington attracts many African immigrants, and is home to the largest concentration of Ethiopians in the U.S.

ships. Lagos, Nigeria, is Africa's film capital. Referred to as Nollywood because over 500 films a year are made there, most are shot in a few days and with budgets of $10,000. These pulp movies are often criticized for being exploitive imitations of Hollywood B-movies. Yet the African movies touch on themes that resonate with Africans such as religion, ethnicity, corruption, witchcraft, and ritual killings. They can be seen all over English-speaking Africa.

Music in West Africa Nigeria is the musical center of West Africa, with a well-developed and cosmopolitan recording industry. Modern Nigerian styles such as juju, highlife, and Afro-beat are influenced by jazz, rock, reggae, and gospel, but they are driven by an easily recognizable African sound. Further up the Niger River, lies the country of Mali. Bamako, the capital, is also a music center that has produced scores of recording artists. Many Malian musicians descend from a traditional caste of musical storytellers performing on either the traditional kora (a cross between a harp and a lute) or the guitar. The musical style is strikingly similar to that of Blues from the Mississippi Delta. So much so that Ali Farka Touré, from northern Mali, was referred to as the Bluesman of Africa because of his distinctive, yet familiar, guitar work. Each January, not far from Timbuktu, music fans from West Africa and Europe gather for the Festival in the Desert. In this remote Saharan locale, a celebration of Malian music and Touareg nomadic culture draws together western tourists, African musicians, and nomads (Figure 6.32).

Contemporary African music can be both commercially and politically important. Nigerian singer Fela Kuti became a voice of political conscience for Nigerians struggling for true democracy. From an elite family and educated in England, Kuti borrowed from jazz, traditional, and popular music to produce the Afro-beat sound in the 1970s. Yet it was his searing and angry lyrics that attracted the most at-

tention. Acutely critical of the military government, he sang of police harassment, the inequities of the international economic order, and even Lagos's infamous traffic. Singing in English and Yoruba, his message was transmitted to a larger audience, and he became a target of state harassment. At times self-exiled in Ghana, in the 1980s Kuti was jailed briefly by the Nigerian government, but widespread protests eventually led to his early release. Though Fela Kuti's protest music is unpopular with the state, it has been copied by other groups, making music an important form of political expression in Nigeria as well as in other Sub-Saharan states. Sadly, Kuti died in Lagos in 1997 from complications of AIDS; he was 58 years old. His son, however, is now an important recording artist in Nigeria.

For many African emigrants, music can also be deeply nostalgic. No singer expresses this longing for home better than Cesária Evora from Cape Verde. A Grammy-winning singer, Evora is known for a style of singing called *mornas*, ballads that express sadness and yearning. Her need to sing is rooted in the emotion of *sodade*—a longing to find a better life elsewhere combined with the hope of returning to live among one's people. This need to leave one's home in order to support one's family is an experience that has shaped Cape Verdeans since the late 1800s when mass emigration began. As more Africans emigrate from their countries of origin in response to dire economic or political conditions, their music is reflective of this experience.

The Pride of Runners Ethiopia and Kenya have produced many of the world's greatest distance runners. Abebe Dikila won Ethiopia's and Africa's first Olympic gold medal running barefoot at the Rome games in 1960. Since then nearly every Olympic games has yielded medals for Ethiopia and Kenya. At the Beijing Olympics in 2008, Kenyan runners won 14 medals and Ethiopians 7 (4 of them gold). These states were the top medal winners for Africa in Beijing (Figure 6.33).

Running is a national pastime in Kenya and Ethiopia, where elevation—Addis Ababa sits at 7,300 feet (2,200 meters) and Nairobi at 5,300 feet (1,600 meters)—increases oxygen carrying capacity. Past medalists Haile Gebrselassie and Derartu Tulu are national celebrities in Ethiopia who are idealized by the country's youth. Tulu, the first black African woman to win a gold medal in distance running, is a forceful voice for women's rights in a country where women are discouraged from putting on running shorts. There is talk of a political career for Gebrselassie after he hangs up his running shoes.

Sub-Saharan Africa has shared many of its cultural practices with the world, and the creative and athletic vitality of its people continues to be recognized. In contrast to the fairly peaceful coexistence of diverse religious traditions in Sub-Saharan Africa, ethnic tensions have often boiled over into violent disputes. To understand the roots of ethnic conflict in the region, it is necessary first to examine the region's political history, paying particular attention to the legacy of European colonization.

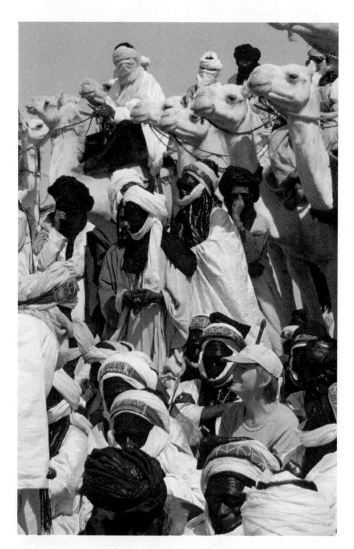

Figure 6.32 Festival in the Desert Every January, thousands of Touareg nomads, Malian musicians, and Western tourists gather in the oasis town of Essakane, Mali, to attend the Festival in the Desert. In this image a Western tourist sits among the Touareg at the festival.

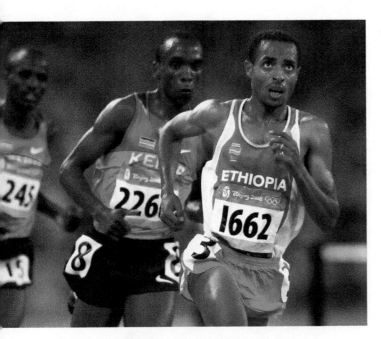

Figure 6.33 Ethiopian or Kenyan Distance Runners Kenenisa Bekele of Ethiopia, right, leads Eliud Kipchoge and Edwin Soi of Kenya on the last lap of the 5000 meters race at the Beijing Olympic Games. Kenyans and Ethiopians take pride in their elite distance runners.

GEOPOLITICAL FRAMEWORK: Legacies of Colonialism and Conflict

The duration of human settlement in Sub-Saharan Africa is unmatched by any other region. Evidence shows that humankind originated there, evidently evolving from a rather apelike *Australopithicus* all the way to modern *Homo sapiens*. Over the millennia, many diverse ethnic groups formed in the region. Although conflicts among these groups have existed, cooperation and coexistence among different peoples has also occurred.

With the arrival of Europeans, patterns of human relatedness and ethnic relations were changed forever. As Europeans rushed to carve up the continent to serve their imperial ambitions, they instituted various policies that heightened ethnic tensions and promoted hostility. Many of the region's modern conflicts can trace their roots back to the colonial era, especially the arbitrary drawing of political boundaries. Others are attributed to struggles over national identity and political control over limited resources among different ethnic groups.

Indigenous Kingdoms and European Encounters

The first significant state to emerge in Sub-Saharan Africa was Nubia, which controlled a large territory in central and northern Sudan some 3,000 years ago (Figure 6.34); 1,000 years later the Kingdom of Axum arose in northern Ethiopia and Eritrea. Both of these states were strongly influenced by political models derived from Egypt and Arabia. The first wholly indigenous African states were founded in the Sahel around 700 CE. Kingdoms such as Ghana, Mali, Songhai, and Kanem-Bornu grew rich by exporting gold to the Mediterranean and importing salt from the Sahara, and they maintained power over lands to the south by monopolizing horse breeding and mastering cavalry warfare.

Over the next several centuries, a variety of other states emerged in West Africa. Some were large but diffuse empires organized through elaborate hierarchies of local kings and chiefs; others were centralized states focused on small centers of power. The Yoruba of southwestern Nigeria, for example, developed a city-state form of government, and their homeland is still one of the most urbanized and densely populated parts of Africa. The most powerful Sub-Saharan states continued to be located in the Sahel until the 1600s, when European coastal trade undercut the lucrative trans-Saharan networks. Subsequently, the focus of power moved to the Gulf of Guinea, where well-organized African states (such as Dahomey and Ashanti) as well as Europeans took advantage of the lucrative opportunities presented by the slave trade and in the process increased their military and economic power.

Early European Encounters Unlike the relatively rapid colonization of the Americas, Europeans needed centuries to gain effective control of Sub-Saharan Africa. Portuguese traders arrived along the coast of West Africa in the 1400s, and by the 1500s they were well established in East Africa as well. Initially, the Portuguese made large profits, converted a few local rulers to Christianity, established several fortified trading posts, and acquired dominion over the Swahili trading cities of the east. They stretched themselves too thin, however, and many of their settlements failed or were lost to other colonizers. Only where a sizable population of mixed African and Portuguese descent emerged, as along the coasts of modern Angola and Mozambique as well as the islands of Cape Verde, could Portugal maintain power. Along the Swahili, or eastern, coast they were eventually expelled by Arabs from Oman, who subsequently established their own mercantile empire in the area.

The Disease Factor One of the main reasons for the Portuguese failure was the disease environment of Africa. With no resistance to malaria and other tropical diseases, roughly half of all Europeans who remained on the African mainland died within a year. Protected both by their formidable armies and by the diseases of their native lands, African states were able to maintain an upper hand over European traders and adventurers well into the 1800s. Unlike the Americas, where European conquest was facilitated by the introduction of Old World diseases that devastated native populations (see Chapters 4 and 5), Sub-Saharan Africa's native diseases limited European settlement until the mid-19th century.

The hazards of malaria and other tropical diseases such as sleeping sickness were compensated by the lure of profit, and other European traders soon followed the Portuguese.

Figure 6.34 Early Sub-Saharan States and Empires
Lost in the current political boundaries of Sub-Saharan Africa are the many African states and empires that existed long before Europeans advanced their territorial claims in the region. Most African kingdoms ceased to exist by 1900, but Buganda (in Uganda) and Abyssinia (in Ethiopia), existed well into the mid-20th century. (From Aryeetey-Attoh, 1997, *Geography of Sub-Saharan Africa,* Upper Saddle River, NJ: Prentice Hall, 63; and Stock, 1995, *Africa South of the Sahara,* New York: Guilford Press, 62)

By the 1600s, Dutch, British, and French firms dominated the lucrative export of slaves, gold, and ivory from the Gulf of Guinea. The Dutch also established a settler colony in South Africa, safely outside of the tropical disease zone, to supply their ships bound for Indonesia. For the next 200 years, European traders came and went, occasionally building fortified coastal posts, but they almost never ventured inland and seldom had any real influence on African rulers. By exporting millions of slaves, however, they had a profoundly negative impact on African society.

In the 1850s, European doctors discovered that a daily dose of quinine would offer protection against malaria, radically changing the balance of power in Africa. Explorers immediately began to penetrate the interior of the conti-

nent, while merchants and expeditionary forces began to move inland from the coast. The first imperial claims soon followed. The French quickly grabbed power along the easily navigated Senegal River, while the British established protectorates over the indigenous states of the Gold Coast (modern-day Ghana), in which the British guaranteed protection for these territories in exchange for various trade preferences.

European Colonization

In the 1880s, European colonization of the region quickly accelerated, leading to the so-called scramble for Africa. By this time, after the invention of the machine gun, no African state could long resist European force. The exact reasons for the abrupt division of Africa among the colonial powers remain controversial, but several developments seem to have been crucial. One was the British seizure in 1882 of Egypt, a territory that the French had long coveted. In return, the infuriated French began to seize additional lands in West Africa, equatorial Africa, and Madagascar.

Another contributing factor was the desire of several new European countries to join the game of empire-building. Because Asia was either occupied by established European powers or controlled by still-formidable indigenous empires, Africa emerged as the main arena of rivalry and expansion. Even though Belgium had been a country only since 1830, its king quickly began to carve out a personal empire along the Congo River, using particularly brutal techniques. The German government—which itself dated back only to 1871—began to claim territories wherever German missionaries were active, and it soon staked out the colonies of Togo, Cameroon, Namibia, and Tanganyika (modern Tanzania minus the island of Zanzibar). The Italians eyed the Horn of Africa, while Spain acquired a small coastal foothold in equatorial West Africa. Alarmed by such activity, the Portuguese began to push inland from their coastal possessions in Angola and Mozambique.

Also in the early 1800s, two small territories were established in West Africa so that freed and runaway slaves would have a place to return to in Africa. The territory that was to become Liberia was set up by the American Colonization Society in 1822 to settle former African American slaves. By 1847, it was the independent and free state of Liberia. Sierra Leone served a similar function for ex-slaves from the British Caribbean, but it remained a protectorate of Britain until the 1960s. Despite the good intentions behind the creation of these territories, they too were colonies. Liberia, in particular, was imposed on existing indigenous groups who viewed their new "African" leaders with contempt.

The Berlin Conference As the scramble intensified, tensions among the participating countries mounted. Rather than risk war, 13 countries convened in Berlin at the invitation of the German chancellor Bismarck in 1884 in a gathering known as the **Berlin Conference**. During the conference, which no African leaders attended, rules were established as to what constituted "effective control" of a territory, and Sub-Saharan Africa was carved up and traded like properties in a game of Monopoly® (Figure 6.35). Exact boundaries in the interior, which was still poorly known, were not determined, and a decade of "orderly" competition remained as imperial armies marched inland. Although European arms were by the 1880s far superior to anything found in Africa, several indigenous states did mount effective resistance campaigns. For example, in central Sudan, an Islamic-inspired force held out against the British until 1900, and as late as 1914, the Darfur region of western Sudan maintained tenuous independence.

Eventually European forces prevailed everywhere, with one major exception: Ethiopia. The Italians had conquered the Red Sea coast and the northern highlands (modern Eritrea) by 1890, and they quickly set their sights on the large Ethiopian kingdom, called Abyssinia, which had itself been vigorously expanding for several decades. In 1896, however, Abyssinia defeated the invading Italian army, earning the respect of and recognition by the European powers. In the 1930s, fascist Italy launched a major invasion of the country, now renamed Ethiopia, to redeem its earlier defeat, and with the help of poison gas and aerial bombardment, it quickly prevailed. By 1942, Ethiopia had regained its freedom.

Although Germany was a principal instigator of the scramble for Africa, it lost its own colonies after suffering defeat in World War I. Britain and France then partitioned most of Germany's African empire between them. Figure 6.35 shows the colonial status of the region in 1913, prior to Germany's territorial loss. The French held most of West Africa, but the British controlled populous Nigeria and several other coastal territories. The French also colonized Gabon in western equatorial Africa, Madagascar, and the small but strategic enclave of Djibouti at the southern end of the Red Sea. The British holdings were larger still, covering a continuous swath of territory in the east from Sudan to South Africa. Belgium and Portugal were the other main colonial powers. The government of Belgium had taken direct control over the personal domain of King Leopold II and had extended it to the south, eventually reaching the mineral-rich copper belt. Portugal, the weakest European power, controlled huge territories in southwestern and southeastern Africa (Angola and Mozambique). Britain's drive to the north from South Africa, organized by imperial dreamer and diamond magnate Cecil Rhodes, thwarted the Portuguese effort to bridge the continent.

Establishment of South Africa While the Europeans were cementing their rule over Africa after World War I, South Africa was inching toward political freedom, at least for its white population. South Africa was one of the oldest colonies in Sub-Saharan Africa, and it became the first to obtain its political independence from Europe in 1910. Its economy is the most productive and influential of the region, yet the legacy of apartheid made it an international outcast, especially within Africa.

The original body of Dutch settlers in South Africa grew slowly, expanding to the north and east of its original nucleus around Cape Town. As a farming and pastoral people largely isolated from the European world, these Afrikaners, or Boers, developed an extremely conservative cultural outlook marked by an intensifying belief in their racial superiority over the native population. In 1806 the British, then the world's unchallenged maritime power, seized the Cape district from the Dutch. Relations between the British rulers and their new Afrikaner subjects quickly soured, in part because the British attempted to restrict the enslavement of Africans as part of a larger abolitionist movement. In the 1830s, the bulk of the Afrikaner community opted to leave British territory and strike out for new lands. After being rebuffed by the powerful Zulu state in the Natal area, they set-

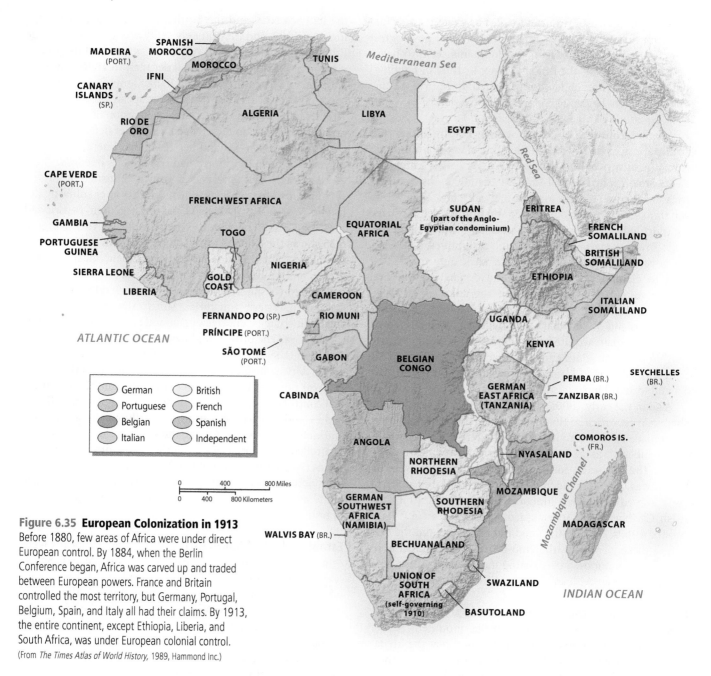

Figure 6.35 European Colonization in 1913
Before 1880, few areas of Africa were under direct European control. By 1884, when the Berlin Conference began, Africa was carved up and traded between European powers. France and Britain controlled the most territory, but Germany, Portugal, Belgium, Spain, and Italy all had their claims. By 1913, the entire continent, except Ethiopia, Liberia, and South Africa, was under European colonial control.
(From *The Times Atlas of World History*, 1989, Hammond Inc.)

tled on the northeastern plateau, known as the highveld. By the 1850s, they had established two "republics" in the area: the South African Republic (commonly called the *Transvaal*) and the Orange Free State (Figure 6.36).

Once relocated on the highveld, the Afrikaners found themselves threatened by Zulu armies. The Zulus had been a relatively minor group until a Zulu king introduced centralized rule and new military techniques in the 1820s. From then on Zulu armies were virtually invincible. After a series of inconclusive wars, the British intervened in 1878 on behalf of the Dutch settlers. The first British army sent into Zululand was annihilated; the second, equipped with machine guns, prevailed. By 1900, the British had incorporated the Zulu into South Africa's Natal province.

The British had more difficulty subduing the Afrikaners. By the late 1800s, it had become clear that the two Boer republics were sitting above one of the world's greatest troves of mineral wealth. The British were increasingly drawn to the area, and they grew resentful of Afrikaner power. The result was the Boer War, which turned into a protracted and brutal guerrilla struggle between the British Army and mobile Afrikaner bands. By 1905, the Boers relented, after which the British joined the two former republics to Cape Province and Natal to form the Union of South Africa. Five years later South Africa was given its independence from Britain. Britons and other Europeans continued to settle there, but the Afrikaners remained the majority white group. Black and coloured South Africans, however, greatly outnumbered whites.

Figure 6.36 The Evolution of South African Political Boundaries
South Africa's internal political boundaries have been redrawn several times in the past century. To appease the Afrikaans (Dutch) settlers, a Boer republic was established in the late nineteenth century with British approval. It was later reabsorbed into the Union of South Africa when gold and diamonds were discovered. During the apartheid years, homelands were created with the intent of having all black South Africans live in these ethnic-based rural settings. In order to accomplish this, 3 million black South Africans were forcibly relocated. Lastly, in the new South Africa, homelands were eliminated and new province boundaries were drawn. (From Christopher, 1994, *The Atlas of Apartheid,* London: Routledge, 16, 83)

It was not until 1948, when the Afrikaner's National Party gained control of the government, that they introduced the policy of "separateness" known as *apartheid*. British South Africans had enacted a series of laws that were prejudicial to nonwhite groups, but it was under Afrikaner leadership that racial separation become more formalized and systematic. Operating on three scales—petite, meso-, and grand—apartheid managed social interaction by controlling space. Petite apartheid, like Jim Crow laws in the United States, created separate service entrances for government buildings, bus stops, and restrooms based on skin color. Meso-apartheid divided the city into residential sectors by race, giving whites the best and largest urban zones. Finally, grand apartheid was the construction of black **homelands** by ethnic group. Technically, blacks were to become citizens of the nominally independent homelands (see the 1970 map in Figure 6.36). Likened to the reservations created for Native Americans in the United States, homelands were rural, overcrowded, and on marginal land. Moreover, to ensure the notion that every black had a homeland, some 3 million blacks were forcibly relocated into homelands during apartheid, and residence outside of the homelands was strictly regulated.

Granted its independence in 1910, South Africa was the first state in the region freed from colonial rule. Yet because of its formalized system of discrimination and racism, it was hardly a symbol of liberty. Ironically, at the same time that the Afrikaners tightened their political and social control over the nonwhite population, the rest of the continent was preparing for political independence from Europe.

Decolonization and Independence

Decolonization of the region happened rather quickly and peacefully beginning in 1957. Independence movements, however, had sprung up throughout the continent, some dating back to the early 1900s. Workers' unions and independent newspapers became voices for African discontent and the hope for freedom. Black intellectuals, who had typically studied abroad, were influenced by the ideas of the **Pan-African Movement** led by W. E. B. Du Bois and Marcus Garvey in the United States. Founded in 1900, the movement's slogan of "Africa for Africans" encouraged a trans-Atlantic liberation effort. Nevertheless, Europe's hold on Africa remained secure through the 1940s and early 1950s, even as other colonies in South and Southeast Asia gained their independence.

By the late 1950s, Britain, France, and Belgium decided that they could no longer maintain their African empires and began to withdraw. (Italy had already lost its colonies during World War II, and Britain gained Somalia and Eritrea.) Once started, the decolonization process moved rapidly. By the mid-1960s, virtually the entire region had achieved independence. In most cases, the transition was relatively peaceful and smooth with the exception of southern Africa.

Dynamic African leaders put their mark on the region during the early independence period. Men such as Kenya's Jomo Kenyatta, Ivory Coast's Felix Houphuët-Boigney, Julius Nyerere of Tanzania, and Ghana's Kwame Nkrumah became powerful father figures who molded their new nations (Figure 6.37). President Nkrumah's vision for Africa was the most expansive. After helping to secure independence for Ghana in 1957, his ultimate aspiration was the political unity of Africa. While his dream was never realized, it set the stage for the founding of the Organization of African Unity (OAU) in 1963, which was renamed the **African Union** (AU) in 2002. The AU is a continent-wide organization headquartered in Addis Ababa, Ethiopia, whose main role has been to mediate disputes between neighbors. Certainly in the 1970s and 1980s it was a constant voice of opposition to South Africa's minority rule, and the AU intervened in some of the more violent independence movements in southern Africa.

Given the scale of the African continent, it is not surprising that groups of states formed regional organizations to facilitate intraregional exchange and development. The two most active regional organizations are the Southern African

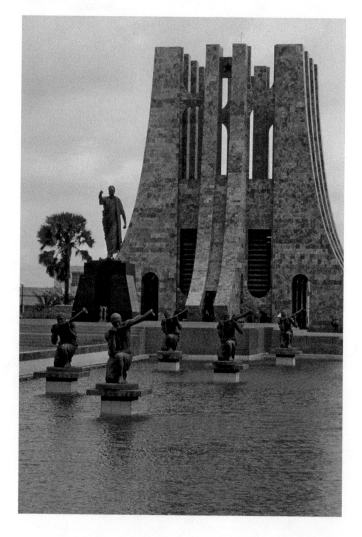

Figure 6.37 A Monument to Kwame Nkrumah Charismatic independence leader Kwame Nkrumah is remembered with this monument in Accra, Ghana. Nkrumah led Ghana to an early independence in 1957; he was also a founder of the Organization of African Unity (OAU), now called the African Union.

Figure 6.38 Supranational Organizations of Sub-Saharan Africa Political affiliations in Sub-Saharan Africa are both continental and regional. The African Union includes all African countries. Smaller organizations, such as SADC, ECCAS, and ECOWAS, represent regional affiliations. Of these, SADC shows the most economic promise.

Development Community (SADC) and the Economic Community of West African States (ECOWAS). Both were founded in the 1970s but became more prominent in the 1990s (Figure 6.38). SADC and ECOWAS are anchored by the region's two largest economies: South Africa and Nigeria. The Economic Community of Central African States (ECCAS) was founded in the mid-1980s and is headquartered in Libreville, Gabon. Its effectiveness has been hampered by the political instability of the area. Several ECCAS members also are members of SADC.

Southern Africa's Independence Battles

Independence did not come easily to southern Africa. In Southern Rhodesia (modern-day Zimbabwe), the problem was the presence of some 250,000 white residents, most of whom owned large farms. Unwilling to see power pass to the country's black majority, then some 6 million strong, these settlers declared themselves the rulers of an independent, white-supremacist state in 1965. The black population continued to resist, however, and in 1978 the Rhodesian government was forced to give up power. The renamed country of Zimbabwe was, henceforth, ruled by the black majority, although the remaining whites still formed an economically privileged community. Since the mid-1990s, disputes over government land reform (splitting up the large commercial farms mostly owned by whites and giving the land to black farmers) and President Robert Mugabe's strongman politics have resulted in serious racial and political tensions as well as the collapse of the country's economy.

In the former Portuguese colonies, independence came violently. Unlike the other imperial powers, Portugal refused to relinquish its colonies in the 1960s. As a result, the people of Angola and Mozambique turned to armed resistance. The most powerful rebel movements adopted a socialist orientation and received support from the Soviet Union and Cuba. A new Portuguese government came to power in 1974, however, and it withdrew abruptly from its African colonies. At this point, Marxist regimes quickly came to power in both Angola and Mozambique. The United States, and especially South Africa, responded to this perceived threat by supplying arms to rebel groups that opposed the new governments. Fighting dragged on for nearly three decades in Angola and Mozambique. The countryside in both states is now so heavily laden with land mines that it is risky to use. Efforts to clear the mines and make the land usable are ongoing but uneven. With the end of the Cold War, however, outsiders lost interest in continuing these conflicts, and sustained efforts began to negotiate a peace settlement. Mozambique has been at peace since the mid-1990s. After several failed attempts at peace in Angola, the Angolan army signed a peace treaty with rebels in 2002 that ended a 27-year conflict in which more than 300,000 people died and 3 million Angolans were displaced.

Apartheid's Demise in South Africa While fighting continued in the former Portuguese zone, South Africa underwent a remarkable transformation. Through the 1980s, its government had remained firmly committed to white supremacy. Under apartheid only whites enjoyed real political freedom, while blacks were denied even citizenship in their own country—technically, they were citizens of homelands.

Opposition to apartheid began in the 1960s, intensifying and becoming more violent by the 1980s. Blacks led the opposition, but coloureds and Asians (who suffered severe, but less extreme, discrimination) also opposed the Afrikaner government. As international pressure mounted, white South Africans found themselves ostracized. Many corporations refused to do business there, and South African athletes (regardless of color) were banned from most international competitions, such as the Olympics and World Cup Soccer. Increasing numbers of whites also opposed the apartheid system, and many businesspeople began to believe that apartheid threatened to undermine their economic endeavors.

The first major change came in 1990, when South Africa withdrew from Namibia, which it had controlled as a protectorate since the end of World War I. South Africa now stood alone as the single white-dominated state in Africa. A few years later, the leaders of the Afrikaner-dominated political party decided they could no longer resist the pressure for change. In 1994, free elections were held in which Nelson Mandela, a black leader who had been imprisoned for 27 years by the old regime, emerged as the new president. Black and white leaders pledged to put the past behind them and work together to build a new, multiracial South Africa. The homelands themselves were the first to be eliminated from the political map of the new South Africa (see the 1999 map in Figure 6.36). Since Mandela's presidency, orderly elections have been held and South Africans have elected Thabo Mbeki for two terms (1999–2009) and Jacob Zuma in 2009.

Unfortunately, the legacy of apartheid is not so easily erased. Residential segregation is officially illegal, but neighborhoods are still sharply divided along race lines. Under the multiracial political system, a black middle class emerged, but most blacks remain extremely poor (and most whites remain prosperous). Violent crime has increased, and rural migrants and immigrants have poured into South African cities, producing a xenophobic anti-immigrant backlash. Because the political change was not matched by a significant economic transformation, the hopes of many people are frustrated.

Enduring Political Conflict

Although most Sub-Saharan countries made a relatively peaceful transition to independence, virtually all of them immediately faced a difficult set of institutional and political problems. In several cases, the old authorities had done virtually nothing to prepare their colonies for independence. Lacking an institutional framework for independent government, countries such as the Democratic Republic of the Congo confronted a chaotic situation from the beginning. Only a handful of Congolese had received higher education, let alone been trained for administrative posts. The indigenous African political framework had been essentially destroyed by colonization, and in most cases very little had been built in its place.

Even more problematic in the long run was the political geography of the newly independent states. Civil servants could always be trained and administrative systems built, but little could be done to rework the region's basic political map. The problem was the fact that the European colonial powers had essentially ignored indigenous cultural and political patterns, both in dividing Africa among themselves and in creating administrative subdivisions within their own imperial territories.

The Tyranny of the Map All over Africa, different ethnic groups found themselves forced into the same state with peoples of different linguistic and religious backgrounds, many of whom had recently been their enemies. At the same time, a number of the larger ethnic groups of the region found their territories split between two or more countries. The Hausa people of West Africa, for example, were divided between Niger (formerly French) and Nigeria (formerly British), each of which they had to share with several former enemy groups.

Given the imposed political boundaries, it is no wonder that many African countries struggled to generate a common sense of national identity or establish stable political institutions. **Tribalism**, or loyalty to the ethnic group rather than to the state, has emerged as the bane of African political life. Especially in rural areas, tribal identities usually supersede national ones. Because virtually all of Africa's countries

Figure 6.39 Geopolitical Issues—Conflict and Refugees
Many Sub-Saharan countries have experienced wars or serious insurrections since 1995. These same states are also likely to produce refugees (red circles) and internally displaced persons (yellow circles). As of 2009, nearly 3 million Africans were refugees and 13 million were internally displaced. (Data from U.S. Committee for Refugees, 2009, *World Refugee Survey*)

inherited an inappropriate set of colonial borders, one might assume that they would have been better redrawing a new political map based on indigenous identities. Such a strategy was impossible, as all the leaders of the newly independent states realized. Any new territorial divisions would have created winners and losers, and thus would have resulted in more conflict. Moreover, because ethnicity in Sub-Saharan Africa was traditionally fluid, and because many groups were territorially intermixed, it would have been difficult to generate a clear-cut system of division. Finally, most African ethnic groups were considered too small to form viable countries. With these complications in mind, the new African leaders meeting in 1963 to form the Organization of African Unity agreed that colonial boundaries should remain. The violation

of this principle, they argued, would lead to pointless wars between states and endless civil struggles within them.

Despite the determination of Africa's leaders to build their new nations within existing boundaries, challenges to the states began soon after independence. Figure 6.39 maps the ethnic and political conflicts that have disabled parts of Africa since 1995. The human cost of this turmoil is several million refugees and internally displaced persons. **Refugees** are people who flee their state because of a well-founded fear of persecution based on race, ethnicity, religion, or political orientation. Nearly 3 million Africans were considered refugees in 2009. Added to this figure are another 13 million internally displaced persons. **Internally displaced persons** have fled from conflict but still reside in their country of origin. Sudan had the largest number of internally displaced people (5 to 6 million), followed by the Democratic Republic of the Congo and Uganda (over 1 million each). These populations are not technically considered refugees, making it difficult for humanitarian nongovernmental organizations and the United Nations to assist them.

Over the past decade, the number of internally displaced people has risen, while the total number of refugees has declined. This decline is due, in part, to the reluctance of neighboring states to take on the burden of hosting refugees. Tanzania had more than 300,000 refugees (mostly from Burundi and the Democratic Republic of the Congo), and Chad had 300,000 (mostly from Sudan) in 2009. With international support of refugees on the decline, it is understandable that poor African states that struggle to serve their own people are disinclined to respond to the needs of refugees. Yet the region's many ethnic conflicts continue to produce many vulnerable and needy people fleeing persecution.

Ethnic Conflicts As Figure 6.39 suggests, more than half of the states in the region have experienced wars or serious insurrections since 1995. Fortunately, in the past few years peace has returned to Sierra Leone, Liberia, Ivory Coast, and Angola, states that produced large numbers of refugees in the 1990s. For the countries of Sierra Leone and Liberia, many attributed the availability of diamonds in these countries as financing cycles of violence. While the relationship between resources and conflict is complex, the term conflict diamonds was employed when discussing the diamond trade in West Africa (see Environment and Politics: Africa's Conflict Diamonds). Currently, the two states with the most deadly conflicts are Sudan and the Democratic Republic of the Congo. Each of these will be discussed in turn.

Darfur, a Sahelian province in Sudan, is the size of France. In 2003, an ethnic conflict between Arab nomads and herders and non-Arab "black" farmers ignited. Since the fighting began, an estimated 300,000 people have died and more than 2.5 million have been displaced. In 2004, the U.S. government accused the Sudanese government of **genocide**—the deliberate and systematic killing of a racial, political, or cultural group. The African Union and the United Nations have sent peacekeeping troops to assist the displaced and reduce the violence. In 2009, the International Criminal Court issued a warrant for the arrest of Sudanese President Bashir for war crimes, but as of 2010 Bashir remains in office and denies the charges.

The conflict began when a non-Arab rebel group (later called the Sudan Liberation Movement) attacked a Sudanese military base. The SLM complained of economic marginalization and wanted a power-sharing arrangement with the Sudanese government. The Sudanese government responded to the rebels by encouraging Arab militiamen (called *janjaweed*—an Arabic term meaning "horse and gun") to attack non-Arab civilians in Darfur. The janjaweed storm villages on horseback and camelback, destroying grain supplies and livestock, killing villagers, and setting buildings on fire. Human rights groups are especially alarmed by the systematic use of rape by the janjaweed as a weapon of ethnic cleansing and terror. The government of Khartoum claims it has been unable to stop the janjaweed atrocities, yet international observers continue to produce evidence that the gov-

ernment is supporting the Arab militiamen through aerial bombardment and attacks on civilians. More than 500 villages were completely or substantially destroyed in Darfur.

The deadliest ethnic and political conflict in the region has been in the Democratic Republic of the Congo. Between 1998 and 2008, nearly 5 million people died, although many of the deaths were from war-induced starvation and diseases rather than bullets or machetes. In 1996 and 1997, a loose alliance of armed groups from Rwanda (led by Tutsis) and Uganda joined forces with other groups in the Congo and marched their way across the country, installing Laurent Kabila as president. Under Kabila's rocky and ruthless leadership, which ended in assassination in 2001, rebel groups again invaded from Uganda and Rwanda and soon controlled the northern and eastern portion of the country while the Kinshasa-based government loosely controlled the western and southern portions.

Figure 6.40 Chukudus in the Democratic Republic of the Congo A Congolese boy with his chukudu (wooden scooter) delivers onions to a Goma market in the Democratic Republic of the Congo. Locally made chukudus are rugged symbols of improvisation and invention in this war-weary region of Central Africa.

With Kabila's death in 2001, his son Joseph took power and signed a peace accord with the rebels in 2002. In 2003 rebel leaders were part of a transitional government and an unsteady peace was in place with help from the UN, the African Union, and support by western donors. Remarkably, elections were held in 2006, Joseph Kabila was elected president. The country has no real experience with democracy, a civil service that barely functions, and virtually no roads or working infrastructure for the 70 million people who live there. In 2008, foreign aid accounted for 15 percent of the country's GNI, down from 20 percent in 2005. For now, continuing peace and the ability of the Congo's people to improvise and cope under such adversity may gradually bring about social and economic improvements. A symbol of this improvisation is the rugged wooden scooters (called *chukudus*) that move cargo and people around in the eastern Congo (Figure 6.40).

Secessionist Movements Problematic African political boundaries have occasionally led to attempts by territories to secede and form new states. The Shaba (or Katanga) province in what was then the state of Zaire tried to leave its national territory soon after independence. The rebellion was crushed a couple of years after it started with the help of France and Belgium. Zaire was unwilling to give up its copper-rich territory, and the former colonialists had economic interests in the territory worth defending. Similarly, the Igbo in oil-rich southeastern Nigeria declared an independent state of Biafra in 1967. After a short but brutal war during which Biafra was essentially starved into submission, Nigeria was reunited.

In 1991, the government of Somalia disintegrated. The territory has since been ruled by clan-based warlords and their militias, who have informally divided the country into clan-based units. **Clans** are social units that are branches of a tribe or ethnic group larger than a family. Early in the conflict, the northern portion of the country declared its independence as a new country—Somaliland (Figure 6.41). Somaliland has a constitution, a functioning parliament, government ministries, a police force, a judiciary, and a president. The territory produces its own currency and passports. Yet no country has recognized this territory, in part because no government exists in Somalia to negotiate the secession. In 1998, neighboring Puntland also declared itself an autonomous state. Although it does not seek outright independence like Somaliland, Puntland is creating its own administration. Meanwhile, Islamic courts with their well-armed militias control the south, where Al Qaeda operatives are believed to reside, along with pirates who seize ships for ransom in the Indian Ocean and Gulf of Aden.

Only one territory in the region has successfully seceded. In 1993, Eritrea gained independence from Ethiopia after two decades of civil conflict. This territorial secession is striking because Ethiopia forfeited its access to the Red Sea, making it landlocked. Yet the creation of Eritrea still did not bring about peace. After years of fighting, the transition

Figure 6.41 Somalia Divided A state in name only, Somalia has had no central government since 1991. Two areas in the north—Somaliland and Puntland—seek political autonomy or independence. Meanwhile, Islamic courts have controlled areas in the south.

to Eritrean independence began remarkably well. Unfortunately, border disputes between the two countries erupted in 1998, resulting in some 100,000 troop deaths. In 2000, a peace accord was reached and the fighting stopped. As Ethiopia comes to accept Eritrea's independence, it might be possible for other areas torn by ethnic warfare to find peace as well. Still, major transformations of Africa's political map should not be expected.

ECONOMIC AND SOCIAL DEVELOPMENT: The Struggle to Rebuild

By almost any measure, Sub-Saharan Africa is the poorest and least-developed world region. While other regions have experienced significant improvements in life expectancy and per capita income since 1990, many Sub-Saharan African states have experienced declines in life expectancy, and income levels have remained stubbornly low. The average GNI per capita figure using purchasing power parity is about $1,950. Some states such as Botswana, Equatorial

ENVIRONMENT AND POLITICS   Africa's Conflict Diamonds

The term 'conflict diamond' is used to link African diamond exports with armed conflict. In the 1990s in countries such as Liberia, Sierra Leone, Angola and the Democratic Republic of the Congo, there was clear evidence that diamonds were used to purchase arms and perpetuate conflict. Yet, there are also several African states that are major diamond producers, such as South Africa, Botswana, and Namibia, where a link between diamond extraction and armed conflict is not clear.

Geographer Philippe Le Billon has researched the linkages between natural resources such as diamonds and armed conflict from a geographical perspective in a recent study in the *Annals of the Association of American Geographers*. He concludes that the relationship is not predetermined but has much to do with the materiality of production, locational aspects of the resource, the commodity chains that support the trade, and the political economic context. That said there are particular aspects in diamond extraction and trade that are well suited for funding conflict.

In the media the idea of 'blood diamonds' caught on in the late 1990s and was used to explain the actions of greedy warlords manipulating easily looted resources for nefarious purposes. Diamonds are small in size and highly valuable. They can be easily smuggled, traded, and used as currency. Moreover, where they come from is not easily determined. Most rough diamonds from Africa are bound for two places, Antwerp and London, so controls higher up the commodity chain could be effective if applied.

Yet subtleties of diamond extraction were lost in most media portrayals. One important distinction is the extraction of diamonds from primary deposits where capital-intensive industrial mining techniques are used, versus secondary alluvial deposits were artisanal mining occurs that is spatially more diffuse and politically harder to regulate. These artisanal practices also can have deleteri-

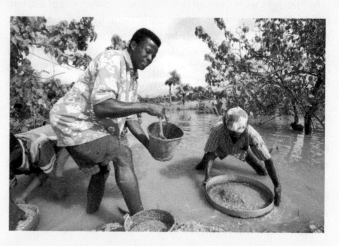

Figure 6.4.1 Diamond Miners in Sierra Leone Men sieve gravel looking for diamonds in the Kono District of Sierra Leone. Alluvial diamond deposits exist throughout Sierra Leone and are often extracted using simple artisanal methods.

ous environmental impacts as watersheds are disturbed and contaminated. It is usually artisanal mining that is most associated with conflict diamonds (Figure 6.4.1)

The relationship between diamonds and conflict is most acute in the West African countries of Sierra Leone and Liberia. Sierra Leone has significant alluvial deposits of diamonds and a long tradition of artisanal mining that goes back to the 1930s. In the 1990s, the Revolutionary United Front (RUF) supported by former Liberian president and warlord Charles Taylor, gained control of the eastern and northern sections of Sierra Leone where there are significant diamond deposits. During the war in Sierra Leone that lasted from 1991 to 2000,

Guinea, Mauritius, the Seychelles, and South Africa have much higher per capita GNI-PPP (Table 6.2). Purchasing power parity is a relative income figure; when absolute income is measured, over 70 percent of the population have average incomes of less than $2 a day. Nearly all the states in the region are ranked at the bottom of most lists comparing per capita GNI or the Human Development Index.

In the 1990s, most countries in Sub-Saharan Africa saw their economic productivity decline, with low or negative growth rates between 1990 and 1999. The economic and debt crisis of the 1980s and 1990s prompted the introduction of **structural adjustment programs**. Promoted by the International Monetary Fund (IMF) and the World Bank, structural adjustment programs typically reduce government spending, cut food subsidies, and encourage private-sector initiatives. Yet these same policies have caused immediate hardships for the poor, especially women and children, and have led to social protest, most notably in the cities. The idea of debt forgiveness for Africa's poorest states, argued for by the unlikely duo of economist Jeffrey

Sachs and U2 rock star Bono, has gradually gained acceptance as a strategy to reduce human suffering by redirecting monies that would have gone to debt repayment to the provision of services and the building of infrastructure. Sachs argues that in order for the region to get out of the poverty trap, it will need substantial sums of new foreign aid and investment.

On the positive side, there are signs of economic growth since 2000. For most states, the average annual growth rates from 2000 to 2008 are positive. Several countries have seen average annual growth rates of 5 percent or more (see Table 6.2). While good news overall, such figures can be deceptive. Some are due to soaring oil prices during this time period (notably so for Angola, Chad, Nigeria, and Sudan), whereas others are due to countries beginning from a very low base after years of conflict (Mozambique, Sierra Leone, Rwanda). Still, for the first time in many years, Sub-Saharan African economies are growing at a faster rate than their populations. It appears that the global financial crisis of 2008–09 did not greatly impact these growth trends.

Figure 6.4.2 Armed Conflict and Diamonds in Sierra Leone
During the 1990s the Revolutionary United Front (RUF) lead by Charles Taylor from Liberia, controlled much of northern Sierra Leone and its diamond trade. Funds from illicit diamond sales funded armed conflict in Sierra Leone and Liberia. (Source: Philippe Le Billion, 2008, "Diamond Wars? Conflict Diamonds and Geographies of Resource Wars" *Annals of the Association of American Geographers* 98(2): p 362)

it is estimated that diamond sales funneled $25 to 75 million per year to rebel forces. Liberia was also engulfed in conflict, with arms bought by RUF from diamond sales. War-related deaths in these two states approached 300,000 from 1989 to 2000. Diamonds were a significant resource that provided capital and arms to fuel the conflicts (Figure 6.4.2). As of 2010 Charles Taylor, who was president of Liberia from 1997 until 2003, is detained and under investigation through United Nations courts for his role in the civil wars.

One result of public concern about conflict diamonds was the establishment of the Kimberly Process Certification Scheme, adopted in 2002, to keep conflict diamonds out of the market. Corporate leaders, such as DeBeers, were initially resistant to the certification process but later came to support it as a means protect this valuable luxury product from the possibility of wider boycotts due to its tainted image. The process is voluntary and requires participating nations to agree not to trade in diamonds from non-participating countries.

Overall the certification process has been seen as a positive step for diamond-dependent countries in Africa. As a result of the Kimberly Process, diamond exports flow from Sierra Leone and are viewed as critical for the country's post-conflict development. Ironically, industrial approaches to mining (with tighter controls) are preferred over artisanal methods when it comes to certification. This has the unintended consequence of making it difficult for small-scale producers to have their diamonds certified even when there is no evidence of conflict.

Adapted from Philippe Le Billon, 2008, "Diamond Wars? Conflict Diamonds and Geographies of Resource Wars" *Annals of the Association of American Geographers* 98(2): 345-372.

Roots of African Poverty

In the past, outside observers often attributed Africa's poverty to its environment. Favored explanations included the infertility of its soils, the erratic patterns of its rainfall, the lack of navigable rivers, and the virulence of its tropical diseases. Most contemporary scholars, however, argue that such handicaps are not prevalent throughout the region and that even where they do exist they can be—and have often been—overcome by human labor and ingenuity. The favored explanations for African poverty today look much more to historical and institutional factors than to environmental circumstances.

Numerous scholars have singled out the slave trade for its debilitating effect on Sub-Saharan African economic life. Large areas of the region were effectively depopulated, and many people were forced to flee into poor, inaccessible refuges. Colonization was another blow to Africa's economy. European powers invested little in infrastructure, education, and public health and were instead interested mainly in extracting mineral and agricultural resources for their own

benefit. Several plantation and mining zones did achieve a degree of prosperity under colonial regimes, but strong national economies failed to develop. In almost all cases, the rudimentary transport and communications systems were designed to link administration centers and zones of extraction directly to the colonial powers rather than to their own surrounding areas. As a result, upon achieving independence, Sub-Saharan African countries thus faced economic and infrastructural challenges that were as daunting as their political problems (Figure 6.42). Today, the average amount of paved road per person in countries such as Ghana, Ethiopia, Kenya, Tanzania, and Uganda is just 33 feet (10 meters) per person. The average for the non-African developing world is 2.8 miles (4.5 kilometers) per person. South Africa is the only African state with a developed national road network.

Failed Development Policies The first decade or so of independence was a time of relative prosperity and optimism for many African countries. Most of them relied heavily on

TABLE 6.2 Development Indicators

Country	GNI per capita, PPP 2008	GDP Average Annual % Growth 2000–08	Human Development Index (2007)[a]	Percent Population Living Below $2 a Day	Life Expectancy (2010)[b]	Under Age 5 Mortality Rate (1990)	Under Age 5 Mortality Rate (2008)	Gender Equity (2008)[c]
Angola	4,820	13.5	0.564		47	260	220	
Benin	1,470	3.9	0.492		59	184	121	
Botswana	13,300	4.5	0.699	49.4	55	50	31	100
Burkina Faso	1,160	5.6	0.389	81.2	53	201	169	85
Burundi	380	2.9	0.394	93.4	50	189	168	91
Cameroon	2,170	3.5	0.523	57.7	51	149	131	84
Cape Verde	3,080		0.708		73			
Central African Republic	730	0.5	0.369	81.9	49	178	173	
Chad	1,070	11.9	0.392		49	201	209	64
Comoros	1,170		0.576		64			
Congo	2,800	3.9	0.601		53	104	127	
Dem. Rep. of Congo	280	5.2	0.389		48	199	199	76
Djibouti	2,320		0.520	41.2	55			
Equatorial Guinea	21,700		0.719		49			
Eritrea	640	1.3	0.472		59	150	58	77
Ethiopia	870	8.2	0.414	77.5	55	210	109	85
Gabon	12,390	2.2	0.755		60	92	77	
Gambia	1,280	5.1	0.456	56.7	55	153	106	102
Ghana	1,320	5.6	0.526	53.6	60	118	76	96
Guinea	970	3.2	0.435	87.2	57	231	146	77
Guinea-Bissau	520	0.6	0.396	77.9	46	240	195	
Ivory Coast	1,580	0.5	0.484		73	150	114	
Kenya	1,550	4.5	0.541	39.9	57	105	128	96
Lesotho	1,970	3.9	0.514	62.2	41	101	79	105
Liberia	310	−1.1	0.442		56	219	145	86
Madagascar	1,050	3.8	0.543	89.6	60	167	106	97
Malawi	810	4.2	0.493	90.4	49	225	100	99
Mali	1,090	5.2	0.371	77.1	51	250	194	78
Mauritania	1,990	5.1	0.520	44.1	57	129	118	104
Mauritius	12,570	3.7	0.804		73	24	17	100
Mozambique	770	8.0	0.402	90.0	48	249	130	87
Namibia	6,240	5.6	0.686		61	72	42	104
Niger	680	4.4	0.340	85.6	48	305	167	74
Nigeria	1,980	6.6	0.511	83.9	47	230	186	85
Reunion					78			
Rwanda	1,110	6.7	0.460	90.3	51	174	112	100
São Tomé and Principe	1,790		0.651		66			
Senegal	1,780	4.5	0.464	60.3	55	149	108	96
Seychelles	19,630		0.845	<2	73			
Sierra Leone	770	10.3	0.365	76.1	47	278	194	84
Somalia					49	200	200	
South Africa	9,780	4.3	0.683	42.9	55	56	67	100
Sudan	1,920	7.4	0.531		58	124	109	89
Swaziland	5,000	2.6	0.572	81.0	46	84	83	92
Tanzania	1,260	6.8	0.530	96.6	55	157	104	
Togo	830	2.4	0.499		61	150	98	75
Uganda	1,140	7.5	0.514	75.6	52	186	135	99
Zambia	1,230	5.3	0.481	81.5	42	172	148	95
Zimbabwe		−5.7			43	79	96	97

[a]United Nations, Human Development Report, 2009.

[b]Population Reference Bureau, World Population Data Sheet, 2010.

[c]Gender Equity—Ratio of female to male enrollments in primary and secondary school. Numbers below 100 have more males in primary/secondary school, numbers above 100 have more females in primary/secondary schools.

Source: World Bank, World Development Indicators, 2010.

serious economic decline. By the early 1990s, the region's foreign debt was around $200 billion. Although low compared to that of other developing regions (such as Latin America), Sub-Saharan Africa's debt was the highest in the world as a percentage of its economic output.

Many economists contend that Sub-Saharan African governments enacted counterproductive economic policies and thus brought some of their misery on themselves. Keen to build their own economies and reduce their dependency on the former colonial powers, most African countries followed a course of economic nationalism. More specifically, they set about building steel mills and other forms of heavy industry in which they were simply not competitive (Figure 6.43). Local currencies also were often maintained at artificially elevated levels, which benefited the elite who consume imported products but undercut exports. Some former French colonies kept their currencies pegged to the franc, which made successful export strategies almost impossible.

The largest blunders made by Sub-Saharan leaders were in agricultural and food policies in the post-independence period. The main objective was to retain a cheap supply of staple foods in the urban areas. A modern industrial economy could emerge, or so it was argued, only if manufacturing wages remained lower, which in turn was feasible only if food could remain inexpensive. The main problem with this policy was that the majority of Africans were farmers, who could not make money from their crops because prices were kept artificially low. Thus they opted to grow food mainly for subsistence, rather than to sell—often at a loss—to national marketing boards. At the same time, they were encouraged to shift into export crops, such as coffee, cocoa, peanuts, and cotton. The end result was the failure to meet staple food needs at a time when the population was growing explosively. In the 1980s famine occurred in 22 African states, partly as a result of failed agricultural policies com-

Figure 6.42 Lack of Infrastructure Aid workers in the Republic of the Congo push their vehicles out of the mud along the main road from Kinkala to the capital of Brazzaville. Basic infrastructure, such as paved roads, is limited in Central Africa. During the rainy season, many dirt roads are not passable.

the export of mineral and agricultural products, and through the 1970s commodity prices generally remained high. Some foreign capital was attracted to the region, and in many cases the European economic presence actually increased after decolonization. (This is one reason critics refer to the period as one of "neocolonialism.")

In the 1980s, as most commodity prices began to decline, foreign debt began to weigh down many Sub-Saharan countries. By the end of the 1980s, most of the region was in

Figure 6.43 Industrialization Heavy industry, such as this chemical plant in Kafue, Zambia, has failed to deliver Sub-Saharan Africa from poverty. In the worst cases, these industrial enterprises were unable to produce competitive products for world and domestic markets.

bined with drought. As a result of these events, most countries began to reform their agricultural policies in the 1980s, but they met with resistance from the urban poor who had grown dependent upon low prices for staple goods.

Millennium Development Goals By the 1990s, after two decades of stymied economic development, a different approach was sought. The implementation of the **Millennium Development Goals** is one example of global effort to foster development in Sub-Saharan Africa, as well as other poor areas of the developing world. The Millennium Development Goals (MDG) are part of a United Nations effort to reduce extreme poverty by 2015. The goals are to:

- Halve the proportion of people living on incomes of less than $1 a day between 1990 and 2015;
- Ensure universal primary schooling and promote gender equity in school enrollment by 2015;
- Reduce child mortality by two-thirds from 1990 to 2015;
- Reduce by three-quarters the maternal mortality rate between 1990 and 2015;
- Halt the growing prevalence of HIV/AIDS and malaria, and begin to reduce their spread by 2015;
- Halve the proportion of the population without sustainable access to safe drinking water and sanitation by 2015.

As of 2010, several regions of the world are on track to meet many of these goals, although it appears that Sub-Saharan Africa will not meet many of its 2015 goals, especially in terms of reducing extreme poverty and achieving universal primary education. The region has made gains in fighting disease, especially HIV/AIDS. That said, individual countries in Sub-Saharan Africa have made impressive gains towards achieving some of these goals.

International interest in Africa's overall development seems to be growing: Between 2000 and 2008 net development assistance to the region tripled from $13 billion to $40 billion. Some argue that aid increased as a result of having stated MDG benchmarks and agreed-upon measures for assessment. Most of the new aid is directed towards fighting disease, improving health care, and providing basic education. There are still pressing needs for infrastructure development. Now, as in the past, some donated funds do end up in the hands of corrupt officials.

Corruption Although prevalent throughout the world, corruption also seems to have been particularly rampant in several African countries. Civil servants typically are not paid a living wage and are thus virtually forced to solicit bribes. Teachers solicit informal fees from students in order to get paid. According to a recent poll of international business-people, Nigeria ranks as the world's most corrupt country. (Skeptical observers, however, point out that several Asian nations with highly successful economies, such as China, also are noted for high levels of corruption, so that corrup-

tion alone may not be an explanation for Africa's economic problems.)

With millions of dollars in loans and aid pouring into the region, officials at various levels were tempted to skim from the top. Some African states, such as the Democratic Republic of the Congo (DRC), were dubbed kleptocracies. A **kleptocracy** is a state in which corruption is so institutionalized that politicians and government bureaucrats siphon off a huge percentage of the country's wealth. President Mobutu of the DRC was a legendary kleptocrat. While his country was saddled with an enormous foreign debt, he reportedly skimmed several billion dollars and deposited them in Belgian banks during his presidency from 1965 to 1997.

Links to the World Economy

Sub-Saharan Africa's trade connection with the world is limited, accounting for less than 2 percent of global trade. The level of overall trade is low both within the region and outside it. Traditionally, most exports went to the European Union, especially the former colonial powers. The United States is the second most common destination. These trade patterns are changing, especially as trade with China and India grows. As of 2007, exports to Asia nearly equaled exports to the United States. The pattern of imports is also changing. The majority of African countries still turn to Europe for imports but Asia (particularly China) now accounts for one-third of all imports.

By most measures of connectivity, Sub-Saharan Africa lags behind other developing regions. Telephone lines are scarce; Nigeria has only one landline per 100 people. The regional average is slightly better, at two lines per 100 people. Communication via cellular phones, however, is soaring. According to World Bank estimates for every 100 Nigerians, there were 42 mobile phone subscriptions in 2008, and for the region as a whole there were 36 mobile phone subscriptions for every 100 people. By comparison, in 2000 the regional average was just 2 subscriptions per 100 people. No longer reliant on expensive fixed telephone lines for communication, multinational providers now are competing for mobile-phone customers. Internet use is also on the rise; recent World Bank estimates show that 6.5 percent of the population uses the Internet. The growth of mobile telephones and Internet access are a powerful indicator of Africans' desire to acquire modern telecommunication systems long denied to them due to limited landlines (Figure 6.44).

Africa lacks the infrastructure to facilitate more trade. Only southern Africa has a telecommunications and road network of any note. Of the few roads that exist in Central and West Africa, the majority are not paved. This, too, is a legacy of colonialism, and one that keeps Africans from nurturing economic linkages with each other and with the outside world. Trade groups, such as the Southern African Development Community, have the potential to build up regional economies and infrastructure but have yet to achieve the influence of similar groups such as Mercosur in South America.

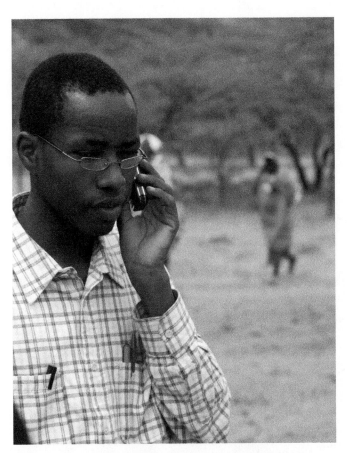

Figure 6.44 Mobile Phones for Africa A young Maasai man in Eremit, Kenya uses his cell phone. Since 2000 mobile phone access and use has surged in the region, greatly improving telecommunications.

Aid Versus Investment In many ways, Sub-Saharan Africa is linked to the global economy more through the flow of financial aid and loans than through the flow of goods. As Figure 6.45 reveals, aid for several states equals 20 percent or more of the GNI. In the extreme case of Liberia, official development assistance in 2008 was estimated to be 185 percent of the GNI; in Burundi it was 44 percent in the same time period. Most of this aid comes from a handful of developed countries (see the inset in Figure 6.45). The United States and the European Commission provided the most aid to the region in 2008, followed by France, the United Kingdom, and Germany.

While aid is extremely important for many African states, foreign direct investment in the region substantially increased from only $4.5 billion in 1995 to $34 billion in 2008. The largest recipients of this foreign investment were the region's major mineral and oil producers. South Africa received nearly 30 percent of the region's foreign investment, but Nigeria, the Republic of the Congo, Sudan, and Ghana also experienced foreign investment growth. The poorer states—without minerals or oil to export—were largely bypassed by foreign investors. Yet the overall level of foreign investment remains low. Consider that all of the foreign direct investment in Sub-Saharan Africa in 2008 was just three-quarters of the foreign investment in Brazil alone.

The reasons foreign investors avoid Africa are fairly obvious. The region is generally perceived to be too poor and unstable to merit much attention, and most foreign investors eager to take advantage of low wages put their money in Asia or Latin America. Sub-Saharan Africa, some economists contend, is therefore starved for capital. Other scholars, however, see foreign investment as more of a trap—and one that the region would be wise to avoid. Recently in countries such as the Republic of the Congo, Chad, Equatorial Guinea, and Angola, investment in oil exploration and production has attracted considerable overseas interest. It is not just the oil producing states attracting foreign capital, copper-rich Zambia saw its foreign investment increase 10-fold between 1995 and 2008. Optimists interpret this as a sign of Africa's economic renewal, but others counter that in the past, mineral extraction has failed to lead to broad-based and lasting economic gains (see "Exploring Global Connections: China's Investment in Africa").

Debt Relief Another development strategy making a difference in the region is debt relief. The World Bank and the IMF proposed in 1996 to reduce debt levels for heavily indebted poor countries, many of which are in Sub-Saharan Africa. Most Sub-Saharan states are indebted to official creditors such as the World Bank, not to commercial banks (as is the case in Latin America and Southeast Asia). Under this World Bank/IMF program, substantial debt reduction is given to Sub-Saharan countries that are determined to have "unsustainable" debt burdens. Mauritania, for example, spends six times more money on repaying its debts than it does on health care.

States qualify for different levels of debt relief provided they present a poverty reduction strategy. Uganda was the first state to qualify for the program, using the money it saved on debt repayment to expand primary schooling. Ghana qualified for debt relief in 2004 and received a $3.5 billion relief package. Other countries that have benefited from debt reduction are Tanzania, Mozambique, Ethiopia, Mauritania, Mali, Niger, Nigeria, Senegal, Burkina Faso, and Benin. More African countries may qualify in the future to redirect debt payments toward building infrastructure and improving basic health and education.

Economic Differentiation Within Africa

As in most regions, considerable differences in levels of economic and social development persist in Sub-Saharan Africa. In many respects, the small island nations of Mauritius and the Seychelles have little in common with the mainland. With a high per capita GNI, life expectancies averaging in the low 70s, and economies built on tourism, they could more easily fit into the Caribbean were it not for their Indian Ocean location. Only a few states, such as Botswana, South Africa, Gabon, Namibia, and Equatorial Guinea, have a per

Figure 6.45 Global Linkages: Aid Dependency Many states in Sub-Saharan Africa are dependent on foreign aid as their primary link to the global economy. This figure maps aid as a percentage of GNI, which ranges from less than 1 percent to 186 percent in Liberia. (From *World Development Indicators*, 2010, Washington, DC: World Bank)

capita GNI-PPP of over $5,000. In the developed world, where a latte at Starbucks costs $3, it is hard to imagine existence on $2 a day, but such is the case for nearly three-quarters of all people living South of the Sahara.

There are millions of Africans living in extreme poverty in every state in the region. In rural areas many of the very poor still practice subsistence farming and are barely a part of the formal economy. In the rapidly growing urban areas, massive slums are homes to millions with inadequate shelter and no regular access to clean water. Most make their living through the informal economy. These are the people that the Millennium Development Goals hope to reach, although securing the resources and finding the right programs to ease this poverty is both a difficult and long-term proposition.

There are places and people experiencing real social and economic gains in Sub-Saharan Africa. South Africa is the unchallenged economic powerhouse of the region. The per capita GNI-PPP of Nigeria, the next largest economy, is just one-fifth of South Africa's. Only South Africa has a well-developed and well-balanced industrial economy. It also boasts a healthy agricultural sector and, more importantly, it stands as one of the world's mining superpowers. South Africa remains unchallenged in gold production, and is a leader in many other minerals and precious gems, including diamonds. In the summer of 2010 South Africa hosted the World Cup, the first African country to do so, symbolizing its arrival as a developed and modern nation.

While South Africa is undeniably a wealthy country by African standards, and while its white minority is prosperous by any standard, it is also a country beset by severe and widespread poverty. In the former townships lying on the outskirts of the major cities and in the rural districts of the former homelands, employment opportunities remain limited and living standards marginal. Despite the end of apartheid in 1994, South Africa still has one of the most unequal income distributions in the world measured by the Gini index.

Oil and Mineral Producers Another group of relatively prosperous Sub-Saharan countries benefits from substantial oil and mineral reserves and small populations. The prime example is Gabon, a country of noted oil wealth that is inhabited by nearly 2 million people. Its neighbors, the Republic of the Congo and Equatorial Guinea, have also experienced steady growth in income and foreign invest-

ment due to oil finds in the 1980s and 1990s respectively. Equatorial Guinea, a former Spanish colony, began producing significant amounts of oil in 1998. Today it has the distinction of having the region's highest per capita GNI at $21,700. Yet after a decade of oil production, these newfound revenues have not been invested in the country's citizens but, as is often the case, seem to have fallen into the hands of few elites (Figure 6.46). Farther south, Namibia and Botswana also have the advantage of small populations and abundant mineral resources, especially diamonds. Over the past few years, both countries have enjoyed sound government and experienced significant economic and social development reflected in their relatively high human development index figures.

The Leaders of ECOWAS The most populous country in Africa, Nigeria is the core member of the Economic Community of West African States (ECOWAS). Nigeria has the

---

EXPLORING GLOBAL CONNECTIONS   China's Investment in Africa

In 2006, China hosted nearly every African head of state at the China–Africa Forum. The event signaled China's growing economic investment in the region at a time when U.S. and European interests were (and still are) focused on proffering aid or fighting terrorism. China wants to secure the oil and ore it needs for its massive industrial economy. In exchange, it offers African nations money for roads, railways, and schools, with relatively few strings attached. Some African leaders see China as a new kind of global partner, one that wants straight commercial relations without an ideological or political agenda. China's trade with Africa is growing faster than with any other region except Southwest Asia, increasing 10-fold in the past decade. Angola, a country where China has invested heavily, is now China's largest foreign supplier of oil—beating out Saudi Arabia. Sudan, with its largely untapped oil reserves, has also received substantial Chinese investment, despite international pressure not to negotiate with the Sudanese government due to the genocide in Darfur (Figure 6.5.1).

China's engagement with Africa is not new. In the 1960s and 1970s, China supported the socialist governments of postcolonial Africa with development assistance. In the 1970s, Beijing funded and built the Tan-Zam railroad that gave landlocked Zambia an outlet to the sea via Tanzania, bypassing the need for Zambia to use apartheid South Africa's ports. China's investment today is strictly commercial and substantially larger. In addition to buying up oil, China purchases copper from Zambia and wood from the Democratic Republic of the Congo. It also sells cheap manufactured goods and clothing in record quantities.

The biggest complaint about Chinese investment in Africa comes from the West. There is frustration that China readily invests in states that have wretched human rights records (Sudan and Zim-

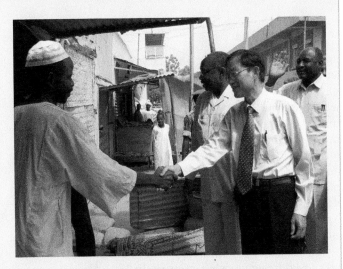

Figure 6.5.1 Chinese investment in Sudan Liu Guijin, the Chinese special representative for African Affairs, shakes hands with a man in a market in al-Fashir, Sudan. China has invested heavily in Sudan arguing that economic development is the best way to end the bloodshed there. Meanwhile, western states disagree with this approach.

babwe). China mostly ignores the lending standards that have been used in the region to curb corruption. Some Africans complain that China is only interested in exporting raw materials and importing manufactured goods back to Africa. Yet through its investments, China has also gained diplomatic friends, as well as access to raw materials. Interestingly, Chinese officials see themselves as the developing world's biggest beneficiary of globalization, and by partnering with the region most ignored by globalization, they will foster more development in Sub-Saharan Africa.

Figure 6.46 Oil Production in Equatorial Guinea A tanker approaches the liquefied natural gas (LNG) loading jetty in Equatorial Guinea. Gas and oil exports from Equatorial Guinea have soared in the past decade, contributing to the country's high per capita GNI.

largest oil reserves in the region and it is an OPEC member. Yet despite its natural resources, its per capita GNI-PPP is a relatively low $1,980. It has been argued that oil money has helped to make Nigeria notoriously inefficient. A small minority of its population has grown fantastically wealthy more by manipulating the system than by engaging in productive activities. Sixty percent of Nigerians, however, remain trapped in poverty earning less than $2 per day. Oil money led to the explosive growth of the former capital city of Lagos, which by the 1980s had become one of the most expensive—and least livable—cities in the region. As a result, the Nigerian government opted to build a new capital city in Abuja, located near the country's center, a move that has proved tremendously expensive. In 1991 Abuja became the national capital and it now has 1.5 million residents. The southwestern corner of the country, in the Niger delta where most of the oil is produced, has seen few of the benefits of oil production but bears the burden of the environmental costs and related social unrest.

The second and third most populous states in ECOWAS, Ivory Coast and Ghana, are also important West African commercial centers. These states rely upon a mix of agricultural and mineral exports. In the mid-1990s, the Ivorian economy began to take off. Boosters within the country called it an emerging "African elephant" (comparing it to the successful "economic tigers" of eastern Asia). Yet a destructive civil war began in 2002 in which rebel forces controlled the northern half of the county and over half a million Ivorians were displaced. A peace agreement was signed in 2007, but the economic growth of the 1990s has yet to return.

Ghana, a former British colony, began its economic recovery in the 1990s. In 2001, it negotiated with the IMF and World Bank for debt relief and in 2004 it qualified for $3.5 billion in relief. The country's average annual growth from 2000 to 2008 was an impressive 5.6 percent.

East Africa Long the commercial and communications center of East Africa, Kenya experienced economic decline and political tension throughout the 1990s. In recent years the economy has grown at 4 percent per year and per capita GNI-PPP is at $1,550. Kenya boasts good infrastructure by African standards, and about 1 million foreign tourists come each year to marvel at its wildlife and natural beauty. Traditional agricultural exports of coffee and tea, as well as nontraditional exports such as cut flowers, dominate the economy (see "Global to Local: Roses for Europe, Thanks to Kenya"). As for social indicators, Kenyan women are having fewer children now than in the late 1970s (down from an average of 8 to 5 children per woman), and those children are better educated and less likely to be in extreme poverty compared to other countries in the region. If Kenya can avoid political implosion due to ethnic rivalries, it could lead East Africa into better economic integration with the southern and western parts of the continent.

The political and economic indicators for Kenya's neighbors, Uganda and Tanzania, are also improving with average annual growth rates in the 2000s of 7.5 percent and 6.8 percent respectively (see Table 6.2). When compared with Kenya, both countries have a much higher proportion of their populations living on less than $2 a day. Both coun-

GLOBAL TO LOCAL   Roses to Europe, Thanks to Kenya

When Europeans give roses on Valentine's Day, they often have Kenyans to thank. Kenya produces about one-third of the cut flowers sold in Europe, especially roses. In the middle of the Northern Hemisphere winter, fresh roses usually come from tropical Africa or America. Cut flowers are now Kenya's second largest source of foreign exchange in agriculture after traditional tea exports. The industry employs some 50,000 workers, the majority of them women.

This was not always the case. Beginning the 1970s the highland tropical flower business began to bloom. Kenya's floriculture trade took off in the 1990s. Today the two largest producers of cut flowers in the world are Colombia and Kenya. Near the equator, with growing areas above 5,000 ft, year-round spring-like conditions and 12-hour days perfect for growing roses, these environmental and locational attributes contribute to their prominence in the global flower trade. Environmental conditions are not enough; to succeed in floriculture a country needs near-by international airports, refrigerated warehouses and transport, capital intensive greenhouse technology, and knowledge of the cultural demands of different national markets (for example Mother's Days are celebrated on different dates throughout the world).

Due to the seasonality of the cut flower trade (with peaks at Christmas, Valentine's Day and various Mother's Days) hours can be irregular and peak-season days long. Women dominate this industry, both in the greenhouses and in the assembly areas where flowers are sorted and arranged (Figure 6.6.1). There have been many reports of abuses in this industry. The workers (often young women) are poorly paid, work long-hours with limited benefits, and are exposed to dangerous agricultural chemicals. After numerous national and international campaigns, it appears

Figure 6.6.2 Lake Naivasha Landscape Irrigated vegetables and flowers grow on the shore of Lake Naivasha, Kenya. A combination of elevation, good soils, irrigation, and access to Nairobi International Airport, makes Naivasha the hub of Kenya's floriculture industry.

that some of the more abusive aspects of this industry are being addressed.

Around the shores of Lake Naivasha, in Kenya's Rift Valley and about a one-hour drive from Nairobi International Airport, lies the country's major production area (Figure 6.6.2). Greenhouses now dominate the lakeshore, and water pollution has become a serious issue. Consequently, growers are now being forced to recycle wastewater and purify it for reuse in their operations, but environmentalists are still concerned about the decline in water levels and quality in Naivasha. Also, as European demand for socially and economically sustainable *fair trade* products has increased, some Kenya producers have switched over to fair trade programs in which workers receive more benefits (housing, childcare, and medical treatment) in exchange for premium prices in the market.

In April 2010 when a volcanic eruption in Iceland closed airspace over Europe for several days, Kenyan flower producers lost tens of thousands of dollars. Unable to ship their crop, spoiled flowers were returned to growers for composting. Fortunately, air traffic returned to normal before various Mother's Day celebrations in Europe. Under normal conditions, harvested, packed and chilled flowers are trucked to Nairobi airport, air freighted to Europe, distributed (usually through the Netherlands), and in shops for sale within 72 hours of being cut in Kenya. Such commodity chains were unthinkable several decades ago but are now a part of everyday consumption.

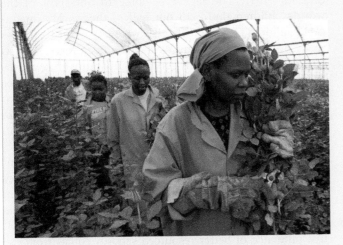

Figure 6.6.1 Kenyan Greenhouse Workers Workers cut roses for export at a flower farm in Naivasha. Floriculture is a vital contributor to Kenya's agricultural exports and has grown dramatically in the past decade.

For further study see Lone Riisgaard (2009) "Global Value Chains, Labor Organization and Private Social Standards: Lessons from East Africa Cut Flower Industries" *World Development* 37(2): 326-340.)

tries rely heavily upon agricultural exports and mining (especially gold). Uganda and Tanzania both benefited from debt reduction agreements that redirected funds from debt repayment to education and health care.

Measuring Social Development

By world standards, measures of social development in Africa are extremely low. Yet there are some positive trends, especially with regard to child survival, education, and gender equity. Also, many governments in the region have reached out to the modern African diaspora (economic migrants who have left the region for employment in Europe and North America). As in other parts of the world, African immigrant organizations have worked to improve schools and health care, and immigrants themselves have returned to invest in businesses and real estate. The economic impact of remittances on this region is relatively small when compared to Latin America, South Asia, or the Caribbean, but it is growing.

Reductions in child mortality are often a surrogate measure for improved social development because if most children make it to their fifth birthday there is usually adequate primary care and nutrition. In a country where the child mortality rate is above 200, it means that one out of five children die before their fifth birthday. As Table 6.2 shows, most of the states in the region saw modest to significant improvements in child survival between 1990 and 2008. Angola, Ethiopia, and Malawi actually experienced dramatic gains in child survival rates. Yet in countries undergoing prolonged conflict (Sierra Leone) or with high HIV/AIDS infection rates (Swaziland), child mortality increased or barely improved over the time period. With a regional child mortality rate of 144 per 1,000 in 2008, the region is a long way from cutting child mortality by two-thirds, as stated in the MDG goals.

Life Expectancy and Health Issues Live expectancy for Sub-Saharan Africa is only 52 years, whereas life expectancy for Latin America is 73. Countries hit hard by HIV/AIDS or conflict have seen life expectancies tumble to 40 years. Despite these statistics, there are indications that access to basic health care is improving and, eventually, so will life expectancies. Keep in mind that while high infant- and child-hood-mortality figures depress the overall life expectancy figures; average life expectancies for people who make it to adulthood are much better. States such as Botswana, Kenya, and Zimbabwe achieved relatively good life expectancy figures in the 1980s but the AIDS epidemic undercut those achievements.

The causes of short life expectancy generally are related to extreme poverty, environmental hazards (such as drought), and various environmental and infectious diseases (cholera, measles, malaria, schistosomiasis, and AIDS). Often these factors work in combination. The effects of disease are exacerbated by poverty, with undernourished children being the most vulnerable to the effects of high fevers. For example, cholera outbreaks occur in crowded slums and villages where food or water is contaminated by the feces of infected persons and basic infrastructure is lacking. Tragically, diseases that are preventable, such as measles, occur when people have no access to or cannot afford vaccines. Funding from the Gates Foundation in particular has targeted fighting such diseases as a critical first step in overall development, and some diseases have seen dramatic declines in incidence due to the availability of relatively simple treatments.

The scarcity of doctors and health facilities, especially in rural areas, also helps to explain Sub-Saharan Africa's short life expectancies and high child mortality levels. The more successful countries in the region have discovered that inexpensive rural clinics dispensing basic treatments, such as oral rehydration therapy for infants with severe diarrhea, can substantially improve survival rates. Another problem is the severity of the African disease environment itself. Malaria, which kills a half-million African children each year, is reappearing in many areas as the disease-causing organisms develop resistance to common drugs and the mosquito carriers develop resistance to insecticides. While most Africans have partial immunity to malaria, it remains a major killer, and many who survive infections remain debilitated. Collectively, national and international health agencies, along with local NGOs, have improved the availability of basic health care in Sub-Saharan Africa, but much work remains to be done.

Meeting Educational Needs Basic education is another obstacle confronting the region. The goal of universal access to primary education is a daunting one for a region in which 43 percent of the population is less than 15 years old. World Bank estimates show that 62 percent of African children have access to primary education (up from just 51 percent in 1991). The region is home to one-sixth of the world's children under 15 but half of the world's uneducated children. Traditionally girls were less likely than boys to attend school. But many West African countries, such as Niger, have improved their gender equity ratios (Niger's was 53 percent in 1999 and rose to 74 percent in 2008) (see Table 6.2). For the region as a whole, the ratio of girls to boys in school is 88 to 100, which is an improvement in terms of greater equity of access for those with schools to attend.

In part, the Millennium Development Goals contributed to a greater emphasis on universal education since 2000. More resources have been directed to schools from the state (through restructured foreign debt) and private donors and organizations. One example of the transformative influence of better resourced schools comes from the village of Bumwalukani, Uganda. This remote village in eastern Uganda has government schools that accommodate hundreds of children but classes are crowded, teachers are poorly trained and paid, and educational materials are scarce. Malaria and hunger keep overall attendance low. A new school in Bumawalukani, the Arlington Academy of

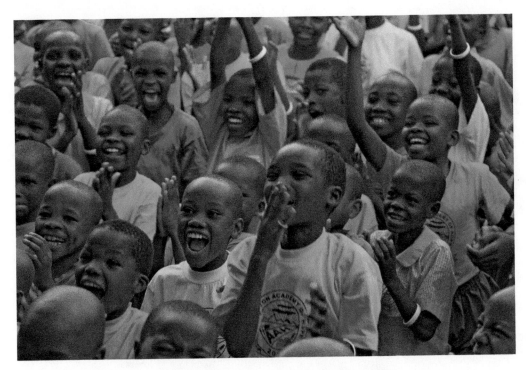

Figure 6.47 Ugandan School Children Cheering at a school event, these children in rural Bumwalukani, Uganda, are receiving a good education as a result of efforts by a U.S.-based NGO founded by a Ugandan emigrant from this village. Educating the region's many children is one of the most pressing challenges.

Hope, was built in 2003 and funded by a U.S. NGO started by a Ugandan migrant who grew up in this rural mountain village. Students pay a small fee to attend the school and are given hot lunches, uniforms, and incomparable educational resources compared to the government schools (Figure 6.47). Teachers are recruited from the best teaching schools in Kampala and are well paid by Ugandan standards. All classes are in English. In Uganda, students who excel receive scholarships to attend residential high schools in the capital. Many of the students from Arlington Academy are able to continue their education because of the foundation received in their model village school.

Women and Development

Development gains cannot be made in Africa unless the economic contributions of African women are recognized. Officially, women are the invisible contributors to local and national economies. In agriculture, women account for 75 percent of the labor that produces more than half the food consumed in the region. Tending subsistence plots, taking in extra laundry, and selling surplus produce in local markets all contribute to household income. Yet because many of these activities are considered informal economic activities, they are not counted. For many of Africa's poorest people, however, the informal sector is the economy, and within this sector women dominate.

Status of Women The social position of women is difficult to gauge for Sub-Saharan Africa. Women traders in West Africa, for example, have considerable political and economic power. By such measures as female labor force participation, many Sub-Saharan African countries show relative

gender equality. And women in most Sub-Saharan societies do not suffer the kinds of traditional social liabilities encountered in much of South Asia, Southwest Asia, and North Africa. In 2006, Mrs. Johnson-Sirleaf, was sworn in as Liberia's president, making her Africa's first elected female leader. A former World Bank economist and grandmother, she beat out a Liberian soccer star in a runoff election. In fact, throughout the region women occupied 18 percent of all seats in national parliaments in 2009. In the country of Rwanda, over half the parliamentary seats are filled by women (Figure 6.48).

By other measures, however, such as the prevalence of polygamy, the practice of the "bride-price," and the denial of property inheritance, African women do suffer discrimination. Perhaps the most controversial issue regarding women's status is the practice of female circumcision, or genital mutilation. In Sudan, Ethiopia, Somalia, and Eritrea, as well as parts of West Africa, almost 80 percent of girls are subjected to this practice, which is extremely painful and can have serious health consequences. Yet because the practice is considered traditional, most African states are unwilling to ban it.

Regardless of their social position, most African women still live in remote villages where educational and wage-earning opportunities remain limited and bearing numerous children remains a major economic contribution to the family. As educational levels increase and urban society expands—and as reduced infant mortality provides greater security—one can expect fertility in the region to gradually decrease. Governments can speed up the process by providing birth control information and cheap contraceptives—and by investing more money in health and educational efforts aimed at women. As the economic importance of

Figure 6.48 Development Issues: African Women in the Work Force and Politics Female participation in the work force is comparable to that of developed countries, as 70 percent of women over the age of 15 are in the labor force. Another significant change for the region is the increase of women holding seats in national parliaments. While the national average is 18 percent, in South Africa 45 percent of parliamentary seats are held by women, and 56 percent of the seats in Rwanda are held by women. In Africa's largest country, Nigeria, only 7 percent of the parliamentry seats are held by women.

women receives greater attention from national and international organizations, more programs are being directed exclusively toward them.

Building from Within Major shifts in the way development agencies view women and women view themselves have the potential to transform the region. All across the continent, support groups and networks have formed, raising women's consciousness, offering women micro-credit loans for small businesses, and harnessing their economic power. From farm-labor groups to women's market associ-

ations, investment in the organization of women has paid off. In Kenya, for example, hundreds of women's groups organize tree plantings to prevent soil erosion and ensure future biofuel supplies.

Whether inspired by feminism, African socialism, or the free market, community organizations have made a difference in meeting basic needs in sustainable ways. No doubt the majority of the groups fall short of all of their objectives. Yet for many people, especially women, the message of creating local networks to solve community problems is an empowering one.

Summary

- The largest landmass straddling the equator, Africa is called the plateau continent because it is dominated by extensive uplifted plains. Key environmental issues facing this tropical region are desertification, deforestation, and drought. Global warming is likely to make these problems worse. At the same time, the region supports a tremendous diversity of wildlife, especially large mammals.

- With 865 million people, Sub-Saharan Africa is the fastest growing region in terms of population. Yet it is also the poorest region, with three-quarters of the population living on less than $2 a day. In addition, it has the lowest average life expectancy at 52 years. Disease, especially the scourge of HIV/AIDS, has driven down life expectancy in the region.

- Culturally, Sub-Saharan Africa is an extremely diverse region, where multi-ethnic and multi-religious societies are the norm. With a few exceptions, religious diversity and tolerance has been a distinctive feature of the region. Most states have been independent for 50 years, and in that time, pluralistic but distinct national identities have been forged. Many African cultural expressions such as music, dance, religion, and film have had an influence well beyond the region.

- Since 1995 there have been numerous bloody ethnic and political conflicts in the region. Fortunately, peace now exists in many former conflict-ridden states such as Angola, Liberia, Sierra Leone, and the Democratic Republic of the Congo. However, ongoing ethnic and territorial disputes in Darfur, Sudan, northern Uganda, and Somalia have produced millions of internally displaced persons and refugees.

- In terms of contemporary economic globalization, Sub-Saharan Africa's connections to the global economy are weak. With 12 percent of the world's population, the region only accounts for less than 2 percent of the world's economic activity. Most of the region's economic ties are through international aid and loans rather than trade. Foreign direct investment, especially from China, is increasing in the region. Economic growth also improved in the 2000s, from the low to negative rates in the 1990s.

- Poverty is the region's most pressing issue. Since 2000, economic growth has occurred, led in part by debt forgiveness policies, higher commodity prices, and the end of some of the longest running conflicts in the region. Foreign aid to the region tripled from 2000 to 2008, in part due to the targets set by the Millennium Development Goals. It remains to be seen if the international community is truly committed to helping millions of Africans out of extreme poverty and into longer and healthier lives.

Key Terms

African Union (AU) (*page 264*)
agricultural density (*page 239*)
apartheid (*page 248*)
Berlin Conference (*page 261*)
biofuels (*page 235*)
clan (*page 269*)
coloured (*page 248*)
desertification (*page 233*)
genocide (*page 268*)
Gondwanaland (*page 228*)

Great Escarpment (*page 228*)
homelands (*page 264*)
Horn of Africa (*page 232*)
internally displaced persons (*page 267*)
kleptocracy (*page 274*)
Millennium Development Goals (*page 274*)
Pan-African Movement (*page 264*)
pastoralists (*page 245*)
physiological density (*page 239*)
refugee (*page 267*)

Sahel (*page 233*)
structural adjustment programs (*page 270*)
swidden (*page 243*)
township (*page 249*)
transhumance (*page 233*)
tribalism (*page 266*)
tribe (*page 252*)
tsetse fly (*page 245*)

Review Questions

1. Describe the relationship between soil types and patterns of settlement in Sub-Saharan Africa.

2. Is desertification a natural or a human-induced process? Where does it occur? How might global warming impact desertification trends?

3. What are the demographic, social, and economic consequences of AIDS in Sub-Saharan Africa?

4. Explain the factors that contribute to high population growth rates in the region.

5. What was the political significance of the 1884 Berlin Conference for Africa?

6. Why have there been relatively few boundary changes since African nations won their independence?

7. How are private and grassroots organizations shaping African development?

8. Explain the history and policies that make South Africa distinct from other states in the region.

9. How might the food policies of African governments have undermined the region's ability to feed itself?

10. What are the region's key economic resources that may facilitate its integration into the global economy?

Thinking Geographically

1. What factors might explain why European conquest and settlement occurred much earlier in tropical America than in tropical Africa?

2. What are some of the cultural and political ties that unite Africa with the Americas? With Southwest Asia? With South Asia?

3. Discuss how increasing urbanization in the 21st century might affect the overall structure of the population of Sub-Saharan Africa.

4. More than any other region, Sub-Saharan Africa is noted for its wildlife, especially large mammals. What environmental and historical processes explain the existence of so much fauna? Why are there relatively fewer large mammals in other world regions?

5. Compare and contrast the role of tribalism in Sub-Saharan Africa with that of nationalism in Europe.

6. Historically, how was Sub-Saharan Africa integrated into the global economy? Was its role similar to or different from that of other developing regions?

7. The northern boundary of the region of Sub-Saharan Africa is particularly problematic because of its relationship to North Africa. Should the Sahara be considered a cultural divide between these two regions? Why or why not?

8. Compare the contrasting development model put forward by the United States and Europe with that of China. Will Chinese influence in the region alter the course of development for the region?

9. Why is the political map of Africa blamed for the region's many ethnic conflicts? Is it the map at fault or are other factors more significant?

10. How useful are the Millennium Development Goals in measuring development? What are the problems in tracking Sub-Saharan Africa's relative progress given the lack of infrastructure and data?

Regional Novels and Films

Novels

Chinua Achebe, *Things Fall Apart* (1959, Fawcett Crest)

Ishmael Beah, *A Long Way Gone* (2007, Sarah Crichton Books)

Chris Cleave, *Little Bee: A Novel* (2010, Simon & Schuster)

Nuruddin Farah, *Knots* (2007, Riverhead Books)

Nadine Gordimer, *Burger's Daughter* (1979, Viking)

Barbara Kingsolver, *The Poisonwood Bible* (1998, Harper)

Doris Lessing, *African Laughter: Four Visits to Zimbabwe* (1992, Harper)

Alexander McCall Smith, *The No. 1 Ladies' Detective Agency* (2002, Anchor Books)

Alan Paton, *Cry, the Beloved Country* (1948, Scribner's)

Ngugi Wa Thiong'o, *A Grain of Wheat* (1967, Heinemann)

Ngugi Wa Thiong'o, *Petals of Blood* (1977, Heinemann)

Films

Daresalam (2000, Chad)

The Gods Must Be Crazy (1981, Botswana/South Africa)

Hotel Rwanda (2004, U.S.)

The Last King of Scotland (2006, U.S./U.K)

Live and Become (2005, France/Israel)

Lumumba (2000, France)

Masai: The Rain Warriors (2005, Kenya/France)

Thunderbolt (2000, Nigeria)

Tsotsi (2005, South Africa)

Youssou N'Dour: Return to Gorée (2006, Senegal/Switzerland)

Bibliography

Aryeetey-Attoh, Samuel, ed. 2009. *Geography of Sub-Saharan Africa, 3rd ed.* Upper Saddle River, NJ: Prentice Hall.

Christopher, A. J. 1984. *Colonial Africa: A Historical Geography.* Totowa, NJ: Barnes & Noble.

Carney, Judith. 2002. *Black Rice: The African Origins of Rice Cultivation in the Americas.* Cambridge, MA: Harvard University Press.

Curtin, Philip D. 1969. *The Atlantic Slave Trade.* Madison: University of Wisconsin Press.

Grant, Richard. 2009. *Globalizing City: The Urban and Economic Transformation of Accra, Ghana.* Syracuse: Syracuse University Press.

Le Billion, Philippe. 2008. "Diamond Wars? Conflict Diamonds and Geographies of Resource Wars." *Annals of the Association of American Geographers* 98(2): 345–372.

Ndegwa, Stephen N. 1996. *The Two Faces of Civil Society: NGOs and Politics in Africa.* West Hartford, CT: Kumarian Press.

Newman, James L. 1995. *The Peopling of Africa: A Geographical Interpretation.* New Haven: Yale University Press.

Rain, David. 1999. *Eaters of the Dry Season: Circular Labor Migration in the West African Sahel.* Boulder, CO: Westview Press.

United Nations and World Health Organization. 2009. *'09 AIDS Epidemic Update.* Geneva, Switzerland: United Nations.

Stock, Robert. 2004. *Africa South of the Sahara: A Geographical Interpretation,* 2nd ed. New York: Guilford Press.

Mastering Geography

MapMaster™

Log in to www.masteringgeography.com for MapMaster™ interactive maps, geography videos, RSS feeds, flashcards, web links, an eText version of *Diversity Amid Globalization,* and self-study quizzes to enhance your study of Sub-Saharan Africa.

MapMaster™ presents 13 Place Name and 13 Layered Thematic interactive maps to help students practice and master their geographic literacy, spatial reasoning, and critical thinking skills.

7
Southwest Asia and North Africa

Home to a large Palestinian community, the West Bank city of Hebron is an important center of trade and industry within the region and it contains key sites of religious significance for Muslim, Jewish, and Christian populations.

DIVERSITY AMID GLOBALIZATION

Globalization has played out across Southwest Asia and North Africa in complex ways. Energy-rich nations have reaped the greatest economic rewards in satisfying global demands for oil and natural gas, but varied cultural and political elements of the outside world have not been embraced by many residents of the region.

ENVIRONMENTAL GEOGRAPHY

Water shortages are likely to increase across this arid region in the early 21st century as growing populations, rapid urbanization, and increasing demands for agricultural land consume limited water supplies.

POPULATION AND SETTLEMENT

Rapid population growth in North African cities such as Algiers and Cairo is far outpacing the ability of these urban places to supply adequate housing and services.

CULTURAL COHERENCE AND DIVERSITY

The heart of the Islamic world, this region finds itself at the center of the global rise of Islamist movements that often come into conflict with Western values and traditions.

GEOPOLITICAL FRAMEWORK

Ongoing political instability is a fact of life across much of the region. Religious and ethnic differences, shifting political allegiances, and persistent economic problems all contribute to the region's geopolitical challenges.

ECONOMIC AND SOCIAL DEVELOPMENT

Changing world oil prices have a tremendous economic impact on this region, which holds almost two-thirds of all petroleum reserves on the planet. The economic crisis of 2008–2010 produced widespread unemployment in the energy, tourism, and manufacturing sectors of the regional economy and selectively contributed to more political instability across the region.

Climate, culture, and oil all help define the Southwest Asia and North Africa world region. Straddling the historic meeting ground between Europe, Asia, and Africa, the region sprawls across thousands of miles of parched deserts, rugged plateaus, and oasis-like river valleys. It extends 4,000 miles (6,400 kilometers) between Morocco's Atlantic coastline and Iran's eastern boundary with Pakistan. More than two dozen nations are included within its borders, with the largest populations found in Egypt, Turkey, and Iran (Figure 7.1). Generally, its climates are arid, although the region's diverse physical geography causes precipitation to vary considerably.

Regional boundaries and terminology defy easy definition. Often the same broad area is simply called the *Middle East,* but most experts would exclude the western parts of North Africa as well as Turkey and Iran from such a region. In addition, the *Middle East* carries with it a peculiarly European vantage point—Lebanon is in the "middle of the east" only from the perspective of the western Europeans who colonized the region. Instead, *Southwest Asia and North Africa* offers a useful and straightforward way to describe the general limits of the region.

There also are problems with simply defining the geographical limits of the region. To the northwest, a small piece of Turkey actually sits west of the Bosporus Strait, generally considered to be the dividing line between Europe and Asia (see Figure 7.1). The addition of Cyprus (off the coast of Turkey) to the European Union in 2004 effectively removed it from the region, and that country is treated in the chapter on Europe (see Chapter 8). To the northeast, the largely Islamic peoples of Central Asia share many religious and linguistic ties with Turkey and Iran, but we have chosen to treat these groups in a separate chapter on Central Asia (see Chapter 10).

African borders also are problematic. The conventional regional division of "North Africa" from "Sub-Saharan Africa" often cuts directly through the middle of modern Mauritania, Mali, Niger, Chad, and Sudan. We place all of these transitional countries in Chapter 6, Sub-Saharan Africa, but also include some discussion of Sudan within our Southwest Asia and North Africa material because of its status as an "Islamic republic," a political and cultural designation that ties it strongly to the Muslim world.

Culturally, diverse languages, religions, and ethnic identities have molded land and life within the region for

centuries. One traditional zone of conflict is in the eastern Mediterranean, where Jewish, Christian, and Islamic peoples have yet to resolve long-standing cultural tensions and political differences, particularly as they relate to the state of Israel and various Palestinian groups within the region. Iraq also has been a setting for recent violence as an American-led invasion toppled the regime of Saddam Hussein and various religious, ethnic, and political factions have divided the

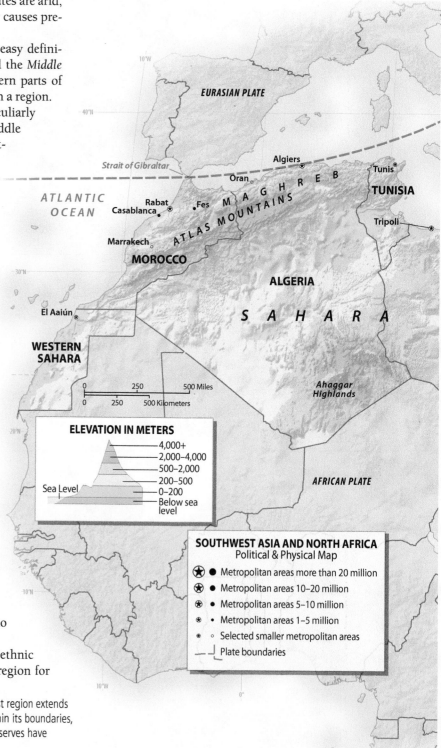

Figure 7.1 Southwest Asia and North Africa This vast region extends from the shores of the Atlantic Ocean to the Caspian Sea. Within its boundaries, major cultural differences and globally important petroleum reserves have contributed to recent political tensions.

country. Nearby Iran and its ongoing development of a nuclear capability have also increased tensions. In addition, Southwest Asia and North Africa's extraordinary petroleum resources place the area in the global economic spotlight. The strategic value of oil has combined with ongoing ethnic and religious conflicts to produce one of the world's least stable political settings, one prone to geopolitical conflict both within and between the countries of the region.

No world region has better exemplified the theme of globalization throughout history than Southwest Asia and North Africa. A key global **culture hearth**, the region witnessed many cultural innovations that subsequently diffused widely to other portions of the world. As an early center for agriculture, several great civilizations, and three major world religions, the region has been a key human crossroads for thousands of years. Important trade routes have connected North Africa with the Mediterranean and Sub-Saharan Africa. Southwest Asia also has had historical ties to Europe, the Indian subcontinent, and Central Asia. As a result, innovations within the region

Figure 7.2 Man at Livestock Market, Al Ayn, United Arab Emirates Longtime residents of Southwest Asia have witnessed incredible change in their lifetimes. In many localities, traditional ways have been radically transformed by urbanization, foreign investment, and external cultural influences.

Figure 7.3 Saudi Arabian Oil Refinery Eastern Saudi Arabia's Ras Tanuna Oil Refinery links the oil-rich country to the world beyond. Huge foreign and domestic investments since 1960 have dramatically transformed many other settings in the region.

have often spread far beyond its bounds. For example, the domestication of wheat and cattle in Southwest Asia had far-reaching global impacts. In addition, religions born within the region (Judaism, Christianity, and Islam) have shaped many other parts of the world.

Particularly within the past century, globalization also has operated in the opposite direction: The region's strategic importance has made it increasingly vulnerable to outside influences. Traditional lifeways have been transformed (Figure 7.2). The 20th-century development of the petroleum industry, largely initiated by U.S. and European investment, has had enormous, but selective, consequences for economic development. Global demand for oil and natural gas has powered rapid industrial change within the region, defining its pivotal role in world trade (Figure 7.3). Many key members of the **Organization of the Petroleum Exporting Countries (OPEC)** are found within the region, and these countries strongly influence global prices and production levels for petroleum. Regional dependence on the petroleum industry has also made the area especially vulnerable to global recessions, and the recent downturn of 2008–2010 was no exception. Once-booming cities such as Dubai in the United Arab Emirates (U.A.E.) witnessed soaring unemployment rates, stalled construction projects, and real financial crises. Future growth in such settings continues to be wed to the health of

global oil demand. Still, the regional patterns are complex. Oil-rich nations such as the United Arab Emirates, Saudi Arabia, and Kuwait have been fundamentally transformed by the global fossil fuel economy, while petroleum-poor neighbors such as Jordan, Lebanon, and Tunisia have seen less dramatic impacts. Politically, petroleum resources also have elevated the region's strategic importance, adding to many traditional cultural tensions.

More recently, **Islamic fundamentalism** has advocated a return across the region to more traditional practices within the Muslim religion. Fundamentalists in any religion advocate a conservative loyalty to enduring beliefs within their faith and they strongly resist change. A related political movement within Islam known as **Islamism** challenges the encroachment of global popular culture and blames colonial, imperial, and Western elements for many of the region's political, economic, and social problems. Islamists resent the role they claim the West has played in creating poverty in their world, and many Islamists advocate merging civil and religious authority and rejecting modern, Western-style consumer culture. While often demonized in the Western press, particularly when associated with terrorist acts of violence, Islamic fundamentalism and Islamism can be seen as cultural and political reactions to the disruptive role that forces of globalization have played across the region.

The region's environment provides additional challenges for the populations of Southwest Asia and North Africa. The availability of water in this largely dry portion of the world has shaped the region's physical and human geographies. Biologically, the region's plants and animals must adapt to the aridity of long dry seasons and short, often unpredictable rainy periods. Human settlement is linked to water in similar ways. Whether it comes from precipitation, underground aquifers, or rivers, water has shaped settlement patterns and has placed severe limits on agricultural development across huge portions of the region. In the future, the region's growing population of more than 400 million people will stress these available resources even further, and water issues will no doubt increase economic and political instability.

ENVIRONMENTAL GEOGRAPHY: Life in a Fragile World

In the popular imagination, much of Southwest Asia and North Africa is a land of shifting sand dunes, searing heat, and scattered oases. Although examples of those stereotypes certainly can be found across the region, the actual physical setting, in both landforms and climate, is considerably more complex (see Figure 7.1). In reality, the regional terrain varies greatly, with rocky plateaus and mountain ranges more common than sandy deserts. Even the climate, although dominated by aridity, varies remarkably from the dry heart of North Africa's Sahara Desert to the well-watered highlands of northern Morocco, coastal Turkey, and western Iran. One theme is pervasive; however, a lengthy legacy of human settlement has left its mark on a fragile environment, and the entire region will be faced with increasingly daunting ecological problems in the decades ahead.

Legacies of a Vulnerable Landscape

The island of Socotra illustrates the region's fragile and vulnerable environment and suggests how processes of globalization may threaten the area's long-term ecological health. Socotra's stony slopes rise out of the shimmering waters of the Indian Ocean about 230 miles (368 kilometers) southeast of Yemen. The island's unique natural and cultural history has recently caught the world's attention. Separated for millions of years from the mainland of the Arabian Peninsula, Socotra's environment evolved in isolation. More than 30 percent of the island's 850 plants are found nowhere else on Earth. Exotic dragon's blood trees dot many of the is-

land's dry and rocky hillsides, and dozens of other species have only recently been catalogued by botanists (Figures 7.4 and 7.5). Offshore, equally rare coral reefs and unusual fish populations have evolved as a part of the island's unique environmental setting in the wet–dry tropics of the northwestern Indian Ocean.

Socotra's unique environmental heritage now hangs in the balance. Global participants in the 1992 environmental summit at Rio de Janeiro established a $5 million international biodiversity project on Socotra, and Edinburgh's Royal Botanic Garden has conducted extensive studies on the island. In 2008, the island was recognized as a United Nations World Natural Heritage Site, and the European Union has officially supported the idea of preserving the area's unique biogeography.

At the same time, global pharmaceutical companies have already been allowed to harvest some of the island's unique plant species and other plants and animals have been illegally taken by visitors. In addition, the Yemeni government has invited international petroleum companies to explore the island's offshore oil and gas potential, and it has considered a grand scheme for developing a series of luxury tourist hotels that would forever change the island's character. In 2009, an environmental expert noted that even well-meaning ecotourists on the island are already damaging coral reefs and their growing numbers have led to increased firewood gathering and road construction. Only time will tell how Socotra, which is often cited as the Galápagos of the Indian Ocean, will fare in the 21st century. A recently developed mixed-use zoning plan and a newly paved airstrip suggest development is inevitable.

The larger environmental history of Southwest Asia and North Africa contains many examples of the clever but short-sighted legacies of its human occupants. Lengthy human settlement in a marginal land has resulted in deforestation, soil salinization and erosion, and depleted water resources (see Figure 7.5). Indeed, the pace of population growth and technological change during the past century suggests that the region's vulnerable environment is destined to face even greater challenges in the 21st century.

Deforestation and Overgrazing Deforestation is an ancient problem in Southwest Asia and North Africa. Although much of the region is too dry for trees, the more humid and elevated lands that ring the Mediterranean once supported heavy forests. Included in these woodlands are the cedars of Lebanon, cut during ancient times and now reduced to a few scattered groves in a largely denuded landscape. In many settings, growing demands for agricultural land caused upland forests to be removed and replaced with grain fields, orchards, and pastures.

Human activities have conspired with natural conditions to reduce most of the region's forests to grass and scrub. Mediterranean forests grow slowly, are highly vulnerable to fire, and usually fare poorly if subjected to heavy grazing. Browsing by goats in particular often has been blamed for much of the region's forest loss, but other live-

Figure 7.4 Socotra's Dragon's Blood Tree Unique to Socotra, the rare dragon's blood tree reflects the island's environmental isolation. Evolving as a part of the island's ecosystem, the tree survives in the region's dry tropical climate.

Figure 7.5 Environmental Issues in Southwest Asia and North Africa Growing populations, pressures for economic development, and pervasive aridity combine to create environmental hazards across the region. Long human occupance has contributed to deforestation, irrigation-induced salinization, and expanding desertification. Saudi Arabia's deep-water wells, Egypt's Aswan High Dam, and Libya's Great Man-made River are all recent technological attempts to expand settlement, but they may carry a high long-term environmental price tag.

stock have also impacted the vegetative cover, especially in steeply sloping semiarid settings that are slow to recover from grazing. Deforestation also has resulted in a millennia-long deterioration of the region's water supplies and in accelerated soil erosion.

Some forests survive in the mountains of northern and southern Turkey, and northern Iran also retains considerable tree cover. Scattered forests can be found in western Iran, the eastern Mediterranean, and the Atlas Mountains. Moreover, several governments have launched reforestation drives and forest preservation efforts in recent years. For example, both Israel and Syria have expanded their coverage of wooded lands since the 1980s. In nearby Lebanon, more than 5 percent of the country's total area was included in the Shouf Cedar Reserve in 1996 to protect old-growth cedars, junipers, and oak forests. An even larger area (including the Shouf Cedar Reserve) was declared the Shouf Biosphere Reserve by the United Nations in 2005 and is designed to protect both the rare trees as well as endangered mammals such as the wolf and Lebanese jungle cat.

Salinization Salinization, or the buildup of toxic salts in the soil, is another ancient environmental issue in a region where irrigation has been practiced for centuries (see Figure 7.5). The accumulation of salt in the topsoil is a common problem wherever desert lands are subjected to extensive irrigation. All freshwater contains a small amount of dissolved salt, and when water is diverted from streams into fields, salt remains in the soil after the moisture is absorbed by the plants and evaporated by the sun. In humid climates, accumulated salts are washed away by saturating rains, but in arid climates this rarely occurs. Where irrigation is practiced, salt concentrations build up over time, leading to lower crop yields and eventually to land abandonment.

Hundreds of thousands of acres of once-fertile farmland within the region have been destroyed or degraded by salinization. The problem has been particularly acute in Iraq, where centuries of canal irrigation along the Tigris and Euphrates rivers has seriously degraded land quality. Similar conditions plague central Iran, Egypt, and irrigated portions of the Maghreb.

Managing Water Residents of the region are continually challenged by many other problems related to managing water in one of the driest portions of Earth. As technological change has accelerated, the scale and impact of water management schemes have had a growing effect on the region's environment. Sometimes the costs are justified if large new areas are brought into productive and sustainable agricultural use. In other cases, the long-term environmental price will far outweigh any immediate and perhaps short-lived gains in agricultural production.

Regional populations have been modifying drainage systems and water flows for thousands of years. The Iranian **qanat system** of tapping into groundwater through a series of gently sloping tunnels was widely replicated on the Arabian Peninsula and in North Africa. With simple technology, farmers directed the downslope flow of underground water to fields and villages where it could be efficiently utilized.

In the past half century, however, the scope of environmental change has been greatly magnified. Water management schemes have become huge engineering projects, major budget expenditures, and even political issues, both within and between countries of the region. One remarkable example is Egypt's Aswan High Dam, completed in 1970 on the Nile River south of Cairo (see Figure 7.5). Many benefits came with the dam's completion. Most important, greatly increased storage capacity in the upstream reservoir promoted more year-round cropping and an expansion of cultivated lands along the Nile, critical changes in a country that continues to experience rapid population growth. The dam also generates large amounts of clean electricity for the region. But the environmental costs have been high. The dam has changed methods of irrigation along the Nile, greatly increasing salinization. While fresh sediments and soil nutrients once annually washed across the valley floor with high river flows, more controlled irrigation has meant greatly increased inputs of costly fertilizers. Sediments that used to move downstream now accumulate behind the dam, infilling Lake Nasser. Other problems with the dam include an increased incidence of schistosomiasis (a debilitating parasitic disease spread by waterborne snails in irrigation canals) and the collapse of the Mediterranean fishing industry near the Nile Delta, an area previously nourished by the river's silt.

Israel's "Peace Corridor" project is another potential massive engineering venture within the region. Designed to stimulate the regional economy and bring Red Sea water north into the Dead Sea, the effort received increased government backing in 2007. The ambitious plan calls for a 120-mile (200-kilometer) conduit to be built from near Aqaba to the southern end of the Dead Sea (Figure 7.6). The water could be desalinated, generate hydroelectricity, and help save the Dead Sea and its major tourist resorts from literally drying up.

Elsewhere, **fossil water**, or water supplies stored underground during earlier and wetter climatic periods, has also been put to use by modern technology. Libya's "Great Man-

Figure 7.6 Water Issues in the Middle East Many water-related issues complicate the geopolitical setting in the Middle East. The Jordan River system has been a particular focus of conflict. (Modified from *Soffer, Arnon, Rivers of Fire: The Conflict over Water in the Middle East*, 1999, p. 180. Reprinted by permission of Rowman and Littlefield Publishers, Inc.)

made River" scheme taps underground water in the southern part of the country, transports it 600 miles (965 kilometers) to northern coastal zones, and uses the precious resource to expand agricultural production in one of North Africa's driest countries (see Figure 7.5). Similarly, Saudi Arabia has invested huge sums to develop deep-water wells, allowing it to expand its food output greatly (Figure 7.7). Unfortunately, these underground supplies are being depleted much more rapidly than they are being recharged, thus limiting the long-term sustainability of such ventures.

Most dramatically, **hydropolitics**, or the interplay of water resource issues and politics, has raised tensions between countries that share drainage basins. For example, in 2007, with the help of Chinese capital and engineering expertise, Ethiopia began construction of its huge Tekeze Dam project on the Nile. Already referred to by its promoters as the equivalent of "China's Three Gorges Dam in Africa," the controversial project threatens to disrupt downstream fisheries and irrigation in North Africa. Similarly Sudan's Merowe Dam project (on another stretch of the Nile) has raised major concerns in nearby Egypt. In Southwest Asia, Turkey's growing development of the upper Tigris and Euphrates rivers (the Southeast Anatolia Project or "GAP"), complete with 22 dams and 19 power plants, has raised issues with Iraq and Syria, who argue that capturing "their" water might be considered a provocative political act. Hydropolitics also has played into negotiations between Israel, the Palestinians, and other neighboring states, particularly in the Golan Heights area (an important headwaters zone for multiple nations) and within the Jordan River drainage (see Figure 7.6). Israelis fear Palestinian and Syrian pollution; nearby Jordanians argue for more water from Syria; and all regional residents must deal with the uncomfortable reality that, regardless of their political differences, they must drink from the same limited supplies of freshwater. In addition, a 2009 report by Amnesty International suggested that Israeli water restrictions harshly discriminated against Palestinians in both Gaza and the West Bank (see "Environment and Politics: Water and the Palestinians in the Middle East").

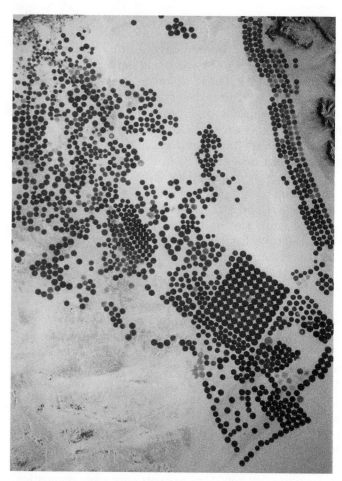

Figure 7.7 Saudi Arabian Irrigation These irrigated fields in the Saudi Desert draw from wells over 4,000 feet deep. While significantly expanding the country's food production, such efforts are rapidly depleting underground supplies of fossil water.

Figure 7.8 Atlas Mountains The rugged Atlas Mountains dominate a broad area of interior Morocco. Steep slopes and narrow canyons can make travel slow and hazardous across the region.

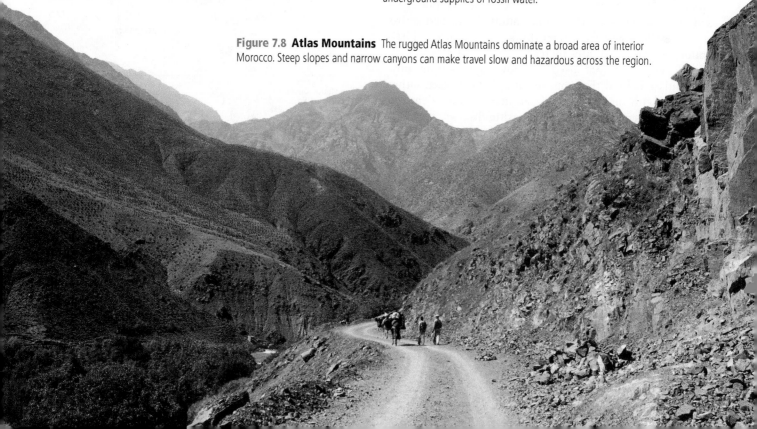

ENVIRONMENT AND POLITICS   Water and the Palestinians in the Middle East

Inevitably, water and politics are intertwined in the Middle East. Not surprisingly, fundamental disagreements over water have trickled into the long-standing conflict between the Israelis and the Palestinians, both in Gaza and in the West Bank. Palestinian authorities argue that the Israelis have used water as a weapon of control and that Palestinian settlements are often left high and dry because of Israel's discriminatory policies. On the other hand, Israelis argue that the Palestinians often waste water or fail to utilize it fully and that they have no right to complain about Israel's own brand of "hydropolitics."

Take the small, overcrowded, poverty-stricken lands of the Gaza Strip (see Figure 7.6 and 7.1.1). In a 2009 report, Amnesty Interna-

tional observed that most Gaza residents survived on only 20–70 liters of water per day, compared to the Israeli average of 300 liters. Much of Gaza's water storage and delivery infrastructure has been damaged or destroyed in recent military operations, and Israeli blockades along the Gaza border have severely limited efforts to rebuild the system. The report noted that both the area's water and sewage systems had reached a "crisis point." But it also criticized local Palestinian leaders, suggesting their own management of the existing system was in "total chaos."

In the nearby West Bank area (see Figure 7.6), water is also at the center of many political tensions between Palestinian and Jewish settlers. Palestinians point to lush gardens and swimming pools in Israeli-controlled areas that stand in sharp contrast to thirsty Palestinian towns that often end up severely restricted in their access to underground aquifers or to water flowing in the nearby Jordan River (which is largely appropriated for Israeli uses). Palestinians also complain that well-drilling permits are difficult to obtain from Israeli authorities and that cisterns used to store rainwater are often used for target practice by the Israeli army. Israeli authorities argue that many of the criticisms leveled against them are nonsense. They point to the fact that many well permits have not even been used by Palestinians and that international aid that Palestinians have received for investments in water infrastructure has been spent elsewhere.

Regardless of whose claims can be believed, water remains a politically charged resource in the Middle East. There will never be enough of it, and its resulting scarcity creates inevitable conflicts between those who control it and those who need it.

Figure 7.1.1 Gaza Strip Basic water storage and delivery systems are often heavily damaged or destroyed in settings such as this Palestinian refugee camp north of Gaza City in the war-torn Gaza Strip.

Regional Landforms

A quick tour of the region reveals a surprising diversity of environmental settings and landforms (see Figure 7.1). In North Africa, the **Maghreb** region (meaning "western island") includes the nations of Morocco, Algeria, and Tunisia and is dominated near the Mediterranean coastline by the Atlas Mountains. The rugged flanks of the Atlas rise like a series of islands above the narrow coastal plains to the north and the vast stretches of the lower Saharan deserts to the south (Figure 7.8). South and east of the Atlas Mountains, interior North Africa varies between rocky plateaus and extensive lowlands. In northeast Africa, the Nile River dominates the scene as it flows north through Sudan and Egypt.

Southwest Asia is more mountainous than North Africa. In the **Levant**, or eastern Mediterranean region,

mountains rise within 20 miles (32 kilometers) of the sea, and the highlands of Lebanon reach heights of more than 10,000 feet (3,048 meters). Farther south, the Arabian Peninsula forms a massive tilted plateau, with western highlands higher than 5,000 feet (1,524 meters) gradually sloping eastward to extensive lowlands in the Persian Gulf area. North and east of the Arabian Peninsula lie the two great upland areas of Southwest Asia: the Iranian and Anatolian plateaus (*Anatolia* refers to the large peninsula of Turkey, sometimes called Asia Minor) (see Figures 7.1 and 7.9). Both of these plateaus, averaging between 3,000 and 5,000 feet (915 to 1,524 meters) in elevation, are geologically active and prone to earthquakes. One dramatic quake in western Turkey (1999) measured 7.8 on the Richter scale, killed more than 17,000 people, and left 350,000 residents homeless. Another quake near the Iranian city of Bam (2003) claimed more than 30,000 lives.

Figure 7.9 Satellite View of Turkey
This satellite image of Turkey suggests the varied, quake-prone terrain encountered across the Anatolian Plateau. The Black Sea coastline is visible near the top of the image, and the island-studded Aegean Sea borders Turkey on the west.

Smaller lowlands characterize other portions of Southwest Asia. Narrow coastal strips are common in the Levant, along both the southern (Mediterranean) and northern (Black Sea) Turkish coastlines, and north of the Iranian Elburz Mountains near the Caspian Sea. Iraq contains the most extensive alluvial lowlands in Southwest Asia, dominated by the Tigris and Euphrates rivers, which flow southeast to empty into the Persian Gulf. Although much smaller, the distinctive Jordan River Valley is also a notable lowland that straddles the strategic borderlands of Israel, Jordan, and Syria and drains southward to the Dead Sea (Figure 7.10).

Patterns of Climate

Although often termed the *dry world*, a closer look at Southwest Asia and North Africa reveals a more complex climatic pattern (Figure 7.11). Both latitude and altitude come into play. Aridity dominates large portions of the region. A nearly continuous belt of desert lands stretches eastward from the Atlantic coast of southern Morocco across the continent of Africa, through the Arabian Peninsula, and into central and eastern Iran. Throughout this vast dry zone, plant and animal life have adapted to extreme conditions. Deep or extensive root systems and rapid life cycles allow desert plants to benefit from the limited moisture they receive. Similarly, animals adjust by efficiently storing water, hunting nocturnally, or migrating seasonally to avoid the worst of the dry cycle.

Some of the driest conditions are found across North Africa. Away from the Atlas Mountains, the Sahara Desert dominates much of the region. Much of the central Sahara receives less than 1 inch (2.5 centimeters) of rain a year and can thus support only the most meager forms of vegetation. Saharan summers feature extremely hot days and warm evenings (the world's record high, 136°F [58°C] was recorded in Libya), but winters are generally pleasant, even cool at night. Only in the tropical latitudes of southern

Figure 7.10 Jordan Valley This view of the Jordan Valley shows a fertile mix of irrigated vineyards and date palm plantations.

Figure 7.11 **Climate Map of Southwest Asia and North Africa** Dry climates dominate from western Morocco to eastern Iran. Within these zones, persistent subtropical high-pressure systems offer only limited opportunities for precipitation. Elsewhere, mild midlatitude climates with wet winters are found near the Mediterranean Basin and Black Sea. To the south, tropical savanna climates provide summer moisture to southern Sudan.

Sudan do precipitation levels rise significantly. Here, summer rains produce between 20 and 50 inches (51 to 127 centimeters) of precipitation, and tropical savannas and woodlands replace the desert vegetation to the north.

Across the Red Sea, deserts also dominate Southwest Asia. Most of the Arabian Desert is not quite as dry as the Sahara proper, although the Rub-al-Khali along Saudi Arabia's

southern border is one of the world's most desolate areas. On the fringe of the summer-monsoon belt, the Yemen Highlands along the southwestern edge of the Arabian Peninsula receive much more rain than the rest of the region and thus form a more favorable site for human habitation. To the northwest, precipitation also increases slightly in the central Tigris and Euphrates river valleys, with Baghdad, Iraq, aver-

Figure 7.12 Arid Iran Only sparse vegetation dots this arid scene from central Iran, a landscape characterized by isolated mountain ranges and dry interior plateaus.

aging just over 5 inches (13 centimeters) of rain annually. Another major arid zone lies across Iran, a country divided into a series of minor mountain ranges and desert basins (Figure 7.12).

Elsewhere, altitude and latitude dramatically alter the desert environment and produce a surprising amount of climatic variety. For example, the Atlas Mountains and the nearby lowlands of northern Morocco, Algeria, and Tunisia experience a distinctly Mediterranean climate in which hot, dry summers alternate with cooler, relatively wet winters. In these areas, the landscape resembles that found in nearby southern Spain or Italy (Figure 7.13). A second zone of Mediterranean climate extends along the Levant coastline into the nearby mountains and northward across large portions of northern Syria, Turkey, and northwestern Iran.

Global Warming in Southwest Asia and North Africa

Projected changes in global climate will tend to aggravate already-existing environmental issues within North Africa and Southwest Asia. Temperature changes are predicted to have a greater impact on the region than changes in precipitation. The already arid and semiarid region will likely remain relatively dry, but warmer average temperatures are likely to have several major consequences. First, higher overall evaporation rates and lower overall soil moisture across the region will more likely stress crops, grasslands, and other vegetation. Semiarid lands are particularly vulnerable, especially dryland cropping systems that cannot depend on irrigation. Even in irrigated zones, higher temperatures are likely to reduce yields for crops such as wheat and maize. Second, warmer temperatures will likely reduce net runoff into the region's already stressed streams and rivers, potentially reducing hydroelectric potential and water that is available for the region's increasingly urban population. Third, there will be a higher likelihood of ex-

treme weather events, such as record-setting summertime temperatures. These extreme events will undoubtedly lead to more heat-related deaths as residents struggle to adapt, particularly in urban settings where many people cannot afford air conditioning.

Sea level changes will pose special threats to the Nile Delta. This portion of northern Egypt is a vast, low-lying landscape of settlements, farms, and marshland. Studies that simulate rising sea levels reveal that much of the region will be lost, either to inundation, erosion, or salinization. Farmland losses of more than 250,000 acres (100,000 hectares) are quite possible with even modest sea level changes. For

Figure 7.13 Algerian Orange Harvest The Mediterranean moisture in northern Algeria produces an agricultural landscape similar to that of southern Spain or Italy. Winter rains create a scene that contrasts sharply with deserts found elsewhere in the region.

Figure 7.14 Alexandria, Egypt This beachside view along northern Egypt's low-lying coastline at Alexandria could change significantly if global sea levels were to rise.

example, estimates are that a 1-meter (3.3 feet) sea-level rise could affect 15 percent of Egypt's habitable land and displace 8 million Egyptians in coastal and delta settings. In the Egyptian city of Alexandria, $30 billion in losses have been projected because sea level changes will devastate the city's huge resort industry as well as nearby residential and commercial areas (Figure 7.14).

Some experts have also attempted to estimate the broader political and economic costs associated with potential climate changes within the region. For example, given the political instability of the Middle East, even relatively small changes in water supplies, particularly where they might involve several nations, could significantly add to the potential for conflict within the region. Projected economic implications of climate change may depend on the relative importance of agriculture within different nations. In addition, wealthier nations such as Israel and Saudi Arabia may have more available resources to plan, adjust, and adapt to climate shifts and extreme events versus poorer, less-developed countries such as Yemen, Syria, or Sudan.

POPULATION AND SETTLEMENT: Changing Rural and Urban Worlds

The geography of human population across Southwest Asia and North Africa demonstrates the intimate tie between water and life in this part of the world. The pattern is complex: Large areas of the population map remain almost devoid of permanent settlement, while more moisture-favored lands suffer increasingly from problems of crowding and overpopulation (Figure 7.15). Almost everywhere across the

region, humans have uniquely adapted themselves to living within arid or semiarid settings.

The Geography of Population

Today, about 450 million people live in Southwest Asia and North Africa (Table 7.1). The distribution of that population is strikingly varied. In countries such as Egypt, large zones of almost empty desert land stand in sharp contrast to crowded, well-watered locations, such as those along the Nile River. While the overall population density in such countries appears modest, the **physiological density**, which is the number of people per unit of arable land, is among the highest on Earth. Patterns of urban geography also are highly uneven: Although less than two-thirds of the overall population is urban, many nations are overwhelmingly dominated by huge and sprawling cities that produce the same problems of urban crowding found elsewhere in the developing world. Rates of recent urban growth have been phenomenal: Cairo, a modest-sized city of 3.5 million people in the 1960s, has quadrupled in population in the past 40 years.

Across North Africa, two dominant clusters of settlement, both shaped by the availability of water, account for most of the region's population (see Figure 7.15). In the Maghreb, the moister slopes of the Atlas Mountains and nearby better-watered coastal districts have accommodated denser populations for centuries. Today, concentrations of both rural and urban settlement extend from south of Casablanca in Morocco to Algiers and Tunis on the shores of the southern Mediterranean. Indeed, most of the populations of Morocco, Algeria, and Tunisia crowd into this crescent, a stark contrast to the almost empty lands south and east of the Atlas Mountains. Casablanca and Algiers are the largest cities

Figure 7.15 Population Map of Southwest Asia and North Africa The striking contrasts between large, sparsely occupied desert zones and much more densely settled regions where water is available are clearly evident. The Nile Valley and the Maghreb region contain most of North Africa's people, while Southwest Asian populations cluster in the highlands and along the better-watered shores of the Mediterranean.

in the Maghreb. They have rapidly growing metropolitan populations of 3 to 4 million residents each. Farther east, much of Libya and western Egypt is very thinly settled. Egypt's Nile Valley, however, is home to the other great North African population cluster. The vast majority of Egypt's 80 million people live within 10 miles of the river. Optimistic politicians and planners are creating a second corridor of denser settlement in Egypt's "New Valley" west of the Nile by diverting water from Lake Nasser into the Western Desert.

Most Southwest Asian residents are clustered in favored coastal zones, moister highland settings, and desert localities where water is available from nearby rivers or subsurface aquifers. High population densities are found in better-watered portions of the eastern Mediterranean (Israel, Lebanon, and Syria) and Turkey. Nearby Iran is home to more than 70 million residents, but population densities vary considerably from thinly occupied deserts in the east to more concentrated

settlements near the Caspian Sea and across the more humid highlands of the northwest. Turkey's Istanbul, formerly Constantinople, (12.8 million) and Iran's Tehran (8.4 million) are Southwest Asia's largest urban areas, and both have grown in recent years as rural populations gravitate toward the economic opportunities of these cities (Figure 7.16). Elsewhere, sizable populations are scattered through the Tigris and Euphrates valley, the Yemen Highlands, and near oases where groundwater can be tapped to support agricultural or industrial activities.

Water and Life: Rural Settlement Patterns

Water and life are closely linked across the rural settlement landscapes of Southwest Asia and North Africa. Indeed, the diverse environments of Southwest Asia, in particular, are home to one of the world's earliest hearths of **domestication**,

TABLE 7.1   Population Indicators

Country	Population (Millions) 2010	Population Density (per Square Kilometer)	Rate of Natural Inrease (RNI)	Total Fertility Rate	Percent Urban	Percent <15	Percent >65	Net Migration (per 1,000, 2005–10)[a]
Algeria	36.0	15	1.8	2.3	63	28	5	–0.8
Bahrain	1.3	1,807	1.3	1.9	100	20	2	5.2
Egypt	80.4	80	2.1	3.0	43	33	4	–0.8
Gaza and West Bank	4.0	672	2.8	4.6	83	44	3	–0.5
Iran	75.1	46	1.3	1.8	69	28	5	–1.4
Iraq	31.5	72	2.6	4.1	67	41	3	–3.9
Israel	7.6	342	1.6	3.0	92	28	10	2.4
Jordan	6.5	73	2.6	3.8	83	37	3	8.3
Kuwait	3.1	175	2.0	2.2	98	23	2	8.3
Lebanon	4.3	409	1.5	2.3	87	25	10	–0.6
Libya	6.5	4	1.9	2.7	77	30	4	0.6
Morocco	31.9	71	1.5	2.4	57	29	5	–2.7
Oman	3.1	10	1.8	2.6	72	29	2	1.7
Qatar	1.7	152	0.8	1.8	100	15	1	93.9
Saudi Arabia	29.2	14	2.6	3.8	81	38	2	1.2
Sudan	43.2	17	2.2	4.5	38	41	3	0.7
Syria	22.5	122	2.5	3.3	54	36	3	7.7
Tunisia	10.5	64	1.2	2.1	66	24	7	–0.4
Turkey	73.6	94	1.2	2.1	76	26	7	–0.1
United Arab Emirates	5.4	64	1.4	2.0	83	19	1	15.6
Western Sahara	0.5	2	2.5	4.5	81`	40	3	19.6
Yemen	23.6	45	3.0	5.5	29	45	3	–1.2

[a]*Net Migration Rate from the United Nations, Population Division, World Population Prospects: The 2008 Revision Population Database.*
Source: Population Reference Bureau, World Population Data Sheet, 2010.

where plants and animals were purposefully selected and bred for their desirable characteristics. Beginning around 10,000 years ago, increased experimentation with wild varieties of wheat and barley led to agricultural settlements that later included domesticated animals, such as cattle, sheep, and goats. Much of the early agricultural activity focused on the **Fertile Crescent**, an ecologically diverse zone that stretches from the Levant inland through the fertile hill country of northern Syria into Iraq. Between 5,000 and 6,000 years ago, better knowledge of irrigation techniques and increasingly centralized political states promoted the spread of agriculture into nearby valleys such as the Tigris and Euphrates (Mesopotamia) and North Africa's Nile Valley. Since then, different peoples of the region have adapted to its environmental diversity and limitations in distinctive ways. In the process, they have practiced forms of agriculture appropriate to their settings and have left their own unique imprints upon the landscape (Figure 7.17).

Pastoral Nomadism Most common in the drier portions of the region, **pastoral nomadism** is a traditional form of subsistence agriculture in which practitioners depend on the seasonal movement of livestock for a large part of their livelihood. Arabian Bedouins, North African Berbers, and Iranian Bakhtiaris provide surviving examples of nomadism within the region. Today, however, with fewer than 10 million nomads remaining, the lifestyle is in decline, the victim of constricting political borders, a reduced demand for traditional beasts of burden such as camels, competing land uses, and selective overgrazing. In addition, government resettlement programs in Saudi Arabia, Syria, Egypt, and elsewhere are actively promoting a more settled lifestyle for many nomadic groups (see "People on the Move: Jordanian Bedouins and the Badia Project").

The settlement landscape of pastoral nomads reflects their need for mobility and flexibility as they seasonally move camels, sheep, and goats from place to place. Near highland zones such as the Atlas Mountains or the Anatolian Plateau, nomads practice **transhumance** (the seasonal movement of animals between wet-season and dry-season pastures) by herding their livestock to cooler, greener high country pastures in the summer and then returning them to valley and lowland settings for fall and winter grazing. Elsewhere, seasonal movements often involve huge territories of desert to support small groups of a few dozen families. In addition, nomads trade with sedentary agricultural populations, a mutu-

Figure 7.16 Tehran, Iran With a population of more than 8 million people, Iran's capital city of Tehran sprawls in all directions and is facing many of the same urban challenges as cities in North America.

ally beneficial relationship in which they exchange meat, milk, hides, and wool for cereal and orchard crops available at desert oases.

Oasis Life Permanent oasis settlements dot the arid landscape where high groundwater levels or modern deep-water wells provide reliable moisture in otherwise arid locales

(Figure 7.18). Tightly clustered, often walled villages, their sun-baked mud houses blending into the surrounding scene, sit adjacent to small but intensely utilized fields where underground water is carefully applied to tree and cereal crops. In more recently created oases, concrete blocks and prefabricated housing add a contemporary look. Surrounded by large zones of desert, these green islands of rural

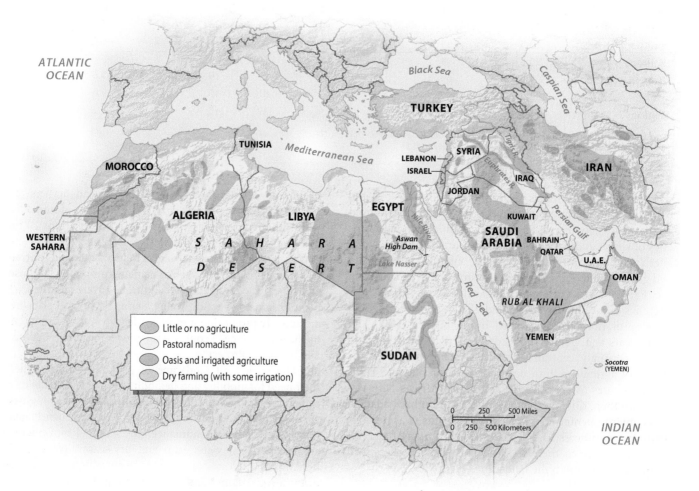

Figure 7.17 Agricultural Regions of Southwest Asia and North Africa Important agricultural zones include oases and irrigated farming where water is available. Elsewhere, dry farming supplemented with irrigation is practiced in midlatitude settings. (Modified from Clawson and Fisher, 2004, *World Regional Geography*, 8th ed., Upper Saddle River, NJ: Prentice Hall, and Bergman and Renwick, 1999, *Introduction to Geography*, Upper Saddle River, NJ: Prentice Hall)

Figure 7.18 Oasis Agriculture The green fields and trees of Morocco's Tinghir oasis contrast dramatically with the surrounding desert landscape.

activity stand out in sharp contrast to the sand- and rock-strewn landscape.

Traditional oasis settlements are composed of close-knit families who work their own irrigated plots or, more commonly, work for absentee landowners. Although oases are usually small, eastern Saudi Arabia's Hofuf oasis covers more than 30,000 acres (12,150 hectares). While some crops are raised for local consumption, commercial trade always has played a role in such settings. In the past century, the expanding world demand for products such as figs and dates has included even these remote oases in the global economy, and many products end up on the tables of hungry Europeans or North Americans. New drilling and pumping technologies, particularly in Saudi Arabia, have added to the size and number of oasis settlements. But oasis life across the region faces major challenges. Population growth, groundwater depletion, and the pressures of global cultural change threaten the economic and social integrity of these settlements.

Settlement Along Exotic Rivers For centuries, the region's densest rural settlement has been tied to its great river valleys and their seasonal floods of water and enriching nutrients. In such settings, **exotic rivers** transport precious water and nutrients from distant, more humid lands into drier regions, where the resources are utilized for irrigated farming (Figure 7.19). The Nile and the Tigris and Euphrates rivers are the largest regional examples of such activity, and both systems have large, densely settled deltas. Other linear irrigated settlements can be found near the Jordan River in Israel and Jordan, along short streams originating in North Africa's Atlas Mountains, and on the more arid peripheries of the Anatolian and Iranian plateaus. These settings, although capable of supporting sizable rural populations, also are among the most vulnerable to overuse, particularly if irrigation results in salinization.

Farming in such localities supports much higher population densities than is the case with pastoral nomadism or traditional desert oases. Fields are small, intensely utilized, and connected with closely managed irrigation systems designed to store and move water efficiently through the settle-

ment. In Egypt, farmers of the Nile Valley live in densely settled, clustered villages near their fields, work much of their land with the same tools and technologies their ancestors used, and grow a mix of cotton, rice, wheat, and forage crops. The scale and persistence of their agricultural imprint is dramatically visible from space (Figure 7.19). But rural

Figure 7.19 Nile Valley This satellite image of the Nile Valley dramatically reveals the impact of water on the North African desert. Cairo lies at the southern end of the delta, where it begins to widen toward the Mediterranean Sea. The coastal city of Alexandria sits on the northwest edge of the low-lying Nile Delta.

PEOPLE ON THE MOVE   Jordanian Bedouins and the Badia Project

Jordan's Prince Hassan Bin Talal (uncle of the country's ruling King Abdullah) has recently created the Badia Project, an initiative designed to keep the country's mobile Bedouin population viable and free. The "Badia" refers to the nation's large desert and semidesert zones which sprawl south and east of the capital city of Amman. For centuries, the Badia has been home to Bedouin populations who depend on a nomadic lifestyle and seasonal pastures to survive with their herds of camels, sheep, and goats (Figure 7.2.1).

But pressures upon the Bedouin lifestyle have steadily mounted in recent years. Droughts have reduced the amount of pasture land available for grazing. The attraction of urban amenities and the promise of better jobs have also drawn younger Bedouins away to the bright lights of Amman. Finally, political tensions have conspired to limit Bedouin mobility, further restricting their access to potential grazing pastures. For example, the eastern border zone with Iraq has often been closed and subject to political instability. The Saudi government has also gotten more restrictive and no longer permits unregulated Bedouin movements across the border to the south and southeast. The result is a growing crisis in the Bedouin community.

Prince Hassan has called attention to the problem and has vowed to support a traditional lifestyle he believes is worth preserving throughout the region. He has worked with religious leaders to cultivate Islamic environmentalism, a movement that uses traditional passages and interpretations from the Quran to encourage cooperation, better pasture management, water conservation, and the revegetation of overgrazed areas. Indeed, the Muslim concept of "haema" or protected area has been applied to encourage better use of the land. Local imams detail practices designed to help the Bedouins survive, and they use traditional texts to encourage cooperation among the clans. In addition the Prince is working with Jordan's financial institutions to increase Bedouin access to capital to build up their herds and improve the efficiency of their operations, thus encouraging them to remain on the land. Optimistically, the Prince even believes the initiative can lead towards more pan-Arab cooperation. He is lobbying nearby Arab nations to allow for more trans-boundary movement between countries, an initiative the Prince believes might help Bedouin populations throughout the region and might contribute to greater cooperation among the region's Arab countries.

Longer term, the survival of the Bedouin's mobile lifestyle remains in doubt, but Prince Hassan's initiative suggests some of the ways in which ancient cultural practices might be preserved and enhanced through a creative blend of tradition and innovation that combines local and global knowledge.

Figure 7.2.1 **Jordan's Bedouins** This Bedouin weaver is helping to preserve important cultural traditions in her Jordanian community.

life is also changing in such settings. New dam- and canal-building schemes in Egypt, Israel, Syria, Turkey, and elsewhere are increasing the storage capacity of river systems, which allows for more year-round agricultural activity. Higher-yielding rice and wheat varieties and more mechanized agricultural methods also have raised food output, particularly in places such as Egypt and Israel. Some of the most efficient farms in the region are associated with Israeli **kibbutzim**, collectively worked settlements that produce grain, vegetable, and orchard crops irrigated by waters from

the Jordan River and from the country's elaborate feeder canals. For example, Israel's National Water Carrier system takes water from the Sea of Galilee and moves it south and west, where intensively worked agricultural operations produce key food crops for nearby Tel Aviv and Jerusalem.

The Challenge of Dryland Agriculture Mediterranean climates in portions of the region permit varied forms of dryland agriculture that depend largely on seasonal moisture to support farming. These zones include the better-watered valleys and coastal lowlands of the northern Maghreb, lands along the shore of the eastern Mediterranean, and favored uplands across the Anatolian and Iranian plateaus. A regional variant of dry farming is practiced across Yemen's terraced highlands in the moister corners of the southern Arabian Peninsula (Figure 7.20).

Often, a variety of crops and livestock surrounds the Mediterranean villages of the region. Drought-resistant tree crops are common, with olive groves, almond trees, and citrus orchards producing output for both local consumption and commercial sale. Elsewhere, favored locations support grape vineyards, while more marginal settings are used to grow wheat and barley or to raise forage crops to feed cattle, sheep, and goats. Vulnerability to drought and the availability of more sophisticated water management strategies are leading some Mediterranean farmers to utilize more irrigated cropping, thus improving production of cotton, wheat, citrus fruits, and tobacco across portions of the region. More mechanization, crop specialization, and fertilizer use are also transforming such agricultural settings, following a pattern set earlier in nearby areas of southern Europe. One commercial adaptation of growing regional and global importance is Morocco's flourishing hashish crop. More than 200,000 acres (80,000 hectares) of cannabis are cultivated in the hill country near Ketama in northern Morocco, generating more than $2 billion annually in illegal exports (mostly to Europe).

Many-Layered Landscapes: The Urban Imprint

Cities have played a pivotal role in the region's human geography. Indeed, some of the world's oldest urban places are located in the region. Today, enduring political, religious, and economic ties link the city and countryside.

A Long Urban Legacy Cities in the region traditionally have played important functional roles as centers of political and religious authority, as well as key focal points of local and long-distance trade. Urbanization in Mesopotamia (modern Iraq) began by 3500 BCE, and cities such as Eridu and Ur reached populations of 25,000 to 35,000 residents. Similar centers appeared in Egypt by 3000 BCE, with Memphis and Thebes assuming major importance amid the dense populations of the middle Nile Valley. These ancient cities were key centers of political and religious control. Temples, palaces, tombs, and public buildings dominated the urban landscapes of such settlements, and surrounding walls (particularly in Mesopotamia) offered protection from outside invasion. By 2000 BCE, however, a different kind of city was emerging, particularly along the shores of the eastern Mediterranean and at the junction points of important caravan routes. Centers such as Beirut, Tyre, and Sidon, all in modern Lebanon, as well as Damascus in nearby Syria, exemplified the growing role of trade in creating urban landscapes. Expanding port facilities, warehouse districts, and commercial thoroughfares suggested how trade and commerce shaped these urban settlements, and many of these early Middle Eastern trading towns have survived to the present.

Islam also left a lasting mark because cities traditionally served as centers of Islamic religious power and education. By the 8th century, Baghdad had emerged as a religious center, followed soon thereafter by the appearance of Cairo as a seat of religious authority and expansion. Urban settlements from North Africa to Turkey felt the influences of Islam. Indeed, the Islamic Moors carried its characteristic Muslim signature to Spain, where it shaped urban centers such as Córdoba and Málaga. Islam's impact upon the settlement landscape merged with older urban traditions across the region and established a characteristic Islamic cityscape that

Figure 7.20 Rural Yemen This isolated hilltop village in the rugged mountains of northern Yemen is surrounded by small, terraced fields and livestock pastures.

exists to this day. Its traditional attributes include a walled urban core, or **medina**, dominated by the central mosque and its associated religious, educational, and administrative functions (Figure 7.21). A nearby bazaar, or *suq*, functions as a marketplace where products from city and countryside are traded (Figure 7.22). Housing districts feature an intricate maze of narrow, twisting streets that maximize shade and accentuate the privacy of residents, particularly women. Houses have small windows, frequently are situated on dead-end streets, and typically open inward to private courtyards often shared by extended families with similar ethnic or occupational backgrounds.

More recently, European colonialism added another layer of urban landscape features in selected cities. Particularly in North Africa, coastal and administrative centers during the late 19th century added dozens of architectural features from Britain and France. Victorian building blocks, French mansard roofs, suburban housing districts, and wide European-style commercial boulevards complicated the settlement landscapes of dozens of cities, both old and new. Centers such as Algiers (French), Fes (French), and Cairo

Figure 7.22 The Old City of Fes, Morocco These narrow streets in the old city of Fes are lined with shops and commercial stalls. The winding labyrinth of alleyways and cul-de-sacs forms an almost impenetrable maze to visitors, and it exemplifies the complex urban landscapes of the traditional Islamic city.

(British) vividly displayed the effects of colonial control, and many of these urban signatures remain today (Figure 7.23).

Signatures of Globalization Since 1950, dramatic new forces have transformed the urban landscape. Cities have become key gateways to the global economy. As the region has been opened to new investment, industrialization, and tourism, the urban landscape reflects the fundamental changes taking place. Expanded airports, commercial and financial districts, industrial parks, and luxury tourist facilities all mark the impress of the global economy.

Further, as urban centers become focal points of economic growth, surrounding rural populations are drawn to the new employment opportunities, thus fueling rapid population increases. The results are both impressive and problematic. Many traditional urban centers, such as Algiers and Istanbul, have more than doubled in size in recent years. Booming demand for homes has produced ugly, cramped high-rise apartment houses in some government-planned neighborhoods, while elsewhere sprawling squatter settlements provide little in the way of quality housing or municipal services.

Crowded Cairo, now with 15 million people, exemplifies the pattern of urban expansion. The city is now much more densely settled, as well as larger in size. Its legendary "City of the Dead" neighborhood, home to almost 1 million residents, is an urban cemetery intermingled with homes and apartment houses, a vivid acknowledgment of the premium put on living space. Many central-city neighborhoods have become so crowded and congested that wealthier urbanites have left, moving to outlying suburbs with large villas and lower population densities. Other suburbs are sites for major industrial expansion, often financed through foreign investment. In some cases, entirely new industrial centers are being established, part of Egypt's ambitious New-Town Program.

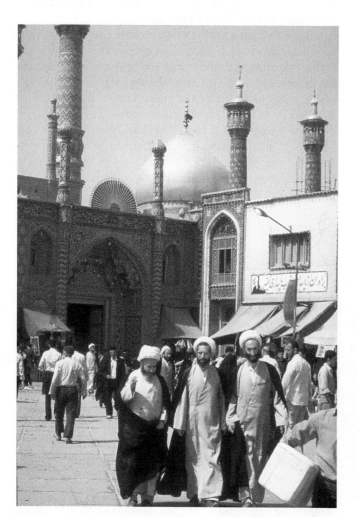

Figure 7.21 The Islamic Landscape Iranian mullahs discuss the religious questions of the day beneath the minarets of the Moussavi Mosque in Qom. Islam has left a widespread mark on the region's cultural landscapes.

Figure 7.23 Map of Fes, Morocco The tiny neighborhoods and twisting lanes of the old walled city reveal features of the traditional Islamic urban center. To the west, however, the rectangular street patterns, open spaces, and broad avenues suggest colonial European influences.

Figure 7.24 Modern Doha, Qatar The rapidly changing urban landscapes of the oil-rich Persian Gulf region are illustrated in the modern architecture seen in Doha's West Bay district.

Certainly, the oil-rich states of the Persian Gulf display the most extraordinary changes in the urban landscape (Figure 7.24). Before the 20th century, urban traditions were relatively weak in the area, and even as late as 1950 only 18 percent of Saudi Arabia's population lived in cities. All that changed, however, as the global economy's demand for petroleum mushroomed. Today, the Saudi Arabian population is more urban than those of many industrialized nations, including the United States, and the capital city of Riyadh has grown to about 5 million people. Particularly after 1970, other cities, such as Abu Dhabi (United Arab Emirates), Doha (Qatar), and Kuwait City (Kuwait), grew in size and took on modern Western characteristics, including futuristic architecture and new transportation infrastructure. In addition, investments in petrochemical industries have fueled the creation of new urban centers, such as Jubail along Saudi Arabia's Persian Gulf coastline. The result is an urban settlement landscape in which traditional and global influences intermingle, producing cityscapes where domed mosques, resort complexes, mirrored bank buildings, and oil refineries coexist beneath the dusty skies and desert sun.

Recent Migration Patterns

While pastoral nomads have crisscrossed the region for ages, entirely new patterns of migration have been sparked by the dynamic global economy and by recent political events. Several major migration streams have profoundly reshaped the human geography of the region. First, the rural-to-urban shift seen so widely in many parts of the less-developed world is also reworking population patterns across Southwest Asia and North Africa. The Saudi Arabian example is echoed in many other countries within the region. Cities from Casablanca to Tehran are experiencing phenomenal growth rates, spurred by in-migration from rural areas.

Second, large numbers of workers are migrating within the region to areas with growing job opportunities. Labor-poor countries such as Saudi Arabia, Kuwait, and the United Arab Emirates, for example, have attracted thousands of Jordanians, Palestinians, Yemenis, and Iranians to construction and service jobs within their borders. Indeed, the demand for workers has been so strong that large numbers of South Asians, Southeast Asians, and East Africans, particularly from Muslim nations, have flooded into the region. Today, for instance, more than 85 percent of Saudi Arabia's labor force is foreign and they annually export more than $20 billion in wages. In Dubai (United Arab Emirates), Pakistani cab drivers, Filipino nannies, and Indian shop clerks typify a foreign workforce that currently makes up a large majority of the city's 1.4 million inhabitants (Figure 7.25). Job-related movements, however, can be fickle. In the economic downturn of 2008–2010, many workers left Dubai and returned to their home countries, leaving thousands of abandoned cars in the airport parking lot.

A third major pattern of movement involves residents migrating to job opportunities elsewhere in the world. Because of its strong economy and close location, Europe has been a particularly powerful draw. More than 2 million Turkish guest workers live in Germany. Both Algeria and Morocco also have seen large out-migrations to western Europe, particularly France. Only 8 miles separates Africa from Europe, and illegal northbound boat traffic has reached unprecedented levels. Many Lebanese, often skilled workers and business owners, have also emigrated. Thousands of migrants have journeyed to North America, particularly more educated professionals who seek high-paying jobs.

Political forces have also encouraged migrations. Thousands of wealthier residents, for example, left Lebanon and Iran during the political turmoil of the 1980s and are today living in cities such as Toronto, Los Angeles, and Paris. Elsewhere, more recent political instability has provoked other refugee movements. Although Iraq's political situation has stabilized some since 2009, hundreds of thousands of Iraqi refugees are still in nearby Syria and Jordan and sev-

Figure 7.25 Labor Camp in Shariah City, United Arab Emirates These South Asian workers live a few miles outside wealthy Dubai and enjoy a card game during their time off from work. Over 80 percent of the country's population is foreign-born and many immigrants work in the construction and service sectors of the economy.

eral million remain displaced from their homes within Iraq. More than 35,000 Iraqis have resettled in the United States since 2003.

Elsewhere, thousands of displaced Afghans remain in eastern Iran. In the Middle East, the movement of more than 500,000 Russian Jewish immigrants to Israel after the 1991 breakup of the Soviet Union has also reshaped the cultural and political geography of that country. To the south, huge numbers of people in western Sudan's unsettled Darfur region have been forced from their land and forced to move to dozens of ill-prepared refugee camps in nearby Chad.

Shifting Demographic Patterns

While high population growth remains a critical issue throughout the region, the demographic picture is shifting. Uniformly high rates of population growth in the 1950s and 1960s have been replaced by more varied regional patterns, and many nations are seeing birthrates fall fairly rapidly. For example, women in Tunisia and Turkey are now averaging fewer than three births, representing a large decline in the total fertility rate (see Table 7.1). Indeed, some experts now predict that fertility rates on the European and North African sides of the Mediterranean will almost converge (at just over two births per woman) by 2030. Many factors help explain the changes. More urban, consumer-oriented populations have opted for fewer children. Many Arab women now are delaying marriage into the middle 20s and even early 30s. Even in more traditional Bahrain, the average marriage age of women has risen from 15 to 23 years of age since the early 1970s.

Intriguingly, fundamentalist Iran has witnessed the fastest decline in fertility in the past two decades, producing a pronounced "youth bulge" in its population pyramid (Figure 7.26). Fertility has declined by more than two-thirds since the mid-1970s (from an average of 6.6 births per woman to 2.0 births per woman). While Iran's family planning program was initially dismantled after the fundamentalist revolution in 1979 (it was seen as a Western idea), more recent Iranian leaders have recognized the wisdom in containing the country's large population. As a result, Iran has one of the most successful family planning programs in the world, according to a 2009 report by the Population Reference Bureau.

Still, demographic challenges loom. Areas such as the West Bank, Gaza, and Yemen experience some of the highest rates of natural increase on the planet. In some localities, persisting patterns of poverty and traditional ways of rural life contribute to the large rates of population increase, and even in more urban and industrialized Saudi Arabia, annual growth rates remain very high. Such growth rates result from the combination of high birthrates and low death rates.

Elsewhere, even as new births are declining, already existing populations pose problems. For most countries in the region, more than 35 percent of the present population is younger than 15 years old, promising another large generation of people in need of food, jobs, and housing. In Egypt, for example, even though birthrates are likely to decline, the labor market will need to absorb more than 500,000 new workers annually over the next 10 to 15 years just to keep up with the country's large, youthful population. As that population ages in the mid-21st century, it will continue to demand jobs, housing, and social services. Given recent trends in job growth and migration, the region's large cities probably will bear the brunt of future population increases. Growing populations will also impose new demands on the region's already limited water resources.

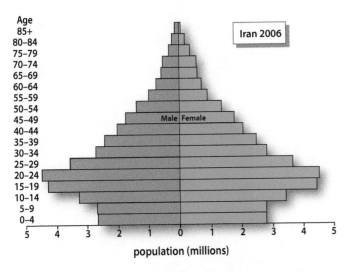

Figure 7.26 Iran's Population Pyramid, 2006 Iran's annual population growth rates have slowed considerably, thanks to an effective national family planning program. A pronounced youth bulge (ages 15–29) has been followed more recently by much lower birthrates. (Population Reference Bureau, 2009)

CULTURAL COHERENCE AND DIVERSITY: Signatures of Complexity

While Southwest Asia and North Africa clearly define the heart of the Islamic and Arab worlds, a surprising degree of cultural diversity characterizes the region. Muslims practice their religion in varied ways, often disagreeing profoundly on basic religious views as well as on how much of the modern world and its mass consumer culture should be incorporated into their daily lives. In addition, diverse religious minorities complicate the region's contemporary cultural geography. Linguistically, Arabic languages form an important cultural core historically centered on the region. However, different Arab dialects can mean that a Syrian may struggle to comprehend an Algerian. In addition, many non-Arab peoples, including Persians, Kurds, and Turks, populate important homelands. Understanding these varied patterns of cultural geography is essential to comprehending many of the region's political tensions, as well as appreciating why many of its residents resist processes of globalization and celebrate the lasting cultural identity of their home neighborhoods and communities.

Patterns of Religion

Religion permeates the lives of most people within the region. Its centrality stands in sharp contrast to largely secular cultures in many other parts of the world. Whether it is the quiet ritual of morning prayers or profound discussions about contemporary political and social issues, religion is part of the daily routine of most regional residents from Casablanca to Tehran. The geographies of religion—their points of origin, paths of diffusion, and patterns of modern regional distribution—are essential elements in understanding cultural and political conflicts within the region.

Hearth of the Judeo-Christian Tradition Both Jews and Christians trace their religious roots to the eastern Mediterranean, and while neither group is numerically dominant across the area, each plays a key cultural role. The roots of Judaism lie deep in the past: Abraham, an early patriarch in the Jewish tradition, lived some 4,000 years ago and led his people from Mesopotamia to Canaan (modern-day Israel), near the shores of the Mediterranean. From Jewish history, recounted in the Old Testament of the Holy Bible, springs a rich religious heritage focused on a belief in one God (or **monotheism**), a strong code of ethical conduct, and a powerful ethnic identity that continues to the present. Around 70 CE, during the time of the Roman Empire, most Jews were forced to leave the eastern Mediterranean after they challenged Roman authority. The resulting forced migration, or diaspora, of the Jews took them to the far corners of Europe and North Africa. Only in the past century have many of the world's far-flung Jewish populations returned to the religion's hearth area, a process that accelerated greatly with the formation of the Jewish state of Israel in 1948.

Christianity also emerged in the vicinity of modern-day Israel and has left a lasting legacy across the region. An outgrowth of Judaism, Christianity was based on the teachings of Jesus and his disciples, who lived and traveled in the eastern Mediterranean about 2,000 years ago. While many Christian traditions became associated with European history, some forms of early Christianity remained strong near the religion's original hearth. To the south, one stream of Christian influences linked with the Coptic Church diffused into northern Africa, shaping the culture of places such as Egypt and Ethiopia. In the Levant, another group of early Christians, known as the Maronites, retained a separate cultural identity that survives today. The region remains the "Holy Land" in the Christian tradition and attracts millions of the faithful annually, as they visit the most sacred sites in the Christian world.

The Emergence of Islam Islam originated in Southwest Asia in 622 CE, forming yet another cultural hearth of global significance. Muslims can be found today from North America to the southern Philippines; however, the Islamic world is still centered on its Southwest Asian origins. Most Southwest Asian and North African peoples still follow its religious

teachings and moral doctrines. Muhammad, the founder of Islam, was born in Makkah (Mecca) in 570 CE and taught in nearby Medinah (Medina) (Figure 7.27). In many respects, his creed parallels the Judeo-Christian tradition. Muslims believe that both Moses and Jesus were true prophets and that both the Hebrew Bible (or Old Testament) and the Christian New Testament, while incomplete, are basically accurate. Ultimately, however, Muslims hold that the **Quran** (or Koran), a book of revelations received by Muhammad from Allah (God), represents God's highest religious and moral revelations to humankind.

The basic teachings of Islam offer an elaborate blueprint for leading an ethical and religious life. Islam literally means "submission to the will of God," and the creed rests on five essential pillars: (1) repeating the basic creed ("There is no God but God, and Muhammad is his prophet"); (2) praying facing Makkah five times daily; (3) giving charitable contributions; (4) fasting between sunup and sundown during the month of Ramadan; and (5) making at least one religious pilgrimage, or **Hajj**, to Muhammad's birthplace of Makkah (Figure 7.28). Islam is a more austere religion than most forms of Christianity, and its modes of worship and forms of organization are generally less ornate. Muslims avoid the use

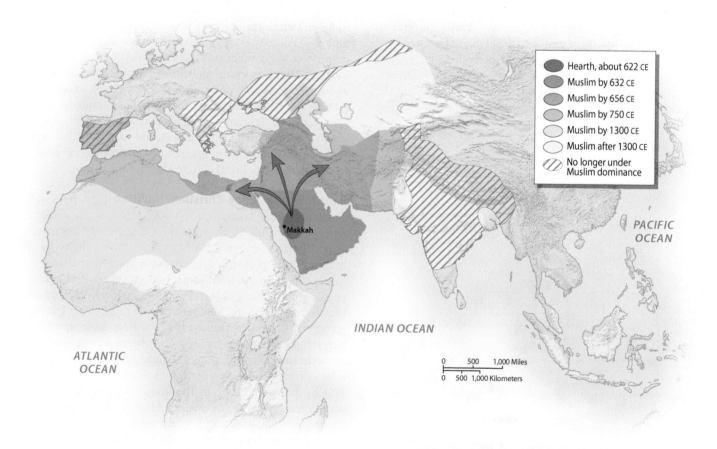

Figure 7.27 Diffusion of Islam The rapid expansion of Islam that followed its birth is shown here. From Spain to Southeast Asia, Islam's legacy remains strongest nearest its Southwest Asian hearth. In some settings, its influence has ebbed or has come into conflict with other religions, such as Christianity, Judaism, and Hinduism. (Modified from Rubenstein, 2005, *An Introduction to Human Geography*, 8th ed., Upper Saddle River, NJ: Prentice Hall)

Figure 7.28 Makkah Thousands of faithful Muslims gather at the Grand Mosque in central Makkah, part of the pilgrimage to this sacred place that draws several million visitors annually. Portions of the city's commercial district are in the distance.

of religious images, and the strictest interpretations even forbid the depiction of the human form. Followers of Islam are prohibited from drinking alcohol and are instructed to lead moderate lives, avoiding excess. Many Islamic fundamentalists still argue for a **theocratic state**, such as modern-day Iran, in which religious leaders (ayatollahs) guide policy.

A major religious schism divided Islam early on, and the differences endure to the present. The breakup occurred almost immediately after the death of Muhammad in 632 CE. Key questions surrounded the succession of religious power. One group, now called the **Shiites**, favored passing on power within Muhammad's own family, specifically to Ali, his son-in-law. Most Muslims, later known as **Sunnis**, advocated passing power down through the established clergy. This group emerged victorious. Ali was killed, and his Shiite supporters went underground. Ever since, Sunni Islam has formed the mainstream branch of the religion, to which Shiite Islam has presented a recurring, and sometimes powerful, challenge. The Shiites argue that a successor to Ali will someday return to reestablish the pure, original form of Islam. The Shiites also are more hierarchically organized than the Sunnis. Iran's ayatollahs, for example, have overriding religious and political power.

In a very short period of time, Islam diffused widely from its Arabian hearth, often following camel caravan routes and Arab military campaigns as it expanded its geo-

graphical range and converted thousands to its beliefs. By the time of Muhammad's death in 632 CE, the peoples of the Arabian Peninsula were united under its banner. Shortly thereafter, the Persian Empire fell to Muslim forces and the Eastern Roman (or Byzantine) Empire lost most of its territory to Islamic influences. By 750 CE, Arab armies had swept across North Africa, conquered most of Spain and Portugal, and established footholds in Central and South Asia. At first, only the Arab conquerors followed Islam, but the diverse inhabitants of Southwest Asia and North Africa gradually were absorbed into the religion, although with many distinct local variants. By the 13th century, most people in the region were Muslims, while older religions such as Christianity and Judaism became minority faiths or disappeared altogether.

Between 1200 and 1500, Islamic influences expanded in some areas and contracted in others. The Iberian Peninsula (Spain and Portugal) returned to Christianity by 1492, although many Moorish (Islamic) cultural and architectural features remained behind and still shape the region today. At the same time, Muslims expanded their influence southward and eastward into Africa. In addition, Muslim Turks largely replaced Christian Greek influences in Southwest Asia after 1100. One group of Turks moved into the Anatolian Plateau and finally conquered the last vestiges of the Byzantine Empire in 1453. These Turks soon created the vast **Ottoman Empire** (named after one of its leaders, Osman), which included southeastern Europe (including modern-day Albania, Bosnia, and Serbia) and most of Southwest Asia and North Africa. The legacy of the Ottoman Empire was considerable. It offered a new, distinctly Turkish interpretation of Islam, and it provided a focus of Muslim political power within the region until the empire's disintegration in the late 19th and early 20th centuries.

Modern Religious Diversity Today, Muslims form the majority population in all of the countries of Southwest Asia and North Africa except Israel, where Judaism is the dominant religion (Figure 7.29). Still, divisions within Islam have created key cultural differences within the region. While most (73 percent) of the region is dominated by Sunni Muslims, the Shiites (23 percent) remain an important element in the contemporary cultural mix. In Iraq, for example, the majority Shiite population in the southern portion of the country (around Najaf, Karbala, and Basra) set its own cultural and political course following the fall of Saddam Hussein. Many Shiites saw the departure of Hussein (who gathered most of his support from Sunnis in the central and western parts of Iraq) as an opportunity for increasing their cultural and political influence within the country. Shiites claim a majority in nearby Iran, as well, where their religious fervor has fundamentally shaped government policies since the late 1970s. In Yemen, important Shiite minorities claim the government has neglected their needs and that has led to increased political instability in that impoverished nation. In addition, they form a major religious minority in Lebanon, Bahrain, Algeria, and Egypt.

Figure 7.29 Modern Religions Islam remains the dominant religion across the region. Most Muslims are tied to the Sunni branch, while Shiites are found in places such as Iran and southern Iraq. In some locales, however, Christianity and Judaism remain important. African animism is found in southern portions of Sudan.
(Modified from Rubenstein, 2011, *An Introduction to Human Geography*, 10th ed., Upper Saddle River, NJ: Prentice Hall, and National Geographic Society, 2003, *Atlas of the Middle East*, Washington, DC)

Strongly associated with the recent flowering of Islamist movements, the Shiites also have benefited from rapid growth rates because their brand of Islam is particularly appealing to the poorer, powerless, and more rural populations of the region. While some Sunnis have been attracted to Islamist tendencies as well, many reject its more radical cultural and political teachings and argue for a more modern Islam that accommodates some Western values and traditions.

Whereas the Sunni–Shiite split is the great divide within the Muslim world, other variations of Islam also can be found in the region. One division, for example, separates the mystically inclined form of Islam—known as *Sufism*—from the mainstream tradition (see Figure 7.29). Sufism is especially prominent in the peripheries of the Islamic world, including the Atlas Mountains of Morocco and Algeria. Other well-established examples of Sufism are found across northwestern Iran and portions of Turkey. The Druze of Lebanon practice another variant of Islam, and they form a cohesive religious minority in the Shouf Mountains east of the Lebanese capital of Beirut.

Southwest Asia also is home to many non-Islamic communities. Israel has a Muslim minority (16 percent) that is dominated by that nation's Jewish population (77 percent), while Christians make up another 2 percent of the total. Even within Israel's Jewish community, increasing cultural differences divide Jewish fundamentalists from more reform-minded Jews. Indeed, this cultural diversity within Judaism has shaped the way Israel has dealt with political and social issues involving Muslims within and beyond its borders. In neighboring Lebanon, there was a slight Christian (Maronite and Orthodox) majority as recently as 1950. Christian out-migration and differential birthrates, however, have created a nation that today is 60 percent Muslim. Christians also form approximately 10 percent of Syria's population; Iraqi Christians, concentrated mostly in the rugged northern uplands, make up about 3 percent of its population.

Within the Middle East, the city of Jerusalem (now the Israeli capital) holds special religious significance for several groups and also stands at the core of the region's political problems (Figure 7.30). Indeed, the sacred space of this ancient Middle Eastern city remains deeply scarred and divided as different groups argue for more control of contested neighborhoods and nearby suburbs. Historically, Jews particularly revere the city's old Western Wall (the site of a Roman-era temple); Christians honor the Church of the Holy Sepulchre (the burial site of Jesus); and Muslims hold sacred religious sites in the city's eastern quarter (including the place from which the prophet Mohammad reputedly ascended to heaven).

Important Jewish and Christian communities also have left a long legacy across North Africa. Roman Catholicism was once dominant in much of the Maghreb, but it disappeared several hundred years after the Muslim conquest. The Maghreb's Jewish population, on the other hand, remained prominent until the post–World War II period, when most of the region's Jews migrated to the new state of Israel. In Egypt, Coptic Christianity has maintained a stable presence through the centuries and today includes approximately 9 per-

cent of the country's population. In earlier years the Coptic community had a secure place in Egyptian society, and numerous Copts held high-level posts in government and business. Today, however, Egypt's Christians are being increasingly marginalized, and some of their communities have been put under pressure, even subjected to physical attack, by extremist Islamic elements. Other Christian communities are located in southern Sudan, but unlike those of Egypt, these are mostly recent converts from traditional African religions.

Geographies of Language

Although the region is often referred to as the "Arab World," linguistic complexity creates many important cultural divisions across Southwest Asia and North Africa (Figure 7.31). The geography of language offers insights into regional patterns of ethnic identity and potential cultural conflicts that exist at linguistic borders. While the language map is useful in identifying the major families found across the region, it is important to remember that there are many local variations in language not seen on the map that represent distinctive dialects and well-defined islands of cultural and ethnic identity. For example, more than 70 separate languages are recognized in Iran, 36 in Turkey, and 23 in Iraq.

Semites and Berbers Afro-Asiatic languages dominate much of the region. Within that family, Arabic-speaking Semitic peoples can be found from Morocco to Saudi Arabia. Before the expansion of Islam, Arabic was limited to the Arabian Peninsula. Today, however, Arabic is spoken from the Persian Gulf to the Atlantic and reaches southward into Sudan, where it borders the Nilo-Saharan speaking peoples of Sub-Saharan Africa. As the language has diffused, it has slowly diverged into local dialects. As a result, the everyday Arabic spoken on the streets of Fes, Morocco, is quite distinct from Arabic spoken in the United Arab Emirates. The Arabic language also has a special religious significance for all Muslims because it was the sacred language in which God delivered his message to Muhammad. While most of the world's Muslims do not speak Arabic, the faithful often memorize

Figure 7.30 Old Jerusalem Jerusalem's historic center reflects its varied religious legacy. Sacred sites for Jews, Christians, and Muslims all cluster within the Old City. The Western Wall, a remnant of the ancient Jewish temple, stands at the base of the Dome of the Rock and Islam's Al Aqsa Mosque. (Reprinted from Rubenstein, 2011, *An Introduction to Human Geography*, 10th ed., Upper Saddle River, NJ: Prentice Hall)

Figure 7.31 Modern Languages Arabic is a Semitic Afro-Asiatic language, and it dominates the region's cultural geography. Turkish, Persian, and Kurdish, however, remain important exceptions, and such differences within the region often have had lasting political consequences. Israel's more recent reintroduction of Hebrew further complicates the region's linguistic geography. (Modified from Rubenstein, 2011, *An Introduction to Human Geography*, 10th ed., Upper Saddle River, NJ: Prentice Hall and National Geographic Society, 2003, *Atlas of the Middle East*, Washington, DC)

certain prayers in the language, and many Arabic words have entered the other important languages of the Islamic world. Advanced Islamic learning, moreover, demands competence in Arabic.

Hebrew, another traditional Semitic language of Southwest Asia, was recently reintroduced into the region with the creation of Israel. Hebrew originated in the Levant and was used by the ancient Israelites 3,000 years ago. Today its modern version survives as the sacred tongue of the Jewish people and is the official language of Israel, although the country's non-Jewish population largely speaks Arabic. English is also widely used as a second or third language throughout the country.

While Arabic eventually spread across North Africa, several older languages survive in more remote areas. Older Afro-Asiatic tongues endure in the Atlas Mountains and in certain parts of the Sahara. Collectively known as Berber, these languages are related to each other but are not mutually intelligible. Most Berber languages have never been written, and none has generated a significant literature. Indeed, a Berber-language version of the Quran was not completed until 1999. The decline in pastoral no-

madism and pressures of modernization threaten the integrity of these Berber languages. Scattered Berber-speaking communities are found as far to the east as Egypt, but Morocco is the center of this language group, where it plays an important role in shaping that nation's cultural identity.

Persians and Kurds Although Arabic spread readily through portions of Southwest Asia, much of the Iranian Plateau and nearby mountains are dominated by older Indo-European languages. Here the principal tongue remains Persian, although, since the 10th century, the language has been enriched with Arabic words and written in the Arabic script. Persian, like other languages, developed distinct local dialects. Today Iran's official language is called *Farsi*, which denotes the form of Persian spoken in Fars, the area around the city of Shiraz. Thus, although both Iran and neighboring Iraq are Islamic nations, their ethnic identities spring from quite different linguistic and cultural traditions.

The Kurdish speakers of northern Iraq, northern Iran, and eastern Turkey add further complexity to the regional pattern of languages. Kurdish, also an Indo-European language, is spoken by 10 to 15 million people in the region. Kurdish has not historically been a written language, but the Kurds do have a strong sense of shared cultural identity. Indeed, "Kurdistan" has sometimes been called the world's largest nation without its own political state because the group remains a minority in several countries of the region. In the 2003 war in Iraq, the Kurds emerged as a cohesive group in the northern part of the country that was opposed to Saddam Hussein. Iraqi Kurds have gained more political autonomy in a post-Saddam Iraq state and are also intent on maintaining control of important oil resources found in their portion of the country. Their leading city of Kirkuk has been called the "Kurdish Jerusalem" because its history and settlement so richly capture the group's cultural identity. Nearby Kurds in eastern Turkey, however, still complain that their ethnic identity is frequently challenged by the majority Turks, leaving some to wonder if they will attempt to join forces with their Iraqi neighbors.

The Turkish Imprint Turkish languages provide more variety across much of modern Turkey and in portions of far northern Iran. The Turkish languages are a part of the larger Altaic language family that originated in Central Asia. Turkey remains the largest nation in Southwest Asia dominated by that family. Tens of millions of people in other countries of Southwest and Central Asia speak related Altaic languages, such as Azeri, Uzbek, and Uighur. During the era of the Ottoman Empire, Turkish speakers ruled much of Southwest Asia and North Africa, but Iran is the only other large country in the region today where Turkic languages persist, particularly in the northwest part of the country.

Regional Cultures in Global Context

Many cultural connections tie the region with the world beyond. Islam links the region with a Muslim population that now lives in many different settings around the world. In addition, European and American cultural influences have multiplied greatly across the region since the mid-19th century. Colonialism, the boom in petroleum investment, and the growing presence of Western-style popular culture have had enduring impacts from the Atlas Mountains to the Indian Ocean. These global cultural connections are nuanced and complex, linking this region with the rest of the world in fascinating, often unanticipated ways (see "Global to Local: How Morocco Went Hollywood in Ouarzazate").

Islamic Internationalism While Islam is geographically and theologically divided, all Muslims recognize the fundamental unity of their religion. This religious unity extends far beyond Southwest Asia and North Africa. Islamic communities are well established in such distant places as central China, European Russia, central Africa, and the southern Philippines. Today, Muslim congregations also are expanding rapidly in the major urban areas of western Europe and North America, largely through migration but also through local conversions. Islam is thus emerging as a truly global religion. Even with its global reach, however, Islam remains centered on Southwest Asia and North Africa, the site of its origins and its most holy places. As Islam expands in number of followers and geographical scope, the religion's tradition of pilgrimage ensures that Makkah will become a city of increasing global significance in the 21st century. The global growth of Islamist fundamentalism and Islamism also focuses attention on the region, where these contemporary movements recently burst upon the scene. In addition, the oil wealth accumulated by many Islamic nations is used to sustain and promote the religion. Countries such as Saudi Arabia and Libya invest in Islamic banks and economic ventures and make donations to Islamic cultural causes, colleges, and hospitals worldwide. Indeed, geographers have studied new flows of global capital in an "Islamic financial services sector" that promotes economic development through the application of Islamic religious principles (see "Geographic Tools: Measuring the Urban Impact of Islamic Banking").

Globalization and Cultural Change The region also is struggling with how its growing role in the global economy is changing traditional cultural values. European colonialism left its own cultural legacy not only in the architectural landscapes still found in the old colonial centers, but also in the widespread use of English and French among the Western-educated elite across the region. In oil-rich countries, huge capital investments have had important cultural implications as the number of foreign workers has grown and as more affluent young people have embraced elements of Western-style music, literature, and clothing. The expansion of Islamic fundamentalism and Islamism are in many ways reactions to the threat posed by external cultural influences, particularly the supposed evils of European colonialism, American and Israeli power, and local governments and cultural institutions that are seen as selling out to the West.

Technology has also contributed to cultural change. Educated and more affluent residents in the region have been embracing the Internet and its power to access a global wealth of information and entertainment. Cell phone use also has increased rapidly. In Morocco, for example, while less than 6 percent of the country's population is served by fixed phone lines, more than 85 percent is within the reach of cellular phones. Widespread television-viewing has transformed the region, with viewers offered everything from Islamist religious programming to American-style reality TV and talent shows. For some, these technological transformations bring problems, particularly in conservative Islamic nations. Sudan's government has attempted to limit the influx of global cultural media and television programming.

GLOBAL TO LOCAL   How Morocco Went Hollywood in Ouarzazate

The global movie-making industry has carved out a unique niche in the North African desert. Filmmakers have been drawn to Morocco for over a century, beginning during its French colonial period and accelerating in the 1980s. Orson Welles filmed *Othello* there in the 1940s, and David Lean shot the epic *Lawrence of Arabia* in Morocco in the 1960s. More recently, Martin Scorsese filmed *Kundun* and *The Last Temptation of Christ*, while Ridley Scott filmed *Gladiator, Black Hawk Down*, and *Kingdom of Heaven* in this North African country.

In the early days of cinematography it was Morocco's fabulous light and dry desert climate that attracted filmmakers dependent upon outdoor locations and natural lighting. The country's rugged coastline, high Atlas Mountains, desert dunes, arid valleys, and historic architecture also became a lure, as its varied physical and cultural landscapes inspired location scouts to transform exotic Moroccan settings into other places in the world such as Saudi Arabia, Somalia, the biblical Holy Land, or even Tibet (Figure 7.3.1).

Economics and regional politics also contribute to Morocco's attractiveness as a destination. Close to Europe and easily accessible from North America, the cost of crews and local "extras" is considerably less in Morocco. For directors who want to set their films in desert environments, other countries in North Africa and Southwest Asia (such as Saudi Arabia, Iran, or Libya) are off limits to Western production companies. In contrast, the Moroccan government has courted foreign filmmakers and created government agencies that facilitate logistics. Over the years, Morocco has financially supported its own burgeoning film industry and film schools. Indeed, the country has reaped the economic benefits of the policy. In 2009 global movie-making productions injected over $100 million into the Moroccan economy, employing numerous local workers.

In the center of the country, just south of the high Atlas Mountains on a barren plateau, is the city of Ouarzazate. This modern Berber city of only 70,000 residents is now the center of the country's movie industry and nearby landscapes such as the traditional mud-brick Kasbah of Ait Benhaddou have ended up as part of the backdrop in both *Lawrence of Arabia* and *Gladiator* (Figure 7.3.2). Isolated from the distractions of major cities, with lots of open arid space, the location enables production companies to build the massive sets they need as well as exploit nearby historic structures. A gateway city to the Sahara desert with modern amenities, Ouarzazate caters to filmmakers and desert-seeking tourists. Ouarzazate is the Hollywood of Morocco, but it is relatively unknown to those outside of the country. Yet it is likely that moviegoers have seen this city's environs, only they might have thought they were looking at Tibet, Somalia, Jerusalem, Egypt, or the Arabian Peninsula.

Figure 7.3.1 Movie Production in the Desert, Ouarzazate, Morocco Visitors tour a movie set at Atlas Film Corporation Studios in Ouarzazate, Morocco.

Figure 7.3.2 Filming at the Kasbah, Ouarzazate, Morocco The traditional mud-brick kasbah at Ait Benhaddou near Ouarzazate has been used as a movie set for many films, including *Lawrence of Arabia* and *Gladiator*. This walled city, once situated on an important caravan route between Marrakesh and Timbuktu, has been designated a UNESCO World Heritage Site.

Figure 7.32 Desert Heat Rappers Salim and Abdullah Dahman from the United Arab Emirates created the group Desert Heat, and they celebrate many aspects of Arab culture in their music.

Similarly, Iran has restricted the use of satellite dishes and has prevented access to many Internet Websites.

Hybrid forms of popular culture also express the shaping power of globalization. Recently, for example, both within the region and beyond, Arab hip-hop music has offered a form of artistic and political expression that represents the fusion of several cultural traditions. Tune in MTV Arabia and you are liable to hear the newest cut from Desert Heat (United Arab Emirates), Malikah (Lebanon), or MWR (Palestine). These young artists represent a generation of rappers that spits out lyrics challenging many of the cultural and political stereotypes within the region. The global vibe is hard to miss: The African-American roots of rap remain a fixture in the strong beats and bops that set the tone amid the Arabic ouds (lutes), clangs of Asian pop, and soulful lyrics that might emerge in Arabic, English, or French.

The social roots of hip-hop help explain its resonance in the region. Just as urban African Americans used rap to vent frustration and offer commentary on their lives, beginning in the 1970s, this newer generation of Arab artists tells a similar social and cultural story. For Salim and Abdullah Dahman (aka Desert Heat), their pioneering venture into hip-hop within the United Arab Emirates was designed to cultivate Arab unity and to offer to the world a more positive view of the Arab experience after the painful events of September 11, 2001 (Figure 7.32). They were a recent star attraction at the Red Bull Air Race in Abu Dhabi and their first album, "When the Desert Speaks," was released in 2008 along with their debut video, "Keep It Desert." Their aim is clear. As Salim noted in 2009 to a *Gulf News* (published in the United Arab Emirates) reporter: "We just want to fight two stereotypes. Firstly that Arabs and Muslims are not all terrorists or ignorant people, and secondly that hip-hop is not all negative. Hip-hop was born out of positivity; out of struggle and freedom of speech." These new connec-

tions forged in music between younger generations of Arabs, Jews, Europeans, North Americans, and others may be powerful stimulants to redefining traditional cultural and political narratives. In this way, the global leanings and nontraditional messages of Arab hip-hop may be much more than entertainment.

But cultural changes among younger residents of the region are not going unchallenged. In the culturally conservative Persian Gulf states of Qatar and the United Arab Emirates, a new penchant for cross-dressing among young women has produced a considerable backlash amongst more orthodox Muslims. Many young women in those countries (particularly on university campuses) have donned western-style baggy trousers and wear short-cropped hair. Termed *boyats,* or "tomboys," the women have been accused of adopting a "foreign trend" in dress brought about by globalization. Their "deviant behavior" has been seen as a menace to society. The same clothing style and look that would go unnoticed on North American college campuses has provoked calls among conservatives for the death penalty, "medical treatment," or reeducation workshops in femininity.

Elsewhere, conservative cultural influences are gaining strength and visibility. For example, in Tunisia, long known for its more Western-leaning, modernized brand of Islam, the growing use of headscarves and veils among conservative women has caused a stir. A ban on such traditional practices was enacted in 1981 by a Tunisian government that described it as a "sectarian form of dress." More recently, such clothing has been seen by some as promoting the political agenda of extremist Islamist elements within the country. Interestingly, European human rights advocates have come to the aid of the women as they are increasingly harassed by police to remove the scarves and sign pledges that they will not go back to wearing them. In Turkey, a growing

GEOGRAPHIC TOOLS   Measuring the Urban Impact of Islamic Banking

Urban and economic geographers often utilize various forms of "network analysis" to measure how effectively one locality is connected to another. A study published in 2010, completed by a group of geographers in Belgium, illustrates the technique and suggests how the unique cultural character of the Islamic financial sector is linked in special ways with the rest of the world's cities and how it may be contributing to urban and economic growth within the Islamic world.

Unlike dominant banks and financial institutions based in Europe or North America, the Islamic financial services (IFS) sector operates on religious principles that are consistent with the Quran and the Muslim religion. For example, based on teachings within Sunni Islam, conventional interest-bearing loans are prohibited because the simple idea that money should make money is considered immoral. Instead, the loan recipient may agree to pay back the principal in the form of profits. In addition, these institutions ban

Figure 7.4.1 Persian Gulf City of Manama, Bahrain The 2010 view of Manama's Financial Harbor was taken from Muharraq Island. Towering construction cranes in the distance suggest the city's role as one of the centers of the Islamic financial world is likely to continue.

anything that could be considered as gambling or speculation since these activities are also prohibited in Islam. Indeed, the IFS sector would not advocate participating in any activity associated with prohibitions within traditional Islam.

The Belgian geographers wanted to know how these special characteristics influenced how the IFS interacted at the global level and within the Islamic world. They also wanted to explore a different way to examine the world-city system which often is based on the singular dominance of localities such as New York City, London, or Tokyo. The geographers identified dozens of leading IFS sector firms and mapped their headquarters as well as their linkages to various global branch offices. They analyzed the resulting networks to assess where these firms fit into more traditional interpretations of world city rankings and where their activities seemed most directly linked with economic development. Drawing upon spatial interaction models to measure linkages between places, the geographers examined the top 100 IFS firms and their urban-based location strategies.

The results of the study show how the IFS sector is strongly centered in Southwest Asia. The Gulf State of Bahrain and its capital city of Manama emerged as the undisputed global leader of the IFS (Figure 7.4.1). Fully one-quarter of all the major IFS firms were headquartered there, and many other firms had branch offices in the city.

Indeed, Manama has been a well-established center of regional banking and relative economic stability for decades, making it an attractive financial center for the Saudis and many other regional Islamic interests. Dubai and Abu Dhabi, both within the nearby United Arab Emirates, were also major participants in the global IFS network. Both Tehran and Istanbul were key participants, although the Iranian city's greater dominance was somewhat surprising and probably indicates the impact of its explicitly Islamist regime. Beyond the region, London and Paris are important European participants in the system as is Kuala Lumpur (in Muslim-friendly Malaysia) in Southeast Asia. New York, however, barely made it into the top 20 cities on the list.

The innovative use of network analysis offered these geographers a fresh way to look at how the world city-system works and it provided a reminder how a cultural lens can often inform traditional economic analysis and complicate our understanding of how future development in the Islamic world will inevitably be tied to both Western flows of capital as well as to the blossoming IFS sector that remains firmly based within the region as well as its religion.

Source: Adapted from David Bassens, Ben Derudder, and Frank Witlox, "Searching for the Mecca of finance: Islamic financial services and the world city network," *Area* 42, 1 (2010): 35–46.

traditional Islamist presence in the government and in the civil service bureaucracy has allowed for more religious study and prayers in that country's public school system. Science textbooks are also being changed, deemphasizing Western interpretations in favor of more traditional religiously based explanations.

GEOPOLITICAL FRAMEWORK: Never-Ending Tensions

Geopolitical tensions remain high in Southwest Asia and North Africa (Figure 7.33). Some of the tensions surround the struggle of different ethnic, religious, and linguistic

Figure 7.33 Geopolitical Issues in Southwest Asia and North Africa Political tensions continue across much of the region, including those surrounding events in Iraq and Iran. Although regional conflict remains oriented around Israel, its neighboring states, and the rights of resident Palestinians, other regional trouble spots periodically erupt into violence. Islamist political movements have challenged political stability in settings from Algeria to Saudi Arabia. Several large American military bases are found in the region.

groups to live with one another in a rapidly changing world of political relationships. The region's brief but complex ties to the era of European colonialism also contribute to present difficulties, because the boundaries of many countries were imposed by colonial powers. American political power has been repeatedly exercised throughout the region, evident in its multiple military bases and in its recent involvement in Iraq. Geographies of wealth and poverty also enter the geopolitical mix: Some residents profit from petroleum resources and industrial expansion, while others struggle just to feed their families. Islamist elements in many countries such as Iran, Egypt, Algeria, Turkey, and Saudi Arabia have changed the political atmosphere dramatically in the past 20 years. The result is a political climate charged with tension, a region in which the sounds of bomb blasts and gunfire remain for many a common characteristic of everyday life.

The Colonial Legacy

European colonialism arrived relatively late in Southwest Asia and North Africa, but the era left an important impact upon the modern political landscape. The Turks were one reason for Europe's late participation in imposing colonial rule. Between 1550 and 1850, much of the region was dominated by the Turkish Ottoman Empire, which expanded from its Anatolian hearth to engulf much of North Africa as well as nearby areas of the Levant, the western Arabian Peninsula, and modern-day Iraq. Ottoman rule imposed an outside political order and economic framework that had lasting consequences. The tide began to turn, however, in the early 19th century as the European presence increased and Ottoman power ebbed. Still, it took a century for Ottoman influences to be replaced with largely European colonial dominance after World War I (1918). While much of that direct European control ended by the 1950s, old colonial ties persist in a variety of economic, political, and cultural contexts. It is still common to encounter British English on the streets of Cairo, and French still can be heard in Algiers and Beirut. Indeed, the persistence of terms such as "Middle East" and "Levant" (a French term meaning "east" or "the Orient") within our 21st-century geographical vocabulary is a reminder of the long-standing linkages that tied this "eastern" land to western European influences.

Imposing European Power French colonial ties have long been a part of the region's history. Beginning around 1800, France became committed to a colonial presence in North Africa which included an expedition to Egypt by Napoleon. By the 1830s, France moved more directly into Algeria, forcing that region into its colonial sphere of influence. In the next 120 years, several million French, Italian, and other European immigrants poured into the country, taking the best lands from the Algerian people. The French government expected this territory to become an integral part of France, dominated by the growing French-speaking immigrant population. Indeed, the landscape of modern Algiers still reflects these colonial connections (Figure 7.34). France also established its influence in Tunisia (1881) and Morocco (1912), ensuring a lasting French political and cultural presence in the Maghreb. These **protectorates** in Tunisia and Morocco retained some political autonomy, but remained under a broader sphere of French influence and protection from other competing colonial powers. Finally, France's victory over the German–Ottoman Turk alliance in World War I produced additional territorial gains in the Levant, as France gained control of the northern zone, encompassing the modern nations of Syria and Lebanon.

Great Britain's colonial fortunes also grew within the region before 1900. To control its sea-lanes to India, Britain established a series of 19th-century protectorates over the small coastal states of the southern Arabian Peninsula and the Persian Gulf. In this manner, such places as Kuwait, Bahrain, Qatar, the United Arab Emirates, and Aden (in southern Yemen) were loosely incorporated into the British Empire. Nearby Egypt also caught Britain's attention. Once the European-engineered **Suez Canal** linked the Mediterranean and Red seas in 1869, foreign banks and trading companies gained more influence over the Egyptian economy. The British took more direct control in 1883. In the process, Britain also inherited a direct stake in Sudan, since Egyptian soldiers and traders had been pushing south along the Nile for decades.

Another series of British colonial gains within the region came at the close of World War I. In Southwest Asia, British and Arab forces had joined to expel the Turks during the war. To obtain Arab trust, Britain promised that an independent Arab state would be created in the former Ottoman territories. At roughly the same time, however, Britain and France signed a secret agreement to partition the area. When the war ended, Britain opted to slight its Arab allies and honor its treaty with France, with one exception: The Saud family convinced the British that a smaller country (Saudi Arabia) should be established, focused on the desert wastes of the Arabian Peninsula. Saudi Arabia became fully independent in 1932. Elsewhere, however, Britain carried out its plan to partition lands with France. Britain divided its new territories into three entities: Palestine (now Israel, Gaza, and the West Bank) along the Mediterranean coast; Transjordan to the east of the Jordan River (now Jordan); and a third zone that later became Iraq. Iraq, in particular, was a territory contrived by the British that combined three dissimilar former Ottoman provinces. It included the centers of Basra in the south (an Arabic-speaking Shiite area), Baghdad in the center (an Arabic-speaking Sunni area), and Mosul in the north (a Kurd-dominated zone).

Other settings within the region felt more marginal colonial impacts. Libya, for example, was long regarded by Europeans as a desert wasteland. Italy, never a dominant colonial power, expelled Turkish forces from the coastal districts by 1911 and its colonial influence continued until 1947. Spain also carved out its own territorial stake within the region, gaining control over southern Morocco (now Western Sahara) in 1912. To the east, Persia and Turkey never were directly oc-

Figure 7.34 Algiers European colonial influences still abound in the old French capital of Algiers in northern Algeria. The city's modern streets have witnessed periodic political and religious tensions since 1992.

cupied by European powers. In Persia, the British and Russians agreed to establish mutual spheres of economic influence (the British in the south, the Russians in the north), while respecting Persian independence. In 1935, Persia's modernizing ruler, Reza Shah, changed the country's name to Iran.

In nearby Turkey, the old core of the Ottoman Empire was almost partitioned by European powers following World War I. After several years of fighting, however, the Turks expelled the French from southern Turkey and the Greeks from western Turkey. The key to the successful Turkish resistance was the spread of a new modern, nationalist ideology under the leadership of Kemal Ataturk. Ataturk decided to emulate the European countries and establish a culturally unified and resolutely secular state. He was successful, and Turkey was quickly able to stand up to European power.

Decolonization and Independence European colonial powers began their withdrawal from several Southwest Asian and North African colonies before World War II. By the 1950s, most of the countries in the region were independent, although many maintained political and economic ties with their former colonial rulers. In North Africa, Britain finally withdrew its troops from Sudan and Egypt in 1956. Libya (1951), Tunisia (1956), and Morocco (1956) achieved independence peacefully during the same era, but the French colony of Algeria became a major problem. Since several million French citizens resided there, France had no intention of simply withdrawing. A bloody war for independence began in 1954, and France agreed to an independent Algeria in 1962, but the two nations continued to share a close—if not always harmonious—relationship thereafter.

Southwest Asia also lost its colonial status between 1930 and 1971, although many of the imposed colonial-era boundaries continue to shape the regional geopolitical setting. While Iraq became independent from Britain in 1932, its later instability in part resulted from its artificial borders, which never recognized much of its cultural diversity. Similarly, the French division of its Levant territories into the two independent states of Syria and Lebanon (1946) greatly angered local Arab populations and set the stage for future political instability in the region. As a favor to its small Maronite Christian majority, France carved out a separate Lebanese state from largely Arab Syria, even guaranteeing the Maronites constitutional control of the national government. The action created a culturally divided Lebanon as well as a Syrian state that repeatedly has asserted its influence over its Lebanese neighbors.

Modern Geopolitical Issues

The geopolitical instability in Southwest Asia and North Africa continues in the 21st century. It remains difficult to predict political boundaries that seem certain to change as a result of negotiated settlements or political conflict. A quick regional transect from the shores of the Atlantic to the borders of Central Asia suggests how these forces are playing out in different settings early in the century.

Across North Africa Varied North African settings threaten the region's political stability. Libya's leader, Colonel Muammar al-Qaddafi, has intermittently fomented regional tensions since he took power in 1969. Libya has financed violent political movements directed against Israel, western Europe, and the United States. Since 2004, however, Qaddafi has vowed to disarm, winning praise and growing diplomatic recognition from both the European Union and the United States.

Elsewhere in North Africa, Islamist political movements have reshaped the political landscape in several states. Most notably, Algeria was plunged into an escalating cycle of Islamist-led violence and protests for much of the 1990s, and more than 150,000 Algerians and foreign visitors were killed in the process. Since 1999, an amnesty has encouraged some rebel groups to lay down their arms, but the government still faces active opposition from Islamist extremists who are linked with Al Qaeda. Nearby Egypt has found itself ensnared in Islamist-initiated instability, and groups such as the Muslim Brotherhood have pushed for more radical political change.

Sudan faces some of the most daunting political issues in North Africa. A Sunni Islamist state since a military coup in 1989, Sudan imposed Islamic law across the country and in the process antagonized both moderate Sunni Muslims as well as the nation's large non-Muslim (mostly Christian and animist) population in the south. A long civil war between the Muslim north and the Christian and animist south produced more than 2 million casualties (mostly in the south) in the past 20 years. The carnage in the south has lessened since 2001 and a tentative peace agreement was signed in 2005. The agreement opened the way for a 2011 referendum on independence in southern Sudan, but intertribal squabbles and government corruption in the south have clouded hopes for a new, stable, independent state of South Sudan. Meanwhile, a newer conflict erupted in the Darfur region in the western portion of the country (see Figure 7.33). Ethnicity, race, and control of territory seem to be at the center of the struggle in the largely Muslim region as a well-armed Arab-led militia group (with many ties to the central government in Khartoum) has attacked hundreds of black-populated villages, driving more than 2.5 million people from their homes and leading to the deaths (through violence, starvation, and disease) of more than 300,000 Sudanese.

The Arab–Israeli Conflict The 1948 creation of the Jewish state of Israel produced another enduring zone of cultural and political tensions within the eastern Mediterranean. Jewish migration to Palestine increased after the defeat of the Ottoman Empire. In 1917 Britain issued the Balfour Declaration, a pledge to encourage the creation of a Jewish homeland in the region. After World War II, the United Nations divided the region into two states, one to be predominantly Jewish, the other primarily Muslim (Figure 7.35). Indigenous Arab Palestinians rejected the partition, and war erupted. Jewish forces proved victorious, and by 1949 Israel had actually grown in size. The remainder of Palestine, in-

Figure 7.35 Evolution of Israel Modern Israel's complex evolution began with an earlier British colonial presence and a UN partition plan in the late 1940s. Thereafter, multiple wars with nearby Arab states produced Israeli territorial victories in settings such as Gaza, the West Bank, and the Golan Heights. Each of these regions continues to figure importantly in the country's recent relations with nearby states and with resident Palestinian populations. (Modified from Rubenstein, 2011, *An Introduction to Human Geography*, 10th ed., Upper Saddle River, NJ: Prentice Hall)

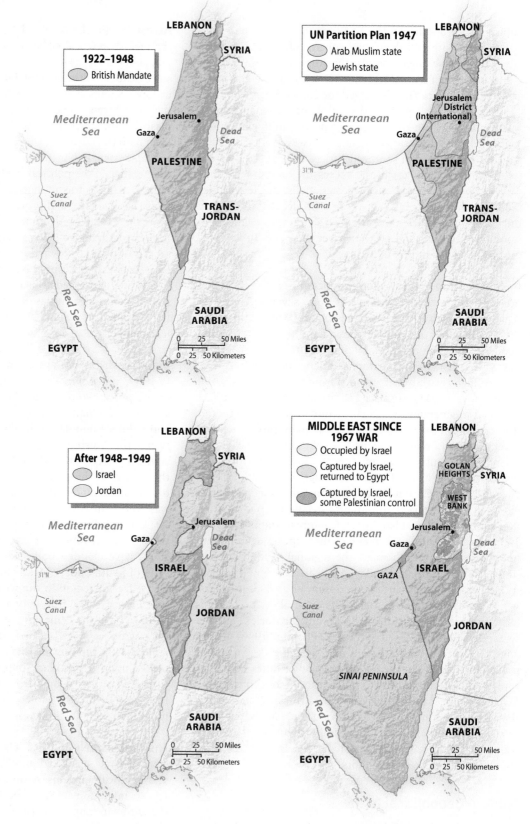

cluding the West Bank and the Gaza Strip, passed to Jordan and Egypt, respectively. Hundreds of thousands of Palestinian refugees fled from Israel to neighboring countries, where many of them remained in makeshift camps. Under these conditions, Palestinians nurtured the idea of creating their own state on land that had become Israel.

Israel's relations with neighboring countries remained poor. Supporters of Arab unity and Muslim solidarity sympathized with the Palestinians, while their antipathy toward Israel grew. Israel fought additional wars in 1956, 1967, and 1973. In territorial terms, the Six-Day War of 1967 was the most important conflict (see Figure 7.35). In this struggle

Figure 7.36 West Bank Portions of the West Bank were returned to Palestinian control in the 1990s, but Israel has partially reasserted its authority in some of these areas since 2000, citing the increased violence in the region. New Israeli settlements also are scattered through the West Bank in areas still under their nominal control. (Modified from Rubenstein, 2011, *An Introduction to Human Geography*, 10th ed., Upper Saddle River, NJ: Prentice Hall)

strengthened the potential control of the ruling **Palestinian Authority (PA)** in the Gaza Strip and portions of the West Bank (Figure 7.36). But a new cycle of heightened violence erupted late in 2000 as Palestinian attacks against Jews increased and as the Israelis continued with the construction of new settlements in occupied lands (especially in the West Bank) (Figure 7.37). In 2010, with about 500,000 Israeli settlers already living in these West Bank settlements, the Israeli government pledged to continue its support for new construction, including developments in and near Jerusalem. Palestinian authorities continue to strongly protest these new West Bank Jewish settlements.

Even more daunting has been construction of the Israeli security barrier, a partially completed series of concrete walls, electronic fences, trenches, and watchtowers designed to effectively separate the Israelis from Palestinians across

Figure 7.37 Jewish Settlement, West Bank The new houses and well-planned neighborhoods of the West Bank Jewish settlement of Eli (foreground) contrast with the older Palestinian settlement in the distance. Many Palestinians resent the construction of these controversial Israeli settlements in the West Bank region.

against Egypt, Syria, and Jordan, Israel occupied substantial new territories in the Sinai Peninsula, the Gaza Strip, the West Bank, and the Golan Heights. Israel annexed the eastern part of the formerly divided city of Jerusalem, arousing particular bitterness among the Palestinians, since Jerusalem is a sacred city in the Muslim tradition (it contains the Dome of the Rock and the holy Al-Aqsa Mosque) (see Figure 7.30). Jerusalem is sacred in Judaism as well (it contains the Temple Mount and the holy Western Wall of the ancient Jewish temple), and Israel remains adamant in its claims to the entire city. A peace treaty with Egypt resulted in the return of the Sinai Peninsula in 1982, but tensions focused on other occupied territories that remained under Israeli control. To strengthen its geopolitical claims, Israel also built additional Jewish settlements in the West Bank and in the Golan Heights, further angering Palestinian residents.

Palestinians and Israelis began to negotiate a settlement in the 1990s. Preliminary agreements called for a quasi-independent Palestinian state in the Gaza Strip and across much of the West Bank. A tentative agreement late in 1998 much of the West Bank region (Figure 7.38). Israeli supporters of the barrier (to be more than 400 miles long when completed) see it as the only way they can protect their citizens from suicide bombings and more terrorist attacks. Palestinians see it as a land grab, an "apartheid wall" designed to socially and economically isolate many of their settlements along the Israeli border.

Nearby, Israel withdrew troops and settlers from the Gaza Strip in 2005, but political instability thereafter resulted in repeated and violent Israeli incursions and reoccupations of the small, war-torn region. Today, Gaza remains a poor and isolated portion of the Middle East. Some of its most effective links to the outside world are a series of tunnels that connect it with settlements in nearby Egypt. But its hostile Palestinian leadership combined with Israeli fears of continued terrorist attacks suggest tensions in the area will remain very high.

The political fragmentation of the Palestinians has added further uncertainty. In 2006, control of the Palestinian government was split between the Fatah and Hamas political parties. Hamas has long been seen by many Israelis as an extremist and violent Palestinian political party, whereas the Fatah party has shown more of a willingness to work peacefully with the state of Israel. In 2007, the split between these rival Palestinian factions became violent, with Hamas gaining effective control of the PA within Gaza and with Fatah maintaining its greatest influence across the West Bank region. Further complicating this political geography is the emergent Islamist movement among some Palestinians. Often, Islamists have challenged the more secular orientation of both Hamas and Fatah. These growing complexities within the Palestinian movement make an eventual peace treaty with Israel seem even more difficult to achieve.

Instability also continues along Israel's northern border with Lebanon. In 2006, a Shiite militia group known as Hezbollah increased its rocket attacks into northern Israel, prompting an armed response by the Israelis. Along with Hamas, Hezbollah represents a radicalized Arab political element within the region that shows little inclination to negotiate with Israel (or vice versa).

One thing is certain: Geographical issues will remain at the center of the regional conflict. Palestinians hope for a land they can call their own, and Israelis continue their search

for more secure borders that guarantee their political integrity in a region where they are surrounded by potentially hostile neighbors. Ultimately, the sacred geography of Jerusalem, a mere 220 acres of land within the Old City, stands at the center of the conflict (see Figure 7.30). Imaginative compromises in defining that political space will need to recognize its special value to both its Israeli and Palestinian residents.

Devastated Iraq Iraq is another multinational state born during the colonial era that has yet to escape the consequences of its geopolitical origins. When the country was carved out of the British Empire in 1932, it contained the cultural seeds of its later troubles decades before Saddam Hus-

Figure 7.38 Israeli Security Barrier The map (a) shows the completed and planned portions of the Israeli security barrier as well as many of the Israeli settlements located in the West Bank region. The photo (b) shows a segment of the Israeli security barrier passing near Bethlehem, south of Jerusalem.

sein came to power. Iraq remains culturally complex today (Figure 7.39). Most of the country's Shiite population lives in the lower Tigris and Euphrates valleys near and south of Baghdad. Indeed, the region focused around the city of Basra contains some of the holiest Shiite shrines in the world. In northern Iraq, the culturally distinctive Kurds have their own ethnic identity and political aspirations. Many Kurds want complete independence from Baghdad, and they have managed to establish a federal region that already enjoys a great deal of autonomy from the central Iraqi government. A third major subregion is dominated by the Sunnis and includes part of the Baghdad area as well as a triangle of territory to the north and west that includes Sunni strongholds such as Falujah and Tikrit. After enjoying a great deal of power under Saddam Hussein, many Sunnis feel they may get the short end of any future power-sharing agreement within the country.

Led by Saddam Hussein, Iraq created a major source of instability in the region before he was removed in 2003. In 1980, Hussein invaded oil-rich but politically weakened Iran to gain a better foothold in the Persian Gulf. Eight years of bloody fighting resulted in a stalemate, and the conflict left Iraq's finances in disarray. Iraq then invaded and overran Kuwait in 1990, claiming it as an Iraqi province. A U.S.-led UN coalition, receiving substantial support from Saudi Arabia, expelled Iraq from Kuwait in early 1991. Twelve years later, the 2003 American-led invasion of the country replaced one set of uncertainties with another.

When Iraqi leaders assumed control of their new state on June 28, 2004, more than 135,000 American troops remained in the country. Thereafter, growing religious and ethnic violence between different Iraqi factions threw portions of the nation into civil war. Rival Sunni and Shiite groups forced many Iraqis from their communities. American troops within the country in 2007 and 2008 worked with Iraqi officials to reduce the level of violence. New parliamentary elections in 2010 confirmed the ongoing political uncertainties within Iraq. Both the leading Shiite and Sunni candidates proved about equally popular, largely splitting the vote along regional lines (Shiites winning in the south and narrowly in Baghdad; Sunnis winning in central and western provinces). Complicating matters further, the Kurdish Alliance remained dominant in many of the country's Kurdish areas. An enduring geopolitical solution for a stable Iraqi state has yet to take shape, but it will need to recognize these cultural differences that continue to divide the country, as well as allow for an ongoing revival of the country's oil industry. One challenge to the notion of shared political power and economic wealth is the uneven distribution of oil resources within the country. By far, the country's dominant oil fields are located in Shiite- and Kurdish-controlled por-

Figure 7.39 Multicultural Iraq Iraq's complex colonial origins produced a state with varying ethnic characteristics. Shiites dominate south of Baghdad, Sunnis hold sway in the western triangle zone, and Kurds are most numerous in the north near oil-rich Kirkuk and Mosul.

tions of Iraq, an uneasy fact of resource geography that has long troubled the nation's sizable Sunni population.

Instability in the Arabian Peninsula Saudi Arabia, the region's greatest oil power, is led by a conservative monarchy (the Saud family) that has been unwilling to promote many democratic reforms. On the surface, it has supported U.S. efforts in the region to provide stable flows of petroleum, but beneath the surface certain elements of the regime may have financed radically anti-American groups such as Al Qaeda. The Saudi people themselves, largely Sunni Arabs, are torn between an allegiance to their royal family (and the economic stability it brings), the lure of a more democratic, open Saudi society, and an enduring distrust of foreigners, particularly Westerners. Furthermore, the Sunni majority includes many Wahhabi sect members, whose radical Islamist philosophy has fostered anti-American sentiment. Add to this a large number of foreign laborers and a persisting American military and economic presence within the country (one of the chief complaints of Al Qaeda leader Osama bin Laden) and you have a setting ripe for political instability. Economic declines between 2008 and 2010 only made matters worse as many Saudis saw fewer job opportunities within their energy-dependent economy.

In nearby Yemen, a growing rebel movement along the country's northwest border with Saudi Arabia has destabilized that rugged, isolated portion of the peninsula (see Figure 7.33). Since 2004, the area's Houthis, a group of Shiite militants, have protested the policies and dominance of the Yemeni government. Both Yemen and Saudi Arabia claim the Houthis have received extensive support from Iran and that the disputed area plays host to Iranian-sponsored terrorist training camps. The Saudi government has stepped up its own attacks on the Houthis across the ill-defined border zone and American experts have monitored the area with increased concern.

Tensions in Turkey Turkey continues to find itself strategically positioned between diverse, often contradictory geopolitical forces. Many pro-Westerners within Turkey, for example, are committed to joining the European Union (EU). To do so, the country has embarked on an active agenda of reforms designed to demonstrate its commitment to democracy. Press freedoms and multiparty elections have been permitted, the role of the military downplayed, and minority groups (particularly the Kurds) have gained greater recognition from the central government. At the same time, anti-Western Islamist political elements have been on the rise, linked to a growing number of terrorist bombings in the country since 2003. Moderate Turks are hoping that its road to the EU will not be interrupted with the violence, but Islamists and ultra-nationalists are suspicious of the EU pledge to move the country in a radically different direction. Turkey also has continuing tensions with nearby Greece and Cyprus, two countries that are now both in the EU. Final approval of Turkey's admission still remains clouded by all of these concerns.

Iranian Geopolitics Nearby Iran also garners a great deal of international attention. Islamic fundamentalism dramatically appeared on the political scene in 1978 as Shiite Muslim clerics overthrew the shah, an authoritarian, pro-Western ruler friendly to U.S. political and economic interests. The new leaders proclaimed an Islamic republic in which religious officials ruled both clerical and political affairs.

Today, Iran supports Shiite Islamist elements throughout the region (such as Hezbollah) and has repeatedly threatened the state of Israel. The country has also been seen as a growing threat by many moderate Arab states. In 2009, the nearby United Arab Emirates, for example, invited the French to open their first new military base in decades on foreign soil and French leaders pledged to defend against Iranian expansion within the region. Adding uncertainty has been Iran's ongoing nuclear development program, an initiative its government claims is solely related to the peaceful construction of power plants (see Figure 7.33). Many in the West, how-

ever, remain unconvinced of the government's motives and demand that its program be stopped or opened to more outside inspections before allowing for greater international cooperation with the Iranian regime. Israel, in particular, has suggested it may destroy these Iranian nuclear sites before Iranian leaders have an opportunity to attack Israel with a nuclear-tipped missile. In addition, hotly contested and controversial presidential elections in 2009 and further street demonstrations in 2010 reveal growing frustration with the status quo within the country, suggesting more internal political instability is on the horizon. Many of Iran's middle-class intellectuals, well-educated youth, and human-rights advocates are harsh critics of a government they feel is increasingly intolerant and guilty of isolating the country on the world stage.

An Uncertain Political Future

Few areas of the world pose more geopolitical questions than Southwest Asia and North Africa. Twenty years from now, the region's political map could look quite different from the one today. The region's strategic global importance increased greatly after World War II, propelled into the international spotlight by the creation of Israel, the tremendous growth in the world's petroleum economy, Cold War tensions between the United States and the Soviet Union, and, more recently, the rise of Islamic fundamentalism and Islamist political movements. Now that the Cold War between global superpowers has ended, the region is experiencing a geopolitical reorientation.

One key question that remains is what geopolitical role should the United States play in Southwest Asia? That simple question continues to confound policymakers in the United States as well as residents of that ever-troubled part of the world. The 2003 Iraqi invasion put large numbers of American troops in the region. Even as many of those troops gradually return home, the American role remains central to the region's geopolitical future. How does the United States identify and deal with hostile elements? Should the United States go it alone in these efforts ("unilateralism"), or depend on sharing the responsibilities with other countries or international organizations ("multilateralism")? Regional resistance movements directed against the United States also have grown more powerful in many countries within the region, drawing on growing popular suspicion of American motives and on the heated religious rhetoric of Islamist elements.

Four interrelated settings appear destined to hold continuing U.S. attention within the region. First, the U.S. involvement in Iraq remains important even as the country struggles to find its own, more independent political identity. Iraq's fragile political structure and its globally significant oil economy, all cast amid the country's complex ethnic and religious geography, seem likely to remain key concerns for American policymakers. A second question mark is oil-rich Saudi Arabia. Of particular concern are domestic challenges to the all-powerful al-Saud royal family. U.S. observers fret that a sudden change in Saudi Arabian politics would have global ramifications, particularly if oil exports are disrupted. Third, the growing geopolitical presence of Iran challenges American, Israeli, and many moderate Arab (particularly Saudi Arabian) interests within the region. Iran's regional aspirations and its always murky nuclear installations remain key question marks for this portion of the world. Finally, recent events in Israel, Gaza, and the West Bank continue to make global headlines. Palestinian infighting, continuing attacks on Israel, and Israeli reprisals (including the construction of its security barrier) continue to fracture and enflame the region. What is an appropriate role for the United States in tactically improving short-term relationships between Israel and its Palestinian populations and in crafting a longer-term strategic policy aimed at achieving a permanent peace in the region? How the United States responds to Southwest Asia's shifting geopolitics seems destined to shape the region for decades to come.

ECONOMIC AND SOCIAL DEVELOPMENT: Lands of Wealth and Poverty

Southwest Asia and North Africa is a region of both incredible wealth and disheartening poverty. While a few of its countries enjoy great prosperity, due mainly to rich reserves of petroleum and natural gas, other nations within the region are among the least developed in the world (Table 7.2). Overall, recent economic growth rates have lagged behind those of many other parts of the developing world. The global recession of 2008–2010 also hit many economies within the region hard. Persistent political instability also has contributed greatly to the regional economic malaise. These economic stumbling blocks have had profound social consequences: Investments in education, health care, and new employment opportunities have slowed considerably in many countries from the heady

TABLE 7.2   Development Indicators

Country	GNI per Capita, PPP (2008)	GDP Average Annual % Growth (2000–08)	Human Development Index (2007)[a]	Percent Population Living Below $2 a Day	Life Expectancy (2007)[b]	Under Age 5 Mortality Rate (1990)	Under Age 5 Mortality Rate (2005)	Gender Equity[c]
Algeria	7,880	4.3	0.754	23.6	72	64	41	102
Bahrain	33,400		0.895		75			
Egypt	5,470	4.7	0.703	18.4	72	90	23	
Gaza and West Bank		−0.9	0.737		72	40	23	
Iran	10,840	5.9	0.782	8.0	71	73	32	116
Iraq		−11.4			67	53	44	
Israel	27,450	3.5	0.935		81	11	5	101
Jordan	5,710	7.2	0.775	3.5	73	38	20	103
Kuwait	53,430	8.4	0.916		78	15	11	100
Lebanon	11,740	4.0	0.803		72	40	13	103
Libya	16,260	5.6	0.847		74	38	17	105
Morocco	4,180	5.0	0.654	14.0	71	88	36	88
Oman	22,150	4.0	0.846		72	31	12	99
Qatar		9.0	0.910		76	20	10	120
Saudi Arabia	24,490	4.1	0.843		76	43	21	91
Sudan	1,920	7.4	0.531		58	124	109	89
Syria	4,490	4.4	0.742		74	37	16	97
Tunisia	7,450	4.9	0.769	12.8	74	50	21	103
Turkey	13,420	5.7	0.806	8.2	72	84	22	89
United Arab Emirates		7.8	0.903		77	17	8	101
Western Sahara					60			
Yemen	2,220	3.9	0.575	46.6	63	127	69	

[a]United Nations, *Human Development Report, 2009.*

[b]*Population Reference Bureau, World Population Data Sheet, 2010.*

[c]*Gender Equity—Ratio of female to male enrollments in primary and secondary school. Numbers below 100 have more males in primary/secondary. school, numbers above 100 have more females in primary/secondary schools.*

Sources: *World Bank, World Development Indicators, 2010.*

gains of the late 1970s and 1980s. Petroleum will no doubt figure prominently into the region's future economic relationships with the rest of the world, but many countries in the area also have focused on increasing agricultural output, investing in new industries, and promoting tourism as important ways to broaden the regional economic base. In addition, development within the region will be shaped by its access to information and how well it is connected with the rest of the world. Cell phone and Internet use, for example, vary widely across North Africa and Southwest Asia (Figure 7.40). Lower penetration of cell phone technology in some settings (Egypt, Sudan, and Iran) suggests basic investments in infrastructure remain lacking, while areas of very high cell phone usage (Israel, many Persian Gulf states) are correlated with greater affluence as well as highly mobile, foreign-born populations. Internet use is also highly variable, ranging from 1 percent in Yemen to more than half the population of the United Arab Emirates. In some settings such as Iran (18 percent), official government resistance to the Internet plays a role, as well.

The Geography of Fossil Fuels

The striking global geographies of oil and natural gas reveal the region's persistent importance in the world oil economy, as well as the extremely uneven distribution of these resources within the region (Figure 7.41). Higher oil prices early in the new century have once again highlighted the economic clout of this region of the world. Saudi Arabia remains one of the major producers of petroleum in the world, and Iran, the United Arab Emirates, Libya, and Algeria also contribute significantly. The region plays an important though less dominant role in natural gas production. The distribution of fossil fuel reserves suggests that regional supplies will not be exhausted anytime soon. Overall, with only 7 percent of the world's population, the region holds a staggering 60 percent of the world's proven oil reserves. Saudi Arabia's pivotal position, both regionally and globally, is clear: Its 30 million residents live atop 20 percent of the planet's known oil supplies.

Several major geological zones supply much of the region's output of fossil fuels. The world's largest concentration

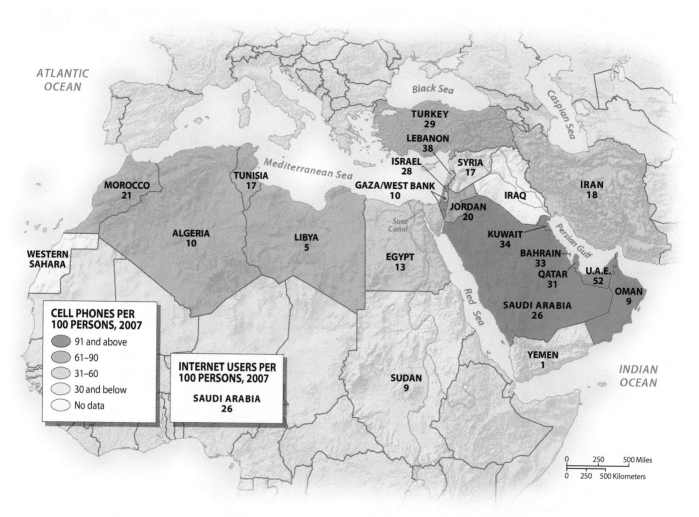

Figure 7.40 Development Issues: Cell Phone and Internet Use (per 100 in the population), 2007 The map illustrates how access to information technology can be used as a measure of development within the region. The oil-rich United Arab Emirates emerge as far more connected to global information flows than are Egypt, Yemen, or Sudan. (World Bank Development Indicators, 2007)

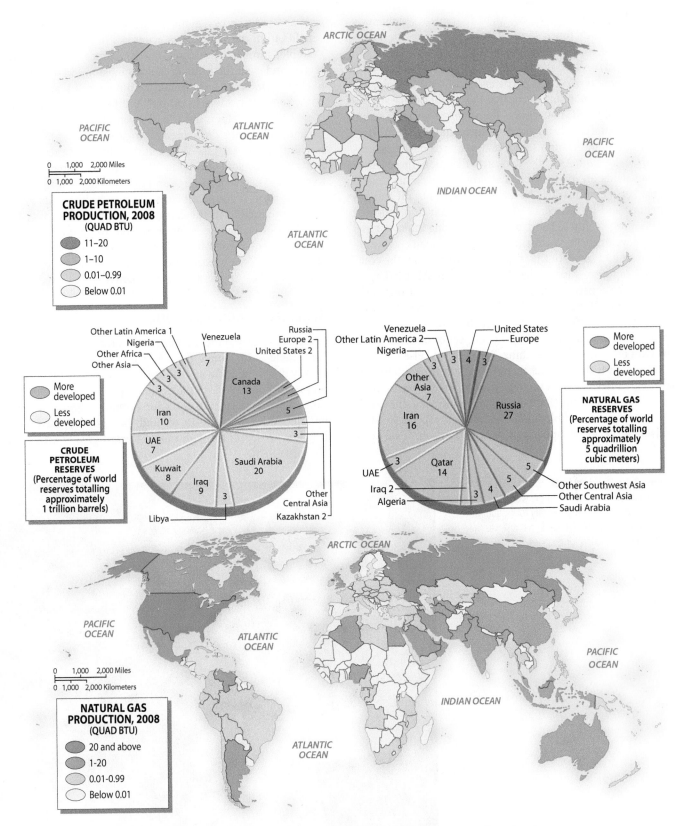

Figure 7.41 Crude Petroleum and Natural Gas Production and Reserves The region plays a central role in the global geography of fossil fuels. Abundant regional reserves suggest that the pattern will continue. (Modified from Rubenstein, 2011, *An Introduction to Human Geography*, 10th ed., Upper Saddle River, NJ: Prentice Hall)

of petroleum lies within the Arabian–Iranian sedimentary basin, a geological formation that extends from northern Iraq and western Iran to Oman and the lower Persian Gulf (Figure 7.42). All of the states bordering the Persian Gulf reap the benefits of oil and gas deposits within this geological basin, and it is not surprising that the world's densest concentration of OPEC members is found in the area. A second important zone of oil and gas deposits includes eastern Algeria, northern and central Libya, and scattered developments in northern Egypt. As in the Persian Gulf region, these North African fields are tied to regional processing points and to global petroleum markets by a complex series of oil and gas pipelines and by networks of technologically sophisticated oil shipping facilities. Third, a zone of growing importance is being developed in the African nation of Sudan, including areas near and south of Khartoum. Near Khartoum, the commercial center of Alsunut has become one of Africa's largest commercial construction sites. Home to regional oil giants Petrodar and the Greater Nile Petroleum Operating Company, the new city of Alsunut is being built on Sudan's petroleum riches and is financed by a global set of investors from the Gulf region, Malaysia, China, Pakistan, and elsewhere.

Even with all these riches, the geography of fossil fuels is strikingly uneven across the region. Some states—even those with tiny populations (Bahrain, Qatar, and Kuwait, for example)—contain incredible fossil fuel reserves, especially when considered on a per capita basis. Many other countries, however, and millions of regional inhabitants, reap relatively few benefits from the oil and gas economy. In North Africa, for example, Morocco possesses few developed petroleum reserves, and even the fruits of Sudan's blossoming wealth will likely remain very concentrated within a small segment of a large, poor population. In oil-rich Southwest Asia, the distribution of fossil fuels is also uneven: Israel, Jordan, and Lebanon all lie outside favored geological zones for either petroleum or natural gas. While Turkey has some developed fields in the far southeast, it must import substantial supplies to meet the needs of its large and industrializing population.

The region's abundant sunshine may be key to its future energy production in the centuries to come. Long after the last drop of oil has been pumped from the ground, the region's vast solar potential will be critical to the world's energy budget (see "Exploring Global Connections: Sunny Side Up: North Africa's Desertec Initiative").

Regional Economic Patterns

Remarkable economic differences characterize the region (see Table 7.2). Some oil-rich countries have prospered greatly since the early 1970s, but in many cases fluctuating oil prices, political disruptions, and rapidly growing populations have reduced prospects for economic growth. Other nations, although poor in oil and gas reserves, have seen brighter prospects through moves toward greater economic

Figure 7.42 Persian Gulf This satellite view of the Persian Gulf reveals one of the world's richest sources of petroleum. Sedimentary rocks, both on land and offshore, contain additional reserves that can sustain production for decades.

diversification. Finally, some countries in the region are subject to persistent poverty, where rapid population growth and the basic challenges of economic development combine with political instability to produce very low standards of living.

Higher-Income Oil Exporters The richest countries of Southwest Asia and North Africa owe their wealth to massive oil reserves. Nations such as Saudi Arabia, Kuwait, Qatar, Bahrain, and the United Arab Emirates benefit from fossil fuel production, as well as from their relatively small populations. Large investments in transportation networks, urban centers, and in other petroleum-related industries have reshaped the cultural landscape. Billions of dollars have also poured into new schools, medical facilities, low-cost housing, and modernized agriculture, significantly raising the standard of living in the past 40 years.

The Saudi petroleum-processing and shipping centers of Jubail (on the Persian Gulf) and Yanbu (on the Red Sea) are examples of this commitment to expand the region's economic base beyond the simple extraction of crude oil. Other oil-rich cities have cultivated an even more cosmopolitan image, with globalized Dubai in the United Arab Emirates appealing both to international tourists and business interests (see "Cityscapes: Dubai's Rocky Road to Urbanization").

Still, problems remain. Dependence on oil and gas revenues produces economic pain in times of falling prices, such as those seen in the recent economic downturn (2008–2010). Such fluctuations in world oil markets will inevitably continue in the future, disrupting construction projects, producing large layoffs of immigrant populations, and slowing investment in the region's economic and social infrastructure. In addition, countries such as Bahrain and Oman are faced with the problem of rapidly depleting their reserves over the next 20 to 30 years.

Lower-Income Oil Exporters Other states in the region are important secondary players in the oil trade, but different political and economic variables have hampered sustained economic growth. In North Africa for example, Algerian oil and natural gas overwhelmingly dominate its exports, but the past 15 years have also brought political instability and increasing shortages of consumer goods. While the country contains some excellent agricultural lands in the north, the overall amount of arable land has increased little over the past 25 years, even as the country's population has grown by more than 50 percent.

In Southwest Asia, Iraq faces huge economic and political challenges. The war crippled much of Iraq's already deteriorated infrastructure, and continuing political instability has made the task of rebuilding its economy more difficult. Iraq suffers from extremely high unemployment, more than 20 percent of the population remains malnourished, and only 25 percent of the country is served by dependable electricity. The country's economic leaders do have an ambitious plan for increasing oil output, and in 2009 the Iraqi cabinet

Figure 7.43 Israeli High-Tech Industry These Israeli workers are employees of the Telrad factory, a high-tech division of the Koor conglomerate.

endorsed a plan to reorganize its domestic oil industry under a single national oil company.

The situation in Iran also is challenging. The country is large and populous, and has a relatively diverse economy. Iran's oil and gas reserves are huge and have seen active commercial development since 1912. The country also has a sizable industrial base, much of it built in the 20 years prior to the fundamentalist revolution of 1979. But today Iran is relatively poor, burdened with a stagnating if not declining standard of living. Since 1980, the country's fundamentalist leaders have downplayed the role of international trade in consumer goods and services, fearing they would import unwanted cultural influences from abroad. There are economic bright spots, as well: The country benefits from energy developments in Central Asia. In addition, Iran's literacy rate (particularly for women) has risen, reflecting a new emphasis on rural education in the country. Political differences with potential Western trading partners are vast, however, and Iran's recent nuclear development program isolated the country from many nations, including the United States.

Prospering Without Oil Some countries, while lacking petroleum resources, have nevertheless found paths to increasing economic prosperity. Israel, for example, supports one of the highest standards of living in the region, even with its political challenges (see Table 7.2). The Israelis and many foreigners have invested large amounts of capital to create a highly productive agricultural and industrial base. The country also is emerging as a global center for high-tech computer and telecommunications products. The country is known for its fast-paced and highly entrepreneurial business culture, which resembles California's Silicon Valley (Figure 7.43). Israel also has daunting economic problems. Its persistent struggles with the Palestinians and with neighboring states have sapped much of its potential vitality. Defense spending absorbs a large share of total gross national

EXPLORING GLOBAL CONNECTIONS   Sunny Side Up: North Africa's Desertec Initiative

One of the planet's most ambitious renewable energy schemes, co-ordinated by the Desertec Foundation, is taking shape across North Africa and the Middle East. If successful, it will supply nearby portions of western and central Europe with at least 15 percent of its energy needs by 2050. While the initiative also includes wind, biomass, geothermal, and hydroelectric components, the key source in the green energy network will be thousands of concentrating solar thermal power (CSP) collectors that will be built across vast portions of North Africa and southwest Asia (Figure 7.5.1). The parabolic mirrors concentrate the sun's energy to heat a liquid that can be used to power steam turbines to generate safe and clean electricity. Once the electricity is produced, a sprawling network of long-distance transmission cables will take the energy to local sources of consumption within the region as well as to distant European users.

One plan calls for a major axis of collecting panels to extend through Morocco with other portions of the network gathering energy from Algeria, Tunisia, Libya, and Egypt (Figure 7.5.2). Eventually, the network might be extended further into the Sahara Desert as well as across the Arabian Peninsula and other portions of the Middle East. The transmission network will include huge underwater connections across the bottom of the Mediterranean Sea. Once in Europe, the electricity will be targeted to consumers in settings such as Germany, Spain, Italy, France, and Great Britain.

Backers of the proposal formed the Desertec Industrial Initiative in 2009 and include help from the German government as well as a growing collection of European and North American renewable energy companies. Both public and private utility interests in settings such as Morocco, Tunisia, and Israel are also keen to see their por-

Figure 7.5.1 Solar Energy Collectors If the Desertec project is successful, North Africa's sun-drenched deserts will be populated by thousands of cylindrical parabolic solar collectors, such as these in southern Spain.

income, necessitating high tax rates. Poverty among the Palestinians is also widespread, and the gap between rich and poor within the country has widened considerably.

Turkey also has a diversified economy even though its per capita income is modest by regional standards. Lacking petroleum, Turkey produces varied agricultural and industrial goods for export. About 35 percent of the population remains employed in agriculture, and the country's principal commercial products include cotton, tobacco, wheat, and fruit. The industrial economy has grown since 1980, including exports of textiles, food, and chemicals. Turkey remains an important tourist destination in the region, as well, attracting more than 6 million visitors annually in recent years. Some Turkish leaders hope to bolster the economy by eventually joining the EU.

Regional Patterns of Poverty Poorer countries of the region share the problems of much of the less-developed world. For example, Sudan, Egypt, and Yemen each face unique economic challenges. For Sudan, continuing political problems have stood in the way of progress. Civil war has resulted in major food shortages. The country's transportation and communications systems have seen little new investment and secondary school enrollments remain very low. On the other hand, Sudan's fertile soils could support more farming, and its new oil production suggests petroleum's expanding role in the economy. However, the country's sustained economic development appears delayed by continuing political instability.

Egypt's economic prospects are also unclear. On the one hand, the country experienced real economic growth during tion of the world connected to Europe in this new way. Germany's Deutsche Bank is helping to coordinate the $400 billion investment that will be necessary to fund the first phase of the project. Pilot projects are already underway and larger flows of solar-generated electricity are planned by 2015. Renewable energy enthusiasts

argue the technology will soon be available to make every part of the plan feasible, even the challenging task of economically transmitting electricity across long distances. Ironically, if they are right, the region's greatest contribution to the planet's long-term energy needs may have nothing to do with fossil fuels.

Figure 7.5.2 Desertec Solar Energy Project This map of North Africa and nearby portions of Europe suggests one planned scenario by which desert solar energy can contribute to Europe's future energy budget.

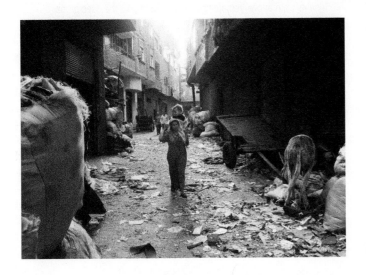

the 1990s as President Hosni Mubarak pushed for more foreign investment, smaller government deficits, and a multibillion-dollar privatization program to put government-controlled assets under more efficient management. Even so, many Egyptians live in poverty, and the gap between rich and poor continues to widen (Figure 7.44). Illiteracy is widespread, and the country suffers from the **brain drain** phenomenon as some of its brightest young people leave for better jobs in western Europe or the United States. Egypt's 80 million people already make it the region's most heavily

Figure 7.44 Cairo Slums One distinctive group of Cairo's population is the Zabbaleen, a community of Coptic Christians who collect the city's trash and live along the narrow streets of Manshiet Nasser, one of the city's most poverty-stricken neighborhoods.

CITYSCAPES   Dubai's Rocky Road to Urbanization

It was a somewhat tarnished celebration. Early in 2010, the Burj Dubai was officially completed in the United Arab Emirates. The tallest free-standing structure in the world at over 2,625 feet (800m), the 160-story building dominates the urban skyline of a city that has struggled mightily in the global economic downturn between 2008 and 2010 (Figure 7.6.1). After booming for years, the city witnessed a spectacular crash in real estate values. Construction projects folded, workers exited the city as fast as they had arrived, and the entire regional economy teetered, awash in a debt crisis that threatened the very stability of regional banks and governments.

Before the crash, Dubai's rise along the sandy shoreline of the Persian Gulf had been nothing short of spectacular. Studded with eye-popping skyscrapers and famous for its fabricated islands in the shapes of palm trees and the world map, Dubai got its start with oil dollars (Figure 7.6.2). The city became a major financial and commercial hub of the Middle East. Its leaders, the ruling al-Maktoum family, still aspire to make it a global city that competes with London, Tokyo, New York, and Hong Kong. In less than a lifetime, Dubai grew from a small fishing village of 40,000 in 1960, to a metropolis of 1.4 million residents today. Clustered developments such as

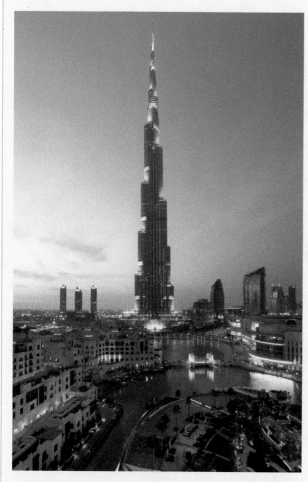

Figure 7.6.1 Burj Dubai, Dubai, United Arab Emirates Dubai's soaring Burj Khalifa, completed in 2010, became the world's tallest free-standing structure, but it towered over a city still struggling with profound economic challenges.

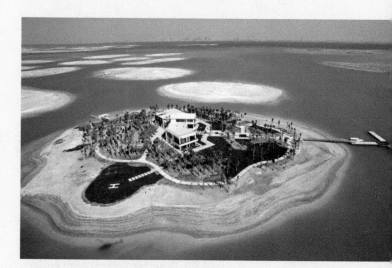

Figure 7.6.2 Dubai's Offshore Real Estate Dubai's island-studded shoreline includes the ambitious "World" real estate venture, but many of the archipelago's pricey properties (which resemble an outline of the world's continents from above) remain vacant, a testimony to the deep global economic downturn that hit this region hard between 2008 and 2010.

populated state, and recent efforts to expand the nation's farmland have met with numerous environmental, economic, and political problems.

In Southwest Asia, Yemen remains the poorest country on the Arabian Peninsula. Positioned far from most of the region's principal oil fields, Yemen's low per capita GNI puts it on par with many nations in impoverished Sub-Saharan Africa. The largely rural country relies mostly on marginally productive subsistence agriculture, and much of its mountain and desert interior lacks effective links to the outside world. The present state emerged in 1990 with the political union of North and South Yemen, but political instability also remains a fact of life for many within the country. Coffee, cotton, and fruits are commercial agricultural products and modest oil exports bring in needed foreign currency. Overall, however, high unemployment and marginal subsistence farming remain widespread across the country.

Unique problems afflict the Palestinian populations of Gaza and the West Bank. Continued declines have devastated the economy as political disruptions discourage investment and conflicts with the Israelis destroy infrastructure. In many

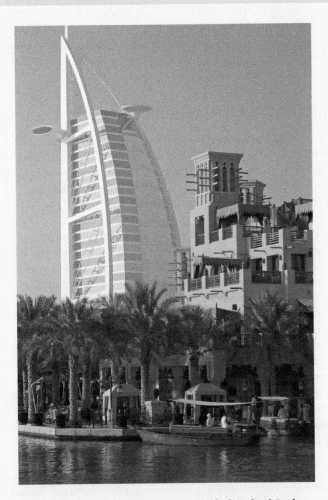

Figure 7.6.3 Landscapes of Luxury, Dubai, United Arab Emirates The canals of the elite Madinat Jumeirah Arabian Resort are visible in the foreground. In the background, the telltale sail of the luxurious Burj Al Arab Hotel is one of the most dramatic visual symbols of affluence in the region. The hotel bills itself as the world's first seven-star hotel.

Internet City, Media City, Healthcare City (partnered with Harvard University), and the Dubai International Financial Center blossomed to serve 21st-century needs of the Middle East.

Millions of tourists from the Middle East, Russia, and Europe still pour into the city. The Burj al Arab, a seven-star hotel in the shape of a sail, serves a jet-set elite from Moscow to Riyadh (Figure 7.6.3). International tourists, glitzy sporting events, and major corporation headquarters (including Haliburton) find this Arab boomtown irresistible. In 2005, Dubai added indoor skiing to the Mall of the Emirates (the largest mall in the Middle East, naturally). City billboards proclaim, in both English and Arabic, "If you can dream it, it can happen."

But Dubai's rise and subsequent stumble are emblematic of the integrating yet uneven forces of globalization. Oil and ambition created the city and it also benefited indirectly from post–September 11 geopolitics. Arab investors flush with cash began to invest more in the Middle East—Dubai was ready and waiting. In addition, Dubai promoters attracted global investors who were keen to get in on the appeal of ever-rising real estate prices. When the tide turned in 2008, Dubai investors and government-controlled companies had run up a debt of over $80 billion. The resulting downturn has meant unfinished golf courses, half-empty office buildings, and an exit of thousands of foreign workers, many of them from South Asia.

Dubai's promoters argue persuasively that the city is down, but not out. Recovering oil prices have improved the region's economic prospects. Investment capital is once again flowing into the city. Immigrant workers are returning. Longer term, the city's exclusive offshore island real estate market may bloom again. In the process, Dubai is creating one of the world's most globalized cities, a place where four out of five residents are foreign-born, where wealthy people from around the world come to shop and play, and where the price of oil continues to shape the fortunes of a landscape that reflects both the best and worst of an unpredictable global economy.

cases, when Israeli forces suspect political dissidents and terrorist elements in a given Palestinian town or urban neighborhood, they destroy the settlement, leveling houses and shops in the process. Poverty grips two-thirds of the Palestinian population, unemployment hovers above 40 percent, and the ongoing construction of the Israeli security barrier promises to further disrupt the Palestinian economy in the years to come. The isolated Gaza Strip has been particularly hard hit, although local Hamas leaders have proven effective in helping to organize the informal economy and providing basic social services.

A Woman's Changing World

The role of women in the largely Islamic region also remains a major social issue. Female labor participation rates in the workforce are among the lowest in the world, and large gaps typically exist between male and female literacy (see Table 7.2). In the most conservative parts of the region, few women are allowed to work outside the home. Even in parts of Turkey, where Western influences are widespread, it is rare to see rural women selling goods in the marketplace or driving cars in the street. More orthodox Islamic states impose legal restrictions on the activities of women. In Saudi Arabia, for example, women are not allowed to drive, although a growing flurry of recent protests (including highly publicized convoys of renegade women drivers) may lead to lifting that limitation. In Iran, full veiling remains mandatory in more conservative parts of the country and women are restricted from serving as judges and as political leaders. Generally, Islamic women lead more private lives than men: Much of their domestic space is shielded from the world by walls and shuttered windows, and their public appearances are filtered through the use of the face veil or chador (full-body veil).

Yet in some places women's roles are changing, even within the norms of more conservative, Islamic societies. Many young Algerian women demonstrate the pattern (Figure 7.45). Most studies suggest the younger generation are more religious than their parents and are more likely to cover their heads and drape their bodies with traditional religious clothing. At the same time, they are more likely to be educated and employed than ever before. Today, 70 percent of Algeria's lawyers and 60 percent of its judges are women. A majority of university students are women and women dominate the health-care field. These new social and economic roles also help explain why the birthrates in such settings are declining and are likely to continue doing so. The Algerian case also demonstrates how complex social processes actually unfold, rarely following simple models for how "traditional" societies might evolve.

Women's roles are shifting elsewhere in the region. In Sudan and Saudi Arabia, a growing number of women pursue high-level careers. Education may be segregated, but it is available. Libya's Qaddafi has singled out the modernization of women as a high priority, and today more women than men graduate from the country's university system. In the Western Sahara, Saharawi women play a leading role in the

country's political fight for independence from Morocco and their broader educational backgrounds and social freedoms (including the right to divorce their husbands) further separate them from Moroccan women. Women also have a more visible social position in Israel, except in fundamentalist Jewish communities where conservative social customs require more traditional domestic roles.

Global Economic Relationships

Southwest Asia and North Africa share close economic ties with the world. While oil and gas remain critical commodities that dominate international economic linkages, the growth of manufacturing and tourism are also redefining the region's role in the world.

OPEC's Changing Fortunes While OPEC no longer controls oil and gas prices globally, it still influences the cost and availability of these pivotal products within the developed and less-developed worlds. Western Europe, the United States, Japan, China, and many less industrialized countries depend on the region's fossil fuels. In the case of Saudi Arabia, for example, petroleum and its related products make up more than 90 percent of its exports. One recent trend evident in oil-producing countries (such as Saudi Arabia) is their willingness to form partnerships with foreign corporations, accelerating the economic integration of the region with the rest of the world. Even so, the region's major energy producers will be particularly vulnerable to global-scale recessions, such as the downturn which hit the region hard between 2008 and 2010.

Beyond key OPEC producers, other economic activities have also contributed to global economic integration. Turkey, for example, ships textiles, food products, and manufactured goods to its principal trading partners: Germany, the United

Figure 7.45 Algerian Women Even within the norms of a more conservative Islamic society, Algerian women are increasingly visible and highly productive contributors to that nation's workforce.

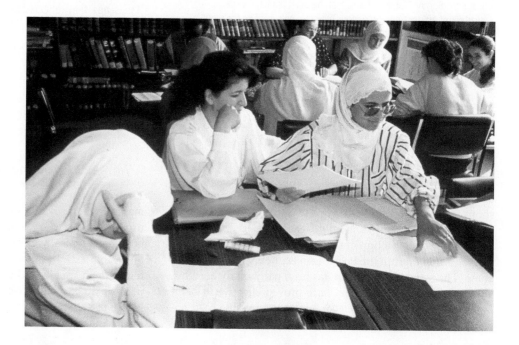

States, Italy, France, and Russia. Tunisia sends more than 60 percent of its exports (mostly clothing, food products, and petroleum) to nearby France and Italy. Israeli exports emphasize the country's highly skilled workforce: Products such as cut diamonds, electronics, and machinery parts are exported to the United States, western Europe, and Japan.

Regional and International Linkages Future interconnections with the global economy may depend increasingly on cooperative economic initiatives far beyond OPEC. Relations with the EU are critical. Since 1996, Turkey has enjoyed closer economic ties with the EU, but recent attempts at full membership in the organization have failed. Other so-called Euro-Med agreements also have been signed between the EU and countries across North Africa and Southwest Asia that border the Mediterranean Sea.

Most Arab countries, however, are wary of too much European dominance. They formed a regional political organization known as the Arab League in 1945. Seventeen league members established the Greater Arab Free-Trade Area (GAFTA) in 2005, designed to eliminate all intraregional trade barriers and spur economic cooperation. In addition, Saudi Arabia plays a pivotal role in regional economic development through organizations such as the Islamic Development Bank and the Arab Fund for Economic and Social Development.

The Geography of Tourism Tourists are another link to the global economy. Traditional magnets such as ancient historical sites and globally significant religious areas (for a multitude of faiths) draw millions of visitors annually. As the developed world becomes wealthier, there is also a growing global demand for recreational spots that can offer beaches, sunshine, and novel entertainment. Indeed, many miles of the Mediterranean, Black, and Red Sea coastlines are now lined with the upscale, but often ticky-tacky, landscapes of resort hotels and condominiums dedicated to serving travelers' needs. More adventurous travelers seek ecotourist activities such as snorkeling in Naama Bay on Egypt's Sinai Coast or four-wheeling among the Berbers in the Moroccan backcountry. Endangered wildlife also beckons photographers and poachers hoping to catch a glimpse of a South Arabian grey wolf, Nubian ibex, or a darting Persian squirrel.

All of this activity means big business to many countries in the region, and the economic impacts of tourism seem likely to grow during the 21st century. Tourism already is a huge part of the regional economy in settings such as Turkey, Israel, and Egypt. Elsewhere, smaller inflows of tourist dollars still have an extraordinary impact on the economies of, for example, northern Morocco and Tunisia, Lebanon (near Beirut), and the holy Saudi Arabian cities of Makkah and Medinah. In some cases, tourism remains much less developed, but the small existing inflows in such places as Libya and Jordan may be the beginning of a much larger economic trend in future years, depending on the region's political stability.

The growth of tourism, while further connecting the region to the global economy, has come at a considerable price. In addition to the visual blight of high-rise hotels, real environmental damage is increasingly the product of the growing human presence in many fragile regional settings. Various archeological and sacred sites have been negatively impacted across the region. More broadly, the economic realities of the tourist economy have produced a local underclass of poorly paid service workers, a growing sense of social distance between the haves and have-nots in tourist settings, and a consumption-oriented lifestyle that contrasts sharply with many traditional ways of life. Still, these changes appear inevitable for a region that, even in uncertain political times, seems to irresistibly attract tourists from every corner of the globe.

Summary

- Positioned at the meeting ground of Earth's largest land masses, the Southwest Asia and North Africa region historically has played a central role in world history and in processes of globalization. In ancient times, the region's inhabitants were early contributors to the agricultural revolution, a long process of plant and animal domestication destined to reshape world cultures. The region also served as a birthplace for some of the world's earliest urban civilizations, offering in the process a fundamentally new way of human settlement that continues to reshape the distribution of global populations today. Three of the world's great religions—Judaism, Christianity, and Islam—emerged beneath its desert skies.

- Many nations within the region suffer from significant environmental challenges. Twentieth-century population growth across the region was dramatic. At the same time, it has been difficult and costly to expand the region's limited supplies of agricultural land and water resources. The results, apparent from the eroded soils of the Atlas Mountains to overworked garden plots along the Nile, are a classic illustration of the environmental price paid when population growth outstrips the ability of the land to support it.

- Culturally, the region remains the hearth of Christianity, the spatial and spiritual core of Islam, and the political and territorial salvation of modern Judaism. Muslims worldwide are influenced by its cultural and political evolution, and the Arab–Israeli conflict will continue to be a critical element in global geopolitics.

- Political conflicts have disrupted economic development across the region. Civil wars, conflicts between states, and regional tensions have worked against initiatives for greater cooperation and trade. Perhaps most important, the region must deal with the conflict between modernity and more fundamentalist interpretations of Islam. One thing is certain: Future cultural change will be guided by a complex response to Western influences.

- Abundant reserves of oil and natural gas, coupled with the global economy's reliance on fossil fuels, dictate that the region will remain prominent in world petroleum markets. Also

likely are moves toward economic diversification and integration, which will gradually draw the region closer to Europe and other participants in the global economy.

Key Terms

brain drain (*page 333*)
culture hearth (*page 289*)
domestication (*page 300*)
exotic rivers (*page 303*)
Fertile Crescent (*page 301*)
fossil water (*page 293*)
Hajj (*page 310*)
hydropolitics (*page 294*)
Islamic fundamentalism (*page 290*)
Islamism (*page 290*)

kibbutzim (*page 304*)
Levant (*page 295*)
Maghreb (*page 295*)
medina (*page 306*)
monotheism (*page 309*)
Organization of the Petroleum Exporting Countries (OPEC) (*page 290*)
Ottoman Empire (*page 311*)
Palestinian Authority (PA) (*page 323*)
pastoral nomadism (*page 314*)

physiological density (*page 299*)
protectorates (*page 320*)
qanat system (*page 293*)
Quran (*page 310*)
Shiites (*page 311*)
Suez Canal (*page 320*)
Sunnis (*page 299*)
theocratic state (*page 311*)
transhumance (*page 301*)

Review Questions

1. Why do Southwest Asia and North Africa form a useful world region? What are some of the problems associated with defining the region?

2. Describe the climatic changes you might experience as you traveled from the eastern Mediterranean coast to the highlands of Yemen. What are some of the key climatic variables that explain these variations?

3. Discuss five important human modifications of the Southwest Asian and North African environment, and assess whether these changes have benefited the region.

4. Discuss how pastoral nomadism, oasis agriculture, and dryland wheat farming represent distinctive adaptations to the regional environments of Southwest Asia and North Africa. How do these rural lifeways create distinctive patterns of settlement?

5. Compare the modern maps of religion and language for the region, and identify three major examples where Islam dominates non-Arabic-speaking areas. Explain why that is the case.

6. Describe the role played by the French and British in shaping the modern political map of Southwest Asia and North Africa. Provide specific examples of their lasting legacy.

7. Define Islamic fundamentalism and Islamism. Outline three regional examples where Islamic fundamentalism or Islamism redefined the domestic geopolitical setting since the late 1970s.

8. Explain how ethnic differences have shaped Iraq's political conflicts in the past 50 years.

9. Describe the basic geography of oil reserves across the region, and compare the pattern with the geography of natural gas reserves.

10. What strategies for economic development have recently been employed by nations such as Turkey, Israel, Egypt, and Morocco? How successful have they been, and how do they relate to the theme of globalization?

Thinking Geographically

1. How might a major project for transferring water from Turkey to the Arabian Peninsula affect the development of Saudi Arabia? What would be some of the potential political and ecological ramifications of such a project?

2. Why are birthrates declining in selected countries within the region? Despite the cultural differences with North America, what common processes seem to be at work in both regions that have contributed to this demographic transition?

3. What economic changes could occur if Israel and the Palestinians were to reach a lasting peace? What kinds of general connections might be found between political conflict and economic conditions throughout the region?

4. Are relations between the region's Muslim societies and the United States likely to improve or worsen? What factors would you cite to defend your answer?

5. What might be some of the reasons for Southwest Asia and North Africa's general failure to match the rates of economic and industrial growth found in China or India?

6. Why has the idea of Arab nationalism failed to achieve any lasting geopolitical changes in the region?

7. Imagine you are a ruler of a conservative, Islamist Arab state. What might be the advantages and disadvantages of opening up your country to the Internet?

Regional Novels and Films

Novels

Shmuel Agnon, *Shira* (1989, Schocken)

Hanan Al-Shaykh, *Beirut Blues: A Novel* (1995, Doubleday)

Murid Barghuthi, *I Saw Ramallah* (2003, Doubleday)

Simin Daneshvar, *Savushun: A Novel About Modern Iran* (1990, Mage)

Kahlil Gibran, *Broken Wings: A Novel* (1957, Citadel)

Barbara Hodgson, *The Tattooed Map* (1995, Chronicle Books)

Yasar Kemal, *Salman the Solitary* (1998, Harvill)

Naguib Mahfouz, *Palace of Desire* (1991, Doubleday)

Naguib Mahfouz, *Palace Walk* (1991, Doubleday)

Abdelrahman Munif, *Cities of Salt: A Novel* (1987, Random House)

Films

Casablanca (1942, U.S.)

The Children of Heaven (1999, Iran)

The English Patient (1996, U.S.)

The House on Chelouche Street (1973, Israel)

Kadosh (1999, Israel)

Lawrence of Arabia (1962, U.S.)

Lion of the Desert (1981, U.K.)

The Lizard (Marmoulak) (2004, Iran)

The Ten Commandments (1956, U.S.)

Time of Favor (2000, Israel)

Bibliography

Cramer, Richard Ben. 2004. *How Israel Lost: The Four Questions*. New York: Simon and Schuster.

Esposito, John L., ed. 1999. *The Oxford History of Islam*. Oxford, UK: Oxford University Press.

Ibrahim, Fouad, and Ibrahim, Barbara. 2003. *Egypt: An Economic Geography*. New York: Macmillan.

Keyder, Caglar, ed. 1999. *Istanbul: Between the Global and the Local*. Lanham, MD: Rowman and Littlefield.

Lewis, Bernard. 2004. *The Crisis of Islam: Holy War and Unholy Terror*. New York: Random House.

Rodenbeck, Max. 1999. *Cairo: The City Victorious*. New York: Knopf.

Rogan, Eugene. 2009. *The Arabs: A History*. New York: Basic Books.

Smith, Dan. 2006. *The State of the Middle East: An Atlas of Conflict and Resolution*. Berkeley: University of California Press.

Soffer, Arnon. 1999. *Rivers of Fire: The Conflict over Water in the Middle East*. Lanham, MD: Rowman and Littlefield.

Swearingen, Will D., and Bencherifa, Abdellatif, eds. 1996. *The North African Environment at Risk*. Boulder, CO: Westview Press.

 Mastering Geography

 MapMaster™

Log in to www.masteringgeography.com for MapMaster™ interactive maps, geography videos, RSS feeds, flashcards, web links, an eText version of *Diversity Amid Globalization*, and self-study quizzes to enhance your study of Southwest Asia and North Africa.

MapMaster™ presents 13 Place Name and 13 Layered Thematic interactive maps to help students practice and master their geographic literacy, spatial reasoning, and critical thinking skills.

10
Central Asia

Azerbaijan's capital of Baku is noted for its arresting contrasts. Here a forest of oil derricks can be seen behind the Bibi Heybat Mosque. The current mosque, built in the 1990s, was designed to replicate a structure from the 1200s that had been destroyed by the communist government of the Soviet Union in 1936.

DIVERSITY AMID GLOBALIZATION

Although it was once a power center as well as one of the main conduits of global trade, the landlocked region of Central Asia has been relatively isolated for most of the past 200 years, geopolitically dominated by countries in other world regions. Since the downfall of the Soviet Union in 1991, however, it has emerged as a key player in the global oil and natural gas trade and a focus of international geopolitical rivalry.

ENVIRONMENTAL GEOGRAPHY
Intensive agriculture along the rivers that flow into the deserts of Central Asia has resulted in water shortages, leading to the desiccation of many of the region's lakes and wetlands.

POPULATION AND SETTLEMENT
Pastoral nomadism, the traditional way of life across much of Central Asia, is gradually disappearing as people settle in towns and cities.

CULTURAL COHERENCE AND DIVERSITY
In much of eastern Central Asia, the growing Han Chinese population threatens the indigenous culture of the Tibetan and Uyghur people; in the west, the role of Islam in social and political life remains a major issue.

GEOPOLITICAL FRAMEWORK
Due to its rich resource base and strategic position, Central Asia has become a zone of geopolitical rivalry in which the United States, Russia, China, India, Pakistan, and Iran vie for influence.

ECONOMIC AND SOCIAL DEVELOPMENT
Despite its abundant resources, Central Asia remains a relatively poor region, although much of it does enjoy relatively high levels of social development.

Central Asia does not appear in most books on world regional geography (Figure 10.1). Although it covers a larger expanse than the United States, it is a remote and lightly populated area dominated by high mountains, barren deserts, and semiarid steppes (grasslands). Geopolitically, Central Asia was long ruled by external powers. Until 1991, most of the region was controlled by the Soviet Union. When the Soviet Union collapsed, Central Asia began to reappear in discussions of global geography. Suddenly a number of new countries appeared on the international scene, prompting scholars to reexamine the position of Central Asia in human affairs

The term *Central Asia* is defined in various ways by different writers. Most authorities agree that it includes five newly independent former-Soviet republics: Kazakhstan, Kyrgyzstan, Uzbekistan, Tajikistan, and Turkmenistan. This chapter also includes other territories—Mongolia, Afghanistan, Azerbaijan, and the autonomous regions of western China (Tibet, Xinjiang, and Inner Mongolia [Nei Mongol]). The inclusion of these additional territories within Central Asia is controversial. Azerbaijan is often classified with its neighbors in the Caucasus region (Georgia and Armenia); western China is obviously part of East Asia by political criteria; and Mongolia is also often placed within East Asia because of both its location and its historical connections with China. Afghanistan can alternatively be located within either South Asia or Southwest Asia.

But considering Central Asia's historical unity, its common environmental circumstances, and its reentry onto the stage of global geopolitics, we think that it deserves consideration in its own right. It also makes sense to define its limits rather broadly. For example, Azerbaijan is linked both culturally (language and religion) and economically (oil) more to Central Asia than to Armenia and Georgia.

Figure 10.1 Central Asia Central Asia, a vast, sprawling region in the center of the Eurasian continent, is dominated by arid plains and basins and lofty mountain ranges and plateaus. Eight independent countries—Kazakhstan, Turkmenistan, Uzbekistan, Kyrgyzstan, Tajikistan, Azerbaijan, Afghanistan, and Mongolia—form Central Asia's core. China's lightly populated far west and north are often placed within Central Asia as well, due to patterns of cultural and physical geography.

At the same time, any unity that Central Asia possesses is far from stable. Continuing Chinese political control over southeastern Central Asia and Han Chinese (meaning people of Chinese cultural heritage) migration into that region threatens any claims for regional coherence. Moreover, Central Asia itself remains deeply divided along cultural lines. Most of the region is Muslim in religious orientation and Turkic in language, but both the northeastern and southeastern sections (Mongolia and Tibet) are traditionally Buddhist. Only time will tell whether Central Asia will continue to merit recognition as a distinct world region in its own right.

One reason for Central Asia's former lack of prominence is that it was poorly integrated into international trade networks. This situation began to change in the 1990s as large oil and gas reserves were found, especially in Kazakhstan, Turkmenistan, and Azerbaijan. Moreover, a number of external countries are seeking to exert geopolitical influence over Central Asia, in-cluding Iran, Pakistan, India, the United States, and Russia. Controversies surrounding China's strict control of its Central Asian lands also highlight the significance of the region.

Central Asia forms a large, compact region in the center of the Eurasian landmass. Alone among the world regions, it lacks ocean access. Owing to its continental position in the center of the world's largest landmass, Central Asia is noted for its rigorous climate. High mountains, deep basins, and extensive plateaus magnify its climatic extremes. The aridity of the region, as we shall see, has also contributed to some of the most severe environmental problems in the world.

ENVIRONMENTAL GEOGRAPHY: Steppes, Deserts, and Threatened Lakes of the Eurasian Heartland

Much of Central Asia has a relatively clean environment, owing mainly to low population density. Some parts of Central Asia, such as northwestern Tibet, remain almost pristine, with little human impact of any kind. Industrial pollution, however, is a serious problem in the larger cities, such as Uzbekistan's Tashkent and Azerbaijan's Baku. Elsewhere, the typical environmental dilemmas of arid environments plague the region: desertification (the spread of deserts), salinization (the accumulation of salt in the soil), and desiccation (the drying up of lakes and wetlands). The destruction of the Aral Sea, located on the boundary of Kazakhstan and Uzbekistan in western Central Asia, has been particularly tragic.

The Shrinking Aral Sea

In April 2010, U.N. Secretary General Ban-Ki Moon examined the remains of the Aral Sea by helicopter. He later told reporters that he had been shocked by what he saw. "It is clearly one of the worst environmental disasters of the world," he said. "It really left with me a profound impression, one of sadness that such a mighty sea has disappeared."

Until the late 20th century the Aral Sea was the world's fourth largest lake. Its only significant sources of water are the Amu Darya and Syr Darya rivers, which flow out of the Pamir Mountains, some 600 miles (960 kilometers) to the southeast. For thousands of years, water diversions for irrigation have lowered flows in both of these rivers, but after 1950 the scale of diversion vastly expanded. The valleys of the two rivers formed the southernmost farming districts of the Soviet Union, and thus the rivers are vital suppliers of water for warm-season crops, especially cotton. The largest of these projects was the Kara Kum Canal, which carries water from the Amu Darya across the deserts of southern Turkmenistan.

Unfortunately, the more river water was diverted for crop production, the less freshwater was available for the Aral Sea. The Aral proved to be particularly sensitive because

CENTRAL ASIA
Political & Physical Map

- ⊛ ● Metropolitan areas more than 20 million
- ⊛ ● Metropolitan areas 10–20 million
- ⊛ • Metropolitan areas 5–10 million
- ⊛ · Metropolitan areas 1–5 million
- ⊛ ○ Selected smaller metropolitan areas
- ⌐ Plate boundaries

The gorge country of eastern Tibet. *Several extremely steep canyons alternate with lofty ridges, making eastern Tibet one of the most topographically forbidding places in the world.*

it is relatively shallow. By the 1970s the shoreline was retreating at an unprecedented rate; eventually a number of "seaside" villages found themselves stranded more than 40 miles (64 kilometers) inland. As salinity levels increased, most fish species disappeared. New islands began to emerge, and by the 1990s the Aral Sea consisted of two separate lakes (see "Geographical Tools: Remote Sensing, GIS, and the Tragedy of the Aral Sea").

The destruction of the Aral Sea resulted in economic and cultural damage, as well as ecological devastation. Fisheries were wiped out and even local agriculture suffered. The retreating lake left large salt flats on its exposed beds; wind-

---

GEOGRAPHIC TOOLS   Remote Sensing, GIS, and the Tragedy of the Aral Sea

Remote sensing technology is directly relevant to the study of the Aral Sea; satellite images clearly and immediately reveal the extensive and rapid reduction of the lake (Figure 10.1.1). But remote sensing and other technologically sophisticated geographical tools, such as geographic information system (or GIS, which allows spatially organized databases to generate numerous maps and map overlays), have also allowed geographers and other environmental scientists to more fully understand both the processes that have caused the tragedy and the broader social and environmental effects. Such tools are also invaluable for designing plans to reduce the damage.

Geographers Elena Lioubimtseva (Grand Valley State University) and Grigoriy Kapustin (Geography Institute, Russian Academy of Sciences) have recently used several sequences of medium-resolution satellite images to determine the spatial patterns and the underlying processes behind desertification in the Amu Darya Delta along the southern edge of the lake—one of the most devastated environments of the world. Their work shows the significance of overgrazing, wind erosion, and the salinization of soils, revealing as well local changes in microclimate caused by the shrinkage of the lake.

An even more comprehensive project, "GIS of the Aral Sea," is led by Rainer Ressl (German Aerospace Center), Andrei Ptichnikov (Institute of Geography, Russian Academy of Sciences), and Philip Micklin (USAID advisor on water management policy for the Uzbek government). As its Website (http://igras.geonet.ru/igras_e/project/aral/index.htm) explains, this project, under development since 1993, uses "dozens of georeferenced cartographic layers and a huge data base. It covers topics of physical geography and topography, social, demographic, health, water management and irrigation, ecological problems, desertification and biodiversity of the region around the Aral Sea, and the Sea itself. Satellite imagery of different resolution . . . is widely used to update the map layers. Models of optimal water and land use of irrigated lands, of ecosystem transformation and desertification are under construction."

If the problems of the Aral Sea are to be genuinely addressed at any level, the concerted efforts of a number of both national and international agencies will be required. Despite the overwhelming severity of those problems, it is heartening to learn that geographers have responded by devising such internationally focused projects, using the best and most up-to-date technologies at their disposal.

Figure 10.1.1 The Shrinking of the Aral Sea These satellite images show the dramatic shrinkage of the Aral Sea. A 90-percent reduction of the lake's size has occurred since the 1960s, resulting in severe economic damage and environmental degradation.

storms pick up the salt, along with the agricultural chemicals that have accumulated in the lake's shallows, and deposit it in nearby fields. Crop yields have thus declined; desertification has accelerated; and public health has been undermined. Particularly hard hit by this destruction are the Karakalpak people, members of a relatively powerless ethnic group who inhabit the formerly rich delta of the Amu Darya River.

In 2001, the oil-rich government of Kazakhstan decided to save what was left of its portion of the Aral Sea. By reconstructing canals, sluices, and other waterworks along the Syr Darya River, it doubled the flow of water reaching the northern Aral, which correspondingly began to rise (Figure 10.2 on page xxx). A large dam built across the lakebed prevented the extra water from flowing south into the salty waters and onto the extensive salt flats of the southern Aral Sea. By 2010, the area of the northern lake had increased by 50 percent, and its salt content had dropped low enough to allow the return of indigenous fish species. Currently, the World Bank and the government of Kazakhstan are discussing an extension of the project, hoping to extend the lake as far as the former port city of Aralsk.

The southern Aral Sea, meanwhile, continues to shrink, and its water quality continues to deteriorate. It too has been divided into two water bodies, and its eastern basin now dries up completely during the summer. Thus far, the oil-poor, agriculture-dependent government of Uzbekistan has done little to salvage what remains of its portion of the Aral Sea. It is worried, however, that Tajikistan will further reduce the flow of local rivers by its own water development projects, resulting in significant tension between the two countries (see "Environment and Politics: Tajikistan and Uzbekistan's Environmental Cold War").

ENVIRONMENT AND POLITICS Tajikistan and Uzbekistan's Environmental Cold War

In August 2008, the *New York Times* described Tajikistan and Uzbekistan as being in a "cold war." More recently, the conflict has warmed up; in early 2010, Uzbekistan imposed a partial blockade on Tajikistan. Uzbek authorities held freight cars at the border, stifling Tajikistan's economy. Uzbekistan's government claimed that technical and logistical difficulties merely slowed traffic over the border. Tajik authorities, however, grew so concerned that they threatened to take Uzbekistan to international courts, and they began talking about building alternative transportation routes. As anger against Uzbekistan mounted in Tajikistan, anger at Tajikistan mounted in Uzbekistan. In March 2010, around 1,000 university students and professors marched in the Uzbek city of Termez to protest Tajikistan's plans to expand a highly polluting aluminum smelter near the Uzbek border.

A root cause of the Tajikistan-Uzbekistan feud is water. Former Soviet Central Asia is a dry region that depends on the snow-fed rivers flowing out of the Pamir and Tien Shan mountains. Mountainous Tajikistan and Kyrgyzstan contain its major headwaters, thus potentially controlling the water supply. Downstream Uzbekistan is water-short yet dependent on irrigated agriculture. It is thus hardly surprising that its government fears potential upstream water development diversions. Energy-poor Tajikistan wants to build dams primarily to generate hydroelectricity. In 2009, Uzbekistan partially cut-off natural gas supplies to debt-strapped Tajikistan, almost shutting down its aluminum smelters—one of the country's few profitable industries. Dam-building would not just protect the industry but would allow its expansion.

The dam in question is Rogun on the Vakhsh River, an important tributary of the Amu Darya (Figure 10.2.1). If and when it is ever completed, Rogun will be the world's highest dam. Work began in 1976, but the unfinished project sank with the Soviet Union in 1991. In 2007, Russia partnered with Tajikistan to complete the dam, but the two parties soon fell out. The Tajik government announced in early 2010 that it would try to raise by itself the $1.4 billion needed to finish the dam. Uzbekistan demanded an inde-

Figure 10.2.1 Blasting on the Vakhsh River in Preparation for the Construction of the Rogun Dam As Tajikistan moves ahead with ambitious water development projects, Uzbekistan fears that its own water resources, already in limited supply, will be further reduced.

pendent study to prove that its own water supplies would not be adversely affected, and when Tajikistan refused, the traffic came to a crawl. To complete Rogun Dam, Tajikistan needs to import vast quantities of construction supplies and heavy equipment through Uzbekistan.

Central Asia obviously has major water problems. The downstream countries, particularly agriculture-dependant Uzbekistan, have proposed the creation of a regional water authority that could coordinate development plans among all of the countries of the region. Water-rich Tajikistan and Kyrgyzstan, however, have been reluctant to enter in to such agreements. Considering as well the problems posed by global warming, Central Asia's hydropolitical problems are likely to become more extreme in the near future.

Figure 10.2 The Northern Aral Sea
Due to water diversions from the Amu Darya and Syr Darya rivers, the Aral Sea has lost most of its volume and now forms two separate lakes. The government of Kazakhstan has recently built dikes to protect the water of the smaller Northern Aral, which is fed by the flow of the Syr Darya River.

Other Environmental Issues

Although the desiccation of the Aral Sea represents Central Asia's worst environmental crisis, other lakes in the region are also endangered. In addition, large areas of Central Asia suffer from extensive desertification and deforestation.

Fluctuating Lakes Western Central Asia supports large lakes because it forms a low-lying basin, without drainage to the ocean, that is virtually surrounded by mountains and other more humid areas. The world's largest lake, by a huge margin, is the Caspian Sea, located along the region's western boundary; and the 15th largest is Lake Balkhash in eastern Kazakhstan. Several other large lakes, such as Kyrgyzstan's spectacular Ysyk-Kol, are also located in the region.

Neither the Aral nor the Caspian are true seas because they are not connected with the ocean. The Caspian is less salty than the ocean (particularly in the north), while until the 1970s the Aral was only slightly brackish (salty). Lake Balkhash is almost fresh in the west but its long eastern extension is quite salty. Because none of these lakes are drained by rivers, all naturally fluctuate in size, depending on how much precipitation falls in their drainage basin in a given year. Like the Aral Sea, a number of Central Asia's lakes have suffered from reduced water flow and hence increasing salinity; Balkhash, for example, has recently shrunk by some 770 square miles (2,000 square kilometers).

Figure 10.3 Environmental Issues in Central Asia Central Asia has experienced some of the world's most severe desertification problems. Soil erosion and overgrazing have led to the advance of desertlike conditions in much of western China and Kazakhstan. In western Central Asia, the most serious environmental problems are associated with the diversion of rivers for irrigation and the corresponding desiccation of lakes. Oil pollution is a particularly serious issue in the Caspian Sea area.

Northern Kazakhstan. "Virgin Lands Campaign" in 1950s resulted in the cultivation of steppe lands, leading to pronounced soil erosion.

Aral Sea. This large lake has been virtually destroyed by the diversion of fresh water out of the Amu Darya and Syr Darya rivers.

The story of the Caspian is more complicated. The Caspian Sea receives most of its water from the large rivers of the north, the Ural and the Volga, which drain much of European Russia. Owing to the development of extensive irrigation facilities in the lower Volga basin, the volume of freshwater reaching the Caspian began to decline in the second half of the 20th century. With a reduced influx of water, the level of the great lake dropped, exposing as much as 15,000 square miles (39,000 square kilometers) of former lake bed. A reduced volume of water resulted in increased salinity levels, undermining fisheries. The Russian caviar industry, centered in the northern Caspian, suffered extensive damage.

After reaching a low point in the late 1970s, the Caspian began to rise, presumably because of higher than normal precipitation in its drainage basin. By the mid 1990s it had risen some 8.2 feet (2.5 meters). This enlargement, too, has caused problems, inundating, for example, some of the newly reclaimed farmlands in the Volga Delta. Since 1995, the level of the lake has generally stabilized, experiencing only minor fluctuations. The most serious current environmental threat to the Caspian is pollution from the oil industry rather than fluctuation in size.

Water development projects have also begun to impact the Tibetan Plateau. Concerned about water shortages in the North China Plain, China is now diverting part of the flow of the headwaters of the Yangtze River into headwaters of the Huang He (or Yellow River). This and other transfer schemes now threaten several of the Tibetan Plateau's large wetlands, havens for many rare species of migrating waterfowl.

Desertification and Deforestation Desertification is another major concern in Central Asia. In the eastern part of the region, the Gobi and Taklamakan deserts have gradually spread southward, encroaching on settled lands in northeastern China. Farmers sometimes have to relocate their houses three or four times over the course of their lives in order to avoid the sands. The Chinese government has tried to stabilize dune fields with massive tree- and grass-planting campaigns, but such efforts have been only partially successful. As a result, sand and dust storms have increased in frequency, and now often affect much of northern China. In April 2010, sandstorms in the area were so severe that they were clearly visible on satellite images.

Former Soviet Central Asia has also seen extensive desertification. Northern Kazakhstan was one of the main sites of the ambitious Soviet "Virgin Lands Campaign" of the 1950s, in which semiarid grasslands were plowed and planted with wheat. Many of these lands have since returned to native grasses, but not before erosion stripped away much of their productivity. Some reports claim that up to 50 percent of Kazakhstan's farmland has been abandoned since 1990, due in part to desertification. In the irrigated lands of Uzbekistan, salinization has been a major problem, forcing the abandonment of some agricultural areas to the desert. Water quality is also poor through much of the region, due to dissolved agricultural chemicals as well as salts and other minerals.

Deforestation has also harmed the region, resulting in wood shortages and reduced dry-season water supplies. Although most of Central Asia is too dry to support forests, many of its mountains were once well wooded. Today extensive forests can be found only in the wild gorge country of the eastern Tibetan Plateau; in some of the more remote west- and north-facing slopes of the Tien Shan, Altai, and Pamir mountains; and in the mountains of northern Mongolia. Some of Central Asia's woodlands, particularly the walnut forests of Kyrgyzstan, are noted for their high biodiversity, and hence form specific target areas for conservation groups.

Central Asia's Physical Regions

To understand why Central Asia suffers from such environmental problems as lake desiccation, an examination of the region's physical geography is necessary. In general, Central Asia is dominated by grassland plains (or steppes) in the north, desert basins in the southwestern and central areas, and high plateaus and mountains in the south-center and southeastern areas (Figure 10.3). Several mountain ranges also extend into the heart of the region, dividing the

Gobi Desert. *The expansion of the Gobi Desert is causing major problems in China and Mongolia.*

Ulaanbaatar ⊛

Hohhot .

- ⬤ Forest
- ⬤ Desert
- ○ Desertification
- ◌ Oil pollution
- ◎ Lake desiccation and salinization
- — Diverted rivers for irrigation

desert zone into a series of separate basins and giving rise to the rivers that flow into the deserts and hence into the imperiled lakes.

The Central Asian Highlands The highlands of Central Asia originated in one of the great tectonic events of Earth's history: the collision of the Indian subcontinent into the Asian mainland. This ongoing impact has created the highest mountain range in the world, the Himalayas, located along the boundary of South Asia and Central Asia.

Yet the Himalayas are merely one portion of a much larger network of high mountains and plateaus. To the northwest they merge with the Karakoram Range and then the Pamir Mountains. From the so-called Pamir Knot, a complex tangle of mountains situated where Pakistan, Afghanistan, China, and Tajikistan converge, other towering ranges radiate outward in several directions. The Hindu Kush sweeps to the southwest through central Afghanistan; the Kunlun Shan extends to the east (along the northern border of the Tibetan Plateau); and the Tien Shan swings out to the northeast into China's Xinjiang province. All of these ranges have peaks higher than 20,000 feet (6,000 meters) in elevation. Much lower but still significant ranges are found along Turkmenistan's boundary with Iran and Azerbaijan's boundaries with Russia, Armenia, and Iran.

More extensive than these mountain ranges, however, is the Tibetan Plateau (Figure 10.4). This massive upland extends some 1,250 miles (2,000 kilometers) from east to west and 750 miles (1,200 kilometers) from north to south. More

remarkable than its size is its elevation; virtually the entire area is higher than 12,000 feet (3,700 meters) above sea level, and its average height is about 15,000 feet (4,600 meters). Most of the large rivers of South, Southeast, and East Asia originate on the Tibetan Plateau and adjoining mountains, including the Indus, Ganges, Brahmaputra, Mekong, Yangtze, and Huang He.

The greater part of the Tibetan Plateau, at about 15,000 feet (4,600 meters) of elevation, lies near the maximum height at which human life can exist. Rather than forming a flat, tablelike surface, the plateau is punctuated with east-west-running ranges alternating with undrained basins. Although the southeastern sections of the plateau receive ample precipitation, most of Tibet is arid. Cut off from any source of moisture by high ranges, large areas of the plateau receive only a few inches of rain a year. Winters on the Tibetan Plateau are cold, and while summer afternoons can be warm, summer nights remain chilly.

The Plains and Basins Although the mountains of Central Asia are higher and more extensive than those found anywhere else in the world, most of the region is characterized by plains and basins of low and intermediate elevation. This lower-lying zone can be divided into two main areas: a central belt of deserts punctuated by lush river valleys and a northern swath of semiarid steppe.

Central Asia's desert belt is itself divided into two segments by the Tien Shan and Pamir mountains (Figure 10.5). To the west lie the arid plains of the Caspian and Aral sea basins, located primarily in Turkmenistan, Uzbekistan, and

Figure 10.4 Tibetan Plateau The Tibetan Plateau is dominated by alpine grasslands and tundra interspersed with rugged mountains and saline lakes. In summer the sparse vegetation offers forage for the herds of nomadic Tibetan pastoralists. Much of the northern part of Tibet, however, is too high to sustain even low-intensity land use.

southern Kazakhstan (Figure 10.6). Most of this area is relatively flat and very low, with the surface of the Caspian Sea lying 92 feet (28 meters) below sea level. The climate of this region is continental; summers are dry and hot, whereas winter temperatures average well below freezing. Central Asia's eastern desert region extends for almost 2,000 miles (3,200 kilometers) from the extreme west of China to the southeastern edge of Inner Mongolia. It is conventionally divided into two deserts: the Taklamakan, found in the Tarim Basin of Xinjiang, and the Gobi, which runs along the border between Mongolia proper and the Chinese region of Inner Mongolia.

The environment of western Central Asia is distinguished from that of eastern Central Asia in part by its larger rivers. More snow falls on the western than the eastern slopes of the Pamir Mountains, giving rise to more abundant runoff. The largest of these rivers, as we have seen, flow to the Aral Sea. Others, such as the Helmand of Afghanistan, terminate in shallow lakes or extensive marshes and salt flats. In Xinjiang, one substantial river, the Tarim, flows out of the highlands onto the basin floor, where it frequently shifts course across the sandy lowlands. Before the completion of irrigation projects in the 1960s, it terminated in a salty lake called Lop Nor. Subsequently, the newly dried-out Lop Nor salt flat was used periodically by China for testing nuclear weapons.

North of the desert zone, rainfall gradually increases and desert eventually gives way to the great grasslands, or steppe, of northern Central Asia. Near the region's northern boundary, trees begin to appear in favored locales, outliers of the great Siberian taiga (coniferous forest) of the north. A nearly continuous swath of grasslands extends some 4,000 miles (6,400 kilometers) east to west across the entire region, only partially broken by Mongolia's Altai Mountains. Summers on the northern steppe are usually pleasant, but winters can be brutally cold.

Global Warming in Central Asia

Most climate change experts predict that Central Asia will be hard hit by global warming, largely because the region depends so heavily on snow-fed rivers. The Tibetan Plateau has already seen marked increases in temperature, resulting in the reduction of permafrost and the rapid drawback of mountain glaciers. Eighty percent of Tibet's glaciers are presently retreating, some at rates of up to 7 percent a year, leading to controversial predictions that the region could lose up to half of its ice fields within the next 50 years. It has also been predicted that Tajikistan could lose 20 percent of its ice cover by 2050. Tree-ring data from Mongolia indicate that the last century has been the warmest in more than a thousand years. Overall, Central Asia has experienced a 3.6°F (2°C) temperature increase since the early 1900s.

The retreat of Central Asia's glaciers is especially worrisome because of their role in providing dependable flows of water for local rivers. In some areas, the melting of ice has resulted in the temporary flooding of lowland basins, but the long-term result will be to further reduce freshwater resources in a region already burdened by aridity. Climate change from global warming could also reduce precipitation in the arid lowlands of western Central Asia, compounding the problem. Prolonged and devastating droughts have recently struck Afghanistan and several of its neighbors, indicating a possible shift to a drier climate. As a result, the U.N. Intergovernmental Panel on Climate Change (IPCC) has predicted a 30-percent crop decline for Central Asia as a whole by mid-century.

But as is true elsewhere in the world, global warming will not affect all parts of Central Asia in a uniform manner. Some areas, including the Gobi Desert and the Tibetan Plateau, could possibly see a long-term increase in precipi-

Figure 10.5 Climates of Central Asia Central Asia is a dry region dominated by desert and steppe climates. Even in most of Central Asia's highlands, marked "H" on this map, arid conditions predominate. Truly humid areas in Central Asia are limited to the far north and extreme southeast. As a midlatitude region located in the interior of a vast continent, Central Asia is marked by pronounced continentality, experiencing profound differences between winter and summer temperatures.

A TROPICAL AND HUMID CLIMATES	D CONTINENTAL MIDLATITUDE CLIMATES
Am Tropical monsoon	**Dwa** Humid continental, with dry winter, warm summer
B DRY CLIMATES	**Dwb** Humid continental, with dry winter, cool summer
BWk Midlatitude desert	**Dfb** Humid continental, without dry season, cool summer
BSk Midlatitude steppe	**Dwc** Subarctic
	H HIGHLAND
	H Complex mountain climates

tation. Such forecasts are scant consolation, however, in a region that is experiencing rampant desertification. Some global climate models also indicate increased precipitation in the boreal forest zone of Siberia that extends into the mountains of northern Mongolia. But as the rivers coming out of these mountains generally flow north, few benefits would be reaped by the rest of Central Asia.

Overall, Central Asia is a moderate producer of greenhouse gasses. The oil-rich economies of Kazakhstan and Azerbaijan are noted for their inefficient energy use, as is the mechanized agriculture of Uzbekistan and Turkmenistan. The traditional nomadic pastoralism and peasant agriculture generate little excess carbon dioxide, but such modes of life are steadily declining across the region. Greenhouse gas emis-

Figure 10.6 Central Asian Desert
Much of Central Asia is dominated by deserts and other arid lands. The Karakum Desert of Turkmenistan, seen in this photograph, is especially dry, supporting little vegetation.

sions from the region are rapidly increasing, due mainly to the expansion of the fossil fuel industry and the growth of cities and modern transportation systems, as we shall see in the following section.

POPULATION AND SETTLEMENT:
Densely Settled Oases Amid Vacant Lands

Most of Central Asia is sparsely populated (Figure 10.7). Large areas are essentially uninhabited, either too arid or too high to support human life, while vast expanses are populated by widely scattered groups of nomadic **pastoralists** (people who raise livestock for subsistence purposes). Mongolia, which is more than twice the size of Texas, has only 2.6 million inhabitants. But as is common in arid environments, those few lowland areas with fertile soil and dependable water supplies can be thickly settled. Despite its overall aridity, Central Asia is well endowed with perennial rivers and productive oases. While the nomadic pastoralists of the steppe and desert zones have dominated the history of Central Asia, the sedentary peoples of the river valleys have always been more numerous.

Highland Population and Subsistence Patterns

The environment of the Tibetan Plateau is particularly harsh. Not only is the climate cold and water often scarce or brackish, but ultraviolet radiation in this high-elevation area is always pronounced. Only sparse grasses and herbaceous plants—so-called mountain tundra—can survive, and human subsistence is obviously difficult under such conditions. The only feasible way of life over much of the Tibetan Plateau is nomadic pastoralism based on the yak, an altitude-adapted relative of the cow. Several hundred thousand people manage to make a living in such a manner, roaming with their herds over vast distances.

Farming in Tibet is possible only in a few favorable locations, generally those that are *relatively* low in elevation and that have good soils and either adequate rain or a dependable irrigation system. The main zone of agricultural settlement lies in the far south, where protected valleys offer favorable conditions. The population of Tibet proper (the Chinese autonomous region of Xizang) is only 2.8 million, a small number indeed considering the vast size of the area.

Population densities are also low in the other highland areas of Central Asia, although densely settled agricultural communities can be found in protected valleys. The complex topography of the Pamir Range in particular offers a large array of small and nearly isolated valleys that are suitable for agriculture and intensive human settlement. Not surprisingly, this area is marked by great cultural and linguistic diversity. Many villages here are noted for their agricultural terraces and well-tended orchards.

Central Asia's mountains are vitally important for people living in the adjacent lowlands, whether they are settled farmers or migratory pastoralists. Many herders use the highlands for summer pasture; when the lowlands are parched, the high meadows provide rich grazing. The Kyrgyz (of Kyrgyzstan) are noted for their traditional economy based on **transhumance**, moving their flocks from lowland pastures in the winter to highland meadows in the summer. The farmers of Central Asia rely on the highlands for their wood supplies and, more important, for their water. Settled agricultural life in most of Central Asia is possible only because of the rivers and streams flowing out of the region's mountains.

Figure 10.7 Population Density in Central Asia Central Asia as a whole remains one of the world's least densely populated regions, although it does contain distinct clusters of higher population density. Most of Central Asia's large cities are located near the region's periphery or in its major river valleys.

Northern Kazakhstan. *A moderate population density characterized by relatively even spacing is found in the agricultural lands of northern Kazakhstan.*

River valleys. *Population concentrations are found in the river valleys and alluvial fans of Uzbekistan. A number of ancient cities are also located here.*

Northern Tibet. *Large areas of northern Tibet are essentially uninhabited; most of Tibet's people live in the lower-elevation lands of the south.*

Lowland Population and Subsistence Patterns

Most of the inhabitants of Central Asia's deserts live in the narrow belt where the mountains meet the basins and plains. Here water supplies are adequate and soils are not contaminated with salt or alkali, as is often the case in the basin interiors. As a result, the population distribution pattern of China's Tarim Basin forms a ringlike structure (Figure 10.8). Streams flowing out of the mountains are diverted to irrigate fields and orchards in the narrow fertile band situated between the steep slopes of the mountains and the nearly empty deserts of the central basin.

The population west of the Pamir Range, in former Soviet Central Asia, is also concentrated in the transitional zone nestled between the highlands and the plains. A series of **alluvial fans**, fan-shaped deposits of sediments dropped by streams flowing out of the mountains, have long been devoted to intensive cultivation. Fertile **loess**, a silty soil deposited by the wind, is widespread, and in a few favored areas winter precipitation is high enough to allow rain-fed agriculture. Several large valleys in this area, such as the Fergana Valley of the upper Syr Darya River, offer fertile and easily irrigated farmland (Figure

10.9). In the far west of the region, Azerbaijan's Kura River Basin also supports intensive agriculture and concentrated settlement.

Unlike the other deserts of the region, the Gobi has few sources of permanent water. Rivers draining Mongolia's highlands flow to the north or terminate in interior basins, while only a few of the larger streams from the Tibetan Plateau reach the Gobi proper. (The Huang He, however, does swing north to reach the desert edge before turning south to flow through the Loess Plateau.) Owing to this scarcity of **exotic rivers** (those originating in more humid areas) and to its own aridity, the Gobi remains one of Asia's least-populated areas.

The steppes of northern Central Asia are the classical land of nomadic pastoralism. Until the 1900s, virtually none of this area had ever been plowed and farmed. To this day, pastoralism remains a common way of life across the grasslands. In northwestern China and the former Soviet republics, however, many pastoral peoples have been forced to adopt sedentary lifestyles. National governments in the region, like those in most other parts of the world, find migratory people hard to control and difficult to provide with social services. Migratory herders are also highly vulnerable to natural disasters. Severe cold in the winter of 2010, for example, killed millions of domesticated animals in Mongolia, resulting in a subsistence crisis over much of the country. Although roughly one-third of Mongolians are still nomadic pastoralists (Figure 10.10), the country's prime minister recently announced that he expected this way of life to essentially disappear over the next few decades.

In northern Kazakhstan, the Soviet regime converted the most productive pastures into farmland in the mid-1900s in order to increase the country's supply of grain. Some of these lands have since reverted to steppe, but large areas remain under the plow; Kazakhstan is a major producer of spring wheat. Consequently, northern Kazakhstan has the highest population density of the steppe belt.

Population Issues

Some portions of Central Asia are growing at a moderately rapid pace. The demographic data on the region show overall fertility rates near the global middle, while exhibiting pro-

Gobi Desert. *Whereas the Gobi Desert along the border of China and Mongolia is virtually uninhabited, many people now inhabit the semiarid southern portion of China's autonomous region of Inner Mongolia.*

PEOPLE PER SQUARE KILOMETER

Fewer than 6
6–25
26–100
101–250
251–500
501–1000
1000–12,801
More than 12,801

POPULATION

Metropolitan areas more than 20 million
Metropolitan areas 10–20 million
Metropolitan areas 5–10 million
Metropolitan areas 1–5 million
Selected smaller metropolitan areas

Figure 10.8 Population Patterns in Xinjiang's Tarim Basin The central portion of the Tarim Basin is a virtually uninhabited expanse of sand dunes and salt flats. Along the edge of the basin, however, dense agricultural and urban settlements are located where streams running out of the surrounding mountains allow for intensive irrigation. The largest of these oasis communities are found along the southwestern fringe of the basin.

ELEVATION IN METERS

4000+
2000–4000
500–2000
Desert
5,000 people

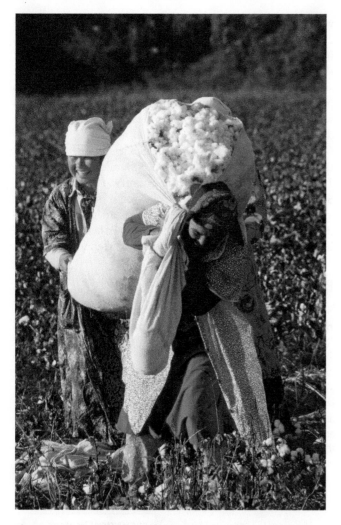

Figure 10.9 Farmland in Uzbekistan The fertile river valleys of Uzbekistan have been intensely cultivated for many centuries, producing large harvests of fruits and vegetables in addition to cotton and grain.

Figure 10.10 Steppe Pastoralism The steppes of northern and central Mongolia offer lush pastures during the summer. Mongolians, some of the world's most skilled horse riders, have traditionally followed their herds of sheep, goats, and cattle, living in collapsible, felt-covered yurts. Many Mongolians still follow this way of life.

nounced variation between different areas (Table 10.1). Afghanistan, the least-developed and most male-dominated country of the region, has the highest birthrate by a substantial margin. Tajikistan, also noted for its low levels of economic development, also has an elevated birthrate.

Low fertility, however, can be counteracted by immigration, as is the case in much of western China. Here substantial population growth over the past 30 years has stemmed from the migration of Han Chinese into the area. While many of the indigenous inhabitants resent this influx, the Chinese government claims that it is necessary for economic development.

Migration has also complicated demographic patterns in the former Soviet zone (Figure 10.11). After the breakup of the

TABLE 10.1	Population Indicators							
Country	Population (Millions, 2010)	Population Density (per Square Kilometer)	Rate of Natural Increase (RNI)	Total Fertility Rate	Percent Urban	Percent <15	Percent >65	Net Migration Rate (per 1,000, 2005–10)[a]
Afghanistan	29.1	45	2.1	5.7	22	44	2	7.5
Azerbaijan	9.0	104	1.1	2.2	54	23	7	−1.2
Kazakhstan	16.3	6	1.4	2.7	54	24	8	−1.3
Kyrgyzstan	5.3	27	1.6	2.8	35	29	5	−2.8
Mongolia	2.8	2	1.9	2.7	61	33	4	−0.8
Tajikistan	7.6	53	2.4	3.4	26	38	4	−5.9
Turkmenistan	5.2	11	1.4	2.5	47	31	4	−1.0
Uzbekistan	28.1	63	1.8	2.8	36	33	5	−3.0

[a]Net Migration Rate from the United Nations, Population Division, World Population Prospects: The 2008 Revision Population Database.
Source: Population Reference Bureau, World Population Data Sheet, 2010.

Soviet Union, millions of Russians and Ukrainians left Central Asia to return to their homelands (see "People on the Move: Migration In and Out of Kazakhstan"). More recently, Russia's economic boom has led many Azerbaijanis, Tajiks, Uzbeks, and other Central Asians to seek employment in Moscow and St. Petersburg, even though they face substantial discrimination and occasional violence. Russian neo-Nazi gangs with names such as "The White Wolves" have specifically targeted Central Asians for attacks. In early 2010, however, nine members of the White Wolvers were sentenced to long prison terms, leading some observers to hope that the Russian government was finally responding seriously to the problem.

Urbanization in Central Asia

Although the steppes of northern Central Asia had no real cities before the modern age, the river valleys and oases have been partially urbanized for millennia. Cities such as

Figure 10.11 Recent Migration and Refugee Flows Since the early 1990s, large numbers of people have been moving out of the former Soviet Central Asia and into the Chinese portions of Central Asia. More recently, workers from Uzbekistan, Kyrgyzstan, and Tajikistan began moving to Kazakhstan. Afghanistan has one of the largest refugee problems in the world.

Samarkand and Bukhara in Uzbekistan were famous even in medieval Europe for their riches and their lavish architecture (see "Cityscapes: The Storied City of Samarkand"). This early urban development was built upon the region's economic and political position. The Amu Darya and Syr Darya valleys lay near the midpoint of the trans-Eurasian silk route, and they formed the core of a number of empires based on the cavalry forces of the steppe. The modern era of steamships and oceanic trade undermined this system, bringing hardship to the cities of Central Asia.

The conquest of Central Asia by the Russian and Chinese empires ushered in a new wave of urban formation. Cities slowly began to appear on the Kazakh steppe, where none had previously existed. The Manchu and Chinese conquerors of Inner Mongolia and Xinjiang built new administrative and garrison cities, often placing them only a few miles from indigenous urban sites. The old indigenous cities of the region are characterized by complex and almost maze-like networks of streets and alleyways, while the neighboring Chinese cities were constructed according to a strict geometrical order. The continuing growth of urban populations along with the establishment of new urban policies is now obscuring this old dualism. In 2009, Beijing announced that the old city of Kashgar (Kashi) in China's Far West would be largely demolished, due mainly to concerns about earth-

PEOPLE ON THE MOVE   Migration In and Out of Kazakhstan

Kazakhstan has experienced several major migration waves over the past century. From the 1920s through the 1960s, large numbers of Russians, Ukrainians, and other people of European background migrated to the Kazakh Soviet Republic, settling in the cities of the south and the farming belt of the north. The 1930s also saw substantial out-migration of Kazakhs, fleeing from Soviet repression into China and Mongolia. At the same time, Soviet authorities exiled members of suspect ethnic groups to the region, including hundreds of thousands of Koreans and Crimean Tatars. Overall, many more people moved in than moved out, with Kazakhstan's population growing from 6 million in 1939 to almost 17 million in 1991.

The independence of Kazakhstan in 1991 ushered in a period of substantial population loss as Russians and other peoples of European ancestry increasingly left the country. In 1989, Kazakhstan recorded 957,518 residents of German background; 10 years later, that number had dropped to 353,441. Russians accounted for 42 percent of the population in 1970 but only 24 percent in 2009. As a result of such emigration, Kazakhstan's total population dropped to under 15 million by 2002.

In the 1990s, the new government of Kazakhstan's grew increasingly concerned about depopulation. The country's birthrate was below the replacement level, yet large numbers of people continued to leave. As a result, it began to encourage the immigration of ethnic Kazakhs living in Mongolia and China, people called Oralmans in Kazakhstan. By 2001, around 180,000 Oralmans had moved into the country. The government continues to subsidize the migration of Oralmans, calling for the resettlement of another 20,000 such families in 2010. Overall, however, the immigration of ethnic Kazakhs is not adequate to replace the ethnic Russians, Ukrainians, and Germans who have emigrated from Kazakhstan in recent years.

Meanwhile, members of other ethnic groups have begun to move to Kazakhstan on their own accord, attracted by its booming economy. More than 500,000 people from other former Soviet countries have entered the Kazakhstan since the turn of the century. More than half are from Uzbekistan, and most the rest come from Kyrgyzstan and Tajikistan (Figure 10.3.1). Work opportunities in the Kazakh oilfields are plentiful, and even farm laborers in Kazakhstan are paid roughly five times more than they would receive in Uzbekistan. Illegal immigrants, however, do not always receive the going wage, and allegations of exploitation are numerous. Roughly three-quarters of the Uzbek migrants into the country are male, many of whom plan to stay only on a temporary basis. Increasingly, however, women and children are migrating as well.

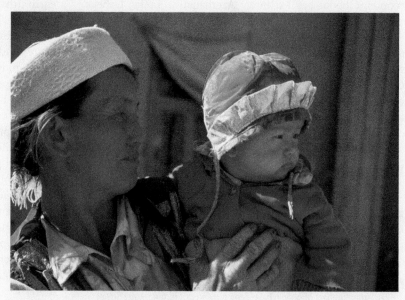

Figure 10.3.1 Uzbek Migrant Laborers in Kazakhstan. Many poor workers from Uzbekistan, Kyrgyzstan, and Tajikistan have recently sought work in booming Kazakhstan. Here an Uzbek grandmother is seen holding her grandchild in a camp in Kazakhstan.

The government of Kazakhstan generally has a positive attitude toward immigration, as it recognizes its need for additional labor. Most of the migrants from the south enter the country illegally, but permanent residency is relatively easy for them to gain. In 2006, the Kazakh Ministry of the Interior announced that it would legalize 100,000 immigrants, but ended up giving out 164,000 residency permits. Many Uzbek, Tajik, and Kyrgyz immigrants are also able to eventually obtain Kazakh citizenship.

The pathway to permanent residence is not so clear for Han Chinese migrants. According to one report, in 2006 alone an estimated 100,000 Chinese entered Kazakhstan for work, with only 5,000 doing so legally. Many Kazakhs are worried about Chinese migration, with only 7 percent of respondents to one poll saying that its effects were positive. Concerns mounted in December 2009, when Kazakh President Nursultan Nazarbaev announced that he was negotiating with Chinese investors who wanted to lease 1 million hectares of Kazakh farmland. Murat Auezov, Kazakhstan's former ambassador to China, was quick to urge caution, asking pointedly, "Who will grow the crops?" He went on to contend that, "If this question is decided in favor of the proposal from China, then it will be the very colonization of Kazakhstan."*

*Bruce Pannier, "Kazakhstan Mulls China Land Deal," *Asia Time Online*, December 19, 2009, http://www.atimes.com/atimes/Central_Asia/KL19Ag01.html)

quake safety. Although China promised to save many of Kashgar's most historic buildings and to build new residences for its inhabitants, some local people view the plan an assault on their cultural identity.

Although it is possible to distinguish Russian/Soviet cities from indigenous cities in the former Soviet zone, this dichotomy is not clear-cut. In Uzbekistan, for example, Tashkent is largely a Soviet creation, while many parts of Bukhara and Samarkand still reflect the older urban patterns. Several major cities, such as Kazakhstan's former capital of Almaty, did not exist before Russian colonization. In Azerbaijan, Baku emerged as a major city in the early 20th century as the first Caspian oil fields began to be intensively exploited. Almost everywhere, one can see the effects of centralized Soviet urban planning and design.

Urbanization is gradually but unevenly spreading across Central Asia. Northcentral Kazakhstan recently witnessed the rise of a major city, Astana, the country's new, centrally located capital. With fewer than 300,000 residents in 1999, Astana had grown to almost 700,000 people by 2010. Even Mongolia, long a land virtually without permanent settlements, now has more people living in cities than in the countryside. In some parts of the region, however, cities remain relatively few and far between. Only 26 percent of the people of Tajikistan, for example, are urban residents. Tibet similarly remains a predominantly rural society, but the influx of Han Chinese into the region is creating a larger urban system. To understand this movement and its broader ramifications, one must examine Central Asia's patterns of cultural geography.

CULTURAL COHERENCE AND DIVERSITY:
A Meeting Ground of Different Traditions

Although Central Asia has a certain environmental unity, its cultural coherence is more questionable. The western half of the region is largely Muslim and is often classified as part of Southwest Asia. Northeastern and southeastern Central Asia—Mongolia and Tibet—are characterized by a distinctive form of Tibetan Buddhism. Tibet is culturally linked to both South and East Asia, and Mongolia is intimately associated with China, but neither fits easily within any world region. Such complexity can best be understood by examining the region's historical geography.

Historical Overview: Steppe Nomads and Silk Road Traders

The river valleys and oases of Central Asia were early sites of agricultural communities. Archaeologists have discovered abundant evidence of farming villages dating back to the Neolithic period (beginning circa 8000 BCE) in the Amu Darya and Syr Darya valleys and along the rim of the Tarim Basin. After the domestication of the horse around 4000 BCE, nomadic pastoralism emerged in the steppe belt as a new

human adaptation. Eventually pastoral peoples gained power over the entire region, transforming not only the history of Central Asia but also that of virtually all of Eurasia. In the premodern period, highly mobile pastoral nomads enjoyed major military advantages over sedentary societies. Not until the age of gunpowder were the benefits of pastoralism offset by the demographic and economic advantages held by the more populous agriculturally based states.

The linguistic geography of Central Asia has undergone major changes over the ages. Into the first millennium CE, the inhabitants of the region spoke Indo-European languages closely related to Persian. Indo-European languages began to be replaced on the steppe by languages in the Altaic family, which include Mongolian and Turkic, more than a thousand years ago. By the second century BCE, a powerful nomadic empire of Turkic-speaking peoples arose in what today is Mongolia. As Turkic power spread through most of Central Asia, Turkic languages gradually began to replace Indo-European tongues in the agricultural communities. This process was never completed, however, and southwestern Central Asia remains a meeting ground of the Persian and Turkic languages. Uzbek, for example, is classified in the Turkic language family, but much of its basic vocabulary is of Persian origin.

The Turks were eventually replaced on the eastern steppes by another group of Altaic speakers, the Mongols. In the late 1100s the Mongols, under the leadership of Genghis Khan, united the pastoral peoples of Central Asia and used the resulting force to conquer nearby sedentary societies. By the late 1200s the Mongol Empire had grown into the largest contiguous empire the world had ever seen, stretching from Korea and southern China in the east to the Carpathian Mountains and the Euphrates River in the west (Figure 10.12). In today's Mongolia, Genghis Khan has reemerged as the country's national hero. China is also trying to claim the same legacy, having recently built a Genghis Khan theme park in Inner Mongolia.

Protected by mountain barriers and by the rigorous conditions of the plateau, Tibet has taken a different course from the rest of Central Asia. Tibet emerged as a strong, unified kingdom around 700 CE. Tibetan unity and power did not persist, however, and the region reverted to its former state of semi-isolation. Tibet was incorporated for a short period in the 1200s into the Mongol Empire, and in later centuries other Mongol states occasionally enjoyed limited powers over the Tibetans. These interactions resulted in the establishment of Mongolian communities in the northeastern portion of the plateau and in the eventual conversion of the Mongolian people to Tibetan Buddhism.

Contemporary Linguistic and Ethnic Geography

Today most of Central Asia is inhabited by peoples speaking Altaic languages, but patterns of linguistic geography remain complex. A few indigenous Indo-European languages are confined to the southwest, while Tibetan remains the main language of the plateau. Russian is also widely spoken

CITYSCAPES   The Storied City of Samarkand

Like all cities of the former Soviet Union, Uzbekistan's Samarkand has its share of drab concrete buildings designed for public housing and government offices. And like all of the older cities of Central Asia, it has its share of crowded traditional neighborhoods with narrow streets (Figure 10.4.1) and houses facing inward toward private courtyards. But in other ways, Samarkand is unique; it contains more sites of historical and religious significance than any other city in the region. Life in the streets of central Samarkand, a city that poets once dubbed the "Rome of the East," forces one to confront and appreciate the past with an unusual intensity. In recognition of its significance, Samarkand was declared a United Nations Educational, Scientific and Cultural Organization (UNESCO) World Heritage Site in 2001.

Samarkand's historical riches derive in part from its physical geography. Located in a fertile valley at roughly the midway point of the Silk Road that once connected China to the Mediterranean, it was an important city as far back as the time of Alexander the Great. Many centuries later, it became the capital city of the famous and feared Turkic-Mongol conqueror, Tamerlane (Timur-i-leng; 1336–1405). Tamerlane and his descendants endeavored to beautify the city, building mosques, tombs, madrassahs (Islamic colleges), and a host of other public buildings. Many of these architectural marvels remain. Muslims from throughout Central Asia and beyond often make pilgrimages to visit the sacred sites of the city, some viewing the trip as second in importance only to the hajj to Mecca.

At the core of historical Samarkand sits Registan Square (Figure 10.4.2), described in the 19th century by Lord George Curzon (Britain's Viceroy of India) as simply "the best central city square in the world." Majestic buildings, including the famous Ulugbek Madrassah, line three sides of the square. Nearby, sitting in the midst of a crowded and colorful market, is the Bibi-Khanum Mosque, which was the largest in the world when built in the 15th century. But it is Tamerlane's final resting place, the Gur-Emir Mausoleum, that is considered by many as the most spectacular example of traditional Central Asian architecture.

As is true of many other Central Asian cities, Samarkand's historical legacy remains vulnerable. In 2008, UNESCO's World Heritage Committee requested "reinforced monitoring" of Samarkand, arguing that its traditional urban fabric was threatened by the poorly regulated construction of new roads and buildings.

Figure 10.4.1 The Narrow Streets of Samarkand The older districts of Samarkand are noted for their tightly packed buildings and narrow streets and alleys. Many of the old city's roads are too narrow for wheeled vehicles.

Figure 10.4.2 Traditional Architecture in Samarkand Samarkand is famous for its lavish Islamic architecture, some of it dating to the 1400s. This photograph shows some of the buildings arrayed around Registan Square, the city's traditional core.

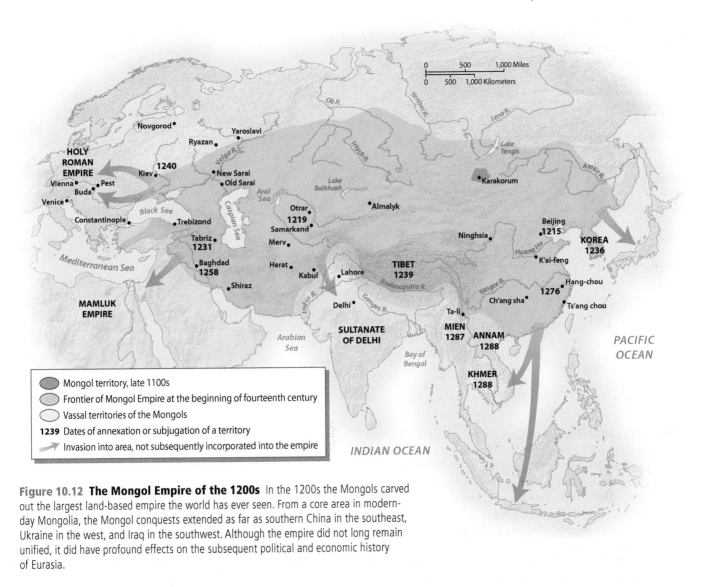

Figure 10.12 The Mongol Empire of the 1200s In the 1200s the Mongols carved out the largest land-based empire the world has ever seen. From a core area in modern-day Mongolia, the Mongol conquests extended as far as southern China in the southeast, Ukraine in the west, and Iraq in the southwest. Although the empire did not long remain unified, it did have profound effects on the subsequent political and economic history of Eurasia.

in the west, and in most former Soviet countries Russian retains an official status, whereas Mandarin Chinese is increasingly important in the east. In both Tibet and Xinjiang, Mandarin Chinese is now the basic language of higher education. In Tibet, most urban merchants are now Chinese-speaking immigrants, causing much concern among the indigenous people (Figure 10.13).

Tibetan Tibetan is divided into a number of distinct dialects that are spoken over almost the entire inhabited portion of the Tibetan Plateau. Approximately 6 million people speak Tibetan; of these, roughly 2.5 million live in Tibet proper, while most of the rest reside in China's provinces of Qinghai and Sichuan. Tibetan is usually placed in the Sino-Tibetan family, implying a shared linguistic ancestry between the Chinese and the Tibetan peoples, but some scholars argue that no definite relationship between the two has been established. Tibetan has an extensive literature written in its own script, most of which is devoted to religious topics.

Mongolian Mongolian is comprised of a cluster of closely related dialects spoken by approximately 5 million people. The standard Mongolian of both the independent country of Mongolia and China's Inner Mongolia is called Khalkha; other Mongolian dialects include Buryat (found in southern Siberia) and Kalmyk (found to the northwest of the Caspian Sea). Mongolian has its own distinctive script, which dates back some 800 years, but Mongolia itself adopted the Cyrillic alphabet of Russia in 1941. In China's region of Inner Mongolia, however, the old script is still widely used.

Although Mongolian speakers form about 90 percent of the population of Mongolia, in China's Inner Mongolian Autonomous Province they have been partly submerged by a wave of Han Chinese migrants over the past 50 years. Today only about 4 million out of the 25 million residents of Inner Mongolia identify themselves as Mongols. There are still more Mongols in China than in Mongolia, as Mongolia's total population is less that 3 million.

Figure 10.13 Linguistic Geography of Central Asia
Most of Central Asia is dominated by languages in the Altaic family, which includes both the Turkic languages (found through most of the center and the west of the region) and Mongolian (found in Central Asia's northeast). Several Indo-European languages, however, are located in both the far northwestern and southcentral regions, while the Tibeto-Burman language of Tibetan covers most of the Tibetan Plateau in southeastern Central Asia.

Turkic Languages Far more Central Asians speak Turkic languages than Mongolian and Tibetan combined. Central Asia's Turkic linguistic sphere extends from Azerbaijan in the west through China's Xinjiang province in the east. The various Turkic languages are not as closely related to each other as are the dialects of Mongolian, but they are still obviously kindred tongues. Six main Turkic languages are found in Central Asia; five are associated with newly independent (former Soviet) republics of the west, while the sixth, Uyghur, is the main indigenous language of northwestern China.

Uyghur is an old and important language. The Uyghur number about 8 million, almost all of whom live in Xinjiang. As recently as 1949, the Uyghur formed about 90 percent of the population of Xinjiang; now, because of Han Chinese immigration, that figure has dropped to 45 percent. Eastern and northern Xinjiang are now largely Chinese-speaking. There are also about 1 million Kazakh speakers in far northern Xinjiang.

Of the six countries of the former Soviet Central Asia, five—Kazakhstan, Uzbekistan, Turkmenistan, Kyrgyzstan, and Azerbaijan—are named after the Turkic languages of their dominant populations. In three of these countries the indigenous people form a substantial majority. Some 82 percent of the people of Azerbaijan are classified as Azeri (there are more Azeris in northern Iran, however, than there are in Azerbaijan); some 80 percent of the people of Uzbekistan are classified as Uzbek; and some 77 percent of the people in Turkmenistan are classified as Turkmen. Most of these people speak their indigenous languages at home, although many Kazakhs are more comfortable speaking Russian than Kazakh.

With more than 23 million speakers, Uzbek is the most widely spoken Central Asian language. In the Amu Darya Delta in the far north of Uzbekistan, however, many people speak a Turkic language more closely related to Kazakh called Karakalpak. Kazakh speakers are widely scattered across Uzbekistan's sparsely populated deserts. Uzbekistan's older cities, such as Samarkand, are still partly Tajik (or Persian) speaking. Tajik activists, moreover, claim that the number of Tajik speakers in Uzbekistan is much greater than what the official statistics indicate, and that many local Tajiks have been pressured into assuming an Uzbek identity.

In the two other Turkic republics, the nationality for which the country is named forms less than two-thirds of the total population. Some 65 percent of the inhabitants of Kyrgyzstan are classified as Kyrgyz, while roughly 63 percent of the people of Kazakhstan are classified as Kazakh. The other residents of these countries identify themselves as Russians, Uzbeks, Ukrainians, and members of a wide assortment of other groups. In general, the Kazakhs and other Turkic peoples live in the center and south of Kazakhstan, while the people of European descent live in the agricultural districts of the north and in the cities of the southeast.

Linguistic Complexity in Tajikistan The sixth republic of the former Soviet Central Asia, Tajikistan, is dominated by people who speak an Indo-European rather than a Turkic language. Tajik is so closely related to Persian that it is considered to be a Persian (or Farsi) dialect. Roughly 5.8 million people in Tajikistan, about 80 percent of the total population, identify themselves as Tajiks. The remote mountains of eastern Tajikistan are populated by peoples speaking a variety of distinctive Indo-European languages, sometimes collectively referred to as "Mountain Tajik."

Tajikistan, like much of the rest of former Soviet portion of Central Asia, is noted for its complex mixture of language and ethnic groups. About 15 percent of its people, for example, are Uzbeks. Today ethnic suspicion pervades much of the region, in part because the governments of Tajikistan and Uzbekistan have poor relations. Before the Soviet period, however, mode of life was as important as language in determining identity; settled farmers and city-dwellers were usually classified as "Sarts" regardless of whether they spoke Tajik or a local Turkic language. Soviet planners essentially created the modern nationalities of Tajik and Uzbek, and they tried to force people into one category or the other. Because the two groups were generally mixed together, the Soviet Union also had to draw extremely convoluted boundaries around the republics of Uzbekistan and Tajikistan. The resulting political geography causes problems today for both countries.

Language and Ethnicity in Afghanistan The linguistic geography of Afghanistan is even more complex than that of Tajikistan (Figure 10.14). Afghanistan was never colonized by outside powers, and it is one of the few countries of the world to have inherited the

Figure 10.14 Afghanistan's Ethnolinguistic Patchwork
Afghanistan is one of the world's more ethnically complex countries. Its largest ethnic group is that of the Pashtuns, a people who inhabit most of the southern portion of the country as well as the adjoining borderlands of Pakistan. Northern Afghanistan is inhabited mostly by Uzbeks, Tajiks, and Turkmens—whose main population centers are located in Uzbekistan, Tajikistan, and Turkmenistan, respectively. The Hazaras of Afghanistan's central mountains, like the Tajiks, speak a form of Persian but are considered to be a separate ethnic group in part because they, unlike other Afghans, follow Shiite rather than Sunni Islam. Smaller groups are found elsewhere in the country.

boundaries of a premodern, indigenous kingdom. This kingdom emerged in the 1700s on traditional dynastic lines that did not reflect ethnic or linguistic divisions ("dynastic" linkages are those based on the family of the monarch). The modern nation-state ideal—that each country should be identified with a particular national group—was never very important in Afghanistan.

The 18th-century creators of Afghanistan were mostly members of the Pashtun ethnic group, but they did not attempt to build a nation-state around Pashtun identity. Indeed, more Pashtuns live in Pakistan than in Afghanistan. In Afghanistan, estimates of the proportion of the populace speaking the Pashto language of the Pashtuns vary from 40 to 60 percent. Most of them live to the south of the Hindu Kush Mountains.

Approximately half of the people of Afghanistan speak Dari, Afghanistan's variant of Persian, as their first language. Dari speakers are concentrated in the north. Three separate ethnicities are ascribed to the Dari-speaking people: the settled farmers and townspeople in the west and north are Tajiks; the traditionally seminomadic people of the west-center are Aimaks; and the East Asian–appearing villagers of the central mountains are Hazaras, reputed to be descendants of medieval Mongol conquerors. Although traditionally forming something of an underclass, Afghanistan's Hazaras are now showing more dedication to modern education than the country's other ethnic groups and as a result are beginning to prosper.

Although Pashto and Dari are Afghanistan's official languages, a variety of other languages are also spoken in the country, creating an especially complex ethnic patchwork. Approximately 11 percent of the people of Afghanistan speak Turkic languages, including both Uzbek and Turkmen. Other ethnolinguistic groups in Afghanistan include the Baluchis, the Nuristanis (who speak five separate languages), and the Pashai, all of whose languages are Indo-European, and the Brahui, who speak a Dravidian language related to the tongues of southern India.

Geography of Religion

An assortment of religions characterized ancient and medieval Central Asia. The major overland trading routes of premodern Eurasia crossed the region, giving easy access to both merchants and missionaries. Several varieties of Buddhism, Islam, Christianity, and Judaism, as well as several minor religions, have all thrived at various times and places within the region. Eventually, however, religious lines hardened, and Central Asia was divided into two opposed spiritual camps: Islam triumphed in the west and center (Figure 10.15), while Tibetan Buddhism prevailed in Tibet and Mongolia.

Islam in Central Asia As is true elsewhere in the Muslim world, different Central Asian peoples are known for their different interpretations of Islamic orthodoxy. The Pashtuns of Afghanistan are noted for their strict Islamic ideals—although critics contend that Pashtun religious practices,

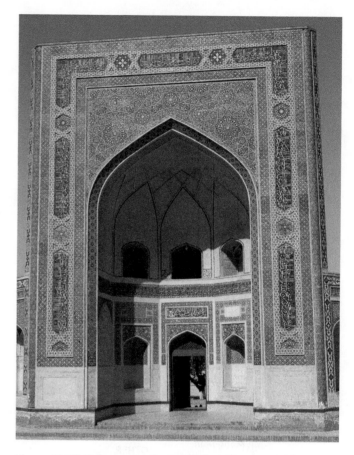

Figure 10.15 Entrance to the Poi-Kalyan Mosque, Bukhara, Uzbekistan With the exceptions of Tibet and Mongolia, most of Central Asia is religiously dominated by Islam. The mosque architecture of Central Asia's older cities, such as Bukhara in Uzbekistan, are noted for their striking architecture.

such as forbidding women's faces to be seen in public, are based mostly on their own customs (Figure 10.16). By contrast, the traditionally nomadic groups of the northern steppes, such as the Kazakhs, have historically been considered lax in their religious practices. Although most of the region's Muslims are Sunnis, Shiism is dominant among the Hazaras of central Afghanistan, the Azeris of Azerbaijan, and the mountain dwellers of eastern Tajikistan.

Under the communist rule of China, the Soviet Union, and Mongolia, all forms of religion were discouraged. Chinese authorities and student radicals suppressed Islam in Xinjiang during the Cultural Revolution of the late 1960s and early 1970s. Mosques were destroyed or converted to museums and religious schools were closed. Periodic persecution of Islam also occurred in Soviet Central Asia, and until the 1970s many observers thought that that religion was slowly diminishing throughout the region.

Religious expression was not so easily discouraged; however, interest in Islam began to grow in former Soviet Central Asia in the 1980s. In the post-Soviet period, Islam continues to revive as people reassert their indigenous heritage and identity. Thus far, however, signs of widespread Islamic political fundamentalism are few. Still, most Central

Figure 10.16 Afghan Women in Public Especially in the Pashtun areas of Afghanistan, women have traditionally been forced to cover their entire bodies when in public areas. In areas that were controlled by the Taliban, such dress codes were strictly enforced. Extremely modest dress still prevails in Afghanistan.

Asian leaders remain wary of any signs of radical Islamic practices. In 2005, for example, Tajikistan banned the wearing of Islamic head-scarves in public schools, and in 2009 it prohibited teachers under the age of 50 from growing beards. In response to widespread religious criticism, Tajikistan's government also banned revealing Western clothing styles—as well as graduation parties and the use of mobile phones and private cars at the country's secondary schools.

In China, Muslims now enjoy basic freedom of worship, but the state still closely monitors religious expression out of fear that it might become entangled with political separatism. Although some evidence suggests that Islam has served as a focal point of an anti-Chinese movement among the Uyghur people, most Uyghur leaders insist that their program is not radically fundamentalist. Still, ethnic relations in northwestern China remain very tense. In 2009, ethnic rioting pitting Uyghurs against Han Chinese took as many as 200 lives in Urumqi, the capital city of Xinjiang province.

In Afghanistan, however, Islamism (or politically radical Islamic fundamentalism) did emerge as a powerful political movement. From the mid-1990s until 2001, most of the country was controlled by the **Taliban**, an extremist organization that insisted that all aspects of society conform to its own harsh version of Islamic orthodoxy. This commitment was demonstrated in early 2001 when Afghanistan's religious authorities oversaw the destruction of Buddhist statues in the country—including some of the world's largest and most magnificent works of art—as symbols of a non-Islamic past. Although the Taliban regime fell in late 2001, Islamism remains a powerful force in Afghanistan, particularly among the Pashtun people of the south.

Islam is not the only religion represented in western Central Asia. Many Russians belong to the Russian Orthodox Church, and Uzbekistan has a small Jewish population. Kazakhstan also counts some 100,000 Catholics, mostly people of Polish or German descent.

Tibetan Buddhism Mongolia and Tibet stand apart from the rest of Central Asia in the adherence of their people to Tibetan Buddhism. Buddhism entered Tibet from India many centuries ago, where it merged with the indigenous religion of the area, called Bon. The resulting faith is more oriented toward mysticism than are other forms of Buddhism, and it is more hierarchically organized. Standing at the apex of Lamaist society is the Dalai Lama, considered to be a reincarnation of the **Bodhisattva** of Compassion (a Bodhisattva is a spiritual being who helps others attain enlightenment). Ranking below him is the Panchen Lama, followed by other religious officials. Until the Chinese conquest, Tibet was essentially a **theocracy**, or religious state, with the Dalai Lama enjoying political as well as religious authority. A substantial proportion of Tibet's male population has traditionally become monks, and monasteries once wielded both economic and political power (Figure 10.17).

Tibetan Buddhism suffered severe persecution in the 1960s. The Dalai Lama fled to India with many of his followers after China invaded Tibet in 1959, and has since been a powerful advocate for the Tibetan cause in international circles. During the 1960s and 1970s, an estimated 6,000 Tibetan Buddhist monasteries were destroyed and thousands of monks were killed. The number of active monks today is only about 5 percent of what it was before the Chinese occupation. Still, the Buddhist faith continues to form the basis of Tibetan identity, and in so doing helps keep alive the dream of independence or at least of real autonomy within China. In 2008, Tibetan monks led a series of protests against the Chinese government that resulted in ethnic riots between Tibetans and Han Chinese breaking out across the Tibetan Plateau. The Chinese government reacted harshly and later blamed the Dalai Lama for inciting the unrest.

Figure 10.17 Lamaist Buddhist Monastery Tibet is well known for its large Buddhist monasteries, buildings that in earlier years served as seats of political as well as religious authority. Lhasa's Jokhang Temple and Monastery, seen in this photograph, dates back to the 7th century.

In Mongolia the downfall of communism has allowed the Tibetan Buddhist faith to experience a renaissance. Several monasteries have been refurbished, and many people are returning to their national religion. The intensity of Buddhist belief, however, is not as strong in Mongolia as it is in Tibet. It is estimated that about half of the people of Mongolia actively follow the Buddhist religion today.

Central Asian Culture in International Context

During the Soviet period, the Russian language spread widely through western Central Asia. Russian served both as a common language and as a means of instruction in higher education. One had to be fluent in Russian in order to reach any position of responsibility. The Cyrillic (or Russian) script, moreover, replaced the modified Arabic script that was previously used for the indigenous languages. After the fall of the Soviet Union, however, most Russians migrated back to Russia, especially from the region's poorer countries. As a result, the use of Russian in education, government, business, and the media has declined in favor of local languages.

But despite its recent decline, Russian remains the common language of former Soviet Central Asia. Even some of the leaders of these countries speak their own languages imperfectly, and Russian is often the only way to communicate across Central Asia's national boundaries. The continuing

prominence of Russia, however, irritates many people. Kazakh nationalists, for example, are upset that Russian remains the country's "official language of communication between different ethnic groups." In early 2010, hundreds of Kazakh students protested their country's language laws, demanding that governmental meetings, sessions of parliament, and presidential speeches be conducted only in Kazakh. In 2007, Tajikistan ordered its citizens to change their names if they sounded too Russian, and in 2009 it announced plans to ban the use of Russian in advertising, business communication, and governmental documents.

Although Central Asia is remote and poorly integrated into global cultural circuits, it is hardly immune to the forces of globalization (Figure 10.18). Even the tensions existing throughout the region between religious and secular orientations, and between ethnic nationalism and multiethnic inclusion, are aspects of the current global condition. So, too, the increased usage of English throughout Central Asia shows that this part of the world is not cut off from global culture. Such influences are especially marked in the oil cities of the Caspian Basin, such as Azerbaijan's Baku.

GEOPOLITICAL FRAMEWORK: Political Reawakening in a Power Void

Central Asia has played a minor role in global political affairs for the past 300 years. Before 1991 the entire region, except Mongolia and Afghanistan, lay under direct Soviet or Chinese control. Mongolia, moreover, was a Soviet satellite, and even Afghanistan came under Soviet domination in the late 1970s. The breakup of the Soviet Union, however, saw the emergence of six new countries, helping to reestablish Central Asia as a world region (Figure 10.19).

Partitioning of the Steppes

Before the 1700s, Central Asia had been a power center whose mobile armies threatened the far more populous, sedentary peoples of the Eurasian rim. Military developments, however, changed the balance of power, allowing the wealthier agricultural states to defeat the nomadic pastoralists and take over their lands by the late 1700s. The winners in this struggle were the two largest states bordering the steppes: Russia and China.

The Manchu conquest of China in 1644 undercut the autonomy of the peoples of the eastern steppe. The Manchus came from Manchuria, the eastern borderlands of Central Asia, and were themselves skilled in the arts of cavalry warfare. By the late 1700s China stood at its greatest territorial extent. Within its grasp lay not only Mongolia and Xinjiang but also Tibet and a slice of modern Kazakhstan. Although Manchu-ruled China declined rapidly after 1800, it was still able to retain most of its Central Asian territories. But by the early 1900s, Chinese authority had begun to diminish in Central Asia as well. When the Manchu (also called Ch'ing or Qing) dynasty fell in 1912, Mongolia became independ-

Figure 10.18 U.S.-Style Restaurant in Baku, Azerbaijan. Baku is a vibrant and increasingly cosmopolitan city closely linked to global economic and cultural networks. The coffee shop and wine bar seen in this photograph caters to both local and international tourists.

Figure 10.19 Central Asian Geopolitics Six of the eight independent states of Central Asia came into existence in 1991 with the dissolution of the Soviet Union. In eastern Central Asia, the most serious difficulties stem from China's maintenance of control over areas in which the indigenous peoples are not Chinese. Afghanistan, scene of a prolonged and brutal civil war, has experienced the most extreme forms of geopolitical tension in the region.

ent, although China did keep the extensive borderlands of Inner Mongolia (Nei Mongol). Tibet had earlier gained de facto independence, and even Xinjiang lay beyond the reach of effective Chinese authority during the 1920s.

Russia began to advance into Central Asia at roughly the same time as China. In the 1700s the Russian Empire undertook the systematic conquest of the Kazakh steppe. Expansion farther to the south, however, was blocked by the agricultural states of Uzbekistan. Only in the late 1800s, when European military techniques and materials raced ahead of those of Asia, was Russia able to conquer the Amu Darya and Syr Darya valleys. Its subjugation of this area was not completed until the early 1900s, just before the Soviet Union replaced the Russian Empire. The Russians advanced

into Central Asia in part because of their concern over possible British influence in the area. Britain attempted to conquer Afghanistan, but was rebuffed by Afghan forces—and by the country's forbidding terrain. Subsequently, Afghanistan's position as an independent "buffer state" between the Russian Empire (later the Soviet Union) and the British Empire in South Asia remained secure.

Central Asia Under Communist Rule

Western Central Asia came under communist rule soon after the foundation of the Soviet Union in 1917, with Mongolia following in 1924. After the Chinese revolution of 1949, the communist system was imposed on Xinjiang, Tibet, and

Inner Mongolia. In all of these areas, major changes in the geopolitical order soon followed.

Soviet Central Asia

Although the Soviet Union inherited the Russian imperial domain in Central Asia virtually intact, it enacted new policies. The Soviet regime sought to create a socialist economy and to build a new society that would eventually knit together all of the massive territories of the country. Central Asia's leaders were replaced by Communist Party officials loyal to the new state; Russian immigration was encouraged; and local languages could no longer be written in Arabic script.

Although Soviet authorities foresaw the emergence of a single Soviet nationality, they realized that local ethnic diversity would not disappear overnight. Early Soviet leaders such as Vladimir Lenin also hoped to insulate non-Russian peoples from Russian domination. The Soviet Union therefore divided the Soviet Union into a series of nationally defined "union republics" in which a certain degree of cultural autonomy would be allowed. They were uncertain, however, what the relevant units in Central Asia should be. Was there a single Turkic-speaking nationality, or were the Turkic peoples divided into a number of separate nationalities, with the Tajiks forming yet another? For several years boundaries shifted as new "republics" appeared on the map. Finally, in the 1920s the modern republics of Kazakhstan, Kyrgyzstan, Tajikistan, Uzbekistan, Turkmenistan, and Azerbaijan assumed their present configurations. In certain areas, such as the fertile Fergana Valley, the political boundaries so drawn remained extremely complex (Figure 10.20).

Some scholars argue that the Soviet nationalities policy backfired severely. Rather than forming a transitional step on the way to a Soviet identity, the constituent republics of the Soviet Union nurtured local nationalisms that ultimately undermined the Soviet system. Identities such as Turkmen, Uzbek, and Tajik that had been vague in the pre-Soviet period were now given real political significance. Another problem undercutting Soviet unity was the fact that the cultural and economic gaps separating Central Asians from Russians did not diminish as much as planned.

The Chinese Geopolitical Order

After China reemerged as a united country in 1949, it too was able to reclaim most of its old Central Asia territories. China's communist leaders promised the non-Chinese peoples a significant degree of political self-determination and cultural autonomy, and thus found much local support in Xinjiang. Tibet, isolated behind its mountain walls and virtually independent for many years, presented a greater obstacle. China occupied Tibet in 1950, but the Tibetans launched a rebellion in 1959. When the rebellion was crushed, the Dalai Lama and some 100,000

Figure 10.20 Political Boundaries Around the Fergana Valley Some of the world's most convoluted political boundaries can be found in the vicinity of the Fergana Valley. The central portion of the valley belongs to Uzbekistan, which is otherwise separated from it by high mountains. The lower valley, on the other hand, is part of Tajikistan, the core area of which is likewise separated from the valley by highlands. The Fergana's upper periphery belongs to Kyrgyzstan. Note also the small exclaves of Uzbekistan within Kyrgyzstan.

followers found refuge in India, where they maintain the "Tibetan Government in Exile."

Loosely following the Soviet nationalities model, China established autonomous regions in areas occupied primarily by non-Han Chinese peoples, including Xinjiang, Tibet proper (called Xizang in Chinese), and Inner Mongolia. Such autonomy, however, often turned out to be more symbolic than real, and it did not prevent the massive immigration of Han Chinese into these areas. Nor were all parts of Chinese Central Asia granted autonomous status. The large and historically Tibetan and Mongolian province of Qinghai, for example, remained an ordinary Chinese province.

Current Geopolitical Tension

Although the former Soviet portion of Central Asia weathered the post-1991 transition to independence relatively smoothly (Figure 10.21), the region suffers from a number of ethnic conflicts as well as from the struggle between radical Islam and secular governments. Much of China's Central Asian territory is troubled, but China retains a firm grip. Such troubles are insignificant, however, compared to what is faced by Afghanistan, where brutal warfare has been going on for decades.

Independence in Former Soviet Lands After 1991, the six newly independent countries of the former Soviet Union did not find it easy to chart their own political courses. They still had to cooperate with Russia on security issues, and all initially opted to join the Commonwealth of Independent States, the rather hollow successor of the Soviet Union. In most cases authoritarian rulers, rooted in the old order, retained power and sought to undermine opposition groups. All told, democracy made less progress in Central Asia than in other parts of the former Soviet Union. Kyrgyzstan seemed to form an exception to this pattern, especially in 2005 when citizens protesting corruption and authoritarianism forced the country's president out of office. Kyrgyzstan's new government, however, quickly followed in the footsteps of the old, resulting in renewed protest and unrest. In April 2010, demonstrators again brought down the government, forcing Kyrgyzstan's president to flee. Three months later, massive ethnic riots broke out in southern Kyrgyzstan as supporters of the country's ousted president attacked ethnic Uzbeks. As many as 2,000 people were killed in the rioting, and up to 300,000 were displaced.

Kazakhstan, Tajikistan, and Azerbaijan faced particular difficulties in the post-Soviet transition. Many Kazakhs wanted to create a national state centered on Kazakh identity, and they resented the presence and power of Russians and other peoples of European background. These Europeans feared what they considered alien Central Asian cultural standards, and for a time there was some concern that northern Kazakhstan, the country's breadbasket, might attempt to join Russia. In the late 1990s, Kazakhstan moved its capital from Almaty in the south to Astana in the Russian-dominated north, partly to forestall any plans for seces-

Figure 10.21 The End of Soviet Rule in Central Asia An old Tajik man looks over a toppled and decapitated statute of Lenin, founder of the Soviet Union, in Dushanbe in 1991. When the Soviet Union collapsed in that year, many emblems of the old regime were destroyed immediately.

sion. The continued out-migration of Russians and other Europeans from Kazakhstan, however, has gradually made this issue irrelevant.

In Tajikistan war broke out almost immediately after independence in 1991. Many members of the smaller ethnic groups of the mountainous east resented the authority of the Tajiks and thus rebelled. They were joined by Islamist groups seeking to overthrow the secular state. The civil war was officially ended in 1997 when the Islamists agreed to work through normal political channels. However, continuing instability led Tajikistan's government to increase its pressure on the Islamic Renaissance Party, the only legal Islamist party in former Soviet Central Asia. The Islamic Renaissance Party responded by modernizing its image to appeal to educated people, youth, and women, but in the 2010 elections it received only 8 percent of the vote.

Azerbaijan also experienced strife following the breakup of the Soviet Union. Armenia invaded and occupied a portion of far-western Azerbaijan, allowing the Armenian-speaking highlands to form the "breakaway republic" of Nagorno-Karabakh. Hostile relations with Armenia make it difficult for Azerbaijan to govern its **exclave** of Nakhchivan, a piece of Azerbaijani territory separated from the rest of the country by Armenia and Iran. The situation remains tense; as recently as 2008, military skirmishes were taking place along the border between Azerbaijan and Nagorno-Karabakh.

Although Uzbekistan and Turkmenistan had relatively easy transitions out of the Soviet Union, both countries are ruled by repressive governments that allow little room for personal freedom or opposition movements. Uzbekistan has recently increased its censorship of the news and cracked down on human rights. Until his death in late 2006, Turkmenistan's authoritarian president, Saparmurat Niyazov—who called himself simply "Turkmenbashi" ("father of the Turkmens")—maintained a lavish personality cult, forcing all students in his country to read and honor his lengthy book on Turkmen history, philosophy, and mythology. Since Niyazov's death, Turkmenistan has gradually reduced its restrictions on daily life while tentatively opening up to the outside world. By 2010, for example, it had allowed the re-opening of cinemas, theaters, and circuses, all of which had previously been banned as representing "alien culture."

Strife in Western China Local opposition to Chinese rule is pronounced in many of the region's indigenous communities. Protests by Tibetans have not been successful, but they have brought the attention of the world to their struggle. China maintains several hundred thousand troops in a region that has only 2.8 million civilian inhabitants. Such an overwhelming military presence is considered necessary because of both Tibetan resistance and the strategic importance of the region. Massive Tibetan protests in 2008 were handled harshly by the Chinese government; in 2009, four Tibetan activists were executed for inciting the unrest, and an estimated 670 were imprisoned.

China's control of Xinjiang is more secure than its hold on Tibet. Although fragmented by deserts and mountains, Xinjiang's terrain is less forbidding than that of Tibet and it is now the home of millions of Han Chinese immigrants. Xinjiang is also an economically vital part of China. It contains a variety of mineral deposits (including oil) essential for Chinese industry, and it has been the site of nuclear weapons tests. Many Uyghurs, not surprisingly, oppose such uses of their homeland, and they resent the periodic suppression of their religion by the communist regime. Ethnic strife between Han Chinese and Uyghurs resulted in massive unrest in 2009, leading to a number of deaths and large-scale destruction of property (Figure 10.22).

China's position is that all of its Central Asian lands are integral portions of its national territory. Those who advocate independence are viewed as traitors and are sometimes considered to be in league with Western political forces that have sought to keep China weak and divided for the past 200 years.

War in Afghanistan None of the conflicts elsewhere in Central Asia compares in intensity to the situation in Afghanistan. Afghanistan's troubles began in 1978 when a Soviet-supported military "revolutionary council" seized power. The new Marxist-oriented government suppressed religion, which resulted in rebellion. When the government was about to collapse, the Soviet Union launched a massive invasion. Despite its power, the Soviet military was never able to gain control of the more rugged parts of the country. Moreover, Pakistan, Saudi Arabia, and the United States ensured that the anti-Soviet forces remained well armed and financed.

The exhausted Soviets finally withdrew their troops in 1989. The puppet government that they installed remained to face the insurgents alone. It managed to hold the country's core around the city of Kabul for a few years, largely because the opposition forces were themselves divided. Local warlords grabbed power in the countryside, destroying any semblance of central authority. Warlords and their forces

Figure 10.22 Ethnic Tension in Xinjiang In 2009, ethnic rioting pitting the indigenous Uyghurs against Han Chinese immigrants broke out in a number of cities in Xinjiang. Chinese security forces reacted harshly to Uyghur protesters.

committed many atrocities, including the shelling of civilian areas, the abduction of noncombatants, and the mass raping of women from enemy communities.

In 1995–96, the Taliban arrived on the Afghan scene. The Taliban was founded by young Muslim religious students disgusted with the anarchy that was consuming their country. They were convinced that only the firm imposition of Islamic law could end corruption and quell the disputes among the country's different ethnic groups. With large numbers of soldiers flocking to their standard and with military support from Pakistan, the Taliban won control of most of Afghanistan by the late 1990s. As their own power grew more secure, they offered refuge in Afghanistan to the radical Islamist organization Al Qaeda, led by Osama bin Laden.

The Taliban acquired power not only from its religious nature, but also from the ethnic divisions of Afghanistan. It gained most of its strength from the Pashtuns of the southern half of the country. The Pashtuns have a reputation for militarism, as well as good connections for military supplies among their relatives across the Pakistan border. The main opposition to the Taliban came from the country's other ethnic groups, especially the Uzbeks and Tajiks of the north and the Shiite Hazaras of the central mountains.

By the end of the century, most of the people of Afghanistan lost faith in the Taliban, largely because of the severe restrictions imposed on daily life. Such constraints were most pronounced for women, but even men were compelled to obey the Taliban's numerous decrees. Most forms of recreation were outlawed, including television, films, music, and even kite-flying. Little escaped the watchful eyes of the Taliban's religious police.

The aftermath of September 11, 2001, completely changed the balance of power in the region. The United States and Britain, working closely with anti-Taliban groups concentrated in northern Afghanistan, launched a war against Al Qaeda and the Taliban government. Within a few months, formal Taliban power collapsed, allowing the emphasis to shift to rebuilding Afghanistan's institutions and establishing an effective central government. Such projects were not very successful, however, as governmental corruption and ethnic animosity have prevented Afghanistan from becoming a stable country. By 2004, the Taliban had regrouped, operating from safe havens in Pakistan tribal areas (see Chapter 12).

Afghanistan's new government has had to rely on the military power of the North Atlantic Treaty Organization (NATO)-led International Security Assistance Force (ISAF). But despite its more than 58,000 troops, the ISAF has been unable to stop the Taliban resurgence (Figure 10.23). By 2008, many observers feared that Afghanistan was on the verge of becoming a failed state, and in 2009, the new administration of the United States responded by sending an additional 17,000 troops to the country. Early 2010 saw major offensives against Taliban strongholds in the Kandahar area. U.S. forces have also targeted high-level Taliban leaders, often by bombing their compounds. This strategy has weakened the Taliban command structure but has also resulted in large numbers of civilian casualties, reducing local support for the war effort. Although many areas of northern Afghanistan are relatively secure, the south remains an extremely dangerous and battle-scarred war zone.

Global Dimensions of Central Asian Geopolitics

As the previous discussion indicates, Central Asia has recently emerged as a key arena of geopolitical tension. Vying for power and influence in the region are a number of important countries, including China, Russia, Pakistan, India, Iran, Turkey, and the United States. In addition, the revival of Islam has generated international geopolitical repercussions.

A Continuing U.S. Role   Afghanistan is not the only Central Asian country to have experienced a substantial U.S. armed presence. After 9/11, the United States established military operations in Uzbekistan, Tajikistan, and Kyrgyzstan (see "Exploring Global Connections: Foreign Military

Bases in Central Asia"). These countries were eager to host the U.S. military because they feared that Islamic fundamentalist movements could overthrow their governments. Already by the late 1990s, the Islamic Movement in Uzbekistan (IMU), a group dedicated initially to the creation of an Islamic state in the Fergana Valley, was engaging the armies of Uzbekistan, Tajikistan, and Kyrgyzstan. As a result, military budgets increased throughout the region, straining governmental finances but also allowing Central Asian governments to get an upper hand on the IMU. The IMU suffered a major blow in early 2007 when a contingent of its fighters operating out of northern Pakistan had a falling-out with local Pashtun tribes, resulting in battles that left over 300 Uzbek militants dead. By 2010, experts had concluded that the IMU was no longer operating in former Soviet Central Asia

Since 2005, the influence of the United States has declined across much of the former Soviet portion of Central Asia. Mongolia, however, has sought closer ties with the United States (as well as with Japan), due largely to its concerns about falling under the influence of China or Russia.

Relations with China and Russia   After the breakup of the Soviet Union, relations between the newly independent countries of Central Asia and China remained tense for a number of years. China objected to the boundary lines separating it from Tajikistan and Kyrgyzstan and asked for adjustments. These boundary disputes were peacefully settled in the early years of the new millennium, with Kyrgyzstan ceding 222,400 acres (90,000 hectares) of disputed land to China. China subsequently initiated a series of diplomatic maneuvers designed to quell tensions, fight Islamic separatism, and gain greater access to the natural resources of Central Asia.

After the fall of the Soviet Union, Russia continued to regard all of the former Soviet territories of Central Asia as lying within its sphere of influence, and as such has resented U.S. military initiatives. Russia has, moreover, retained or built military bases of its own in both Tajikistan and Kyr-

Figure 10.23 War in Afghanistan   Warfare continues in Afghanistan as troops from the United States and other countries attempt to root out remnants of the Taliban and maintain order. Tense encounters with local residents often result when foreign soldiers search for weapons and insurgent fighters.

EXPLORING GLOBAL CONNECTIONS · Foreign Military Bases in Central Asia

After the downfall of the Soviet Union, Russia sought to keep its strategic influence in Central Asia's newly independent countries. The Russian military has thus maintained installations in Azerbaijan and Kazakhstan, while in Tajikistan it retains a division of ground forces as well as a large airbase. After the United States built the Manas Air Base in Kyrgyzstan in 2001 to support its war in Afghanistan (Figure 10.5.1), Russia responded by constructing a new air force station only a few miles away from the American facility.

Outside Afghanistan, the United States has been less successful than Russia in maintaining its military influence. In 2001, the U.S. military established a sizable air base in eastern Uzbekistan, but in 2005, Uzbekistan ordered it to be shut down after the U.S. government harshly criticized that country for its violent response to an anti-government protest. In February 2009, the parliament of Kyrgyzstan voted overwhelmingly to expel U.S. forces from Manas Air Base. This move came after Russia agreed to provide Kyrgyzstan with $2 billion in new loans and $150 million in direct financial aid. Four months later, however, the government of Kyrgyzstan agreed that the United States could continue to use the facility in exchange for tripling its rent payments and referring to it as a "transit center" rather than an "air base." After the collapse of Kyrgyzstan's government in April 2010, some of the country's new leaders expressed anger at the United States, arguing that the U.S. had tolerated the corruption of the previous regime so long as it allowed the base to operate. After some negotiations, however, Kyrgyzstan agreed that the Manas facility could continue to operate for the time being.

Pakistan's military has also long been interested in extending its power into Central Asia, leading it to support the Taliban's efforts to rule Afghanistan before September 11, 2001. Pakistan's maneuvering, in turn, has prompted India to seek influence in the region. In 2004, the governments of India and Tajikistan ratified an agreement allowing India to construct an air base 80 miles (130 kilometers) south of Tajikistan's capital city, and only 1.2 miles (2 kilometers) from the Afghan border. Fully operational since 2007, the Farkhor Air Base, India's only foreign military installation, is thought to hold roughly dozen MiG-29 fighter-bombers. Pakistan, not surprisingly, sees this base as part of an Indian effort to surround Pakistan with hostile forces.

The expulsion of U.S. military bases from Uzbekistan and especially Kyrgyzstan has complicated the war effort in Afghanistan, as have continuing Indian–Pakistani competition and maneuvering in the region. Historians describe competing British and Russian efforts to gain influence in Central Asia in the late 1800s as the "Great Game"; some observers now argue that a "New Great Game" in the region will result in complex geopolitical tensions for some time to come.

Figure 10.5.1 Manas Transit Center A soldier is seen near the entrance of the Manas Transit Center, formerly called the Manas Air Base, in Kyrgyzstan.

gyzstan. Economics and infrastructure also tie Russia to the former Soviet Central Asian sphere. The main transportation line linking European Russia to central Siberia, for example, cuts across northern Kazakhstan, while former Soviet Central Asia's rail and pipeline links to the outside world are still largely oriented toward Russia. Kazakhstan also contains the huge Baikonur Cosmodrome, Russia's main site for rocket launches.

In the early years of the new millennium, most Central Asian leaders concluded that the potential economic and political advantages to be gained by cooperation with Russia and China outweighed the disadvantages. The major consequence of this attitude was the formation of the **Shanghai Cooperation Organization** (or SCO, commonly referred to as the "Shanghai Six"), composed of China, Russia, Kazakhstan, Kyrgyzstan, Tajikistan, and Uzbek-

Figure 10.24 Meeting of the Shanghai Cooperation Organization The leaders of the six countries that make up the Shanghai Cooperation Organization have gathered together to discuss their common concerns. Pictured here are the leaders (or former leaders) of Russia, China, Kazakhstan, Kyrgyzstan, Tajikistan, and Uzbekistan.

istan (Figure 10.24). The SCO seeks cooperation on such security issues as terrorism and separatism, aims to enhance trade, and serves as a counterbalance against the United States. Although not a member, Mongolia does have "observer" status in the SCO (as do Iran, Pakistan, and India); Turkmenistan, on the other hand, has rejected membership. By 2010, some observers were arguing that economic competition between Russia and China would weaken the Shanghai Cooperation Organization, reducing Russian influence in the region. They noted that none of the Central Asian countries supported Russia when it invaded Georgia in 2008, just as none has recognized the independence of the breakaway republics of South Ossetia and Abkhazia.

The Roles of Iran, Pakistan, and Turkey Iran is also interested in the new republics of Central Asia. It is a major trading partner, and it offers a good potential route to the ocean. Since the completion of a rail link between Iran and Turkmenistan in the late 1990s, some of Central Asia's global trade has been reoriented toward Iran's ports. Iran's cultural links with the region are old and deep, particularly in Tajikistan and northern Afghanistan. The Iranian government has gained some influence in Afghanistan, especially in the western region of Herat and among the Shiite Hazaras. Iran's relations with Azerbaijan, on the other hand, remain tense, in part because many Azerbaijanis refer to northwestern Iran—an Azeri-speaking region—as "Southern Azerbaijan."

Pakistan has also strived to gain influence in Central Asia, hoping that pipelines will eventually carry Central Asian oil and natural gas to its new deep-water port at Gwadar. Any such pipelines, however, would have to pass through the rugged topography and perilous political environment of Afghanistan. During the Taliban period, Pak-

istan enjoyed close relations with Afghanistan's government. The aftermath of 9/11 thus put Pakistan in a serious bind. In response to both U.S. pressure and promises, Pakistan joined the anti-Taliban coalition and supplied the U.S. military with valuable intelligence. The subsequent retreat of the Taliban into northwestern Pakistan, however, has resulted in extremely tense relations between the two countries.

Turkey's connections with Central Asia are potentially close. Most Central Asians speak Turkic languages, while Turkey also offers itself as the model—contrary to those of Iran and Pakistan—of the modern, secular state of Muslim heritage. It is unclear, however, whether the Turkish system can be exported easily, even to other Turkic-speaking states. But if Central Asia were to experience substantial Western-oriented economic growth, it seems likely that its relations with Turkey would strengthen.

ECONOMIC AND SOCIAL DEVELOPMENT: Abundant Resources, Struggling Economies

By most measures, Central Asia is one of the poorer regions of the world. Afghanistan in particular stands near the bottom of almost every list of economic and social indicators. Other Central Asian countries, however, have enjoyed relatively high levels of health and education, a legacy of the social programs enacted by their former communist regimes. These same governments, however, built inefficient economic systems, and after the fall of the Soviet Union, western Central Asia experienced a spectacular economic decline. Although much of the region is now economically expanding, growth has been largely based on the extraction of natural resources, particularly oil and natural gas.

Economic Development in Central Asia

Soviet economic planners sought to spread the benefits of economic development widely across their country. This required building large factories even in remote areas such as Tajikistan regardless of the costs involved. Such Central Asian industries relied heavily on subsidies from the Soviet central government. When those subsidies ended, the industrial base of the region began to collapse, leading to plummeting living standards. But as is true elsewhere in the former Soviet Union, certain well-connected individuals have grown very wealthy since the fall of communism. The growing gap between the rich and the poor remains a major concern across most of Central Asia.

The Postcommunist Economies As Table 10.2 shows, no Central Asian country or region could be considered prosperous by global standards. Kazakhstan generally stands as the most developed, and it probably has the best prospects. Kazakhstan has two of the world's largest underutilized deposits of oil and natural gas, the vast Tengiz and Kashagan fields in the northeastern Caspian Basin (Figure 10.25), as well

TABLE 10.2 Development Indicators

Country	GNI per Capita, PPP 2008	GDP Average Annual % Growth 2000–08	Human Development Index (2007)[1]	Percent Population Living Below $2 a Day	Life Expectancy (2010)[2]	Under Age 5 Mortality Rate (1990)	Under Age 5 Mortality Rate (2008)	Gender Equity[3] (2008)
Afghanistan	1,110	11.8	0.352		44	260	257	58
Azerbaijan	7,770	18.1	0.787	<2	72	98	36	98
Kazakhstan	9,710	9.5	0.804	<2	69	60	30	98
Kyrgyzstan	2,150	4.4	0.710	27.5	68	75	38	100
Mongolia	3,470	7.8	0.727	13.6	67	98	41	104
Tajikistan	1,860	8.6	0.688	50.8	67	117	64	91
Turkmenistan	6,120	14.5	0.739	49.6	65	99	48	
Uzbekistan	2,660	6.6	0.710		68	79	38	98

Source: World Bank, World Development Indicators, 2010 World Data Sheet, 2007; gender equity data from Millennium Development Goals.

[1]United Nations, Human Development Report, 2009.

[2]Population Referene Bureau, World Population Data Sheet, 2010.

[3]Gender Equity—Ratio of female to male enrollments in primary and secondary school. Numbers below 100 have more males in primary/secondary school, numbers above 100 have more females in primary/secondary school.

Figure 10.25 Development Issues: Human Development in Central Asia Levels of social development vary significantly across Central Asia. As this Human Development Index map shows, Afghanistan ranks as one of the least developed countries in the world, whereas both Azerbaijan and Kazakhstan rank relatively high.

Figure 10.26 Oil Development in Azerbaijan Although oil has brought a certain amount of wealth to Azerbaijan, it has also resulted in extensive pollution and visual blight. Because most of the petroleum is located either near or under the Caspian Sea, this sea—actually the world's largest lake—is now ecologically endangered.

as sizable deposits of other minerals. Kazakhstan has signed agreements with Western oil companies to exploit its oil reserves, and has received major investments from China. Between 2001 and 2008, Kazakhstan's oil and gas wealth led to one of the world's fastest growing economies, with annual growth averaging more than 8 percent. Like much of the rest of the world, Kazakhstan experienced an economic decline in 2009, but growth resumed in 2010.

Owing to its sizable population, Uzbekistan has the second largest economy in the region. Uzbekistan did not decline as sharply as its neighbors after the fall of the Soviet Union, largely because it retained many aspects of the old command economy (that is, an economy run by governmental planners rather than by private firms responding to the market). Uzbekistan remains the world's second largest exporter of cotton, and it has significant gold and natural gas deposits. However, environmental degradation threatens cotton production, and both inefficient state management and widespread corruption continue to hamper production.

Kyrgyzstan, in contrast, moved aggressively after the fall of the Soviet Union to privatize former state-run industries. Along with Mongolia, it is Central Asia's only member of the World Trade Organization (WTO). But Kyrgyzstan's economy is heavily agricultural, few of its industries are competitive, and political strife has discouraged foreign investment. Kyrgyzstan does, however, enjoy the largest supply of freshwater in Central Asia, which will likely become increasingly valuable in years to come, and its mineral reserves are substantial. Gold exports are particularly important; when gold exports slump, as they did in 2009, Kyrgyzstan experiences economic hardship. Political instability in early 2010 also hurt the country's economy.

Turkmenistan also has a substantial agricultural base, due mainly to Soviet irrigation projects, and it remains a major cotton exporter. It retains a state-run economy and has resisted pressure for economic liberalization. Government planners hope that the development of new oil and gas fields will bring prosperity. China has invested heavily, completing the Central Asia-China Gas Pipeline, which runs from Turkmenistan through Uzbekistan and Kazakhstan, in December 2009. In the same year, China lent Turkmenistan $3 billion to develop new natural gas fields.

Central Asia's oldest fossil fuel industry is located in Azerbaijan (Figure 10.26). Azerbaijan has attracted a great deal of international interest and investment, promising to revitalize its oil industry. Through the 1990s, however, its economy responded slowly, and Azerbaijan remains a poor country. In 2006, however, its oil-fueled economy reportedly grew by 34 percent, the fastest rate of expansion in the world. Even in the recession year of 2009, Azerbaijan's economy managed to expand by 9.3 percent. Critics, however, say that the country has not enacted adequate market reforms and remains far too dependent on its oil industry.

The most economically troubled of the former Soviet republics is Tajikistan. With a per capita GNI of only some $1,860, Tajikistan is poor indeed. It is burdened by its remote location, rugged topography, a lack of natural resources, and political strife. Almost half of Tajikistan's labor force works abroad, mostly in Russia and Kazakhstan, supporting the local economy through their remittances. Tajikistan's government hopes to revive its fortunes by opening new transportation routes to China and by further developing its generation of hydroelectricity. A large new dam was finished in 2009, and others are under construction. Enhanced electricity supplies are allowing

GLOBAL TO LOCAL   The Mongolian Cashmere Industry Readjusts

For centuries, Mongolia has produced high-quality cashmere textiles derived from the soft undercoat of a particular variety of goat. Areas with particularly cold winters—such as Mongolia—produce especially soft and luxurious fibers. Herders in southern Mongolia have relied for hundreds of years on cashmere for their cash needs, raising small herds of goats in a sustainable manner and laboriously combing out the underfur of their animals each spring (Figure 10.6.1).

From the 1920s until 1990, most of Mongolia's goat herds were collectively owned, the cashmere fibers being transformed into tex-

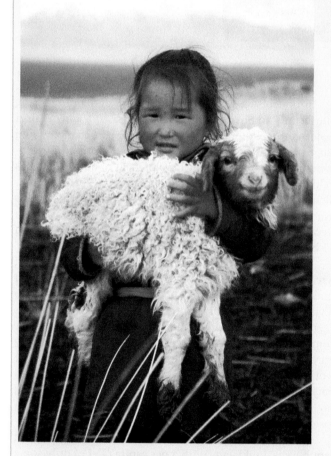

Figure 10.6.1 Mongolia's Cashmere Industry A girl holding a young goat in southern Mongolia.

tiles in state-owned factories. Everything changed, however, when communism collapsed. As unemployment skyrocketed, tens of thousands of urban Mongolians returned to the countryside to herd goats, figuring that they could always earn cash by selling cashmere. Lacking experience, however, many of these new herders stocked too many goats, leading to serious overgrazing hence the degradation of pasturelands. When a series of dry summers followed by brutally cold winters hit in 2000 and 2001, millions of goats died, forcing many of the new cashmere producers back into the urban economy.

Economic as well as environmental disorder has plagued Mongolia's cashmere industry after the fall of communism. In the early 1990s, Mongolia's government sought to earn more foreign exchange by developing a larger textile industry, and was distressed that many herders were sending their cashmere combings to Chinese mills for processing. In 1994, Mongolia banned the export of raw cashmere, resulting in the rapid opening of 50 new Mongolian textile factories. In the following year, however, the Asian Development Bank informed Mongolia that essential new loans would be held back until the ban—regarded by the bank as anticompetitive—was dropped. Mongolia soon complied, putting its newly revived cashmere textile industry in deep trouble.

To revive its cashmere trade, Mongolia needed a new strategy. One problem was that its own textile styles were out-of-date, tending toward neon colors and stodgy designs from the 1950s. In response, a number of local firms joined together under the banner of the Mongolian Fibermark Society and sought assistance from international development organizations. When the United States Agency for International Development (USAID) began an economic reform initiative in Mongolia in 2003, the cashmere producers eagerly sought its support. By 2005, USAID was helping connect Mongolian producers with buyers in wealthy countries and providing information about the kinds of cashmere textiles that would satisfy demanding consumers in North America, Europe, and East Asia.

Within a year, these efforts appeared to be bearing fruit. In early 2006, the Mongolian Fibermark Society's exhibition at a Las Vegas textile trade fair generated considerable interest, as did an exhibit in New York in early 2007. It is still difficult, however, for Mongolia's cashmere textile manufacturers to compete with those of China, just as it is still hard for Mongolia's goat herders to earn a consistent income in an area noted for its periodic droughts and harsh winters. In April 2010, another cause for concern emerged when China announced that it had cloned goats genetically engineered to produce woollier coats.

Tajikistan to expand its aluminum smelting, one of its few competitive industries.

Mongolia, although never part of the Soviet Union, was a close Soviet ally run by a communist party. It too suffered an economic collapse in the 1990s when Soviet subsidies came to an end. (See "Global to Local: The Mongolian Cashmere Industry Readjusts") Mongolia thus emerged in the postcom-

munist period as a poor country. During the early 2000s, however, major mining investments by both Chinese and Western firms resulted in rapid economic expansion. In early 2010, international companies reached an agreement with the Mongolian government to develop the massive Oyu Tolgoi copper-gold project; with production scheduled to begin in 2013, it will be one of the world's largest mines. The mining boom, however, has generated problems of its own. Many Mongolians fear that their Chinese mining companies have too much power. Small-scale, unlicensed "ninja miners," moreover, have caused a significant amount of local environmental degradation.

The Economy of Western China The Chinese portions of Central Asia did not suffer the same economic crash that visited other parts of the region with the fall of the Soviet Union. China has one of the world's fastest-growing economies, although its centers of dynamism are located in the distant coastal zone. Still, even the more remote parts of the country have experienced a significant degree of development in recent years. From 2003 to 2008, Inner Mongolia's economy expanded at a scorching annual rate of around 20 percent, owing in large part to its extensive deposits of rare earth minerals and other valuable mineral resources.

Tibet in particular remains burdened by poverty. Most of the plateau is relatively cut off from the Chinese economy and is even more isolated from the global economy. Hoping to reduce Tibetan separatism, China has been investing large amounts of money in infrastructure projects. In 2006, it inaugurated the monumentally expensive Qinghai-Tibet Railway linking Tibet's capital city of Lhasa to the rest of the country. Reaching heights of over 16,400 feet (5,000 meters), the trains on this railway have to be equipped with supplemental oxygen. As a result of this and other transportation projects, Tibet's tourism economy is booming. Many Tibetans, however, argue that most of the benefits are flowing to Han Chinese immigrants rather than to the indigenous peoples of the region (Figure 10.27). Ethnic unrest in 2008 resulted in a marked slowdown in economic expansion.

Most observers agree that Xinjiang has tremendous economic potential. It boasts significant mineral wealth, including most of China's oil and natural gas reserves, and it has benefited from infrastructural development projects over the

past several decades. The recent completion of oil and natural gas pipelines from Kazakhstan and Turkmenistan have also bolstered the region's petrochemical industries. But as is the case in Tibet, many of the indigenous peoples of Xinjiang believe that the wealth of their region is being monopolized by the Chinese state and the Han Chinese immigrants. Some point to the Xinjiang Production and Construction Corps, a quasi-military firm that runs hundreds of factories, farms, schools, and hospitals. This huge company was initially formed by the army that rejoined Xinjiang to China in 1949, and it is still run almost entirely by Han Chinese.

Economic Misery in Afghanistan Afghanistan is Central Asia's poorest country. Since the late 1970s, it has suffered nearly continuous war, undermining virtually all economic endeavors. Even before the war it had experienced little industrial or commercial development. Its only significant legitimate exports are animal products, handwoven carpets, and a few fruits, nuts, and semiprecious gemstones.

Through all of these years of chaos, Afghanistan remained economically competitive in one area: the production of illicit drugs for the global market. According to the CIA, Afghanistan had emerged by 1999 as the world's largest producer of opium. The country's drug economy has recently grown more sophisticated, as Afghan opium is increasingly processed into heroin within the country. From 2007 to 2009, however, opium production did decline, but pervasive corruption will make any further reductions very difficult.

Since 2003, the economy of Afghanistan has experienced some growth, although much of the gains have come through foreign assistance. From 2001 to 2009, international donors delivered roughly $15 billion to the country. Afghanistan does have substantial mineral deposits, however, and in 2008 China agreed to invest $2.8 billion in a massive copper mining scheme. Genuine economic development in Afghanistan seems unlikely, however, unless the country becomes politically secure.

Central Asian Economies in Global Context Afghanistan—despite its poverty and relative isolation—is thoroughly embedded in the global economy, albeit through illicit products. The overland flow of Afghan opium and heroin to Europe implicates several other Central Asian countries, especially Tajikistan, in the international drug economy. But with the exceptions of the drug trade and the oil and natural gas industries, the overall extent of globalization in Central Asia remains low (Figure 10.28).

In the former Soviet area, the most important international connections remain with Russia, although economic ties with China are rapidly expanding. In the early post-Soviet period, both Russia and the newly independent Central Asian countries were ambivalent about their continuing economic relationships. Disentangling Central Asian economies from that of Russia, however, proved difficult, largely because of infrastructural linkages inherited from the Soviet period. In 2007, two-thirds of Turkmenistan's natural gas exports flowed through Russia's state-owned Gazprom pipelines.

Figure 10.27 Chinese Business in Lhasa, Tibet An elderly Tibetan woman peers into a hair salon in Lhasa, Tibet, in 2006. As Han Chinese immigrants stream into Tibet's cities, rapid cultural change and economic modernization leave many Tibetans behind.

Figure 10.28 **Global Linkages** Although Azerbaijan and Kazakhstan are relatively well connected to the rest of the world through their exports of oil and natural gas, the other countries of Central Asia remain somewhat isolated from the global economy.

Since the creation of the SCO, moreover, Uzbekistan, Kazakhstan, Kyrgyzstan, and Tajikistan have eagerly sought closer linkages with both Russia and China. Connections to China were enhanced in 2006 with the opening of the Kazakhstan–China oil pipeline and again in 2009, with the completion of the Central Asia-China Gas Pipeline.

The United States and other Western countries, as well as India, are also drawn to the area by its oil and natural gas deposits. Many large oil companies operate in Azerbaijan and Kazakhstan. The delivery of Central Asian oil to the west was enhanced in 2006 with the opening of the extraordinarily expensive Baku-Tbilsi-Ceyhan Pipeline—the second longest in the world—which runs from the Caspian Sea to the Turkish Mediterranean at the port of Ceyhan. If the current Nabucco Pipeline plans come to fruition, Azerbaijan will be exporting large quantities of natural gas to Europe by 2015.

Social Development in Central Asia

Social conditions in Central Asia vary more than economic conditions. In the former Soviet territories, levels of health and education remain fairly high but are generally declining.

Not surprisingly, Afghanistan stands at the bottom of the scale by every measure.

Social Conditions and the Status of Women in Afghanistan
Social conditions in Afghanistan are no better than economic circumstances, although reliable information is difficult to obtain. As can be seen in Table 10.2, the average life expectancy in the country is a mere 44 years, one of the lowest figures in the world. Infant and childhood mortality levels remain extremely high. Not only does Afghanistan suffer from constant warfare, but its rugged topography hinders the provision of basic social and medical services. Illiteracy is commonplace and is notably gender-biased. Afghanistan's 21 percent adult female literacy figure is one of the lowest in the world.

Women in most parts of Afghanistan—and especially in Pashtun areas—lead highly constrained lives. In many areas they must completely conceal their bodies, including their faces, when venturing into public. Such restrictions intensified in the 1990s. Dress controls were strictly enforced where the Taliban gained authority. In most areas, Taliban forces prevented women from working, attending school, and often even from obtaining medical care. The assault on women by the Taliban did not go uncontested in Afghanistan. Many women risked their lives to document the horrific abuses that Afghan females were suffering. While Taliban leaders argued that they were upholding Islamic orthodoxy, their opponents contended that they were actually enforcing an extreme version of Pashtun customary law.

The fall of the Taliban brought temporary joy to most of the women of Afghanistan. Many promptly uncovered their faces and began working—or seeking work. The new Afghan constitution proclaimed that henceforth men and women would enjoy equal rights. But in most parts of the country, little actually changed with the coming of the new regime. Social customs continued to force most women into arranged marriages followed by domestic seclusion. Indeed, in some areas of the country the upsurge in both crime and political violence have made the position of women increasingly insecure. In recent years, Taliban forces have physically attacked several girls' schools, demonstrating their determination to thwart any movement toward gender equity. According to some Afghan women's groups, over 70 percent of women in the country face forced marriages, and roughly one third suffer physical, psychological, or sexual violence.

Social Conditions in the Former Soviet Republics and Mongolia Compared to women in Afghanistan, those in the former Soviet portion of Central Asia enjoy a high social position. Traditionally, women had much more autonomy among the northern pastoral peoples than among the farmers and city dwellers of the south, but under Soviet rule the position of women everywhere improved. In the former Soviet republics today, adult women's educational rates are not far behind those of men, and women are well represented in the workplace. Some evidence suggests, however, that the position of women has recently declined in many areas. In Kazakhstan, leaders have blamed feminism for the country's low birthrate, and in much of the region newly rich men are increasingly practicing polygamy. As education becomes more expensive, moreover, girls are increasingly staying at home. Women are also trafficked from the poorer countries of the region, particularly Uzbekistan and Tajikistan, into prostitution in Russia, the United Arab Emirates, and elsewhere.

The figures in Table 10.2 reveal generally favorable levels of social welfare overall for the former Soviet zone. This is especially notable when one considers the dismal state of the region's economy—or contrasts conditions with those of neighboring Afghanistan. Tajikistan, with a per capita GNI of only $1,860 has a female life expectancy of 69 years as well as almost universal adult literacy. The social successes of Tajikistan and its northern and western neighbors reflect investments made during the Soviet period. Health and educational facilities have declined in the face of economic and political turmoil. Certainly the region's relatively high levels of infant and childhood mortality do not bode well. Whereas Tajikistan might hope that its educated workforce will at-

tract foreign investment, its remote location and continued instability make such a scenario unlikely.

Somewhat similar conditions prevail in Mongolia, although the preponderance of its women in professional positions is striking. This is a legacy of both the former socialist system and of traditional Mongol culture, which is noted for its female domestic authority. In 2000, one survey found that women made up 60 percent of Mongolia's lawyers, 77 percent of its doctors, and 84 percent of its university graduates (Figure 10.29). But despite such educational and professional advances, Mongolia's women have gained little political power.

Social Conditions in Western China Although China as a whole has made significant progress in health and education, many reports suggest that the indigenous peoples of Tibet and Xinjiang have been left behind. Some sources claim that more than half of the non-Han people of Xinjiang and Tibet remain illiterate. Chinese sources, on the other hand, maintain that illiteracy has been declining rapidly in both areas. In 2008, China's official media outlets reported that over 95 percent of the young people of Tibet had learned to read and write.

China's minority peoples have, however, been granted certain exemptions from the country's strict population control measures. But there are many reports from Xinjiang and elsewhere of forced sterilization and abortions, adding to the local political tensions.

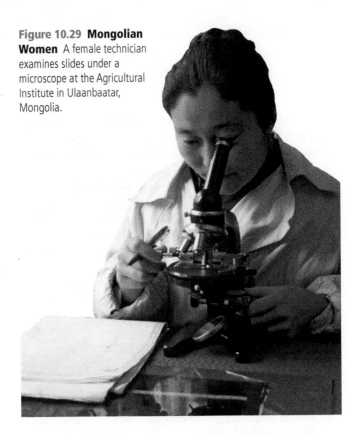

Figure 10.29 Mongolian Women A female technician examines slides under a microscope at the Agricultural Institute in Ulaanbaatar, Mongolia.

Summary

- Central Asia, long hidden by Russian domination, has recently reappeared on the map of the world. Environmental problems, among others, have brought the region to global attention. The destruction of the Aral Sea is one of the worst environmental disasters the world has experienced, and many other lakes in the region have experienced similar problems. Desertification has devastated many areas, and the booming oil and gas industries have created their own environmental disasters.

- Large movements of people in Central Asia have attracted global attention. The migration of Han Chinese into Tibet and Xinjiang is steadily turning the indigenous peoples of these areas into minority groups. The migration of Russian speakers out of the former Soviet areas of Central Asia has also resulted in major transformations. People are currently moving from the poorer countries of the former Soviet zone to oil-rich Kazakhstan. In Afghanistan, war and continuing chaos have generated large refugee populations.

- Religious tension has recently emerged as a major cultural issue through much of western Central Asia. Radical Islamic fundamentalism remains a potent force in southern and western Afghanistan, and to a somewhat lesser extent in the Fergana Valley of Uzbekistan, Tajikistan, and Kyrgyzstan. Although moderate forms of Islam are prevalent through most of the region, Central Asian leaders have used the threat of religiously inspired violence to maintain repressive and antidemocratic policies.

- While China maintains a firm grip on Tibet and Xinjiang, the rest of Central Asia has emerged as a key area of geopolitical competition. Russia, the United States, China, Iran, Turkey, Pakistan, and India all contend for influence. Central Asian countries have attempted to play these powers against each other in order to maintain or increase their world status. Overall, political structures throughout the region remain largely authoritarian, although popular uprisings have brought down two governments in Kyrgyzstan.

- The economies of Central Asia are gradually opening up to global connections, largely because of their substantial fossil fuel reserves. However, Central Asia is likely to face serious economic difficulties for some time, especially since the region is not a significant participant in global trade and has attracted little foreign investment outside the fossil-fuel sector. The growing of opium and the manufacture of heroin remain a serious problem in Afghanistan. Drug trafficking, moreover, has weakened legitimate economic activities in other countries of the region.

Key Terms

alluvial fan (*page 452*)
Bodhisattva (*page 463*)
exclave (*page 467*)
exotic river (*page 452*)

loess (*page 452*)
pastoralist (*page 453*)
Shanghai Cooperation Organization (SCO); "Shanghai Six" (*page 470*)

Taliban (*page 471*)
theocracy (*page 463*)
transhumance (*page 451*)

Review Questions

1. Describe the three major regions of Central Asia as defined by physical geography.

2. Why is lake level a particularly serious concern in Central Asia?

3. Why is the distribution of population in Central Asia so uneven? Why are certain areas virtually uninhabited?

4. Describe the different agricultural patterns that are found on (a) the plains of northern Kazakhstan, (b) the major river valleys of Uzbekistan, and (c) the Tibetan Plateau.

5. Why is much of Central Asia often called "Turkestan"? Why does this label not apply to the entire region?

6. How does religion act as a political force in Central Asia? How does this situation vary in different parts of the region?

7. Why is the United States concerned about the fossil fuel resources of Central Asia? How do transportation routes play into this concern?

8. What role does Russia currently play in Central Asian geopolitics? How has Russian power historically influenced the region?

9. How do social conditions (health, longevity, literacy, etc.) vary across the border between Afghanistan and Uzbekistan? Why are the disparities so pronounced?

10. If western Central Asia is so rich in natural resources, why did the region experience such pronounced economic decline in the 1990s?

Thinking Geographically

1. To what extent will Central Asia's continental location be a disadvantage in years to come? Is coastal access truly significant in determining a country's competitive position in the global economy? Explain.

2. Will the countries of former Soviet Central Asia be able to maintain their high levels of education now that they are independent? If so, will they be able to use education to their own economic advantage? Explain.

3. Is Russia's influence in Central Asia bound to decline now that Russia has no direct political authority in the area? Explain.

4. Which external connection will prove most important for Central Asia in years to come—those based on religion, language, economic ties, or geopolitical connections?

5. Is China's political control over eastern Central Asia justified? Should Han Chinese migration to the area be a concern to the United States? Explain.

6. Is Chinese control over Tibet a legitimate concern of U.S. foreign policy? Should the United States use trade sanctions to attempt to influence Chinese policy in the area? Explain.

7. How might the desiccation of Central Asia's great lakes best be addressed?

Regional Novels and Films

Novels

Chinghiz Aitmatov, *The Day Lasts More Than a Hundred Years* (1983, Indiana University Press)

Rinjing Dorje, *Tales of Uncle Tompa, The Legendary Rascal of Tibet* (1997, Barrytown Ltd.)

Mark Frutkin, *Invading Tibet* (1993, Soho Press)

James Hilton, *Lost Horizon* (1996, Morrow)

Khaled Hosseini, *The Kite Runner* (2003, Riverhead Books)

Amin Maalouf, *Samarkand: A Novel* (1998, Interlink)

Hilary Roe Metternich, ed., *Mongolian Folktales* (1996, Avery Press)

Films

Kandahar (2001, Iran)

Kundun (1997, U.S.)

Mongol (2007, Germany, Kazakhstan, Mongolia, and Russia)

Osama (2003, Afghanistan)

Pure Coolness (2007, Kyrgyzstan)

The Road under the Heavens (2006, Uzbekistan)

The Story of the Weeping Camel (2003, Mongolia)

Tulpan (2008, Kazakhstan)

Urga: Close to Eden (1991, Mongolia)

Bibliography

Adshead, S. A. M. 1993. *Central Asia in World History*. New York: St. Martin's Press.

Beckwith, Christopher. 2009. *The Empires of the Silk Road: A History of Central Eurasia from the Bronze Age to the Present*. Princeton: Princeton University Press.

Bissell, Tom. 2003. *Chasing the Sea: Lost Among the Ghosts of Empire in Central Asia*. New York: Pantheon.

Drompp, Michael. 1989. "Centrifugal Forces in the Inner Asian 'Heartland': History *Versus* Geography." *Journal of Asian History* 23, 135–55.

Ewans, Martin. 2002. *Afghanistan: A Short History of Its People and Politics*. New York: Perennial.

Jones, Seth. 2010. *In the Graveyard of Empires: America's War in Afghanistan*. New York: W.W. Norton.

Kobori, Iwao, and Glantz, Michael. 1998. *Central Eurasian Water Crisis: Caspian, Aral, and Dead Sea*. Tokyo: United Nations University Press.

Mahnovski, Sergei. 2007. *Economic Dimension of Security in Central Asia*. Santa Monica, CA: RAND Corporation.

Rashid, Ahmed. 2001. *Taliban: Militant Islam, Oil, and Fundamentalism in Central Asia*. New Haven, CT: Yale University Press.

Sinor, Denis, ed. 1990. *The Cambridge History of Early Inner Asia*. Cambridge, UK: Cambridge University Press.

  Mastering Geography

 MapMaster™

Log in to www.masteringgeography.com for MapMaster™ interactive maps, geography videos, RSS feeds, flashcards, web links, an eText version of *Diversity Amid Globalization*, and self-study quizzes to enhance your study of Central Asia.

MapMaster™ presents 13 Place Name and 13 Layered Thematic interactive maps to help students practice and master their geographic literacy, spatial reasoning, and critical thinking skills.

11
East Asia

The Balinghe Bridge in China's Guizhou province was opened to traffic in December 2009. Located in the poorest province of China, it is one of the world's highest bridges.

颂陵河大桥

DIVERSITY AMID GLOBALIZATION

East Asia has been an economic core area for several thousand years, attracting merchants from many other parts of the world. After World War II, communist governments in China and North Korea withdrew as much as possible from the global economic system. In the 1980s, however, China opted to reengage with global capitalism, quickly transforming itself into an economic power. Today, East Asia is again a global center of both economic and cultural production.

ENVIRONMENTAL GEOGRAPHY
China has long experienced severe deforestation and soil erosion, and its current economic boom is generating the worst pollution problems in the world.

POPULATION AND SETTLEMENT
China is currently undergoing a major transformation as tens of millions of peasants move from poor villages in the interior to booming cities of the coastal region.

CULTURAL COHERENCE AND DIVERSITY
Despite the presence of several unifying cultural features, East Asia in general and China in particular are divided along several striking cultural lines.

GEOPOLITICAL FRAMEWORK
Both Korea and China remain divided nations, with Taiwan pitted against the People's Republic of China and South Korea set in opposition against North Korea.

ECONOMIC AND SOCIAL DEVELOPMENT
Over the past several decades, East Asia has emerged as a core area of the world economy, with China experiencing one of the most rapid economic expansions the world has ever seen.

East Asia, composed of China, Japan, South Korea, North Korea, and Taiwan (Figure 11.1), is the most populous region of the world. China alone is inhabited by more than 1.3 billion people, more than live in any other region of the world except South Asia. Although East Asia is historically unified by cultural features, in the second half of the 20th century it was divided ideologically and politically, with the capitalist economies of Japan, South Korea, Taiwan, and Hong Kong separated from the communist bloc of China and North Korea. Differences in levels of economic development also remained pronounced. As Japan reached the pinnacle of the global economy, much of China remained mired in extreme poverty.

Since the 1990s, however, divisions with East Asia have been reduced. While China is still governed by the Communist Party, it has embarked on a path of capitalist development. Business ties between its booming coastal zone and Japan, South Korea, and Taiwan have quickly strengthened. Animosity still exists between North Korea and South Korea and between China and Taiwan, but East Asia as a whole has witnessed a gradual reduction in political tension.

East Asia is now a core area of the world economy, and it is becoming a center of geopolitical power as well. Japan, South Korea, and Taiwan are among the world's key trading states. Tokyo, Japan's largest city, stands alongside New York and London as one of the financial centers of the globe, and is noted as both a consumer and producer of global culture. China has more recently emerged as a global trading power. Its coastal zone is now tightly integrated within global networks of information, commerce, and entertainment. China is also developing into a regional military power. This development has caused much concern among its neighbors—and among distant countries, such as the United States.

East Asia is easily marked off on the world map by the territorial extent of its constituent countries. Japan is an island country composed of four main islands and a chain of much smaller islands (the Ryukyus) that extends almost to Taiwan. Taiwan is basically a single-island country, but its political status is ambiguous since China claims it as part of its own territory. China itself is a vast continental state—the third most extensive in the world—that reaches well into Central Asia. It also includes the large island of Hainan in the South China Sea. Korea constitutes a compact peninsula between northern China and Japan, but it is divided into two sovereign states: North Korea and South Korea.

In political terms, such a straightforward definition of East Asia is appropriate. If one turns to cultural considerations, however, the issue becomes more complicated. The main cultural issue concerns the western half of China. This is a huge but lightly populated area; only about 5 percent of the residents of China live in the west. By certain criteria, only the populous eastern half of China (often called "**China proper**") fits into the East Asian world region. The indigenous inhabitants of western China are not Chinese by culture and language, and they have never accepted the

religious and philosophical beliefs that give historical unity to East Asian civilization. In the northwestern quarter of China, called *Xinjiang* in Chinese, most indigenous inhabitants speak Turkic languages and are Muslim in religion. Tibet, in southwestern China, has a highly distinctive culture, and the Tibetans in general resent Chinese authority. Xinjiang and Tibet can thus be classified within both East Asia and Central Asia (covered in Chapter 10). In this chapter we will examine western China largely to the extent that it is politically part of China.

Figure 11.1 East Asia This region includes China, Japan, North Korea, South Korea, and Taiwan. The physical geography of mainland East Asia varies widely from the high plateaus and desert basins of western China to the broad river valleys and vast plains of eastern China. In the island region, landscapes are shaped by the convergence of three major tectonic plates, the Eurasian, Philippine, and Pacific.

ENVIRONMENTAL GEOGRAPHY: Resource Pressures in a Crowded Land

Environmental problems in East Asia are particularly severe owing to a combination of the region's large population, its massive industrial development, and its physical geography (Figure 11.2). The wealthier countries of the region, particularly Japan, have been able to invest heavily in environmental protection. China, in contrast, not only has less money available for conservation but also has more deeply rooted environmental problems. One of China's most controversial environmental issues has been the construction of the Three Gorges Dam on the Yangtze River.

Dams, Flooding, and Soil Erosion in China

The Yangtze River (also called the Chang Jiang) is one of the most important physical features of East Asia. This river, the third largest (by volume) in the world, emerges from the

Figure 11.2 Environmental Issues in East Asia This vast world region has been almost completely transformed from its natural state and continues to have serious environmental problems. In China, some of the more pressing environmental issues involve deforestation, flooding, water control, and soil erosion.

Tibetan highlands onto the rolling lands of the Sichuan Basin, passes through what used to be a magnificent canyon in the Three Gorges area (Figure 11.3), and then meanders across the lowlands of central China before entering into the sea near the city of Shanghai. The Yangtze has historically been the main avenue of entry into the interior of China, and is celebrated in Chinese literature for its beauty and power. Since the 1990s, however, it has become the focal point of an environmental controversy of global proportions.

The Three Gorges Dam Controversy Finished in 2006, the Three Gorges Dam—600 feet (180 meters) high and 1.45 miles (2.3 kilometers) long—is the largest hydroelectric dam in the world, requiring $26 billion to build. The reservoir is 350 miles (563 kilometers) long, has displaced an estimated 1.2 million people while inundating a major scenic attraction (the Three Gorges of the Yangtze for which it is named). The dam will trap sediment and pollutants in the reservoir, as well as disrupt habitat for several endangered species, including the Yangtze River dolphin. The ecological and human rights consequences of the dam are so negative that the World Bank withdrew its support.

The Three Gorges Dam generates massive amounts of electricity, meeting approximately 3 percent of China's needs. As China industrializes, its demand for power is skyrocketing. At present, nearly three-fourths of China's total energy supply comes from burning coal, which results in horren-

Figure 11.3 The Three Gorges of the Yangtze The spectacular Three Gorges landscape of the Yangtze River is now gone, inundated by the reservoir that has formed behind the controversial Three Gorges Dam. Not only are the human costs high, but there may also be significant ecological costs to endangered aquatic species.

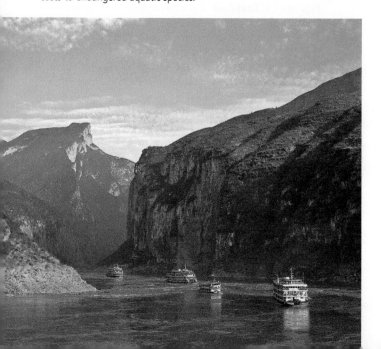

dous air pollution and acid rain. But while dam-building may reduce air pollution, it will not be nearly adequate to supply China's vast energy needs. Most environmentalists therefore argue that the damage caused by the dams is greater than the benefits they confer.

Chinese planners also praise the water-control benefits provided by dams. The lower and middle stretches of the Yangtze periodically suffer from devastating flooding, and planners hope that the Three Gorges Dam will store enough water to help protect 15 million people and over 3 million acres (1.2 million hectares) of farmland on the lower

Soil erosion. *Some of the most severe soil erosion in the world can be found in the Loess Plateau of central China.*

Three Gorges Dam. *This massive dam on the Yangtze River will provide relatively clean power, but will endanger several species and will displace several million people.*

Yangtze flooding. *Deforestation in the uplands coupled with the draining and filling of regulatory lakes in the basins has resulted in increasingly severe floods on the middle and lower reaches of the Yangtze River.*

Deforestation in Southern China. *Most of the uplands of southern China are largely deforested—the results of a process that dates back hundreds of years but which accelerated in the 20th century. Reforestation efforts have been, at best, partially successful.*

Yangtze floodplains. However, flooding has been exacerbated over the past several decades by the declining area of lakes on the Yangtze floodplain, which function as overflow areas during floods. East of Sichuan, the Yangtze passes through several basins (in Hunan, Hubei, and Jiangxi provinces), each containing a group of lakes. During periods of high water, river flows are diverted into these **regulatory lakes**, thus reducing the flow downstream. After the flood season is over, water drains from the lakes and therefore helps maintain the water level in the river downstream. In the 1950s and 1960s, however, the Chinese government drained many of these lakes in order to convert the lake beds to farmland. As a result, flooding downstream intensified.

Flooding in Northern China The North China Plain, which has been deforested for thousands of years, is plagued by both drought and flood. This area is dry most of the year, yet often experiences heavy downpours in summer. Since ancient times, large-scale hydraulic engineering projects have both controlled floods and allowed irrigation. But no matter how much effort has been put into water control, disastrous flooding has never been completely prevented.

Figure 11.4 The Huang He, the World's Muddiest River Tourists are shown visiting the Hukou waterfall, China's second largest cascade. Major flooding, sometimes inundating large sections of the North China Plain, has been a historical problem with the Huang He River. Dam-building is generally unsuccessful here because the reservoirs quickly fill up with silt.

The worst floods in northern China are caused by the Huang He, or Yellow River, which cuts across the North China Plain. Owing to upstream erosion, the Huang He carries a huge **sediment load**, or suspended clay, silt, and sand, making it the world's muddiest major river (Figure 11.4). When the river enters the low-lying plain, its velocity slows and its sediments begin to settle and accumulate in the riverbed. As a result, the level of the riverbed gradually rises above that of the surrounding lands. Eventually the river must break free of its course to find a new route to the sea over lower-lying ground. Twenty-six such course changes have been recorded for the Huang He throughout Chinese history.

Through the process of sediment deposition and periodic course changes, the Huang He has actually created the vast North China Plain. In prehistoric times, the Yellow Sea extended far inland. Even today the sea is retreating as the Huang He's delta expands; one study revealed a 6-mile advance of the land in a 3-year period. Such a process occurs in other alluvial plains, but nowhere else in the world is it so pronounced. Nowhere else, moreover, is it so destructive. The world's two deadliest recorded natural disasters, each of which killed between one and two million people, both involved flooding of the Yellow River (in 1887 and 1931). The North China Plain has been densely populated for millennia and is now home to more than 300 million people. Since ancient times, the Chinese have attempted to keep the river within its banks by building progressively larger dikes. Eventually, however, the riverbed rises so high that the flow can no longer be contained and catastrophic flooding results. While the river has not changed its course since the

1930s, most geographers think that another course correction is inevitable.

Erosion on the Loess Plateau The Huang He's sediment burden is derived from the eroding soils of the Loess Plateau, located to the west of the North China Plain. **Loess** consists of fine, windblown sediment that was deposited on this upland area during the last Ice Age, accumulating in some places to depths of several hundred feet.

Loess forms fertile soil, but it washes away easily when exposed to running water. At the dawn of Chinese civilization, the semiarid Loess Plateau was covered with tough grasses and scrubby forests that retained the soil. Chinese farmers, however, began to clear the land for the abundant crops that it yields when rainfall is adequate. Cultivation required plowing, which, by exposing the soil to water and wind, exacerbated erosion. As the population of the region gradually increased, the remaining areas of woodland diminished, leading to faster rates of soil loss. As the erosion process continued, great gullies cut across the plateau, steadily reducing the extent of arable land.

Today, the Loess Plateau is one of the poorest parts of China. Population is only moderately dense by Chinese standards, but good farmland is limited and drought is common. The Chinese government has long encouraged the construction of terraces to conserve the soil, but such efforts have not been effective everywhere. More recently, the World Bank and the government of China have pushed through the "Loess Plateau Watershed Rehabilitation Project," which has achieved considerable success in some

Figure 11.5 Denuded Hillslopes in China Because of the need to clear forests for wood products and agricultural lands, China's mountain slopes have long been deforested. Without forest cover, soil erosion is a serious issue.

areas. An estimated 133 square kilometers (51 square miles) of degraded land have been fully reforested.

Other East Asian Environmental Problems

The problems associated with the Yangtze and Huang He rivers are by no means the only environmental issues in East Asia. Deforestation, urban pollution, and the loss of wildlife are increasing problems in much of the region.

Deforestation and Desertification Many of the upland regions of China and North Korea support only grass, meager scrub, and stunted trees (Figure 11.5). China lacks the his-

torical tradition of forest conservation that characterizes Japan. During earlier periods of Chinese history, hillsides were often cleared for fuelwood, and in some instances entire forests were burned for ash that could be used as fertilizer. In much of southern China, sweet potatoes, maize, and other crops have been grown on steep and easily eroded hillsides for hundreds of years. After centuries of exploitation, many hillslopes are now so degraded that they cannot easily regenerate forests.

Over the past 50 years, China, unlike North Korea, has initiated a number of reforestation efforts. Millions of people have been mobilized by the government to plant trees. In many areas such projects have failed, but the government claims that overall the area covered by forests has increased from 9 percent in 1949 to 13 percent in 2008. After severe flooding along the Yangtze River in 1998, reforestation efforts in central China were significantly enhanced. Still, it will be many years before such new forests can be logged. At present, substantial timber reserves are found only in China's far northeast, where a cold climate limits tree growth, and along the eastern slopes of the Tibetan Plateau, where rugged terrain restricts commercial forestry. As a result, China suffers a severe shortage of forest resources. China makes up for this shortfall by massively importing lumber and other wood products from other parts of the world.

Desertification is also a major problem for China. In many areas, sand dunes have pushed south from the Gobi Desert, smothering farmlands. Some reports claim that more desertification occurs in China than any other country. The Chinese government has responded with massive dune-stabilization schemes, which usually involve planting grasses to stop sand from blowing away (Figure 11.6). The most ambitious of such projects involved planting more than 300

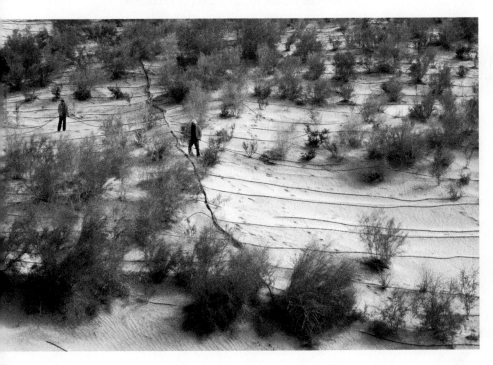

Figure 11.6 Dune Stabilization in China Farmers are shown planting grass on a dune in an effort to keep the sand from blowing toward cultivated fields. China has one of the worst desertification problems in the world, but it has made some progress in slowing the advance of deserts in recent years.

million trees along a 3,000-mile (4,800-kilometer)-long swath of northern China. This "great green wall" was designed both to stop the southward expansion of the desert and reduce the dust storms that often hit northern China. Overall, the rate of desertification in China is reported to have declined from 3,400 square kilometers (1,300 square miles) per year in the 1990s to 1,300 square kilometers (502 square miles) in the early 2000s.

Mounting Pollution As China's industrial base expands, other environmental problems, such as water pollution and toxic-waste dumping, are growing more acute, particularly

ENVIRONMENT AND POLITICS China Embraces Green Energy

As China has undergone breakneck industrialization in recent years, it has emerged as the world's most polluted country. China's pollution extends well beyond its borders. Emissions of particulates, sulphur dioxide, and nitric oxide reach Japan and Korea; even mercury found in California rainwater has been traced to China. China is also the world's largest emitter of carbon dioxide. As a result, China has developed a poor reputation in international environmental circles. Recently, however, China's environmental standing has experienced something of a turnaround. Its government has embraced renewable energy with fervor, planning to become the world leader in green technology. By 2020, China hopes to meet 20 percent of its own energy needs through renewable sources.

China's push for renewable energy stems from political and economic considerations, as well as those of environmental protection. China is dependent on energy from Central and Southwest Asia, areas vulnerable to political instability. Governmental planners also see massive export potential in renewable energy. China is now the world leader in hydroelectric turbines, and produces over 30 percent of the world's solar photovoltaic panels. Chinese renewable energy firms respond to market signals, but the industry as a whole is guided by governmental subsidies and mandates. By law, utility companies in China must purchase renewable energy at prices above the market level.

China's accomplishments in wind power have been especially impressive. China is sometimes said to have the largest wind-power potential in the world, owing both to the southwest monsoon and to stiff breezes that blow out of Central Asia during much of the year. At the end of 2009, the United States produced more wind-generated electricity, but most experts expected that China would soon grab the top position. Between 2004 and 2009, China doubled its installed wind power every year (Figure 11.1.1). A 2009 study showed that China could economically meet all of its additional energy needs through 2030 by wind power alone.

Not surprisingly, China is emerging as a global leader in the manufacture of wind turbines. Chinese firms began by buying technology licenses from European companies but quickly began to develop their own expertise. The Beijing government has pushed forward the development of local technologies, mandating at first that 40 percent of the components used in wind farms be made in China, and then increasing that figure to 70 percent in 2009. China treats wind energy as strategic industry, and thus demands much secrecy. It is difficult for foreigners to obtain permission to visit not just wind turbine factories, but even wind farms themselves. The Chinese government sees the world's energy future as dominated by renewable sources, a market it hopes to dominate.

Figure 11.1.1 Chinese Wind Farm China is currently pushing hard for renewable energy. Wind power development is concentrated in the deserts and grasslands of Inner Mongolia.

in the booming coastal areas. The burning of high-sulfur coal has resulted in severe air pollution, a problem aggravated by the increasing number of automobiles driven by the Chinese. One recent study found that 16 of the world's 20 most polluted cities are located in China. According to a World Health Organization (WHO) report, air pollution kills 656,000 Chinese citizens each year, while another 95,000 die from polluted drinking water. Although Chinese citizens have organized thousands of protests against pollution and other forms of environmental destruction, the government has generally insisted that economic growth remain the top priority. Beginning in 2006, however, China's government has been supporting the development of clean, renewable sources of energy.

Considering its large population and intensive industrialization, Japan's environment is relatively clean. The very density of its population gives certain environmental advantages, allowing, for example, a highly efficient public transportation system. In the 1950s and 1960s, Japan did suffer from some of the world's worst pollution. Soon afterward the Japanese government passed stringent environmental laws covering both air and water pollution.

Japan's cleanup was aided by its insular location, because winds usually carry smog-forming chemicals out to sea. Equally important has been the phenomenon of **pollution exporting**. Because of Japan's high cost of production and its strict environmental laws, many Japanese companies have moved their dirtier factories overseas. In effect, Japan's pollution has been partially displaced to poorer countries. Of course, the same argument can also be made about the United States and western Europe, but to a somewhat lesser extent.

Serious air and water pollution problems also emerged early in other East Asian countries. But Taiwan and South Korea, which have large chemical, steel, and other heavy industries, responded by imposing more stringent environmental controls as they grew wealthier. These two countries have also followed Japan's footsteps by setting up new factories in poorer countries—including China—that have less strict environmental standards.

Endangered Species The growing number of endangered species in East Asia has been linked to the region's economic rise. Many forms of traditional Chinese medicine are based on products derived from rare and exotic animals. Deer antlers, bear gallbladders, snake blood, tiger penises, and rhinoceros horns are believed to have medical effectiveness, and certain individuals will pay fantastic sums of money to purchase them. As wealth has accumulated, trade in such substances has expanded. China itself has relatively little remaining wildlife, but other areas of the world help supply its demand for wildlife products.

China has, however, moved strongly to protect some of its remaining areas of habitat. Among the most important of these are the high-altitude forests and bamboo thickets of western Sichuan province, home of the panda bear. Efforts are also being made to preserve wildlands in northern Manchuria, where evidence of a surviving population of Siberian tigers was discovered in 1997, and in the canyon lands of northwestern Yunnan, which were declared off-limits to loggers in 1999.

Wildlife is also scarce in Korea. Ironically, however, the so-called demilitarized zone that separates North from South Korea functions as an unintentional wildlife sanctuary, supporting populations of several endangered species, including the Asiatic black bear.

Global Warming in East Asia

East Asia has come to occupy a central position in global warming debates, largely because of China's rapid increases in carbon emissions. From levels only about half those of the United States in 2000, China's total production of greenhouse gases surpassed those of the United States in 2007. This staggering rise has been caused both by China's explosive economic growth and by the fact that it relies on burning coal to meet most of its energy needs (Figure 11.7).

The potential effects of global warming in China have serious implications for human populations. According to the 2007 Chinese National Climate Change Assessment, the country's production of wheat, corn, and rice could fall by as much as 37 percent if average temperatures increase by 3.5 to 5.5°F (2 or 3°C) over the next 50 to 80 years. Increased evaporation rates, coupled with the melting of glaciers on the Tibetan Plateau, could greatly intensify the water shortages that already plague much of northern China. Officials believe that by the middle of the 21st century, even Shanghai, located in the humid Yangtze Delta, will either have to use desalinized water or build an expensive network of canals, dams, and pumps to import water from south-central China for municipal use. In the wet zones of southeastern China, global

Figure 11.7 Coal-Fired Power Plant in China A coal-fired power plant emits large quantities of pollution in northwestern China. As China industrializes, it is building many such plants, damaging local air quality and contributing to global warming.

warming concerns center on the possibility of more intense storms in this already flood-prone region.

Despite these concerns, the Chinese government has insisted that economic growth take priority over reducing greenhouse gas emissions. Officials argue that China's per capita emissions are still far below those of the United States and most other wealthy countries, and that Chinese industries have been learning how to use energy more efficiently. Government officials also maintain that wealthier countries should take the lead on reducing emissions and figuring out other ways to combat global warming.

In June 2007, China released its first national plan on climate change, which called for a 20-percent gain in energy efficiency by 2010. China's new strategy also includes a major expansion of nuclear power, increased use of renewable energy sources, and the continuation of ambitious reforestation efforts. Current plans call for a target of producing 15 percent of the country's electricity through renewable sources by 2020 (see "Environment and Politics: China Embraces Green Energy"). While environmentalists were pleased to see China addressing these issues, most feel that the country has not gone nearly far enough, and they have been disappointed that it has not embraced the goal of halving carbon emissions by 2050.

China's contribution to the causes of global warming has overshadowed that of other East Asian countries. Japan, South Korea, and Taiwan are all major emitters of greenhouse gases, but all also have energy-efficient economies, releasing far less carbon than the United States on a per capita basis. Overall, Japan has been a strong proponent of international treaties, such as the Kyoto Protocol, designed to force reductions in greenhouse gas emissions. But while its total emissions have been relatively flat in recent years, Japan has not achieved the reductions that it promised in Kyoto. Increasingly, however, Japanese high-tech companies, like those of South Korea and Taiwan, realize that it could be very good business to develop more efficient forms of energy production. Japan is widely regarded as the world leader in a broad range of climate-friendly technologies.

East Asia's Physical Geography

East Asia is situated in the same general latitudinal range as the United States, although it extends considerably farther north and south. The northernmost tip of China lies as far north as central Quebec, while China's southernmost point is at the same latitude as Mexico City. The climate of southern China is thus roughly comparable to southern Florida and the Caribbean, whereas that of northern China is more similar to south-central Canada (Figure 11.8).

The island belt of East Asia, extending from northern Japan through Taiwan, is situated at the intersection of three tectonic plates (the basic building blocks of Earth's crust): the Eurasian, the Pacific, and the Philippine. This area, particularly Japan, is therefore geologically active, experiencing numerous earthquakes and dotted with volcanoes (Figure 11.9).

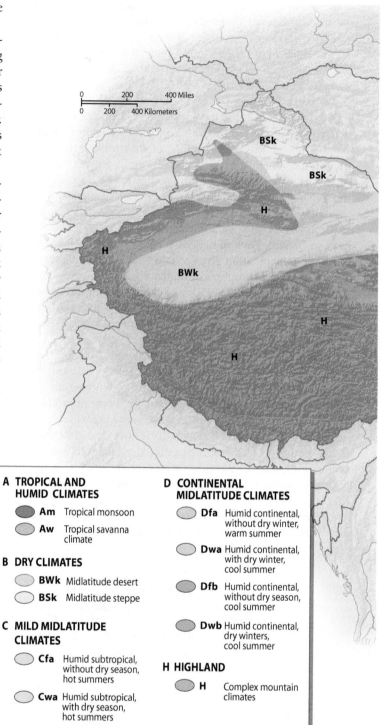

A TROPICAL AND HUMID CLIMATES

Am Tropical monsoon

Aw Tropical savanna climate

B DRY CLIMATES

BWk Midlatitude desert

BSk Midlatitude steppe

C MILD MIDLATITUDE CLIMATES

Cfa Humid subtropical, without dry season, hot summers

Cwa Humid subtropical, with dry season, hot summers

D CONTINENTAL MIDLATITUDE CLIMATES

Dfa Humid continental, without dry winter, warm summer

Dwa Humid continental, with dry winter, cool summer

Dfb Humid continental, without dry season, cool summer

Dwb Humid continental, dry winters, cool summer

H HIGHLAND

H Complex mountain climates

Japan's Physical Environment Although slightly smaller than California, Japan extends farther north and south. As a result, Japan's extreme south, in southern Kyushu and the Ryukyu Archipelago, is subtropical, while northern Hokkaido is almost subarctic. Most of the country, however, is temperate. The climate of Tokyo is not unlike that of Washington, DC—although Tokyo is distinctly rainier.

Japan's climate varies not only from north to south, but also from southeast to northwest across the main axis of the

Figure 11.8 Climate Map of East Asia East Asia is located in roughly the same latitudinal zone as North America, and climatic parallels exist between the two world regions. The northernmost tip of China lies at about the same latitude as Quebec and shares a similar climate, whereas southern China approximates the climate of Florida. In Japan, maritime influences produce a milder climate.

archipelago. In the winter, the area facing the Sea of Japan receives much more snow than the Pacific Ocean coastline. During this time of the year, cold winds from the Asian mainland blow across the relatively warm waters of the Sea of Japan. The air picks up moisture over the sea and deposits it, usually as snow, when it hits land (Figure 11.10). The Pacific

coast of Japan, on the other hand, is far more vulnerable to typhoons (hurricanes), which frequently strike the country.

The Pacific coast of Japan is separated from the Sea of Japan coast by a series of mountain ranges. Japan is one of the world's most rugged countries, with mountainous terrain covering some 85 percent of its territory. Most of these

EARTHQUAKES AND VOLCANOES			
Number	City/Location	Date	Richter Magnitude
1	Fukui	1948	7.3
2	Kobe	1995	7.2
3	Kwanto	1923	7.9
4	Mino-Owari	1891	8.4
5	Mt. Asama	1783,1982	
6	Mt. Aso	867	
7	Mt. Bandai	1880	
8	Mt. Fuji	864,1707	
9	Mt. Komagatake	1640	
10	Mt. Unzen	1792,1991	
11	Myojin	1952	
12	Niigata	1964	7.7
13	Oga	1983	7.7
14	Sakurajima	1779,1914	
15	Sanriku	1896	7.6
16	Sanriku	1933	8.5
17	Senda City	1978	
18	Tango	1927	8.0
19	Sendai City	2005	7.2
20	Kashiwazaki	2007	6.8

- Hill land and mountains
- Diluvial plains and lowlands of new alluvium
- Tsunami activity
- Plate boundaries
- • Earthquake epicenters
- ＊ Major volcanic eruptions

Figure 11.9 Japan's Physical Geography Japan has several sizable lowland plains, primarily along the coastline, but they are interspersed among rugged mountains and uplands. Because of its location at the convergence of three major tectonic plates, Japan experiences numerous earthquakes. Volcanic eruptions can also be hazardous and are linked directly to Japan's location on tectonic plate boundaries. Additionally, much of Japan's coast is vulnerable to devastating tsunamis (tidal waves) caused by earthquakes in the Pacific Basin.

intensive agriculture. The largest Japanese lowland is the Kanto Plain to the north of Tokyo, but even it is only some 80 miles wide and 100 miles long (130 by 160 kilometers). The country's other main lowland basins are the Kansai, located around Osaka, and the Nobi, centered on Nagoya. In the mountainous province of Nagano, smaller basins are sandwiched between the imposing peaks of the Japanese Alps.

Taiwan's Environment Taiwan, an island about the size of Maryland, sits at the edge of the continental land mass. To the west, the Taiwan Strait is only about 200 feet (60 meters) deep; to the east, ocean depths of many thousands of feet are found 10 to 20 miles (16 to 32 kilometers) offshore.

Taiwan itself forms a large tilted block. Its central and eastern regions are rugged and mountainous, while the west is dominated by an alluvial plain. Bisected by the tropic of Cancer, Taiwan has a mild winter climate, but it is sometimes battered by typhoons in the early autumn. Unlike nearby areas of China proper, Taiwan still has extensive forests, concentrated in its eastern upland areas.

uplands are thickly wooded, making Japan also one of the world's most heavily forested countries (Figure 11.11). Japan owes its lush forests both to its mild, rainy climate and to its long history of forest conservation. For hundreds of years, both the Japanese state and its village communities have enforced strict conservation rules, ensuring that timber and firewood extraction would be balanced by tree growth.

Along Japan's coastline and interspersed among its mountains are limited areas of alluvial plains (see Figure 11.9). Although these lowlands were once covered by forests and wetlands, they have long since been cleared and drained for

Figure 11.10 Heavy Snow in Japan's Mountains Cold, moist air moving off the Sea of Japan produces heavy snows in northwestern Japan and along the country's mountainous spine. Numerous major ski areas dot the Japanese Alps, several of which have hosted world-class sports competitions.

Figure 11.11 Forested Landscapes of Japan Although much of Japan is heavily forested and supports a viable wood products industry, the yield is not large enough to satisfy demand. As a result, Japan imports timber extensively from North America, Southeast Asia, and Latin America.

Chinese Environments Even if one excludes its Central Asian provinces of Tibet and Xinjiang, China is a vast country with diverse environmental regions. For the sake of convenience, China proper can be divided into two main areas, one lying to the north of the Yangtze River valley, the other including the Yangtze and all areas to the south. As Figure 11.12 shows, each of these divisions can be subdivided into a number of distinctive regions.

Southern China is a land of rugged mountains and hills interspersed with lowland basins. The lowlands of southern China are far larger than those of Japan. One of the most distinctive is the former lake bed of central Sichuan (in the central Upper Yangtze region of Figure 11.12). Protected by imposing mountains, Sichuan is noted for its mild winter climate. Eastward from Sichuan, the Yangtze River passes through several other broad basins (in the Middle Yangtze region), partially separated from each other by hills and low mountains, before flowing into a large delta near Shanghai.

Figure 11.12 Landscape Regions of China The term *China proper* denotes the densely populated, culturally Han Chinese areas to the east of the blue line. The Yangtze Valley divides China proper into two general areas. Immediately to the north is the large fertile area of the North China Plain, bisected by the Huang He (or Yellow) River. To the west is the Loess Plateau, an upland area of soil derived from wind-deposited silt after the prehistoric glacial period, about 15,000 years ago.

South of the Yangtze Valley, the mountains are higher (up to 7,000 feet, or 2,150 meters, in elevation), but they are still interspersed with alluvial lowlands. Sizable valleys are found in the far south, such as the Xi Basin in Guangdong province. Here the climate is truly tropical, free of frost. West of Guangdong lie the moderate-elevation plateaus of Yunnan and Guizhou, the former noted for its perennial springlike weather. Finally, to the northeast of Guangdong lies the rugged coastal province of Fujian (Figure 11.13). With its narrow coastal plain and deeply indented coastline, Fujian's landscape does not support a productive agricultural economy; as a result, the Fujianese people have often sought a maritime way of life, many of them working in the fishing and shipping industries.

North of the Yangtze Valley, the climate is both colder and drier than it is to the south. Summer rainfall is generally abundant except along the edge of the Gobi Desert, but the other seasons are dry. Desertification is a major threat in parts of the North China Plain, which have experienced prolonged droughts in recent years. With the exception of a few low mountains in Shandong province, the entire area is a virtually flat plain. Seasonal water shortages in this area are growing increasingly severe as withdrawals for irrigation and industry increase, leading to concerns about an impending crisis.

West of the North China Plain sits the Loess Plateau. This is a fairly rough upland of moderate elevation and uncertain precipitation. It does, however, have fertile soil—as well as huge coal deposits. Farther west one finds the semiarid plains and uplands of Gansu province, situated at the foot of the great Tibetan Plateau.

China's far northeastern region is called *Dongbei* in Chinese and Manchuria in English. Manchuria is dominated by a broad, fertile lowland basin sandwiched between moun-

Figure 11.14 The Mountains and Lowlands of Korea Like Japan, Korea has extensive uplands interspersed with lowland plains. The country's highest mountains are in the north, whereas its most extensive alluvial plains are in the south. South Korea's provinces, shown here, are culturally as well as physically distinctive.

Figure 11.13 The Fujian Coast of China In southeastern China lies the rugged coastal province of Fujian. Here the coastal plain is narrow and the shoreline deeply indented, producing a picturesque landscape. Because of limited agricultural opportunities along this rugged coastline, many Fujianese people work in maritime activities.

tains stretching along China's borders with North Korea, Russia, and Mongolia. Although winters here can be brutal, summers are usually warm and moist. Manchuria's peripheral uplands have some of China's best-preserved forests and wildlife refuges.

Korean Landscapes Korea forms a well-demarcated peninsula, partially cut off from Manchuria by rugged mountains and sizable rivers (Figure 11.14). Like Japan, its latitudinal range is pronounced. The far north, which just touches Russia's Far East, has a climate not unlike that of Maine, whereas the southern tip is more reminiscent of the Carolinas. Korea is a mountainous country with scattered alluvial basins, a landscape that has, as in many other parts of East Asia, deeply influenced its demographic and agricultural development. The lowlands of the southern portion of the peninsula are more extensive than those of the north, giving South Korea a distinct agricultural advantage over North Korea. However, North Korea has more abundant mineral deposits, forests, and hydroelectric resources.

POPULATION AND SETTLEMENT: A Realm of Crowded Lowland Basins

East Asia, along with South Asia, is the most densely populated region of the world (Table 11.1). The lowlands of Japan, Korea, and China are among the most intensely used portions of Earth, containing East Asia's major cities and most of its agricultural lands (Figure 11.15). Although the population density of East Asia is extremely high, the region's demographic growth rate has plummeted since the 1970s. In Japan especially, the current concern is impending population loss, hence an aging population that will need to be supported by a shrinking number of younger workers.

Agriculture and Settlement in Japan

Japan is a highly urbanized country, supporting two of the largest urban agglomerations in the world. Yet it is also one of the world's most mountainous countries, with lightly inhabited uplands. Agriculture must therefore share the limited lowlands with cities and suburbs, resulting in extremely intensive farming practices.

Japan's Agriculture Lands Japanese agriculture is largely limited to the country's coastal plains and interior basins. Japanese rice farming has long been one of the most productive forms of agriculture in the world, helping support a population of 127 million people on a relatively small and rugged land. Although rice is grown in almost all Japanese lowlands, the country's premier rice-growing districts lie along the Sea of Japan coast in Honshu. Vegetables and even rice crops are cultivated intensively on tiny patches within suburban and urban neighborhoods (Figure 11.16). The valleys of central and northern Honshu are famous for their temperate-climate fruit, while citrus comes from the milder southwestern reaches of the country. Crops that thrive in a cooler climate, such as potatoes, are produced mainly in Hokkaido and northern Honshu.

Settlement Patterns All Japanese cities—and the vast majority of the Japanese people—are located in the same lowlands that support the country's agriculture. Not surprisingly, the three largest metropolitan areas—Tokyo, Osaka, and Nagoya—sit near the centers of the three largest plains.

The fact that Japan's settlements are largely restricted to roughly 15 percent of its land area means that the country's effective population density—the actual crowding it experiences—is one of the highest in the world. This is especially notable in the main industrial belt, which extends from Tokyo through Nagoya and Osaka, hence along the Inland Sea (the maritime region sandwiched between Shikoku, western Honshu, and Kyushu) to the northern coast of Kyushu. This area is perhaps the most intensively used part of the world for human habitation, industry, and agriculture.

Japan's Urban–Agricultural Dilemma Due to such space limitations, all Japanese cities are characterized by dense settlement patterns. In the major urban areas, the amount of available living space is highly restricted for all but the most affluent families. Many observers—especially American ones—argue that Japan should allow its cities and suburbs to expand into nearby rural areas. However, because most uplands are too steep for residential use, such expansion would have to come at the expense of farmland.

As it now stands, the wholesale conversion of farmland to neighborhoods would be difficult. Although most farms are extremely small (the average is only several acres) and only marginally viable, farmers are politically powerful and croplands are often protected by the tax code. Moreover,

TABLE 11.1	Population Indicators							
Country	Population (millions) 2010	Population Density (per square kilometer)	Rate of Natural Increase (RNI)	Total Fertility Rate	Percent Urban	Percent <15	Percent >65	Net Migration (Rate per 1,000) 2005–10[a]
China	1,338.1	140	0.5	1.5	47	18	8	−0.3
Hong Kong	7.0	6,410	0.6	1.0	100	12	13	3.3
Japan	127.4	337	−0.0	1.4	86	13	23	0.2
North Korea	22.8	189	0.5	2.0	60	22	9	0.0
South Korea	48.9	491	0.4	1.2	82	17	11	−0.1
Taiwan	23.2	644	0.2	1.0	78	16	11	

[a]Net Migration Rate from the United Nations, Population Division, World Population Prospects: The 2008 Revision Population Database.
Source: Population Reference Bureau, World Population Data Sheet, 2010.

Figure 11.15 Population Map of East Asia Parts of East Asia are extraordinarily densely settled, particularly in the coastal lowlands of China and Japan. This contrasts with the sparsely settled lands of western China, North Korea, and northern Japan. Although the total population of this world region is high, as is the overall density, the rate of natural population increase has slowed rather dramatically in the last several decades.

most Japanese citizens believe that it is vitally important for their country to remain self-sufficient at least in rice. Rice imports are therefore highly restricted.

U.S. economic interests, along with certain Japanese consumer advocates, stress the fact that the present system forces Japanese consumers to pay several times the world market price for rice, their staple food. Critics also point out that Japan relies on imports for more than half of its overall food needs as well as for the energy that is required to grow rice. But whatever arguments are made, change will only come gradually, if at all. For the moment, Japan must live with the tensions resulting from the fact that its affluent population is forced to live in tight proximity and to pay high prices for basic staples.

Agriculture and Settlement in China, Korea, and Taiwan

Like Japan, Taiwan and Korea are urban societies. Although China remains predominantly rural, with an urbanization rate of only some 47 percent, its cities are growing rapidly. Chinese cities are rather evenly distributed across the plains and valleys of China proper. As a result, the overall pattern of population distribution in China closely follows the geography of agricultural productivity.

China's Agricultural Regions A line drawn just to the north of the Yangtze Valley divides China into two main agricultural regions. To the south, rice is the dominant crop. To the north, wheat, millet, and sorghum are the most common.

In southern and central China, population is highly concentrated in the broad lowlands, which are famous for their fertile soil and intensive agriculture. More than 100 million people live in the Sichuan Basin, while more than 70 million reside in deltaic Jiangsu, a province smaller than Ohio. Crop-

PEOPLE PER SQUARE KILOMETER

- Fewer than 6
- 6–25
- 26–100
- 101–250
- 251–500
- 501–1000
- 1000–12,801
- More than 12,801

POPULATION

- Metropolitan areas more than 20 million
- Metropolitan areas 10–20 million
- Metropolitan areas 5–10 million
- Metropolitan areas 1–5 million
- Selected smaller metropolitan areas

Figure 11.16 Japanese Urban Farm Japanese landscapes often combine dense urban settlement with small patches of intensively farmed agriculture. Here a tiny farm coexists with an urban neighborhood.

The North China Plain and the Loess Plateau. *The North China Plain is one of the most densely settled agricultural landscapes in the world. To the west, the Loess Plateau is less densely settled, but it is often still considered overpopulated, due to its environmental limitations.*

The Sichuan Basin. *The Sichuan Basin holds well over 100 million people, making it one of the most densely populated parts of East Asia—and the world.*

Japan and South Korea. *Japan and South Korea are more densely populated than they appear on this map. The populations of both countries are highly concentrated in major cities, with most upland areas remaining relatively sparsely populated.*

ping occurs year-round in most of southern and central China; summer rice alternates with winter barley or vegetables in the north, whereas two rice crops can be harvested in the far south. Southern China also produces a wide variety of tropical and subtropical crops, and moderate slopes throughout the area supply sweet potatoes, corn, and other upland crops.

The North China Plain is one of the world's most thoroughly **anthropogenic landscapes**; that is, it has been heavily transformed by human activities. Virtually its entire extent is either cultivated or occupied by houses, factories, and other structures of human society. Too dry in most areas for rice, the North China Plain supports the main crops of wheat, millet, and sorghum.

Manchuria was a lightly populated frontier zone as recently as the mid-1800s. Today, with a population of more than 100 million, its central plain is thoroughly settled. Still, Manchuria remains less crowded than many other parts of China, and it is one of the few parts of China to produce a consistent food surplus.

The Loess Plateau is more thinly settled yet, supporting only some 70 million inhabitants. But considering the area's aridity and widespread soil erosion, this is a high figure. Like other portions of northern China, the Loess Plateau produces wheat and millet. One of its unique settlement features is subterranean housing. Although loess erodes quickly under the impact of running water, it holds together well in other circumstances. For millennia, villagers have excavated pits on the surface of the plateau, from which they have tunneled into the earth to form underground houses (Figure 11.17). These subterranean dwellings are cool in the summer and warm in the winter. Unfortunately, they tend to collapse during earthquakes. One quake in 1920 killed an estimated 100,000 persons; another in 1932 killed some 70,000.

Patterns in Korea and Taiwan Like China and Japan, Korea is a densely populated country. It contains some 72 million persons (23 million in the north and 49 million in the south) in an area smaller than Minnesota. South Korea's population density is approximately 1,200 per square mile (491 per square kilometer), a higher density than Japan's. Most of South Korea's people are crowded into the alluvial plains and basins of the west and south. South Korean agriculture is dominated by rice. North Korea, in contrast, relies heavily on corn and other upland crops that do not require irrigation.

Taiwan is the most densely populated state in East Asia. Roughly the size of the Netherlands, it contains more than 22 million inhabitants. Its overall population density is more than 1,500 people per square mile (644 per square kilometer), one of the highest figures in the world. Because mountains cover most of central and eastern Taiwan, virtually the entire population is concentrated in the narrow lowland belt in the north and west. Large cities and numerous factories are scattered here amid lush farmlands. Despite its highly productive agriculture, Taiwan, like other East Asian countries, is forced to obtain much of its food from abroad.

Agriculture and Resources in Global Context

Japan, South Korea, and Taiwan are major food importers, and China has recently moved in the same direction. Other resources also are being drawn in from all quarters of the world by the powerful economies of East Asia.

Global Dimensions of Japanese Agriculture and Forestry

Japan may be mostly self-sufficient in rice, but it is still one of the world's largest food importers. As the Japanese have grown more prosperous over the past 60 years, their diet has grown more diverse. That diversity is made possible largely by importation of food.

Japan imports food from a wide array of other countries. It procures both meat and the feed used in its domestic livestock industry from the United States, Canada, and Australia. These same countries supply wheat needed to produce bread and noodles. Japan is now the world's second largest wheat importer. Even soybeans, long a staple of the Japanese diet, must be purchased from Brazil and the United States. Japan has one of the highest rates of fish consumption in the world, and the Japanese fishing fleet scours the world's oceans to supply the demand (Figure 11.18). Japan also purchases prawns and other seafood, much of it farm-raised in former mangrove swamps, from Southeast Asia and Latin America.

Japan also depends on imports to supply its demand for forest resources. While its own forests produce high-quality cedar and cypress logs, it obtains most of its construction lumber and pulp (for papermaking) from western North America and Southeast Asia. As the rain forests of Malaysia, Indonesia, and the Philippines diminish, Japanese interests are beginning to turn to Latin America and Africa as sources of tropical hardwoods. Japanese and South Korean firms also are looking to eastern Russia, a nearby and previously little-exploited forest zone.

Japan is able to support its large and prosperous population on such a restricted land base because it can purchase resources from abroad. Almost all of the oil, coal, and other minerals that it consumes are imported. Although geographers once looked at resource endowments as a main support of each country's economy, such a view is no longer supportable. As long as a country can export products of value, it can obtain whatever imports it requires. This also means, however, that the environmental degradation gener-

Figure 11.17 Loess Settlement A typical subterranean dwelling carved out the soft loess sediment in central China. Approximately 70 million people live similarly in the Loess Plateau region. Unfortunately, this region is prone to major earthquakes that take a high toll on the local population because of dwelling collapse.

Figure 11.18 Japanese Fishing Boat A Japanese whaling ship leaves the port of Shimonoseki in southwestern Japan. While Japanese whaling is particularly controversial, the larger Japanese fishing fleet covers much of the world's ocean surface in search of high-quality seafood.

ated by a successful economy, such as that of Japan, becomes globalized as well.

Global Dimensions of Chinese Agriculture Until the late 1990s, China was self-sufficient in food, despite its huge population and crowded lands. But rapid economic growth has resulted in an increased consumption of meat, which requires large amounts of feed grain. Growth also has brought about the loss of agricultural lands to residential and industrial development. China is now the world's largest importer of soybeans and vegetable oil, and it imports significant quantities of wheat and other grains in most years. China's government aims to be 95 percent self-sufficient in food, but planners have recently discussed lowering that figure to 90 percent.

Although China is a net food importer when it comes to total calories, the situation is not so clear in regard to total value. China exports many high-value specialty crops and processed foods, such as garlic, apples, farm-raised fish, and many vegetables. Farmers in both wealthy countries such as the United States and poor countries such as the Philippines often complain that China sells its fruit and vegetables abroad at below-market rates, seeking to build export dominance. Consumers in foreign markets are concerned about the safety of Chinese exports. In 2007, the United States prohibited the import of a number of Chinese seafood products until they could be proved safe. China responded by banning chicken and pork products from Tyson Foods, a U.S. company. At the same time, however, the Chinese government shut down more than 100 food-processing plants, and went so far as to execute the former

head of its own food and drug agency after he was convicted of corruption.

Korean Agriculture in a Global Context South Korea has also made the transition, like Japan and Taiwan, to a global food and resource procurement pattern. It is now one of the world's main importers of wheat, corn, and soybeans. South Korea also imports large quantities of beef, particularly from Australia. In 2003, it banned beef imports from the United States due to fears about mad cow disease. U.S. beef was again allowed into the country in 2008, but the decision prompted massive protests by South Korean farmers and others concerned about food safety.

North Korea, on the other hand, has pursued a goal of self-sufficiency. While relatively successful for a number of years, in the mid-1990s this policy resulted in widespread famine after a series of floods, followed by drought, destroyed most of the country's rice and corn crops. Since then, North Korea has relied heavily on international aid—much of it coming from South Korea—to feed its people, but malnutrition and even starvation remain widespread. North Korea also purchases food from China, buying more than 13,000 tons of grain in January 2010 alone.

Urbanization in East Asia

China has one of the world's oldest urban foundations, dating back more than 3,500 years. In medieval and early modern times, East Asia supported a well-developed system of cities. In the early 1700s, Tokyo, then called Edo, probably overshadowed all other cities, with a population of more than 1 million.

But despite this early start, East Asia was largely rural at the end of World War II. Some 90 percent of China's people then lived in the countryside, and even Japan was only about 50 percent urbanized. But as the region's economy began to grow after the war, so did its cities. Japan, Taiwan, and South Korea are now between 78 and 86 percent urban, which is typical for advanced industrial countries. Most of China's people still live in rural areas, but within a few years the country will have an urban majority.

Chinese Cities Traditional Chinese cities were clearly separated from the countryside by defensive walls. Most were planned in accordance with strict geometrical principles that were thought to reflect the cosmic order. The old-style Chinese city was dominated by low buildings and characterized by straight streets. Houses were typically built around courtyards, and narrow alleyways served both commercial and residential functions.

China's urban fabric began to change during the colonial period. A group of port cities was taken over by European interests, which proceeded to build Western-style buildings and modern business districts. By far the most important of these semicolonial cities was Shanghai, built near the mouth of the Yangtze River, the main gateway to interior China.

When the communists came to power in 1949, Shanghai, with a population of more than 10 million, was the second-largest city in the world. The new authorities, however, viewed it as a decadent, foreign creation. They therefore milked it for taxes, which they invested elsewhere. Most of the wealthy people fled to Hong Kong, and relatively few migrants were allowed in. As a result, much of the city began to decay.

Since the late 1980s, Shanghai has experienced a major revival and is again in many respects China's premier city. Migrants are now pouring into the city, even though the state still tries to restrict the flow, and building cranes crowd the skyline. Official statistics now put the population of the municipality at more than 19 million, but the actual number is greater, as Shanghai probably holds around 3 million undocumented migrants from other parts of China (see "People on the Move: Rural Migrants Flock to China's Cities). The new Shanghai is a city of massive high-rise apartments and concentrated industrial developments (Figure 11.19). In 2008, Shanghai had the second busiest port in the world (after Singapore) and boasted the world's fastest train. But despite Shanghai's revived economic fortunes, the city remains politically secondary to Beijing, China's capital.

Beijing was China's capital during the Manchu period (1644–1912), a status it regained in 1949. Under communist rule, Beijing was radically transformed; old buildings were razed and broad avenues were plowed through neighborhoods (Figure 11.20). Crowded residential districts gave way to large blocks of apartment buildings and massive government offices. Some historically significant structures were saved; the buildings of the Forbidden City, for example, where the Manchu rulers once lived, survived as a complex of museums. The area immediately in front of the Palace Museum, however, was cleared. The resulting plaza, Tiananmen Square, is reputed to be the largest open square in any city of the world. The Chinese government invested large amounts of money into Beijing's urban infrastructure in preparation for the city's 2008 Summer Olympics.

The Chinese Urban System China's urban system as a whole is fairly well balanced, with sizable cities relatively evenly spaced across the landscape and with no city overshadowing all others. This balance stems from China's heritage of urbanism, its vast size and distinctive physical–geographical regions, and its legacy of socialist planning. In the early 1960s, noted China scholar G. William Skinner argued that the distribution of Chinese cities is best explained through the use of **central place theory**. Central place theory holds that an evenly distributed rural population will give rise to a regular hierarchy of urban places, with uniformly spaced larger cities surrounded by constellations of smaller cities, each of which, in turn, will be surrounded by smaller towns.

In the 1990s, Beijing and Shanghai vied for the first position among Chinese cities, with Tianjin, serving as Beijing's port, coming in third. All three of these cities, along with Chongqing in the Sichuan Basin, have been removed from the regular provincial structure of the country and granted their own metropolitan governments. In 1997, another major city, Hong Kong, passed from British to Chinese control. Rather than becoming an ordinary part of China, Hong Kong was granted a unique status as an autonomous "special administrative region," and allowed to largely manage its own affairs. Although not as populous as Beijing or Shanghai, Hong Kong is far wealthier. The greater metropolitan area of the Xi Delta, composed of Hong Kong, Shenzhen, and Guangzhou (called Canton in the

Figure 11.19 Contemporary Shanghai This vibrant city of approximately 20 million embodies the new China with its massive high-rise apartments, industrial developments, and office towers.

Figure 11.20 Beijing, China The historic capital during the Manchu period (1644–1912), Beijing regained its status as capital city in 1949. Under communist rule, much of Beijing's historical landscape was razed and replaced with large blocks of government offices and massive apartment buildings. Only the historically significant Forbidden City, home to the Manchu rulers, was saved from this transformation of the urban landscape. Tiananmen Square, reputed to be the largest open square in any city, was created by clearing buildings away from the area in front of the Palace Museum.

Population of Beijing in selected years	
Year	Population
1953	2.8 million
1973	7.6 million
1994	12.6 million
2008	15.0 million

West), is certainly one of China's premier urban areas. In addition to these four primary Chinese cities are several dozen large and growing urban centers. By 2010, more than 40 of them had more than 1 million inhabitants.

Urban Patterns in Japan, Korea, and Taiwan Unlike China, South Korea and Taiwan are noted for their **urban primacy**, with their urban population concentrated in a single city. Japan supports a more extensive urban phenomenon called a **superconurbation**, or megalopolis, which is a huge zone of coalesced metropolitan areas (Figure 11.21).

Seoul, the capital of South Korea, overwhelms all other cities in the country. Seoul itself is home to more than 10 million people, and its metropolitan area contains between 20 and 24 million, almost half of South Korea's population. All of South Korea's major governmental, economic, and cultural institutions are concentrated there. Seoul's explosive and generally unplanned growth has resulted in severe congestion. The South Korean government is promoting industrial growth in other cities, but none of its actions has yet challenged the primacy of the capital.

Taiwan is similarly characterized by a high degree of urban primacy. The capital city of Taipei, located in the far north, mushroomed from some 300,000 people during the Japanese colonial period (from 1895 to 1945) to more than 6 million in the metropolitan area today.

Japan has traditionally been characterized by urban "bipolarity" rather than urban primacy. Until the 1960s, Tokyo, the capital and main business and educational center, together with the neighboring port of Yokohama, was balanced by the mercantile center of Osaka and its port of Kobe. Kyoto, the former imperial capital and the traditional

TOKYO'S GROWTH
- 1914
- 1946
- 1975

POPULATION OF JAPAN'S MAIN URBAN CONCENTRATIONS

Region	Population
Tokyo	27.5 million
Osaka/Kobe/Kyoto	13.9 million
Nagoya	4.9 million

65% of Japan's total population lives in the Tokkaido corridor

- Primary area of population concentration (Tokkaido corridor)
- Secondary area of population concentration
- Rail trunk line

Figure 11.21 Urban Concentration in Japan The inset map shows the rapid expansion of Tokyo in the postwar decades. Today the Greater Tokyo metropolitan area is home to almost 30 million people. The larger map shows the cluster of urban settlements along Japan's southeastern coast. The major area of urban concentration is between Tokyo and Osaka, a distance of some 300 miles (482 kilometers), known as the Tokkaido corridor. By some accounts, 65 percent of Japan's population lives in this area.

cultural center, is also situated in the Osaka region. A host of secondary and tertiary cities balance Japan's urban structure. Nagoya, with a metropolitan area of some 5 million persons, remains the center of the automobile industry and is one of the few large Japanese cities in which it is more efficient to travel by car than by public transportation.

As Japan's economy boomed in the 1960s, 1970s, and 1980s, so did Tokyo (see "Cityscapes: The Varied Neighborhoods of Tokyo"). The capital city then outpaced all other urban areas in almost every urban function. While Tokyo itself has about 13 million inhabitants, the Greater Tokyo area now contains 35 to 39 million people, making it the world's most populous urbanized area. The Osaka–Kobe–Kyoto metropolitan area stands second, with 18 million inhabitants. Concerned about the increasing primacy of Tokyo, the

Japanese government has been trying to steer new developments to other parts of the country.

Most of Japan's other main cities have seen modest population gains over the past several decades. Urban growth, in general, has been supported by rural depopulation. Metropolitan expansion has been particularly pronounced in the cities linking Tokyo to Osaka, an area known as the Tokkaido corridor. Transportation connections are superb along this route, and proximity to Tokyo, Osaka, and Nagoya encourages development. The result has been the creation of a superconurbation (see Figure 11.21). One can travel from Tokyo to Osaka on the main rail line, a distance of almost 300 miles (480 kilometers), and never leave the urbanized area. By some accounts, 65 percent of Japan's people are crowded into this narrow supercity.

PEOPLE ON THE MOVE   Rural Migrants Flock to China's Cities

China is currently the site of the largest migration stream in human history. Over the last several decades, more than 100 million rural Chinese have moved to the country's burgeoning cities, a number that is expected to increase to nearly 250 million by 2025. According to recent census data, most of these migrants remain in their home provinces. As a result, midsized cities across China are rapidly growing. More than a third of such migrants, however, cross provincial lines, most of them heading from the interior to the booming cities of the coastal zone.

Several factors contribute to this remarkable process of relocation. Agricultural wages have been relatively stagnant for years, whereas those in the urban sector have been rising steadily. China's farms tend to be too small to use labor efficiently; as a result, the country has up to 300 million "surplus" agricultural workers. The rapid growth of urban infrastructure, meanwhile, generates a large demand for unskilled workers. Rural areas also tend to have higher birthrates than cities, as China's one-child policy is not rigorously enforced in the countryside. With few opportunities at home, young people from rural environments often head to the cities when they come of age.

Although the Chinese economy benefits in many ways from such migration, the government is concerned that the process could get out of hand, generating squatter settlements and other forms of urban blight. China also wants to maintain close control over its citizens, and is thus wary of granting the freedom to relocate. Such policies stem both from the authoritarian nature of the Chinese state and from traditional patterns of government. China has long maintained a comprehensive system of household registration, known as the *hukou* system. Registration papers include information about a person's age, family background, marital status, and legal place of residence. Rural migrants in urban areas often have no legal standing in the city; as far as the government is concerned, they are mere visitors (Figure 11.2.1). To obtain governmental services, such people must either return to their home villages or pay hefty bribes.

The hukou system is especially burdensome in regard to education. The estimated 200 million Chinese citizens who live outside of their areas of registration usually have difficulty enrolling their children in schools. If they are to be educated, such children must either move back to the countryside and live with relatives or their parents must find a away around the registration system. But rural schools are often poor in quality, and many migrant parents are too poor to get their children enrolled in urban schools. And even if they are able to attend school in the city, students from unregistered rural backgrounds must return to their home villages to take college entrance exams.

The hukou system has been the subject of intense discussion in China in recent years. Critics contend that it creates a two-tier system of the "haves" (registered urban dwellers) and "have nots" (those registered in the countryside). Some fear that vast numbers of migrant children are not receiving adequate education, thus imperilling the future of the country. As a result, China has recently eased education restrictions on rural migrants. Some voices are calling for the registration system to be abolished altogether, but thus far the government shows no signs of contemplating such a radical reform.

Figure 11.2.1 Rural Migrants in a Chinese City Rural migrants are often unable to acquire official residency in China's cities. As a result, they are often forced to perform difficult and dangerous work for low wages.

Japanese cities sometimes strike foreign visitors as rather gray and monotonous places, lacking historical interest (Figure 11.22). Little of the country's premodern architecture remains intact. Traditional Japanese buildings were made of wood, which survives earthquakes much better than stone or brick. Fires have therefore been a long-standing hazard, and in World War II the U.S. Air Force fire-bombed most Japanese cities, virtually obliterating them. In addition, Hiroshima and Nagasaki were completely destroyed by atomic bombs. The one exception was Kyoto, the old imperial capital, which was spared devastation. As a result, Kyoto is famous for its beautiful (wooden) Buddhist monasteries and Shinto temples, which ring the basin in which central Kyoto lies.

Other Japanese cities were largely reconstructed in the 1950s and 1960s, a period when Japan was still relatively poor and could afford only inexpensive concrete buildings. In the boom years of the 1980s, however, modern skyscrapers rose in many of the larger cities, and postmodernist architecture began to lend variety, especially to the wealthier

Figure 11.22 Tokyo Apartments The extremely high population density of Tokyo and other large Japanese cities forces most people to live in crowded apartment blocks. The photograph depicts Tokyo's Danchi high-rise apartment complex.

neighborhoods. Critics sometimes contend that Japanese cities still have relatively few features that show a distinctive cultural flavor. Others disagree, noting that if one looks closely, one may see aspects of Japanese and, more generally, East Asian culture everywhere.

CULTURAL COHERENCE AND DIVERSITY: A Confucian Realm?

East Asia is in some respects one of the world's most unified cultural regions. Although different parts of East Asia have their own unique cultural features, the entire region shares certain historically rooted ways of life and systems of ideas.

Most of these East Asian commonalties can be traced back to ancient Chinese civilization. Chinese civilization emerged roughly 4,000 years ago, largely in isolation from the Eastern Hemisphere's other early centers of civilization in the valleys of the Indus, Tigris-Euphrates, and Nile rivers. As a result, East Asian civilization developed along several unique lines.

Unifying Cultural Characteristics

The most important unifying cultural characteristics of East Asia are related to religious and philosophical beliefs. Throughout the region, Buddhism and Confucianism have shaped not only individual beliefs but also social and political structures. Although the role of traditional belief systems has been seriously challenged over the past 50 years, especially in China, historically grounded cultural patterns have not disappeared.

Writing Systems The clearest distinction between East Asia and the world's other cultural regions is found in written language. Existing writing systems elsewhere in the world are based on the alphabetic principle, in which each symbol represents a distinct sound. East Asia, in contrast, evolved an entirely different system, **ideographic writing**. In ideographic writing, each symbol (commonly called a character) primarily represents an idea rather than a sound (although the symbols can denote sounds in certain circumstances). As a result, ideographic writing requires the use of a large number of distinct symbols.

The East Asian writing system can be traced to the dawn of Chinese civilization, some 3,200 years ago. As the Chinese Empire expanded and the prestige of Chinese civilization carried its culture to other lands, the Chinese writing system spread. Japan, Korea, and Vietnam all came to use the same system, although in Japan it was substantially modified, while in Korea and Vietnam it was much later largely replaced by alphabetic systems.

The Chinese ideographic writing system has one major disadvantage and one major advantage when compared with alphabetic systems, both of which stem from the fact that it is largely divorced from spoken language. The disadvantage

Although Tokyo is a huge city in a vast metropolitan area, it can feel like a small, intimate place. This is partly because it is divided into 23 districts (or *ku*, in Japanese), each of which has its own distinctive character and specializes in specific goods and services (Figure 11.3.1). Fortunately, Tokyo has a superb system of public transportation, making it relatively easy to get from one neighborhood to another (Figure 11.3.2).

Several Tokyo neighborhoods are noted as entertainment districts. For people looking for exciting nightlife and a cosmopolitan atmosphere, Roppongi is the place to go. Emerging around a now-defunct U.S. military base, Roppongi is the most Westernized part of Japan, and thus appeals to many tourists and expatriates. Younger Japanese looking for fun and fashion more often head for Harajuku, famous for its boutiques and sidewalk cafes. Well-heeled business executives, on the other hand, tend to favor the Akasaka nightlife district, celebrated for its expensive hotels and "hostess bars."

Other Tokyo neighborhoods are better known for their shopping potential. Some are highly specialized. Akihabara, for example, has more than 600 stores focused on electronics. Tsukiji, on the other hand, boasts the largest fish market in Japan and perhaps the world. The most expensive shops—and some of the world's most

Figure 11.3.2 Tokyo Train Station Tokyo boasts an extremely efficient public transportation system, based largely on subways and commuter rail lines. Trains and train stations, however, can be very crowded during rush hours.

Figure 11.3.1 Neighborhoods and Districts of Tokyo Tokyo is divided into numerous administrative districts, each of which has an individual personality. Each district, in turn, contains a number of distinctive neighborhoods.

expensive real estate—are found in the Ginza, a swanky neighborhood also noted for its art galleries and exclusive clubs. Tokyo's department store center is found in Shibuya, which also has an active and rather hip nightlife scene. One also can shop, and do much more, in Shinjuku, Tokyo's main business district. Reminiscent of midtown Manhattan, Shinjuku boasts a collection of impressive skyscrapers.

Other Tokyo neighborhoods are better known for their historical significance. Although Hibiya is an important financial district, it is more famous as the site of the Imperial Palace and the center of the old city. Ueno, also part of the old downtown, supports the National Museum, which has the world's largest collection of Japanese art.

Tourists less often venture into Tokyo's other districts, but many are worth the effort. If one wants to see the rougher side of the city—which, by U.S. standards, is not very rough at all—head for Ikebukuro, which has aptly been described as "working man's Tokyo." For the geographically inclined, one can do no better than simply walk the narrow back streets and encounter the unexpected. Turn one corner, and you might find an entire street of small-scale machine shops, each of which is relatively open to visual inspection; turn another, and you might come across a large assemblage of tiny printing establishments. For a pedestrian's encounter of diversity amid globalization, few places are more interesting and accessible than Tokyo.

is that it is difficult to learn; to be literate, a person must memorize thousands of characters. The advantage is that two literate people do not have to speak the same language to be able to communicate, because the written symbols that they use to express their ideas are the same.

In Korea, Chinese characters were adopted at an early date and were used exclusively for hundreds of years. In the 1400s, however, Korean officials decided that Korea needed its own alphabet. They wanted to allow more widespread literacy, hoping also to more clearly differentiate Korean culture from that of China. The use of the new script spread quickly through the country. Korean scholars and officials, however, continued to use Chinese characters, regarding their own script as suitable only for popular writings. Today the Korean script is used for almost all purposes, but scholarly works still contain scattered Chinese characters.

The writing system of Japan is even more complex (Figure 11.23). Initially the Japanese simply borrowed Chinese characters, referred to in Japanese as kanji. Owing to the grammatical differences between Japanese and Chinese, the exclusive use of kanji resulted in awkward sentence construction. The Japanese solved this quandary by developing a quasi-alphabet known as hiragana that allowed the expression of words and parts of speech not easily represented by Chinese characters. In hiragana, each symbol represents a distinct syllable, or combination of a consonant and a vowel sound. (A different but essentially parallel system, called katakana, is used in Japan for spelling words of foreign origin.) Eventually the two styles of writing merged, and written Japanese came to employ a complex mixture of symbols. Japanese kanji today differ slightly from Chinese characters.

The Confucian Legacy Just as the use of a common writing system helped forge cultural linkages throughout East Asia, so too **Confucianism** (the philosophy developed by Confucius) came to occupy a significant position in all of the societies of the region. So strong is the heritage of Confucius that some writers refer to East Asia as the "Confucian world."

The premier philosopher of Chinese history, Confucius (or *Kongfuzi,* in Mandarin Chinese) lived during the 6th century BCE, a period of marked political instability. Confucius's goal was to create a philosophy that could generate stability. Although Confucianism is often considered to be a religion, Confucius himself was mostly interested in the "here and now," focusing his attention on how to lead a correct life and organize a proper society. Confucian thought does not deny the existence of a deity or an afterlife, but neither does it give them much consideration.

Confucius stressed deference to the proper authority figures, but he also thought that authority has a responsibility to act in a benevolent manner. The most basic level of the traditional Confucian moral order is the family unit, considered the bedrock of society. The ideal family structure is patriarchal, and children are told to obey and respect their parents—especially their fathers—as well as their elder brothers.

Confucian philosophy also stresses the need for a well-rounded and broadly humanistic education. To a certain extent, Confucianism advocates a kind of meritocracy, holding that an individual should be judged on the basis of behavior and education, rather than on family background. The high officials of Imperial China (pre-1912)—the powerful **Mandarins**—were thus selected by competitive examinations. Only wealthy families, however, could afford to give their sons the education needed for success on those grueling tests.

In Japan, Confucianism was never as important as it was on the mainland. Japanese officials were actually able to exclude certain Confucian beliefs that they considered dangerous. The most important of these was the revocable "mandate of heaven." According to this notion, the emperor of China derived his authority from the principle of cosmic harmony, but such a mandate could be withdrawn if he failed to fulfill his duties. This idea was used both to explain and to legitimize the rebellions that occasionally resulted in a change of China's ruling dynasty. In Japan, on the other hand, a single imperial dynasty has persisted throughout the entire period of written history. Although the emperor of Japan has had little real power for more than a thousand years, the sanctity of his family lineage continues to form a basic principle of Japanese society.

The Modern Role of Confucian Ideology The significance of Confucianism in East Asian development has been hotly debated for the past hundred years. In the early 1900s, many observers believed that the conservatism of the philosophy,

Figure 11.23 Japanese Writing The writing system of Japan was originally based on Chinese characters, known in Japan as kanji. Because of grammatical differences, however, the Japanese developed two unique "alphabets" of syllables, known as katakana and hiragana. Here kanji and katakana symbols are visible.

derived from its respect for tradition and authority, was responsible for the economically backward position of China and Korea. But because East Asia has enjoyed the world's fastest rates of economic growth over the past several decades, such a position is no longer supportable. Some scholars now argue that Confucianism's respect for education and the social stability that it generates give East Asia an advantage in international competition.

Over the past 100 years, Confucianism has lost much of the hold that it once had on public morality throughout East Asia, especially in China. After the communist revolution, China's rulers sought for decades to discourage if not eliminate Confucian thought. Currently, however, Chinese officials are pushing for a revival of the philosophy, hoping that it will lead to enhanced social stability. Confucian schools are multiplying, and recent books, films, and television shows about Confucius have been popular. The Chinese government also maintains 145 Confucius Institutes in more than 50 countries, designed to promote Chinese culture and language.

Religious Unity and Diversity

Certain religious beliefs have worked alongside Confucianism to cement together cultures of the East Asian region. The most important culturally unifying beliefs are associated with Mahayana Buddhism. Other religious practices, however, have had a more divisive role.

Mahayana Buddhism Originating in India in the 6th century BCE, Buddhism stresses escape from an endless cycle of rebirths to reach union with the divine cosmic principle (or nirvana). By the 2nd century CE, Buddhism was spreading through China, and within a few hundred years it had expanded throughout East Asia. Today Buddhism remains widespread everywhere in the region, although it is far less significant here than it is in mainland Southeast Asia and Sri Lanka.

The variety of Buddhism practiced in East Asia—Mahayana, or Greater Vehicle—is distinct from the Theravada Buddhism of Sri Lanka and Southeast Asia (Figure 11.24). Most important, Mahayana Buddhism simplifies the quest for nirvana, in part by suggesting that entities (boddhisatvas) exist who refuse divine union for themselves in order to help others spiritually. Mahayana Buddhism is also nonexclusive; in other words, one may follow it while simultaneously practicing other faiths. Thus, many Chinese consider themselves to be both Buddhists and Taoists, whereas most Japanese are at some level both Buddhists and followers of Shinto.

As Mahayana Buddhism spread through East Asia in the medieval period, many different sects emerged. Probably the best known is Zen, which demands that its followers engage in the rigorous practice of "mind emptying." At one time, Buddhist monasteries associated with Zen and other sects were rich and powerful. In all East Asian countries, however, periodic reactions against Buddhism resulted in the persecution of monks and the suppression of monasteries. One rea-

Figure 11.24 The Buddhist Landscape Mahayana Buddhism has been traditionally practiced throughout East Asia. This Golden Buddha statue is located in Baomo Park in Chi Lei Village, Guangdong Province, China.

son for this opposition was the fact that government officials often viewed Buddhism as a foreign religion that placed India—rather than China—at the center of the world.

Despite such hardships, East Asian Buddhism was never extinguished. But it also never became the focal point of society that it did in mainland Southeast Asia. In Japan, that position was partially captured by a different religion, Shinto.

Shinto The religious practice of Shinto is so closely bound to the idea of Japanese nationality that it is questionable whether a non-Japanese person can follow it. Shinto began as the animistic worship of nature spirits, but it was gradually refined into a subtle set of beliefs about the harmony of nature and its connections with human existence. Until the late 1800s, Buddhism and Shinto were complexly intertwined. Subsequently, the Japanese government began to disentangle the two faiths while elevating Shinto into a nationalistic cult focused on the divinity of the Japanese imperial family. After World War II, the more excessive aspects of nationalism were removed from the religion.

Shinto is still a place- and nature-centered religion. Certain mountains, particularly the volcanic Mount Fuji, are considered sacred and are thus climbed by large numbers of people. Major Shinto shrines, often located in scenic places, attract numerous pilgrims; most notable is the Ise Shrine south of Nagoya, site of the cult of the emperor. Local Shinto shrines, as well as Buddhist temples, offer leafy oases in otherwise largely treeless Japanese urban neighborhoods.

Taoism and Other Chinese Belief Systems The Chinese religion of Taoism (or Daoism) is similarly rooted in nature worship. Like Shinto, it stresses the acquisition of spiritual harmony and the pursuit of a balanced life. Taoism is indi-

Figure 11.25 The Language Geography of East Asia The linguistic geography of Korea and Japan is very straightforward, as the vast majority of people in those countries speak Korean and Japanese, respectively. In China, the dominant Han Chinese speak a variety of closely related Sinitic languages, the most important of which is Mandarin Chinese. In the peripheral regions of China, a large number of languages—belonging to several different linguistic families—can be found.

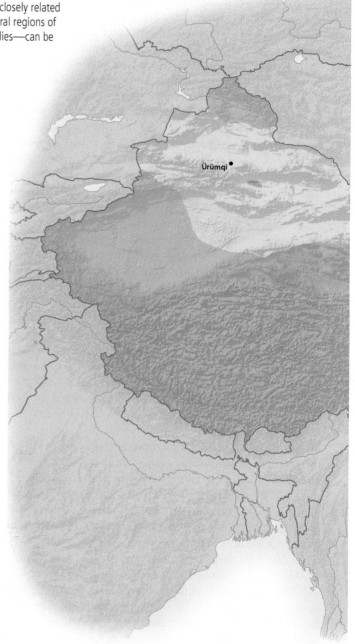

rectly associated with feng shui, also called **geomancy**, the Chinese and Korean practice of designing buildings in accordance with the spiritual powers that supposedly course through the local topography. Even in hypermodern Hong Kong, skyscrapers worth millions of dollars have occasionally gone unoccupied because their construction failed to accord with geomantic principles. The government of China officially recognizes Taoism as a religion, and seeks to regulate it through the state-run China Taoist Association.

Despite the fact that both Taoism and Buddhism were historically followed throughout the country, traditional religious practice in China has always embraced local particularism; in other words, it has focused on the unique attributes of particular places. Many minor gods were traditionally associated with single cities or other specific areas. In modern-day rural China, village gods are often still honored.

Minority Religions Followers of virtually all world religions can be found in the increasingly cosmopolitan cities of East Asia. Christianity is well represented. Over a million Japanese belong to Christian churches, whereas South Korea is roughly 30 percent Christian (mostly Protestant). South Korea reportedly sends more missionaries abroad than any country except the United States. Some reports indicate that Christianity is growing rapidly in China—despite state discouragement—but reliable information is scarce. In 2008, official statistics put the number of Chinese Protestants at 20 million and Chinese Catholics at 10 million; some experts think that an additional 50 million or so Chinese belong to unofficial "house churches."

China also has a long-established Muslim community, estimated as having between 20 and 60 million adherents. Most Chinese Muslims are members of minority ethnic groups living in the far west. The roughly 10 million Chinese-speaking Muslims, called *Hui*, are concentrated in Gansu and Ningxia in the northwest and in Yunnan province in the south. Smaller clusters of Hui, often segregated in their own villages, live in almost every province of China. The only Muslim congregations in Japan and South Korea, on the other hand, are associated with recent and often temporary immigrants from South, Southeast, and Southwest Asia.

Secularism in East Asia For all of these varied forms of religious expression, East Asia is one of the most secular regions of the world. In Japan, most people occasionally observe Shinto or Buddhist rituals and maintain a small shrine for their ancestors, but only a small segment of the population is deeply religious. As a result, statistics on religious affiliation in Japan vary tremendously, with estimates of the followers of Shinto ranging between 4 million and 119 million! Japan also has a number of "new religions," sometimes called cults, a few of which are noted for their fanaticism. But for Japanese society as a whole, religion is not tremendously important.

After the communist regime took power over China in 1949, all forms of religion and traditional philosophy were discouraged and sometimes severely repressed. Under the new regime, atheistic Marxist philosophy—the communistic belief system developed by Karl Marx—became the official ideology. In the 1960s, many observers thought that traditional forms of Chinese religion would survive only in overseas Chinese communities. With the easing of Marxist orthodoxy during the

1980s and 1990s, however, many forms of spiritual expression began to return.

Like China, North Korea adopted communist ideology when it became independent after World War II. As a result, religious beliefs were severely repressed. North Korean leaders also supplemented **Marxism** with a unique official ideology called *juche,* or "self-reliance." Ironically, juche demands absolute loyalty to North Korea's political leaders. It also involves intense nationalism based on the idea of Korean racial purity. Over time, Marxist beliefs have gradually been supplanted by those of juche; in North Korea's revised 2009 constitution, all references to communism were removed.

Linguistic and Ethnic Diversity

Japanese and Mandarin Chinese may partially share a system of writing, but the two languages bear no direct relationship (Figure 11.25). In their grammatical structures, Chinese and Japanese are more different from each other than are Chinese and English. Japanese, however, has adopted many words of Chinese origin.

Language and National Identity in Japan According to most scholars, Japanese is not related to any other language. Korean is also usually classified as the only member of its language family. Many linguists, however, think that Japanese and Korean should be grouped together because they share many grammatical features. Only the mutual distrust between the Japanese and the Koreans, some suggest, has prevented this linguistic relationship from being acknowledged.

From several perspectives, the Japanese form one of the world's most homogeneous peoples, and they tend to regard themselves in such a manner. To be sure, minor cultural and linguistic distinctions are noted between the people of western Japan (centered on Osaka) and eastern Japan (centered on Tokyo), and many individual regions have distinctive customs and lifeways. Overall, however, such differences are of little significance. Only in the Ryukyu Islands does one encounter variants of Japanese so distinct that they can be considered separate languages. Ethnically, this region of Japan is also distinct. In fact, many Ryukyu people believe that they have not been treated as full members of the Japanese nation, and that they have suffered from discrimination.

Minority Groups in Japan In earlier centuries, the Japanese archipelago was divided between two very different peoples: the Japanese living to the south, and the Ainu inhabiting the north. The Ainu are completely distinct from the Japanese. They possess their own language and have a distinct physical appearance (Figure 11.26). Owing to their facial features, the Ainu were once categorized as members of the "Caucasian race." However, few scholars now believe that humankind is divided into separate races, and Ainu do not appear to be closely related to Europeans by genetic criteria.

For centuries the Japanese and the Ainu competed for land, and by the 10th century CE the Ainu had been largely driven off the main island of Honshu. Until the 1800s, however, Hokkaido largely remained Ainu territory. The Japanese people subsequently began to colonize Hokkaido, putting renewed pressure on the Ainu. Today, according to official statistics, around 25,000 Ainu remain, although some sources put the actual number as high as 200,000. Fewer than 100 people, however, speak the Ainu language, although efforts are being made to revive it.

The approximately 800,000 people of Korean descent living in Japan today also have felt discrimination. Many of them were born in Japan (their parents and grandparents having left Korea early in the 1900s) and speak Japanese rather than Korean as their primary language. But despite their deep bonds to Japan, such individuals are not easily able to obtain Japanese citizenship. Perhaps as a result of such treatment, many Japanese Koreans hold radical political views and support North Korea.

Starting in the 1980s, other immigrants began to arrive in Japan, mostly from the poorer countries of Asia. Most do not have legal status. Men from China and southern Asia typically work in the construction industry and in other dirty and dangerous jobs; women from Thailand and the Philippines often work as entertainers and sometimes as prostitutes. Roughly 200,000 Brazilians of Japanese ancestry have returned to Japan for the relatively high wages they can earn. However, immigration is less pronounced in Japan

Figure 11.26 Ainu Men The indigenous Ainu people of northern Japan are much reduced in population, but they still maintain a number of their cultural traditions. In this photograph, Ainu men participate in the Marimo Festival on the northern Japanese island of Hokkaido.

than in most other wealthy countries, and relatively few migrants acquire permanent residency, let alone citizenship. Because of Japan's impending population loss, however, some scholars estimate that it may need to import several million foreign workers over the next decade.

The most victimized people in Japan could be the **Burakumin**, or *Eta*, an outcast group of Japanese whose ancestors worked in "polluting" industries such as leathercraft. While discrimination is now illegal, the Burakumin are still among the poorest and least-educated people in Japan. Private detective agencies do a brisk business checking prospective marriage partners and employees for possible Burakumin ancestries. The Burakumin, however, have banded together to demand their rights; the Buraku Liberation League is politically powerful and is reputed to have close connections with the Yakuza (the Japanese mafia). The Burakumin usually live in separate neighborhoods and are concentrated in the Osaka region of western Japan.

Language and Identity in Korea The Koreans, like the Japanese, are a relatively homogeneous people. The vast majority of people in both North and South Korea speak Korean and unquestioningly consider themselves to be members of the Korean nation.

South Korea does, however, have a strong sense of regional identity, which can be traced back to the medieval

Figure 11.27 The Hakka Diaspora
The Hakka form an important and distinctive subgroup of the Han Chinese. They seem to have originated in north-central China but long ago migrated to the area where Fujian, Guangdong, and Jiangxi provinces converge. Here they developed distinctive agricultural patterns well suited to the rough uplands of the region. Later movements took Hakka communities to upland areas throughout much of southern China. In the 1800s and early 1900s, many Hakka moved to Southeast Asia, where they still form important communities.

period when the peninsula was divided into three separate kingdoms. The people of southwestern South Korea, centered on the city of Kwangju, tend to be viewed as distinctive, and many southwesterners believe that they have suffered periodic discrimination. In contract, the Kyongsang region of southeastern South Korea has supplied most of the country's political leaders and has received more than its share of development funds.

Korean identity also has an international component. Several million Korean speakers reside directly across the border in northern China. Because of deportations ordered by the Soviet Union in the mid-20th century, substantial Korean communities also can be found in Kazakhstan in Central Asia. Over the past several decades, a Korean **diaspora**—the scattering of a particular group of people over a vast geographical area—has brought hundreds of thousands of Koreans to the United States, Canada, Australia, and New Zealand.

Language and Ethnicity Among the Han Chinese The geography of language and ethnicity in China is far more complex than that of Korea or Japan. This is true even if one considers only the eastern half of the country, so-called China proper. The most important distinction is that of separating the Han Chinese from the non-Han peoples. The Han, who form the vast majority, are those people who have long been incorporated into the Chinese cultural and political systems and whose languages are expressed through Chinese writing. The Han do not, however, all speak the same language.

Northern, central, and southwestern China—a vast area extending from Manchuria through the middle and upper Yangtze Valley to the valleys and plateaus of Yunnan in the far south—constitute a single linguistic zone. The spoken language here is generally called *Mandarin Chinese*. Mandarin is divided into a number of dialects, but the standard dialect of the Beijing area is gradually spreading. Standard Mandarin—called *Pŭtōnghuà* locally—is China's official national language.

In southeastern China, from the Yangtze Delta to China's border with Vietnam, a number of separate languages are spoken. Peoples speaking these languages are Han Chinese, but they are not native Mandarin speakers. Traveling from south to north, one encounters Cantonese (or Yue) spoken in Guangdong, Fujianese (alternatively Hokkienese, or Min, locally) spoken in Fujian, and Shanghaiese (or Wu), spoken in and around the city of Shanghai and in Zhejiang province. These are true languages, not dialects, since they are not mutually intelligible. They are usually called dialects, however, because they have no distinctive written form.

The Hakka are one group of people speaking a southern Chinese language that are occasionally not considered to be Han Chinese. Evidently, their ancestors fled northern China roughly a thousand years ago to settle in the rough upland area where Guangdong, Fujian, and Jiangxi provinces meet. Later migrations took them throughout southern China, where they typically settled in hilly wastelands (Figure 11.27). The Hakka traditionally made their living by growing upland crops such as sweet potatoes and by working as loggers, stonecutters, and metalworkers. Today they form one of the poorest communities of southern China.

Despite their many differences, all of the languages of the Han Chinese (including Hakka) are closely related to each other and belong to the same Sinitic language subfamily. Since their basic grammars and sound systems are similar, a person speaking one of these languages can learn another relatively easily. It is usually difficult, however, for speakers of European languages—or of Japanese or Korean—to gain fluency in these tongues. All Sinitic languages are **tonal** and monosyllabic; their words are all composed of a single syllable (although compound words can be formed from several syllables), and the meaning of each basic syllable changes according to the pitch in which it is uttered.

The Non-Han Peoples Many of the more remote upland districts of China proper are inhabited by groups of non-Han peoples speaking non-Sinitic languages. According to the Chinese government, the country contains 55 such ethnic groups. Most of these peoples are classified as tribal, implying that they have a traditional social order based on self-governing village communities (Figure 11.28). Such a view is not entirely accurate, however, because some of these groups once had their own kingdoms. What they do have in common is a heritage of cultural and sometimes political tension with the Han Chinese.

Over the course of many centuries, the territory occupied by these non-Han communities has steadily declined in size, caused by the continued expansion of the Han as well as by non-Han emigration. Acculturation into Chinese society and intermarriage with the Han also have reduced many non-Han groups. Their main concentrations today are in the rougher lands of the far north and the far south.

As many as 11 million Manchus live in the more remote portions of Manchuria. The Manchu language is related to those of the tribal peoples of central and southeastern Siberia. Fewer than 100 Manchus, however, still speak their own language, the rest having abandoned it for Mandarin Chinese. This is an ironic situation, because the Manchus ruled the Chinese Empire from 1644 to 1912. Until the end of this period, the Manchus prevented the Han from settling in central and northern Manchuria, which they hoped to preserve as their homeland. Once Chinese were allowed to settle in Manchuria in the 1800s—in part to prevent Russian expansion—the Manchus soon found themselves vastly outnumbered. As they began to intermarry with and adopt the language and customs of the newcomers, their own culture began to disappear.

Larger and more secure communities of non-Han peoples are found in the far south, especially in Guangxi. Most of the inhabitants of Guangxi's more remote areas speak languages of the Tai family, closely related to those of Thailand. Because as many as 18 million non-Han people live in Guangxi, it has been designated an **autonomous region**. Such autonomy was designed to allow non-Han peoples to experience "socialist modernization" at a different pace from that expected of the rest of the country. Critics contend that very little real autonomy has ever existed. (In addition to Guangxi, there are four other autonomous regions in China. Three of these, Xizang [Tibet], Nei Monggol [Inner Mongolia], and Xinjiang, are located in Central Asia and are discussed in Chapter 10. The final autonomous region, Ningxia, located in northwestern China, is distinguished by its large concentration of Hui [Mandarin-speaking Muslims].)

Other areas with sizable numbers of non-Han peoples are Yunnan and Guizhou, in southwestern China, and western Sichuan. Most tribal peoples here practice swidden agriculture (also called "slash and burn"; see Chapters 6 and 13) on rough slopes; flatter lands are generally occupied by rice-growing Han Chinese. A wide variety of separate languages, falling into several linguistic families, are found among the ethnic groups

Figure 11.28 Tribal Villages in South China Non-Han people are usually classified as "tribal" in China, which assumes they have a traditional social order based upon autonomous village communities. The photograph shows a Miao village in the Xiangxi Tujia and Miao Autonomous Prefecture, Hunan province.

living in the uplands. Figure 11.29 shows that in Yunnan, the resulting ethnic mosaic is staggeringly complex.

Language and Ethnicity in Taiwan   Taiwan is also noted for its linguistic and ethnic complexity. In the island's mountainous eastern region, several small groups of "tribal" peoples speak languages related to those of Indonesia (belonging to the Austronesian language family). These peoples resided throughout Taiwan before the 16th century. At that time, however, Han migrants began to arrive in large numbers. Most of the newcomers spoke the Fujianese dialect, which evolved into the distinctive language of Taiwanese.

Taiwan was transformed almost overnight in 1949, when China's nationalist forces, defeated by the communists, sought refuge on the island. Most of the nationalist leaders spoke Mandarin, which they made the official language. Taiwan's new leadership discouraged Taiwanese, viewing it as a mere local dialect. As a result, tension developed between the Taiwanese and the Mandarin communities. Only in the 1990s did Taiwanese speakers begin to reassert their language rights, a movement that accelerated after 2000. Interestingly, as Taiwan has become more fully global, its own cultural framework has grown more locally specific.

East Asian Cultures in Global Context

East Asia has long exhibited tensions between an internal orientation and tendencies toward cosmopolitanism. This dichotomy has both a cultural and an economic dimension. Until the mid-1800s, East Asian countries attempted to insulate themselves from Western cultural influences. Japan subsequently opened its doors but remained ambivalent about foreign ideas. Only after its defeat in 1945 did Japan really opt for a globalist orientation. It was followed in this regard by South Korea, Taiwan, and Hong Kong (then a British colony). The Chinese and North Korean governments, to the contrary, decided during the early **Cold War** decades of the 1950s and 1960s to isolate themselves as much as possible from Western and global culture.

The Cosmopolitan Fringe   Japan, South Korea, Taiwan, and Hong Kong are characterized by a vibrant internationalism, which coexists with strong national and local cultural identity. Virtually all Japanese, for example, study English for 6 to 10 years, and, although relatively few learn to speak it fluently, most can read and understand a good deal. Business meetings among Japanese, Chinese, and Korean firms are

Figure 11.29 Language Groups in Yunnan   China's Yunnan Province is the most linguistically complex area in East Asia. In Yunnan's broad valleys and relatively level plateau areas and in its cities, most people speak Mandarin Chinese. In the hills, mountains, and steep-sided valleys, however, a wide variety of tribal languages, falling into several linguistic families, are spoken. In certain areas, several different languages can be found in very close proximity.

GLOBAL TO LOCAL   The Korean Wave

A century ago, Korea was commonly referred to as a "hermit king-dom," in reference to its relative isolation from global cultural and political currents. Today, North Korea retains the tradition, largely cutting itself off from the rest of the world. South Korea has taken the opposite approach, and is today one of Asia's most globalized countries. Cultural products as well as technological devices from all over the world are readily available in the streets of Seoul and other large South Korean cities.

In recent years, however, South Korea's most notable contribution to cultural globalization has been as an exporter rather than importer. In the 1990s, South Korean music, movies, television shows and even cuisine began to follow the country's electronic exports into markets throughout East and Southeast Asia and beyond. The Chinese media was so taken by the phenomenon that they dubbed it the *Hallyu*, or "Korean Wave." By 2004, some two-thirds of all television viewers in Japan were tuning into the popular Korean television drama, *Winter Sonata*. By 2006, Chinese television stations devoted more time to South Korean shows than to those of all other foreign countries put together. The Hallyu movement has in turn prompted massive tourism into South Korea, with the number of tourist arrivals going from 2.8 million in 2003 to 3.7 million in 2004. By 2010, Korean hair salons were spreading across the major cities of China, both due to the skill of Korean hairdressers and to the fact that many young Chinese want to look like Korean pop stars.

Not surprisingly, the Korean Wave has generated resentment in other Asian countries. Both Vietnam and Taiwan have threatened to ban or at least limit Korean broadcasting, while in Japan a comic book called "Halting the Korean Wave" was a minor hit. Still, considering the animosity that so often marks relations between Japan and Korea, it is remarkable that Korean popular culture is so well-liked and has generated so little overt opposition in Japan.

Scholars are not sure how to explain the Hallyu phenomenon. Some argue that Korean films and TV shows are popular because they tend to deal with themes of family life and obligations during a period of technological change, incorporating Confucian values that resonate strongly in other East Asian countries. Others look more to issues of business and showmanship. In the 1900s, Korean shows tended to be much cheaper than those produced in North America, Europe, or Japan, yet were almost as sophisticated in terms of production techniques. Since then, Korean cultural prod-

ucts have grown more technologically advanced, enhancing their appeal.

But whatever the explanation, it is undeniable that South Korean popular culture is big business. South Korean stars are now among the highest paid entertainers in the world, with at least 10 actors earning more than $10 million a year (Figure 11.4.1).

Figure 11.4.1 South Korean Film Star South Korea's noted film star Yi-Hyun So attends a press conference in regard to her new film "Jung" at the Pusan International Film Festival.

often conducted in English. Relatively large numbers of advanced students, especially from Taiwan, study in the United States and other English-speaking countries, and thus bring home a kind of cultural bilingualism.

The current cultural flow is not merely from a globalist West to a previously isolated East Asia. Instead, the exchange is growing more reciprocal. Hong Kong's action films are popular throughout most of the world and have influenced filmmaking techniques in Hollywood. Over the past few years, South Korean popular culture has spread throughout East Asia and in much of the rest of the world (see "Global to Local: The Korean Wave"). Japan almost dominates the world market in video games, and its ubiquitous comic-book culture and animation techniques are now following its karaoke bars in their overseas march.

Cultural globalization is, of course, as controversial in Japan as it is elsewhere. Japanese ultranationalists are few but vocal, calling their fellow citizens to resist the decadence of the West and to return to the military traditions of the **samurai**, the warrior class of premodern Japan. Many other Japanese people, however, contend that their country is too insular, worrying that they do not possess

Figure 11.30 Chinese Theme Park As China's economy grows, its people are spending increasing amounts of money on entertainment. Theme parks, which now number over 2,000, are particularly popular. Happy Valley Theme Park in Beijing, shown here, was China's largest when it opened in 2006.

the English-language and global cultural skills necessary to operate effectively in the world economy.

The Chinese Heartland In one sense, Japan is more culturally predisposed to cosmopolitanism than is China. The Japanese have always borrowed heavily from other cultures (particularly from China itself), whereas the Chinese have historically been more self-sufficient. However, the southern coastal Chinese have long tended to be more international in their orientation, with close linkages to the Chinese diaspora communities of Southeast Asia and ultimately to maritime trading circuits extending over much of the globe.

In most periods of Chinese history, the interior orientation of the center prevailed over the external orientation of the southern coast. After the communist victory of 1949, only the small British enclave of Hong Kong was able to pursue international cultural connections. In the rest of the country, a dour and puritanical cultural order was rigidly enforced. While this culture was largely founded on the norms of Chinese peasant society, it was also influenced by the communist-oriented cultural system that had emerged in the Soviet Union.

After China began to liberalize its economy and open its doors to foreign influences in the late 1970s and early 1980s, the southern coastal region suddenly assumed a new prominence. Through this gateway, global cultural patterns began to penetrate the rest of the country. The result has been the emergence of a vibrant but somewhat showy urban popular culture throughout China that is replete with such global features as nightclubs, karaoke bars, fast-food franchises, and theme parks (Figure 11.30).

GEOPOLITICAL FRAMEWORK: Enduring Cold War Tensions

Much of the political history of East Asia revolves around the centrality of China and the ability of Japan to remain outside China's grasp. The traditional Chinese conception of geopolitics was based on the idea of a universal empire: All territories were either supposed to be a part of the Chinese Empire, pay tribute to it and acknowledge its supremacy, or stand outside the system altogether. Until the 1800s, the Chinese government would not recognize any other as its diplomatic equal. When China could no longer maintain its power in the face of European aggression, the East Asian political system fell into disarray. As European power declined in the 1900s, China and Japan contended for regional leadership. After World War II, East Asia was split by larger Cold War rivalries (Figure 11.31).

The Evolution of China

The original core of Chinese civilization was the North China Plain and the Loess Plateau. For many centuries, periods of unification alternated with times of division into competing states. The most important episode of unification occurred in the 3rd century BCE. Once political unity was achieved, the Chinese Empire began to expand vigorously to the south of the Yangtze Valley. Subsequently, the ideal of the imperial unity of China triumphed, with periods of division seen as indicating disorder. This ideology helped cement the Han Chinese into a single people.

Several Chinese dynasties rose and fell between 219 BCE and 1912, most of them controlling roughly the same territory (Figure 11.32). The core of the Chinese Empire remained China proper, excluding Manchuria. Other lands, however, were sometimes ruled as well. The most important of these was a western projection extending north of the Tibetan Plateau into the desert basins of Central Asia (modern Xinjiang). China valued this area primarily because the vital trading route to western Eurasia (the "Silk Road") passed through it.

Various Chinese dynasties attempted to conquer Korea, but the Koreans resisted. Eventually China and Korea worked out an arrangement whereby Korea paid token tribute and acknowledged the supremacy of the Chinese Empire, and in return Korea received trading privileges and retained independence. When foreign armies invaded Korea—as did those of Japan in the late 1500s—China sent troops to support its "vassal kingdom."

For most of the past 2,000 years, the Chinese Empire was Earth's wealthiest and most powerful state. Its only real threat came from the pastoral peoples of Mongolia and Manchuria. Although vastly outnumbered by China, these societies were organized on a highly effective military basis. Usually the Chinese and the Mongols enjoyed a mutually beneficial trading relationship. Periodically, however, they waged war, and on several occasions the northern nomads conquered China (see Chapter 10). The Great Wall along

Figure 11.31 Geopolitical Issues in East Asia East Asia remains one of the world's geopolitical hot spots. Tensions are particularly severe between capitalist, democratic South Korea and the isolated communist regime of North Korea, and between China and Taiwan. China has had several border disputes, whereas Japan and Russia have not been able to resolve their quarrel over the southern Kuril Islands.

China's border did not, in other words, provide adequate defense. In time, the conquering armies adopted Chinese customs in order to govern the far more numerous Han people.

The Manchu Qing Dynasty The final and most significant conquest of China occurred in 1644, when the Manchus toppled the Ming Dynasty and replaced it with the Qing (also spelled Ch'ing) Dynasty. Like earlier conquerors, the Manchus retained the Chinese bureaucracy and made few

institutional changes. Their strategy was to adapt themselves to Chinese culture, yet at the same time to preserve their own identity as an elite military group. Their system functioned well until the mid-19th century, when the empire began to crumble before the onslaught of European and, later, Japanese power.

China's most significant legacy from the Manchu Qing Dynasty was the extension of its territory to include much of Central Asia. The Manchus subdued the Mongols and eventually established control over eastern Central Asia, including Tibet. Even the states of mainland Southeast Asia sent tribute and acknowledged Chinese supremacy. Never before had the Chinese Empire been so extensive or so powerful (Figure 11.33).

The Modern Era From its height of power and extent in the 1700s, the Chinese Empire descended rapidly in the 1800s as it failed to keep pace with the technological progress of Europe. Threats to the empire had always come from the north, and Chinese and Manchu officials saw little peril from European merchants operating along their coastline. The Europeans were distressed by the amount of silver needed to obtain Chinese silk, tea, and other products, and by the fact that the Chinese disdained their manufactured goods. In response, the British began to sell opium, which

Chinese authorities viewed as a threat. When the imperial government tried to suppress the opium trade in the 1839, the British attacked and quickly prevailed.

This first "opium war" ushered in a century of political and economic chaos in China. The British demanded free trade in selected Chinese ports, and in the process overturned the traditional policy of managed trade based on the acknowledgment of Chinese supremacy. As European enterprises penetrated China and undermined local economic interests, anti-Manchu rebellions began to break out. In the 1800s, all such uprisings were crushed, but not before causing tremendous destruction. Meanwhile, European power continued to advance. In 1858, Russia annexed the northernmost reaches of Manchuria, and by 1900 China had been divided into separate "**spheres of influence**" where the in-

Figure 11.32 The Historical Extent of China China is usually regarded as the world's oldest country, but the territorial extent of the Chinese state has varied greatly over the centuries. The earliest states were limited to the Loess Plateau and North China Plain, but most historical Chinese dynasties controlled the entire core area of modern China as well as the Tarim Basin in Xinjiang. Before the 1600s, however, China seldom held control of Tibet, Inner Mongolia, or central and northern Manchuria.

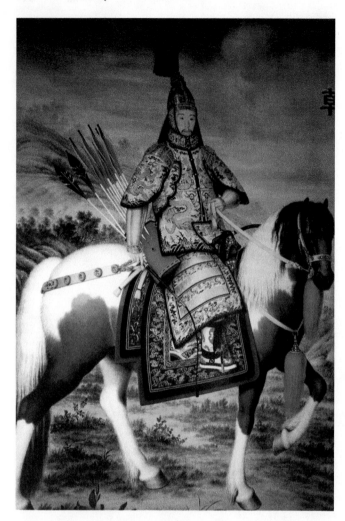

Figure 11.33 The Qianlong Emperor of China Under the Qianlong Emperor, who reigned from 1736 to 1795, the Manchu-ruled Chinese empire reached its greatest territorial extent.

terests of different European countries prevailed (Figure 11.34). (In a sphere of influence, the colonial power had no formal political authority but did enjoy informal influence and tremendous economic clout.)

A successful rebellion launched in 1911 finally toppled the Manchus, but subsequent efforts to establish a unified Chinese Republic were not successful. In many parts of the country, local military leaders, or "warlords," grabbed power for themselves. By the 1920s, it appeared that China might be completely dismembered. The Tibetans had regained autonomy; Xinjiang was under Russian influence; and in China proper Europeans and local warlords vied with the weak Chinese Republic for power. In addition, Japan was increasing its demands and seeking to expand its territory.

The Rise of Japan

Japan did not emerge as a strong, unified state until the 7th century. From its earliest days, Japan looked to China (and, at first, to Korea as well) for intellectual and political models. Its offshore location insulated Japan from the threat of

rule by the Chinese Empire. At the same time, the Japanese conceptualized their islands as a separate empire, equivalent in certain respects to China. Between 1000 and 1580, however, Japan was usually divided into a number of mutually hostile feudal realms.

The Closing and Opening of Japan Around 1600, Japan was reunited by the armies of the Tokugawa **Shogunate** (a shogun was a supreme military leader who theoretically remained under the emperor). Shortly afterward, Japan attempted to isolate itself from the rest of the world. Until the 1850s, Japan traded with China mostly through the Ryukyu islanders and with Russia through Ainu intermediaries. The only Westerners allowed to trade in Japan were the Dutch, and their activities were strictly limited.

Japan remained largely closed to foreign commerce and influence until U.S. gunboats sailed into Tokyo Bay to demand access in 1853. Aware that they could no longer keep the Westerners out, Japanese leaders set about modernizing their economic, administrative, and military systems. This effort accelerated when the Tokugawa Shogunate was toppled in 1868 by the Meiji Restoration. (It is called a restoration because it was carried out in the emperor's name, but it did not give the emperor any real power.) Unlike China, Japan successfully accomplished most of its reform efforts.

The Japanese Empire Japan's new rulers realized that their country remained threatened by European imperial power. They therefore nurtured the development of a silk export industry, which gave them the funds needed to buy modern equipment (see "Geographic Tools: The East Asian Gazetteer and the Reconstruction of Historical Geography"). They also decided that the only way to meet the European challenge was to become expansionistic themselves. Japan therefore took control over Hokkaido and began to move farther north into the Kuril Islands and Sakhalin.

In 1895, the Japanese government tested its newly modernized army against China, winning a quick and profitable victory that gave it authority over Taiwan. Tensions then mounted with Russia as the two countries vied for power in Manchuria and Korea. The Japanese defeated the Russians in 1905, giving them considerable influence in northern China. With no strong rival in the area, Japan annexed Korea in 1910. Alliance with Britain, France, and the United States during World War I brought further gains, as Japan was awarded Germany's island colonies in Micronesia.

The 1930s brought a global depression, putting a resource-dependent Japan in a difficult situation. The country's leaders sought a military solution, and in 1931 Japan conquered Manchuria. In 1937, Japanese armies moved south, occupying the North China Plain and the coastal cities of southern China. The Chinese government withdrew to the relatively inaccessible Sichuan Basin to continue the struggle. During this period, Japan's relations with the United States steadily deteriorated. When the United States cut off the export of scrap iron, Japan began to experience a resource crunch.

Figure 11.34 Imperialism in East Asia
The Chinese lost influence and territory in the 19th century as European power expanded. Although China regained its autonomy and most of its territory in the 1900s, Russia retained large areas that were formerly under Chinese control. The first half of the 20th century saw the rapid expansion of the Japanese Empire, which ended with the defeat of Japan in World War II.

GEOGRAPHIC TOOLS   The East Asian Gazetteer and the Reconstruction of Historical Geography

East Asia is a particularly good place in which to conduct research in historical geography because of its gazetteer tradition. In common usage, a gazetteer is simply a kind of index: a list of place-names and their spatial coordinates found at the back of most comprehensive atlases. But a gazetteer can also be a geographical encyclopedia, providing detailed information about a large array of particular places. Gazetteers of this sort have historically been used most extensively in East Asia, as they were believed to be essential tools for government. Using gazetteer data, geographers and historians literally can map out landscape transformations in East Asia over periods of hundreds of years.

One geographer who has used gazetteer data extensively is Kären Wigen, especially in her award-winning book *The Making of a Japanese Periphery, 1750–1920* (University of California Press, 1995). Here she examined how the region around the city of Ina, located in a sizable valley in the heart of the Japanese Alps, has repeatedly been transformed. In the 1700s, Ina was a minor feudal domain that formed a key node in the packhorse trains that carried goods across the mountainous central region of Japan. It also supported its own major handicraft industry focused on high-quality paper goods. As Wigen discovered by mapping out gazetteer data (see Figure 11.5.1), the paper industry entailed a complex spatial organization; although the entire Ina region supplied the paper-mulberry bark from which paper was made, different villages specialized in the manufacture of different paper-craft items.

As Wigen discovered by examining gazetteers from later decades, the economic geography of the Ina region was completely transformed during the mid- and late 1800s. In part because of changing fash-

ions, decorative paper goods no longer commanded high prices, and as a result the industry underwent a rapid decline. Simultaneously, the regional economy was subordinated to that of the rapidly centralizing Japanese state. To obtain foreign exchange, the state began to export silk thread. As a result, Ina's paper mulberries were ripped out, to be replaced by a different species of mulberry used to feed the voracious silkworms.

The prosperity silk brought to Ina did not prove sustainable. The depression of the 1930s, followed by World War II, combined to destroy the industry. In the postwar period, mulberries were again uprooted, this time to be replaced by apple and other fruit trees. By the turn of the century, however, fruit growing was no longer very profitable, and the farmers of Ina were again looking for alternative crops.

Figure 11.5.1 Ina's Paper Industry In the early 1800s, before Japan's modernization, the area around Ina in central Japan supported a sizable and highly specialized paper-craft industry. Different villages focused on the production of different paper objects.

In 1941, Japan's leaders decided to destroy the American Pacific fleet in order to clear the way for the conquest of resource-rich Southeast Asia. Their grand strategy was to unite East and Southeast Asia into a "Greater East Asia Co-Prosperity Sphere." This "sphere" was to be ruled by Japan, however, and was designed to keep the Americans and Europeans out. Japanese forces elsewhere in East Asia sometimes engaged in brutal acts. In Korea, the colonial government evidently planned to extinguish the Korean language

in favor of Japanese. As a result, serious tensions emerged between the Japanese and the other East Asians—tensions that persist to this day.

Postwar Geopolitics

With the defeat of Japan at the end of World War II, East Asia became an arena of rivalry between the United States and the Soviet Union. Initially, American interests prevailed in the maritime fringe, while Soviet influence advanced on the mainland. Soon, however, East Asia began to experience its own revival.

Japan's Revival Japan lost its colonial empire when it lost World War II. Its territory was reduced to the four main islands plus the Ryukyu Archipelago and a few minor outliers. In general, the Japanese government accepted this loss of land. The only remaining territorial conflict concerns the four southernmost islands of the Kuril chain, which were taken by the Soviet Union in 1945. Although Japan still claims these islands, Russia refuses even to discuss relinquishing control, straining Russo-Japanese relations.

After losing its overseas possessions, Japan had to turn to trade to obtain the resources needed for its economy. Japan's military power was strictly limited by the constitution imposed on it by the United States, forcing Japan to rely on the U.S. military for much of its defense needs. The U.S. Navy continues to patrol many of Japan's vital sea-lanes, and U.S. armed forces maintain several bases within the country. This U.S. military presence, however, is controversial. Particularly contentious are the U.S. bases on Okinawa, which take up much of the island's territory. In 2009, the new Japanese prime minister Yukio Hatoyama pledged to force the U.S. military off of Okinawa, but in May 2010, as tensions mounted between Japan and North Korea, he decided to let the bases remain. The resulting controversy, however, was so intense that Hatoyama resigned his position.

Slowly but steadily, Japan's own military has emerged as a strong regional force despite the constitutional limits imposed on it. In recent years, fears about North Korea's nuclear program and China's military growth have led the Japanese government to reconsider its constitutionally imposed limitations on military spending. In 2007, Japan announced that it would make international peacekeeping a military priority, strengthen its missile defenses, and enhance its coordination with U.S. troops.

Other East Asian countries are concerned about the potential threat posed by a remilitarized Japan. Such a perception was strengthened in the early years of the new millennium when Japan's former prime minister visited the Yasukuni Shrine, which contains a military cemetery in which several war criminals from World War II are buried. Anti-Japanese sentiments in China—which have occasionally boiled over into huge public protests—have also been encouraged by the publication of Japanese textbooks that minimize the country's atrocities during the war.

The Division of Korea The aftermath of World War II brought much greater changes to Korea than to Japan. As the end of the war approached, the Soviet Union and the United States agreed to divide Korea at the 38th parallel. Soon two separate regimes were established, the northern one allied with the Soviet Union, the southern one with the United States. In 1950, North Korea invaded South Korea, seeking to reunify the country. The United States, with support from the United Nations, supported the south, while

China aided the north. The war ended in a stalemate, and Korea has remained a divided country, its two governments locked in a continuing Cold War (Figure 11.35).

Large numbers of U.S. troops remained in the south after the war. South Korea in the 1960s was a poor, agrarian country that could not defend itself. Over the past 30 years, however, the south has emerged as a wealthy trading nation while the fortunes of the north have plummeted. The southerners' fear of the north gradually lessened, especially among the members of the younger generation. Many South Korean students have resented the presence of U.S. forces, seeking instead to build friendly relations with North Korea. Changing military priorities, meanwhile, led the United States to reduce its presence in Korea, dropping its troop strength in 2004 from roughly 37,000 to 28,500.

In the late 1990s, the South Korean government began to pursue better relations with North Korea, giving it large amounts of food aid and industrial investment in exchange for reduced hostility. In 2008, however, a new South Korean government concluded that this so-called Sunshine Policy had not restrained North Korean belligerency. North Korean nuclear testing further strained relations, as did the

Figure 11.35 The Demilitarized Zone in Korea North and South Korea were divided along the 38th parallel after World War II. Today, even after the conflict of the early 1950s, the demilitarized zone, or DMZ (which runs near the parallel), separates these two states. U.S. armed forces are active in patrolling the DMZ.

Figure 11.36 Chinese Soldiers in Tibet Following a full-scale invasion of Tibet in 1959, China continues to increase its presence through its military forces, the relocation of migrants into the area from other parts of China, and rebuilding programs that mask the traditional Tibetan landscape. Here a Chinese soldier watches Tibetan Buddhist monks in robes at a horse festival.

March 2010 sinking of a South Korean naval vessel. Although North Korea denied attacking the ship and killing 46 of its crew members, South Korea presented strong evidence of its guilt. As a result of the attack, tensions in the Korean peninsula reached their highest levels in decades, with the North temporarily cutting off most relations with the South.

The Division of China World War II brought tremendous destruction and loss of life to China. Even before the war began, China had been engaged in a civil conflict between nationalists (who favored an authoritarian capitalist economy) and communists. The communists had originally been based in the middle Yangtze region, but in 1934 nationalist pressure forced them out. Under the leadership of Mao Zedong, they retreated in the "Long March," which took them to the Loess Plateau, an area close to both the traditional power center of northern China and the industrialized zones of Manchuria. After the Japanese invaded China proper in 1937, the two camps cooperated, but as soon as Japan was defeated, China was again embroiled in civil war. In 1949, the communists proved victorious, forcing the nationalists to retreat to Taiwan.

A latent state of war has persisted ever since between China and Taiwan. Although no battles have been fought, gunfire has periodically been exchanged over the Matsu Islands, several small Taiwanese islands just off the mainland. The Beijing government still claims Taiwan as an integral part of China and vows eventually to reclaim it. The nation-

alists who gained power in Taiwan long maintained that they represented the true government of China. It was actually made a crime in Taiwan to advocate formal Taiwanese independence, because the fiction had to be maintained that Taiwan was merely one province of a temporarily divided China.

The idea of the intrinsic unity of China continues to be influential. In the 1950s and 1960s, the United States recognized Taiwan as the only legitimate government of China, but its policy changed in the 1970s after U.S. leaders decided that it would be more useful and realistic to recognize Mainland China. Soon China entered the United Nations, and Taiwan found itself diplomatically isolated. As of 2010, only 23 countries, mostly small African, Pacific, and Caribbean states, continued to recognize Taiwan and, in return, to receive Taiwanese aid (see Exploring Global Connections: Taiwan Seeks Diplomatic Recognition). In reality, however, Taiwan is a fully separate country. In 2000, after Taiwan elected a former advocate of Taiwanese independence, China threatened to invade if Taiwan were to declare itself a separate country. In 2001, both China and Taiwan entered the World Trade Organization (WTO), but Taiwan was forced to join under the awkward name of "Chinese Taipei," to avoid the suggestion that it is a sovereign country.

In the early years of the new century, Taiwan seemed to be moving toward formal separation from China. The year 2007 also saw the systematic purging of words and phrases suggesting unity with China in Taiwanese textbooks. Thus the common term "cross-strait ties" was replaced with "China–Taiwan ties." In the 2008 Taiwanese election, however, the anti-independence Kuomingtang party returned to power. The new president Ma Ying-Jeou made it clear that he regarded Taiwan and China as two separately governed areas of a single country.

The election of Ma greatly reduced tensions between China and Taiwan. Trade between the island and the mainland is booming, as is tourism. But the de facto independence of Taiwan continues to irritate Beijing. In 2010, China harshly criticized the United States for agreeing to sell $6.4 billion worth of military equipment to the Taiwanese government.

Chinese Territorial Issues Despite the fact that it has been unable to regain Taiwan, China has successfully retained the Manchu territorial legacy. In the case of Tibet, this has required considerable force; resistance by the Tibetans compelled China to launch a full-scale invasion in 1959. The Tibetans, however, have continued to struggle for real autonomy if not actual independence, as they fear that the Han Chinese now moving to Tibet will eventually outnumber them (Figure 11.36; also see Chapter 10).

The postwar Chinese government also retained control over Xinjiang in the northwest, as well as Inner Mongolia (or Nei Monggol), a vast territory stretching along the Mongolian border. Like Tibet, Nei Monggol and Xinjiang

EXPLORING GLOBAL CONNECTIONS   Taiwan Seeks Diplomatic Recognition

On March 15, 2010, newspapers across the world announced that Taiwanese President Ma Ying-Jeou would visit his country's allies in the South Pacific: Nauru, Kiribati, Marshall Islands, Palau, Tuvalu, and Solomon Islands. Such headlines were somewhat misleading, as the countries mentioned are not exactly allies of Taiwan.

An ally, according to the common definition, is a "state formally cooperating with another for military or other purposes." It is difficult to imagine Nauru, a mined-out semiwasteland of eight square miles and 14 thousand people, coming to the aid of Taiwan for military or any other purposes. The relationship between these countries and Taiwan is actually one of clientage rather than alliance. In essence, Nauru, Kiribati, Marshall Islands, Tuvalu, Palau, and Solomon Islands sell their diplomatic recognition to Taiwan in exchange for aid. Taiwan thereby gains a small measure of international legitimacy, while these small Pacific countries gain much needed financial resources. They are not alone in the practice, as Taiwan maintains diplomatic recognition with 23 countries (Figure 11.6.1).

Most of Taiwan's diplomatic partners are small countries in the Pacific, the Caribbean, and Central America. Taiwan has had no success in securing recognition by other Asian countries. Most Asian states are too large to be swayed by aid incentives—and too close to China to deny Beijing's power. But Taiwan is also disadvantaged in its quest for recognition by the fact that it claims not just the whole of China but also parts of Russia, Tajikistan, Pakistan, India,

Afghanistan, Bhutan, and Burma—as well as Mongolia in its entirety. Officially, Taiwan maintains that all territories controlled by China at the time of the 1911 revolution are rightfully its own.

Despite its formal claims, Taiwan has bent to the demands of reality to informally recognize Mongolia's independence. In 2002, it opened an unofficial embassy in Mongolia called the "Taipei Trade and Economic Representative Office in Ulaanbataar." Taiwan's government simultaneously excluded Mongolia from the oversight of its Mainland Affairs Council, in effect recognizing Mongolia's sovereignty. As a result, Mongolians wanting to visit Taiwan now have to obtain visas, which were not necessary so long as Taipei regarded Mongolia as one of its (temporarily) lost provinces. Still, Taiwan has never formally dropped its constitutional claims to Mongolia. The situation remains ambiguous to say the least.

Nonetheless, Taiwan and Mongolia have developed reasonably close relations. As a sign of friendship, Taiwan recently gave Mongolia a three-story high portrait of Genghis Khan, made out of 437,000 mosaic tiles, based on a rare portrait of the world conqueror held in Taipei's National Palace Museum. But the potential for discord has not vanished. In 2008, a Hong Kong-based company posted a map on its Website showing Mongolia as part of China; when Mongolia protested, China's embarrassed government responded by claiming that the original map had been made in Taiwan.

Figure 11.6.1 Warner Park Sporting Complex, St. Kitts and Nevis Taiwan often rewards its diplomatic partners with lavish subsidies. The Warner Park Sporting Complex, site of the 2007 Cricket World Cup, was mostly financed by Taiwan.

are classified as autonomous regions. The peoples of Xinjiang are asserting their religious and ethnic identities, and separatist sentiments are widespread. However, most Han Chinese regard Nei Monggol and Xinjiang as integral parts of their country, and they regard any talk of secession as treasonous.

China claims several other areas that it does not control. It contends that former Chinese territories in the Himalayas were illegally annexed by Britain when it controlled South Asia, resulting in a border dispute with India. The two countries went to war in 1962 when China occupied an uninhabited highland district in northeastern Kashmir. Tensions between India and China have eased over the past decade, but their territorial disagreement remains unresolved. China also asserts its rights over a number of tiny islands in the East and South China seas. In September 2010, relations between China and Japan reached a crisis point after Japan seized a Chinese ship near the Japanese-controlled Senkaku Islands, which China claims under the name Diaoyu Islands. Japan eventually released the ship's captain, but refused to apologize, angering the Chinese government.

One territorial issue was finally resolved in 1997 when China reclaimed Hong Kong. In the 1950s, 1960s, and 1970s, Hong Kong acted as China's window on the outside world, and it grew prosperous as a capitalist enclave. As Chinese relations with the outer world opened in the 1980s, Britain decided to honor its treaty provisions and return Hong Kong to China. China in turn promised that Hong Kong would retain its fully capitalist economic system and its partially democratic political system for at least 50 years. Civil liberties not enjoyed in China itself were to remain protected in Hong Kong (Figure 11.37).

Hong Kong's autonomy, however, remains insecure. Over the past several years, China has thwarted efforts by its people to install a more representative government. As a result of such incidents, hundreds of thousands of people have taken to the streets of Hong Kong in protest. In 2010, several members of the Legislative Council of Hong Kong resigned in protest against the limitations on democratic governance. Their resignation forced a new election, in which they won back their seats. The Beijing government was angered by this maneuver, which it saw as a waste of taxpayer money.

In 1999 Macao, the last colonial territory in East Asia, was returned to China (Figure 11.38). Like Hong Kong, it is classified as Special Administrative Region, under its own autonomous government and subject to its own laws. This small former Portuguese enclave, located across the estuary from Hong Kong, has functioned largely as a gambling refuge. Now the largest betting center in the world, Macao derives 40 percent of its gross domestic product from gambling.

Global Dimensions of East Asian Geopolitics

In the early 1950s, East Asia was divided into two hostile Cold War camps: China and North Korea were allied with the Soviet Union, while Japan, Taiwan, and South Korea were linked to the United States. The Chinese–Soviet alliance soon deteriorated into mutual hostility, and in the 1970s China and the United States found that they could accommodate each other, sharing an enemy in the Soviet Union. In contrast, North Korea's relations with the United States and many other countries have only grown more heated during the same period.

The North Korean Crisis In 1994, North Korea refused to allow international inspections of its nuclear power facilities—which many countries believed were being used for weapons production—provoking an international crisis. It eventually relented, however, in exchange for energy assistance from the United States. But by 2002, the agreement had fallen apart, as evidence mounted that North Korea was continuing to pursue nuclear weapons. Other complaints by the international community focused on North Korea's traf-

Figure 11.37 Distinctive Hong Kong Although part of China since 1997, Hong Kong remains both politically and culturally distinctive from the rest of China. In this Hong Kong scene, a bride is posing for photographs in front of a sexually suggestive advertisement.

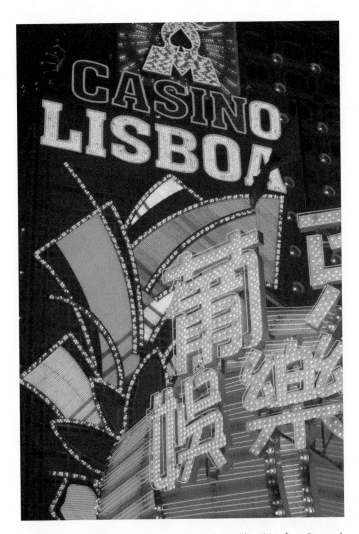

Figure 11.38 Macao Casino Macao, reclaimed by China from Portugal in 1999, retains a unique mixture of Chinese and Portuguese cultural influences. Its economic mainstay remains gambling, which is prohibited in the rest of China.

ficking in illegal drugs and the fact that it reportedly holds more than 200,000 of its own citizens in brutal labor-camp prisons.

In response to North Korea's nuclear ambitions, the United States has advocated multilateral negotiations involving South Korea, China, Japan, and Russia. North Korea, however, insisted for years that it would negotiate only with the United States. Owing in part to pressure from China, its main trading partner, North Korea finally agreed to the broader framework, participating in five rounds of talks between 2003 and 2007. Little progress was made, however, and in 2009 North Korea pulled out of the negotiations, expelled all nuclear inspectors, and resumed nuclear enrichment. In the same year, it detonated a nuclear weapon, launched a partially successful space booster rocket, and tested a series of ballistic missiles. Such actions have greatly increased tensions in the region and have put China, North Korea's main supporter, in a difficult diplomatic situation.

China on the Global Stage The end of the Cold War, coupled with the rapid economic growth of China, reconfigured the balance of power in East Asia. The United States no longer needed China to offset the Soviet Union, and the U.S. military became increasingly worried about the growing power of the Chinese armed forces. China's neighbors also have become more concerned. China now has the largest army in the world, as well as nuclear capability, and sophisticated missile technology. Through the early years of the new century, China's military budget grew at an average annual rate of about 10 percent, creating one of the world's most powerful armed forces. China is also rapidly building up its navy, buying advanced ships from Russia and beginning to construct its own. Like Japan, China is concerned about the vulnerability generated by its reliance on foreign oil, and as a result it is enhancing its naval capacity.

China is thus coming of age as a major force in global politics. Whether it is a force to be feared by other countries is a matter of considerable debate. Chinese leaders insist that they have no expansionistic designs and no intention of interfering in the internal affairs of other countries. They regard concerns expressed by the United States and other countries about their human rights record, as well as their activities in Tibet, as undue meddling in their own internal affairs.

Current opinions on China in the United States vary tremendously. Many U.S. leaders, particularly those in the business community, contend that the two countries should ignore their political differences and develop closer economic and cultural ties. Some East Asian experts similarly argue that the United States must respect China's sovereignty more carefully—or risk a future conflict in the region. Critics, on the other hand, think that China's trade practices are unfair; its labor, human-rights, and environmental records appalling; and its actions in Tibet unsupportable.

Regardless of what one thinks about East Asia's international relations, its economic ascent is undeniable. Yet East Asia does have a number of serious economic problems.

ECONOMIC AND SOCIAL DEVELOPMENT:
An Emerging Core of the Global Economy

East Asia exhibits extreme differences in economic and social development. Japan's urban belt contains one of the world's greatest concentrations of wealth, whereas North Korea is one of the world's most impoverished societies. Overall, however, East Asia has experienced rapid economic growth since the 1970s, with two of its economies, those of Taiwan and South Korea, jumping from the ranks of underdeveloped to developed (Table 11.2). Over the past two decades, China has experienced extraordinarily rapid economic growth, and now has the world's second largest economy (Figure 11.39).

TABLE 11.2	Development Indicators							
Country	GNI per capita, PPP 2008	GDP Average Annual % Growth 2000–08	Human Development Index (2007)[a]	Percent Population Living Below $2 a Day	Life Expectancy (2010)[b]	Under Age 5 Mortality Rate (1990)	Under Age 5 Mortality Rate (2008)	Gender Equity (2008)[c]
China	6,010	10.4	0.772	36	74	46	21	103
Hong Kong	43,960	5.2	0.944		83			100
Japan	35,190	1.6	0.960		83	6	4	100
North Korea					63	55	55	
South Korea	27,840	4.5	0.937		80	9	5	97
Taiwan					79			

[a]United Nations, Human Development Report, 2009.

[b]Population Reference Bureau, World Population Data Sheet, 2010.

[c]Gender Equity—Ratio of female to male enrollments in primary and secondary school. Numbers below 100 have more males in primary/secondary school, numbers above 100 have more females in primary/secondary schools.

Source: World Bank, World Development Indicators, 2010.

Figure 11.39 East Asia's Global Ties As this map shows, much of East Asia is highly integrated into global economic networks, receiving large amounts of direct foreign investment from other countries and exporting massive quantities of goods. North Korea, however, is a major exception to this pattern.

Figure 11.40 Automated Japanese Auto Factory Part of Japan's economic success has resulted from automation of its factory assembly lines. Here Mazda automobiles are assembled in a Hiroshima plant. These cars are destined for the east coast of the United States.

Japan's Economy and Society

Japan was the pacesetter of the world economy in the 1960s, 1970s, and 1980s. In the early 1990s, however, the Japanese economy experienced a major setback, and growth has been slow ever since. But despite its recent problems, Japan is still the world's third largest economic power.

Japan's Boom and Bust Although Japan's heavy industrialization began in the late 1800s, most of its people remained poor. The 1950s, however, saw the beginnings of the Japanese "economic miracle." Shorn of its empire, Japan was forced to export manufactured products. Beginning with inexpensive consumer goods, Japanese industry moved to more sophisticated materials, including automobiles, cameras, electronics, machine tools, and computer equipment (Figure 11.40). By the 1980s, it was the leader in many segments of the global high-tech economy.

In the early 1990s, Japan's inflated real estate market collapsed, leading to a banking crisis. At the same time, many Japanese companies discovered that producing labor-intensive goods at home had become too expensive. They therefore began to relocate factories to Southeast Asia and China. Because of these and related difficulties, Japan's economy slumped through the 1990s and into the new millennium. The Japanese government made several attempts to revitalize the economy through state spending, resulting in a huge government debt, totaling 192 percent of the country's gross domestic product in 2009. In 2007 it looked like the Japanese economy had turned a corner, expanding as a result of large industrial exports to China. The global economic crisis of 2008–2009, however, hit Japan hard, resulting in an economic decline of 5 percent in 2009.

Despite such problems, Japan remains a core country of the global economic system. Its economic system spans the globe, as Japanese multinational firms invest heavily in production facilities in North America and Europe, as well as in poorer countries. Japan is a world leader in a large array of high-tech fields, including robotics, optics, and machine tools for the semiconductor industry. It is also one of the world's largest creditor nations, despite its own debts, owning a large percentage of U.S. government bonds.

The Japanese Economic System The business environments in Japan and the United States are quite different, reflecting distinct versions of the capitalist economic system. In Japan, the bureaucracy maintains far greater control over the economy than it does in the United States. Japanese corporations are also structured differently from those of the United States. Large groups of companies (called keiretsu) are complexly intertwined, owning each other's stock and buying products and services from each other. Because of these interconnections, Japanese firms are less influenced by investors and stockbrokers than are those of the United States. Two other differences are that Japanese workers seldom switch companies, and the core workforce of each corporation is rarely subjected to layoffs.

Proponents of the Japanese system argue that it creates business and social stability and encourages long-term planning. Opponents argue that it reduces flexibility, results in high prices and low profits, and ultimately will prove too costly to maintain. They also point out that Japanese agriculture, wholesaling, and distribution remain relatively inefficient. Japan has only recently begun to see the rise of large-scale discount stores, which offer lower prices but also threaten the viability of small-scale merchants as well as downtown shopping districts in small cities.

Living Standards and Social Conditions in Japan Despite its affluence, living standards in Japan remain somewhat lower than those of the United States. Housing, food, transportation, and services are particularly expensive in Japan. But while the Japanese live in cramped quarters and pay high prices for basic products, they also enjoy many benefits unknown in the United States. Unemployment remains lower than in the United States; health care is provided by the government; and crime rates are extremely low. By such social measures as literacy, infant mortality, and average longevity, Japan surpasses the United States. Japan also lacks the extreme poverty found in certain pockets of American society.

Japan, of course, has its share of social problems. Koreans and alien residents from other Asian countries suffer discrimination, as do members of the indigenous Japanese underclass, the Burakumin. Japan's more remote rural areas have few jobs, and many have seen population decreases. In many small villages, most of the remaining people are elderly. Farming is an increasingly marginal occupation, and many farm families survive only because one family member works in a factory or office. Professional and managerial occupations in Japan's cities are noted for their long hours and high levels of stress.

Women in Japanese Society Critics often contend that Japanese women have not shared the benefits of their country's success. Advanced career opportunities remain limited, especially for those who marry and have children. Mothers are still expected to devote themselves to their families and to their children's education. Japanese business executives often work, or socialize in bars with their coworkers, late every evening, and thus contribute little to child care. Japan's recent economic problems seem to have further reduced career opportunities for women.

One response to the conditions faced by Japanese women has been a drop in the marriage rate. Many Japanese women are delaying marriage, and a sizable number may be abandoning it altogether. Japan has seen an even more dramatic decline in its fertility rate; beginning in 2005, Japan has seen more deaths than births. Whether this is due to the domestic difficulties of Japanese women or merely the result of the pressures of a postindustrial society is an open question. Fertility rates have, after all, dropped even lower in many parts of Europe. In 2009, the population of Japan did grow slightly, but only because more Japanese returned home than left for other countries. Japanese economic planners are concerned about the increasing dependency burden associated with a shrinking population. As Japan's population ages, increasing numbers of retirees will have to be supported by declining numbers of workers.

The Newly Industrialized Countries

In the 1960s, 1970s, and 1980s, the Japanese path to development was successfully followed by its former colonies, South Korea and Taiwan. Hong Kong also emerged as a newly industrialized economy in this period, although its economic and political systems remained distinctive.

The Rise of South Korea The postwar rise of South Korea was even more remarkable than that of Japan. During the period of Japanese occupation, Korean industrial develop-

ment was concentrated in the north, which is rich in natural resources. The south, in contrast, remained a densely populated, poor, agrarian region. South Korea emerged from the bloody Korean War as one of the world's least-developed countries.

In the 1960s, the South Korean government initiated a program of export-led economic growth. It guided the economy with a heavy hand and denied basic political freedom to the Korean people. By the 1970s, such policies had proved highly successful in the economic realm. Huge Korean industrial conglomerates, known as chaebol, moved from manufacturing inexpensive consumer goods to heavy industrial products and then to high-tech equipment.

At first South Korean firms remained dependent on the United States and Japan for basic technology. By the 1990s, however, South Korea emerged as one of the world's main producers of semiconductors as well as the world's largest shipbuilder. South Korean wages also rose at a rapid clip. The country has invested heavily in education (by some measures it has the world's most intensive educational system), which has served it well in the global high-tech economy. Large South Korean companies are themselves now strongly multinational, building new factories in the low-wage countries of Southeast Asia and Latin America, as well as in the United States and Europe.

Contemporary Korea The political and social development of South Korea has not been nearly as smooth as its economic progress. Throughout the 1960s and 1970s, student-led protests against the dictatorial government were brutally repressed. As the South Korean middle class expanded and prospered, pressure for democratization grew, and by the late 1980s it could no longer be denied. But even though democratization has been successful, political tension has not disappeared (Figure 11.41).

South Korea's periodic political crises have been accompanied by economic difficulties. In 1997, for example, with the country's banking system in chaos, its economy entered a deep recession. Although the South Korean economy soon recovered, it remained unstable for several years, with periods of fast growth alternating with slowdowns. Critics contend that the South Korean economy needs substantial

Figure 11.41 Protests in South Korea Massive political protests are common in South Korea. In May 2008, some 10,000 cattle breeders took to the streets of Seoul to burn cow effigies, protesting a new policy that would allow increased beef exports from the United States to South Korea.

reforms, in particular the breaking up of the large conglomerates (chaebol). In recent years, however, the South Korean economy has been characterized by steady growth, moderate inflation, low unemployment, and large export surpluses. Even in the global recession year of 2009, the South Korean economy managed a slight expansion.

Under the Sunshine Policy between 1998 and 2008, South Korea attempted to use its own economic success to help North Korea, encouraging Korean companies to invest in jointly operated factories in the North. During the same period, North Korea allowed the limited emergence of public markets. Joint ventures with South Korea, however, were never particularly successful, and during the Korean crisis of 2010 their future was thrown temporarily into doubt. North Korean industry, suffering from parts shortages and decaying infrastructure, continues to decline. The Pyongyang government also moved to restrict its small private markets. In 2009, it ordered a currency reevaluation, forcing citizens to exchange old bank bills for new, less valuable ones. In the process, most of the meager savings of the North Korean people were wiped out, further undermining the economy. In early 2010, the North Korean government admitted that the currency change had been a mistake by executing the top-level bureaucrat who had been in charge of its implementation.

Taiwan and Hong Kong Like South Korea, Taiwan and Hong Kong also have experienced rapid economic growth since the 1960s. The Taiwanese government, like that of South Korea and Japan, has guided the economic development of the country. Taiwan's economy, however, is based more extensively on small to midsized family firms. This characteristically Chinese form of business organization is sometimes said to give Taiwan greater economic flexibility than its northern neighbors, but it has prevented it from entering certain industries that require huge concentrations of capital.

Hong Kong, unlike its neighbors, has been characterized by one of the most **laissez-faire** economic systems in the world, one with a great amount of market freedom from government interference (laissez-faire is a French term meaning "let it be"). Hong Kong traditionally functioned as a trading center, but in the 1960s and 1970s it emerged as a major producer of textiles, toys, and other consumer goods. By the 1980s, however, such cheap products could no longer be made in such an expensive city. Hong Kong's industrialists subsequently began to move their plants to nearby areas in southern China, while Hong Kong itself increasingly specialized in business services, banking, telecommunications, and entertainment. Fears that its economy would falter after the Chinese takeover in 1997 were not realized. Since 2005, Hong Kong's economy has been strengthened by a number of Chinese companies listing their initial public offerings on the booming Hong Kong stock exchange.

Both Taiwan and Hong Kong have close overseas economic connections. Linkages are particularly tight with Chinese-owned firms located in Southeast Asia. Taiwan's high-technology businesses are also intertwined with those

of the United States; there is a constant back-and-forth flow of talent, technology, and money between Taipei and Silicon Valley. Hong Kong's economy also is closely bound with that of the United States (as well as those of Canada and Britain), but its closest connections are with the rest of China. Taiwan is moving in the same direction; China is now its largest export market and its second-largest source of imports after Japan.

Chinese Development

China dwarfs all of the rest of East Asia in both physical size and population. Its economic takeoff is thus reconfiguring the economy of the entire region and, to some extent, that of the world as a whole. But despite its recent growth, China's economy has a number of weaknesses. The future of the Chinese economy is thus one of the biggest uncertainties facing both the East Asian and the global economies.

China Under Communism More than a century of war, invasion, and near-chaos in China ended in 1949 when the communist forces led by Mao Zedong seized power. The new government, inheriting a weak economy, set about nationalizing private firms and building heavy industries. Certain successes were realized, especially in Manchuria, where a large amount of heavy industrial equipment was inherited from the Japanese colonial regime.

In the late 1950s, however, China experienced an economic disaster ironically called the "Great Leap Forward." One of the main ideas behind this scheme was that small-scale village workshops could produce the large quantities of iron needed for sustained industrial growth. Communist Party officials demanded that these inefficient workshops meet unreasonably high production quotas. In some cases the only way they could do so was to melt peasants' agricultural tools. Peasants also were forced to contribute such a large percentage of their crops to the state that many went hungry. The result was a horrific famine that may have killed 20 million people.

The early 1960s saw a return to more pragmatic policies, but toward the end of the decade a new wave of radicalism swept through China. This "Cultural Revolution" was aimed at mobilizing young people to stamp out the remaining vestiges of capitalism. Thousands of experienced industrial managers and college professors were expelled from their positions. Many were sent to villages to be "reeducated" through hard physical labor; others were simply killed. The economic consequences of such policies were devastating.

Toward a Postcommunist Economy When Mao Zedong, revered as an almost superhuman being, died in 1976, China faced a crucial turning point. Its economy was nearly stagnant and its people were desperately poor. A political struggle ensued between pragmatists hoping for change and dedicated communists. The pragmatists emerged victorious, and by the late 1970s it was clear that China would embark on a different economic path. The new China would seek closer connections with the world economy and take a modified capitalist road to development.

China did not, however, transform itself into a fully capitalist country. The state continued to run most heavy industries, and the Communist Party retained a monopoly on political power. Instead of suddenly abandoning the communist model, as the former Soviet Union later did, China allowed cracks to appear in which capitalist ventures could take root and thrive. As recently as 1995, almost 80 percent of the Chinese economy was in government hands, but by 2009 over 70 percent was controlled by the private sector.

One of China's first capitalist openings was in agriculture, which had previously been dominated by large-scale communal farms. Individuals were suddenly allowed to act as agricultural entrepreneurs, selling produce in the open market. Owing to this change, the income of many farmers rose dramatically. By the late 1980s, however, the focus of growth had shifted to the urban-industrial sector. As the government became concerned about inflation, it placed price caps on agricultural products and increased taxes on farmers. By the early years of the new millennium, many rural areas in China's interior provinces were experiencing economic distress, prompting many people to relocate to China's coastal cities or to foreign countries.

Industrial Reform One of China's most important early industrial reforms involved opening **Special Economic Zones (SEZs)** in which foreign investment was welcome and state interference minimal. The Shenzhen SEZ, adjacent to Hong Kong, proved particularly successful after Hong Kong manufacturers found it a convenient source of cheap land and labor (Figure 11.42). Additional SEZs soon were opened, mostly in the coastal region. The basic strategy was to attract foreign investment that could generate exports, the income from which would supply China with the capital it needed to build its infrastructure and thus achieve conditions for sustained economic growth.

Other market-oriented reforms followed. Former agricultural cooperatives were allowed to transform themselves into capitalist entities. Many of these "township and village enterprises" proved highly successful. From 1980 to 2010, the Chinese economy grew at an average rate of roughly 10 percent a year, perhaps the fastest rate of expansion the world has ever seen. China emerged as a major trading nation, amassing large trade surpluses and foreign reserves. In 2010 China's foreign exchange reserves stood at $2,447 billion, dwarfing second-place Japan's figure of $990 billion.

China's economy has grown so quickly in recent years that many economists have feared that it would overheat, leading to unsustainably high rates of inflation. Thus far, however, inflation has remained moderate. Other critics contend that China must fully abandon centralized planning if its expansion is to be sustainable over the long run. China's leadership, however, has made it clear that reform will be a gradual process, maintaining that it has proved quite successful at managing its economic expansion.

Figure 11.42 Shenzhen The city of Shenzhen, adjacent to Hong Kong, was one of China's first Special Economic Zones. It has more recently emerged as a major city in its own right.

China's economic growth has resulted in increased tensions with the United States. China exports far more to the United States than it imports, leading some U.S. politicians to demand that China allow its currency, the yuan, to rise against the dollar. In 2005, China officially unhooked its currency from the U.S. dollar; by 2008 it had appreciated 21 percent. Since then, the Chinese government has prevented the yuan from rising further. U.S. critics accuse China of unfairly keeping its currency undervalued in order to enhance its exports. China's large and growing holdings of U.S. treasury bonds, however, make it tricky for the United States to exert pressure on this issue.

Social and Regional Differentiation The Chinese economic surge unleashed by the reforms of the late 1970s and 1980s resulted in growing **social and regional differentiation**. In other words, certain groups of people—and certain portions of the country—prospered far more than others. Despite its official socialism, the Chinese state encouraged the formation of an economic elite, concluding that wealthy individuals are necessary to transform the economy. The least-fortunate Chinese citizens were sometimes left without work, and many millions have migrated to the booming coastal cities. The government has tried to control the transfer of population, but with only partial success. As China's economic boom accelerated, economic disparities mounted. The rapid growth of the elite population made China the world's fastest-growing market for luxury automobiles and even golf-course developments. At the same time, vulnerable state-owned enterprises have increasingly abandoned their provision of housing, medical care, and other social services, leaving many people destitute—particularly the elderly.

Economic disparities in China, as in other countries, are geographically structured. Before the reform period, the communist government attempted to equalize the fortunes of the different regions, giving special privileges to individuals from poor places. Such efforts were not wholly successful, and some provinces continued to be deprived. Since the coming of market reforms, moreover, the process of regional economic differentiation has accelerated (Figure 11.43).

The Booming Coastal Region Most of the benefits from China's economic transformation have flowed to the coastal region and to the capital city of Beijing. The first beneficiaries were the southern provinces of Guangdong and Fujian. This region was perhaps predisposed to the new economy, because the southern Chinese have long been noted for engaging in overseas trade. Guangdong and Fujian have also benefited from their close connections with the overseas Chinese communities of Southeast Asia and North America. Proximity to Taiwan and especially Hong Kong also proved helpful. Vast amounts of capital have flowed to the south coastal region from foreign (and Hong Kong-based) Chinese business networks.

**GROSS DOMESTIC PRODUCT
(per person, by administrative division, 2009, U.S. $, Purchasing Power Parity)**

- Over 40,000
- 20,000–40,000
- 10,000–20,000
- 7,000–10,000
- 5,000–7,000
- Below 5,000

Figure 11.43 Development Issues: Economic Differentiation in China Although China has seen rapid economic expansion since the late 1970s, the benefits of growth have not been evenly distributed throughout the country. Economic prosperity and social development are concentrated on and near the coast. Most of the interior remains relatively poor. The poorest part of China is the upland region of Guizhou in the south-central part of the country.

By the early 2000s, the Yangtze Delta, centered on the city of Shanghai, reemerged as the most dynamic region of China. The delta was the traditional economic (and intellectual) core of China, and before the communist takeover Shanghai was its premier industrial and financial center. The Chinese government, moreover, has encouraged the development of huge industrial, commercial, and residential complexes, hoping to take advantage of the region's dynamism. In 2010, Shanghai was the site of the world's largest and most expensive world's fair, Expo 2010, designed to showcase the "next great world city."

Interior and Northern China The interior regions of China have seen much less economic expansion. Central and northern Manchuria were formerly quite prosperous, owing to fertile soils and early industrialization, but have not participated much in the recent boom. Many of the state-owned heavy industries of the Manchurian "**rust belt**," or zone of decaying factories, are not efficient. Manchuria's once-productive oil wells, moreover, are largely exhausted. China and Russia have, however, recently constructed an oil pipeline from Siberia to Daqing in Manchuria, hoping to revive the economy of this decaying oil town.

Most of the interior provinces of China likewise largely missed the initial wave of growth in the 1980s and '90s. In many areas, rural populations continued to grow while the natural environment deteriorated. One consequence has been high levels of underemployment and outmigration. By most measures, poverty increases with distance from the coast. As a result of such discrepancies, China is now encouraging development in the west (including Tibet and Xinjiang as well as the western provinces of China proper), focusing on transportation improvement and natural resource extraction. As labor shortages begin to appear in the booming coastal areas, industrialists are responding by building new factories in the interior portions of the country.

Scholars debate the conditions found in the poorer parts of interior China. Some believe that China's official statistics are too positive, hiding significant poverty. Others think that the country's economic boom has substantially raised living standards even in the poorest districts. According to official statistics, China's poverty rate fell from 53 percent in 1981 to less than 3 percent in 2009. Critics note, however, that more than 30 percent of the Chinese population still lives on less than $2 a day.

Rising Tensions China's explosive but uneven economic growth has generated a number of problems. Inflation has made planning difficult and created hardship for those on fixed incomes. Corruption by state officials is by some accounts rampant; success often seems to depend on knowing the right people and having the right connections. In 2009 alone, more than 100,000 public officials were convicted on corruption charges. China's crime rate, moreover, which was extremely low, is rising rapidly. Organized crime in particular is emerging as a major problem in many areas.

An equally significant issue has been the struggle for free expression and political openness. The desire for reform has been enhanced by rising incomes and the development of a sizable middle class. In 1989, however, the state crushed a movement for government accountability and democracy, and forced the opposition to go underground. Whether most Chinese people really want democracy is a controversial issue. If they do, tensions will probably mount as long as China's economy prospers while its rulers deny basic freedoms. An estimated 3 million Chinese citizens took part in some 58,000 separate public protests in 2004, mostly focused on wage disputes, evictions, pension issues, and environmental degradation.

China has responded to such protest movements in part by increasing its restrictions on free speech. Internet censorship has become a particularly contentious issue. The Chinese government is currently estimated to employ an "Internet police force" roughly 30,000 strong. In 2010, in response to such interference, Google temporarily pulled out of China proper, redirecting its Chinese traffic to its servers in Hong Kong. Many Chinese Internet users, however, have learned to use sophisticated techniques to avoid official censorship.

China's political and human-rights policies have complicated its international relations. Tension with the United States and other wealthy countries also stems from economic issues. China's large and growing trade surplus and its reluctance to enforce copyright and patent law irritate many of its trading partners. Numerous U.S. firms have accused Chinese businesses of pirating music, software, and brand names. In 2010, the Unites States accused China of doing to little to control copyright violations; China responded by calling such accusations "groundless." As the global market grows and as popular culture becomes globalized, copyright and trademark infringement are becoming increasingly profitable and hence increasingly difficult to control.

Social Conditions in China

Despite its pockets of persistent poverty, China has achieved significant progress in social development. Since coming to power in 1949, the communist government has made large investments in medical care and education, and today China boasts fairly impressive health and longevity figures. But as China has moved to a market-based economy, its formerly extensive system of rural medical clinics has deteriorated. Some observes fear that levels of both health and education may be declining for the poorest segments of China's population.

Human well-being in China is also geographically structured. The literacy rate, for example, remains lower in many of the poorer parts of China, including the uplands of Yunnan and Guizhou and the interior portions of the North China Plain, than in the most prosperous coastal regions of the country. Increasingly, the largest gap is that which separates the booming cities from the languishing rural areas.

Population policy also remains an unsettling issue for China. With 1.3 billion people highly concentrated in less than half of its territory, China has one of the world's highest effective population densities. By the 1980s, its government had become so concerned that it instituted the famous "one-child policy." Under this plan, couples in normal circumstances are expected to have only a single offspring and can suffer financial and other penalties if they do not comply (Figure 11.44). Although the one-child policy was never fully implemented in many rural areas, China's demographic strategy has been generally successful; the average fertility level is now only 1.6, and the population is growing at the relatively slow rate of 0.6 percent a year. China will likely reach roughly 1.5 billion persons before stabilization occurs.

The decline in Chinese fertility, however, has brought about problems of its own. China is now worried about impending labor shortages as well as its aging population. Thus far, China has not provided adequate facilities for caring for its elderly population. As a result, the government is increasingly allowing couples to have more than one child, hoping that the additional children will care for their parents as they grow old.

China's population policy has also has generated social tensions and human-rights abuses. Particularly troubling is the growing gender imbalance in the Chinese population. In 2009, 119 boys were born for every 100 girls. This asymmetry reflects the practice of honoring one's ancestors; because family lines are traced through male offspring, one must produce a male heir to maintain one's lineage. Many couples are therefore desperate to produce a son. Some opt to bear more than one child regardless of penalties. Another option is gender-selective abortion; if ultrasound reveals a female fetus, the pregnancy is sometimes terminated. Baby girls also are commonly abandoned, and well-substantiated rumors of female infanticide circulate. International women's organizations, as well as antiabortion groups, are concerned about these effects of China's population policy.

The Position of Women Women have historically had a relatively low position in Chinese society, as is true in most other civilizations. One particularly blatant traditional expression of this was the practice of foot binding: the feet of elite girls were usually deformed by breaking and binding them in order to produce a dainty appearance. This crippling and painful practice was eliminated only in the 20th century. In certain areas of southern China it was also common in earlier times for girls to be married, hence to leave their own families, when they were mere toddlers (such marriages, of course, would not be consummated for many years).

Not all women suffered such disabilities in premodern China. Some individuals achieved fame and fortune—a few

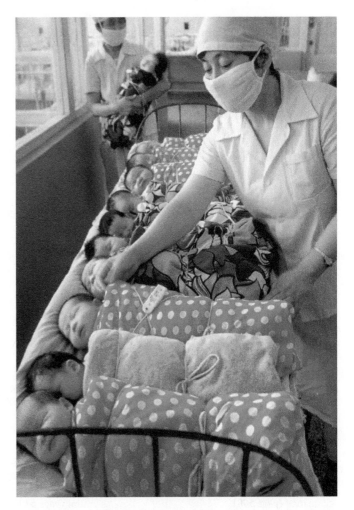

Figure 11.44 China's Population Policies One aspect of China's population policy is the expansion of child-care facilities so that mothers can be near their children while at work. This enables women to resume participating in the workforce soon after giving birth. This photo shows a typical day-care center attached to an industrial plant in Guangdong province in coastal China.

even through military service. Among the Hakka, women enjoyed a relatively high social position and were seldom subjected to foot binding. Both the nationalist and communist governments have, moreover, sought to begin equalizing the relations between the sexes. Many of their measures have been successful, and women now have a relatively high level of participation in the Chinese workforce. But it is still true that throughout East Asia—in Japan no less than in China—few women have achieved positions of power in either business or government.

Summary

- The economic success of East Asia has been accompanied by severe environmental degradation. Japan, South Korea, and Taiwan have responded by enacting strict environmental laws and by moving many of their most polluting industries overseas. The major environmental issue in the region today concerns the rapid growth of the Chinese economy. Pollution in Chinese cities is so serious that it has major negative effects on human health, while much of the Chinese countryside suffers from such problems as soil erosion and desertification. China is responding, however, with a major program for renewable energy.

- East Asia is a densely populated region, but its birthrates have plummeted in recent decades. Japan is now experiencing population decline, which will put pressure on the Japanese economy. In China, the biggest demographic challenge results from the massive movement of people from the interior to the coast and from rural villages to the rapidly expanding cities. China has been trying to redirect development toward the interior, but thus far has had little success.

- East Asia is united by deep cultural and historical bonds. China has the largest influence because, at one time or another, it ruled most of the region. Although Japan has never been under Chinese rule, it still has profound historical connections to Chinese civilization. The more prosperous parts of East Asia have welcomed cultural globalization over the several past decades.

- Geopolitically, East Asia has been characterized by much strife since the end of World War II. China and Korea are still suspicious of Japan, and they worry that it might rebuild a strong military force. Japan is concerned about the growing military power of China and especially about the nuclear arms and missiles of North Korea. Relations between North and South Korea improved between 2000 and 2008, but subsequently deteriorated. North Korean weapons development is also a major concern in Japan and the United States.

- With the notable exception of North Korea, all East Asian countries have experienced rapid economic growth since the end of World War II. In the 2000s, the most important story has been the rise of China. China's economic expansion has reduced poverty nationwide, but has also generated serious tensions between the wealthier, more globally oriented coastal regions and the less-prosperous interior provinces. The rise of China also has global implications, as many countries in all regions of the world have profited by exporting the raw materials needed by China's booming industries.

Key Terms

anthropogenic landscape *(page 497)*
autonomous region *(page 512)*
Burakumin *(page 510)*
central place theory *(page 500)*
China proper *(page 511)*
Cold War *(page 513)*
Confucianism *(page 506)*
diaspora *(page 511)*
geomancy *(page 508)*

ideographic writing *(page 504)*
laissez-faire *(page 529)*
loess *(page 486)*
Mandarin *(page 506)*
Marxism *(page 509)*
pollution exporting *(page 489)*
regulatory lakes *(page 485)*
rust belt *(page 532)*
samurai *(page 514)*

sediment load *(page 486)*
Shogunate *(page 518)*
social and regional differentiation
  (page 530)
Special Economic Zones (SEZs) *(page 530)*
spheres of influence *(page 517)*
superconurbation *(page 501)*
tonal language *(page 512)*
urban primacy *(page 501)*

Review Questions

1. How does the physiography of the Huang He River valley differ from that of the valley of the Yangtze?

2. Why is Japan so much more heavily forested than China?

3. Why has Shanghai emerged as the most populous urban area in China?

4. What are the major ways in which Japanese cities differ from those of the United States?

5. Where are the non-Han peoples of China concentrated? Why are they concentrated in these areas?

6. What have been the main consequences of the geographical division of Korea into two states?

7. Historically speaking, how did China and Japan act differently as imperial powers?

8. How have the different countries of East Asia followed different paths to economic development?

9. Where in China would one find the most rapid economic development, and why would one find it there?

10. How does the position of women in Japan compare to the position of women in other wealthy, industrialized countries?

Thinking Geographically

1. Discuss the advantages and disadvantages of China's building of major dams.

2. Discuss the ramifications, both positive and negative, of Japan's allowing the importation of rice and opening its agricultural lands to urban development.

3. What might be the consequences of China's granting true autonomy to the Tibetans and other non-Han peoples? Independence?

4. What are the potential implications of Taiwan's declaring itself an independent country?

5. Discuss the potential ramifications of the United States' restricting the importation of Chinese goods in order to put pressure on the Chinese government for human-rights reforms.

6. Discuss the advantages and disadvantages of China's current population policies.

7. Do you think that East Asia will emerge as the center of the world economy in the next century?

Regional Novels and Films

Novels

Sawako Ariyoshi, *The River Ki* (1982, Kodansha)

Xingjian Gao, *Soul Mountain* (2000, Flamingo)

Kazuo Ishiguro, *An Artist of the Floating World* (1989, Vintage Books)

Ho Soo Kim, *Den Haag* (2008, Philmac)

Peter H. Lee, *Flowers of Fire* (1986, University of Hawaii Press)

Wang Shuo, *Playing for Thrills* (1998, Penguin)

Hsueh-Chin Tsao, *The Dream of the Red Chamber* (1958, Doubleday)

Films

The Banquet (2006, China)

Farewell, My Concubine (1993, China)

The Gate of Heavenly Peace (1995, China)

The Host (2006, South Korea)

Little Red Flowers (2006, China)

Nomugi Pass (1979, Japan)

The Old Garden (2006, South Korea)

Princess Mononoke (1997, Japan)

Pulgasari (1985, North Korea)

Seven Samurai (1954, Japan)

A Taxing Woman (1987, Japan)

301, 302 (1995, South Korea)

Twilight Samurai (2002, Japan)

Why Has Bodi-Darma Left for the East? (1989, Korea)

Bibliography

Brown, Melissa. 2004. *Is Taiwan Chinese?: The Impact of Culture, Power, and Migration on Changing Identities.* Berkeley: University of California Press.

The Contemporary Atlas of China. 1988. Boston: Houghton Mifflin.

Cybriwsky, Roman A. 1998. *Tokyo: The Shogun's City and the Twenty-First Century.* New York: Wiley.

Elvin, Mark. 2004. *The Retreat of the Elephant: An Environmental History of China.* New Haven, CT: Yale University Press.

Harris, Mark Edward. 2007. *Inside North Korea.* San Francisco: Chronicle Books.

Knapp, Ronald G., ed. 1992. *Chinese Landscapes: The Village as Place.* Honolulu: University of Hawaii Press.

Kynge, James. 2006. *China Shakes the World: A Titan's Rise and Troubled Future—and the Challenge for America.* Boston: Houghton Mifflin.

Myers, B.R. 2010. *The Cleanest Race: How North Koreans See Themselves and Why It Matters.* New York: Melville House.

Ryu, Je-Hun. 2004. *Reading the Korean Cultural Landscape.* Elizabeth, NJ: Hollym International.

Smil, Vaclav. 2004. *China's Past, China's Future: Energy, Food, Environment.* London: Curzon Press.

Totman, Conrad. 1989. *The Green Archipelago: Forestry in Preindustrial Japan.* Berkeley: University of California Press.

MG Mastering Geography

MapMaster™

Log in to www.masteringgeography.com for MapMaster™ interactive maps, geography videos, RSS feeds, flashcards, web links, an eText version of *Diversity Amid Globalization*, and self-study quizzes to enhance your study of East Asia.

MapMaster™ presents 13 Place Name and 13 Layered Thematic interactive maps to help students practice and master their geographic literacy, spatial reasoning, and critical thinking skills.

The Gateway to India is a favored place for relaxation in hectic Mumbai (Bombay), India's largest city. The stone structure was built in 1911 to commemorate the visit of George V, King of Great Britain and Emperor of India.

DIVERSITY AMID GLOBALIZATION

From the late 1940s through the 1980s, South Asia was one of the world's least globalized regions. Over the last two decades, however, a number of South Asian cities have emerged as crucial players in worldwide trade, exporting vast quantities of textiles, information technology products, and cultural goods such as films and television shows.

ENVIRONMENTAL GEOGRAPHY

While the arid parts of South Asia suffer from water shortages and the salinization of the soil, the humid areas often experience devastating floods.

POPULATION AND SETTLEMENT

South Asia will soon become the most populous region in the world; although birthrates have come down substantially in India and Bangladesh, they remain high in Pakistan.

CULTURAL COHERENCE AND DIVERSITY

South Asia is one of the most culturally diverse regions of the world, with India alone having more than a dozen official languages as well as numerous followers of most major religions.

GEOPOLITICAL FRAMEWORK

South Asia is burdened not only by a large number of violent secession movements, but also by the struggle between the nuclear-armed countries of India and Pakistan, which threatens both regional and global stability.

ECONOMIC AND SOCIAL DEVELOPMENT

Although South Asia as a whole is one of the poorest regions of the world, parts of India are experiencing rapid economic development based on the high-tech skills of the educated segment of its population.

537

Figure 12.1 South Asia The second most populous region in the world, South Asia is dominated by India, Pakistan, and Bangladesh. The two Himalayan countries of Nepal and Bhutan, along with the island nations of Sri Lanka and the Maldives, round out the region. Four extensive physical subregions cover most of South Asia: the high Himalayan mountains in the north; the expansive Indus–Ganges lowland that reaches from Pakistan to the delta lands of Bangladesh; peninsular India, dominated by the Deccan Plateau; and the island realm that includes Sri Lanka and the Maldives. Many of this seismically active region's landscapes are products of the slow northward movement of the Indo–Australian tectonic plate against the Eurasian plate. Typhoons from the Bay of Bengal pose a significant risk to parts of eastern South Asia.

South Asia, a land of deep historical and cultural interconnections, has experienced intense political conflict for decades. Since independence from Britain in 1947, India and Pakistan, South Asia's two largest countries, have fought several wars and remain locked in a bitter conflict concerning possession of the disputed territory of Kashmir in the northern reaches of the region. Religious divisions are linked to this geopolitical turmoil, for India is primarily a Hindu country with a large Muslim minority, while Pakistan is almost entirely Muslim. Religious and ethnic tensions also abound within both countries, and in the neighboring countries of Bangladesh, Nepal, and Sri Lanka as well.

Parallel to these geopolitical tensions are demographic and economic concerns. Given its current rate of growth, South Asia soon will surpass East Asia as the world's most populous region. Although fertility levels have dropped dramatically in recent years across much of the region, they remain elevated in other areas, leading to concerns about how South Asia will be able to sustain its population. Although agricultural production has kept pace with population growth over the past four decades, many South Asian environments are experiencing pronounced stress. Poverty compounds such problems. Along with Sub-Saharan Africa, South Asia is the poorest part of the world. Roughly one-third of India's people subsist on less than $1 a day.

Despite its poverty, political tensions, and environmental problems, South Asia has also exhibited a significant degree of vitality in recent decades. India's economy in particular has been expanding at a rapid pace, lifting tens of millions of people into the middle class. Since the early 1990s, most South Asian countries have integrated their economies into the global system. Although such globalization has generated a number of controversies, it has brought major benefits to certain areas and groups of people. Parts of India, for example, have recently become major players in information technology (IT), tightly linked to California's Silicon Valley and other centers of the global IT industry.

The bulk of South Asia forms a subcontinent–often called the **Indian Subcontinent**–separated from the rest of Asia by formidable mountain ranges. Located here are the region's major countries, India, Pakistan, and Bangladesh, as well as the smaller mountainous states of Nepal and Bhutan. Also placed within South Asia are a number of islands in the Indian Ocean, including the countries of Sri Lanka and the Maldives, as well as the Indian territories of the Lakshadweep, and the Andaman and Nicobar islands.

India is by far the largest South Asian country, both in size and in population. Covering more than 1 million square miles (2,590,000 square kilometers), India is the world's seventh largest country in area and, with more than 1.1 billion inhabitants, second only to China in population. Pakistan and Bangladesh are next largest in size and population, each with more than 160 million inhabitants. A compact country about the size of Wisconsin, Bangladesh is one of the most densely populated places in the world. Bangladesh has a short border with Burma (Myanmar), but it is otherwise virtually engulfed by India, which wraps around the country to the north and the northeast.

ENVIRONMENTAL GEOGRAPHY: Diverse Landscapes, from Tropical Islands to Mountain Rim

South Asia's environmental geography covers a wide spectrum that ranges from the highest mountains in the world to densely populated delta islands barely above sea level; from one of the wettest places on Earth to dry, scorching deserts; from tropical rain forests to degraded scrublands to coral reefs (Figure 12.1). All of these ecological zones have their own distinct and complex environmental problems. To illustrate the complexity of South Asian environmental issues, let us begin by looking at the building of India's newly constructed "Golden Quadrilateral" highway system.

Building the Quadrilateral Highway

India's need for improved transportation is difficult to deny. As of 2006, the average speed for a trucker traveling between Kolkata (Calcutta) and Mumbai (Bombay) could be as low as 6.8 miles (11 kilometers) per hour. To address the transport needs generated by its booming economy, India has undertaken a massive multi-billion dollar road project designed to connect its four largest cities, New Delhi, Kolkata (Calcutta), Chennai (Madras), and Mumbai (Bombay), with a modern highway (Figure 12.2). The basic four-lane highway was completed in 2010, but a year earlier the Indian government announced that it would begin converting much of it into a

Figure 12.2 The Golden Quadrilateral Highway India's infrastructure is notoriously poor, but the government is now responding with a massive highway construction program. The Golden Quadrilateral Highway, shown here, has generated numerous protests, as villagers object to the destruction of houses, temples, and trees that lie in its path.

six-lane roadway. Although it only makes up about two percent of India's total road network, the Golden Quadrilateral Highway carries roughly 40 percent of India's vehicular traffic.

Building and expanding the new highway system has not proved easy. Truckers have protested the higher taxes and tolls that are needed to finance it, while citizen groups have stopped construction on several occasions with large protests demanding more underpasses, overpasses, and cattle crossings. Some concessions have been made, but many rural Indians are infuriated that their homes have been destroyed and their farms bisected by the massive project. Environmentalists worry that an expanded road system will lead to an increased reliance on trucks and cars, rather than the more environmentally responsible railroad system.

Highway construction has also generated both religious and environmental conflicts. Several Hindu temples have had to be relocated, prompting local worshippers to try to stop the project. Thousands of trees have been destroyed, generating further opposition. Not only are large trees rare in many parts of India, but they are also often regarded as sa-cred by devout Hindus. As a result, contractors have sometimes been forced to hire Muslims to cut down trees under the cover of night. Such actions, not surprisingly, anger local villagers. Villagers must also worry about a number of other environmental problems, a few of which are examined in the following section.

Environmental Issues in South Asia

As is true in other poor and densely settled regions of the world, a raft of serious ecological issues plague South Asia. The region also suffers from the usual environmental problems of water and air pollution that accompany early industrialization and manufacturing (Figure 12.3). Compounding all of these problems are the immense numbers of new people added each year through natural population growth.

Natural Hazards in Bangladesh The link between population pressure and environmental problems is nowhere clearer than in the delta area of Bangladesh, where the

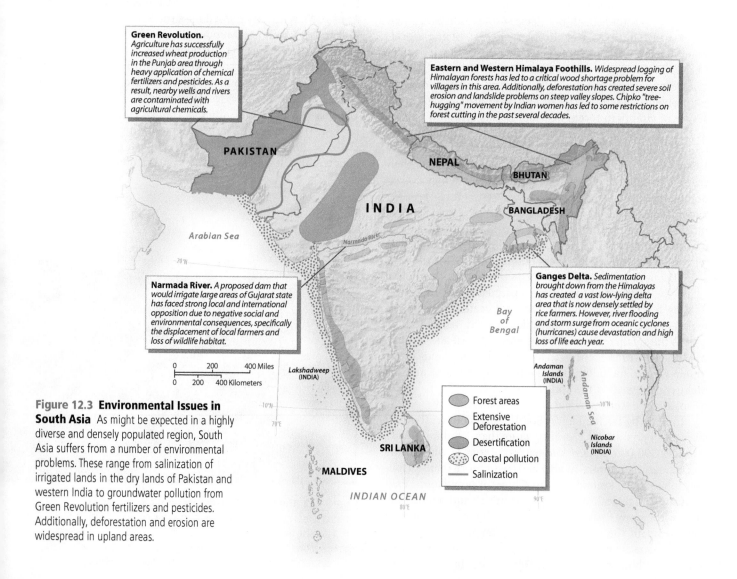

Figure 12.3 Environmental Issues in South Asia As might be expected in a highly diverse and densely populated region, South Asia suffers from a number of environmental problems. These range from salinization of irrigated lands in the dry lands of Pakistan and western India to groundwater pollution from Green Revolution fertilizers and pesticides. Additionally, deforestation and erosion are widespread in upland areas.

Green Revolution. *Agriculture has successfully increased wheat production in the Punjab area through heavy application of chemical fertilizers and pesticides. As a result, nearby wells and rivers are contaminated with agricultural chemicals.*

Eastern and Western Himalaya Foothills. *Widespread logging of Himalayan forests has led to a critical wood shortage problem for villagers in this area. Additionally, deforestation has created severe soil erosion and landslide problems on steep valley slopes. Chipko "tree-hugging" movement by Indian women has led to some restrictions on forest cutting in the past several decades.*

Narmada River. *A proposed dam that would irrigate large areas of Gujarat state has faced strong local and international opposition due to negative social and environmental consequences, specifically the displacement of local farmers and loss of wildlife habitat.*

Ganges Delta. *Sedimentation brought down from the Himalayas has created a vast low-lying delta area that is now densely settled by rice farmers. However, river flooding and storm surge from oceanic cyclones (hurricanes) cause devastation and high loss of life each year.*

Forest areas
Extensive Deforestation
Desertification
Coastal pollution
Salinization

mented by groundwater. Bangladesh's water problems are further magnified by the fact that many of its aquifers are contaminated with arsenic, threatening the health of as many as 80 million people.

Forests and Deforestation Forests and woodlands once covered most of South Asia, except for the desert areas in the northeast, but in most places tree cover has vanished as a result of human activities. The Ganges Valley and coastal plains of India, for example, were largely deforested thousands of years ago to make room for agriculture. Elsewhere, forests were cleared more gradually for agricultural, urban, and industrial expansion. Railroad construction in the 19th century was especially destructive. More recently, hill slopes in the Himalayas and in the remote lands of eastern India have been logged for commercial purposes.

Beginning in the 1970s, India has embarked on a number of reforestation projects. Some of these have efforts been successful; according to some sources, Indian forest coverage actually increased by almost 6 percent between 1990 and 2005. As is true in many parts of the world, however, reforested areas are often covered by non-native trees, such as eucalyptus, that support little wildlife (Figure 12.5). According to a 2010 report, India's single-species tree plantations are

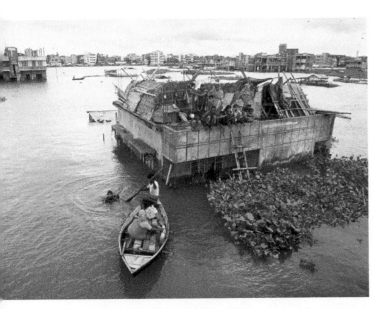

Figure 12.4 Flooding in Bangladesh Devastating floods are common in the low-lying delta lands of Bangladesh. Heavy rains come with the southwest monsoon, especially to the Himalayas, and powerful cyclones often develop over the Bay of Bengal.

Figure 12.5 Logging in India A even-aged stand of small trees is being logged off in the southern Indian state of Kerala. Such forestry practices leave little habitat for wildlife.

search for fertile land has driven people into hazardous areas, putting millions at risk from seasonal flooding as well as from the powerful **cyclones** that form over the Bay of Bengal. For millennia, drenching monsoon rains have eroded and transported huge quantities of sediment from the Himalayan slopes to the Bay of Bengal by the Ganges and Brahmaputra rivers, gradually building this low-lying and fertile deltaic environment. With continual population growth, people have gradually moved into the swamps to transform them into highly productive rice fields. While this agricultural activity has supported Bangladesh's vast population, it has intensified the effects of the area's natural hazards.

Although periodic floods are a natural, even beneficial, phenomenon that enlarges deltas by depositing fertile riverborne sediment, flooding has become a serious problem for people inhabiting these low-lying areas. In September 1998, for example, more than 22 million Bangladeshis were made homeless when water covered two-thirds of the country (Figure 12.4). In June 2010, fairly typical monsoon downpours killed dozens of people and marooned more than 150,000.

With the populations of both Bangladesh and northern India continuing to grow, there is a strong possibility that flooding will take even higher tolls in the coming decade as desperate farmers relocate into the hazardous lower floodplains. Deforestation of the Ganges and Brahmaputra headwaters magnifies the problem. When forest cover and ground vegetation are removed, rainfall does not soak into the ground to slow runoff and replenish groundwater supplies. Thus deforestation in river headwaters results in increased flooding in the wet season, as well as a lower water level during the dry season when river flows are suppleexpanding by up to 18,000 square kilometers (7,000 square miles) every year. And in India's standing natural forests, wood removal is estimated to exceed growth by a substantial margin.

As a result of deforestation, many villages of South Asia suffer from a shortage of fuelwood for household cooking, forcing people to burn dung cakes from cattle. While this low-grade fuel provides adequate heat, it diverts nutrients that could be used as fertilizers to household fires. It also results in high levels of air pollution, both indoors and outside. Where wood is available, collecting it may involve many hours of female labor because the remaining sources of wood are often far from the villages.

Villagers living in India's forest areas have suffered extensively from deforestation. As early as the 1970s, social movements designed to protect remaining groves gained prominence in some areas. The most noted of these movements, Chipko, mobilized women in northern India to engage in "tree-hugging" campaigns to stop logging. As a result of such social pressure, India began to involve local residents in forestry and conservation projects. Increasingly, villagers have been demanding their own rights to land and resources in wooded areas. In the landmark 2006 Forest Rights Act, the Indian government granted extensive rights to members of forest-dwelling communities. Many urban environmentalists, however, argue that this legislation could actually increase deforestation, as expanding villages often seek to convert wooded lands to agricultural fields. Some also fear that it could harm the efforts to preserve tigers and other large animal species.

Wildlife: Extinction and Protection Although the overall environmental situation in South Asia is rather bleak, wildlife protection inspires some optimism. The region has managed to retain a diverse assemblage of wildlife despite population pressure and intense poverty. The only remaining Asiatic lions live in India's Gujarat state, and even Bangladesh retains a viable population of tigers in the Sundarbans, the mangrove forests of the Ganges Delta. Wild elephants still roam several large reserves in India, Sri Lanka, and Nepal.

The protection of wildlife in India far exceeds that in most other parts of Asia. The official Project Tiger, which currently operates more than 40 preserves, is credited with increasing the country's tiger population from 1,200 in the 1970s to roughly 3,500 by the 1990s. A 2008 wildlife census, however, revealed a sharp drop in numbers, prompting the Indian government to pledge $153 million in further funding, and to consider relocating up to 200,000 villagers to make more room for tiger populations.

As the situation with tigers demonstrates, wildlife conservation in a country as poor and crowded as India is not easy. In many areas, pressure is mounting to convert remaining wildlands to farmlands. The best remaining zone of extensive wildlife habitat is in India's far northeast, an area subjected to rapid immigration and political unrest (see "Environment and Politics: Insurgency and National Parks in Northeastern India"). Moreover, wild animals, particularly tigers and elephants, threaten crops, livestock, and even people living near the reserves. When a rogue elephant herd ruins a crop or a tiger kills livestock, government agents are usually forced to destroy the animal.

The Four Subregions of South Asia

South Asia is separated from the rest of the Eurasian continent by a series of sweeping mountain ranges, including the Himalayas—the highest in the world. To better understand environmental conditions in this vast region, the Indian subcontinent can be broken down into four physical subregions, starting with the high mountain ranges of its northern fringe and extending to the tropical islands of the far south.

Mountains of the North South Asia's northern rim of mountains is dominated by the great Himalayan Range, forming the northern borders of India, Nepal, and Bhutan. These mountains are linked to the equally high Karakoram Range to the west, extending through northern Pakistan. More than two dozen peaks exceed 25,000 feet (7,620 meters), including the world's highest mountain, Everest, on the Nepal–China (Tibet) border at 29,028 feet (8,848 meters). To the east are the lower Arakan Yoma Mountains, forming the border between India and Myanmar (Burma) and separating South Asia from Southeast Asia.

These formidable mountain ranges were produced by tectonic activity caused by peninsular India pushing northward into the larger Eurasia Continental Plate; as a result of the collision between these two tectonic plates, great mountain ranges were folded and upthrust. The entire region is seismically active, putting all of northern South Asia in serious earthquake danger (see Figure 12.1). A massive earthquake in the Pakistani-controlled section of Kashmir on October 8, 2005, for example, resulted in roughly 80,000 deaths and left more than 3 million people homeless.

Indus-Ganges-Brahmaputra Lowlands South of the northern highlands lie vast lowlands created by three major river systems that have carried sediments eroded off the mountains through millions of years, building vast alluvial plains of fertile and easily farmed soils. These lowlands are densely settled and constitute the population core areas of Pakistan, India, and Bangladesh.

Of these three rivers, the Indus is the longest, covering more than 1,800 miles (2,880 kilometers) as it flows southward from the Himalayas through Pakistan to the Arabian Sea, providing much-needed irrigation waters to Pakistan's desert areas. The broad band of cultivated land in the desert zone of central and southern Pakistan that is

Figure 12.6 South Asia from Space The four physical subregions of South Asia are clearly seen in this satellite photograph, from the snow-clad Himalayas in the north to the islands of the south. The Deccan Plateau is dark, fringed by white clouds as moist air is lifted over the uplands of the Western Ghats.

made possible by the Indus is clearly visible on satellite images (Figure 12.6). Pakistan is currently concerned about India's plans to build dams on several tributaries of the Indus, which could reduce the flow of this all-important river.

Even more densely settled is the vast lowland of the Ganges, which, after flowing out of the Himalayas, travels southeasterly some 1,500 miles (2,400 kilometers) to empty into the Bay of Bengal. The Ganges not only provides the fertile alluvial soil that has made northern India a densely settled area for thousands of years, but has also long served as a vital transportation corridor. Given the central role of this river in South Asia's past and present, it is understandable that Hindus consider the Ganges sacred. But while the waters of the Ganges are reputed to have healing powers, the river is considered to be one of the world's most polluted watercourses.

Although this large South Asian lowland often is referred to as the Indus–Ganges Plain, this term neglects the Brahmaputra River. This river rises on the Tibetan Plateau and flows easterly, then southward and westerly over 1,700 miles (2,720 kilometers), joining the Ganges in central Bangladesh and spreading out over the vast delta, the largest in the world. Unlike the sparsely populated Indus Delta in Pakistan, the Ganges–Brahmaputra Delta is very densely set-

tled, containing more than 3,000 people per square mile (1,200 per square kilometer).

Peninsular India Jutting southward from the Indus-Ganges Plain is the familiar shape of peninsular India, made up primarily of the Deccan Plateau. This plateau zone is bordered on each coast by narrow coastal plains backed by elongated north–south mountain ranges. On the west are the higher Western Ghats, which are generally about 5,000 feet (1,524 meters) but reach more than 8,000 feet (2,438 meters) near the peninsula's southern tip; to the east, the Eastern Ghats are lower and discontinuous, thus forming less of a transportation barrier to the broader eastern coastal plains. On both coastal plains, fertile soils and an adequate water supply support population densities comparable to those of the Ganges lowlands.

Soils are poor or average over much of the Deccan, but in Maharashtra state basaltic lava flows have produced fertile black soils. A reliable water supply for agriculture is a major problem in most areas. Much of the western plateau lies in the rain shadow of the Western Ghats, giving it a semiarid climate. Small reservoirs or tanks have been the traditional method for collecting monsoon rainfall for use during the dry season. More recently, deep wells and powerful pumps have mined groundwater to support irrigated crops and village water needs.

Partly because of the overuse of these aquifers, the Indian government is building a series of large dams to allow more extensive irrigation. These projects are highly controversial, largely because the reservoirs will displace hundreds of thousands of rural residents. A case in point is the Narmada Project, which involves the construction of 30 major dams along the Narmada River. Proponents claims that the scheme will allow India to feed an additional 20 to 30 million people, while opponents claim that the human costs are too high, pointing out that as of 2010 some 200,000 displaced people had not yet received compensation by the Indian government.

The Southern Islands At the southern tip of peninsular India lies the island country of Sri Lanka, which is almost linked to India by a series of small islands called Adam's Bridge. Sri Lanka is ringed by extensive coastal plains and low hills, but mountains reaching more than 8,000 feet (2,438 meters) cover the southern interior, providing a cool, moist climate. Because the main winds arrive from the southwest, that portion of the island is much wetter than the rain-shadow area of the north and east.

Forming a separate country are the Maldives, a chain of more than 1,200 islands stretching south to the equator some 400 miles (640 kilometers) off the southwestern tip of India. The combined land area of these islands is only about 116 square miles (290 square kilometers), and only a quarter of the islands are actually inhabited. The islands of the Maldives are flat, low coral atolls, with a maximum elevation of just over 6 feet (2 meters) above sea level.

ENVIRONMENT AND POLITICS Insurgency and National Parks in Northeastern India

Many of India's best-preserved natural environments are located in its northeastern region, a land with many rugged landscapes and relatively low population density. Unfortunately, it is also a politically troubled region. Northeastern India stands out for its sheer diversity of insurgent groups. The state of Manipur alone has 15 active or proscribed "terrorist/insurgent groups," while nearby Assam has 11, Meghalaya 4, Nagaland and Tripura 3 each, and Mizoram 2. No such groups are listed for Arunachal Pradesh, but it too has seen insurgent violence in recent years—and it is claimed in its entirety by China, greatly complicating Indo-Chinese relations. Insurgent groups in northeastern India have a strong tendency to divide and proliferate. The Kuki people of Manipur, for example, are "represented" by the Kuki Liberation Army, the Kuki National Army, the Kuki Liberation Front, and the United Kuki Liberation Front.

Insurgent activity certainly complicates the preservation of the natural ecosystem, but it does not always make it impossible. Consider, for example, Kaziranga National Park in Assam (Figure 12.1.1).

Figure 12.1.1 Kaziranga National Park. Kazinaga has some of South Asia's best-preserved natural habitats. Two-thirds of the world's Indian rhinoceroses live in this park.

Kaziranga, one of India's largest parks, boasts two-thirds of the world's Indian rhinoceroses as well as the highest density of tigers. The rebel army called the United Liberation Front of Asom has devastated the local economy, attacking oil pipelines, freight trains, and governmental buildings. Its fighters, however, not only respect the park but actually seek to protect it, killing poachers on more than one occasion. Despite rebel activity in the area, tourists have continued to be able to visit Kaziranga.

Through most of northeastern India, insurgency long made tourism impossible. Recently, however, violence has receded. Whereas Nagaland saw 154 insurgency-related deaths in 2007, the 2009 total was only 17; in Meghalaya, the death count dropped from 79 in 2003 to just 4 in 2009. Only in Manipur and Assam have body counts remained high (369 and 371, respectively, in 2009). Due to improved security, India has been opening parts of the northeast to travelers. For those interested in visiting the area, Northeast India Diary (www.northeastindiadiary.com/meghalaya-travel/wildlife-in-meghalaya.html) provides information on local attractions. On a trip to Meghalaya's Balpakram National Park, it claims, one might see "elephants, wild buffaloes, gaur (Indian bison), sambar, barking deer, wild boar, slow loris, capped langur as well as predators such as tigers, leopards, clouded leopards, and the rare golden cat."

In Nagaland and Mizoram, some observers attribute the recent decline in fighting to peacemaking efforts by local church organizations. Owing to successful missionary activities during the colonial period, both states are now strongly Christian: more than 75 percent of the population of Nagaland is Baptist, whereas Mizoram is more than 90 percent Christian (mostly Presbyterian). Missionary schooling has led to high levels of education. Mizoram boasts India's second highest literacy rate (91 percent), trailing only Kerala. Education, however, has not led to economic prosperity. Lack of infrastructure and insecurity are the major problems, but so too are the famines that occur every few decades after the synchronous flowering and then death of the state's massive bamboo groves. When the bamboo flowers and seeds, rodent and insect populations explode; when the plants subsequently perish, rats and bugs invade fields and granaries. The most recent such famines occurred in 2006–2007.

South Asia's Monsoon Climates

The dominant climatic factor for most of South Asia is the **monsoon,** the distinct seasonal change of wind direction that corresponds to wet and dry periods. Most of South Asia has three distinct seasons. First is the warm and rainy season of the southwest monsoon from June through October. This is followed by a relatively cool and dry season, extending from November until February, when the dominant winds are from the northeast. Only a few areas in far northwestern and southeastern South Asia get substantial rainfall during this period. Next comes the hot season from March to early June, which builds up with great heat and humidity until the monsoon's much anticipated and rather sudden "burst."

This monsoon pattern is caused by large-scale meteorological processes that affect much of Asia (Figure 12.7). During the Northern Hemisphere's winter, a large high-pressure system forms over the cold Asian landmass. Cold, dry winds flow outward from the interior of this high-pressure cell, over the Himalayas and down across South Asia. As winter turns to spring, these winds diminish, resulting in the hot, dry season. Eventually this buildup of heat over South and Southwest Asia produces a large thermal low-pressure cell. By early June this low-pressure cell is strong enough to draw in warm, moist air from the Indian Ocean.

Heavy **orographic rainfall** results from the uplifting and cooling of moist monsoon winds over the Western Ghats. As a result, some stations receive more than 200 inches (508 centimeters) of rain during the 4-month wet season. On the climate map (Figure 12.8), these are the areas of Am, or tropical monsoon, climate. Inland, however, a strong rain-shadow effect dramatically reduces rainfall on the Deccan Plateau. Farther north, as the monsoon winds are forced up and over the mountains, copious amounts of rainfall are characteristic. Cherrapunji, India, at 4,000 feet (1,220 meters), is a strong contender for the title of world's wettest place, with an average rainfall of 450 inches (1,143 centimeters).

Not all of South Asia receives substantial rainfall from the southwest monsoon. In much of Pakistan and the Indian state of Rajasthan, precipitation is low and variable, resulting in steppe and desert climates. In Karachi, the annual total is less than 10 inches (25 centimeters). But even in the drier parts of South Asia, heavy monsoonal rain sometimes hits. In the summer of 2010, for example, prolonged downpours resulted in devastating flooding across much of Pakistan.

Regardless of whether rainfall is heavy or light, the monsoon rhythm affects all of South Asia in many different ways, from the delivery of much-needed water for crops and villages, to the mood of millions of people as they eagerly await relief from oppressive heat (Figure 12.9). Some years the monsoon delivers its promise with abundant moisture; in other years, though, it brings scant rainfall, resulting in crop failure and hardship. A severe drought in northern and central India in 2009, for example, led to a

7 percent decrease in the country's grain harvest. In the near future, the monsoonal patterns may change due to global warming.

Global Warming in South Asia

Many areas of South Asia are particularly vulnerable to the effects of global warming. Even a minor rise in sea level will inundate large areas of the Ganges–Brahmaputra Delta in Bangladesh. Already, over 18,500 acres (7,500 hectares) of swampland in the Sunderbans have been submerged. Several small islands in this area have recently disappeared, due to a combination of sea level rise and subsidence. A 2007 report from the India government suggests that up to 7 million people could be displaced by the end of the century due to a predicted 3.3-foot (1-meter) rise in sea level. If the most severe sea level forecasts come to pass, the atoll nation of the

Figure 12.7 The Summer and Winter Monsoons Low pressure centered over South and Southwest Asia draws in warm, moist air masses during the summer that bring heavy monsoon rains to most of the region. Usually these rains begin in June and last for several months. During the winter, high pressure forms over northern Asia. As a result, winds are reversed from those of the summer. During this season, only a few coastal locations along India's east coast and in eastern Sri Lanka receive substantial rain.

Figure 12.8 Climates of South Asia Except for the extensive Himalayas, South Asia is dominated by tropical and subtropical climates. Many of these climates show a distinct summer rainfall season that is associated with the southwest monsoon. The climographs for Mumbai (Bombay) and Delhi are excellent illustrations. However, the climographs for east-coast locations such as Madras, India, and Colombo, Sri Lanka, show how some locations also receive rains from the northeast monsoon of the winter.

Maldives will simply vanish beneath the waves. Warmer water in the Bay of Bengal has already resulted in the destruction of many coral reefs.

South Asian agriculture is likely to suffer from a number of problems linked to global climate change. Most Himalayan glaciers are rapidly retreating, threatening the dry-season water supplies of the Indus–Ganges Plain, an area that already suffers from overuse of groundwater resources. Increased winter temperatures of up to 6.4°F (3°C) could destroy the vital wheat crop of Pakistan and northwestern India, undermining the food security of both countries. In parts of South Asia, however, global warming could result in increased rainfall due to an intensification of the summer monsoon. Unfortunately, such a new precipitation regime

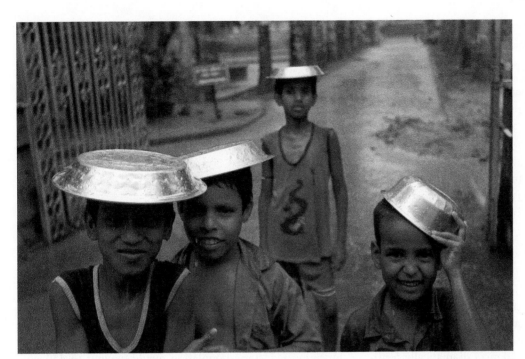

Figure 12.9 Monsoon Rain
During the summer monsoon, some Indian cities such as Mumbai (Bombay) receive more than 70 inches (178 centimeters) of rain in just 3 months. These daily torrents cause floods, power outages, and daily inconvenience. However, the monsoon rains are crucial to India's agriculture. If the rains are late or abnormally weak, crop failure often results.

will likely be characterized by more intense cloudbursts coupled with fewer episodes of gentle, prolonged rain. As a result, more flooding—as well as more soil erosion—may be expected.

India signed the Kyoto Protocol in 2002, but as a developing country has been exempt from the main provisions of the treaty. With its poor and still largely nonindustrial economies, South Asia still has a low per capita output of greenhouse gases. But India's economy in particular is not only growing rapidly, but is heavily dependent on burning coal to generate electricity. According to a 2010 report, India's annual greenhouse gas emissions increased 58 percent between 1994 and 2007. Further increases seem likely; according to official estimates, if India is to maintain an economic growth rate of 8 percent over the next quarter century, it will need to triple or even quadruple its primary energy supply.

South Asia's vulnerability to global warming coupled with its rapidly growing emissions of greenhouse gases has prompted numerous calls to action. Experts were heartened in early 2007 when India's government signed an agreement with Japan aimed at encouraging Japanese companies to invest in India's energy sector and to transfer energy-saving technology. Many South Asian officials, however, argue that the responsibility for addressing global climate change lies with the already industrialized countries, and that local attempts to reduce emissions could undermine economic growth. Some Indian scientists are also skeptical about climate change reports originating in the developed world. In 2010, the Indian government announced that it would create its own organization to monitor global warming, arguing that the United Nations' Intergovernmental Panel on Climate Change could not be fully trusted.

POPULATION AND SETTLEMENT: Continuing Growth in a Crowded Land

South Asia soon will surpass East Asia as the world's most populous region (Table 12.1). Overall, fertility levels have dropped markedly in recent years, but population continues to grow rapidly over much of the region. And although South Asia has made remarkable agricultural gains since the 1960s, there is still widespread concern about the region's ability to feed itself. The threat of crop failure remains, in part because much South Asian farming is vulnerable to the unpredictable monsoon rains.

The Geography of Population Expansion

South Asia's recent decline in human fertility shows distinct geographical patterns. Most of southern and western India, along with Sri Lanka should soon see population stabilization. Over most of northern South Asia, however, the birthrate remains elevated. While all South Asian countries have established family planning programs, the commitment to these policies varies widely from place to place.

India Widespread concern over India's population growth began in the 1960s. To a significant extent, family planning measures, along with general economic and social development, have been successful; the total fertility rate (TFR) dropped from 6 in the 1950s to the current rate of 2.6. Fertility rates vary widely within India, from below 2.0 in the states of Goa, Kerala, Tamil Nadu, Andhra Pradesh, and Himachal Pradesh, to a problematic high of 3.8 in Uttar Pradesh and 4.0 Bihar. (Uttar Pradesh, with more than 183

TABLE 12.1	**Population Indicators**							
Country	Population (millions) 2010	Population Density (per square kilometer)	Rate of Natural Increase (RNI)	Total Fertility Rate	Percent Urban	Percent <15	Percent >65	Net Migration (Rate per 1000) 2005–10[a]
Bangladesh	164.4	1,142	1.5	2.4	25	32	4	−0.7
Bhutan	0.7	15	1.7	3.1	32	31	5	2.9
India	1,188.8	362	1.5	2.6	29	32	5	−0.2
Maldives	0.3	1,070	1.9	2.5	35	30	5	0.0
Nepal	28.0	191	1.9	3.0	17	37	4	−0.7
Pakistan	184.8	232	2.3	4.0	35	38	4	−1.6
Sri Lanka	20.7	315	1.2	2.4	15	26	6	−3.0

[a]*Net Migration Rate from the United Nations, Population Division, World Population Prospects: The 2008 Revision Population Database.*
Source: Population Reference Bureau, World Population Data Sheet, 2010.

million people, would be the sixth largest country in the world if it were independent.) A strong relationship is evident between women's education and family planning; where female literacy has increased most dramatically, fertility levels have rapidly declined (see "Geographic Tools: Survey Work on Contraceptive Use in West Bengal").

A distinct cultural preference for male children is found in most of South Asia, a tradition that complicates family planning. Abortion rates of female fetuses are much higher than those of males, even though the practice of sex-selective abortion is illegal. In northern India, a lower fertility rate seems to be accompanied by an even lower ratio of female-to-male infants. India's prosperous northwestern state of Punjab has recently seen its TFR drop to just below the replacement level, but at the same time its population has grown increasingly male dominated. In 2006, Punjab's sex ratio at birth was only 776 girls for every 1,000 boys.

Pakistan and Bangladesh Pakistan, with a population of more than 184 million, has long had a somewhat ambivalent attitude toward family planning. Although the government's official position is that the birthrate is excessive, the country still lacks an effective, coordinated family planning program. As a result, the TFR remains just under 4.0. At its current birthrate, Pakistan's population would expand to 450 million by 2050. Its concerned government recently launched the National Population Policy 2010 program, which aims to reduce the fertility rate to 3.0 by 2015. The program aims to make family planning more accessible and effective and seeks to recruit religious leaders for support.

Densely settled Bangladesh, with a population about half that of the United States packed into an area smaller than the state of Wisconsin, has made significant strides in population stabilization. As recently as 1975, its TFR was 6.3, but it had dropped to 2.4 by 2010. Its family planning success can be attributed to strong support from the Bangladesh government for advertising through radio and billboards. Also important are more than 35,000 women fieldworkers who take information about family planning into every village in the country (Figure 12.10). In 2010, the president of Bangladesh urged the entire country to adopt the slogan, "Not more than two children, one is better."

Figure 12.10 Family Planning in Bangladesh Bangladesh has been one of the most successful nations in South Asia in reducing its fertility rate through family planning. Many women in Bangladesh use oral contraceptives. This photo shows community health worker Hashina Akhtar giving child nutrition and family planning advice to local villagers.

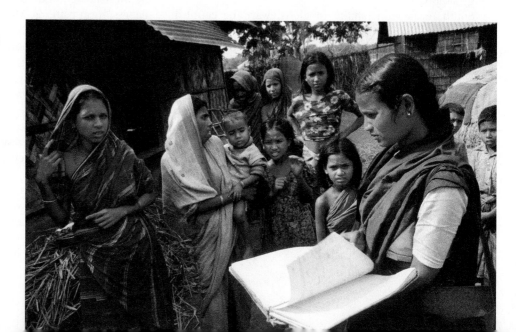

GEOGRAPHIC TOOLS   Survey Work on Contraceptive Use in West Bengal

Geographers, like other social scientists, often make extensive use of surveys in order to acquire raw data. Standardized surveys, in which sizable numbers of local people are asked identical and relatively easily answered questions, allow scholars to build quantitative databases. Statistical tests can then be conducted to determine correlations and to find relationships. Geographers often use such surveys to identify spatial patterns.

Geographers also sometimes follow anthropologists in using informal, open-ended interviews with select people who live in the area under investigation. Such a technique can give a deeper understanding of local attitudes and cultural perceptions and practices. They do not allow, however, for the kinds of statistical testing obtainable with standardized survey methods. As a result, geographers sometimes use both methods to obtain both quantitative and qualitative information.

One geographer who has effectively used both methods is Elizabeth Chacko, of George Washington University, in her study of women's use of contraception in four villages in West Bengal, India. Determining why women in rural South Asia chose to use, or not to use, contraception is particularly important considering the demographic strains faced by the region. But it is a difficult subject to investigate, as women are often reluctant to discuss such issues, particularly with outsiders. Dr. Chacko therefore decided to use both the quantitative method of the formal survey and the qualitative method of in-depth personal conversations and interviews.

In the end, Dr. Chacko discovered that the most important determinants of a woman's contraceptive decisions were age, number of living sons, and religious affiliation. She also found that availability of permanent, village-based government health-care clinics increased the use of contraceptives. Observations and interviews also pointed to the need to provide low-cost, culturally acceptable methods for achieving greater contraceptive usage in the community

(Figure 12.2.1). These findings should be of great help to local health-care workers seeking both to empower rural women and to address India's demographic problems.

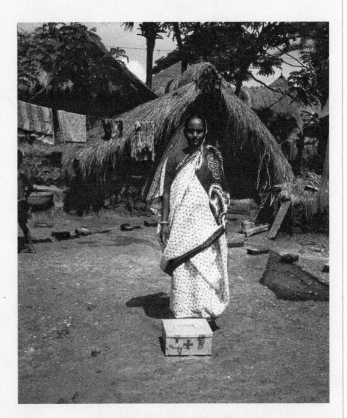

Figure 12.2.1 Village-Based Health-Care Clinics A rural health-care worker poses behind her medical kit in rural West Bengal. Such local outreach efforts have resulted in a reduced birthrate in much of this area.

Migration and the Settlement Landscape

The most densely settled areas of South Asia still coincide with zones of fertile soils and dependable water supplies (Figure 12.11). The largest rural populations are found in the core area of the Ganges and Indus river valleys and on the coastal plains of India. Settlement is less dense on the Deccan Plateau and is relatively sparse in the arid lands of the northwest. While most of South Asia's northern mountains are too rugged and high to support dense human settlement, there are major population clusters in the Katmandu Valley of Nepal, situated at 4,400 feet (1,341 meters), and the Valley, or Vale, of Kashmir in northern India, at 5,200 feet (1,585 meters).

As is true in most other parts of the world, South Asians have migrated for hundreds of years from poor and densely populated areas to places that are either less densely populated or wealthier. This process is ubiquitous in South Asia today, but several areas stand out as zones of intensive out-migration: Bangladesh, the northern Indian states of Bihar, Punjab, and Rajasthan, and the northern portion of India's Andhra Pradesh (Figure 12.12). Migrants from Bangladesh are settling in large numbers in rural portions of adjacent Indian states, exacerbating ethnic and religious tensions. In Nepal, migrants have been moving over the past 50 years from crowded mountain valleys to formerly malaria-infested lowlands along the Indian border, again generating ethnic strife. Sometimes migrants are forced out by war; sizable streams of people from northern Sri Lanka and from Kashmir have sought security away from their battle-scarred homelands over the past 20 years.

South Asia is one of the least urbanized regions in the world, with only about 35 percent of its population living in

Figure 12.11 Population Map of South Asia
Except for the desert areas of the west and the high mountains of the north, South Asia is a densely populated region. Particularly high densities are found on the fertile plains along the Indus and Ganges rivers and in India's coastal lowlands. In rural areas, the population is typically clustered in villages, often located near water sources, such as streams, wells, canals, or small tanks that store water between monsoon rains.

cities. Most South Asians still reside in compact rural villages, but large numbers are streaming into the region's rapidly growing cities. Such urbanization often stems more from desperate conditions in the countryside than from the attractions of city life. As farms begin to mechanize, farm laborers often have no choice but to migrate to urban areas.

Many small farmers, moreover, have difficulty competing with their wealthier neighbors, who can more easily afford modern fertilizers and other agricultural inputs. The agricultural situation over much of India has become so desperate that the country is experiencing an epidemic of farmer suicides. In the single month of April 2009, the Indian state

Figure 12.12 Major Migration Streams in South Asia Large-scale movements of people occur in all parts of South Asia. Despite the region's poverty, it has still attracted large numbers of refugees from war and oppression in Afghanistan and Burma, although many people are now returning to Afghanistan from refugee camps in Pakistan. Within the region, most movement directs people away from particularly poor and overcrowded areas to large cities, more prosperous areas, and less densely populated districts.

MAJOR MIGRATION STREAMS WITHIN SOUTH ASIA

① Afghans returning from refugee camps in northwestern Pakistan

② Kashmir: Hindus to northern Punjab and Delhi

③ Nepalis to Nepals lowlands

③a Nepalis to Delhi

④ Bangladeshis to northeastern India

⑤ Bangladeshis to West Bengal, India

⑥ Pashtuns moving to Karachi

⑦ Biharis to Mumbai, Calcutta, and Delhi

⑧ People from northern Andhra Pradesh to Calcutta, Mumbai, and Bangalore

⑨ People from Karnataka to Goa

⑩ People from Tamil Nadu to Kerala

⑪ Tamils from Sri Lanka to Tamil Nadu

⑫ People from Rajasthan to Delhi and Mumbai

⑬ People from Uttar Pradesh moving to Punjab

of Chattisgarh reported some 1,500 farmer suicides, due largely to debt and crop failures.

Agricultural Regions and Activities

South Asian agriculture has historically been much less productive than that of East Asia. Although the reasons behind such poor yields are complex, many experts cite the rela-

tively low social status of most cultivators and the fact that much farmland has long been controlled by wealthy landlords who hire others to work their plots. Some scholars also blame British colonialism, which emphasized export crops for European markets.

Regardless of the causes, low agricultural yields in the context of a huge, hungry, and rapidly growing population constitute a pressing problem. Since the 1970s, however, agricultural production has grown faster than the population, primarily because of the **Green Revolution**, agricultural cultivation techniques based on hybrid crop strains and the heavy use of industrial fertilizers and pesticides. Because the Green Revolution also carries significant social and environmental costs, it remains controversial, as will be discussed shortly.

Crop Zones   South Asia can be divided into several distinct agricultural regions, all with different problems and potentials. The most fundamental division is between the three primary subsistence crops of rice, wheat, and millet.

Rice is the main crop and foodstuff in the lower Ganges Valley, along the lowlands of India's eastern and western coasts, in the delta lands of Bangladesh, along Pakistan's lower Indus Valley, and in Sri Lanka. This distribution reflects the large volume of irrigation water needed to grow rice (Figure 12.13). The amount of rice grown in South Asia is impressive: India ranks behind only China in world rice production, and Bangladesh is the fourth largest producer.

Wheat is the principal crop of the northern Indus Valley and in the western half of India's Ganges Valley. South Asia's "breadbasket" lies in the northwestern Indian states of Punjab and Haryana along with adjacent areas in Pakistan. Here the Green Revolution has been particularly successful in increasing grain yields. In the less-fertile areas of central India, millet and sorghum are the main crops, along with root crops such as manioc. In general, wheat and rice are the preferred staples throughout South Asia, and it is generally poorer people who consume "rough" grains such as the various millets.

Many other crops are widely cultivated in South Asia, some commercially, others for local subsistence. Oil seeds, such as sesame and peanuts, for example, are grown in semi-arid districts, while Sri Lanka and the Indian state of Kerala are noted for their coconut groves, spice gardens, and tea plantations. In both Pakistan and west central India, cotton is widely cultivated, while Bangladesh has long supplied most of the world's jute, a tough fiber used in the manufacture of rope.

Many if not most South Asians receive inadequate protein, as meat consumption is extremely low. This partly reflects the region's poverty, because meat is expensive to produce. In India, religion is equally important, as most Hindus are vegetarians. Despite this prohibition against eating meat, animal husbandry is vitally important throughout South Asia. India has the world's largest cattle population, in part because cattle are sacred in Hinduism but also because milk is one of South Asia's main sources of protein. While the cattle of India have traditionally yielded little milk, a so-called white revolution has increased dairy efficiency. In 2010, India produced more dairy products than any other country by a substantial margin, while Pakistan ranked third, trailing only India and the United States.

The Green Revolution   The main reason South Asian agriculture has kept up with population growth is the Green Revolution, which originated during the 1960s in agricultural research stations established by international development agencies. One of the major problems researchers faced was the fact that higher yields could not be attained by simply fertilizing local seed strains, because the plants would grow taller and then fall to the ground before the grain could mature. The solution was to cross-breed new "dwarf" crop strains that would respond to heavy chemical fertilization by producing extra grain rather than longer stems.

By the 1970s, it was clear that these efforts had succeeded in reaching their initial goals. The more prosperous farmers of the Punjab quickly adopted the new "miracle wheat" varieties, solidifying the Punjab's position as the region's breadbasket (Figure 12.14). Green Revolution rice strains also were adopted in the more humid areas. As a result, South Asia was transformed from a region of chronic food deficiency to one of self-sufficiency. India more than doubled its annual grain production between 1970 and the mid-1990s, from 80 to 191 million tons.

While the Green Revolution was clearly an agricultural success, many argue that it has been an ecological and social

Figure 12.13 Rice Cultivation   A large amount of irrigation water is needed to grow rice, as is apparent from this photo from Sri Lanka. Rice also is the main crop in the lower Ganges Valley and Delta, along the lower Indus River of Pakistan, and on India's coastal plains.

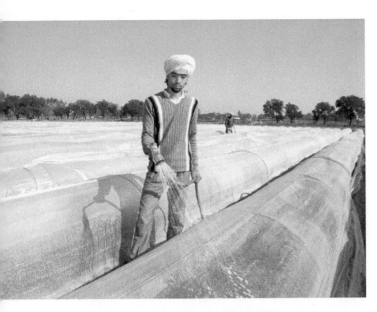

Figure 12.14 Green Revolution Farming Because of "miracle" wheat strains that have increased yields in the Punjab area, this region has become the breadbasket of South Asia. India more than doubled its wheat production in the last 25 years and has moved from chronic food shortages to self-sufficiency. Increased production, however, has led to both social and environmental problems.

disaster. Serious environmental problems result from the chemical dependency of the new crop strains. Not only do they typically need large quantities of industrial fertilizer, which is both expensive and polluting, but they also require frequent pesticide applications because they often lack natural resistance to local plant diseases and insects. A 2009 study showed that 20 percent of the wells in India's Punjab are seriously contaminated by nitrates, derived largely from artificial fertilizers.

Social problems have also followed the Green Revolution. In many areas, only the more prosperous farmers are able to afford the new seed strains, irrigation equipment, farm machinery, fertilizers, and pesticides necessary to support this new high-technology agriculture. As a result, poorer farmers often go deeply into debt and are then forced off the land when they fail to repay their loans.

Future Food Supply The Green Revolution has fed South Asia's expanding population over the past several decades, but whether it will be able to continue doing so remains unclear. Many of the crop improvements have seemingly exhausted their potential, and much of South Asia's agricultural economy is currently in a state of crisis as farmers fail to make ends meet.

Optimists believe, however, that South Asia's food production could be substantially increased. Further improvements in highways and railroads, for example, would result in less wastage as well as higher profit margins for struggling farmers. Green Revolution techniques, moreover, might be profitably applied to secondary grain crops, and genetic engineering might provide another breakthrough,

ushering in a second wave of increased crop yields. Most environmentalists, however, see serious dangers in this new technology.

Another option is expanded water delivery, because many fields remain unirrigated in South Asia's semiarid areas. Even in the humid zone, dry-season fallow is usually the norm. Irrigation, however, brings its own problems. In much of Pakistan and northwestern India, where irrigation has been practiced for generations, soil **salinization** (see Figure 12.3), or the buildup of salt in agricultural fields, is already a major constraint. An estimated 27 million acres (11 million hectares) of land in Pakistan is now too salty for normal farming. Additionally, groundwater levels are falling in the Punjab, India's breadbasket, because double-cropping has pushed water use beyond the sustainable yield of the underlying aquifers.

Urban South Asia

Although South Asia is one of the least urbanized regions of the world (see Table 12.1), it still has some of the largest urban agglomerations in the world. India alone lists more than 43 cities with populations greater than a million, most of which are growing rapidly. Mumbai's (Bombay) population is now roughly 14 million, with up to 22 million living in the city's metropolitan area (see "Cityscapes: Life on the Streets of Mumbai [Bombay]").

Because of this rapid growth, most South Asian cities have staggering problems with homelessness, poverty, congestion, water shortages, air pollution, and sewage disposal. Kolkata's (Calcutta) homeless are legendary, with perhaps half a million sleeping on the streets each night. In that city and others, sprawling squatter settlements, or *bustees*, mushroom in and around urban areas, providing temporary shelter for many urban migrants (Figure 12.15). A brief survey of the region's major cities gives clues to the problems and prospects of the region's urban areas.

Figure 12.15 Mumbai (Bombay) Hutments Hundreds of thousands of people in Mumbai (Bombay) live in crude hutments, with no sanitary facilities, built on formerly busy sidewalks. Hutment construction is forbidden in many areas, but wherever it is allowed, sidewalks quickly disappear.

CITYSCAPES   Life on the Streets of Mumbai (Bombay)

The largest city in South Asia, Mumbai (Bombay) is India's financial, industrial, and commercial center. The major port on the Arabian Sea, Mumbai is responsible for a disproportionate share of the country's foreign trade. Long noted as the center of India's textile manufacturing, the city also is the hub of its film industry, the largest in the world.

Mumbai occupies a peninsular site originally composed of seven small islands (Figure 12.3.1). Since the 17th century, drainage and reclamation projects have joined the islands into a larger body known as Bombay Island, which basically formed the city area through the colonial period. Two parallel ridges of 100 feet (30 meters) form the spines of the inner city, one occupied by the historic colonial fort, now the commercial center, the other, Malabar Hill, an exclusive residential area. India's financial center is found near the southern end of the island, around Nariman Point, as are many of the city's most exclusive hotels. Another nearby expensive area is Kemps Corner, noted for its boutiques and restaurants.

Bombay Island, only 12 miles long, is notoriously congested. As a result, most growth has taken place to the north and east of the historic peninsula so that now the metropolitan region occupies an area 10 times the size of the original city. Spatial restrictions in downtown

Figure 12.3.1 Map of Mumbai (Bombay) Originally composed of seven separate islands, the core of Mumbai (called Bombay Island) now essentially forms a narrow peninsula some 12 miles (19.3 kilometers) long. Recent urban growth is concentrated in the suburbs to the north and east.

Delhi Delhi, the sprawling capital of India, has roughly 19 million people in its metropolitan area. It consists of two contrasting landscapes expressing its past: Delhi (or old Delhi), a former Muslim capital, is a congested town of tight neighborhoods; New Delhi, in contrast, is a city of wide boulevards, monuments, parks, and expansive residential areas. It was born as a planned city when the British decided to move the colonial capital from Calcutta in 1911. Located here are the embassies, luxury hotels, government office buildings, and airline offices necessary for a vibrant political capital. South of the government area are more expensive residential areas, some of which are focused on expansive parks and ornamental gardens. Rapid growth, along with the government's inability to control auto and industrial emissions, made Delhi one of the world's 10 most polluted cities in the late 1990. As a result, the government began to shut down many of the city's small-scale industries, although local residents have banded together to protect their livelihoods. Overall, significant environmental progress has been made.

Kolkata (Calcutta) To many, Kolkata is emblematic of the problems faced by rapidly growing cities in developing countries. Not only is homelessness widespread, but this metropolitan area of some 15 million falls far short of supplying its residents with water, power, or sewage treatment. Electrical power is so inadequate that every hotel, restaurant, shop, and small business has to have some sort of standby power system. During the wet season, many streets are routinely flooded.

With continued rapid growth as migrants drain in from the countryside, a mixed Hindu-Muslim population that generates ethnic rivalry, a troubled economic base, and an overloaded infrastructure, Kolkata faces a problematic future. Yet it remains a culturally vibrant city noted for its fine educational institutions, theaters, and publishing firms.

Dhaka As the capital and major city of Bangladesh, Dhaka (also spelled *Dacca*) has experienced rapid growth due to migration from the surrounding countryside. In 1971, when the country gained independence from Pakistan, Dhaka had

Mumbai also have resulted in skyrocketing commercial and residential rents, which now are some of the highest in the world (Figure 12.3.2). Even members of the city's thriving middle class find it difficult to secure adequate housing. Hundreds of thousands of less-fortunate immigrants, eager for work in central Mumbai, live in "hutments," crude shelters built on formerly busy sidewalks. The least

Figure 12.3.2 Mumbai (Bombay) Central City The heart of this metropolitan area of 16 million is highly congested. Some of the world's highest office and apartment rents are found here, despite the overall poverty of the city.

fortunate sleep on the street or in simple plastic tents, often placed along busy roadways. Meanwhile, slums expand around the city's outskirts, providing crude homes for an estimated 60 percent of Mumbai's population.

Relatively few tourists venture out of the historic and relatively wealthy areas of southern Bombay Island. Thus, they miss much of what Mumbai has to offer. As is true in most other major cities, specific areas have distinctive personalities that must be seen—and heard and smelled—to be appreciated. Turn one corner and you might find yourself in a Muslim neighborhood, with all signs suddenly appearing in Urdu, hence looking much like Arabic. Turn another and you might encounter a several-mile-long stretch of stalled trucks, each waiting to cross a bridge or unload its cargo. The mushrooming suburbs offer their own discoveries. Juhu Beach, for example, offers quality hotels and restaurants that are significantly less expensive than those of the city center, as well as a Sunday night carnival. The ocean here, however, is much too polluted for safe swimming.

Despite Mumbai's extraordinary contrasts of wealth and poverty, it remains in many ways an orderly and relatively crime-free city. In 2007, its crime rate was roughly half of that of other Indian cities with more than one million inhabitants. It is less dangerous to walk the streets of central Mumbai than those of many major North American cities. Organized crime is a problem, especially in the massive film industry, but it has few effects on the lives of the average people.

about 1 million inhabitants; today its metropolitan area numbers almost 13 million (Figure 12.16). Dhaka's economic vitality has increased since independence because it combines the administrative functions of government with the largest industrial concentration in Bangladesh. Cheap and abundant labor in Dhaka has made the city a global center for clothing, shoe, and sports equipment manufacturing. North American shoppers are readily reminded of this new role when looking through clothing tags at any department store.

Karachi Karachi, a rapidly growing port city of approximately 18 million people, is Pakistan's largest urban area and commercial core (Figure 12.17). It also served as the country's capital until 1963, when the new city of Islamabad was created in the northeast. Karachi, however, has suffered little from the exodus of government functions; it is the most cosmopolitan city in Pakistan, with its checkerboard street pattern lined with high-rise buildings, hotels, banks, and travel agencies. In many ways, its landscape conveys the sense that Karachi is a model metropolis for a developing country.

Figure 12.16 Dhaka City View Dhaka, the capital of Bangladesh, has emerged as a vibrant metropolis in recent decades. Although its slums are extensive, its central commercial district is relatively orderly and prosperous.

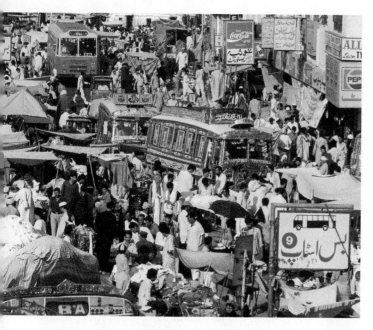

Figure 12.17 Karachi Landscape Karachi, Pakistan's largest city and main port, is noted for both its economic power and its ethnic violence. Congestion, as seen in this photo, can be severe.

Karachi, however, suffers from serious political and ethnic tensions that have turned parts of the city into armed camps. During the worst of the violence in 1995, more than 200 people were killed on the city's streets each month, and army bunkers were lodged at major urban crossroads. Ethnic conflicts have generally pitted Sindis, the region's indigenous inhabitants, against the Muhajirs, Muslim refugees from India who settled in and around the city after independence in 1947. More recently, the migration of Pashtuns from the tribal areas of northwest Pakistan has further destabilized the situation, as have clashes between Sunni and Shiite Muslims. A number of radical Islamist groups, including the Taliban and Al Qaeda, are reputed to have important bases in the city.

Islamabad Upon independence, Pakistan's leaders determined that Karachi was too far from the center of the country and that an entirely new capital was necessary. This planned city would make a statement through its name—Islamabad—about the religious foundation of Pakistan. Located close to the contested region of Kashmir, it would also make a geopolitical statement. In geographic terms, such a city is referred to as a **forward capital** because it signals—both symbolically and geographically—the intentions of the country. By building its new capital in the north, Pakistan sent a clear message that it would not abandon its claims to the portion of Kashmir controlled by India. Islamabad is closely linked to the historic city of Rawalpindi, once a major British encampment, a few miles away. While these two cities form a single metropolitan region of about 4.5 million people, they are completely different in appearance and character. To avoid congestion, planners designed Is-

lamabad around self-sufficient sectors, each with its own government buildings, residences, and shops.

The closest parallel in India to Islamabad is Chandigarh, the modern, planned city that serves as the capital of two Indian states: Punjab and Haryana. All told, the cities of India and Pakistan have a similar feel, as would be expected considering the two countries' common historical and cultural backgrounds.

CULTURAL COHERENCE AND DIVERSITY: A Common Heritage Undermined by Religious Rivalries

Historically, South Asia forms a well-defined cultural region. A thousand years ago, virtually the entire area was united by ideas and social institutions associated with Hinduism. The subsequent arrival of Islam added a new religious dimension without undercutting the region's cultural unity. British imperialism subsequently imposed a number of cultural features over the entire region, from the widespread use of English to a common passion for cricket. Since the mid-20th century, however, religious and political strife have intensified, leading some to question whether South Asia can still be conceptualized as a culturally coherent world region.

India has been a secular country since its inception, with the Congress Party, its early guiding political organization, struggling to keep politics and religion separate. In doing so, it relied heavily on support from Muslims as well as the lower castes. Since the 1980s, this secular political tradition has come under increasing pressure from Hindu "fundamentalism," which is probably better referred to as **Hindu nationalism**. Hindu nationalists promote the religious values of Hinduism as the essential and fabric of Indian society.

Hindu nationalists gained considerable political power both at the federal level and in many Indian states through the Bharatiya Janata Party (BJP), leading to widespread agitation against the country's Muslim minority in the mid-1990s. In several high-profile instances, Hindu mobs demolished Muslim mosques that were allegedly built on the sites of ancient Hindu temples. The destruction of a mosque in Ayodhya in the Ganges Valley galvanized the nationalistic BJP membership in 1992 (Figure 12.18). In 2002, more than 2,000 people—mostly Muslims—were killed during religious riots in India's state of Gujarat. Two years later, however, India's Hindu nationalist movement suffered a huge electoral defeat, perhaps indicating that the wave of religious strife had peaked.

In predominantly Muslim Pakistan, rising Islamic fundamentalism has generated severe conflict. Radical fundamentalist leaders want to make Pakistan a fully religious state under Islamic law, a plan rejected by the country's secular intellectuals and international businesspeople. The government has attempted to intercede between the two groups, but is often viewed as biased toward the Islamists. Anti-blasphemy laws, for example, have been used to persecute

Figure 12.18 Destruction of the Ayodhya Mosque A group of Hindu nationalists are seen listening to speeches urging them to demolish the mosque at Ayodhya, allegedly built on the site of a former Hindu temple. In 2010, an Indian court decided that two-thirds of the contested site should be given to two Hindu groups, and one-third should be awarded to a Muslim foundation.

members of the country's small Hindu and Christian communities, as well as liberal Muslim writers. Large amounts of money from Saudi Arabia, moreover, have gone into the development of fundamentalist religious schools that are reputed to encourage extremism.

Religious and political extremists in South Asia argue that the current struggles reflect deeply rooted historical divisions. Most scholars disagree, regarding religious conflict as a recent development. To weigh these contrasting claims, it is necessary to examine the cultural history of South Asian civilization.

Origins of South Asian Civilizations

Many scholars think that the roots of South Asian culture extend back to the Indus Valley civilization, which flourished more than 4,000 years ago in what is now Pakistan. This remarkable urban-oriented society vanished almost entirely in the second millennium BCE, after which the record grows dim. By 800 BCE, however, a new urban focus had emerged in the middle Ganges Valley (Figure 12.19). The social, religious, and intellectual cus-

toms associated with this civilization eventually spread throughout the lowlands of South Asia.

Hindu Civilization The religious complex of this early South Asian civilization was an early form of Hinduism, a complicated faith that incorporates diverse forms of worship and that lacks any standard system of beliefs (Figure 12.20). Certain deities are recognized, however, by all believers, as is the notion that these various gods are all manifestations of a single divine entity. All Hindus, moreover, share a common set of epic stories, usually written in the sacred language of Sanskrit. Hinduism is noted for its mystical tendencies, which have long inspired many men (and a few women) to seek an ascetic lifestyle, renouncing property and sometimes all regular human relations. One of its hallmarks is a belief in the transmigration of souls from being to being through reincarnation, wherein the nature of one's acts in the physical world influences the courses of these future lives.

Scholars once confidently argued that Hinduism originated from the fusion of two distinct religious traditions: the mystical beliefs of the subcontinent's indigenous inhabitants (including the people of the ill-fated Indus Valley civilization) and the sky-god religion of the Indo-European invaders who swept into the region sometime in the second millen-

Figure 12.19 Early South Asian Civilizations The roots of South Asian culture may extend back 5,000 years to an Indus Valley civilization based on irrigated agriculture and vibrant urban centers. What happened to that civilization remains a topic of conjecture, because the archaeological record grows dim by 1800 BCE. Later, a new urban focus emerged in the Ganges Valley, from which social, religious, and intellectual influences spread throughout lowland South Asia.

Figure 12.20 Hindu Temple Although India has long been noted for its ancient temples, lavish new Hindu religious complexes continue to be constructed. Visible in this photo is the Akshardham Temple, inaugurated in New Delhi in 2005. Expected to be a major tourist attraction, Akshardham also serves as an educational center focused on the culture of India.

nium BCE from Central Asia. Such a scenario also proved convenient for explaining India's **caste system**, the strict division of society into different hierarchically ranked hereditary groups. The elite invaders, according to this theory, wished to remain separate from the people they had defeated, resulting in an elaborate system of social division. Recent research, however, indicates that the caste system, like Hinduism itself, emerged through more gradual processes of social and cultural evolution.

Buddhism While a caste system of some sort seems to have existed in the early Ganges Valley civilization, it was soon challenged from within by Buddhism. Siddhartha Gautama, the Buddha, was born in 563 BCE in an elite caste. He rejected the life of wealth and power that was laid out before him, however, and sought instead to attain enlightenment, or mystical union with the cosmos. He preached that the path to such "nirvana" was open to all, regardless of social position. His followers eventually established Buddhism as a new religion. Buddhism spread through most of South Asia, becoming something of an official faith under the Mauryan Empire, which ruled much of the subcontinent in the 3rd century BCE. Later centuries saw Buddhism expand through most of East, Southeast, and Central Asia.

But for all of its successes abroad, Buddhism never replaced Hinduism in India. It remained focused on monasteries rather than spreading through the wider society. Many Hindu priests, moreover, struggled against the new faith. One of their techniques was to embrace many of Buddhism's philosophical ideas and enfold them within the intellectual system of Hinduism. By 500 CE, Buddhism was on the retreat throughout South Asia, and within another 500 years it had virtually disappeared from the region. The only major

exceptions were the island of Sri Lanka and the high Himalayas, both of which remain mostly Buddhist to this day.

Arrival of Islam The next major challenge to Hindu society—Islam—came from the outside. Arab armies conquered the lower Indus Valley around 700 CE but advanced no farther. Then around the year 1000, Turkish-speaking Muslims began to invade from Central Asia. At first they merely raided, but eventually they began to settle and rule on a permanent basis. By the 1300s, most of South Asia lay under Muslim power, although Hindu kingdoms persisted in southern India and in the arid lands of Rajasthan. Later, during the 16th and 17th centuries, the **Mughal Empire** (also spelled *Mogul*) dominated much of the region from its power center in the upper Indus–Ganges Basin (Figure 12.21).

At first Muslims formed a small ruling elite, but over time increasing numbers of Hindus converted to the new religion, particularly those from lower castes who sought freedom from the rigid social order. Conversions were most pronounced in the northwest and northeast, and eventually the areas now known as Pakistan and Bangladesh became predominantly Muslim.

At first glance, Islam and Hinduism are strikingly divergent faiths. Islam is resolutely monotheistic, austere in its ceremonies, and spiritually egalitarian (all believers stand in the same relationship to God). Hinduism, by contrast, is polytheistic (at least on the surface), lavish in its rituals, and caste structured. Because of these profound differences, Hindu and Muslim communities in South Asia are sometimes viewed as utterly distinct, living in the same region, but not sharing the same culture or civilization. Increasingly, such a view is expressed in South Asia itself. Many residents of modern Pakistan stress the Islamic nature of their country and its complete separation from India.

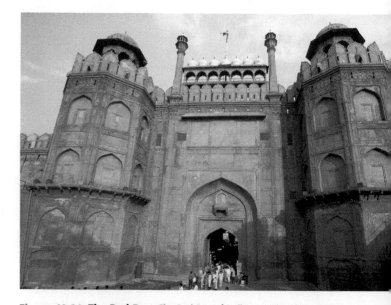

Figure 12.21 The Red Fort The Red Fort of Delhi, completed in 1648, was the military center of the Moghul Empire. Today this massive fortification, one of the largest in the world, is a major tourist destination.

Yet by overemphasizing the separation of Hindu and Muslim communities, one risks missing much of what is historically distinctive about South Asia. Until the 20th century, Hindus and Muslims usually coexisted on friendly terms; the two faiths stood side by side for hundreds of years, during which time they came to influence each other in many ways. Moreover, aspects of caste organization have persisted among South Asian Muslims, just as they have among India's Christians.

The Caste System

Although caste is one of the historically unifying features of South Asia, the system is not uniformly distributed across the subcontinent. It has never been significant in India's tribal areas; in modern Pakistan and Bangladesh its role is fading; and in the Buddhist society of Sri Lanka its influence has long been somewhat marginal. Even in India, caste is now deemphasized, especially among the more urban and educated segments of society. But all said, caste continues to structure day-to-day social existence for hundreds of millions of Indians. It is estimated that roughly 1,000 young Indians are murdered every year by relatives who will not tolerate their marriages across caste lines.

Caste is actually a rather clumsy term for denoting the complex social order of the Hindu world. The word itself, of Portuguese origin, combines two distinct local concepts: *varna* and *jati*. *Varna* refers to the ancient fourfold social hierarchy of the Hindu world, whereas *jati* refers to the hundreds of local endogamous ("marrying within") groups that exist at each varna level (different jati groups are thus usually called *subcastes*). Jati, like varna, are hierarchically arranged, although the exact order of precedence is not so clear-cut.

It often has been argued that the essence of the caste system is the notion of social pollution. The lower one's position in the hierarchy, the more potentially polluting one's body supposedly is. Members of higher castes were traditionally not supposed to eat or drink with, or even use the same utensils as, members of lower castes.

The Main Caste Groups   Three varna groups constitute the traditional elite of Hindu society. At the apex sit the Brahmins, members of the traditional priestly caste. Brahmins perform the high rituals of Hinduism, and they form the traditional intellectual elite of India. Most Brahmins value education highly, and today they are disproportionately represented among India's professional classes. Below the Brahmins in the traditional hierarchy are the Kshatriyas, members of the warrior or princely caste. In premodern India, this group actually had more power and wealth than did the Brahmins; it was they who ruled the old Hindu kingdoms. Next stand the Vaishyas, members of the traditional merchant caste. In earlier centuries, a near monopolization of long-distance trade and money lending in northern India gave many Vaishyas ample opportunities to accumulate wealth. The precepts of vegetarianism and non-

violence are particularly strong among certain merchant subcastes of western India. One prominent representative of this tradition was Mohandas Gandhi, the founder of modern India and one of the 20th century's greatest leaders.

The majority of India's population fits into the fourth varna category, that of the Sudras. The Sudra caste is composed of an especially large array of subcastes (jati), most of which originally reflected occupational groupings. Most Sudra subcastes were traditionally associated with peasant farming, but others were based on craft occupations, including those of barbers, smiths, and potters.

While the Brahmins, Kshatriyas, Vaishyas, and Sudras form the basic fourfold scheme of caste society, another sizable group stands outside the varna system altogether. These are the so-called *untouchables,* or **dalits,** as they are now preferably called. Dalits were not traditionally allowed to enter Hindu temples. Such low-status positions were derived historically from "unclean" occupations, such as those of leather workers (who dispose of dead animals), scavengers, latrine cleaners, and swine herders. In the southern Indian state of Kerala until the 19th century, some groups were actually considered "unseeable"; these unfortunate persons had to hide in bushes and avoid walking on the main roads to protect members of higher castes from "visual pollution." Not surprisingly, many Indian dalits have converted to Islam, Christianity, and Buddhism in an attempt to escape from the caste system. Even so, they continue to suffer discrimination.

The Changing Caste System   The caste system is clearly in a state of flux in India today. Its original occupational structure has long been undermined by the necessities of a modern economy, and various social reforms have chipped away at the discrimination that it embodies. The dalit community itself has produced several notable national leaders who have waged partially successful political struggles. Owing to such efforts, the very concept of "untouchability" is now technically illegal in India. The Indian central government also insists that 27 percent of university seats be reserved for students from low caste backgrounds, while a number of Indian states have set higher quotas, both for education and governmental employment. Such "reservations," as they are called, are controversial, as many people think that they unfairly penalize people of higher caste background. In May 2006, some 100,000 people took to the streets of New Delhi to protest a proposal by India's government to increase the number of reserved positions in several of the country's most prestigious universities.

Contemporary Geographies of Religion

South Asia, as we have seen, has a predominantly Hindu heritage overlain by a substantial Muslim imprint. Such a picture fails, however, to capture the enormous diversity of modern religious expression in contemporary South Asia. The following discussion looks specifically at the geographical patterns of the region's main faiths (Figure 12.22).

Figure 12.22 South Asia's Geography of Religion Hindu-dominated India is bracketed by the two important Muslim countries of Pakistan and Bangladesh. Some 150 million Muslims, however, live within India, constituting roughly 15 percent of the total population. Of particular note are the Muslims in northwestern Kashmir and in the Ganges Valley. Sikhs form the majority population in India's state of Punjab. Also note the Buddhist populations in Sri Lanka, Bhutan, and northern Nepal, the areas of tribal religion in the east, and the centers of Christianity in the southwest.

Hinduism Less than 1 percent of the people of Pakistan are Hindu, and in Bangladesh and Sri Lanka Hinduism is a distinctly minority religion. Almost everywhere in India, however—and in Nepal, as well—Hinduism is very much the faith of the majority. In east-central India, more than 95 percent of the population is Hindu. Hinduism is itself a geographically complicated religion, with aspects of faith varying in different parts of India. Even within a given Indian state, forms of worship often differ from region to region and from caste to caste.

Islam Islam may be considered a "minority" religion for the region as a whole, but such a designation obscures the tremendous importance of this religion in South Asia. With more than 400 million members, the South Asian Muslim community is the largest in the world. Bangladesh and especially Pakistan are overwhelmingly Muslim. India's Islamic community, although constituting only some 13 to 15 percent of the country's population, is still roughly 160 million strong, making it the world's third largest Muslim group.

Although Muslims live in almost every part of India, they are concentrated in four main areas: in most of India's cities; in Kashmir, particularly in the densely populated Vale of Kashmir; in the upper and central Ganges plain; and in the southwestern state of Kerala. In northern India especially, Muslims tend to be poorer and less educated than their Hindu neighbors, leading some observers to call them the country's "new dalits."

Interestingly, the state of Kerala is about 25 percent Muslim even though it was one of the few parts of India that never experienced prolonged Muslim rule. Islam in Kerala is historically connected not to Central Asia, but rather to trade across the Arabian Sea. Kerala's Malabar Coast long supplied spices and other luxury products to Southwest Asia, enticing many Arabian traders to settle in this part of India. Gradually many of Kerala's native inhabitants converted to the new religion as well. Owing to a similar process, Sri Lanka is approximately 9 percent Muslim, and the Maldives is almost entirely Muslim.

As an overwhelmingly Muslim country, Pakistan officially calls itself an Islamic Republic. As such, Islamic law is technically supposed to override the country's secular laws, although in actuality the situation remains ambiguous. In Pakistan's two most conservative provinces, Balochistan and Khyber Pakhtunkhwa (previously known as the North-West Frontier Province), Islamic law tends to be much more strictly enforced.

Sikhism The tension between Hinduism and Islam in medieval northern South Asia helped give rise to a new religion called **Sikhism**. Sikhism originated in the late 1400s in Punjab, near the modern boundary between India and Pakistan. The Punjab was the site of religious fervor at the time; Islam was gaining converts and Hinduism was increasingly on the defensive. The new faith combined elements of both religions and thus appealed to many who felt trapped between their competing claims. Many orthodox Muslims, however, viewed Sikhism as a heresy precisely because it incorporated elements of their own religion. Periodic bouts of persecution led the Sikhs to adopt a militantly defensive stance, and in the political chaos of the early 1800s they were able to carve out a powerful kingdom for themselves. Even today, Sikh men are noted for their work as soldiers and bodyguards.

At present, the Indian state of Punjab is approximately 60 percent Sikh. Small but often influential groups of Sikhs are scattered across the rest of India. Devout Sikh men are immediately visible, because they do not cut their hair or their beards. Instead, they wear their hair wrapped in a turban and often tie their beards close to their faces.

Buddhism and Jainism Although Buddhism virtually disappeared from India in medieval times, it persisted in Sri Lanka. Among the island's dominant Sinhalese people, Theravada Buddhism developed into a virtual national religion, fostering close connections between Sri Lanka and mainland

Figure 12.23 Dharmasala, India The small highland city of Dharmasala in northern India is noted as the base of the Tibetan government-in-exile. It also boasts a growing tourist industry.

Southeast Asia. In the high valleys of the Himalayas, Buddhism also survived as the majority religion. Tibetan Buddhism, with its esoteric beliefs and huge monasteries, has been better preserved in Bhutan and in the Ladakh region of northeastern Kashmir than in Chinese-controlled Tibet itself. The small city of Dharmsala in the northern Indian state of Himachal Pradesh is the seat of Tibet's government-in-exile and of its spiritual leader, the Dalai Lama, who fled Tibet in 1959 (Figure 12.23). Another group of Buddhists is found in central India, where 20th-century efforts to convert Hindu dalits to the faith were particularly successful.

At roughly the same time as the birth of Buddhism (circa 500 BCE), another religion emerged in northern India as a protest against orthodox Hinduism: **Jainism**. This religion took nonviolence to its ultimate extreme. Jains are forbidden to kill any living creatures, and as a result the most devout adherents wear gauze masks to prevent the inhalation of small insects. Agriculture is forbidden to Jains because plowing can kill small creatures. As a result, most members of the faith have looked to trade for their livelihoods. Many have prospered, aided no doubt by the frugal lifestyles required by their religion. Today Jains are concentrated in northwestern India, particularly Gujarat.

Other Religious Groups Even more prosperous than the Jains are the Parsis, or Zoroastrians, concentrated in the Mumbai area. The Parsis arrived as refugees, fleeing from Iran after the arrival of Islam in the 7th century. Zoroastrianism is an ancient religion that focuses on the cosmic struggle between good and evil. Although numbering only a few hundred thousand, the Parsi community has had a major impact on the Indian economy. Several of the country's largest industrial firms were founded by Parsi families, including the giant

EXPLORING GLOBAL CONNECTIONS The Tata Group's Global Network

Most large multinational corporations, which produce goods and services in many different countries, are based in the core areas of the world economy. Such companies generally rely on the financial and technological resources of wealthy cities yet often seek out production sites in poor countries with low wages and few regulations. As a result, multinational corporations have been criticized for their role in maintaining a stark global division between the developed and the underdeveloped worlds. As globalization proceeds, however, such a view is becoming outmoded. Increasing numbers of powerful multinational corporations are based in relatively poor areas, and several are now investing heavily in wealthy countries.

No company illustrates these trends as well as India's Tata Group. Founded in 1868 by Jamshedji Tata, the son of a Parsi Zoroastrian priest, the firm began as an opium-trading firm in Bombay (Mumbai) India. The Tata Group now includes 114 companies operating in 85 companies. Despite its global reach, the company is still headquartered in Mumbai; its current chairman, Ratan Tata, is the fifth generation of the Tata family to exercise control. According to a 2009 survey, international business leaders ranked the Tata Group as the word's 11th most reputable company.

The Tata Group is a classical conglomerate, operating businesses in the steel, motor, consultancy, electrical, chemical, medical, retail, hotel, and information technology industries. Over the past 15 years, it has aggressively expanded its global reach by purchasing foreign companies. In 2008 alone, it acquired firms based in Britain, Spain, Italy, China, South Africa, Norway, and Morocco. Such well-known brands as Tetley Tea and the Taj Hotels now belong to the Tata Group.

One of the most global members of the group is Tata Motors. Although only the world's 11th largest automaker, Tata is the second largest producer of commercial vehicles. It has reached that position in large part through joint ventures and foreign acquisitions. In 2005, for example, it purchased Daewoo Commercial Vehicle, South Korea's second largest bus manufacturer. Tata Motors' most daring international move was probably its 2008 acquisition of British Jaguar Land Rover (JLR) from Ford Motor Corporation for $2 billion. With this purchase, Tata Motors gained control of three manufacturing plants and two design centers in the United Kingdom, as well as two of the best-known luxury car brands.

While targeting high-end automobile consumers with Jaguar, Tata Motors has also taken a greater interest in the opposite end of the market. Its signal product here is the Tata Nano, a "supermini" car that get 73 miles to the gallon and sells for as little as $2,160 (Figure 12.4.1). The two-seater Nano is marketed in a number of African and Asian countries. In 2009, Tata unveiled an upgraded version for the European market that sells for around $6,000, and in 2010 it announced the development of an electric version, the Nano EV, which will be made jointly with a Norwegian company.

Figure 12.4.1 Tata Nano The Tata Nano is the world's least expensive car, selling in India for a little over $2,000.

Tata Group (see "Exploring Global Connections: The Tata Group's Global Network"). Intermarriage and low fertility, however, threaten the survival of the community.

Indian Christians are more numerous than either Parsis or Jains. Their religion arrived some 1,800 years ago; early contact between the Malabar Coast and Southwest Asia brought Christian as well as Muslim traders. A Jewish population also established itself but later declined; today it numbers only a few hundred. Kerala's Christians, by contrast, are counted in the millions, constituting some 20 percent of the state's population. Several Christian sects are represented, but the largest are historically affiliated with the Syrian Church of Southwest Asia. Another stronghold of Christianity is the small Indian state of Goa, a former Portuguese colony, where Roman Catholics make up a little more than a quarter of the population.

During the colonial period, British missionaries went to great efforts to convert South Asians to Christianity. They had very little success, however, in Hindu, Muslim, and Buddhist communities. The remote tribal districts of British India, on the other hand, proved to be more receptive to missionary activity. In the uplands of India's extreme northeast, entire communities abandoned their traditional animist faith in favor of Protestant Christianity. Christian missionaries are still active in many parts of India, but during the 1990s they began to experience severe pressure in many areas from Hindu nationalists. Pakistan's Christian community, some 2.8 million strong, has also been under pressure, in this case from Muslim radicals. In 2009, Pakistani Muslim extremists attacked the Christian community of the town of Gogra, burning 40 houses and a church and killing eight people.

Geographies of Language

South Asia's linguistic diversity matches its religious diversity. In fact, one of the world's most important linguistic boundaries runs directly across India (Figure 12.24). North of the line, languages belong to the Indo-European group, the world's largest linguistic family. The languages of southern India belong to the **Dravidian** family, a linguistic group unique to South Asia. Along the mountainous northern rim of the region, a third linguistic family, Tibeto-Burman, pre-vails, but this area is marginal to the South Asian cultural sphere. Scattered tribal groups in eastern India speak Austro-Asiatic languages related to those of mainland Southeast Asia. South Asia can thus be divided into two major linguistic zones, the Indo-European north and the Dravidian south. But within these broad divisions there are many different languages, each associated with a distinct culture. In most of South Asia, several languages are spoken within the same region or even city, and multilingualism is common everywhere.

Figure 12.24 Language Map of South Asia A major linguistic divide separates the Indo-European languages of the north from the Dravidian languages of the south. In the Himalayan areas, most languages instead belong to the Tibeto-Burman family. Of the Indo-European languages, Hindi is the most widely spoken, with some 480 million speakers, which makes it the second most widely spoken language in the world. Most other major languages are closely associated with states in India.

How or when Indo-European languages came to South Asia is uncertain, but scholars have traditionally argued that they arrived when pastoral peoples from Central Asia invaded the **subcontinent** in the second millennium BCE, largely supplanting the indigenous Dravidian peoples. According to this hypothesis, offshoots of the same original cattle-herding people also swept across both Iran and Europe, bringing their language to all three places. Supposedly, the ancestral Indo-European tongue introduced to India was similar to Sanskrit. This rather simplistic scenario, however, is now regarded with some suspicion, and many scholars argue for a more gradual infiltration of Indo-European speakers from the northwest.

Any modern Indo-European language of India, such as Hindi or Bengali, is more closely related to English than it is to any **Dravidian language** of southern India, such as Tamil. But South Asian languages on both sides of this linguistic divide do share a number of superficial features. Dravidian languages, for example, have borrowed many words from Sanskrit, particularly those associated with religion and scholarship.

The Indo-European North South Asia's Indo-European languages are themselves divided into two subfamilies: Iranian and Indo-Aryan. Iranian languages, such as Baluchi and Pashto, are found in western Pakistan, near the border with Iran and Afghanistan. Languages of the strictly South Asian Indo-Aryan groups are closely related to each other, yet are still quite distinctive, often written in different scripts. Each of the major languages of India is associated with one or more Indian states. One thus finds Gujarati in Gujarat, Marathi in Maharashtra, Oriya in Orissa, and so on. Two of these languages, Punjabi and Bengali, span India's international boundaries to extend into Pakistan and Bangladesh, respectively, as these borders were established on religious rather than linguistic lines.

The most widely spoken language of South Asia is Hindi—not to be confused with the Hindu religion. With almost 500 million speakers, Hindi is the second most widely spoken language in the world. It occupies a prominent role in contemporary India, both because so many people speak it and because it is the main language of the Ganges Valley, the historical and demographic core of India. Hindi is the dominant tongue of a number of Indian states, including Uttar Pradesh, Madhya Pradesh, and Haryana. In addition, the main forms of speech found in Rajasthan and Bihar are often considered to be dialects of Hindi. Most Indian students learn some Hindi, often as their second or third language.

Bengali is the second most widely spoken language in South Asia. It is the national language of Bangladesh and the main language of the Indian state of West Bengal. Spoken by more than 200 million persons, Bengali is the world's eighth or ninth most widely spoken language. Its significance extends beyond its official status in Bangladesh and its total numerical strength. Equally important is its extensive literature. West Bengal, particularly its capital of Kolkata (Cal-

Figure 12.25 Kolkata (Calcutta) Bookstore Although Kolkata (Calcutta) is noted in the West mostly for its abject poverty, the city is also known in India for its vibrant cultural and intellectual life, illustrated by its large number of bookstores, theaters, and publishing firms.

cutta), has long been one of South Asia's main literary and intellectual centers. Kolkata may be noted for its appalling poverty, but it also has one of the highest levels of cultural production in the world, as measured by the output of drama, poetry, novels, and film (Figure 12.25).

The Punjabi-speaking zone in the west was similarly split at the time of independence, in this case between Pakistan and the Indian state of Punjab. While an estimated 90 million persons speak Punjabi, it does not have the significance of Bengali. Although Punjabi is the main vehicle of Sikh religious writings, it lacks an extensive literary tradition. In recent years, moreover, the people of the southern half of Pakistan's province of Punjab have successfully insisted that their dialect forms a separate language, called Saraiki. And even though Punjabi is the most widely spoken language in Pakistan, did not become the country's national language. Instead, that position was given to Urdu.

Urdu, like Hindi, originated on the plains of northern India. The difference between the two was largely one of religion: Hindi was the language of the Hindu majority, Urdu that of the Muslim minority, including the former ruling class. Owing to this distinction, Hindi and Urdu are written differently—the former in the Devanagari script (derived from Sanskrit) and the latter in a modified version of the Arabic script. Although Urdu contains many words borrowed from Persian, its basic grammar and vocabulary are almost identical to those of Hindi.

With independence in 1947, millions of Urdu-speaking Muslims from the Ganges Valley fled to the new state of Pakistan. Since Urdu had a higher status than Pakistan's indigenous tongues, it was quickly established as the new country's official language. Karachi, Pakistan's largest city, is now largely Urdu-speaking, but elsewhere other languages, such as Punjabi and Sindhi, remain primary. Most Pakistanis, however, do speak Urdu as their common language.

Languages of the South Four thousand years ago, Dravidian languages were probably spoken across most of South Asia. As Figure 12.24 indicates, a Dravidian tongue called *Brahui* is still found in the uplands of western Pakistan. The four main Dravidian languages, however, are confined to the south. As in the north, each language is closely associated with an Indian state: Kannada in Karnataka, Malayalam in Kerala, Telugu in Andhra Pradesh, and Tamil in Tamil Nadu. Tamil is usually considered the most important member of the family because it has the longest history and the largest literature. Tamil poetry dates back to the first century CE, making it one of the world's oldest written languages.

Although Tamil is spoken in northern Sri Lanka, the country's majority population, the Sinhalese, speak an Indo-European language. Apparently the Sinhalese migrated from northern South Asia several thousand years ago. Although this movement is lost to history, the migrants evidently settled on the island's fertile and moist southwestern coastal and central highland areas, which formed the core of a succession of Sinhalese kingdoms. These same people also migrated to the Maldives, where the national language, Divehi, is essentially a Sinhalese dialect. The drier north and east of Sri Lanka, on the other hand, were settled hundreds of years ago by Tamils. In the 1800s, British landowners imported Tamil peasants from the mainland to work on their tea plantations in the central highlands, giving rise to a second population of Tamil-speakers in Sri Lanka.

Linguistic Dilemmas The multilingual countries Sri Lanka, Pakistan, and India are all troubled by linguistic conflicts. Such problems are most complex in India, simply because India is so large and has so many different languages. India's linguistic environment is changing in complicated ways, pushed along by modern economic and political forces.

Indian nationalists have long dreamed of a national language that could help forge the different communities of the country into a more unified nation. But this **linguistic nationalism,** or the linking of a specific language with nationalistic goals, meets the stiff resistance of provincial loyalty, which itself is intertwined with local languages. The obvious choice for a national language would be Hindi, and Hindi was indeed declared as such in 1947. Raising Hindi to this position, however, alienated speakers of important northern languages such as Bengali and Marathi, and even more so the speakers of the Dravidian tongues. As a result of this cultural tension, in the 1950 Indian constitution Hindi was demoted to sharing the position of "official language" of India with 14 other languages. Over time, additional languages were added to this list, such that India now has 23 separate languages with an official status.

Regardless of opposition, the role of Hindi is expanding, especially in the Indo-European-speaking north. Here local languages are closely related to Hindi, which can therefore be learned without too much difficulty. Hindi is spreading through education, but even more significantly through popular media, especially television and motion pictures.

Films and television programs are made in several Indian languages, but Hindi remains the primary vehicle. The most popular movies coming out of Mumbai's "Bollywood" film industry actually tend to be delivered in a neutral dialect that is as close to Urdu as to Hindi—and with a good deal of English thrown in as well.

The Role of English Even if Hindi is spreading, it still cannot be considered anything like a common Indian language, even in the north. In the Dravidian south, more importantly, its role remains secondary. National-level political, journalistic, and academic communication thus cannot be conducted in Hindi, or in any other indigenous language. Only English, an "associate official language" of contemporary India, serves this function.

Before independence, many educated South Asians learned English for its political and economic benefits under British colonialism. It therefore emerged as the de facto common tongue of the upper and middle classes. Today a few extreme nationalists want to deemphasize English, but most Indians, and particularly those of the south, advocate it as a neutral national language because all parts of the country have an equal stake in it. Furthermore, English confers substantial international benefits.

English is thus the main integrating language of India, and it remains widely used elsewhere in South Asia. Roughly a third of the people of India are able to carry out a conversation in English. English-medium schools abound in all parts of the region, and many children of the elite learn this global language well before they begin their schooling.

The English spoken in South Asia has forms and vocabulary elements that sometimes make cross-cultural communication difficult. As a result, IT companies in India, particularly those that run international call centers, sometimes ask their employees to watch reruns of popular television shows from the United States in order to gain fluency in American pronunciation and slang.

South Asians in a Global Cultural Context

The widespread use of English in South Asia has not only facilitated the spread of global culture into the region, but it has also helped South Asian cultural production to reach a global audience. The global spread of South Asian literature, however, is nothing new. As early as the turn of the 20th century, Rabindranath Tagore gained international acclaim for his poetry and fiction, earning the Nobel Prize for Literature in 1913. In the 1980s and 1990s, such Indian novelists as Salman Rushdie and Vikram Seth became major literary figures in Europe and North America.

The spread of South Asian culture abroad has been accompanied by the spread of South Asians themselves. Migration from South Asia during the time of the British Empire led to the establishment of large communities in such far-flung places as eastern Africa, Fiji, and the southern Caribbean (Figure 12.26). Subsequent migration targeted the developed world; there are now several million people of

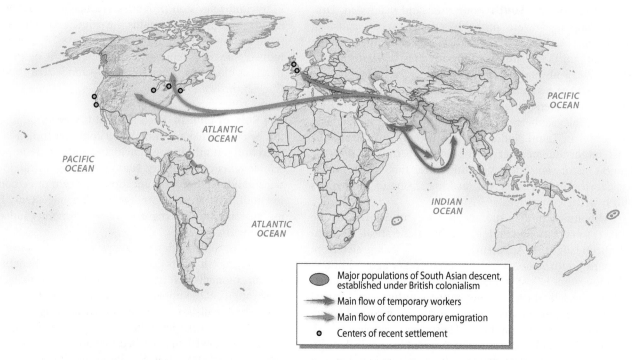

Figure 12.26 The South Asian Global Diaspora During the British imperial period, large numbers of South Asian workers settled in other colonies. Today, roughly 50 percent of the population of such places as Fiji and Mauritius are of South Asian descent. More recently, large numbers have settled, and are still settling, in Europe (particularly Britain) and North America. Large numbers of temporary workers, both laborers and professionals, are employed in the wealthy oil-producing countries of the Persian Gulf.

South Asian descent living in Britain (mostly Pakistani), and a similar number in North America (mostly Indian). Many contemporary migrants to the United States are doctors, software engineers, and other professionals, making Indian Americans one of the country's wealthiest ethnic groups.

In South Asia itself, the globalization of culture has brought tensions as severe as those felt anywhere in the world. Traditional Hindu and Muslim religious customs frown on any overt display of sexuality—a staple feature of global popular culture. While romance is a recurrent theme in the often melodramatic Bollywood films of Mumbai, even kissing is considered risqué. In April 2007, actor Richard Gere sparked massive public protests when he kissed the Indian actress Shilpa Shetty at an AIDS awareness rally in New Delhi (Figure 12.27). Still, the pressures of internationalization are hard to resist. In the tourism-oriented Indian state of Goa, such cultural tensions are on full display. There, German and British sun-worshipers often wear nothing but thong bikini bottoms, whereas Indian women tourists go into the ocean fully clad. Young Indian men, for their part, often simply walk the beach and gawk, good-naturedly, at the outlandish foreigners.

Contemporary popular culture in South Asia thus reveals both global linkages as well as divisions. The same tensions can be seen, and in much stronger form, in the region's geopolitical framework.

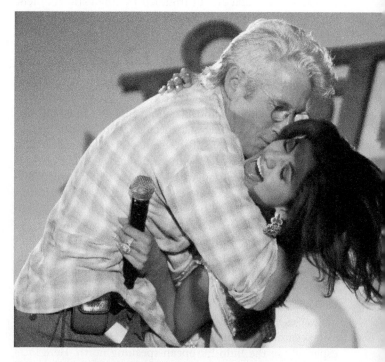

Figure 12.27 A Controversial Kiss Actor Richard Gere embraces and then kisses Indian actress Shilpa Shetty during an AIDS awareness program in 2007. Conservative Indian citizens were shocked by this act, which resulted in large-scale protests.

GEOPOLITICAL FRAMEWORK: A Deeply Divided Region

Before the 1800s, South Asia had never been politically united. While a few empires at various times covered most of the subcontinent, none spanned its entire extent. Whatever unity the region had was cultural, not political. The British, however, brought the region into a single political system by the middle of the 19th century. Independence in 1947 witnessed the traumatic separation of Pakistan from India; in 1971, Pakistan itself was divided with the independence of Bangladesh, formerly East Pakistan. Serious in-

ternal tensions, moreover, began to rise in several South Asian countries in the late 1900s (Figure 12.28). The most important geopolitical issue is the continuing tension between Pakistan and India, both of which are nuclear powers.

South Asia Before and After Independence in 1947

During the 1500s, when Europeans began to arrive on the coasts of South Asia, most of the northern subcontinent came under the power of the Mughal Empire, a powerful Muslim state ruled by people of Central Asian descent

Jammu and Kashmir. *Both Pakistan and India claim the state of Jammu and Kashmir. Pakistan controls the area to the north and west of the red line ("Azad Kashmir"), while India controls the area to the south and west. Much fighting has recently occurred in the area controlled by India.*

Ethnic conflict. *Conflict between indigenous tribal peoples and recent migrants from Bangladesh and India.*

Civil war. *Northeastern Sri Lanka proclaimed as homeland by Tamil independence movement. This led to a prolonged civil war that ended in 2009.*

Map legend:
- Areas claimed by India, controlled by China
- Areas claimed by China, controlled by India
- Areas experiencing serious separatist movements in the past twenty-five years
- New Indian states, emerging after 2000
- Pre-partition Jammu and Kashmir
- Federally administered Tribal Areas of Pakistan
- Areas experiencing serious Maoist revolutionary movements

Figure 12.28 Geopolitical Issues in South Asia Given the cultural mosaic of South Asia, it is not surprising that ethnic tensions have created numerous geopolitical problems in the region. Particularly vexing are ethnic tensions in Sri Lanka and Kashmir.

Figure 12.29 Geopolitical Change At the onset of European colonialism before 1700, much of South Asia was dominated by the powerful Mughal Empire. Under Britain, the wealthiest parts of the region were ruled directly, but other lands remained under the partial authority of indigenous rulers. Independence for the region came after 1947, when the British abandoned their extensive colonial territory. Bangladesh, formerly East Pakistan, gained its independence in 1971 after a short struggle against centralized Pakistani rule from the west.

was the control of land. The Portuguese carved out an enclave in Goa on the west coast, while the Dutch gained control over much of Sri Lanka in the 1600s, but neither was a threat to the Mughals.

The Mughal Empire grew stronger in the 1600s, whereas Hindu power declined until it was limited to the peninsula's extreme south. In the early 1700s, however, the Mughal Empire weakened rapidly. A number of contending states, some ruled by Muslims, others by Hindus, and a few by Sikhs, emerged in former Mughal territories. As a result, the 18th century in South Asia was a time of political and military turmoil.

The British Conquest These unsettled conditions provided an opening for European imperialism. The British and French, having largely displaced the Dutch and Portuguese, competed for trading posts. Because Indian cotton textiles were the best in the world prior to the Industrial Revolution, British and French merchants needed to obtain huge quantities for their global trading networks. With Britain's overwhelming victory over France in the Seven

(Figure 12.29). Southern India remained under the control of a Hindu kingdom called Vijayanagara. European merchants, keen to obtain spices, textiles, and other Indian products, established a series of coastal trading posts. The Mughals and other South Asian rulers were little concerned with the growing European naval power, as their own focus

Years' War (1756–63), France was reduced to a few marginal coastal possessions in southern India. Britain, or more specifically the **British East India Company**, the private firm that acted as an arm of the British government, now monopolized overseas trade in the area and began to stake out a South Asian empire of its own.

The company's usual method was to make strategic alliances with Indian states to defeat the latter's enemies, most of whose territories it would then grab for itself. As time passed, its army, largely composed of South Asian mercenaries, grew ever more powerful. Several Indian states put up strong resistance, but none could ultimately resist the immense resources of the East India Company. Valuable local allies, as well as a few former enemies, were allowed to remain in power, provided that they no longer threatened British interests. The territories of these indigenous states, however, were gradually whittled back, and British advisors increasingly dictated their policies.

From Company Control to British Colony

The continuing reduction in size of the Indian states, coupled with the growing arrogance of British officials, led to a rebellion in 1857 across much of South Asia. When this uprising (called the *Sepoy Mutiny* by the British) was finally crushed, a new political order was implemented. South Asia was now to be ruled by the British government, with the monarch of England serving as its head of state.

Until 1947, the British government maintained direct control over South Asia's most productive and densely populated areas, including virtually the entire Indus-Ganges Valley and most of the coastal plains. The British also ruled Sri Lanka, having supplanted the Dutch in the 1700s. The major areas of indirect rule, where Indian rulers retained their princely states under British advisors, were in Rajasthan, the uplands of central India, southern Kerala, and along the frontiers. The British administered this vast empire through three coastal cities that were largely their own creation: Bombay (Mumbai), Madras (Chennai), and, above all, Calcutta (Kolkata). In 1911, they began building a new capital in New Delhi, near the strategic divide between the Indus and Ganges drainage systems.

While the political geography of British India stabilized after 1857, the empire's frontiers remained unsettled. British officials worried about threats to their immensely profitable colony, particularly from the Russians advancing across Central Asia. In response, they attempted to expand as far to the north as possible. In some cases this merely entailed making alliances with local rulers. In such a manner Nepal and Bhutan retained their independence. In the extreme northeast, a number of small states and tribal territories, most of which had never been part of the South Asian cultural sphere, were more directly brought into the British Empire, hence into India. A similar policy was conducted on the vulnerable northwestern frontier. Here, however, local resistance was much more effective, and the British-Indian army suffered defeat at the hands of the Afghans. Afghanistan thus retained its independence, forming an effective buffer between the British and Russian empires. The British also allowed the tribal Pashto-speaking areas of what is now northwestern Pakistan to retain almost complete autonomy, thus forming a secondary buffer.

Independence and Partition

The framework of British India began to unravel in the early 20th century as the people of South Asia increasingly demanded independence. The British, however, were equally determined to stay, and by the 1920s the region was embroiled in massive political protests.

The rising nationalist movement's leaders faced a major dilemma in attempting to organize a potentially independent regime. Many leaders, including Mohandas Gandhi—the main figure of Indian independence—favored a unified state that would encompass all British territories in mainland South Asia. Most Muslim leaders feared that a unified India would leave their people in a vulnerable position. They therefore argued for the division of British India into two new countries: a Hindu-majority India and a Muslim-majority Pakistan. In several parts of northern South Asia, however, Muslims and Hindus were settled in roughly equal proportions. A more significant obstacle was the fact that the areas of clear Muslim majority were located on opposite sides of the subcontinent, in present-day Pakistan and Bangladesh.

No longer able to maintain their world empire after World War II, the British withdrew from South Asia in 1947. As this occurred, the region was indeed divided into two countries: India and Pakistan. Partition itself was a horrific event, resulting in the death of some 200,000 to 1 million people. Roughly 7 million Hindus and Sikhs fled Pakistan, to be replaced by roughly 7 million Muslims fleeing India (Figure 12.30).

The Pakistan that emerged from partition was for several decades a clumsy two-part country, its western section in the Indus Valley, its eastern portion in the Ganges Delta. The Bengalis, occupying the poorer eastern section, complained that they were treated as second-class citizens. In 1971, they launched a rebellion, and, with the help of India, quickly prevailed. Bangladesh then emerged as a new country.

This second partition did not solve Pakistan's problems, however, as it remained politically unstable and prone to military rule. Pakistan retained the British policy of allowing almost full autonomy to the Pashtun tribes of the Federally Administered Tribal Areas of the northwest, a relatively lawless region marked by clan fighting and vengeance feuds. The large and poor province of Balochistan in southwestern Pakistan has been another problem for the national government, as a long-simmering separatist movement continues to fight against Pakistan's military forces.

Bangladesh has also had a troubled political career since achieving independence in 1971. High levels of corruption, growing Islamic radicalism, and street-level fighting between members its two major political parties have undermined its democratic institutions. As tensions mounted, the Bangladeshi army seized power in January 2007, declared a

Figure 12.30 Partition, 1947 Following Britain's decision to leave South Asia, violence and bloodshed broke out between Hindus and Muslims in much of the region. With the creation of Pakistan (originally in two different sectors, west and east), millions of people relocated both to and from the new states. Many were killed in the process, embittering relations between India and Pakistan.

state of emergency, and detained up to 100,000 individuals. Relatively free elections brought Sheikh Hasina to the office of prime minister in 2009, even though she had been arrested and charged with corruption and extortion 2 years earlier.

Geopolitical Structure of India With independence in 1947, the leaders of India, committed to democracy, faced a major challenge in organizing such a large and culturally diverse country. They decided to chart a middle ground between centralization and local autonomy. India itself was thus organized as a **federal state**, with a significant amount of power being given to its individual states. The national government, however, retained full control over foreign affairs and a large degree of economic authority.

Following independence, India's constituent states were reorganized to match the country's linguistic geography. The idea was that each major language group should have its own state (with the massive Hindi-speaking population having several), hence a degree of political and cultural autonomy. Yet only the largest groups received their own territories, which has led to recurring demands from smaller groups that have felt politically excluded. Over time, several new states have been added to the map. Goa, after the Portuguese were forced out in 1961, became a separate state in 1987 over the objection of its large northern neighbor of Maharashtra. In 2000, three new states were added: Jharkand, Uttaranchal, and Chhattisgarh.

Ethnic Conflicts in South Asia

The movement for new states in India has been largely rooted in ethnic tensions. Unfortunately, violent ethnic conflicts persist in many parts of South Asia. Of these conflicts, the most complex—and perilous—is that in Kashmir.

Kashmir Relations between India and Pakistan were hostile from the start, and the situation in Kashmir has kept the conflict burning (Figure 12.31). During the British period, Kashmir was a large state with a primarily Muslim core joined to a Hindu district in the south (Jammu) and a Tibetan Buddhist district in the far northeast (Ladakh). Kashmir was then ruled by a Hindu **maharaja**, or a king subject to British advisors. During partition, Kashmir came under severe pressure from both India and Pakistan. Troops linked to Pakistan gained control of western and much of northern Kashmir, at which point the maharaja opted for union with India. India thus retained the core areas of the state, but neither country would accept the other's control over any portion of Kashmir. As a result, India and Pakistan have fought several inconclusive wars over the issue.

Although the Indo-Pakistani boundary has remained fixed, the struggle in Kashmir intensified, flaming out into an open insurgency in 1989. Although some Kashmiris would like to join their homeland to Pakistan, a 2007 poll indicated that 87 percent of the people of Kashmir Valley preferred independence. Opposition to Kashmir's independence is one of the few things on which India and Pakistan can agree. India accuses Pakistan of supporting training camps for Islamist militants and of helping them sneak across the border. As a result, India began the construction of a fortified fence along the so-called line of control that divides Kashmir. The result of all of this activity has been a low-level but periodically brutal war that has claimed over 40,000 lives and displaced one out of every six inhabitants of Kashmir.

The situation in Kashmir began to improve in 2004 when India and Pakistan initiated a serious round of negotiations. India agreed that Pakistan must play a role in any Kashmir peace settlement, whereas Pakistan's government reduced its support of Muslim militants. As a result, the daily death toll from political violence dropped from 10 in 2002 to 2 in early 2007. But in 2010, tensions again increased as massive protests followed allegations that the Indian army had killed 15 Kashmiri civilians, many of them teenagers. The Vale of Kashmir, once one of South Asia's premier tourist destinations with its lush gardens and orchards nestled among some of the world's most spectacular mountains, is now a battle-scarred war zone.

The Punjab Religious conflict has also caused political tensions in India's Punjab. The original Punjab, an area of intermixed Hindu, Muslim, and Sikh communities, was divided between India and Pakistan in 1947. During partition, virtually all Hindus and Sikhs fled from Pakistan's allotted portion, just as Muslims were forced out of the zone awarded to India.

Partition did not solve the problems of India's portion of the Punjab. Most Sikhs resented the fact that the Indian government refused to recognize Sikhism as a separate religion, instead classifying it as a sect of Hinduism. In the 1970s and 1980s, as the area grew increasingly prosperous due to the Green Revolution, Sikh leaders began to strive for autonomy and Sikh radicals began to press for outright independence. Since many Sikh men had maintained the military traditions of their ancestors, this secession movement soon became a formidable fighting force. The Indian government reacted firmly, and tensions mounted. An open rupture occurred in 1984 when the Indian army raided the main Sikh temple at Amritsar, in which a group of militants had barricaded themselves (Figure 12.32). As hostility escalated, the Indian government placed the Punjab under martial law ar-

Figure 12.31 Conflict in Kashmir Unrest in Kashmir inflames the continually hostile relationships between the two nuclear powers of India and Pakistan. Today many Kashmiris wish to join Pakistan, while many others argue for an independent state. Note also Pakistan's Federally Administered Tribal Areas (including the Islamic Emirate of Waziristan) and its North-West Frontier Province, areas that have experienced much recent fighting.

resting many militants and driving others out of the country. This policy eventually proved successful in quelling political violence.

Current concerns in the Indian state of Punjab focus on migration. Many Punjabis have been moving out of the state

Figure 12.32 Sikh Temple at Amritsar
Separatism in Indian's Punjab region emerged because of hostility between the Sikh majority and the Indian government. These tensions were magnified in 1984 when the Indian army raided the Golden Temple in Amritsar, shown in this photograph, to dislodge Sikh militants.

PEOPLE ON THE MOVE — Punjabis Leaving Agriculture and Leaving India

Punjab is not only India's breadbasket but also one of its most prosperous states. Many landless people from the poorer states of India, such as Bihar, continue to move to Punjab to find work as farm laborers. But despite their relative prosperity, Punjabis have proved eager to migrate, either to India's growing cities or to foreign countries (Figure 12.5.1). Entire villages in central Punjab's "migration belt" are now almost empty, while illegal migration scandals continue to provide stories for local newspapers. Such scandals reached a peak in April 2007, when a member of the Indian Parliament, Babubhai Katara, was arrested for his involvement in a scheme to smuggle Punjabis to other countries in cooperation with a well-known human-trafficking mafia.

India's recent agricultural distress has hit Punjab hard, leading to massive migration of the state's less successful farmers. As the Green Revolution gained momentum, many farmers went deeply into debt to buy tractors, water pumps, and large quantities of agricultural chemicals. As a result, an estimated 120,000 Punjabi farm families were forced off the land between 1991 and 2001. Since that time, the exodus has apparently accelerated.

Caste issues have also contributed to migration out of Punjab. Dalits often have few, if any, other options locally than to work as farm laborers, a marginal and low-paying occupation. Abroad, however, caste barriers disappear, allowing many low-caste families to prosper. The money that they send home—an estimated $3 billion annually for Punjab as a whole—seems to be changing local caste dynamics. The fact that some members of Punjab's artisan castes have taken greater advantage of technical education—highly useful for finding work abroad—than have the higher-ranked land-owning castes has generated upheavals in the traditional social structure.

Migration patterns from the agricultural areas of Punjab have a pronounced gender dimension. Punjab has a highly male-biased population, with only 874 females for every 1,000 males. Sex-selective abortion is generally considered to be the primary cause, but differential migration also plays a role. On one hand, men from the poorest parts of India continue to move into Punjab's farming districts. On other hand, rural Punjabi men tend to move to the region's cities. These patterns combine to further skew local sex ratios. In April 2007, local leaders were shocked to discover that Chandigarh, a relatively prosperous and sophisticated city that serves as the capital of both Punjab and neighboring Haryana, had a sex ratio of only 777 females to 1,000 males, one of the lowest figures in the world. A 2009 survey, however, discovered that the city's sex ratio was improving, with 882 girls born for every 1000 boys.

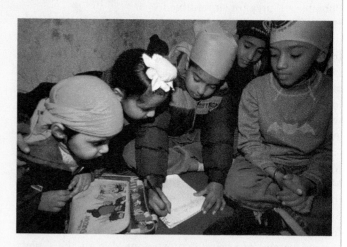

Figure 12.5.1 Punjabi Emigration Young Punjabi children in Paris congregate every Sunday to study the Punjabi language and the Sikh religion. Although one of India's most prosperous states, Punjab has recently experienced pronounced rural economic distress. Partly as a result, it sends many immigrants to other parts of India and to foreign countries.

(see "People on the Move: Punjabis Leaving Agriculture and Leaving India"), but many people from other parts of India have been moving in, attracted by relatively high wages. If presents trends continue, Sikhs could become a minority in Punjab.

The Northeastern Fringe A more complicated ethnic conflict emerged in the late 1900s in the uplands of India's extreme northeast, particularly in the states of Arunachal Pradesh, Nagaland, Manipur, and portions of Assam. One underlying problem stems from demographic change and cultural collision. Much of this area is still relatively lightly populated, and as a result has attracted many migrants from Bangladesh and adjacent provinces of India. Many local inhabitants consider this movement a threat to both their lands and their cultural integrity.

Through much of the northeast, insurgent groups continue to seek autonomy if not statehood. After 2000, the In-dian government began to invest more money in this troubled region, hoping to reduce popular support for separatist movements. India is also eager to expand trade with Burma, and has been working with the Burmese government to secure the border zone. As a result of these and other initiatives, a number of local rebel movements have signed cease-fires with the Indian government. Several insurgent groups have even agreed to cooperate with the Indian army against those groups that continue to fight for independence.

Sri Lanka Interethnic violence in Sri Lanka has also been severe. Here the conflict has roots in both religious and linguistic differences. Northern Sri Lanka and parts of its eastern coast are dominated by Hindu Tamils, while the island's majority group is Buddhist in religion and Sinhalese in language. Relations between the two communities have historically been fairly good, but tensions mounted soon after independence.

The basic problem is that Sinhalese nationalists favor a unitary government, some of them going so far as to argue that Sri Lanka ought to be defined as a Buddhist state. Most Tamils, on the other hand, support political and cultural autonomy, and they have accused the government of discriminating against them. Overall, levels of education are higher among the Tamils, but the government has favored the Sinhalese majority. In 1983, war erupted when the rebel force known as the **Tamil Tigers** (or the *Liberation Tigers of Tamil Eelam*) attacked the Sri Lankan army. Both extreme Tamil and extreme Sinhalese nationalists remained unwilling to compromise, prolonging the war (Figure 12.33).

In the early years of the new millennium, a Norwegian-backed peace process achieved some progress in the area, culminating in a 2003 cease-fire. Within a few years, however, fighting resumed and soon intensified. In March 2007, the Tamil Tigers managed to cobble together a rudimentary air force and bomb Sri Lanka's main airbase, adjacent to the country's international airport. The Sri Lankan government subsequently abandoned negotiations, launching instead an all-out offensive. In May 2009, government forces crushingly defeated the Tamil Tiger army, killing the organiza-

tion's leaders. The defeat of the Tamil Tigers also brought about a humanitarian disaster, as many civilians were killed and over 300,000 were displaced. Sri Lanka is now finally at peace, but ethnic tensions are still pronounced.

The Maoist Challenge

Not all of South Asia's current conflicts are rooted in ethnic or religious differences. Poverty and inequality in east-central India, for example, have generated a persistent revolutionary movement that finds inspiration in the former Chinese communist leader Mao Zedong. Violence associated with this movement resulted in over 1,100 deaths in 2009 alone. In April 2010, Maoist rebels killed 76 Indian troops in the state of Chattisgarh, the largest single death toll of the insurgency. Such persistent violence has prevented investment in some of India's least-developed areas, intensifying the underlying economic and social problems that gave rise to the insurgency in the first place.

While India's Maoist rebellion is too small to effectively challenge the state, the same cannot be said in regard to Nepal. Nepalese Maoists, frustrated by the lack of development in rural areas, emerged as a significant force in the 1990s. In 2002, Nepal's king, citing the communist threat, dissolved parliament and took over total control of the country's government. This move only intensified the struggle, however, and within a few years the rebels had gained control over 70 percent of the country. Both sides committed atrocities, resulting in more than 13,000 deaths. By 2005, Nepal's urban population also turned against the monarchy, launching massive protests in Katmandu. In 2008, the king stepped down, and Nepal became a republic, with the leader of the former Maoist rebels serving as prime minister. But a year later, he resigned after quarrelling with army leaders about the still-armed Maoist militias. By mid 2010, Nepal's parliament was still unable to form a new government, putting the country under the threat of renewed fighting.

Hopes that including the Maoists in Nepal's political mainstream would bring stability have thus been frustrated. Ethnic conflicts also plague other parts of Nepal. In 2007, a new round of political violence broke out in the Terai, a lowland region along the border with India, associated with a group called the Madhesi Peoples' Right Forum. This group claims that the Nepalese lowlanders have been exploited by both Nepal's political elite and its Maoist rebels, and it deeply resents the migration of people from Nepal's mountains and hills into the narrow but fertile lowland belt. Although many Nepalis are working hard to reestablish peace and democratic rule, success will obviously not come easily.

International Geopolitics

South Asia's major international geopolitical problem continues to be the struggle between India and Pakistan (Figure 12.34). Since independence, these two countries have regarded each other as enemies. The stakes now are particu-

Figure 12.33 Civil War in Sri Lanka The majority of Sri Lankans are Sinhalese Buddhist, many of whom maintain that their country should be a Buddhist state. A Tamil-speaking Hindu minority in the northeast strenuously resists this idea. Tamil militants, who have waged war against the Sri Lankan government for several decades until defeated in 2009, hoped to create an independent country in their northern homeland.

Figure 12.34 Border Tensions An Indian officer looks through binoculars in war-torn Kashmir. Relationships between India and Pakistan have remained extremely tense since independence in 1947. Moreover, with both countries now nuclear powers, the fear that border hostilities will escalate into wider warfare has become a nightmarish possibility.

larly high as both India and Pakistan have nuclear capabilities. Tensions were reduced in 2003 and 2004, however, after India initiated a series of talks with Pakistan. Concrete measures have been slow to emerge, but "confidence-building measures"— including cricket matches and the establishment of bus service between the two countries—have led to hopes that an understanding between these rival states might eventually be reached.

During the global Cold War, Pakistan allied itself with the United States and India remained neutral while leaning slightly toward the Soviet Union. Such entanglements fell apart with the end of the superpower conflict in the early 1990s. Subsequently, Pakistan forged an informal alliance with China, from which Pakistan obtained sophisticated military equipment.

China's military connection with Pakistan is rooted in its own animosity toward India. In 1962, China defeated India in a brief war, gaining control over the virtually uninhabited territory of Aksai Chin in northern Kashmir. Growing trade, however, has resulted in a gradual easing of hostilities between India and China. A declaration that 2006 would be an official "year of friendship," however, was undermined when China announced that it still claimed India's northeastern state of Arunachal Pradesh. Most observers think that an eventual settlement will entail India recognizing Chinese sovereignty over Aksai Chin and China giving up its claims in the northeast. But as long as China maintains close military ties with Pakistan, its relationship with India will remain tense.

Pakistan Pakistan's geopolitical situation became more complex in the aftermath of the attacks in the United States on September 11, 2001. Until that time, Pakistan had strongly supported Afghanistan's Taliban regime (see Chapter 10). After the attack on the World Trade Center and Pentagon (orchestrated from Afghanistan by Osama bin Laden), the United States gave Pakistan a stark choice: either it would assist the United States in its fight against the Taliban and receive in return debt reductions and other forms of aid, or it would lose favor. Pakistan's president, Pervez Musharraf, quickly agreed to help, and Pakistan offered both military bases and valuable intelligence to the U.S. military.

Pakistan's decision to help the United States came with large risks. Both Osama bin Laden and the Taliban enjoy substantial support among the Pashtun people of northwestern Pakistan. After suffering several military reversals, Pakistan decided to negotiate with these radical Islamists, and on several occasions it gave them virtual control over sizable areas. From these bases, militants have launched numerous attacks on U.S. forces in Afghanistan and have attempted to gain control over broader swaths of Pakistan's territory. The United States has responded mainly by using unstaffed drones to attack insurgent leaders, a tactic that has resulted in large numbers of civilian casualties and much anti-American sentiment throughout Pakistan.

The security crisis in Pakistan intensified from 2007 to 2010. In November 2008, Pakistan's president declared a state of emergency, and in the following month, Benazir Bhutto, Pakistan's former prime minister, was assassinated as she campaigned for the 2008 election. Although the elections went on relatively smoothly, the new government faced severe challenges as hard-line Islamists expanded their control over remote areas. Islamic militants increasingly gained power not only in the peripheral tribal areas, but also in South Punjab. In April 2009, Pakistan's army launched a major invasion of Swat, a former vacation zone 100 miles (160 kilometers) northwest of the capital city of Islamabad that had been turned over to Islamic militants a few months earlier. As the military advanced, hundreds of thousands of civilians fled, generating a humanitarian catastrophe. The government soon reclaimed Swat as militants retreated, but the entire area remains highly unstable.

Pakistan is a troubled country, facing not only a deep Islamist insurgency and a seemingly unsolvable geopolitical conflict with India but also a low-level ethnic rebellion in its southwestern province (Balochistan). Its relations with India, moreover, deteriorated in November 2008, when terrorists operating from Pakistan launched a series of coordinated attacks on tourist facilities and public places in Mumbai, killing 173 people. Pakistan responded by investigating the event and arresting a number of alleged plotters, but many Indians suspect that the attack had the support of certain elements within Pakistan's government and military. Both Indian and Pakistani leaders, however, decided that it would be in their own best interests to reduce tensions, and in July 2009, they agreed to renew their stalled peace negotiations. In 2010, Pakistan announced that it would crack down on Islamist militants in its core province of Punjab.

Figure 12.35 India-Bangladesh Border Fence India began building a border fence between its territory and that of Bangladesh in 2003 in order to reduce illegal immigration and to stop the influx of militants. Members of the Indian Border Security Force visible in this photograph are patrolling a segment of the fence.

Sceptics, however, fear that Pakistan's security forces have been deeply infiltrated by Islamist radicals, undermining any such moves.

India's Changing Geopolitical Situation The tension between India and Pakistan, and the complex relationships that this entails with China and the United States, overshadows all other international geopolitical issues in South Asia. Elsewhere in the region, the power of India is often overwhelming, if resented. Bangladesh, which owes its very existence to Indian support, long enjoyed relatively cordial relations with India. Their relations began to deteriorate in the late 1990s, however, owing to India's concerns about illegal Bangladeshi immigration and to its fears that Bangladesh was providing refuge to separatist fighters from India's northeastern periphery. As a result, India is building a $1.2 billion security fence along the border between the two countries (Figure 12.35). In other parts of South Asia, India has used its power even more forcefully. For example, in 1975, it annexed the formerly semi-independent country of Sikkim in the Himalayas.

ECONOMIC AND SOCIAL DEVELOPMENT: Burdened by Poverty

South Asia is a land of developmental paradoxes. It is, along with Sub-Saharan Africa, the poorest world region, yet it is also the site of some immense fortunes. Many of South Asia's scientific and technological accomplishments are world-class, but it also has some of the world's highest illiteracy rates. While South Asia's high-tech businesses are closely integrated with centers of the global information economy, the South Asian economy as a whole was long one of the world's most self-contained and inward looking.

It is difficult to exaggerate South Asia's poverty. Roughly 300 million Indians live below their country's official poverty line, which is set at a very meager level (Figure 12.36). Approximately 20 percent of India's citizens are seriously undernourished, as are 30 percent of the people of Bangladesh. By measures such as infant mortality and average longevity, Nepal is in even worse condition. In urban slums throughout South Asia, rapidly growing populations have little chance of finding housing or basic social services. Estimates indicate that up to half a million South Asian children work as virtual slaves in carpet-weaving workshops and other small-scale factories.

Despite such deep and widespread poverty, South Asia should not be regarded as a zone of uniform misery. India especially has a large and growing middle class, as well as a small but wealthy upper class. More than 250 million Indians are able to purchase such modern consumer items as televisions, motor scooters, and washing machines. India's economy grew from the 1950s to the 1990s at a moderate but accelerating pace, and by the new millennium it was booming. Even in the global recession years of 2008 and 2009, the Indian economy expanded at an annual rate of roughly 7 percent. But if a number of Indian states have shown marked economic vitality (Figure 12.37), others have stagnated.

Figure 12.36 Poverty in India India's rampant poverty results in a significant amount of child labor. In this photo, a 10-year-old boy is moving a large burden of plastic waste by bicycle.

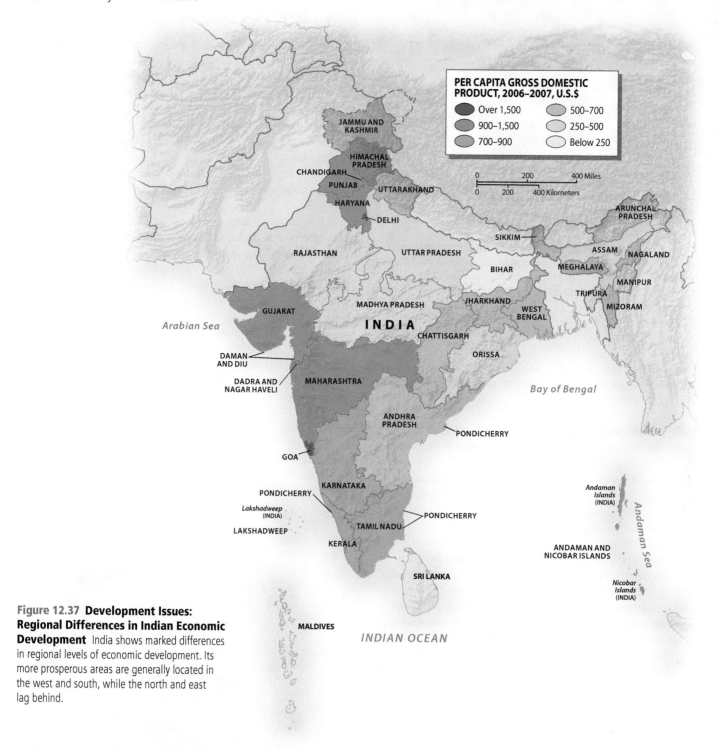

Figure 12.37 Development Issues: Regional Differences in Indian Economic Development India shows marked differences in regional levels of economic development. Its more prosperous areas are generally located in the west and south, while the north and east lag behind.

Geographies of Economic Development

After independence, the governments of South Asia attempted to create new economic systems that would benefit their own people rather than foreign countries or corporations. As in most other parts of the world, planners stressed heavy industry and economic autonomy. While some major gains were realized, the overall pace of development remained slow. Since the 1990s, governments in the region, and especially that of India, have gradually

opened their economies to the global economic system. In the process, core areas of economic development have emerged, surrounded by peripheral areas that have lagged behind, creating landscapes of striking economic disparity (Table 12.2).

The Himalayan Countries Both Nepal and Bhutan are disadvantaged by their rugged terrain and remote locations, as well as by the fact that they remain relatively isolated from modern technology and infrastructure. But such measure-

TABLE 12.2   Development Indicators

Country	GNI per capita, PPP 2008	GDP Average Annual % Growth 2000-08	Human Development Index (2007)[a]	Percent Population Living Below $2 a Day	Life Expectancy (2010)[b]	Under Age 5 Mortality Rate (1990)	Under Age 5 Mortality Rate (2008)	Gender Equity (2008)[c]
Bangladesh	1,450	5.8	0.543	81.3	66	149	54	106
Bhutan	4,820		0.619		68			
India	2,930	7.9	0.612	75.6	64	116	69	92
Maldives	5,290		0.771		73			
Nepal	1,110	3.5	0.553	77.6	64	142	51	93
Pakistan	2,590	5.4	0.572	60.3	66	130	89	80
Sri Lanka	4,460	5.5	0.759	39.7	74	29	15	

[a]*United Nations, Human Development Report, 2009.*

[b]*Population Reference Bureau, World Population Data Sheet, 2010.*

[c]*Gender Equity—Ratio of female to male enrollments in primary and secondary school. Numbers below 100 have more males in primary/secondary school, numbers above 100 have more females in primary/secondary schools.*

Source: World Bank, World Development Indicators, 2010.

ments are somewhat misleading, especially for Bhutan, because they fail to take into account the fact that many areas in the Himalayas are still subsistence-oriented.

Bhutan has purposely remained somewhat disconnected from the modern world economy, its small population living in a relatively pristine natural environment. Bhutan is so isolationist that it has only recently allowed tourists to enter—provided that they agree to spend substantial amounts of money while in the country. Its government has made the unusual move of downplaying conventional measures of economic development, attempting to substitute "gross national happiness" for "gross national product."

Bhutan is not, however, completely cut off from the rest of the world. It exports substantial amounts of hydroelectric power to India, helping its economy grow by 19 percent in 2008 and 5 percent in 2009. Such growth has brought immigrants; approximately 100,000 Indian laborers are now working on roads and other infrastructural projects in Bhutan. Local resentment against these and other newcomers from India and especially Nepal has resulted in ethnic tensions, forcing up to 60,000 people to flee from Bhutan to refugee camps in Nepal.

Nepal is more heavily populated and suffers much more severe environmental degradation than Bhutan. It also is more closely integrated with the Indian, and ultimately the world, economy, although three-quarters of its people still depend on small-scale agriculture for their livelihoods. Nepal's economy relies heavily on international tourism (Figure 12.38). Tourism has brought some prosperity to a few favored locations, but often at the cost of heightened ecological damage. Tourism in Nepal began to suffer, moreover, after the country entered a period of political turmoil in 2002. Remittances from Nepalese workers living abroad currently help sustain the country's fragile economy.

Bangladesh The economic figures for Bangladesh are not as low as those of the Himalayan countries, but they are more indicative of widespread hardship because most people there require cash to meet their basic needs. Partly because of the country's massive population, poverty is extreme and widespread.

Environmental degradation has contributed to Bangladesh's impoverishment, as did the partition of 1947. Most of prepartition Bengal's businesses were located in the western area, which went to India. The division of Bengal tore apart an integrated economic region, much to the detriment of the poorer and mainly rural eastern section. Bangladesh also has suffered because of its agricultural emphasis on jute, a plant that yields tough fibers useful for making ropes and burlap bags. Bangladesh failed to

Figure 12.38 Tourism in Nepal. Nepal has long been one of the world's main destinations for adventure tourism, although business has suffered in recent years d to the county's political instability. Many tourists in Nepal stay in rustic lodges, such the one shown in this photograph.

discover any major alternative export crops as synthetic materials undercut the global jute market.

Not all of the economic news coming from Bangladesh is negative. The country is internationally competitive in textile and clothing manufacture, in part because its wage rate is so low. Low-interest credit provided by the internationally noted Grameen Bank has given hope to many poor women in Bangladesh, allowing the emergence of a number of vibrant small-scale enterprises. By 2000, with the country's birthrate steadily falling, the Bangladeshi economy was finally beginning to grow substantially faster than its population. Even through the global recession of 2008–2009, it continued to grow by 5 to 6 percent a year.

Pakistan Pakistan also suffered the effects of partition in 1947. But unlike Bangladesh, Pakistan at least inherited a reasonably well-developed urban infrastructure. It has a productive agricultural sector, as it shares the fertile Punjab with India. Pakistan also boasts a large textile industry, based in part on its huge cotton crop. Several Pakistani cities, moreover, have developed important niches in the global economy (see "Global to Local: The Sialkot Industrial Complex"). Pakistan's economic growth accelerated after 2001, due in part to the concessions given to it by United States and international economic institutions.

By 2008–2009, however, Pakistan's economy was again faltering, hampered by an inflation rate of over 20 percent. The Pakistani economy is less dynamic than that of India, with a lower potential for growth. Part of the problem is that Pakistan is burdened by extremely high levels of military spending, yet at the same time it has experienced growing internal strife. Additionally, a small but powerful landlord class that pays virtually no taxes to the central government controls many of its best agricultural lands. Unlike India, moreover, Pakistan has not been able to develop a successful IT industry.

Like India, Pakistan has inadequate energy supplies, which has led it to look to both Central Asia and Southwest Asia for fossil fuels. One consequence of this policy has been the construction of a huge new deep-water port at Gwadar near the border with Iran, adjacent to some of the world's most important oil-tanker routes. Built with massive Chinese engineering and financial assistance, the port of Gwadar was turned over to be managed by the Port of Singapore when completed in 2007, showing the increasingly globalized nature of Pakistan's economic planning.

Sri Lanka and the Maldives As can be seen in Table 12.2, Sri Lanka's economy is the second most highly developed in South Asia by conventional criteria. Its exports are concentrated in textiles and agricultural products such as rubber and tea. By global standards, however, it is still a very poor country. Its progress, moreover, was long undercut by its civil war. In 2009, when the war finally ended, the Sri Lankan stock market posted gains of over 100 percent, reflecting renewed confidence in the country's economy. Sri Lanka hopes to benefit more from the prime location of its port of Colombo, from its high levels of education, and from its great tourism potential. To do so, however, it will need to attract large quantities of foreign investment. Sri Lanka currently depends heavily on the remittances sent home by its workers living abroad, estimated to total some $3 billion a year.

The Maldives is the most prosperous South Asian country based on per capita GNI, but its total economy, like its population, is tiny. Most of its revenues are gained from fishing and international tourism. Eighty-eight of the Maldives' otherwise uninhabited islands have been turned over entirely to resorts, which are visited by some 600,000 tourists a year. The benefits from the tourist economy, however, flow mainly to the country's small elite population, resulting in large-scale public discontent and political repression. Tourism is also highly vulnerable to international recessions; in 2009, the economy of the Maldives declined by 4 percent.

India's Less-Developed Areas India's economy, like its population, dwarfs those of the other South Asian countries. While India's per capita GNI is roughly comparable to that of Pakistan, its total economy is many times larger. As the region's largest country, India also exhibits far more internal variation in economic development than its neighbors. The most basic economic division is that between India's more prosperous west and south and its poorer districts in the north and east.

The so-called tribal states of India's northeastern fringe rank low on the economic ladder, as measured by per capita GNI, but the prevalence of subsistence economies makes such statistics misleading. More extreme deprivation is found in the lower Ganges Valley, where cash economies generally prevail. Bihar is India's poorest state by virtually all economic indicators, as well as its most politically corrupt. Neighboring Uttar Pradesh, India's most populous state, also is poverty-stricken. Like Bihar, it is densely populated and has experienced little industrial development. Although both Bihar and Uttar Pradesh have fertile soils, their agricultural systems have not profited as much from the Green Revolution as have those of Punjab. In both states the **caste system** is deeply entrenched, tensions between Hindus and Muslims are bitter, and opportunities for most peasants are limited. Ironically, South Asia's wealth was historically concentrated in the fertile lowlands of the Ganges Valley, yet today the area ranks among the poorest parts of an impoverished world region.

Other eastern India states such as Orissa and Assam are also quite poor, but the large and important state of West Bengal ranks about average for India as a whole. Some of the worst slums in the world are located in West Bengal's Kolkata (Calcutta). But Kolkata also supports a substantial and well-educated middle class, and it is the site of a sizable industrial complex. For most of the period of Indian independence, West Bengal has been governed by a leftist party that has fostered, with little success, heavy, state-led industry. In a dramatic turn-around in the 1990s, West Bengal's Marxist leaders began to advocate internationalization, encouraging large multinational firms to build new factories in

GLOBAL TO LOCAL   The Sialkot Industrial Complex

Pakistan does not have a highly globalized economy. Its exports are dominated by bulk cotton goods, mostly yarn, cloth, sheets, and towels rather than clothing, with rice, leather goods, and low-value chemicals rounding out the list. But one Pakistani city, Sialkot, stands out from all the rest, having carved a unique niche in the global economic system though its production of surgical steel implements and sporting goods (Figure 12.6.1). As a result, Sialkot is noted as Pakistan's most entrepreneurial city, enjoying a per capita income roughly double the national average.

During the Mughal period, Sialkot's weapon-makers were famous for their fine steel swords, but changes in warfare put them out of business by the late 1800s. When an American mission hospital was opened in the city, however, local artisans saw an opportunity to supply it with scalpels and other specialized implements. Before long, Sialkot was exporting such goods throughout British India, and then to the rest of the world.

The rise of the city's sporting goods industry is more difficult to explain. Legend says that it began in the late 1800s when an English tennis player broke his racket and asked a local artisan to repair it. He was evidently so impressed with the product that he commissioned additional replacements, and by 1895 a thriving new industry had emerged.

Today Sialkot's sporting goods industry is most famous for its hand-stitched soccer balls, exporting roughly 60 million each year.

The city's highly competitive businesses, however, produce a huge array of other athletic goods, including equipment for horseback riding, motorcycle racing, boxing, and martial arts. The global nature of the industry is fully apparent in the production line of Saeed Classical Works (http://sportzbiz.pk/), which advertises such products as "Brazilian Jiu-Jitsu Kimonos" sold under the "Bararian" brand name.

Despite its general success, Sialkot's sporting-goods business has faced a number of serious problems. In the 1990s, international criticism mounted over the use of child labor, particularly for hand-sewing soccer balls, an activity that rarely paid more than $1.50 a day. Since then, increased monitoring of factories has reduced labor violations, but abuses remain widespread. Another threat comes from China, which produces machine-assembled balls that dominate the lower end of the market. In response, Sialkot's producers have been striving to widen their product lines and to move into higher-end merchandise. The government of Pakistan offered help by opening a technical university in 2007. As befits the globalized nature of Sialkot's industrial complex, this new University of Engineering Science and Technology has been established in collaboration with Sweden's Royal Institute of Technology. In 2010, Sialkot firms announced that they would soon begin producing machine-made soccer balls in order to compete with Chinese firms in the global market.

Figure 12.6.1 Sialkot Sporting Goods Firm Young employees work at a soccer-ball factory in Sialkot, Pakistan. Sialkot is noted for its exports of sporting goods and medical implements, but it has also been the site of much exploitative child labor.

"special economic zones" subjected to low levels of taxation. Such programs have generated substantial opposition that occasionally become violent.

Although western India is in general much more prosperous than eastern India, the large western state of Ra-

jasthan ranks well below average. Rajasthan suffers from an arid climate; nowhere else in the world are deserts and semi-deserts so densely populated. It also is noted for its social conservatism. During the British period, almost all of this large state remained outside the sphere of direct imperial power. Here, in the courts of maharajas, the military and political traditions of Hindu India persisted up until recent times. Rajasthan's rulers not only maintained elaborate courts and fortifications, but also supported many traditional Indian arts. Because of this political and cultural legacy, Rajasthan is one of India's most important destinations for international tourists.

India's Centers of Economic Growth North of Rajasthan lie the Indian states of Punjab and Haryana, showcases of the Green Revolution. Their economies have relied largely on agriculture, but recent investments in food processing and other industries have been substantial. Punjab has the lowest levels of malnutrition in India and the most highly developed infrastructure. Despite its relative prosperity, this region has seen rural unrest in recent years. On Haryana's eastern border lies the capital district of New Delhi, where India's political power and much of its wealth are concentrated.

India's west-central states of Gujarat and Maharashtra are noted for their industrial and financial clout, as well as for their agricultural productivity. Gujarat was one of the first parts of South Asia to experience substantial industrialization, and its textile mills are still among the most productive in the region. Gujaratis have long been famed as merchants and overseas traders, and they are disproportionately represented in the **Indian diaspora**, the migration of large numbers of Indians to foreign countries. As a result, cash remittances from these emigrants help to bolster the state's economy.

The state of Maharashtra is usually viewed as India's economic pacesetter. The huge city of Mumbai (Bombay) has long been the financial center, media capital, and manufacturing powerhouse of India. According to official figures, the Mumbai metropolitan area accounts for 25 percent of India's industrial output, 40 percent of its maritime trade, and 70 percent of its major financial transactions. Large industrial zones are located in several other cities of Maharashtra, especially Pune and Nagpur. In recent years, Maharashtra's economy has grown more quickly than those of most other Indian states, reinforcing its primacy.

The center of India's fast-growing high-technology sector lies farther to the south, especially in Karnataka's capital of Bangalore, which in 2007 changed its name to Bengaluru. The Indian government selected the upland Bengaluru area for its fledgling aviation industry in the 1950s. Other technologically sophisticated ventures soon followed. In the 1980s and 1990s, a quickly growing computer software industry emerged, earning Bengaluru the label of "Silicon Plateau." In the 1980s, growth was spurred by the investments of U.S. and other foreign corporations eager to hire relatively inexpensive Indian technical talent. Since the 1990s, these multinational companies have been joined by a rapidly expanding group of locally owned firms. Biotechnology is also thriving. Unfortunately, Bengaluru's rapid growth has stretched the city's infrastructure to the breaking point. Roads are commonly jammed, electricity supplies are inadequate, and many parts of the city can only count on three hours of water a day.

Partly because of Bengaluru's problems, other cities in southern India have recently emerged as rival high-tech centers. Hyderabad in Andhra Pradesh, often called "Cyberabad," is well known for its IT and pharmaceutical firms, as well as its film industry, India's second largest. Chennai (Madras) in Tamil Nadu, recently voted as having the highest quality of life among India's major cities, is noted for its software production as well as its financial services and automobile industry.

India has proved especially competitive in software because software development does not require a sophisticated infrastructure; computer code can be exported via wireless telecommunication systems without the use of modern roads or port facilities. What is necessary, of course, is technical talent, and this India has in abundance. Many Indian social groups are highly committed to education, and India has been a scientific power for decades. With the growth of the software industry, India's brainpower has finally begun to translate into economic gains (Figure 12.39). Whether such developments can spread benefits throughout the country remains to be seen. Most of India's rural areas are not prospering, and malnutrition remains widespread. What is certain, however, is that information technology has tightly linked certain parts of India to the global economy.

Globalization and India's Economic Future

South Asia is not one of the world's most globalized regions by conventional economic criteria. The volume of foreign trade is not huge; foreign direct investment is still modest; and (with the exception of the Maldives) international tourists are few (Figure 12.40). But globalization in South Asia is advancing rapidly.

To understand the low globalization indicators for the region, it is necessary to look at its recent economic history. India's postindependence economic policy, like those of other South Asian countries, was based on widespread private ownership combined with high-tariff barriers and governmental control of planning, resource allocation, and certain heavy industrial sectors. This mixed socialist–capitalist system initially brought a fairly rapid development of heavy industry and allowed India to become virtually self-sufficient.

By the 1980s, however, problems with India's economic model were becoming apparent, and frustration was mounting among the business and political elite. While growth was persistent, it remained in most years only a percentage point or two above the rate of population expansion. The percentage of Indians living below the poverty line, moreover, remained virtually constant. At the same time, countries such as China and Thailand were experiencing rapid development after opening their economies to global forces. Many Indian businesspeople were irritated by the governmental regulations that undermined their ability to expand. In the 1980s, foreign indebtedness began to mushroom, putting further pressure on the economy.

In response to these difficulties, the Indian government began to liberalize its economy in 1991. Many regulations

Figure 12.39 India's Silicon Plateau
The Bangalore suburb of Whitefield is usually considered to be the heartland of India's high tech sector. This photograph shows Whitefield's International Technical Park.

were modified and some were eliminated, and the economy was gradually opened to imports and multinational businesses. Other South Asian countries have followed a somewhat similar path. Pakistan, for example, began to privatize many of its state-owned industries in 1994, and in 2000 began to turn over the banking sector to private enterprise.

This gradual internationalization and deregulation of the Indian economy has generated substantial opposition. Foreign competitors are now seriously challenging domestic firms. Cheap manufactured goods from China are seen as an especially serious threat. India has a strong heritage of economic nationalism stemming from the colonial exploitation

Figure 12.40 South Asia's Global Linkages Despite South Asia's growing global connections, the region as a whole is still relatively self-contained, especially in regard to finance. Internet use remains low, especially in Bangladesh and Nepal.

it long suffered. Agricultural liberalization, a central agenda of the World Trade Organization, became an especially contentious issue by the early 2000s because most of India's huge farming sector is not globally competitive. In 2006, mounting opposition led India's government to stall further plans for the privatization of state-controlled economic activities.

Although economic globalization is rapidly advancing in India, the country has not seen the levels of direct foreign investment that have recently transformed the Chinese economy. India also devotes a far smaller percentage of its national budget to infrastructural improvements than does China. Because of such investment shortages, India, like the rest of South Asia, does not have an adequate transportation system to meet its economic needs, and its supply of electricity is woefully short. As a result, many observers doubt that it will be able to match the growth rates that China has achieved. Other, however, are more optimistic, noting that Indian industrial production rose by over 11 percent between mid-2009 and mid-2010, when much of the world was still in an economic crisis.

Social Development

South Asia's social indices show relatively low levels of health and education, which is hardly surprising considering the region's poverty. Levels of social well-being, not surprisingly, vary greatly across the region. As might be expected, people in the more prosperous areas of western India are healthier, live longer, and are better educated, on average, than people in the poorer areas, such as the lower Ganges Valley. Bihar thus stands at the bottom of most social as well as economic measurements, while Punjab, Gujarat, and Maharashtra stand near the top. In much of Bihar, where almost half of the population lives below the poverty line, the situation is dire; considering the fact that over a third of the state's teachers are absent on any given day, progress has not been easy. By 2008, however, Bihar was at long last making considerable gains on both the social and economic fronts, prompting guarded optimism among informed observers.

Several key measurements of social welfare are higher in India than in Pakistan. Pakistan, with a literacy rate of only about 56 percent, has done a particularly poor job of educating its people. Still, it is important to realize how much progress has been made. The province of Balochistan, for example, saw its literacy rate increase from 10 percent in 1981 to 49 percent in 2008. Such gains have not been realized in the Federally Administered Tribal Areas (FATA), where the literacy rate is still below 20 percent overall, and under 5 percent for women. FATA's lack of formal education has provided an opening for radical Islamist organizations, which often offer the only options for schooling.

In several areas of social development, Pakistan is still ahead of India. Pakistan probably suffers less malnutrition, and the average Pakistani lives a few more years than the average Indian. Pakistan also has fewer beggars and people living on the streets than does India, partly due to its widespread Islamic charity system.

Several discrepancies stand out when one compares South Asia's map of economic development with its map of social well-being. Portions of India's extreme northeast, for example, have high literacy rates despite their poverty, owing to the educational efforts of Christian missionaries. In Mizoram, for example, roughly 90 percent of people over the age of 7 can read and write. Kolkata (Calcutta) and its immediate environs also stand out as a relatively well-educated area, despite the general distress of the lower Ganges Basin. The most pronounced discrepancies, however, are found in the southern reaches of South Asia. In health, longevity, and education, the extreme south far outpaces the rest of the region.

The Educated South Southern South Asia's relatively high levels of social welfare are clearly visible when one examines Sri Lanka. Considering its meager economic resources and long-lasting civil war, Sri Lanka must be considered one of the world's great success stories of social development. It demonstrates that a country can achieve significant health and educational gains even in the context of an "undeveloped" economy. Sri Lanka's average longevity of 74 years stands in favorable comparison with some of the world's industrialized countries, as does its literacy rate of more than 90 percent. The Sri Lankan government has achieved these results by funding universal primary education and inexpensive medical clinics.

On the mainland, Kerala in southwestern India has achieved even more impressive results. Kerala is not a particularly prosperous state. It is extremely crowded, has a high rate of unemployment, and has long had difficulty feeding its population. Kerala's indices of social development, however, are the best in India, comparable to those of Sri Lanka (Figure 12.41). Since Kerala is poorer than Sri Lanka, its social accomplishments are all the more impressive.

Some observers attribute Kerala's social successes to its state policies. For most of the period since Indian independence, Kerala has been led by a socialist party that has stressed mass education and community health care. Although no doubt an important factor, this does not seem to offer a complete explanation. West Bengal, for example, also has a socialist political heritage, but it has not been nearly as successful in its social programs. Kerala's neighboring state of Tamil Nadu, on the other hand, also has made significant social progress despite having a different political environment. Some researchers suggest that one of the key variables for explaining the success of the far south is the relatively high social position of its women.

The Status of Women It is often said that South Asian women are accorded a very low social position in both the Hindu and Muslim traditions. In higher-class families of both religions throughout the Indus–Ganges Basin, women traditionally were secluded to a large degree, their social relations with men outside the family being severely restricted.

Some scholars have argued that the Hindu tradition is more limiting to women than the Muslim tradition. Hindu women are forbidden to engage in certain economic activities

Figure 12.41 Education in Kerala
India's southwestern state of Kerala, which has virtually eliminated illiteracy, is South Asia's most highly educated region. It also has the lowest fertility rate in South Asia. Because of this, many argue that women's education and empowerment is the best and most enduring form of contraception.

(such as plowing), and in some areas they are excluded from inheriting land. Throughout northern India, women traditionally leave their own families shortly after puberty to join those of their husbands. As outsiders, often in distant villages, young brides have few opportunities, and it is not uncommon for them to be bullied by their parents-in-law. Widows in the higher castes, moreover, are not supposed to remarry, and instead are encouraged to go into permanent mourning.

Several social indices show that women in the Indus–Ganges Basin still suffer pronounced discrimination. In Pakistan, Bangladesh, and such Indian states as Rajasthan, Bihar, and Uttar Pradesh, female levels of literacy are much lower than those of males. An even more telling statistic is that of gender ratios, the relative proportion of males and females in the population. All things being equal, there should be slightly more women than men in any population because women generally have a longer life expectancy. Northern South Asia, however, contains many more men than women. Nepal is one of the few countries in which men on average live longer than women.

Economics play a major role in India's biased sex ratios. In rural households, boys are usually viewed as a blessing because they typically remain with their families and work for their well-being. In the poorest groups, elderly people (especially widows) subsist largely on what their sons can provide. Girls, on the other hand, marry out of their families at an early age and must be provided with a dowry. They are thus seen as a net economic liability. Considering the economic desperation of the South Asian poor, it is perhaps

not surprising to see such shortages of girls and young women.

Evidence suggests that the social position of women is improving, especially in the more prosperous parts of western India where employment opportunities outside the family context are emerging. But even in many of the region's middle-class households, women still suffer major disabilities. Dowry demands seem to be increasing in many areas, and there have been a number of well-publicized murders of young brides whose families failed to provide enough goods. In some parts of South Asia, gender ratios are growing even more male-biased now that technology allows gender-selective abortion. Laws against this practice have generally been ignored.

While the social bias against women across northern South Asia is striking, it is much less evident in southern India and Sri Lanka. In Kerala especially, women have relatively high status, regardless of whether they are Hindus, Muslims, or Christians. Here the overall gender ratio shows the normal pattern, with a slight predominance of females over males. Female literacy is very high in Kerala, which is one reason the state's overall illiteracy rate is so low. Not surprisingly, the high social position of women in southwestern India has deep historical roots. Among the Nairs—Kerala's traditional military and land-holding caste—all inheritance up to the 1920s had to pass through the female line. By 2000, however, census data showed that even in Kerala the number of girls being born relative to the number of boys was declining, showing some evidence of sex-selective abortion.

Summary

- South Asia, a large and complex area, has in many ways been overshadowed by neighboring world regions: by the uneven globalization of Southeast Asia, by the size and political weight of East Asia, and by the geopolitical tensions of Southwest Asia. Much of that is changing, however, as South Asia now figures prominently in discussions of world problems and issues.

- Environmental degradation and instability pose particular problems for South Asia. The region's monsoon climate causes both floods and droughts to be more problematic here than in most other world regions. Rising sea level associated with global climate change directly threatens the low-lying Maldives, and changes in rainfall may play havoc with the monsoon-dependent agricultural systems of India, Pakistan, and Bangladesh.

- Continuing population growth in this already densely populated region demands attention. Although fertility rates have declined rapidly in recent years, Pakistan and northern India cannot easily meet the demands imposed by their expanding populations.

- South Asia's diverse cultural heritage, shaped by peoples speaking several dozen languages and following several major religions, makes for a particularly rich social environment. Unfortunately, cultural differences have often translated into political conflicts. Ethnically or religiously based separatist movements have severely challenged the governments of Pakistan, India, and Sri Lanka. In India, moreover, religious strife between Hindus and Muslims persists, whereas in Pakistan and Bangladesh Islamic radicals clash with the state.

- Geopolitical tensions within South Asia are particularly severe, again demanding global attention. The long-standing feud between Pakistan and India escalated dangerously in the late 1990s, leading many observers to conclude that this was the most likely part of the world to experience a nuclear war. Although tensions between the two countries have lessened, the underlying sources of conflict—particularly the struggle in Kashmir—remain unresolved.

- Although South Asia remains one of the poorest parts of the world, much of the region has seen rapid economic expansion in recent years. Many argue that India in particular is well positioned to take advantage of economic globalization. Large segments of its huge labor force are well educated and speak excellent English, the major language of global commerce. But will these global connections help the vast numbers of India's poor or merely the small number of its economic elite? Advocates of free markets and globalization tend to see a bright future, while skeptics more often see growing problems.

Key Terms

British East India Company (*page 569*)
caste system (*page 558*)
cyclone (*page 541*)
dalit (*page 559*)
Dravidian language (*page 564*)
federal state (*page 570*)
forward capital (*page 556*)

Green Revolution (*page 552*)
Hindu nationalism (*page 556*)
Indian diaspora (*page 580*)
Jainism (*page 561*)
linguistic nationalism (*page 565*)
maharaja (*page 570*)
monsoon (*page 544*)

Mughal Empire (also spelled *Mogul*) (*page 558*)
orographic rainfall (*page 545*)
salinization (*page 553*)
Sikhism (*page 561*)
subcontinent (*page 564*)
Tamil Tigers (*page 573*)

Review Questions

1. What are the four subregions of South Asia? Describe their similarities and differences.

2. What causes the South Asian monsoon? How does it affect different parts of South Asia?

3. What is orographic rainfall? Where is it important for South Asian agriculture?

4. How and why does the birthrate differ geographically within South Asia?

5. What are some of the infrastructural problems faced by South Asian cities? Give some specific examples.

6. Describe the geography of Islam within India. That is, where are the significant Muslim minorities located in India?

7. What are the major Indo-European languages in South Asia? Where are they located? Where are the non-Indo-European languages located?

8. Describe three different regions of geopolitical and ethnic tension within South Asia.

9. Where are the centers or core areas of economic development within the different South Asian countries?

10. What kinds of relationships are seen between women's literacy and different aspects of economic and social development?

Thinking Geographically

1. As a geographer, suggest different strategies for solving (or at least lessening) the serious flooding problems in Bangladesh. Consider the fact that this crowded country must maximize most of its area for agricultural production.

2. What are the advantages and disadvantages of expanding irrigated agriculture in India and Pakistan? How can the disadvantages be reduced to acceptable levels?

3. What are the pros and cons of the Green Revolution as a means of increasing South Asia's food supplies? What is the outlook for the next decade?

4. Discuss the conflict between wildlife protection and rural villages in India by evaluating the tension between preserving habitat and the needs of the rural poor.

5. What are the drawbacks and benefits of using English as a national language in India? Might it help or hinder unity? Would this increase or decrease India's links to the contemporary world?

6. Choose one of the areas of geopolitical tension (Kashmir, Punjab, Sri Lanka, etc.) and, after becoming better acquainted with the complex issues that underlie this conflict, evaluate

the different proposals currently offered for solving (or at least ameliorating) the problem.

7. As a geographer, you work for an international arms reduction agency that is working to reduce tensions that could lead to nuclear war between Pakistan and India. What would you suggest?

8. From a geographical point of view, what is the best course of action for near-term future economic development in Pakistan, India, and Bangladesh?

9. Acquaint yourself with the environmental, social, and economic implications of Nepal's open-door policy toward trekking and other forms of tourism. Do the benefits seem to outweigh the costs?

10. Is the state of Kerala a good model for economic and social development in other parts of India? Why or why not?

Regional Novels and Films

Novels

Vikram Chandra, *Sacred Games* (2006, HarperCollins)

Anita Desai, *Fasting, Feasting* (1999, Houghton Mifflin)

E. M. Forster, *A Passage to India* (1924, Harcourt, Brace and Company)

Bharti Kirchner, *Darjeeling: A Novel* (2002, St. Martin's Press)

Arundhati Roy, *The God of Small Things* (1997, Random House)

Salman Rushdie, *Midnight's Children* (1981, Knopf)

Paul Scott, *The Raj Quartet* (1980, Morrow)

Vikram Seth, *A Suitable Boy* (1993, HarperCollins)

Bapsi Sidhwa, *Cracking India: A Novel* (1991, Milkweed)

Manil Suri, *The Death of Vishnu* (2001, Norton)

Thirty Umrigar, *Bombay Time* (2001, Picador)

Films

August Sun (Sri Lanka, 2003)

Bandit Queen (1994, India)

City of Joy (1992, UK)

Dasavathaaram (2008, India)

Earth (1998, India)

East Is East (1999, UK)

Matir Moina (2002, Bangladesh)

Monsoon Wedding (2001, India)

Saalam Bombay (1988, India)

A Thousand Dreams Such As These (2003, India)

Travellers and Magicians (2003, Australia/Bhutan)

Bibliography

Bose, Sugata, and Jalal, Ayesha. 2002. *Modern South Asia: History, Culture, and Political Economy.* Delhi: Oxford University Press.

Eaton, Richard M. 1993. *The Rise of Islam and the Bengal Frontier, 1204–1760.* Berkeley: University of California Press.

Fox, Richard G., ed. 1977. *Realm and Region in Traditional India.* Durham, NC: Duke University Program in Comparative Studies on Southern Asia.

Hussain, Zahid. 2007. *Frontline Pakistan: The Struggle with Militant Islam.* New York: Columbia University Press.

Guha, Ramachandra. 2008. *India After Gandhi: The History of the World's Largest Democracy.* New York: Harper Perennial.

Schwartzberg, Joseph E. 1992. *A Historical Atlas of South Asia.* Oxford, UK: Oxford University Press.

Spate, O. H. K., and Learmonth, A. T. A. 1967. *India and Pakistan: A General and Regional Geography.* London: Methuen.

Steven, Stanley F. 1993. *Claiming the High Ground: Sherpas, Subsistence, and Environmental Change in the Highest Himalaya.* Berkeley: University of California Press.

Wolpert, Stanley. 1991. *India.* Berkeley: University of California Press.

Zurick, David, and Karan, P. P. 1999. *Himalaya: Life on the Edge of the World.* Baltimore: Johns Hopkins University Press.

 Mastering Geography

 MapMaster™

Log in to www.masteringgeography.com for MapMaster™ interactive maps, geography videos, RSS feeds, flashcards, web links, an eText version of *Diversity Amid Globalization,* and self-study quizzes to enhance your study of South Asia.

MapMaster™ presents 13 Place Name and 13 Layered Thematic interactive maps to help students practice and master their geographic literacy, spatial reasoning, and critical thinking skills.

13
Southeast Asia

The cascades and rapids of the Khone Falls area on the Mekong in Laos near the Cambodian border are noted for their natural beauty and their abundance of fish and other wildlife species. The fall would be inundated by the proposed Don Sahong Dam in southern Laos, which would stop the movement of fish species that migrate between the lower and middle sections of the Mekong River during the dry season.

DIVERSITY AMID GLOBALIZATION

Southeast Asia has been a key player in global commerce for hundreds of years. It has long attracted migrants from other parts of the world, and has been receptive to foreign cultural influences. In the late 20th century, the Southeast Asia was transformed from a region of Cold War geopolitical struggle to a center of economic globalization. Today Southeast Asian leaders are trying to cope with globalization on their own terms, working to create a more economically and politically united world region.

ENVIRONMENTAL GEOGRAPHY
Southeast Asia's rain forests are vital centers of biological diversity, but they are rapidly diminishing due to commercial logging and agricultural expansion.

POPULATION AND SETTLEMENT
Southeast Asia has a particularly uneven pattern of population distribution, with some areas experiencing serious crowding while others are noted for their sparse settlement.

CULTURAL COHERENCE AND DIVERSITY
Culturally, Southeast Asia is characterized by much more diversity than coherence, hosting significant areas of Muslim, Buddhist, and Christian religions, as well as a vast number of languages.

GEOPOLITICAL FRAMEWORK
Southeast Asia is one of the most geopolitically unified regions of the world, with all but one of its countries belonging to the Association of Southeast Asian Nations (ASEAN).

ECONOMIC AND SOCIAL DEVELOPMENT
Southeast Asia as a whole contains some of the world's most globalized and advanced economies and some of the most isolated and impoverished; it has also experienced marked periods of boom and bust in recent decades.

SOUTHEAST ASIA
Political & Physical Map

⬟● Metropolitan areas more than 20 million
⊛● Metropolitan areas 10–20 million
⊛● Metropolitan areas 5–10 million
⊛• Metropolitan areas 1–5 million
⊛◦ Selected smaller metropolitan areas
⌐ Plate boundaries

Southeast Asia (Figure 13.1) consists of 11 countries that vary widely in spatial extent, population, cultural attributes, and levels of economic and social development. Geographically, the region is commonly divided into an Asian mainland zone and the islands, or the insular realm. The mainland includes Burma (called *Myanmar* by the current government), Thailand, Cambodia, Laos, and Vietnam. Insular Southeast Asia includes the sizable countries of Indonesia, the Philippines, and Malaysia, as well as the small countries of Singapore, Brunei, and East Timor. Although classified as part of the insular realm because of its cultural and historical background, Malaysia actually splits the difference between mainland and islands. Part of its national territory is on the mainland's Malay Peninsula and part is on the large island of Borneo (also known as Kalimantan), some 300 miles (480 kilometers) distant. Borneo also includes the Muslim sultanate of Brunei, a small but oil-rich island country of 400,000 people covering an area slightly larger than Rhode Island. Singapore is essentially a city-state, occupying a small island just to the south of the Malay Peninsula.

Southeast Asia occupies an important place in discussions of globalization. It includes some of the world's most globally networked countries, such as Singapore, as well as some of the countries most resistant to worldwide economic and cultural forces, most notably Burma (Myanmar). Debates about the benefits and drawbacks of economic globalization have often focused on Southeast Asia. Although human well-being has increased across most of the region, the sweatshops associated with low-cost global production are criticized for their low wages and harsh working conditions. Owing to its high levels of economic integration, Southeast Asia is also highly vulnerable to fluctuations in the global economy.

Southeast Asia's involvement with the larger world is not new. Chinese and especially Indian influences date back many centuries. Later, commercial ties with the Middle East opened the doors to Islam, and today Indonesia is the world's most populous country with a Muslim majority. More recently came the heavy imprint of Western colonialism, as Britain, France, the Netherlands, and the United States administered large Southeast Asian colonies. During this period, national territories were rearranged, populations relocated, and new cities built to serve trade and military needs.

Southeast Asia's resources and its strategic location made it a major battlefield during World War II. Yet long after the end of this global conflict in 1945, war continued to be waged in the region. Resistance to imperialism mounted, and after the colonial regimes were replaced by newly independent countries, Southeast Asia became a zone of contention between the world powers and their different philosophical systems. In Vietnam, Laos, and Cambodia, communist forces, supported by China and the Soviet Union, struggled for control of local territory and people. Opposing this movement were the United States and its allies, concerned that communism would rapidly spread throughout Southeast Asia.

Ironically, while communist forces did prevail in Vietnam, Laos, and Cambodia, these countries subsequently opened their economies to global capitalism. With the end of the Cold War, competing political philosophies have taken a back seat to issues of economic integration. Geopolitically, the

ELEVATION IN METERS

- 4000+
- 2000–4000
- 500–2000
- 200–500
- 0–200
- Below sea level

Sea Level

PHILIPPINE PLATE

PACIFIC PLATE

| 0 | 250 | 500 Miles |
| 0 | 250 | 500 Kilometers |

PACIFIC OCEAN

135°E

0°

Sorong

INDONESIA

Papua

PAPUA NEW GUINEA

135°E

AUSTRALIA

Figure 13.1 Southeast Asia This region includes the large peninsula in the southeastern corner of Asia as well as a vast number of islands scattered to the south and east. It is conventionally divided into two subregions: mainland Southeast Asia, which includes Burma (Myanmar), Thailand, Laos, Cambodia, and Vietnam, and insular (or island) Southeast Asia, which includes Indonesia, the Philippines, Malaysia, Brunei, Singapore, and East Timor. Malaysia includes the tip of the mainland peninsula and most of the northern part of the island of Borneo (Kalimantan).

Association of Southeast Asian Nations (ASEAN), which includes 10 of the region's 11 countries, has brought a new level of regional cooperation.

ENVIRONMENTAL GEOGRAPHY: A Once-Forested Region

The mountainous area along the border between northern Thailand and Burma (Myanmar) is a rugged place. Slopes are steep and thickly wooded; rainfall is often torrential; leeches abound; and strains of medicine-resistant malaria are prevalent. These uplands are home to one of the most distinctive Southeast Asian ethnic groups: the Karen, a people numbering roughly 7 million. Unfortunately, the story of the Karen and their homeland in eastern Burma (Myanmar) is not a happy one. The Burmese army has overrun much of their territory, forcing many of the Karen into squalid refugee camps in Thailand. Furthermore, the Karen's loss of land has been accompanied by the logging of the teak forests of upland Burma (Myanmar). In the saga of the Karen, we can see the tragic meshing of cultural, political, economic, and environmental forces.

The Tragedy of the Karen

The Karen, like other tribal peoples of the upland areas of Burma (Myanmar), were never fully incorporated into the Burmese kingdom, which long ruled the lowlands of the country. With the imposition of British colonial rule in the 1800s, however, the Karen territory became part of Burma. Protestant missionaries educated many Karen and converted over 30 percent of them to Christianity. A number of Karen Christians obtained positions in Burma's colonial government. The Burmans of the lowlands, a strongly Buddhist people, resented this deeply, for they had long viewed the Karen as culturally inferior (according to conventional but confusing terminology, the term *Burmese* refers to all of the inhabitants of Burma [Myanmar], whereas *Burmans* refers only to

the country's dominant, Burmese-speaking ethnic group). After independence, the Karen lost their favored position and began to resent Burman cultural and economic domination.

The Karen were soon in open rebellion, building a semi-independent state of their own. They supported their struggle by smuggling goods between Thailand and Burma (Myanmar) and by mining the gemstones of their territory. Because Burma (Myanmar) had one of the world's most protected economies, with high tariffs and governmental controls inhibiting commerce, smuggling was an especially profitable occupation. Some estimates in the 1980s ranked the Karen economy as almost as large as the official Burmese economy.

The Burmese army, however, began to make headway against the rebels in the early 1990s, and by the end of the decade had overrun most of the Karen territory. Although some Karen continue to fight, as a whole they are demoralized and divided. Crucial to Burma's success was an agreement made with Thailand in which the Thai government agreed to prevent Karen soldiers from finding sanctuary on its side of the border, reportedly in exchange for access by Thai timber interests to Burma's teak forests. More than 200,000 Karen people were driven from their homes by the Burmese military between 1994 and 2004 (Figure 13.2). In early 2010, as the Burmese government geared up for national elections, Karen activists living abroad began to press the United Nations to conduct an inquiry on human rights abuses by Burma's armed forces.

Thailand's interests in Burma's forests stems from its own environmental problems. Thailand was once a major exporter of teak and other tropical hardwoods, but by the 1990s the country had been largely deforested. The Thai government responded by banning commercial logging. The only way Thai logging firms could stay in business was to move into the extensive forests of Burma (Myanmar), Laos, and Cambodia, countries that had previously been relatively isolated from the world economy, and therefore little touched by commercial logging. The price of admission in the case of Burma (Myanmar) was for Thailand to crack down on Karen guerrillas on its side of the border.

Figure 13.2 Karen Refugee Camp Many Karen refugees from Burma (Myanmar) still languish in refugee camps in Thailand. Shown here is Tham Hin camp, located 81 miles (130 km) west of Bangkok. The camp is very crowded, but it does have adequate health and education facilities.

The Deforestation of Southeast Asia

While the story of the Karen and Burma's teak forests is unique, deforestation and related environmental problems are major issues throughout most of Southeast Asia (Figure 13.3). Globalization has had a particularly profound effect on the Southeast Asian environment. Export-oriented logging companies have reached deep into the region's forests, cutting trees, damaging watersheds, and reducing biodiversity.

Although colonial powers cut Southeast Asian forests for tropical hardwoods and naval supplies, and indigenous peoples have long cleared small areas of forest for agricultural

Mountains of northern Southeast Asia. *Extensive forests are still found in the mountainous regions of Burma and Laos. These are increasingly threatened, however, by commercial logging and, to a lesser extent, by swidden cultivation.*

Tropical forest
Forest destroyed
Coastal pollution
Poor urban air quality

Kalimantan. *Severe deforestation from commercial logging. After forests are cut, migrants from other Indonesian islands settle on small farming plots. However, soil depletion is a major problem, resulting in many abandoned farms and further environmental deterioration. Meanwhile, forest and field burning contribute to regional smoke pollution.*

Java. *Forests were cleared in most areas decades ago for rice cultivation and plantation crops. Population pressure and overfarming have resulted in serious degradation in many areas.*

Figure 13.3 Environmental Issues in Southeast Asia Southeast Asia was once one of the most heavily forested regions of the world. Most of the tropical forests of Thailand, the Philippines, peninsular Malaysia, Sumatra, and Java, however, have been destroyed by a combination of commercial logging and agricultural settlement. The forests of Borneo (Kalimantan), Burma (Myanmar), Laos, and Vietnam, moreover, are now being rapidly cleared. Water and urban air pollution, as well as soil erosion, are also widespread in Southeast Asia.

use, rampant deforestation came only in the late 1900s with large-scale international commercial logging (Figure 13.4). This activity has largely been driven by the developed world's appetite for wood products such as plywood and paper pulp. Increasingly, China is playing a major role as well. In 2008, it was estimated that over half of forestry exports from Burma and Indonesia went to China.

Although several Southeast Asian countries have been transforming forests into farmlands in order to increase food production and relieve population pressure in their more densely settled areas, agriculture and population growth are not the only cause of deforestation. Most forests are cut so that the wood products can be exported to other parts of the world. Subsequently, some of the logged-off lands are re-planted (often with fast-growing, "weedy" tree species), while others are opened for agricultural settlement. In Malaysia and Indonesia, vast areas of former rain forest have been planted in African oil palms, which yield large quantities of edible oil.

Figure 13.4 Commercial Logging Southeast Asia has long been the world's most important supplier of tropical hardwoods. The logging process has destroyed most of the tropical forests of the Philippines and Thailand, as well as on the Indonesian islands of Java and Sumatra.

Local Patterns of Deforestation Malaysia has long been a leading exporter of tropical hardwoods. Most of the primary forests in western (or peninsular) have already been cut, which has resulted in an acceleration of logging in the states of Sarawak and Sabah on the island of Borneo. In these areas, the granting of forestry concessions to Malaysian and foreign firms has harmed local tribal people by disrupting their traditional resource base. Although Malaysia's conservation policies look good on paper, they are often not enforced. As a result, the World Bank estimates that logging is occurring at several times the sustainable rate.

Indonesia, the largest country in Southeast Asia, has fully two-thirds of the region's forest area, including about 10 percent of the world's true tropical rain forests. Its forest coverage, however, is deeply threatened; between 1990 and 2005, Indonesia lost an estimated 69 million acres (28 million hectares) of forest. Most of Sumatra's primary forests are gone, and those of Borneo (Kalimantan) are rapidly diminishing. Indonesia's last forestry frontier is on the island of New Guinea. But Indonesia, which is still covered in 119 million acres (48 million hectares) of primary forests, is fortunate in comparison to the Philippines, which has lost most of its original forests (see "Geographic Tools: Statistical Comparisons and the Assessment of Philippine Deforestation").

Thailand cut more than 50 percent of its forests between 1960 and 1980. Damage to the landscape was severe; flooding increased in lowland areas, and erosion on hillslopes led to the accumulation of silt in irrigation works and hydroelectric facilities As a result, a series of logging bans in the 1990s severely restricted commercial forestry. Many of Thailand's cutover lands are being reforested with fast-growing Australian eucalyptus trees, a nonnative species that cannot support local wildlife. As the forests of Thailand disappeared, mainland Southeast Asia's logging frontier is moved into Burma (Myanmar), Vietnam, Laos, and Cambodia. A 2005 report by the United Nations Food and Agriculture Organization found that Vietnam and Cambodia had the world's second and third fastest rates of primary deforestation, trailing only Nigeria.

In many parts of Southeast Asia, logged-over lands and other degraded areas are gradually returning to forest coverage. As a result, some experts think that Vietnam's total forest area is actually increasing. Indonesia and other Southeast Asian countries also support reforestation projects, which often try to recruit local people to nurture tree growth. The resulting secondary forests are not nearly as biologically rich as primary forests, but over time their biodiversity does increase.

Throughout the coastal areas of Southeast Asia, a more specific problem is the destruction of the mangrove forests that thrive in shallow and silty marine areas. Often mangrove forests are burned for charcoal, but many are converted to fish and shrimp ponds as well as rice fields and oil palm plantations. As mangrove forests serve as nurseries for many fish species, their destruction threatens to undercut a number of important Southeast Asian fisheries. Mangrove

GEOGRAPHIC TOOLS   Statistical Comparisons and the Assessment of Philippine Deforestation

The Philippines is one of the most thoroughly deforested countries of Southeast Asia. Forest coverage, which was roughly 90 percent at the time of the Spanish conquest in the sixteenth century, is less than 25 percent today (Figure 13.1.1). The remaining forests, most experts agree, are rapidly retreating and may disappear entirely.

Discussions of Philippine deforestation often are supported by precise statistics showing the steady decline of forest area. Whether such statistics are accurate, however, is a different matter. Geographer David Kummer has conducted research on national-level deforestation data in the Philippines by examining how the data were derived, scrutinizing the methodologies used, and comparing the results. Kummer also traveled widely in the Philippines to confer with local experts and to inspect ongoing forestry practices. Through such work he demonstrates that we actually know surprisingly little about Philippine forest coverage. The numbers that are so confidently used by scholars, government agencies, and environmental activists generally turn out to be little better than educated guesswork.

There are several reasons for the poor quality of information on Philippine deforestation. Although we often assume that satellite images give accurate representations of land-use coverage and change, Kummer shows that this simply is not the case. Satellite images are expensive and often hard to obtain, but more importantly they can be difficult to interpret. Cloud coverage, image overlap, shadows in steep areas, and unclear classification categories all create uncertainty. As a result, ground surveys by foresters often result in more accurate data. In the Philippines, much of the survey work done on forests over the past half century has been lost or destroyed. Compounding the problem is the fact that the Philippine government seems to have misstated the extent of deforestation between 1950 and 1987 in order to encourage unregulated logging by politically well-connected firms.

A 2004 government press release indicates that "forest cover" has actually increased since the 1980s. However, the data on which this statement is based may not be reliable, and satellite images remain unverified by on-the-ground investigations. More troubling is the fact that this new survey employs land-cover categories different from those in previous work, making it impossible to evaluate the changes in the Philippines' primary forests—some of the most biologically diverse ecosystems in the world.

Taken as a whole, Kummer's available evidence indicates that primary tropical forests continue to decline as a result of both legal and illegal logging. Poor-quality secondary forests, however, seem to be increasing due to the abandonment of marginal farmland. Biologically impoverished "artificial forests" also are increasing as a result of both governmental reforestation efforts and the planting of fuelwood groves by small-scale farmers. Reforestation with a handful of nonnative, fast-growing tree species has now become a potential threat to biodiversity.

Kummer's work shows that, in poorer parts of the world and especially in countries with high levels of political corruption, official statistics may be questionable. The methods used for this type of statistical evaluation have potential application to other world regions, and to other environmental practices with global implications.

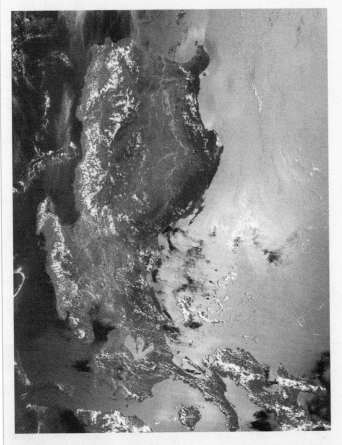

Figure 13.1.1 Luzon, Philippines Part of northeastern Luzon in the Philippines, which appears dark green on this satellite image, is still thickly forested, but most of the rest of the island has experienced extensive deforestation.

forests also protect coastal areas from storm surges associated with the tropical cyclones that often strike the region.

Protected Areas Despite rampant deforestation, Indonesia, like most other Southeast Asian countries, has created a number of large national parks and other protected areas. Kutai National Park in the province of East Kalimantan, for example, covers more than 741,000 acres (300,000 hectares). Southeast Asian rain forests are among the most biologically diverse areas on the planet, containing a large number of species that are found nowhere else. Conservation officials hope that protected areas will allow animals such as the orangutan, which now lives only in a small portion of northern Sumatra and a somewhat larger area of Borneo (Kalimantan), a chance to survive in the wild. Others are less optimistic, noting that Southeast Asian national parks often exist only on paper, receiving little real protection from loggers or immigrant farmers. Much of Kutai National Park, for example, has been logged and burned. According to some sources, over 80 percent of logging activities in Indonesia are illegal in some manner.

Fires, Smoke, and Air Pollution

Logging operations typically leave large quantities of wood (small trees, broken logs, roots, branches, and so on) on the ground. Exposed to the sun, this remaining "slash" becomes highly flammable. Indeed, it is often burned on purpose in order to clear the ground for agriculture or tree replanting. Commercial forest cutting is responsible for most burning, even though the large logging firms commonly blame small-scale farmers. Wildfires also are common in other Southeast Asian habitats. The most thoroughly deforested areas are often covered by rough grasses. Such grasslands often are purposely burned every year so that cattle can graze on the tender shoots that emerge after a fire passes through. Grassland fires, in turn, prevent forest regeneration, further undercutting the region's biodiversity. In drained wetland areas, organic peat soils often burn, causing extensive air pollution (Figure 13.5).

In the late 1990s, wildfires associated with both logging practices and a severe drought raged so intensely across much of insular Southeast Asia that the region suffered from disastrous air pollution. During that period, a commercial airliner crashed because of poor visibility; countless road accidents resulted; two ferries collided in smoke-laden conditions; and hundreds of thousands of people were admitted to hospitals with life-threatening respiratory problems. The smoke crisis of the late 1990s led several Southeast Asian countries to devote more attention to air quality. Deforesta-

tion continues, however, and the fire threat remains. In March 2010, NASA's remote-sensing Aqua satellite noted extremely smoky conditions over northern Thailand, Burma (Myanmar), Laos, and Vietnam.

Efforts to protect Southeast Asia's air quality, moreover, are also hampered by continuing industrial development along with a major increase in vehicular traffic. Southeast Asia's large metropolitan areas have extremely unhealthy levels of pollution, both of air and water. Several cities, including Bangkok and Manila, have built rail-based public transportation systems in order to reduce traffic and vehicular emissions. Bangkok in particular has substantially reduced its levels of ozone and sulfur dioxide, but particulate matter remains at unhealthy levels.

Patterns of Physical Geography

To understand why forestry issues are so important in Southeast Asia, it is necessary to examine its physical geography. The southern portion of the region—insular Southeast Asia—is one of the world's three main zones of tropical rain forest. The northern part of the region—mainland Southeast Asia—is located in the tropical wet-and-dry zone that is noted for particularly valuable timber species, such as teak. Distinguishing between the mainland and the islands is thus one of the keys for understanding the geography of Southeast Asia.

Mainland Environments Mainland Southeast Asia is an area of rugged uplands interspersed with broad lowlands and deltas associated with large rivers. The region's northern boundary lies in a cluster of mountains connected to the highlands of eastern Tibet and south-central China. In the far north of Burma (Myanmar), peaks reach 18,000 feet (5,500 meters). From this point, a series of mountain ranges

Figure 13.5 Burning Peatlands The soil of most wetland areas in Southeast Asia is composed largely of peat, an organic substance that can burn when dry. Draining for agricultural expansion, as well as drought, often results in extensive peat fires. In this photograph, a C130 airplane is dropping water on burning peat in Lampung, Sumatra.

Figure 13.6 Delta Landscape The Mekong Delta in southern Vietnam encompasses a complex maze of waterways. Extensive tracts of fertile farmland can be found between the canals and river channels. The waterways are used for transportation, and provide large quantities of fish and other aquatic resources. This photo shows typical Vietnamese boats in a delta backwater.

radiates out, extending through western Burma (Myanmar), along the Burma–Thailand border, and through Laos into southern Vietnam.

Several large rivers flow southward out of Tibet into mainland Southeast Asia. The longest is the Mekong, which flows through Laos and Thailand, then across Cambodia before entering the South China Sea through an extensive delta in southern Vietnam (Figure 13.6). Second longest is the Irrawaddy, which flows through Burma's central plain before reaching the Bay of Bengal. This river also has a large delta. Two smaller rivers are equally significant: the Red River, which forms a sizable and heavily settled delta in northern Vietnam, and the Chao Phraya, which has created the fertile alluvial plain of central Thailand.

The centermost area of mainland Southeast Asia is Thailand's Khorat Plateau, which is neither a rugged upland nor a fertile river valley. This low, sandstone plateau averages about 500 feet (175 meters) in height and is noted for its thin soils. Water shortages and periodic droughts also plague the area.

Monsoon Climates Mainland Southeast Asia is affected by the seasonally shifting winds known as the monsoon. The climate is characterized by a distinct hot and rainy season from May to October (Figure 13.7). This is followed by dry but still generally warm conditions from November to April. Only the central highlands of Vietnam and a few coastal areas receive significant rainfall during this period. In the far north, the winter months bring mild and sometimes rather cool weather.

Two tropical climate regions are found in mainland Southeast Asia. While both are affected by the monsoon, they differ in the total amount of precipitation. Along the coasts and in the highlands, the tropical monsoon (Am) climate dominates. Rainfall totals for this climate usually register more than 100 inches (254 centimeters) each year. The greater portion of mainland Southeast Asia falls into the tropical savanna (Aw) climate type. Here annual rainfall totals are about half as much. In most cases, this can be explained by interior locations sheltered from the oceanic source of moisture by mountain ranges. A good portion of Thailand receives less than 50 inches (127 centimeters) of annual rainfall. Much of Burma's central Irrawaddy Valley is almost semiarid, with rainfall totals below 30 inches (76 centimeters). Forests in these areas are especially vulnerable, being easily converted by fire and agriculture into rough landscapes of brush and grass.

Insular Environments The signal feature of insular Southeast Asia is its island environment. Indonesia alone is said to contain more than 13,000 islands, while the Philippines supposedly contains 7,000. Borneo (Kalimantan) and Sumatra are the third and sixth largest islands in the world, respectively, while many thousands of others are little more than specks of land rising at low tide from a shallow sea.

Indonesia is dominated by the four great landmasses of Sumatra, Borneo, Java, and the oddly shaped Sulawesi. This island nation also includes the western half of New Guinea and the Lesser Sunda Islands, which extend to the east of Java. A prominent mountain spine runs through these islands as a result of tectonic forces. The two largest and most important islands of the Philippines are Luzon (about the size of Ohio) in the north and Mindanao (the size of South Carolina) in the south. Sandwiched between them are the Visayan Islands, which number roughly a dozen.

Closely related to this impressive collection of islands is the world's largest expanse of shallow seas. These waters cover the **Sunda Shelf**, which is an extension of the continental shelf stretching from the mainland through the Java Sea between Java and Borneo. Here waters are generally less than 200 feet (70 meters) deep. Some local peoples have adopted lifestyles that rely on the rich marine life of this region, essentially living on their boats and setting foot on land only as necessary.

Insular Southeast Asia is less geologically stable than the mainland. Four of Earth's tectonic plates converge here: the Pacific, the Philippine, the Indo-Australian, and the Eurasian. As a result of this tectonic structure, earthquakes occur frequently. Large, often explosive volcanoes are another consequent feature of the insular Southeast Asian landscape. A string of active volcanoes extends the length of eastern Sumatra across Java and into the Lesser Sunda Islands. Volcanic eruptions and earthquakes occasionally result in **tsunamis**, which can devastate coastal regions. A massive earthquake in northern Sumatra on December 26, 2004, for example, caused roughly 100,000 deaths in Indonesia alone. Other geological hazards also confront the region. In late 2006,

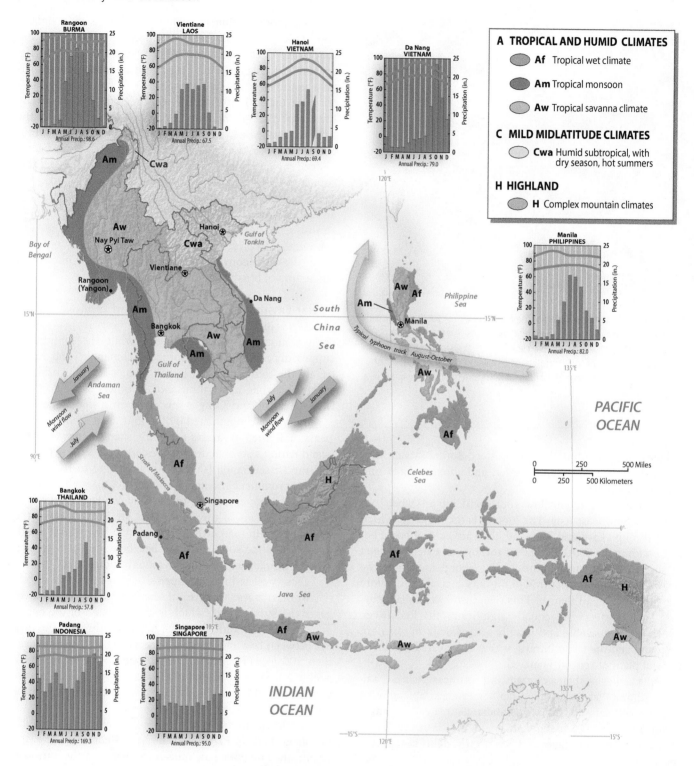

Figure 13.7 Climate Map of Southeast Asia Most of insular Southeast Asia is characterized by the constantly hot and humid climates of the equatorial zone. Mainland Southeast Asia, on the other hand, has the seasonally wet and dry climates of the tropical monsoon and tropical savanna types. Only in the far north are subtropical climates, with relatively cool winters, encountered. The northern half of the region is strongly influenced by the seasonally shifting monsoon winds. Northeastern Southeast Asia—and especially the Philippines—often experiences typhoons from August to October.

13,000 Indonesians had to be evacuated away from a new mud volcano near the city of Surabaya. Roughly 2,500 cubic meters of hot and toxic mud oozes out of the ground every-day, and it is expected to continue flowing for the next 30 years (Figure 13.8).

Island Climates The climates of insular Southeast Asia are more varied than those of the mainland. Most of insular Southeast Asia, unlike the mainland, receives rain during the Northern Hemisphere's winter because the monsoon winds of this season cross large areas of warm equatorial ocean, absorbing moisture. On Sumatra and Java, where north winds blow between November and March, heavy rains occur on the northern side of these east–west-running islands. But during the May–September period, the heaviest rains are found on the southern flanks of these same islands because of the southwesterly winds associated with the Asian summer monsoon.

The climates of Indonesia, Singapore, Malaysia, and Brunei are heavily influenced by their equatorial location, which reduces seasonality. Temperatures remain elevated throughout the year, with little variation. The average high temperature in Singapore, for example, varies between 85°F (29.5°C) in December to 89°F (31.7°C) in April. The equatorial influence also brings high and evenly distributed rainfall to much of the insular realm. As a result, large areas of island Southeast Asia are placed into the tropical rain forest (Af) climate category (see Figure 13.7). The southeastern islands of Indonesia, however, experience a distinct dry season from May to October.

The southern part of the Philippines also has an equatorial climate, but most the country experiences a distinct dry period from December to April. The northern and central Philippines are frequently hit by tropical cyclones, or **typhoons**, especially from August to October. Each year several typhoons strike the Philippines with heavy damage through flooding and landslides. In September 2009, most of central Luzon was declared a "calamity area" after being battered by Typhoon Ketsana, which took almost 500 lives and caused damages of more than $1 billion.

Although typhoons are most pronounced in the Philippines, they do hit mainland Southeast Asia as well. In early May 2008, southern Burma (Myanmar) was slammed by Cyclone Nargis, the worst storm in recent Southeast Asian history. Nargis caused over 150,000 deaths, left as many as 1 million people homeless, and resulted in roughly $10 billion in damages (Figure 13.9). Casualty rates were particularly high because Burma's military government reacted slowly to the crisis, restricting the activities of international aid agencies.

Global Warming in Southeast Asia

Most of Southeast Asia's people live in coastal and delta environments, making the region particularly vulnerable to the rise in sea level associated with global warming. Periodic flooding is already a major problem in many of the regions' low-lying cities. Southeast Asian farmland is also concentrated in delta environments, and thus could suffer from saltwater intrusion and heightened storm surges. A 2009 study by the Asia Development Bank found that Indonesia, Thailand, Vietnam, and the Philippines could suffer climate-change damages of more than twice the global average by the end of the century. Some studies claim that the region's rice harvest could decline by as much as 50 percent by 2100. Sea level rise, moreover, could inundate as many as 2,000 islands in Indonesia alone by the middle of the century.

Figure 13.8 Mud Volcano in Indonesia Villages and farmland in east Java have been devastated by a mud volcano that continues to pour out hot, toxic sludge. The volcano itself was set off when a gas exploration drilling project tapped into a vent of extremely hot mud.

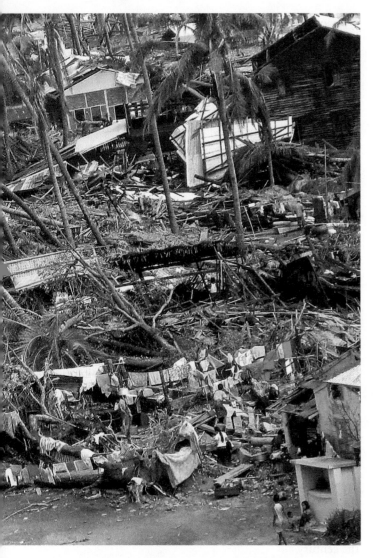

Figure 13.9 Cyclone Nargis Cyclone Nargis slammed into southern Burma (Myanmar) in early May 2008, resulting in the country's worst natural disaster in recorded history. This photograph shows devastated families waiting for relief near their destroyed homes on Haing Guy Island in southwestern Burma.

Changes in precipitation across Southeast Asia brought about by global warming remain highly uncertain. Many experts foresee an intensification of the monsoon pattern, which could bring increased rainfall to much of the mainland. While enhanced precipitation would likely result in more destructive floods, it could bring some agricultural benefits to dry areas such as Burma's central Irrawaddy Valley. Complicating this scenario, however, is the prediction that climate change could intensify the El Niño effect, which would result in more extreme droughts. Some observers think that the prolonged drought that Indonesia experienced in the late 1990s was a harbinger of future conditions.

All Southeast Asian countries have ratified the 1997 Kyoto Accord. But since they are officially classified as developing countries—even wealthy Singapore—none are obligated to reduce their emissions of greenhouse gases. Still, Southeast Asia's overall emissions from conventional sources remain low by global standards. Indonesia, Malaysia, and Vietnam, however, are planning to increase their reliance on coal-fired electricity generation, which would greatly increase the region's emissions. In Thailand, local and international opposition has already led the government to reconsider its coal-based expansion plans. One possible alternative is hydropower, which has significant potential especially in mountainous Laos. But dam building results in its own ecological problems, and is opposed by most environmental groups.

When greenhouse gas emissions associated with deforestation are factored in, Southeast Asia's role in global climate change becomes much larger than it appears at first glance. By some estimates, Indonesia is the world's third largest contributor to the problem, following only China and the United States. Vast quantities of carbon dioxide are released into the atmosphere when slash is burned, a routine practice in many areas. A greater problem, however, is the release of carbon from peat, the partially decayed organic matter that accumulates in perennially saturated soils. The wetlands of coastal Indonesia hold 60 percent of the world's tropical peat, containing roughly 50 billion tons of carbon. During drought periods, peat soils sometimes burn, releasing the stored carbon. More worrisome is the fact that both Indonesia and Malaysia are actively draining coastal wetlands to make room for agricultural expansion, a process that results in the gradual oxidation of the peat. Already some 40 percent of Southeast Asia's peatlands have been lost.

POPULATION AND SETTLEMENT: Densely Settled Lowlands amid Sparsely Settled Uplands

With fewer than 600 million inhabitants, Southeast Asia is not heavily populated by Asian standards. One of the reasons for this relatively low density is the extensive tracts of rugged mountains, which generally remain thinly inhabited. In contrast, relatively dense populations are found in the region's deltas, coastal areas, and zones of fertile volcanic soil (Figure 13.10). Many of the favored lowlands of Southeast Asia have experienced striking population growth over the past half century. Demographic growth and family planning have thus become increasingly important concerns through much of the region. Several countries, especially Singapore and Thailand, have seen rapid reductions in birthrates, but large families are still common in Cambodia and Laos.

Settlement and Agriculture

Much of Insular Southeast Asia has infertile soil, which is unable to support intensive agriculture and high rural population densities. The island rain forests, though lush and biologically rich, typically grow on a poor base. Plant nutrients are locked up in the vegetation itself, rather than being stored in the soil where they would easily benefit agricul-

Figure 13.10 Population Map of Southeast Asia In mainland Southeast Asia, population is concentrated in the valleys and deltas of the region's large rivers. In the intervening uplands, population density remains relatively low. In Indonesia, density is extremely high on Java, an island noted for its fertile soil and large cities. Some of Indonesia's outer islands, especially those of the east, remain lightly settled. Overall, population density is high in the Philippines, especially in central Luzon.

ture. The incessant rain of the equatorial zone also tends to wash nutrients out of the soil. Agriculture must be carefully adapted to this limited fertility by constant field rotation or the application of heavy amounts of fertilizer.

Some notable exceptions can be found to this generalization about soil fertility and settlement density in equatorial Southeast Asia. Unusually rich soils connected to volcanic activity are scattered through much of the region, particularly on the island of Java. Java, with more than 50 volcanoes, is blessed with highly productive agriculture that supports a large array of tropical crops and a very high population density. More than 124 million people live on the island—roughly half the total population of Indonesia—in an area smaller than the state of Iowa. Dense populations also are found in pockets of fertile alluvial soils along the coasts of insular Southeast Asia, where people have traditionally supplemented land-based farming with fishing and other commercial activities.

The demographic patterns in mainland Southeast Asia are less complicated than those of the island realm. In all the mainland countries, population is concentrated in the agriculturally intensive valleys and deltas of the large rivers (see Figure 13.10). The population core of Thailand, for example, clusters around the Chao Phraya River, just as Burma's is focused on the Irrawaddy. Vietnam has two distinct foci: the Red River Delta in the far north and the Mekong Delta in the far south. In contrast to these densely settled areas, the middle reaches of the Mekong River provide only limited lowland areas in Laos, which reduces its population potential. In Cambodia, the population historically is centered around Tonle Sap, a large lake with an unusual seasonal flow reversal. During the rainy summer months the lake receives water from the Mekong drainage, but during the drier winter months it contributes to the river's flow.

Agricultural practices and settlement forms vary widely across the complex environments of Southeast Asia. Generally speaking, however, three farming and settlement patterns are apparent.

Swidden in the Uplands   Also known as shifting cultivation or "slash-and-burn" agriculture, swidden is practiced throughout the uplands of both mainland and island Southeast Asia (Figure 13.11). In the **swidden** system, small plots of tropical forest or brush are periodically cut or "slashed" by hand. The fallen vegetation is then burned to transfer nutrients to the soil before subsistence crops are planted. Yields remain high for several years, then drop off dramatically as the soil nutrients are exhausted and insect pests and plant diseases multiply. These plots are abandoned after a few years and allowed to revert to woody vegetation. The cycle of cutting, burning, and planting is then moved to another small plot not far away—thus the term *shifting cultivation*. Villages generally control a large amount of territory so they can rotate their fields on a regular basis. After a period of 10 to 75 years, farmers must return to the original plot, which once again has accumulated nutrients in the dense vegetation.

Swidden is sustainable when population densities remain low and when upland people control enough territory. Today, however, the swidden system is increasingly threatened. It cannot easily support the increasing population that has re-

Figure 13.11 Swidden Agriculture In the uplands of Southeast Asia, swidden (or slash-and-burn) agriculture is widely practiced. When done by tribal peoples with low population densities, swidden is not environmentally harmful. When practiced by large numbers of immigrants from the lowlands, however, swidden can result in deforestation and extensive soil erosion.

sulted from relatively high birthrates and, in some cases, migration. With greater population density, the rotation period must be shortened, undercutting soil resources. The upland swidden system is also often undermined by commercial logging. Road building presents another threat. Vietnam, for example, is constructing a highway system through its mountainous spine, designed to aid economic development and more fully integrate its national economy. Partly as a result of this activity, lowlanders are streaming into the mountains, disrupting local ecosystems and indigenous societies.

When swidden can no longer support the local population, upland people sometimes adapt by switching to cash crops that will allow them to participate in the commercial economy. In the mountains of northern Southeast Asia, often called the **"Golden Triangle,"** one of the main cash crops is opium, grown by local farmers for the global drug trade. Burma (Myanmar) is the world's second largest opium producer, after Afghanistan. Recent drug eradication programs proved relatively successful, reducing the area of land devoted to opium production by 85 percent between 1998 and 2006. Some experts think, however, that opium growing began expanding again in 2007. Methamphetamine manufacturing has also emerged as a major problem in much of the Golden Triangle.

Plantation Agriculture With European colonization, Southeast Asia became a center of plantation agriculture, producing high-value specialty crops ranging from rice to rubber. Even in the 19th century, Southeast Asia was closely linked to a globalized economy through the plantation system. Forests were cleared and swamps drained to make room for these commercial farms; labor was supplied, often unwillingly, by indigenous people or by contract laborers brought in from India or China.

Plantations are still an important part of Southeast Asia's geography and economy. Most of the world's natural rubber, for example, is grown in Malaysia, Indonesia, and Thailand, while sugarcane has long been a major plantation crop in the Philippines and Indonesia. More recently, pineapple plantations have spread in both the Philippines and Thailand, which are now the world's leading exporters. Indonesia is the region's leading producer of tea (Figure 13.12). Malaysia has traditionally dominated the production of palm oil, but it has recently been surpassed by Indonesia. Coconut oil and **copra** (dried coconut meat) are widely produced in the Philippines, Indonesia, and elsewhere. In the early 2000s, Vietnam rapidly emerged as the world's second-largest coffee producer, its large harvests reducing global coffee prices.

Rice in the Lowlands The lowland basins and deltas of mainland Southeast Asia are largely devoted to intensive rice cultivation. Through most of Southeast Asia, rice is the pre-ferred staple food. Traditionally, rice was mainly cultivated on a subsistence basis by rural farmers. But as the number of wage laborers in Southeast Asia has grown as a result of economic development, so has the demand for commercial rice cultivation. Thailand is currently the world's largest rice exporter, with Vietnam occupying the number two position. In 2008, Thailand spearheaded the creation of OREC, the Organization of Rice Exporting Nations, which also includes Cambodia, Laos, Burma (Myanmar), and Vietnam. Across most of Southeast Asia, the use of agricultural chemicals and high-yield crop varieties, along with improved water control, have allowed rice production to keep pace with population growth. In 2010, however, an El Niño-linked drought reduced rice yields across most of the region.

In those areas without irrigation, yields remain relatively low. Rice growing on Thailand's Khorat Plateau, for example, depends largely on the uncertain rainfall, without the benefits of the more sophisticated water control methods. In some lowland districts lacking irrigation, dry-field crops, especially sweet potatoes and manioc, form the staple foods of people too poor to buy market rice on a regular basis. In some of the poorest parts of Southeast Asia, population growth has combined with economic stagnation to force larger numbers of people into such meager diets. Elsewhere, economic growth and declining birthrates have significantly reduced the burden of poverty.

Recent Demographic Change

Most Southeast Asian countries have seen a sharp decrease in birthrates over the past several decades. Because the region is not facing the same kind of population pressure as East or South Asia, a wide range of government population policies can be found. In countries with highly uneven population distribution, internal relocation away from densely populated areas to outlying districts is a common response.

Population Contrasts The Philippines, the second most populous country in Southeast Asia, has a relatively high growth rate (Table 13.1). When a popular democratic

Figure 13.12 Tea Harvesting in Indonesia Plantation crops, such as tea, are major sources of exports for several Southeast Asian countries. Coconut, rubber, oil palms, and coffee are other major cash crops. Many of these crops require large amounts of labor, particularly at harvest time.

TABLE 13.1   Population Indicators

Country	Population (millions) 2010	Population Density (per square kilometer)	Rate of Natural Increase (RNI)	Total Fertility Rate	Percent Urban	Percent <15	Percent <65	Net Migration (Rate per 1,000) 2005–10)[a]
Burma (Myanmar)	53.4	79	0.9	2.4	31	27	3	−2.0
Brunei	0.4	66	1.3	1.7	72	27	3	1.8
Cambodia	15.1	83	1.6	3.3	20	35	3	−0.1
East Timor	1.2	77	3.1	5.7	22	45	3	1.8
Indonesia	235.5	124	1.4	2.4	43	28	6	−0.6
Laos	6.4	27	2.1	3.5	27	39	4	−2.4
Malaysia	28.9	87	1.6	2.6	63	32	5	−1.0
Philippines	94.0	313	2.1	3.2	63	33	4	−2.0
Singapore	5.1	7,526	0.6	1.2	100	18	9	22.0
Thailand	68.1	133	0.6	1.8	31	22	7	0.9
Vietnam	88.9	268	1.2	2.1	28	25	8	−0.5

[a]Net Migration Rate from the United Nations, Population Division, World Population Prospects: The 2008 Revision Population Database.
Sources: Population Reference Bureau, World Population Data Sheet, 2010.

government replaced a dictatorship in the 1980s, the Philippine Roman Catholic Church pressured the new government to cut funding for family planning programs. As a result, many clinics that had dispensed family planning information were closed. Although high birthrates are not generally associated with Catholicism, the Church's outspoken stand on birth control seems to inhibit the dispersal of family planning information. Still, fertility rates have been declining. In 2010, moreover, the Philippine Secretary of Education came out in favor of teaching family planning in public schools.

Laos and Cambodia, countries of Buddhist religious tradition, also have relatively high fertility rates. Here the elevated birthrate is best explained by the countries' low level of economic and social development. Thailand, which shares cultural traditions with Laos yet is considerably more developed, demonstrates the other end of the spectrum. Here the TFR has dropped from 5.4 in 1970 to 1.8 currently, a figure that will soon bring population stability and then decline. But while economic growth may explain some of this decrease, it is also important to note that the Thai government has promoted family planning for both population and health reasons, including the relatively high incidence of AIDS in the country.

The city-state of Singapore stands out on the demographic charts with its particularly low fertility rate. Unless the deficit is offset by immigration or a dramatic turnabout in the birthrate, Singapore's population will soon begin to decline. The government is concerned about this situation and is actively promoting marriage and childbearing, particularly among the most highly educated segment of its population. As a result, Singaporeans can receive more than $10,000 in direct government subsidies for having a third or fourth child (Figure 13.13). Singapore also encouraged the immigration of highly skilled workers.

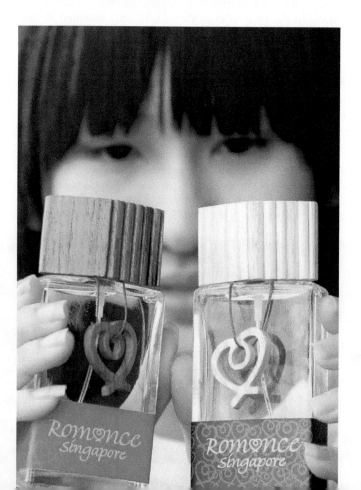

Figure 13.13 Pro-Reproduction Advertisement in Singapore
Due to its extremely low birthrate, the population of Singapore will probably begin to decline soon. Shown here are perfumes created by local students and launched in a government-backed "romance" campaign.

Figure 13.14 Indonesian Transmigration The distribution of population in Indonesia shows a marked imbalance: Java, along with the neighboring island of Madura, is one of the world's most densely settled places, whereas most of the country's other islands remain rather lightly populated. As a result, the Indonesian government has encouraged the resettlement of Javanese and Madurese people to the outer islands, often paying the costs of relocation. This transmigration scheme has resulted in a somewhat more balanced population distribution pattern, but has also caused substantial environmental degradation and intensified several ethnic conflicts.

Indonesia, with the region's largest population at 235 million, also has seen a dramatic decline in fertility in recent decades, with its fertility rate approaching the replacement level. As with Thailand, this drop in fertility seems to have resulted from a strong government family planning effort, coupled with improvements in education.

Growth and Migration Until recently, Indonesia had an official policy of **transmigration**, with the government helping people move from densely populated to lightly populated parts of the country (Figure 13.14). Primarily because of migration from Java and Madura, the population of the outer islands of Indonesia has grown rapidly since the

1970s. The province of East Kalimantan, for example, experienced an astronomical growth rate of 30 percent per year during the last two decades of the 1900s. As a result of this shift in population, many parts of Indonesia outside Java now have moderately high population densities, although many of the more remote districts remain lightly settled (Figure 13.15).

Figure 13.15 Migrant Settlement in Indonesia This sprawling transmigration site in western New Guinea is populated mostly by migrants from Java. Created in the early 1990s, it covers a large area that formerly supported tropical rain forest vegetation. The indigenous inhabitants of the region worry that such schemes will undermine their land rights and traditional subsistence patterns.

High social and environmental costs often accompany these relocation schemes. Javanese peasants, accustomed to working the highly fertile soils of their home island, often fail in their attempts to grow rice in the former rain forest of Borneo (Kalimantan). Field abandonment is common after repeated crop failures. In some areas, farmers have little choice but to adopt a semiswidden form of cultivation, moving to new sites once the old ones have been exhausted. The term **shifted cultivators** is sometimes used for such displaced rural migrants. Partly because of these problems, the Indonesian government restructured and substantially reduced its transmigration program in 2000. It is currently planning, however, a huge new agricultural project in the Merauke region of south-central New Guinea, which could entail the transfer of over half a million people to the area.

The government of the Philippines has also used internal migration to reduce population pressure in the core areas of the country. Beginning in the late 19th century, people began streaming out of central and northwestern central Luzon for the frontier zones. In the early 20th century, this settlement frontier still lay in Luzon; by the postwar years it had moved south to the island of Mindanao. Today, however, internal migration is less appealing, both because the population disparities between the islands have been reduced and

CITYSCAPES   Metro Manila, Primate City of the Philippines

With more than 10 million inhabitants, Manila is one of the world's largest urban areas. But, strictly speaking, Manila itself is a much smaller city, supporting fewer than 2 million inhabitants. The term *Manila* often refers to the urban entity more properly called *Metro Manila* (Figure 13.2.1). Metro Manila, consisting of Manila itself plus 16 other cities and towns, was formally constituted in 1975 as an administrative area, the Philippines' National Capital Region (NCR). Most forms of political power, however, remain decentralized among Metro Manila's constituent units, complicating policy initiatives and planning efforts. When a new mayor of Manila decided to crack down on prostitution in the 1990s, for example, most of the city's "go-go bars" simply relocated to Pasay City.

Metro Manila is economically as well as politically decentralized. Manila itself includes the old central business district, now somewhat decayed, as well as sizable slums, a congested "Chinatown" (Binondo) famous for its discount shopping, and several older, wealthy neighborhoods. It also contains the historic zone of Intramuros, the original fortified city of the Spanish colonial period (Figure 13.2.2). Although Manila was almost completely destroyed during World War II, many of Intramuros's buildings have been rebuilt, lending the area charm and historical significance.

Metro Manila's—and the Philippines'—commercial capital now is located in Makati, southeast of the old urban core. From a rural fringe zone in the 1940s, Makati has grown into a mature city of high-rise office buildings and hotels, shopping plazas, and gated communities that

Figure 13.2.1 Metro Manila The Philippines' National Capital Region (Metro Manila) consists of the city of Manila and a number of neighboring cities and suburbs, which together form a single metropolitan area. Such municipalities as Makati and Quezon City are of significance equal to Manila proper.

because of political instability in the south. The emphasis is now on international migration, resulting in a Filipino overseas population of roughly 8 million.

Population issues and policies thus vary greatly across Southeast Asia. Virtually every part of the region, however, has seen a rapid expansion of its urban population in recent decades.

Urban Settlement

Southeast Asia is a not heavily urbanized region. Even Thailand retains a rural flavor, which is somewhat unusual for a country that has experienced so much industrialization. Currently, however, the region's urban population is growing at 1.75 times the world average. As a result, Southeast Asia's urbanization rate is expected to increase from 45 percent in 2008 to 56.6 percent in 2030.

Several Southeast Asian countries have **primate cities**, single, large urban settlements that overshadow all others. Thailand's urban system, for example, is dominated by Bangkok, just as Manila far surpasses all other cities in the Philippines (see "Cityscapes: Metro Manila, Primate City of the Philippines"). Both have recently grown into megacities of more than 10 million residents. More than half of all city-dwellers in

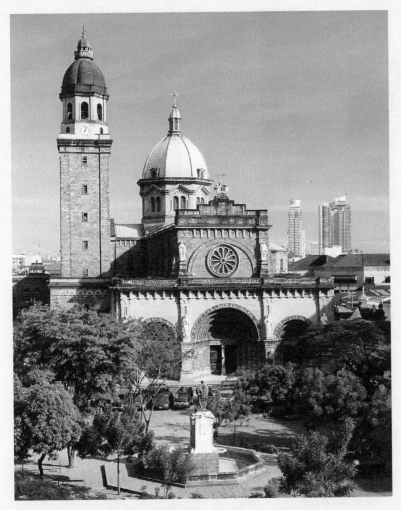

house the country's elite. More recently, Metro Manila has seen the rise of other areas that serve the wealthy, most notably Ortigas Center in neighboring Mandaluyong City. Particularly successful here is the SM Megamall, which opened in 1991. This gargantuan six-story enclosed mall contains 12 cinemas and an ice-skating rink, in addition to hundreds of stores and restaurants. SM Megamall attracts tens of thousands of visitors daily, some of whom come simply to experience the modern ambiance and enjoy the air conditioning.

Official government buildings of the Philippines are concentrated in Quezon City in northeast Metro Manila. Quezon City replaced Manila as the national capital between 1948 and 1976. This sprawling city of widely separated office buildings is also an educational center, supporting the country's two most highly regarded universities, the publicly run University of the Philippines (UP) and the Jesuit-run Ateneo de Manila University.

One of Metro Manila's main problems is an extreme shortage of decent housing. The rapid growth of the city has led to skyrocketing land values and rents, forcing roughly half of the city's residents to live in squatters' shacks. Some squatter settlements emerge almost overnight on vacant lots; others sprawl on for miles and have existed for decades. The inadequate infrastructure found in these communities is also characteristic of the rest of the city. Only an estimated 11 percent of Metro Manila's residences, for example, are connected to fully functioning sewer systems.

Figure 13.2.2 Intramuros Intramuros, the "city between the walls," was the original, fortified capital of the Spanish Philippines. It now is an important historic district.

Figure 13.16 Bangkok Bangkok saw the development of an impressive skyline during its boom years from the late 1970s through the late 1990s. Unfortunately, infrastructure did not keep pace with population and commercial growth, resulting in one of the most congested and polluted urban landscapes in the world.

Thailand live in the Bangkok metropolitan area (Figure 13.16). In both Manila and Bangkok, as with other large Southeast Asian cities, explosive growth has led to housing shortages, congestion, and pollution. In Manila, more than half of the city's population lives in squatter settlements, usually without basic water and electricity service. Both cities also suffer from a lack of parks and other public spaces, enhancing the appeal of massive shopping malls. Bangkok's Paragon Mall has recently emerged as a major urban focus, complete with a conference center and a concert hall.

Thailand, the Philippines, and Indonesia are all making efforts to encourage growth of secondary cities by decentralizing economic functions. The goal is to stabilize the population of the primate cities. In the case of the Philippines, the city of Cebu has emerged in recent years as a relatively dynamic economic center, leading to hopes that a more balanced urban system may be emerging.

Urban primacy is less pronounced in other Southeast Asian countries. Vietnam, for example, has two main cities, Ho Chi Minh City (formerly Saigon) in the south, with 6 million people, and the capital city of Hanoi in the north, with more than 3 million residents. Jakarta is the largest city in Indonesia, but the country has a host of other large and growing metropolitan areas, including Bandung and Surabaya. Rangoon (Yangon), until recently the capital city of Burma (Myanmar), has doubled its population in the last two decades to more than 5 million residents. In Cambodia, the capital of Phnom Penh is still a relatively small city of around 2 million. Vientiane, the capital city of Laos, has only about 200,000 inhabitants.

Kuala Lumpur, the largest city in Malaysia with some 2 million inhabitants, has received heavy investments from

Figure 13.17 Singapore Singapore remains the economic and technological hub of Southeast Asia. It is a very small and extremely crowded country, forming one of the world's few city-states. Despite its high population density, Singapore has devoted almost half of its area to open spaces. The country consists of one main island and some 60 smaller islands.

both the national government and the global business community. This has produced a modern city of grand ambitions that is free of most infrastructural problems plaguing other Southeast Asian cities. The Petronas Towers, owned by the country's national oil company, were the world's tallest buildings at almost 1,500 feet (450 meters) when completed in 1996.

The independent republic of Singapore is essentially a city-state of 5.1 million people on an island of 240 square miles (600 square kilometers) (Figure 13.17). While space is at a premium, Singapore has successfully developed high-tech industries that have brought it great prosperity. Unlike other Southeast Asian cities, Singapore has no squatter settlements or slums. Only in the much diminished Chinatown and historic colonial district does one find older buildings. Otherwise, Singapore is an extremely clean but rather sterile city of modern high-rise skyscrapers, apartment complexes, and space-intensive industry.

Singapore is unique in Southeast Asia not only because it is a city-state, but also because of the Chinese cultural background of most of its people. But as we shall see in the following section, strong Chinese influences also are found in most of the other large cities of the region.

CULTURAL COHERENCE AND DIVERSITY: A Meeting Ground of World Cultures

Unlike many other world regions, Southeast Asia lacks the historical dominance of a single civilization. Instead, the region has been a meeting ground for cultural traditions from South Asia, China, the Middle East, Europe, and even North America. Abundant natural resources, along with the region's strategic location on oceanic trade routes connecting major continents, have long made Southeast Asia attractive to outsiders. As a result, the modern cultural geography of this diverse region reflects a long history of borrowing and combining external influences.

The Introduction and Spread of Major Cultural Traditions

In Southeast Asia, contemporary cultural diversity is embedded in the historical influences connected to the major religions of Hinduism, Buddhism, Islam, and Christianity (Figure 13.18).

South Asian Influences The first major external influence arrived from South Asia roughly 2,000 years ago when small numbers of migrants from South Asia helped local rulers establish Hindu kingdoms in coastal locations in Burma (Myanmar), Thailand, Cambodia, southern Vietnam, Malaysia, and western Indonesia. Although Hinduism faded away in most locations, it persists on the Indonesian islands of Bali and Lombok, and vestiges of the faith remain in many other areas. The ancient Indian script forms the basis for many Southeast Asian writing systems, and in even in Muslim Java the Hindu epic called the **Ramayana** remains a central cultural feature to this day.

A second wave of South Asian religious influence reached mainland Southeast Asia in the 13th century in the form of Theravada Buddhism, which is closely associated with Sri Lanka. Virtually all of the people in lowland Burma (Myanmar), Thailand, Laos, and Cambodia converted to Buddhism at that time. Today this faith forms the foundation for many of the social institutions of Mainland Southeast Asia. Saffron-robed monks, for example, are a common sight in Thailand and Burma (Myanmar), where Buddhist temples abound. In Thailand, the country's revered constitutional monarchy remains closely connected with Buddhism, and in Burma monks have occasionally been politically active (Figure 13.19). While Southeast Asian Theravada Buddhism shares many traits with the Mahayana Buddhism of East Asia, there are enough differences that the two are mapped separately in Figure 13.18.

Chinese Influences Unlike most other mainland peoples, the Vietnamese were not heavily influenced by South Asian civilization. Instead, their early connections were with East Asia. Vietnam was actually a province of China until about a thousand years ago, when the Vietnamese established a kingdom of their own. But while the Vietnamese rejected China's rule, they retained many attributes of Chinese culture. The traditional religious and philosophical beliefs of Vietnam centered around Mahayana Buddhism and Confucianism.

East Asian cultural influences elsewhere in Southeast Asia are linked more directly to immigration from southern China. Although people have been moving to the region from China for hundreds of years, migration reached a peak in the 19th and early 20th centuries. At first, most migrants were single men. Many returned to China after accumulating money, but others married local women and established mixed communities. In the Philippines, the elite population today is often described as "Chinese Mestizo," being of mixed Chinese and Filipino descent. In the 19th century Chinese women begin to migrate in large numbers, allowing the creation of ethnically distinct Chinese settlements. Urban areas throughout much of Southeast Asia still have large and cohesive Chinese communities. In Malaysia, the Chinese minority constitutes a little less than one-third of the population, whereas in the city-state of Singapore three-quarters of the people are of Chinese ancestry.

In much of the region, relationships between the Chinese minority and the indigenous majority are strained. One source of tension is the fact that overseas Chinese communities tend to be relatively prosperous. Chinese emigrants often prospered by becoming merchants, a job that was often ignored by the local people. As a result, they exert a major economic influence on local affairs, which is often resented. In 2000 and 2001, especially severe anti-Chinese rioting broke out in several Indonesian cities.

Figure 13.18 Religion in Southeast Asia Southeast Asia is one of the world's most religiously diverse regions. Most of the mainland is predominantly Buddhist, with Theravada Buddhism prevailing in Burma (Myanmar), Thailand, Laos, and Cambodia, and Mahayana Buddhism (combined with other elements of the so-called Chinese religious complex) prevailing in Vietnam. The Philippines is primarily Christian (Roman Catholic), but the rest of insular Southeast Asia is primarily Muslim. Substantial Muslim minorities are found in the Philippines, Thailand, and Burma (Myanmar). Animist and Christian minorities can be found in remote areas throughout Southeast Asia, especially in Indonesia's portion of the large island of New Guinea.

The Arrival of Islam Muslim merchants from India and Southwest Asia arrived in Southeast Asia more than a thousand years ago, and by the 1200s their religion began to spread. From an initial focus in northern Sumatra, Islam diffused into the Malay Peninsula, through the main population centers in the Indonesian islands, and east to the southern Philippines. By 1650, it had largely replaced Hin-

duism and Buddhism in Malaysia and Indonesia. The only significant holdout was the small but fertile island of Bali. As Islam spread across Java, thousands of Hindu musicians and artists fled to Bali, giving the island an especially strong tradition of arts and crafts. Partly because of this artistic legacy, Bali is now one of the premier destinations of international tourism.

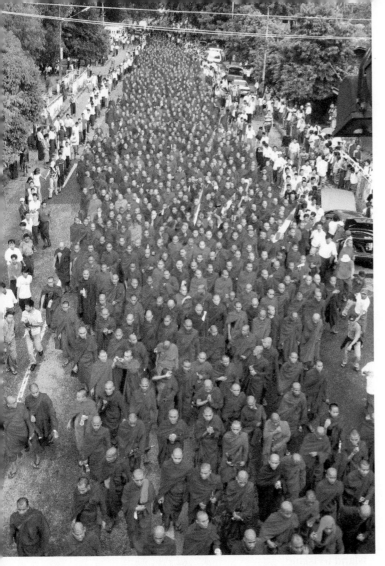

Figure 13.19 Protesting Burmese Monks In September 2007, more than 100,000 people took to the streets to protest Burma's repressive military government. The protests were led by robed monks chanting prayers for peace.

Today the world's most populous Muslim country is Indonesia, where some 88 percent of the people follow Islam. This figure, however, hides a significant amount of internal diversity. In some parts of Indonesia, especially northern Sumatra (Aceh), orthodox forms of Islam took root (Figure 13.20). In others, such as central and eastern Java, a more lax form of worship emerged that retained certain Hindu and even animistic beliefs. Islamic reformers, however, have long been striving to instill more orthodox forms of worship among the Javanese. Today the young people of the island are increasingly turning to mainstream Islam.

In Malaysia and parts of Indonesia, Islamic fundamentalism has recently gained ground. Whereas the current Malaysian government has generally supported the revitalization of Islam, it is wary of the growing power of the fundamentalist movement. Some Malaysian Muslims, moreover, accuse the fundamentalists of advocating social practices derived from the Arabian Peninsula that are not necessarily religious in origin. Adding to Malaysia's religious tension is the fact that almost all ethnic Malays, who narrowly form the country's majority population, follow Islam, whereas most members of the minority communities follow different religions. Religious tensions mounted in 2009, when many Malaysia Muslims were offended by the fact that local Christians were using the term "Allah" to refer to God. In the first three months of 2010, Malaysia witnessed the firebombing or vandalizing of 11 churches, two Muslim prayer halls, a mosque, and a Sikh temple.

Islam was still spreading eastward through insular Southeast Asia when the Europeans arrived in the sixteenth century. When Spain claimed the Philippine Islands in the 1570s, it found the southwestern portion of the archipelago to be thoroughly Islamic. The Muslims resisted the Roman Catholicism introduced by the Spaniards, and much of the southwestern Philippines remains an Islamic stronghold.

Figure 13.20 Indonesian Mosque Indonesia is often said to be the world's largest Muslim country, as more Muslims reside here than in any other country in the world. Islam was first established in northern Sumatra, which is still the most devoutly Islamic part of the Indonesia. In this photo, Acehnese people are praying in front of the Baiturrahman Grand Mosque in the city of Banda Aceh.

The Philippines as a whole is currently about 85 percent Roman Catholic, making it, along with East Timor, the only predominantly Christian country in Asia. Several Protestant sects have been spreading rapidly in the Philippines over the past several decades, however, creating a more complex religious environment.

Christianity and Indigenous Cultures

Christian missions spread through much of Southeast Asia in the late 19th and early 20th century when European colonial powers controlled the region. While French priests converted many people in Vietnam to Catholicism, they had little influence elsewhere. Beyond Vietnam, missions failed to make headway in areas of Hindu, Buddhist, or Islamic heritage.

Missionaries were far more successful in Southeast Asia's highland areas, where they found a wide array of tribal societies that had never accepted the major lowland religions. These peoples retained their indigenous belief systems, which generally focus on the worship of nature spirits and ancestors. Although some modern tribal groups retain such **animist** beliefs, others converted to Christianity. As a result, notable Christian concentrations are found in the Lake Batak area of north-central Sumatra, the mountainous borderlands between southern Burma (Myanmar) and Thailand, the northern peninsula of Sulawesi, and the highlands of southern Vietnam. Animism is still widespread in the mountains of northern Southeast Asia, central Borneo, far eastern Indonesia, and the highlands of northern Luzon in the Philippines. In Indonesia, however, animist practices are technically illegal, as monotheism is one of the country's founding principles. As a result, many Indonesian tribal groups have been gradually converting to either Islam or Christianity.

Indonesia has experienced pronounced religious strife over the past ten years, especially between its Muslim majority and its Christian minority. Inter-faith relations had been relatively good until the late 1990s. Indonesia, despite its Muslim majority, is a secular state that has always emphasized tolerance among its officially recognized religions (Islam, Christianity, Buddhism, Hinduism, and Confucianism). With the Indonesian economic disaster of the late 1990s, however, relations deteriorated. Religious conflicts broke out in many areas, especially in the Maluku Islands of eastern Indonesia and in central Sulawesi. Between 1999 and 2003, an estimated 2,000 people were killed in Christian–Muslim clashes on the island of Sulawesi alone. Transmigration is also implicated in Indonesia's religious conflicts, as in many instances indigenous Christian and animist groups are now competing against Muslim immigrants from Java and Madura. By 2008, however, religious tensions were decreasing in most parts of the country.

Religion and Communism

By 1975, communism had triumphed in Vietnam, Cambodia, and Laos. In all three countries, religious practices were strongly discouraged. At present, Vietnam's officially communist government is struggling against a revival of faith among the country's Buddhist majority and its 8 million Christians. Buddhist monks are frequently detained, and the government reserves for itself the right to appoint all religious leaders. Also expanding is Vietnam's indigenous religion of Cao Dai, a syncretic (or mixed) faith that venerates not only the Buddha, Confucius, and Jesus, but also the French novelist Victor Hugo. Between 3 and 8 million Vietnamese currently belong to this religious community.

Geography of Language and Ethnicity

As with religion, language in Southeast Asia expresses the long history of human movement. The linguistic geography of the region is complicated—too complicated, in fact, to be adequately conveyed in a single map. The several hundred distinct languages of the region can, however, be placed into five major linguistic families. These are *Austronesian,* which covers most of the insular realm; *Tibeto-Burman,* which includes most of the languages of Burma (Myanmar); *Tai-Kadai,* centered on Thailand and Laos; *Mon-Khmer* encompassing most of the languages of Vietnam and Cambodia; and *Papuan,* a Pacific language family found in eastern Indonesia (Figure 13.21).

The Austronesian Languages

Austronesian is one of the world's most widespread language families, extending from Madagascar to Easter Island in the eastern Pacific. Linguists believe that this family originated in Taiwan and adjacent areas of East Asia, and then spread widely across the Indian and Pacific oceans by seafaring people who migrated from island to island.

Today almost all insular Southeast Asian languages fall within the Austronesian family. This means that elements of grammar and vocabulary are widely shared across the islands. As a result, it is relatively easy for a person who speaks one of these languages to learn any other. But despite this linguistic commonality, more than 50 distinct Austronesian languages are spoken in Indonesia alone. And in far eastern Indonesia, a variety of languages fall into the completely separate family of Papuan, closely associated with New Guinea.

One language, however, overshadows all others in insular Southeast Asia: Malay. Malay is indigenous to the Malay Peninsula, eastern Sumatra, and coastal Borneo, and was spread historically by merchants and seafarers. As a result, it became a common trade language, or **lingua franca,** understood and used by peoples speaking different languages throughout much of the insular realm. Dutch colonists in Indonesia eventually employed Malay as an administrative language, although they wrote it with the Roman alphabet, rather than in the Arabic-derived script used by native speakers. When Indonesia became an independent country in 1949, its leaders decided to use the lingua franca version of Malay as the basis for a new national language called *Bahasa Indonesia* (or more simply, *Indonesian*). Although Indonesian is slightly different from Malaysian, they essentially form a single, mutually intelligible language.

The goal of the new Indonesian government was to find a common language that would overcome ethnic differences throughout the far-flung state. In general, this policy has been successful. Indonesian is now used in schools, the government, and the media, and most of the country's people understand it. But regional languages, such as Javanese, Balinese, and Sundanese, continue to be primary languages in most homes. More than 75 million people speak Javanese, which makes it one of the world's major tongues.

The eight major languages of the Philippines also belong in the Austronesian family. Despite more than 300 years of colonization by Spain, Spanish never became a unifying force for the islands. During the American period (1898–1946), English served as the language of administration and education. After independence following World War II, Philippine nationalists decided to create a national language that could replace English and help unify the new country. They selected Tagalog, the language spoken in the Manila region. The first task was to standardize and modernize Tagalog, which had many dialects. After this was accomplished, it was renamed *Filipino* (alternatively, *Pilipino*). Today, mainly because of its use in education, television, and movies, Filipino is emerging as a unifying national language.

Tibeto-Burman Languages

Each country of mainland Southeast Asia is closely identified with the national language spoken in its core territory. This does not mean, however, that all the inhabitants of these countries speak these official languages on a daily basis. In

Figure 13.21 Language Map of Southeast Asia A vast number of languages are found in Southeast Asia, but most are tribal tongues spoken by only a few thousand people. In mainland Southeast Asia—the site of three major language families—the central lowlands of each country are dominated by people speaking the national languages: Burmese in Burma (Myanmar), Thai in Thailand, Lao in Laos, and Vietnamese in Vietnam. Almost all languages in insular Southeast Asia belong to the Austronesian linguistic family. There were no dominant languages here before the creation of such national tongues as Filipino and Bahasa Indonesia in the mid-20th century.

the mountains and other remote districts, other languages remain primary. This linguistic diversity reinforces ethnic divisions despite national educational programs designed to foster unity.

Burma (Myanmar) provides good example of ethnic and linguistic diversity. Its national language is Burmese, which is closely related to Tibetan and perhaps, much more distantly, to Chinese. Today some 32 million people speak Burmese as their first language (Figure 13.22). Although the nationalistic military government of Burma (Myanmar) has attempted to force its version of unity on the entire population, a major schism developed with several non-Burman tribal groups inhabiting the rough uplands that flank the Burmese-speaking Irrawaddy Valley. Although most of these peoples speak languages in the Tibeto-Burman family, they are quite distinct from Burmese.

Tai-Kadai Languages The Tai-Kadai linguistic family probably originated in southern China and then spread into Southeast Asia starting around 1200 CE. Today, closely related languages within the Tai subfamily are found through most of Thailand and Laos, in the uplands of northern Vietnam, in Burma's Shan Plateau, and in parts of southern China. Most Tai languages are quite localized, spoken by small ethnic groups. But two of them, Thai and Lao, are national languages, spoken in Thailand and Laos respectively.

Linguistic terminology here is complicated. Historically, the main language of the Kingdom of Thailand, called *Siamese* (just as the kingdom was called *Siam*), was restricted to the lower Chao Phraya valley, which formed the national core. In the 1930s, however, the country changed its name to Thailand to emphasize the unity of all the peoples speaking closely related Tai languages within its territory. Siamese was similarly renamed *Thai*, and it has gradually become the unifying language for the country. There are still substantial variations in dialect, however, with those of the north often considered separate languages.

Lao, another Tai language, is the national tongue of Laos. More Lao speakers reside in Thailand than in Laos, however, where they form the majority population of the relatively poor Khorat Plateau of the northeast. The dialect of Lao spoken in northeastern Thailand, called Isan locally, seems to be declining in favor of standard Thai. Roughly a third of Thailand's population, however, still speaks Lao (Isan) rather than Thai as their first language.

Mon-Khmer Languages The Mon-Khmer language family probably covered almost all of mainland Southeast Asia 1,500 years ago. It contains two major languages, Vietnamese (the national tongue of Vietnam) and Khmer (the national language of Cambodia), as well as a host of minor languages spoken by hill peoples and a few lowland groups. Because of the historical Chinese influence in Vietnam, Vietnamese was usually written with Chinese characters until the French imposed the Roman alphabet, which remains in use. Khmer, like the other national languages of mainland Southeast Asia, is written in its own script, ultimately derived from India.

The most important aspect of linguistic geography in mainland Southeast Asia is probably the fact that in each country the national language is limited to the core area of densely populated lowlands, whereas the peripheral uplands are inhabited primarily by tribal peoples speaking separate languages. In Laos, up to 40 percent of the population is non-Lao. This linguistic contrast between the lowlands and the uplands poses an obvious problem for national integration. Such problems are most extreme in Burma (Myanmar), where the upland peoples are numerous and well organized—and have strenuously resisted the domination of the lowland Burmans. The Burmese government has, in turn, devoted much of its energies to resisting the influences of global culture.

Figure 13.22 Burmese Script The Burmese script, seen here on posters in Burma's primate city of Rangoon (Yangon), has characters with round shapes, supposedly because the palm leaves that were originally used as writing surfaces would have been split by straight lines. Burma's script, like those of Thailand, Laos, and Cambodia, can be traced back to a writing system from ancient India.

Southeast Asian Culture in Global Context

The imposition of European colonial rule ushered in a new era of globalization in Southeast Asia, bringing with it European languages, Christianity, and new governmental, economic, and educational systems. This period also deprived most Southeast Asians of their cultural autonomy. As a result, with decolonialization after World War II, several countries attempted to isolate themselves from the cultural and economic influences of the emerging global system. Burma (Myanmar) retreated into its own form of Buddhist socialism, placing strict limits on foreign tourism, which the government viewed as a source of cultural contamination. Although the door has opened substantially since the 1980s, the government of Burma remains wary of foreign practices and influences, an attitude that has become a major source of tension within the country. Burma's government is relatively tolerant of music, however, which has resulted in a surge of spontaneous concerts and underground music festivals. At these events, hip-hop and techobeat styles are often mixed with more traditional Burmese musical forms.

Other Southeast Asian countries have been more receptive to foreign cultural influences. This is particularly true in the case of the Philippines, where American colonialism may have predisposed the country to many of the more popular forms of Western culture. As a result, Filipino musicians and other entertainers are in demand throughout East and Southeast Asia (Figure 13.23). Thailand, which was never subjected to colonial rule, is the most receptive country of the mainland to global culture, with its open policy toward tourism, mass media, and economic interdependence.

Cultural globalization has been recently challenged in some Southeast Asian countries. The Malaysian government, for example, is highly critical of many American films and television programs. Islamic revivalism, in both Malaysia and Indonesia, also presents a challenge to global culture. A recent poll, for example, found that that 62 percent of Indone-

sians believe that U.S. culture is "disruptive" to Indonesian society. Singapore's leaders have also criticized cultural influences from the West, but the city–state remains committed to globalization. Singapore is also seeking to enhance tourism and bolster its economy by building Las Vegas–style casinos. A huge gambling complex called Resorts World Sentosa opened its doors in February 2010, welcoming 130,000 visitors in its first week of operation.

As the global language, English causes ambivalence in much of Southeast Asia. On one hand, it is the language of questionable popular culture; yet on the other hand, citizens need proficiency in English if they are to participate in international business and politics. In Malaysia, widespread proficiency in English was challenged in the 1980s as nationalists stressed the importance of their native tongue. This movement distressed the business community, which considers English vital to Malaysia's competitive position, as well as the influential Chinese communities, for which Malaysian is not a native language.

In Singapore, the situation is more complex. Mandarin Chinese, English, Malay, and Tamil (from southeastern India) are all official languages. The local languages of southern China are also common in home environments, as 75 percent of Singapore's population is of southern Chinese ancestry. The Singapore government now encourages Mandarin Chinese and discourages southern Chinese dialects. It also supports English while discouraging *Singlish,* an English-based dialect containing many southern Chinese words and grammatical forms. Singaporean officials have occasionally slapped restrictive ratings on local films for "bad grammar" if they contain too much Singlish dialogue.

In the Philippines, nationalists have long criticized the common use of English, even though widespread fluency has proved beneficial to the millions of Filipinos who have emigrated for better economic conditions or who work as crew members in the globalized shipping industry. The Philippine government has been gradually deemphasizing English in favor of Filipino in public schools and, as a result, some fear that competence in English is slowly declining. Others counter that the spread of cable television, with its many U.S. shows, has enhanced the country's English-language skills.

While the diffusion of global cultural forms is beginning to merge cultures across Southeast Asia, religious revivalism operates in the opposite direction. This same combination of centripetal (merging together) and centrifugal (spreading apart) forces also is found in the geopolitical realm.

GEOPOLITICAL FRAMEWORK: War, Ethnic Strife, and Regional Cooperation

Southeast Asia is sometimes defined as a geopolitical entity composed of the 10 different countries that form the Association of Southeast Asian Nations, or ASEAN (Figure

Figure 13.23 Filipino Entertainers The people of the Philippines have adopted popular forms of Western culture more than most other Southeast Asians, in part because of their long experience with American colonialism. As a result, Filipino performers are often in demand in other Asian countries. This photograph shows a Filipina musician singing in Hong Kong.

13.24). Today ASEAN, more than anything else, gives Southeast Asia regional coherence. East Timor, or Timor-Leste, as the country is officially called, gained independence only in 2002, and is not yet a member of ASEAN. It is expected to gain admission, however, in 2012. Despite the general success of ASEAN in reducing international tensions, several Southeast Asian counties are still struggling with serious ethnic and regional conflicts.

Before European Colonialism

The modern countries of mainland Southeast Asia were all indigenous kingdoms at one time or another before the onset of European colonialism. Cambodia emerged earliest, reaching its height in the twelfth century, when it controlled much of what is now Thailand and southern Vietnam. By the 1300s, independent kingdoms had been established by the Burman, Siamese (Thai), Lao, and Vietnamese people in the major river valleys and deltas. These kingdoms were in a nearly constant state of war with one another, often fighting more for labor than for territory. Victors would typically take home thousands of prisoners to settle their lands, leading to considerable ethnic mixing.

The situation in insular Southeast Asia was different, with the premodern map bearing no resemblance to that of the modern nation-states. Many kingdoms existed on the Malay Peninsula and on the islands of Sumatra and Java, but few were territorially stable. In the

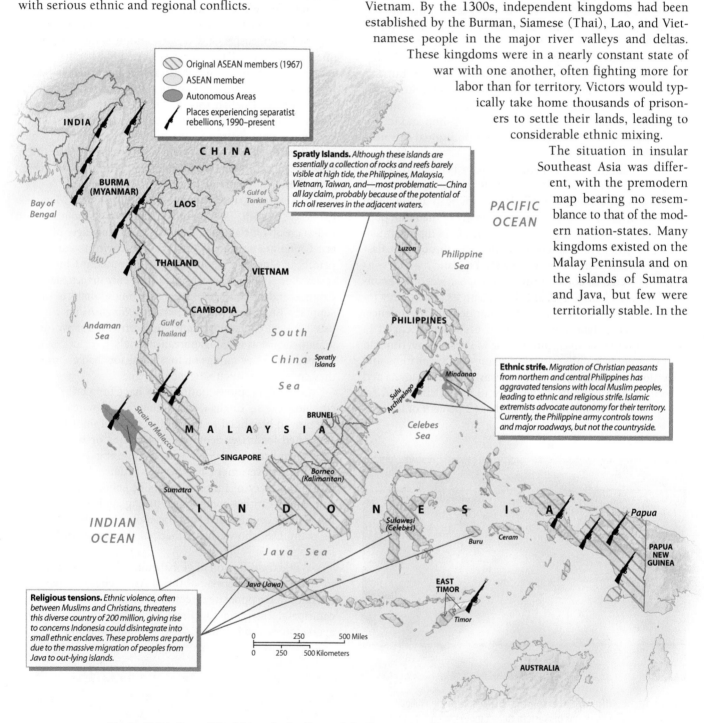

Original ASEAN members (1967)

ASEAN member

Autonomous Areas

Places experiencing separatist rebellions, 1990–present

Spratly Islands. *Although these islands are essentially a collection of rocks and reefs barely visible at high tide, the Philippines, Malaysia, Vietnam, Taiwan, and—most problematic—China all lay claim, probably because of the potential of rich oil reserves in the adjacent waters.*

Ethnic strife. *Migration of Christian peasants from northern and central Philippines has aggravated tensions with local Muslim peoples, leading to ethnic and religious strife. Islamic extremists advocate autonomy for their territory. Currently, the Philippine army controls towns and major roadways, but not the countryside.*

Religious tensions. *Ethnic violence, often between Muslims and Christians, threatens this diverse country of 200 million, giving rise to concerns Indonesia could disintegrate into small ethnic enclaves. These problems are partly due to the massive migration of peoples from Java to out-lying islands.*

Figure 13.24 Geopolitical Issues in Southeast Asia The countries of Southeast Asia have managed to solve most of their border disputes and other sources of potential conflicts through ASEAN (the Association of Southeast Asian Nations). Internal disputes, however, mostly focused on issues of religious and ethnic diversity, continue to plague several of the region's states, particularly Indonesia and Burma (Myanmar). ASEAN also experiences tension with China over the Spratly Islands of the South China Sea.

Philippines, eastern Indonesia, and central Borneo, most societies were organized at the local level. Indonesia, the Philippines, and Malaysia thus owe their modern territorial configuration almost wholly to the European colonial influence (Figure 13.25).

The Colonial Era

The Portuguese were the first Europeans to arrive (around 1500), lured by the cloves and nutmeg of the Maluku region of eastern Indonesia. In the late 1500s, the Spanish conquered most of the Philippines, which they used as a base for their silver and silk trade between China and the Ameri-

cas. By the 1600s, the Dutch had started staking out Southeast Asian territory, followed by the British. With superior naval weaponry, the Europeans were quickly able to conquer key ports and strategic trading locales. Yet for the first 200 years of colonialism, except in the Philippines, the Europeans made no major geopolitical gains.

Dutch Power By the 1700s, the Netherlands had become the most powerful force in the region. As a result, a Dutch Empire in the "East Indies" (or Indonesia) began appearing on world maps. Form its original base in northwestern Java, this empire continued to grow into the early 20th century, when the Dutch defeated their last main adversary, the

Figure 13.25 Colonial Southeast Asia With the exception of Thailand, all of Southeast Asia was under Western colonial rule by the early 1900s. The Netherlands had the largest empire in the region, covering the territory that was later to become Indonesia. France maintained a substantial imperial realm in Vietnam, Laos, and Cambodia, as did Britain in Burma (Myanmar) and Malaysia (including Singapore and Brunei). The Philippines was colonized by Spain, but passed to the control of the United States in 1898.

powerful Islamic sultanate of Aceh in northern Sumatra. Later, the Dutch invaded the western portion of New Guinea in response to German and British advances in the eastern half. In a subsequent treaty, these imperial powers sliced New Guinea down the middle, with the Netherlands taking the west.

British, French, and U.S. Expansion The British, preoccupied with their empire in India, concentrated their attention on the sea-lanes linking South Asia to China. As a result, they established several fortified trading outposts along the vital Strait of Malacca, the most notable being on the island of Singapore, founded in 1819. To avoid conflict, the British and Dutch agreed that the British would limit their attention to the Malay Peninsula and northern Borneo. Britain allowed Muslim sultans to retain limited powers, and their descendants still enjoy token authority in several Malaysian states. When Britain left this area in the early 1960s, Malaysia emerged as an independent state. Two small portions of the former British sphere did not join the new country. In northern Borneo, the Sultanate of Brunei gained independence, backed by its large oil reserves. Singapore briefly joined Malaysia, but then withdrew and became fully independent in 1965. This divorce was carried out partly for ethnic reasons. Malaysia was to be a primarily Malay state, but with Singapore included its population would have been almost half Chinese.

In the 1800s, European colonial power spread through most of mainland Southeast Asia. British forces in India fought several wars against the kingdom of Burma before annexing the entire area in 1885, including considerable upland territories that had never been under Burmese rule. During the same period, the French moved into Vietnam's Mekong Delta, gradually expanding their territorial control to the west into Cambodia and north to China's border. Thailand was the only country to avoid colonial rule, although it did lose substantial territories to the British in Malaysia and the French in Laos. Thai independence was maintained partly because it served British and French interests to have a buffer state between their colonial realms.

The final colonial power to enter the area was the United States, which took the Philippines first from Spain and then, after a bitter war, from Filipino nationalists between 1898 and 1900. The U.S. army subsequently conquered the Muslim areas of the southwest, most of which had never been fully under Spanish authority.

Growing Nationalism Organized resistance to European rule began in the 1920s in mainland countries, but it took the Japanese occupation during World War II to shatter the myth of European invincibility. After Japan's surrender in 1945, agitation for independence was renewed throughout Southeast Asia. As Britain realized that it could no longer control its South Asian empire, it also withdrew from adjacent Burma, which achieved independence in 1948. The Netherlands failed to reconquer Indonesia after WWII, and was forced to acknowledge Indonesian independence in

1949. The United States granted long-promised independence to the Philippines on July 4, 1946, although it retained key military bases, as well as considerable economic influence, for several decades.

The Vietnam War and Its Aftermath

Unlike the United States, France was determined to maintain its Southeast Asian empire. Resistance to French rule was organized primarily by communist groups that were deeply rooted in northern Vietnam. As French forces returned to Southeast Asian in 1946, the leader of this resistance movement, Ho Chi Minh, organized a separatist government in the north. Open warfare between French soldiers and the communist forces went on for almost a decade. After a decisive defeat in 1954, France agreed to withdraw. An international peace council in Geneva decided that Vietnam would be divided into two countries. As a result, communist leaders came to power in North Vietnam, allied with the Soviet Union and China. South Vietnam simultaneously emerged as an independent, capitalist-oriented state with close political ties to the United States.

The Geneva peace accord did not end the war. Communist guerrillas in South Vietnam fought to overthrow the new government and unite it with the north. North Vietnam sent troops and war materials across the border to aid the rebels. Most of these supplies reached the south over the Ho Chi Minh Trail, an ill-defined network of forest passages through Laos and Cambodia that steadily drew these two countries into the conflict. In Laos the communist Pathet Lao forces challenged the government, while in Cambodia the **Khmer Rouge** guerrillas gained considerable power. In South Vietnam, the government gradually lost control of key areas, including much of the Mekong Delta, a region perilously close to the capital city of Saigon.

U.S. Intervention By 1962 the United States was sending large numbers of military advisors to South Vietnam. In Washington, DC, the **domino theory** became accepted foreign policy. According to this notion, if Vietnam fell to the communists, then so would Laos and Cambodia; once those countries were lost, Burma (Myanmar) and Thailand, and perhaps even Malaysia and Indonesia, would join the Soviet-dominated communist bloc. By 1968, over half a million U.S. troops were fighting a ferocious land war against the communist guerrillas (Figure 13.26). But despite superiority in arms and troops—and domination of the air—U.S. forces failed to gain control over much of the countryside. As casualties mounted and the antiwar movement back home strengthened, the United States began secret talks with North Vietnam in search of a negotiated settlement. U.S. troop withdrawals began in earnest by the early 1970s.

Communist Victory With the withdrawal of U.S. forces and financial support, the noncommunist governments of the former French zone began to collapse. Saigon fell in 1975, and in the following year Vietnam was officially reunited

Figure 13.26 U.S. Soldier and Vietcong Prisoners The United States maintained a substantial military presence in Vietnam in the 1960s and early 1970s. Although U.S. forces claimed many victories, they were ultimately forced to withdraw, leading to the victory of North Vietnam and the reunification of the country.

under the government of the north. Reunification was a traumatic event in southern Vietnam. Hundreds of thousands of people fled to other countries, especially the United States. The first wave of refugees consisted primarily of wealthy professionals and businesspeople, but later migrants included many relatively poor ethnic Chinese. Most of these refugees fled on small, rickety boats; large numbers suffered shipwreck or pirate attack.

Vietnam proved fortunate compared with Cambodia. There the Khmer Rouge installed one of the most brutal regimes the world has ever seen. City-dwellers were forced into the countryside to become peasants, and most wealthy and educated persons were summarily executed. The Khmer Rouge's goal was to create a wholly new agrarian society by returning to what they called "year zero." After several years of bloodshed that took an estimated 1.5 million lives, neighboring Vietnam invaded Cambodia and installed a far less brutal, but still repressive, regime. Fighting between different factions continued for more than a decade, but by the late 1980s the United Nations was able to broker a peace settlement. A parliamentary system of government subsequently brought peace to the shattered country. Although Cambodia is officially a constitutional monarchy with an elected government, corruption is widespread and democratic institutions remain weak and unstable (see "Global to Local: Poipet and Southeast Asia's Other 'Sin Cities.'")

Vietnam stationed significant numbers of troops in Laos after 1975. Large numbers of Hmong and other tribal peoples—many of whom had fought on behalf of the United States—fled to Thailand and the United States. The Communist Party still maintains a monopoly over political power in Laos, although much of the economy has been opened to private firms. Many Laotian Hmong refugees who fled to the United States after the war, however, continue to seek political change at home. In 2007, the American Hmong commu-

nity was shocked when U.S. federal agents arrested 11 of their leaders, including the famed general Vang Pao, for plotting to overthrow the government of Laos. In 2009, however, all charges against Vang Pao were dropped.

Geopolitical Tensions in Contemporary Southeast Asia

The most serious geopolitical problems in Southeast Asia today occur within countries rather than between then. In several areas, locally based ethnic groups struggle against centralized national governments that inherited territory from the former colonial powers. Tension also results when tribal groups attempt to preserve their homeland from logging, mining, or interregional migration. Such conflicts are especially pronounced in the large, multiethnic country of Indonesia.

Conflicts in Indonesia When Indonesia gained independence in 1949, it included all the former Dutch possessions in the region except western New Guinea. The Netherlands retained this territory, arguing that its cultural background distinguished it from Indonesia. Although Dutch authorities were preparing western New Guinea for independence, Indonesia demanded the entire territory. Bowing to pressure from the United States, the Netherlands relented and allowed Indonesia to take control in 1963. The Indonesian government formally annexed western New Guinea in 1969.

Tensions in western New Guinea increased in the following decades as Javanese immigrants, along with mining and lumber firms, arrived in the area. Faced with the loss of their land and the degradation of their environment, indigenous residents formed the separatist organization OPM (*Organisesi Papua Merdeka*) and launched a rebellion. Rebel leaders demanded independence, or at least autonomy, but they faced a far stronger force in the Indonesian army. The struggle between the Indonesian government and the OPM is currently a sporadic but occasionally bloody guerrilla affair. Indonesia is determined to maintain control of the region in part because it is home to one of the country's largest taxpayers, the highly polluting Grasberg copper and gold mine run by the Phoenix–based Freeport-McMoRan Corporation (Figure 13.27).

A more intensive war erupted in 1975 on the island of Timor. The eastern half of this poor island had been a Portuguese colony (the only survivor of Portugal's 16th-century foray into the region) and had evolved into a mostly Christian society. The East Timorese expected independence when the Portuguese finally withdrew. Indonesia, however, viewed the area as its own territory and immediately invaded. A ferocious struggle ensued, which the Indonesian army won in part by starving the people of East Timor into submission.

After the economic crisis of 1997, Indonesia's power in the region slipped. A new Indonesian government promised an election in 1999 to see if the East Timorese wanted independence. At the same time, however, Indonesia's army began to organize loyalist militias to intimidate the people of East

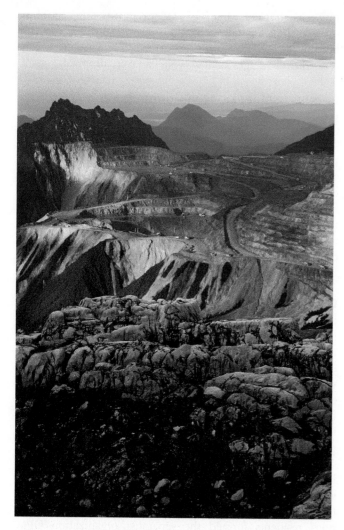

Figure 13.27 Grasberg Mine Grasberg, located in the Indonesian province of Papua, is the world's largest gold mine and third largest copper mine. Employing more than 19,000 people, Grasberg is of great economic importance to Indonesia. It is also highly polluting, generating 253,000 tons (230,000 metric tons) of tailings per day and is thus opposed by many local inhabitants.

Timor into voting to remain within the country. When it was clear that the vote would be for independence, the militias began rioting, looting, and slaughtering civilians. Under international pressure, Indonesia finally withdrew, United Nations forces arrived, and the East Timorese began to build a new country.

Considering the devastation caused by the militias, the reconstruction of East Timor was not easy. Even selecting an official language proved difficult; after some deliberation, both Tetum (one of 16 indigenous languages) and Portuguese were selected. In 2006, ethnic rioting further damaged the country, requiring Australian intervention to reestablish peace. A relatively successful election in 2007 brought hope that East Timor could overcome its divisions, but in 2008 a well-coordinated attack by former soldiers and police officers came close to killing the country's president and prime minister.

Secession struggles have occurred elsewhere in Indonesia. In the late 1950s, central Sumatra and northern Sulawesi rebelled, but they were quickly defeated and eventually reconciled to Indonesian rule. Another small-scale war flared up in the late 1990s in western and southern Borneo (Kalimantan). Here the indigenous Dayaks, a tribal people partly converted to Christianity, began to clash with Muslim migrants from Madura, a densely inhabited island north of Java. The Indonesian military has restored order in Kalimantan's cities, but the countryside remains troubled. The southern Maluku Islands, especially Ambon and Seram, have also seen fighting between Muslims and Christians. Even the area's cities are now divided into Muslim and Christian sectors, and crossing to the wrong side can prove dangerous.

Indonesia's most serious regional conflict has long been that of Aceh in northern Sumatra. Many Acehnese, in general Indonesia's most devout Muslim group, have demanded the creation of an independent Islamic state. While the government has allowed Aceh a high degree of autonomy as a "special territory of Indonesia," it has been determined to prevent actual independence. Ironically, the devastation caused by the December 2004 tsunami, which left over 500,000 Acehnese homeless, allowed a peace settlement to be finally reached, as the needs of the area were so great that the separatist fighters agreed to lay down their weapons. A 2006 election brought former rebel leaders into the heart of Aceh's government. In early 2010, however, violence again broke out after the government discovered a militant training camp in the region.

Indonesia has obviously had difficulties creating a unified nation over its vast, sprawling extent and across its numerous cultural and religious communities. As a creation of the colonial period, Indonesia has a weak historical foundation. Some critics have viewed it as something of a Javanese empire, even though many non-Javanese individuals have risen to high governmental positions. While Indonesia now has the highest degree of political freedom in Southeast Asia, its politically influential military remains hostile to movements for regional autonomy.

Regional Tensions in the Philippines The Philippines has long been struggling against a regional secession movement in its Islamic southwest. Although the government made headway in talks with the main rebel group by creating the Autonomous Region in Muslim Mindanao (ARMM), the more extreme Muslim factions continue to demand greater autonomy over a larger area—if not outright independence. The migration of Christian peasants from northern and central Philippines into the Islamic southwest has exacerbated local tensions. The Philippine army generally maintains control over the area's main cities and roadways, but it has little power in the more remote villages. As radical Islamist groups reportedly have close ties with the Al Qaeda network, the Philippines became a key site in the U.S.-led struggle against global terrorism. Several hundred U.S. military advisors are currently working with Philippine military in the Mindanao region. As a result, some Filipino nationalists argue that their country is again falling under U.S. domination.

GLOBAL TO LOCAL   Poipet and Southeast Asia's Other "Sin Cities"

A number of Southeast Asian cities have prospered by providing socially objectionable services to an international clientele. Foremost among these is the resort city of Pattaya, located on the Gulf of Thailand 102 miles (165 kilometers) southeast of Bangkok. Although many of the approximately 5 million tourists who annually visit this small city (population 100,000) come primarily for the beaches and the shopping, a bigger draw is the hundreds of "go-go bars" that serve as fronts for prostitution. Although technically illegal, Thai prostitution is a big business, netting some $4.3 billion annually.

Pattaya is not the only small Southeast Asian city to find a niche in the global prostitution business. Before 1992, the economy of Angeles City in the Philippines was based on the nearby U.S. Air Force base of Clark Field. When the American military forces pulled out, Angeles City faced an uncertain economic future. Although the Philippine government created a special economic zone to allow businesses to take advantage of the base's extensive facilities, development has been slow. Angeles City's nightclub district, however, has experienced a successful expansion. Built initially to cater to American servicemen, the prostitution-oriented bars (numbering well over 100) now focus on an international clientele.

The exploitation of prostitutes in Thailand and the Philippines may be severe, but much worse conditions are encountered in the comparatively unregulated brothels of Laos, Cambodia, and Burma (Myanmar). In 2004, *New York Times* journalist Nicholas Kristof brought international attention to the horrific situation faced by child prostitutes in the Cambodian city of Poipet. Kristof went so far as to purchase (for $150 and $203, respectively) and then free two prostitute slave-girls. The sale of illegal drugs, especially methamphetamine, is also widespread in this tawdry Cambodian border town (Figure 13.3.1).

The booming city of Poipet, however, owes its most recent growth to casino gambling. Propelling the rise of this city as the "Las Vegas of Southeast Asia" is the fact that casino gambling is extremely popular, although illegal, in neighboring Thailand, where Thais reportedly spend up to $11 billion annually on illegal gambling activities. In response, Cambodian authorities allowed the cre-ation of a gambling enclave in Poipet directly on the Thai border, the first casino opening in 1999. Tourists from Thailand can enter the casino district without passing through Cambodian immigration, and the gambling halls prefer Thai rather than Cambodian currency. Although 90 percent of Poipet's tourists are from Thailand, increasing numbers are arriving from Malaysia, China, and Vietnam. A number of Poipet's casino managers, moreover, hail from North America, and many casino workers are from the Philippines. Overall, the venture is such an economic success that similar gambling reserves are being planned for several Laotian border towns.

Although Poipet has earned huge sums of money for investors and managers, its broader social effects are disastrous. Poipet is a dangerous city with inadequate infrastructure that lures in desperately poor people, many of whom are forced into work as prostitutes or drug dealers. But considering the poverty and corruption found in Cambodia, it is not surprising that the rise of Poipet has met little national resistance.

Figure 13.3.1 Poipet, Cambodia The Holiday Palace casino is one of seven high-end gambling facilities recently constructed in the Cambodian border city of Poipet.

To maintain a degree of authority in the Muslim areas of the south, the Philippine government has allied itself with powerful local clans and their private armies. The Maguindanao Massacre of November 2009, however, showed the limitations of this policy. Fighters associated with the government-allied Ampatuan family attacked a convoy of a rival clan that was heading to register one of its members as a candidate for an upcoming gubernatorial election, killing 51 people, including as many as 32 journalists (Figure 13.28). The Committee to Protect Journalists describes the incident as the largest single attack on news reporters in world history. The Philippine government subsequently arrested the head of the Ampatuan clan, but it was not able to erase the hostility generated by the incident.

The Philippines' political problems are not limited to the south. A long-simmering communist rebellion has affected almost the entire country. In the mid-1980s, the NPA (New People's Army) controlled one-quarter of the country's villages scattered across all the major islands. Although the NPA's strength has declined since then, it remains a potent force in many areas. The Philippine national government, although democratic, is itself far from stable, suffering from continual coup threats, corruption scandals, and mass protests.

The Quagmire of Burma Burma (Myanmar) has also been a war-ravaged country. Its simultaneous wars of the 1970s, 1980s, and 1990s pitted the central government, dominated by the Burmans, against the country's varied non-Burman societies. Fighting intensified gradually after independence in 1948, until almost half of the country's territory had become a combat zone (Figure 13.29). Burma's troubles, moreover, are by no means limited to the country's ethnic minorities. Since 1988, it has been ruled by a repressive military regime that is bitterly resented by much of the population. Democratic opposition to the government, however, has been vigorously suppressed, with its leader, Nobel Peace Prize winner Aung San Suu Kyi, remaining under house arrest (Figure 13.30).

The rebelling ethnic groups of Burma (Myanmar) have sought to maintain authority over their own cultural traditions, lands, and resources. They generally see the national government as something of a Burman empire seeking to impose its language and, in some cases, religion upon them. Most of the insurgent ethnic groups live in rugged and inaccessible terrain, but even some lowland groups have rebelled. The Muslim peoples of the Arakan coast (the Rohingyas) in western Burma have long faced severe discrimination (see "People on the Move: The Rohingyas Seek Sanctuary"). In the 1980s, many were forced to flee to neighboring Bangladesh, while more recently Burmese Muslims have been fleeing to Yunnan Province in China.

Several of Burma's ethnic insurgencies have been financed largely by opium-growing and heroin manufacture. The Shan, a Tai-speaking people inhabiting a plateau area within the Golden Triangle of drug production, formed a breakaway state in the 1980s and 1990s based largely on the narcotics trade. Their efforts faltered in the late 1990s after Burmese agreements with Thailand reduced the Shan heroin trade just as military operations cut off the supply of raw opium reaching the Shan factories. The government's triumph over the Shan was also made possible by alliances with rival ethnic groups that subsequently moved into the drug trade. The most powerful of these groups is the United

Figure 13.28 Massacre in the Southern Philippines In November 2009, a convoy of political activists and journalists heading to register one of its allies for as a candidate for the governorship of Maguindanao province was attacked by gunmen associated with a rival clan. 57 people were killed, including 34 journalists. The photograph shows a backhoe excavating bodies and vehicles from a shallow grave, where they had been deposited by the perpetrators of the massacre.

Eastern and northern uplands. Ethnic groups such as the Chin and Kachin have been in periodic rebellion against Burma the past several decades.

Shan. The Shan have long supported their rebellion against Burma by growing opium and processing and selling heroin. Incursions by the Burmese military in the mid and late 1990s, however, greatly curtailed this trade—as well as Shan autonomy.

Wa. The Wa people have recently assumed leadership of the heroin and amphetamine trade, perhaps with support from elements in the Burmese army who are eager to undermine the Shan.

Karen. The Karen, a people of mixed Christian, animist, and Buddhist faith who live along Burma's border with Thailand, have protested Burmese political domination and have been rebelling against the Burmese majority since the 1970s.

MAJOR ETHNIC GROUPS

TIBETO-BURMAN
- Burman
- Chin
- Kachin
- Rakhine
- Karen
- **TAI** (Shan and others)
- **MON-KHMER**
- **MIXED BURMAN AND MINORITY AREA**

Figure 13.29 Ethnic Conflict in Burma (Myanmar) Although the central lowlands of Burma (Myanmar) are primarily populated by people of the dominant Burman ethnic group, the peripheral highlands and the southeastern lowlands are home to numerous non-Burman peoples. Most of these peoples have been in periodic rebellion against Burma (Myanmar) since the 1970s, owing to their perception that the national government was attempting to impose Burman cultural norms. Economic stagnation and political repression by the central government have intensified these conflicts.

Wa State Army (UWSA), which by 2007 controlled an estimated 50 heroin refineries and methamphetamine factories and maintained over 20,000 heavily armed soldiers. In 2009, the Burmese government felt strong enough to order the UWSA and its other allied ethnic militias to fold their command structure into that of the Burmese Army. The militias

Figure 13.30 Aung San Suu Kyi The noted Burmese democratic opposition leader Aung San Suu Kyi received the Nobel Peace Prize in 1991. As of 2010 she remained under house arrest.

months later, the Thai army seized power in a bloodless coup, apparently with the blessing of King Bhumibol, Thailand's revered constitutional monarch. Although the new military leaders allowed a quick restoration of democracy, they also banned a number of political movements, substantially reducing the freedom of the Thai people. Through early 2010, Thaksin's supporters, known as the "red-shirts" for their distinctive clothing, were organizing massive demonstrations where they called for fresh elections and the resignation of the prime minister. In May 2010, the Thai government began cracking down on the protestors, resulting in several dozen deaths.

The recent political turmoil in Bangkok is connected with the ethnic tensions that have long plagued Thailand's far south, a primarily Malay-speaking, Muslim region. While minor rebellions have flared up in southern Thailand for decades, the violence sharply escalated in 2004. Prime Minister Thaksin Shinawatra responded to the renewed fighting with harsh military measures, a strategy that many Thai military leaders viewed as counterproductive. But the more conciliatory stance taken by the Thai government after the 2006 coup has been no more effective, as a shadowy Islamist group continues to attack Thai-speaking, Buddhist government officials and as well as ordinary civilians. Between 2004 and March 2010, over 4,000 Thai citizens lost their lives in this conflict. The war has also raised tensions between Thailand and Malaysia, as Thailand accuses its southern neighbor of not doing enough to prevent militants from slipping across the border.

International Dimensions of Southeast Asian Geopolitics

As southern Thailand shows, geopolitical conflicts in Southeast Asia can be complex affairs, involving several different countries as well as non-state organizations. In earlier years, some of the most serious tensions emerged when two countries claimed the same territory. More recently, radical Islamist groups have posed the biggest challenge.

Territorial Conflicts In previous decades, several Southeast Asian countries quarreled over their boundaries. The Philippines, for example, still maintains a "dormant" claim to the Malaysian state of Sabah in northeastern Borneo, based on the fact that in the 1800s the Islamic Sultanate of the Sulu Archipelago in the southern Philippines controlled much of its territory. The Philippines suspended this claim as part of a general movement of Southeast Asian countries to reduce regional tensions. With the rise of ASEAN, national leaders concluded that friendly relations with neighbors are more important than the possible gain of additional territory.

More difficult has been the dispute over the Spratly Islands in the South China Sea, a group of rocks, reefs, and tiny islands that may well lie over substantial undersea oil reserves (Figure 13.31). The Philippines, Malaysia, Vietnam,

have resisted such orders. In early 2010, local reports claimed the UWSA was frantically selling heroin and amphetamine stocks in order to purchase weapons as well as gear to protect its fighters against chemical attack.

Burma's repressive government has provoked international opposition. Both the United States and the European Union maintain trade sanctions. Burma's military rulers do not seem very concerned with global opinion, however, and by joining ASEAN in 1997 they gained international credibility and regional support. Growing economic ties with India and especially China have also helped strengthen Burma's government. The other ASEAN countries have expressed frustration with Burma's military government, but they are wary of provoking it for fear of pushing it closer to China.

Overall, Burma's government remains extremely suspicious of the outside world. In 2005 it mandated the creation of a new capital city at Nay Pyi Taw, located in a remote, forested area 200 miles north of the old capital of Rangoon (Yangon). The new capital, which was supposedly picked on the basis of astrological calculations and defense considerations, is largely closed to the outside world. In 2010, however, Burma agreed to hold multiparty elections, largely as a means of gaining international legitimacy. Most experts, however, viewed the elections as a sham, as neither the major opposition groups nor the Buddhist clergy were allowed to participate, and as free media coverage was prohibited.

Trouble in Thailand Compared to that of Burma, Thailand's recent history appears peaceful and stable. Thailand enjoys basic human freedoms and a thriving free press, although it does have a legacy of military takeovers followed by periods of authoritarian rule. In 2006, mass protests in Bangkok led to the resignation of the corruption-plagued prime minister, Thaksin Shinawatra, who had remained very popular among poor Thai voters in rural areas. Several

PEOPLE ON THE MOVE   The Rohingyas Seek Sanctuary

Most contemporary international migrants leave their homeland to seek enhanced opportunity and better economic conditions. Some people, however, move because they are forced out of their own countries by political repression. Although little noted in the global media, the Rohingyas of Burma (Myanmar) have been on the move for some time. A distinct people some 700,000 strong, the Rohingyas appear on few maps of Burma. This erasure of their identity is in keeping with official Burmese policy, which has denied almost all of them Burmese citizenship. Unfortunately, the Rohingyas have been unable to find ready sanctuary elsewhere.

The Rohingyas speak an Indo-European language closely related to Bengali, spoken in Bangladesh and parts of India. Like most eastern Bengali speakers, they follow Islam—the main reason for their persecution by the strongly Buddhist Burmese state. According to Rohingya history, their ancestors began moving to their current homeland as early as the 7th century; Burmese historians contend that they did not arrive until after Burma was conquered by the British, and that they came largely because the British encouraged their migration. As a result, hard-core Burmese nationalists insist that the Rohingyas be regarded as citizens of Bangladesh, not Burma. Bangladesh, not surprisingly, rejects this interpretation.

The persecution of the Rohingyas has been going on for some time. In 1942, after Japanese forces expelled the British from Burma, mob violence took an estimated 100,000 Rohingyas lives. In the late 1970s, renewed harassment sent 250,000 to Bangladesh, where many have continued to languish in wretched refugee camps (Figure 13.4.1). Rohingyas have also fled to refugee camps in Thailand, where an estimated 110,000 currently live. Rohingyas continue to leave Burma, even though they have no place to go. Many have tried to sail to Thailand, but the Thai government tries to prevent them from landing. In 2009, Thai naval authorities reportedly towed five boats loaded with Rohingya refugees out to sea; four of the boats subsequently sank during a storm, and the fifth wrecked on the shore. In March 2010, Malaysian authorities picked up 93 Rohingya refugees in an overcrowded boat who claimed that they had been chased out of Thai waters by the Thai navy.

Bangladeshi authorities also reject Rohingya migrants, arguing that all Rohingyas who entered their country after 1991 are simply illegal immigrants. Tensions between Burma and Bangladesh mounted in the fall of 2009, focused both on the Rohingya issue and on the maritime border between the two countries. The offshore area contains significant energy resources that both countries wish to exploit.

In late December 2009, Burma and Bangladesh finally reached a provisional agreement that involved the "repatriation" of Rohingya refugees. Burma agreed to accept 9,000 out of the estimated 28,000 residing in refugee camps (an additional 300,000 to 400,000 Rohingyas currently live in Bangladesh outside of the camps). But few of the refugees are eager to return. The journalist Nurul Islam quoted one Rohingya man as saying, "We don't have any rights in Myanmar. . . . If we go back, the armed forces will use us as bonded labor. Many will be sent to jail. There are still curbs on practicing our religion or movement from one place to another without the army's permission."

Figure 13.4.1 Rohingya Refugees Thousands of Rohingya refugees live in squalid camps in Bangladesh and Thailand. Many have been expelled from such camps, and must therefore try to seek sanctuary elsewhere. This photo shows the "unregistered" Kutupalong camp near Cox's Bazar in southeastern Bangladesh.

Figure 13.31 The Spratly Islands The Spratly Islands are small and barely above water at high tide, but they are geopolitically important. Oil may exist in large quantities in the vicinity, heightening the competition over the islands. Southeast Asian countries have been especially concerned about China's military activities in the Spratlys.

and Brunei have all advanced territorial claims over the Spratly Islands, as have China and Taiwan. In 2002, all parties pledged to seek a peaceful solution, but in 2010, military analysts highlighted a worrisome naval buildup in the area, particularly on the part of China, Indonesia, Malaysia, and Singapore.

ASEAN and Global Geopolitics The development and enlargement of ASEAN reduced geopolitical tensions across Southeast Asia. Initially, ASEAN was an alliance of nonsocialist countries fearful of communist insurgency. Through the 1980s, the United States maintained naval and air bases in the Philippines, and U.S. military force bolstered the anticommunist coalition. In the early 1990s, however, the United States, under mounting pressure from Filipino nationalists, withdrew from the Philippines. By that time, the struggle between communism and capitalism was no longer an international issue. In 1995, communist Vietnam itself gained membership in ASEAN, followed by Laos and Cambodia.

While ASEAN is on friendly terms with the United States, one purpose of the organization is to prevent the U.S.—or any other country—from gaining undue influence in the region. ASEAN leaders are thus keen to include all Southeast Asian countries within the association. ASEAN's ultimate international policy is to encourage conversation and negotiation over confrontation, and to enhance trade. As a result, the ASEAN Regional Forum (ARF) was established in 1994 as an annual conference in which Southeast Asian leaders could meet with the leaders of both the East Asian and Western powers to attempt to ease tensions. Seeking to further improve relations with East Asia, ASEAN leaders

have also established an annual ASEAN+3 meeting where its foreign ministers confer with those of China, Japan, and South Korea.

Global Terrorism and International Relations ASEAN has not defused all of the international political tensions in Southeast Asia. Most worrisome has been rise of radical Islamic fundamentalism in the Muslim parts of the region. One group, Jemaah Islamiya (JI), which calls for the creation of a single Islamic state across Indonesia, Malaysia, southern Thailand, and the southern Philippines, has cooperated extensively with Al Qaeda. In 2002, JI agents blew up a tourist-oriented nightclub in Bali, killing 202 people. The group followed this by bombing an American-run hotel in Jakarta in 2003, setting off explosions in Australia's Indonesian embassy in 2004, and attacking three tourist restaurants in Bali in 2005.

By 2006, however, Indonesian authorities began to make headway against JI. A number of its leaders were arrested, and in 2009 and 2010 top-level operatives were killed in security raids. As a result, some analysts believe that JI is no longer an effective fighting force. Most evidence shows that few Southeast Asian Muslims support radical groups such as JI. Since 2004, even mainstream Muslim political parties have not done particularly well in national elections in Indonesia and Malaysia. Radical Islamist groups in the southern Philippines and southern Thailand, on the other hand, remain violent and militarily capable.

Although radical Islam has relatively few supporters in Southeast Asia, the people of the region have generally been wary of U.S. foreign policy initiatives designed to combat global terrorism. Resentment against the United States is especially pronounced in Indonesia and Malaysia, where most people see the war in Iraq as an assault on Islam. Perhaps as a result, Indonesia's courts have given lenient prison sentences to several JI operatives. The group's spiritual leader, Abu Bakar Basyir, for example, served only 26 months of a 30-month sentence for his alleged involvement in the 2002 Bali bombing.

ECONOMIC AND SOCIAL DEVELOPMENT: The Roller-Coaster Ride of Globalized Development

Until the Asian economic crisis of the late 1990s, Southeast Asia was often held up as a model for a new globalized capitalism. With investment capital flowing first from Japan and the United States, then from international investment portfolios, Thailand, Malaysia, and Indonesia experienced impressive economic booms. In the summer of 1997, however, regional economies suffered a profound crisis, with the currencies of both Thailand and Indonesia being devalued almost 50 percent. Subsequent years have seen economic ups and downs, with expansion between 2002 and 2007 turning again to recession with the global economic crisis of 2008–2009.

Recent efforts to enhance growth by fostering the integration of the region's economies have met with mixed success. All 10 ASEAN countries are now members of the AFT, or the ASEAN Free Trade Area, and they have agreed to reduce tariffs against products originating in other member states. In 2010, the much larger ACFTA, or ASEAN-China Free Trade Area, came into being. ACFTA has proved highly controversial, however, as many Southeast Asian firms are having a difficult time competing against Chinese companies (see "Exploring Global Connections: The ASEAN-China Free Trade Area.")

Uneven Economic Development

Southeast Asia today is a region of strikingly uneven economic and social development. While some countries, such as Indonesia, have experienced both booms and busts, others, such as Burma (Myanmar), Laos, and East Timor, missed

---

EXPLORING GLOBAL CONNECTIONS   ACFTA: The ASEAN–China Free Trade Area

January 1, 2010, saw the emergence of the world's largest free trade area in terms of population, linking China with the 10 members of the Association of Southeast Asian Nations (ASEAN). Disagreements remain as to what to call the new organization. In the English-language press, the favored term is ACFTA, the ASEAN–China Free Trade Area; Chinese newspapers more often call it CAFTA, the China–ASEAN Free Trade Area. "CAFTA" is a potentially misleading term, as the same acronym was used for the Central American Free Trade Agreement. Officially, however, that CAFTA became CAFTA-DR in 2004, when the Dominican Republic joined the club.

Controversies much deeper than those of naming plague the new free trade pact (Figure 13.5.1). On January 7, 2010, thousands of workers took to the streets of the Indonesian city of Bandung to demand a delay in implementation of the agreement. The protestors, expressed fears about mass layoffs, worrying that Indonesian firms would not be able to compete with Chinese businesses. Similar concerns have been expressed in Thailand and other Southeast Asian countries worried about competing with the Chinese manufacturing juggernaut. In the Philippines, highland vegetable farmers expressed fear that cheap Chinese carrots and cabbages would displace their own produce in Philippine markets. In response to such concerns, China announced on January 22,

2010 that it would work with ASEAN countries to make adjustments to the agreement.

Enthusiasm for ACFTA, on the other hand, runs high in the relatively poor regions along the border between southern China and mainland Southeast Asia. The governments of Laos and the Guangxi Zhuang Autonomous Region of China quickly initiated high-level talks to figure out how to take advantage of the free trade area. On January 7, 2010, direct flights began between Laos and Guangxi's capital, Nanning. Officials in China's Yunnan province are equally excited about the new economic possibilities.

As the Website GoKunming reported, the region will soon see "a vast network of highways and rail which will provide cities in Yunnan with cheap overland access to markets in Myanmar, Laos, Vietnam, Cambodia, Thailand, Malaysia and Singapore." The article goes on to exclaim that, "difficult as it may be to imagine, Yunnan's days as an economic and political backwater are officially over."

Economic ties between southern China and the rugged lands of northern Southeast Asia have already been surging in recent years. Such developments can have both positive and negative consequences, but they almost always generate local controversies. To reduce such tensions, China has promised to cooperate more extensively on such matters as tourism, infrastructural development, business partnerships, and cultural interaction.

Figure 13.5.1 Chinese Exports in Indonesia A mother strolls through a toy shop in Jakarta dominated by goods imported from China. Indonesian manufacturers are concerned that the new China-ASEAN Free Trade Agreement will further undermine their ability to compete with Chinese firms.

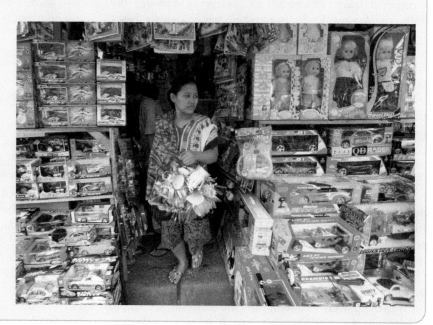

TABLE 13.2	Development Indicators							
Country	GNI per Capita, PPP 2008	GDP Average Annual % Growth (2000–08)	Human Development Index (2007)[a]	Percent of Population Living Below $2 a Day	Life Expectancy (2010)[b]	Under Age 5 Mortality Rate (1990)	Under Age 5 Mortality Rate (2008)	Gender Equity 2008[c]
Burma (Myanmar)			0.586		58	120	98	99
Brunei	50,770		0.920		77			
Cambodia	1,860	9.8	0.593	57.8	61	117	90	90
East Timor	4,690	1.9	0.489	72.8	61	184	93	
Indonesia	3,590	5.2	0.734	60.0	71	86	41	98
Laos	2,050	6.9	0.619	76.8	65	157	61	87
Malaysia	13,730	5.5	0.829	7.8	74	18	6	
Philippines	3,900	5.1	0.751	45.0	72	61	32	102
Singapore	47,940	5.8	0.944		81	7	3	
Thailand	7,760	5.2	0.783	11.5	69	32	14	
Vietnam	2,690	7.7	0.725	48.4	74	56	14	

[a]*United Nations, Human Development Report, 2009.*

[b]*Population Reference Bureau, World Population Data Sheet, 2010.*

[c]*Gender Equity—Ration of female to male enrollments in primary and secondary school. Numbers below 100 have more males in primary/secondary school; numbers above 100 have more females in primary/secondary schools.*

Source: World Bank, World Development Indicators, 2010.

the expansion of the 1980s and 1990s and remain deeply impoverished. Oil-rich Brunei and technologically sophisticated Singapore, on the other hand, remain two of the world's more prosperous countries (Table 13.2). In the Philippines the situation is somewhat more complicated.

The Philippine Decline Fifty years ago, the Philippines was the most highly developed Southeast Asian country and was considered by many to have the brightest prospects in all of Asia. It boasted the best-educated populace in the region, and it seemed to be on the verge of sustained economic development. Per capita GNI in 1960 was higher in the Philippines than in South Korea. By the late 1960s, however, Philippine development had been derailed. Through the 1980s and early 1990s, the country's economy failed to outpace its population growth, resulting in declining living standards. The Philippine people are still well educated and reasonably healthy by world standards, but even the country's educational and health systems declined during the dismal decades of the 1980s and 1990s.

Why did the Philippines fail so spectacularly despite its earlier promise? Although there are no simple answers, it is clear that dictator Ferdinand Marcos (who ruled from 1968 to 1986) squandered billions of dollars while failing to enact programs conducive to genuine development. The Marcos regime instituted a kind of **crony capitalism** in which the president's many friends were granted huge sectors of the economy, while those perceived to be enemies had their properties confiscated. After Marcos declared martial law in 1972 and suspended Philippine democracy, revolutionary activity intensified and the country began to fall into a downward spiral.

While it is tempting to blame the failure of the Philippines on the Marcos regime, such an explanation is only partially adequate. Indonesia and Thailand also saw the development of crony capitalism, yet their economies have proved more competitive. And when the Marcos dictatorship was finally replaced by an elected democratic government in 1986, the Philippine economy continued to languish. Remittances by Filipinos working abroad have kept the economy afloat, but this exodus of labor represents in many respects a tragedy for the country as a whole.

By the beginning of the new millennium, the Philippine economy was showing some signs of revival. The government turned its attention to infrastructural problems, such as electricity generation, and foreign investments began to flow into the country. A vibrant local economy emerged in the former U.S. naval base of Subic Bay. Boasting both world-class facilities and a highly competent local government, Subic Bay has become a major export-processing center. Cebu City, on the central Visayan island of Cebu, also has expanded quickly, giving rise to its local nickname of "Ceboom" (Figure 13.32). Unlike most of its neighbors, the Philippines managed a slight uptick in economic activity in the crisis year of 2009, largely because it had not participated in the financial boom that had preceded the global downturn.

Despite its recent stability, the Philippine economy continues to be undermined by political and social problems. The Philippine political system, modeled on that of the United States, entails elaborate checks and balances between the different branches of government. Critics contend that such "checks" are so effective that little is accomplished. The Philippine government habitually spends far more money than it takes in taxes, leading to a huge public debt

Figure 13.32 Cebu City, Philippines Cebu City in Central Philippines has experienced strong population and economic growth in recent years. The photograph shows a portion of the city's modern central business district.

Figure 13.33 Filipino Seamen Hundreds of thousands of Filipino men work at sea. Many work in the merchant marines, employed by companies all over the world. Others, like those pictured here, serve as crew members of cruise ships.

that consumes a large portion of the national budget. Another obstacle is the fact that the Philippines has the least equitable distribution of wealth in the region. While many members of the elite are fantastically wealthy by any measure, roughly half of the country's people subsist on less than $2 a day. As a result, many Filipinos must seek employment abroad. Women often work as nurses, maids, or nannies, whereas men from the Philippines often work in construction or on ships (Figure 13.33).

The Regional Hub: Singapore Over the past half century, Singapore has been Southeast Asia's greatest developmental success. It has transformed itself from an **entrepôt** port city, a place where goods are imported, stored, and then transshipped, to one of the world's most prosperous and modern states. Singapore, a thriving high-tech manufacturing center, also stands as the communications and financial hub of Southeast Asia. The Singaporean government has played an active role in the development process but has also allowed market forces freedom to operate. Singapore has encouraged investment by multinational companies (especially those involved in technology) and has invested heavily in housing, education, and some social services (Figure 13.34). Although Singapore's economy contracted sharply in 2009, experts see renewed growth in the coming years.

Singapore's political system has nurtured economic development, but it is somewhat repressive and by no means fully democratic. Although elections are held, the government manipulates the process, ensuring that the opposition never gains control of parliament. While many Singaporeans object to such policies, others counter that they have brought fast growth as well as a clean, safe, and remarkably corruption-free society.

Although the Singaporean government has thus far been able to repress dissent, its authoritarian form of capitalism confronts a new challenge in the Internet. National leaders want the communication services that the Net provides, but they are worried about the free expression that it allows, fearing that it will lead to excessive individualism. It will be interesting to see how Singapore responds to this challenge, in part because the governments of China and Vietnam seem to be following the technocratic, authoritarian capitalism pioneered by Singapore.

Malaysia's Insecure Boom Although not nearly as prosperous as Singapore, Malaysia has experienced rapid economic growth over the past several decades and is now generally classified as an upper-middle-income country. Development was initially concentrated in agriculture and natural resource extraction, focused on tropical hardwoods, plantation products (mainly palm oil and rubber), and tin. More recently, manufacturing, especially in labor-intensive high-tech sectors, has become the main engine of growth. As Singapore prospered, many of its enterprises moved their manufacturing operations into neighboring Malaysia. Increasingly, Malaysia's economy is multinational; many Western high-tech firms operate in the country, and several Malaysian companies have themselves established subsidiaries in foreign lands. As a result of its prosperity, Malaysia has attracted hun-

Figure 13.34 Housing in Singapore Despite its free-market approach to economics, the government of Singapore has invested heavily in public housing. Many Singaporeans live in buildings similar to the one depicted in this photograph.

dreds of hundreds of thousands of illegal immigrants, mostly from Indonesia and the Philippines.

Malaysia's economy began to grow rapidly in the 1970s, but it was hard hit by the Asian economic crisis of the late 1990s. The Malaysian government's response to the crisis was different from that of its neighbors. Spurning the advice of the International Monetary Fund, Malaysia instituted temporary currency controls, regulating the flow of international funds in and out of the country. Some observers believe that these policies helped Malaysia recover more rapidly than Thailand and Indonesia, but others are more inclined to credit Malaysia's tight fiscal policies, which have kept its external debt small. Highly dependent on the export of electronic goods, the Malaysian economy remains vulnerable to fluctuations in the North American, European, and Japanese markets. Like Singapore, Malaysia suffered a serious recession in 2009.

The economic geography of modern Malaysia shows large regional variations. Most industrial development has occurred on the west side of peninsular Malaysia, with most of the rest of the country remaining dependent on agriculture and resource extraction. More important, however, are disparities based on ethnicity. The industrial wealth generated in Malaysia has been concentrated in the Chinese community. Ethnic Malays remain less prosperous than Chinese Malaysians, and those of South Asian origin tend to be poorer still. Many of the country's tribal peoples have suffered as development proceeds and their lands are taken away.

The disproportionate prosperity of the local Chinese community is a feature of most Southeast Asian countries. The problem is particularly acute in Malaysia, however, simply because its Chinese minority is so large (some 30 percent of the country's total population). The government's response has been one of aggressive "affirmative action," by

which economic clout is transferred to the numerically dominant Malay, or **Bumiputra** ("sons of the soil"), community. This policy has been reasonably successful, although it has not yet reached its main goal of placing 30 percent of the nation's wealth in the hands of the Bumiputras. Because the Malaysian economy as a whole has grown rapidly since the 1970s, the Chinese community has thrived even as its relative share of the country's wealth declined. Considerable resentment, however, is still felt by the Chinese, many of whom believe that both Malaysia's economic and educational systems are biased against them. More recently, several Malay politicians have been criticizing the system, arguing that it undermines economic incentives for the majority population. In 2009, a number of minor economic sectors were removed from the Bumiputra policy regulations.

Thailand's Ups and Downs Thailand also climbed rapidly during the 1980s and 1990s into the ranks of the world's newly industrialized countries, although it remained much less prosperous than Malaysia. Thailand also experienced a major downturn in the late 1990s that undermined much of this development. Recovery began in earnest after 2000, but the military coup of 2006 coupled with the intensifying insurgency in the far south resulted in another slowdown. Export growth of both agricultural goods and machinery, however, remains strong.

Japanese companies were leading players in the Thai boom of the 1980s and early 1990s. As Japan itself became too expensive for assembly and other manufacturing processes, Japanese firms began to relocate factories to such places as Thailand. They were particularly attracted by the country's low-wage, yet reasonably well-educated workforce. Thailand was also seen as politically stable, lacking the severe ethnic tensions found in many other parts of Asia. Although Thailand's Chinese population is large and economically powerful, relations between the Thai and the local Chinese have generally been good.

Thailand's economic expansion has by no means benefited the entire country to an equal extent. Most industrial development has occurred in the historical core, especially in the greater Bangkok metropolitan area. Yet even in Bangkok, the blessings of progress have been mixed. As the city begins to choke on its own growth, industry has begun to spread outward. The entire Chao Phraya lowland area shares to some extent in the general prosperity due both to its proximity to Bangkok and its rich agricultural resources. In northern Thailand, the Chiang Mai area has profited from its ability to attract large numbers of international tourists.

Other parts of the country have not been so fortunate. Thailand's Lao-speaking northeast (the Khorat Plateau) is the country's poorest regions. Soils here are too thin to support highly productive agriculture, yet the population is sizable. Because of the poverty of their homeland, northeasterners often are forced to seek employment in Bangkok. As Lao-speakers, they often experience ethnic discrimination. Men typically find work in the construction industry; northeastern women more often make their living as prostitutes (Figure 13.35). Not coincidentally, northeastern Thailand has strongly supported the ousted populist prime minister, Thaksin Shinawatra. The Muslim area of southern Thailand also remains very poor, contributing to the region's insurgency.

Indonesian Economic Development At the time of independence (1949), Indonesia was one of the poorest countries in the world. The Dutch had used their colony largely as an extraction zone for tropical crops and mineral resources and had invested little in infrastructure or education. The population of Java mushroomed in the 19th and early 20th centuries, leading to serious land shortages.

The Indonesian economy finally began to expand in the 1970s. Oil exports fueled the early growth, as did the logging of tropical forests. But unlike most other petroleum exporters, Indonesia continued to grow even after prices plummeted in the 1980s. Production subsequently declined, and in 2004 Indonesia had to begin importing oil. But like Thailand and Malaysia, Indonesia proved attractive to multinational companies eager to export from a low-wage economy. Large Indonesian firms, some three-quarters of them owned by local Chinese families, also have capitalized on the country's low wages and abundant resources.

But despite rapid growth in the 1980s and 1990s, Indonesia remains a poor country. Until recently, its pace of economic expansion seldom matched that of Thailand, Singapore, and Malaysia, and it has remained more dependent on the unsustainable exploitation of natural resources. The financial crisis of the late 1990s, moreover, hurt Indonesia more severely than any other country, and political instability continues to hamper economic recovery. Yet Indonesia was one of the few large countries to avoid the recent global economic crisis, with its economy growing by more than 4 percent in 2009.

As in Thailand, development in Indonesia exhibits pronounced geographical disparities. Northwest Java, close to the capital city of Jakarta, has boomed, and much of the resource-rich and moderately populated island of Sumatra has long been relatively prosperous. Eastern Borneo (Kalimantan), another resource area, also is relatively well off. In the overcrowded rural districts of central and eastern Java, however, many peasants have inadequate land and remain near the margins of subsistence. Far eastern Indonesia has experienced little economic or social development, and throughout the remote areas of the "outer islands" tribal peoples have suffered as their resources have been taken and their lands lost to outsiders.

Divergent Economic Paths: Vietnam, Laos, and Cambodia
The three countries of former French Indochina—Vietnam, Cambodia, and Laos—experienced only modest economic expansion during Southeast Asia's boom years of the 1980s and 1990s. This area endured almost continual warfare between 1941 and 1975, which persisted until the mid-1990s in Cambodia. Critics contend that the socialist economic system adopted by these countries prevented sustained economic growth. This debate is now moot, however, since a globalized capitalist model of development has largely been adopted in all three countries.

Vietnam's economy is much stronger than those of Cambodia and Laos. The country's per capita GNI of $2,700, however, is still low by global standards. Postwar reunification in 1975 did not initially bring the anticipated growth, and economic stagnation ensued. Conditions declined in the early 1990s after the fall of the Soviet Union, Vietnam's main supporter and trading partner. Until the mid-1990s, Vietnam remained under embargo by the United States. Frustrated with their country's economic performance, Vietnam's leaders began to embrace the market while retaining the political forms of a communist state. They have, in other words, followed the Chinese model. Vietnam now welcomes multinational corporations, which are attracted by the low wages received by its relatively well-educated workforce (Figure 13.36).

Such efforts seemingly began to pay off after 2000. By 2007, the Vietnamese economy was expanding at roughly 8 percent a year, one of the fastest rates of growth in the world. Foreign investment began to pour into the country, and exports—especially of textiles—began to surge. In January 2007, Vietnam joined the World Trade Organization, which encouraged exports while ensuring the continuation of market-oriented reforms. Like Indonesia, Vietnam continued to grow economically through the global crisis of 2008–2009.

Vietnam's recent economic rise, however, has not been untroubled. Many lowland peasants and upland tribal peoples have been excluded from the boom and are thus growing increasingly discontented. Tensions between the north, center of political authority, and the south, center of economic power, seem to be increasing. Trade disputes have arisen with the United States, which has accused Vietnamese

Figure 13.35 Sex Tourism in Thailand Thailand has one of the highest rates of prostitution in the world. While most prostitutes cater to a local clientele, those working in Bangkok's infamous Patpong district are usually hired by foreign men. Prostitution in Thailand is associated with high rates of HIV infection and with the brutal exploitation of women and girls.

Singapore. *Wealthy Singapore has invested heavily in education and basic social services, giving it a Human Development Index comparable to those of Germany and the United Kingdom.*

East Timor. *The struggling country of East Timor ranks extremely low in regard to basic social development. Outside of sub-Saharan Africa, only Afghanistan has a lower Human Development Index score.*

Figure 13.36 Development Issues: Human Development in Southeast Asia Levels of health, education, and other aspects of human development vary widely across Southeast Asia. As the human development figures shown on the map indicate, Singapore, Brunei, and Malaysia have reached high levels of development, whereas Burma, Cambodia, and East Timor lag well behind.

exporters of dumping such products as farm-raised catfish and shrimp on American markets.

Laos and Cambodia face some of the most serious economic problems in the region. In Cambodia, the ravages of war followed by continuing political instability long undermined economic development. Laos faces special difficulties owing to its rough terrain and relative isolation. Both countries also are hampered by a lack of infrastructure; outside

the few cities, paved roads and reliable electricity are rare. As a result, the economies of both Cambodia and Laos remain largely agricultural in orientation, relying heavily as well on environmentally destructive logging and mining operations. In Laos, subsistence farming still accounts for more than three-quarters of total employment.

The Laotian government is pinning its economic hopes on dam and road building (see "Environment and Politics:

ENVIRONMENT AND POLITICS   Dam Building on the Mekong River

The Mekong is the world's 12th largest river, its average annual discharge being roughly equal to that of the Mississippi. It is also the largest and most important river in Southeast Asia. The Mekong's flow is vital for irrigation and domestic water supplies in Laos, Thailand, Cambodia, and southern Vietnam. The river is also noted for its productive fisheries, worth $2 billion a year, and its diverse fauna. The Mekong has more large fish species that any other river. The Mekong Giant Catfish, which can grow to more than 11 feet (3.3 meters) and 660 pounds (300 kilograms), is usually regarded as the world's largest freshwater fish (Figure 13.6.1).

During the 1950s and 1960s, ambitious plans were developed for "taming" this giant river. Planners wanted to build dams to generate electricity and supply dry-season irrigation water. They also wanted to remove the large rapids that have long impeded navigation. The national governments of the Mekong Basin enthusiastically supported such schemes at first, as did the United States. As a result, local governments created the Mekong River Commission to ensure cooperation and facilitate development. Critics at the time, however, objected to the fact that such dams would displace hundreds of thousands of people in addition to undermining local freshwater fisheries. Their concerns were moot, however, because by the late 1960s all dam-building plans had to be put on hold due to the chaos of the Vietnam War and related conflicts. When peace returned to the region, Mekong River Commission reconsidered its early stance, deciding to focus not on building dams but on managing and preserving existing resources.

Although the Mekong River Commission turned away from a construction-oriented approach to river development, the same cannot be said of China, which is not a member of the Commission even through it controls the river's headwaters and upper reaches. Over the past 30 years, China has constructed three large hydroelectric dams on the river, and is currently building or planning an additional four. China has also been blasting away the rapids that hamper navigation on the upper Mekong.

Most residents of the lower Mekong are not pleased with China's actions. They worry that dam building and rapids blasting will harm fish stocks and reduce the downstream flow of the river. Fish catches have declined, and several endemic animal species, including the Mekong River dolphin and manatee, became endangered shortly after the first Chinese dams were finished. Concerns about the river heated up rapidly in early 2010 when its discharge reached its lowest level in decades. Although scientists claimed that the El Niño-related drought in northern Southeast Asia was the primary culprit, many local people focused their anger on China. As a result, noisy demonstrations were held in front of the Chinese Embassy in Bangkok.

Although the four Southeast Asian countries of the lower Mekong are concerned about the Chinese dams, they are also highly dependent on trade with China, and they certainly do not want to antagonize their giant northern neighbor. The governments of Laos and Cambodia, moreover, are keen to build their own dams so that they can capture hydroelectric and navigation benefits. As they do not have the expertise or the funds to build such dams by themselves, they are currently negotiating with the Chinese government as well as Chinese engineering firms. If these projects go through, the freshwater fisheries of the lower Mekong will be greatly diminished.

Figure 13.6.1 Endangered Species The Mekong Giant Catfish (Pangasianodon gigas), the world's largest freshwater fish, is currently threatened by dam-building projects on the Mekong River. In this photo, taken in 2005, Thai fishermen are measuring the largest fish caught in over 40 years.

Dam Building on the Mekong River"). The country is mountainous and has many large rivers, and could therefore generate large quantities of electricity, in high demand in neighboring Thailand and Vietnam. Up to 100 new dam projects have been proposed for the Mekong River system, most of them to be located in Laos. The Asian Development Bank also is supporting an ambitious road-building program that would pass through Laos in order to link China to Thailand. The Laotian government, however, remains repressive, discouraging foreign investment.

Although still deeply impoverished, Cambodia has experienced a recent economic boom of surprising proportions. Foreign investment has generated an expanding textile sector, tourism is thriving, mining is taking off, and in 2005 important oil and natural gas fields were discovered in Cambodian territorial waters. From 2004 to 2007, the Cambodian grew at an annual rate of over 10 percent. China has recently emerged as Cambodia's closest economic partner. Between 2006 and early 2010, China invested more than $10 billion in Cambodia, a huge figure considering the fact that the country's entire annual economic output is only about $11 billion.

Cambodia's extremely rapid economic expansion was possible only because the country's economic starting point was at such a low level. A lack of both skills and basic infrastructure, as well as problems of political instability and corruption, could easily result in renewed economic difficulties. The recent economic boom has also led to an epidemic of "land-grabbing," in which politically connected elites take over the properties of impoverished peasants in order to develop them (Figure 13.37).

Despite their basic lack of development, Cambodia and Laos are not as poor as one might expect from the official economic statistics. Both countries have relatively low population densities and abundant resources. Their low per capita GNI figures, more importantly, partially reflect the fact that many of their people remain in a subsistence economy. While the Laotian highlanders make few contributions to GNI, most of them at least have adequate shelter and food.

Burma's Troubled Economy Burma (Myanmar) stands near the bottom of the scale of Southeast Asian economic development. For all of its many problems, however, Burma is a land of great potential. It has abundant resources—including natural gas, oil and other minerals, water, and timber—as well as a large expanse of fertile farmland. Its population density is moderate, and its people are reasonably well educated. The country, however, has seen little economic or social development.

Burma's economic woes can be traced in part to the continual warfare that it has experienced. Most observers also blame economic policy. Beginning in earnest in 1962, Burma (Myanmar) attempted to isolate its economic system from global forces in order to achieve self-sufficiency under a system of Buddhist socialism. While its intentions were admirable, the experiment was not successful. Instead of creating a self-contained economy, Burma (Myanmar) found itself burdened by smuggling and black-market activities.

In the early 1990s, Burma began to open its economy to market forces and increase its involvement in foreign trade. By 2000, however, the reform measures had stalled out, and in 2003 a banking crisis resulted in another round of economic havoc. High rates of inflation and worrisome fiscal deficits undermine business confidence, but probably the most damaging economic impediment is Burma's exchange-rate policy. In 2009, when the official exchange rate was 6.4 Burmese kyat to the U.S. dollar, one could get up to 1,090 kyat to the dollar in street markets. The Burmese military and its political allies continue to run much of the economy in a highly inefficient manner. Although Burma's government is now hoping that natural gas exports and increased trade with China and India will help solve its economic problems, its economic policies will probably continue to undermine genuine development.

Figure 13.37 Phnom Penh Severe conflicts have emerged in Cambodia's booming capital city, Phnom Penh, as slum areas are cleared to make way for development projects. In this photograph, a woman wearing a helmet tries to stop a bulldozer from demolishing her home while her daughter tries to pull her away from the dangerous machine.

Globalization and the Southeast Asian Economy

As the previous discussion shows, Southeast Asia has undergone rapid but uneven integration into the global economy (Figure 13.38). Singapore has thoroughly staked its future to the success of multinational capitalism, and several neighboring countries are following suit. According to one measurement, Malaysia and Singapore have, respectively, the fourth and fifth most trade-dependent economies in the world. Even communist Vietnam and once-isolationist Burma (Myanmar) have opened their doors to international commerce, although with far more success in the former case than the latter.

Much debate has arisen among scholars over the roots of Southeast Asia's economic gains, as well as its more recent economic problems. Those who credit primarily the diligence, discipline, and entrepreneurial skills of the Southeast Asian peoples are optimistic about future economic expansion. Skeptics argue, however, that most of the region's growth has come from the application of large quantities of labor and capital unsupported by real advances in productivity. Regardless of how this debate turns out, it is clear that Southeast Asia's globalized economies are heavily dependent upon exports to the international market. In the 1990s, many observers thought that the booming economies of Southeast

Figure 13.38 Southeast Asia's Global Linkages Much of Southeast Asia is tightly integrated into global trade networks, exporting large amounts of both primary products and manufactured goods, and accumulating large reserves of foreign currency and gold. This is particularly true of Malaysia and Singapore. In contrast, Laos, Cambodia, and especially Burma (Myanmar) remain less connected with the global economic system, although their ties are growing.

Asia had become overly dependent on exports to the United States, but in recent years the rise of China has resulted in a more balanced trading regime. In 2009, for example, 10.9 percent of Thailand's exports went to the United States, while 16.8 percent went to China (including Hong Kong) and another 10.3 went to Japan. Currently, the main concern in Southeast Asia is competition from China in exporting inexpensive consumer goods to the rest of the world. As is true in the United States, many people in the region believe that the Chinese currency is undervalued, giving China an unfair advantage in export markets.

Globalized industrial production in Southeast Asia remains controversial. Consumers in the world's wealthy countries worry that many of their basic purchases, such as sneakers and clothing, are produced under exploitative conditions. Movements have thus emerged to pressure both multinational corporations and Southeast Asian governments to improve the working conditions of laborers in the export industries. The multinational firms in question counter that such exploitative conditions occur not in their own factories, but rather in those of local companies that subcontract for them; activists, however, point out that multinationals have tremendous influence over their local subcontractors. Some Southeast Asian leaders object to the entire debate, accusing Westerners of wanting to prevent Southeast Asian development and protect their own home markets, under the pretext of concern over worker rights.

Issues of Social Development

As might be expected, several key indicators of social development in Southeast Asia correlate well with levels of economic development. Singapore thus ranks among the world leaders in regard to health and education, as does the small,

yet oil-rich country of Brunei. East Timor, Laos, and Cambodia, not surprisingly, come out near the bottom for these measures. The people of Vietnam, however, are healthier and better educated than might be expected on the basis of their country's overall economic performance. Burma (Myanmar), on the other hand, has seen a decline in some social indicators. Its per capita health budget is one of the lowest in the world, while its military budget, as a percentage of its overall economic output, is one of the highest.

With the exception of Laos, Cambodia, Burma, and East Timor, Southeast Asia has achieved relatively high levels of social welfare. In Burma, however, life expectancy at birth hovers around a miserable 58 years (as compared to Vietnam's 74 years), and in Laos, female illiteracy rates remain near 40 percent. But even the poorest countries of the region have made improvements in mortality under the age of 5, as is evident from the figures in Table 13.2. Progress has been more pronounced in prosperous countries such as Malaysia and Singapore, whereas war-torn Cambodia has made smaller gains. Thailand has recently begun to provide a social safety net for its citizens, hoping to raise its level of social development to that found in the world's wealthier countries.

Most of the governments of Southeast Asia have placed a high priority on basic education. Literacy rates are relatively high in most countries of the region. Much less success, however, has been realized in university and technical education. As Southeast Asian economies continue to grow, this educational gap is beginning to have negative consequences, forcing many students to study abroad. High levels of basic education, along with general economic and social development, also have led to reduced birthrates through much of Southeast Asia. With population growing much more slowly now than before, economic gains are more easily translated into improved living standards.

Summary

- Some of the most serious problems created by globalization in Southeast Asia are environmental. Given the emphasis placed by global trade on wood products, it is perhaps understandable that Southeast Asia has sacrificed so many of its forests to support economic development. But in most of the region, forests are now seriously depleted. As the Chinese economy expands, market demand for Southeast Asian forest products is increasing rapidly.

- Deforestation in Southeast Asia is also linked to domestic population growth and changes in settlement patterns. As people move from densely populated, fertile lowland areas into remote uplands, both environmental damage and cultural conflicts often follow. Population movements in Southeast Asia also have a global dimension. This is particularly true in regard to the Philippines, which has sent some 8 million workers to more prosperous parts of the world.

- Southeast Asia is characterized today by tremendous cultural diversity. In recent years, conflicts over language and religion have seriously weakened several Southeast Asian countries, including Indonesia, East Timor, and Burma (Myanmar). However, the region has found a new sense of regional identity as expressed through ASEAN, the Association of Southeast Asian Nations.

- The relative success of ASEAN has not solved all of Southeast Asia's political tensions. Many of its countries still argue about geographical, political, and economic issues, while insurgencies remain strong in the Philippines and Thailand. Cambodia, Laos, and especially Burma (Myanmar) have also been held back by repressive and corrupt governments.

- Although ASEAN has played an economic as well as political role, its economic successes have been more limited. Most of the region's trade is still directed outward toward the traditional centers of the global economy: North America, Europe, and East Asia. This orientation is not surprising, considering the export-focused policies of most Southeast Asian countries. A significant question for Southeast Asia's future is whether the region will de-velop an integrated regional economy. A more important issue is whether social and economic development will be able to lift the entire region out of poverty instead of benefiting just the more fortunate areas.

Key Terms

animism (page 610)
Association of Southeast Asian Nations (ASEAN) (page 590)
Bumiputra (page 627)
copra (page 601)
crony capitalism (page 625)
domino theory (page 616)

entrepôt (page 626)
Golden Triangle (page 600)
Khmer Rouge (page 616)
lingua franca (page 610)
primate cities (page 605)
Ramayana (page 607)
shifted cultivators (page 604)

Sunda Shelf (page 595)
swidden (page 600)
transmigration (page 603)
tsunamis (page 595)
typhoons (page 597)

Review Questions

1. Why are river deltas so important in the settlement pattern of Southeast Asia?

2. Explain how and why the monsoon climates of Southeast Asia differ between mainland and islands.

3. What do we mean when we refer to the "globalization of world forestry"?

4. Explain why smoke and air pollution are so pronounced in Southeast Asia.

5. Compare and contrast the three major types of agriculture in the region—swidden, plantation, and rice cultivation.

6. How might "transmigration" solve and also aggravate a country's population problems?

7. What major religions are found in Southeast Asia? Describe the historical and contemporary patterns for each religion.

8. Why is there ambivalence about the English language in some Southeast Asian countries?

9. What are the ethnic tensions facing Indonesia? Locate the different problem areas on a map.

10. What are the goals of ASEAN, and how have those goals changed in the last several decades?

Thinking Geographically

1. Discuss the ramifications of state-sponsored migration in Indonesia from areas of high population density to areas of low population density in both the "sending" and the "receiving" areas.

2. Why should—or should not—citizens of the United States be concerned about deforestation in Southeast Asia? If they should be, what would be the proper ways they might show such concern?

3. What might the fate of animism be in the new millennium? Consider whether it might be doomed to extinction before the forces of modern economics and national integration, or whether it may persist as tribal peoples struggle to retain their cultural identities.

4. What should be the position of the English language in the educational systems of Southeast Asia? What should be the position of each country's national language? What about local languages?

5. How might ethnic tensions in countries such as Burma (Myanmar) and Indonesia be reduced? Does Indonesia have a reasonable claim to such areas as Irian Jaya?

6. What roles might ASEAN play in the coming years? Should it concentrate on economic or political issues?

7. How could Malaysia successfully integrate its economy into the global system and at the same time regulate the flow of global (or Western) culture? Evaluate whether Singapore can continue to experience economic growth while severely limiting basic freedoms.

8. Is the Southeast Asian economic path of integration into the global economy, which is marked by an openness to multinational corporations, going to prove wise in the long run, or do its potential hazards outweigh its benefits?

Regional Novels and Films

Novels

Anthony Burgess, *The Long Day Wanes: A Malaysian Trilogy* (1965, Norton)

Joseph Conrad, *Victory* (1936, Doubleday)

Graham Greene, *The Quiet American* (1956, Viking Press)

Ninfong Ho, *Rice without Rain* (1990, HarperCollins)

F. Sionil Jose, *The Pretenders* (1962, Philippines)

Mochtar Lubis, *A Road with No End* (1982, Graham Bush)

W. Somerset Maugham, *Borneo Stories* (1976, Heinemann)

Paul Theroux, *The Consul's Fire* (1977, Houghton Mifflin)

Films

Anak-Anak Borobudur (2007, Indonesia)

The Bet Collector (2006, Philippines)

The Big Durian (2003, Malaysia)

The Blossoming of Maximo Oliveros (2005, Philippines)

Eliana, Eliana (2002, Indonesia)

Indochine (1992, France)

Jan Dara (2001, Thailand)

King of the Garbage Dump (2002, Vietnam)

Midnight, My Love (2005, Thailand)

Money No Enough 2 (2008, Singapore)

Platoon (1987, U.S.)

The Scent of Green Papaya (1993, Vietnam)

Sunset at Chaopraya (1996, Thailand)

Bibliography

Acharya, Amitav. 2001. *Constructing a Security Community of Southeast Asia: ASEAN and the Problem of Regional Order.* New York: Routledge.

Broad, Robin, and Cavanagh, John. 1993. *Plundering Paradise: The Struggle for the Environment in the Philippines.* Berkeley: University of California Press.

Broek, Jan O. 1944. "Diversity and Unity in Southeast Asia." *Geographical Review* 34, 175–195.

Dixon, Chris. 1991. *South East Asia in the World Economy: A Regional Geography.* Cambridge, UK: Cambridge University Press.

Gupta, Avijit, (ed.). 2005. *The Physical Geography of Southeast Asia.* New York: Oxford University Press.

Hefner, Robert W. 2001. *The Politics of Multiculturalism: Pluralism and Citizenship in Malaysia, Singapore, and Indonesia.* Honolulu: University of Hawaii Press.

Herring, George. 1995. *America's Longest War: The U.S. and Vietnam 1950–1975.* New York: McGraw-Hill.

Peleggi, Maurizio. 2007. *Thailand: The Worldly Kingdom.* London: Reaktion Books.

Rumney, Thomas A. 2010. *The Geography of Southeast Asia: A Scholarly Bibliography and Guide.* Lanham, MD: University Press of America.

Steinberg, David Joel. 2001. *Burma: The State of Myanmar.* Washington, DC: Georgetown University Press.

Taylor, Jean G. 2004. *Indonesia: Peoples and Histories.* New Haven, CT: Yale University Press.

Ulack, Richard, and Pauer, Gyula. 1989. *Atlas of Southeast Asia.* New York: Macmillan.

 Mastering Geography

 MapMaster™

Log in to www.masteringgeography.com for MapMaster™ interactive maps, geography videos, RSS feeds, flashcards, web links, an eText version of *Diversity Amid Globalization*, and self-study quizzes to enhance your study of Southeast Asia.

MapMaster™ presents 13 Place Name and 13 Layered Thematic interactive maps to help students practice and master their geographic literacy, spatial reasoning, and critical thinking skills.

Glossary

Aborigine An indigenous inhabitant of Australia.

acid rain Harmful form of precipitation high in sulfur and nitrogen oxides. Caused by industrial and auto emissions, acid rain damages aquatic and forest ecosystems in regions such as eastern North America and Europe.

African Union (AU) Founded in 1963, the organization grew to include all the states of the continent except South Africa, which finally was asked to join in 1994. In 2004 the body changed its name from the Organization of African Unity (OAU) to the African Union. It is mostly a political body that has tried to resolve regional conflicts.

agrarian reform A popular but controversial strategy to redistribute land to peasant farmers. Throughout the 20th century, various states redistributed land from large estates or granted land titles from vast public lands in order to reallocate resources to the poor and stimulate development. Agrarian reform occurred in various forms, from awarding individual plots or communally held land to creating state-run collective farms.

agribusiness The practice of large-scale, often corporate farming in which business enterprises control closely integrated segments of food production, from farm to grocery store.

agricultural density The number of farmers per unit of arable land. This figure indicates the number of people who directly depend upon agriculture, and it is an important indicator of population pressure in places where rural subsistence dominates.

alluvial fan A fan-shaped deposit of sediments dropped by a river or stream flowing out of a mountain range.

Altiplano The largest intermontane plateau in the Andes, which straddles Peru and Bolivia and ranges in elevation from 10,000 to 13,000 feet (3,000 to 4,000 meters).

altitudinal zonation The relationship between higher elevations, cooler temperatures, and changes in vegetation that result from the environmental lapse rate (averaging 3.5°F for every 1,000 feet [6.5°C for every 1,000 meters]). In Latin America, four general altitudinal zones exist: tierra caliente, tierra templada, tierra fria, and tierra helada.

animism A wide variety of tribal religions based on the worship of nature spirits and human ancestors.

animist One who follows an animist religion.

anthropocentric Human-centered.

anthropogenic Caused by human activities.

anthropogenic landscapes A landscape heavily transformed by humans.

Aotearoa The ancestral Maori word, meaning "Land of the Long White Cloud," for New Zealand.

apartheid The policy of racial separateness that directed separate residential and work spaces for white, blacks, coloreds, and Indians in South Africa for nearly 50 years. It was abolished when the African National Congress came to power in 1994.

archipelagos Island groups, often oriented in an elongated pattern.

areal differentiation The geographic description and explanation of spatial differences on Earth's surface, including both physical as well as human patterns.

areal integration The geographic description and explanation of how places, landscapes, and regions are connected, interact, and are integrated with each other.

Asia-Pacific Economic Cooperation Group (APEC) An international group of Asian and Pacific Basin nations that fosters coordinated economic development within the region.

Association of Southeast Asian Nations (ASEAN) An international organization linking together the 10 most important countries of Southeast Asia.

atoll Low, sandy islands made from coral, often oriented around a central lagoon.

autonomous areas Minor political subunits created in the former Soviet Union and designed to recognize the special status of minority groups within existing republics.

autonomous region In the context of China, provinces that have been granted a certain degree of political and cultural autonomy, or freedom from centralized authority, owing to the fact that they contain large numbers of non-Han Chinese people. Critics contend that they have little true autonomy.

Baikal-Amur Mainline (BAM) Railroad Key central Siberian railroad connection completed in the Soviet era (1984), which links the Yenisey and Amur rivers and parallels the Trans-Siberian Railroad.

balkanization Geopolitical process of fragmentation of larger states into smaller ones through independence of smaller regions and ethnic groups. The term takes its name from the geopolitical fabric of the Balkan region.

Berlin Conference The 1884 conference that divided Africa into European colonial territories. The boundaries created in Berlin satisfied European ambition but ignored indigenous cultural affiliations. Many of Africa's civil conflicts can be traced to ill-conceived territorial divisions crafted in 1884.

biofuels Energy sources derived from plants or animals. Throughout the developing world, wood, charcoal, and dung are primary energy sources for cooking and heating.

biome Ecologically interactive flora and fauna adapted to a specific environment. Examples are deserts or tropical rain forests.

bioregion A spatial unit or region of local plants and animals adapted to a specific environment such as a tropical savanna.

Bodhisattva In the religion of Mahayana Buddhism, a spiritual being that helps others attain enlightenment.

Bolsheviks A faction within the Russian communist movement led by Lenin that successfully took control of the country in 1917.

boreal forest Coniferous forest found in high-latitude or mountainous environments of the Northern Hemisphere.

brain drain Migration of the best-educated people from developing countries to developed nations where economic opportunities are greater.

brain gain The potential of return migrants to contribute to the social and economic development of their country of origin with the experiences they have gained abroad.

British East India Company Private trade organization with its own army that acted as an arm of Britain in monopolizing trade in South Asia until 1857, when it was abolished and replaced by full governmental control.

bubble economy A highly inflated economy that cannot be sustained. Bubble economies usually result from the rapid influx of international capital into a developing country.

buffer zone An array of nonaligned or friendly states that "buffer" a larger country from invasion. In Eurasia, maintaining a buffer zone has been a long-term policy of Russia (and also of the former Soviet Union) to protect its western borders from European invasion.

Bumiputra The name given to native Malays (literally, "sons of the soil"), who are given preference for jobs and schooling by the Malaysian government.

Burakumin The indigenous outcast group of Japan, a people whose ancestors reputedly worked in leathercraft and other "polluting" industries.

cap-and-trade energy policy An energy policy in which overall carbon emissions are limited or *capped* by a central authority within a system that allows polluters to buy and sell carbon credits (or *allowances*) in an emissions-trading marketplace.

capital leakage The gap between the gross receipts an industry (such as tourism) brings into a developing area and the amount of capital retained.

Caribbean Community and Common Market (CARICOM) A regional trade organization established in 1972 that includes mostly former English Caribbean colonies as its members.

caste system Complex division of South Asian society into different hierarchically ranked hereditary groups. Most explicit in Hindu society, the caste system is also found in other South Asian cultures to a lesser degree.

Central American Free Trade Association (CAFTA) A 2004 free trade agreement between the United States and five Central American countries—Guatemala, Nicaragua, El Salvador, Honduras, and Costa Rica—plus the Dominican Republic.

central place theory A theory used to explain the distribution of cities, and the relationships between different cities, based on retail marketing.

centralized economic planning An economic system in which the state sets production targets and controls the means of production.

chain migration A pattern of migration in which a sending area becomes linked to a particular destination, such as Dominicans with New York City.

China proper The eastern half of the country of China where the Han Chinese form the dominant ethnic group. The vast majority of China's population is located in China proper.

circular migration Temporary labor migration, in which an individual seeks short-term employment overseas, earns money, and then returns home.

clan A social unit that is typically smaller than a tribe or ethnic group but larger than a family, based on supposed descent from a common ancestor.

climate region A region of similar climatic conditions. An example would be the marine west-coast climate regions found on the west coasts of North America and Europe.

climographs Graph of average annual temperature and precipitation data by month and season.

Closer Economic Relations (CER) Agreement An agreement signed in 1982 between Australia and New Zealand designed to eliminate all economic and trade barriers between the two countries.

Cold War The ideological struggle between the United States and the Soviet Union that was conducted between 1946 and 1990.

colonialism The formal and established rule over local peoples by a larger imperialist government.

coloured A racial category used throughout South Africa to define people of mixed European and African ancestry.

Columbian exchange An exchange of people, diseases, plants, and animals between the Americas (New World) and Europe/Africa (Old World) initiated by the arrival of Christopher Columbus in 1492.

command economy Centrally planned and controlled economies, generally associated with socialist or communist countries, in which all goods and services, along with agricultural and industrial products, are strictly regulated. This was done during the Soviet era in both the Soviet Union and its eastern European satellites.

Commonwealth of Independent States (CIS) A loose political union of former Soviet republics (without the Baltic states) established in 1992 after the dissolution of the Soviet Union.

concentric zone model A simplified description of urban land use: a well-defined central business district (CBD) is surrounded by concentric zones of residential activity, with higher-income groups living on the urban periphery.

Confucianism The philosophical system developed by Confucius in the 6th century BCE.

connectivity The degree to which different locations are linked with one another through transportation and communication infrastructure.

continentality Inland climates, removed from the ocean, with hot summers and cold winters such as those found in interior North America and Russia.

convection cells Large areas of slow-moving molten rock in Earth's interior that are responsible for moving tectonic plates.

convergent plate boundary Where two tectonic plates converge or are being forced together by convection cells. The Andes Mountains, for example, are formed by the converging Nazca and South America plates.

copra Dried coconut meat.

core-periphery model According to this scheme, the United States, Canada, western Europe, and Japan constitute the global economic core, while other regions make up a less-developed economic periphery from which the core extracts resources.

Cossacks Highly mobile Slavic-speaking Christians of the southern Russian steppe who were pivotal in expanding Russian influence in 16th- and 17th-century Siberia.

creolization The blending of African, European, and even some Amerindian cultural elements into the unique sociocultural systems found in the Caribbean.

crony capitalism A system in which close friends of a political leader are either legally or illegally given business advantages in return for their political support.

cultural assimilation The process in which immigrants are culturally absorbed into the larger host society.

cultural imperialism The active promotion of one cultural system over another, such as the implantation of a new language, school system, or bureaucracy. Historically, this has been primarily associated with European colonialism.

cultural landscape Primarily the visible and tangible expression of human settlement (house architecture, street patterns, field form, etc.), but also includes the intangible, value-laden aspects of a particular place and its association with a group of people.

cultural nationalism A process of protecting, either formally (with laws) or informally (with social values), the primacy of a specific cultural system against influences from another culture.

cultural syncretism or hybridization The blending of two or more cultures, which then produces a synergistic third culture or specific behavior that exhibits traits from all cultural parents.

culture Learned and shared behavior by a group of people empowering them with a distinct "way of life"; it includes both material (technology, tools, etc.) and non-material (speech, religion, values, etc.) components.

culture hearth An area of historical cultural innovation.

cyclones Large storms, marked by well-defined air circulation around a low-pressure center. Tropical cyclones are typically called hurricanes in the Atlantic Ocean and typhoons in the western Pacific.

Cyrillic alphabet Based on the Greek alphabet and used by Slavic languages heavily influenced by the Eastern Orthodox Church. Attributed to the missionary work of St. Cyril in the 9th century.

dacha A Russian country cottage used especially in the summer.

dalits The so-called untouchable population of India; people often considered socially polluting because of their historical connections with occupations classified as unclean, such a leatherworking and latrine-cleaning.

decolonialization The process of a former colony's gaining (or regaining) independence over its territory and establishing (or reestablishing) an independent government.

demographic transition model A four-stage scheme that explains different rates of population growth over time through differing birth and death rates.

denuclearization The process whereby nuclear weapons are removed from an area and dismantled or taken elsewhere.

dependency theory A popular theory to explain patterns of economic development in Latin America. Its central premise is that underdevelopment was created by the expansion of European capitalism into the region that served to develop "core" countries in Europe and to impoverish and make dependent peripheral areas such as Latin America.

desertification The spread of desert conditions into semi-arid areas owing to improper management of the land.

diaspora The scattering of a particular group of people over a vast geographical area. Originally, the term referred to the migration of Jews out of their original homeland, but now it has been generalized to refer to any ethnic dispersion.

divergent plate boundary A place where two tectonic plates move away from each other. Here, magma often flows from Earth's interior, producing volcanoes on the surface such as in Iceland. In other divergent zones large trenches or rift valleys are created.

dollarization An economic strategy in which a country adopts the U.S. dollar as its official currency. A country can be partially dollarized, using U.S. dollars alongside its national currency, or fully dollarized, when the U.S. dollar becomes the only medium of exchange and a country gives up its own national currency. Panama fully dollarized in 1904; more recently, Ecuador became fully dollarized in 2000, followed by El Salvador in 2001.

domestication The purposeful selection and breeding of wild plants and animals for cultural purposes.

domino theory A U.S. geopolitical policy of the 1970s that stemmed from the assumption that if Vietnam fell to the communists, the rest of Southeast Asia would soon follow.

Dravidian language A language that belongs to a large linguistic family that is native to South Asia. Once spoken throughout South Asia, Dravidian languages are now largely confined to southern India and northern Sri Lanka.

Eastern Orthodox Christianity A loose confederation of self-governing churches in eastern Europe and Russia that are historically linked to Byzantine traditions and to the primacy of the patriarch of Constantinople (Istanbul).

economic convergence The notion that globalization will result in the world's poorer countries gradually catching up with more developed economies.

El Niño An abnormally warm current that appears periodically in the eastern Pacific Ocean and usually influences storminess along the western coasts of the Americas. During an El Niño event, which can last several years, torrential rains often bring devastating floods to the Pacific coasts of North, Central, and South America.

entrepôt A city and port that specializes in transshipment of goods.

environmental lapse rate The decline in temperature as one ascends higher in the atmosphere. On average, the temperature declines 3.5°F for every 1,000 feet ascended, or 6.5°C for every 1,000 meters.

ethnicity A shared cultural identity held by a group of people with a common background or history, often as a minority group within a larger society.

ethnic religions A religion closely identified with a specific ethnic or tribal group, often to the point of assuming the role of the major defining characteristic of that group. Normally, ethnic religions do not actively seek new converts.

Euroland The assemblage of European countries belonging to the European Monetary Union (EMU) and using the euro as their currency.

European Union (EU) The current association of 27 European countries that are joined together in an agenda of economic, political, and cultural integration.

exclave A portion of a country's territory that lies outside its contiguous land area.

exotic river A river that issues from a humid area and flows into a dry area otherwise lacking streams.

fair trade An international certification movement to identify primary commodities exported from the developing world in which farmers earn a better price for their product. Commodities such as coffee, tea, and forest products are certified "fair trade" when small-scale producers earn more for their product and production methods are viewed as environmentally and socially sustainable.

federal states Political system in which a significant amount of power is given to individual states. In India, these states were created upon independence in 1947 and were drawn primarily along linguistic lines, so that today state power is often associated with specific ethnic groups within the nation.

Fertile Crescent An ecologically diverse zone of lands in Southwest Asia that extends from Lebanon eastward to Iraq and that is often associated with early forms of agricultural domestication.

free trade zone (FTZ) A duty-free and tax-exempt industrial park created to attract foreign corporations and create industrial jobs.

forward capital A capital city deliberately positioned near a contested territory, signifying the state's interest and presence in this zone of conflict.

fossil water Water supplies that were stored underground during wetter climatic periods.

gender gap A term often used to describe gender differences in salary, working conditions, or political power.

geomancy The traditional Chinese and Korean practice of designing buildings in accordance with the principles of cosmic harmony and discord that supposedly course through the local topography.

genocide The deliberate and systematic killing of a racial, political, or cultural group.

gentrification A process of urban revitalization in which higher income residents displace lower-income residents in central-city neighborhoods.

glasnost A policy of greater political openness initiated during the 1980s by Soviet president Mikhail Gorbachev.

globalization The increasing interconnectedness of people and places throughout the world through converging processes of economic, political, and cultural change.

global warming The increase in global temperatures as a result of the magnification of the natural greenhouse effect due to human-produced pollutants. The resulting climate change could cause profound—and probably damaging—changes to Earth's environments.

Golden Triangle An area of northern Thailand, Burma, and Laos that is known as a major source region for heroin and is plugged into the global drug trade.

Gondwanaland The ancient megacontinent that included Africa, South America, Antarctica, Australia, Madagascar, and Saudi Arabia. Some 250 million years ago, it began to split apart due to plate tectonics.

grassification The conversion of tropical forest into pasture for cattle ranching. Typically, this process involves introducing species of grasses and cattle, mostly from Africa.

Great Escarpment A landform that rims southern Africa from Angola to South Africa. It forms where the narrow coastal plains meet the elevated plateaus in an abrupt break in elevation.

Greater Antilles The four large Caribbean islands of Cuba, Jamaica, Hispaniola, and Puerto Rico.

Green Revolution Term applied to the development of agricultural techniques used in developing countries that involve new, genetically altered seeds that provide higher yields than native seeds when combined with high inputs of chemical fertilizer, irrigation, and pesticides.

greenhouse effect The natural process of lower atmosphere heating that results from the trapping of incoming and reradiated solar energy by water moisture, clouds, and other atmospheric gases.

Group of Eight (G-8) A collection of powerful countries that confer regularly on key global economic and political issues. It includes the United States, Canada, Japan, Great Britain, Germany, France, Italy, and Russia.

gross domestic product (GDP)/gross national product (GNP) GDP is the total value of goods and services produced within a given country (or other geographical unit) in a single year. GNP is a somewhat broader measure that includes the inflow of money from other countries in the form of the repatriation of profits and other returns on investments, as well as the outflow to other countries for the same purposes.

gross national income (GNI) The value of all final goods and services produced within a country's borders (gross domestic product, or GDP), plus the net income from abroad (formerly referred to as gross national product, or GNP).

gross national income (GNI) per capita The figure that results from dividing a country's GNI by the total population.

guest workers Workers from Europe's agricultural periphery—primarily Greece, Turkey, southern Italy, and the former Yugoslavia—solicited to work in Germany, France, Sweden, and Switzerland during chronic labor shortages in Europe's boom years (1950s to 1970s).

Gulag Archipelago A collection of Soviet-era labor camps for political prisoners, made famous by writer Aleksandr Solzhenitsyn.

Hajj An Islamic religious pilgrimage to Makkah. One of the five essential pillars of the Muslim creed to be undertaken once in life, if an individual is physically and financially able to do it.

haoles Light-skinned Europeans or U.S. citizens in the Hawaiian Islands.

high islands Larger, more elevated islands, often focused around recent volcanic activity.

Hindu nationalism A contemporary "fundamental" religious and political movement that promotes Hindu values as the essential—and exclusive—fabric of Indian society. As a political movement, it appears to have less tolerance of India's large Muslim minority than other political movements.

homelands Nominally independent ethnic territories created for blacks under the grand apartheid scheme. Homelands were on marginal land, overcrowded, and poorly serviced. In the post-apartheid era, they were eliminated.

hot spot A supply of magma that produces a chain of midocean volcanoes atop a zone of moving oceanic crust.

Horn of Africa The northeastern corner of Sub-Saharan Africa that includes the states of Somalia, Ethiopia, Eritrea, and Djibouti. Since the 1980s, drought, famine, ethnic conflict, and political turmoil have undermined development efforts in this area.

Human Development Index (HDI) For the past three decades the United Nations has tracked social development in the world's countries through the Human Development Index (HDI), which combines data on life expectancy, literacy, educational attainment, gender equity, and income.

hurricanes Storm systems with an abnormally low-pressure center sustaining winds of 74 mph or higher. Each year during hurricane season (July–October), a half dozen to a dozen hurricanes form in the warm waters of the Atlantic and Caribbean, bringing destructive winds and heavy rain.

ideographic writing A writing system in which each symbol represents not a sound but rather a concept.

indentured labor Foreign workers (usually South Asians) contracted to labor on Caribbean agricultural estates for a set period of time, often several years. Usually the contract stipulated paying off the travel debt incurred by the laborers. Similar indentured labor arrangements have existed in most world regions.

Indian diaspora The historical and contemporary propensity of Indians to migrate to other countries in search of better opportunities. This has led to large Indian populations in South Africa, the Caribbean, and the Pacific islands, along with western Europe and North America.

informal sector A much-debated concept that presupposes a dual economic system consisting of formal and informal sectors. The informal sector includes self-employed, low-wage jobs that are usually unregulated and untaxed. Street vending, shoe shining, artisan manufacturing, and even self-built housing are considered part of the informal sector. Some scholars include illegal activities such as drug smuggling and prostitution in the informal economy.

insolation Incoming solar energy that enters the atmosphere adjacent to Earth.

internally displaced persons Groups and individuals who flee an area due to conflict or famine but still remain in their country of origin. These populations often live in refugee-like conditions but are harder to assist because they technically do not qualify as refugees.

irredentism A state or national policy of reclaiming lost lands or those inhabited by people of the same ethnicity in another nation-state.

Iron Curtain A term coined by British leader Winston Churchill during the Cold War that defined the western border of Soviet power in Europe. The notorious Berlin Wall was a concrete manifestation of the Iron Curtain.

Islamic fundamentalism A movement within both the Shiite and Sunni Muslim traditions to return to a more conservative, religious-based society and state. Often associated with a rejection of Western culture and with a political aim to merge civic and religious authority.

Islamism A political movement within the religion of Islam that challenges the encroachment of global popular culture and blames colonial, imperial, and Western elements for many of the region's problems. Adherents of Islamism advocate merging civil and religious authority.

isolated proximity A concept that explores the contradictory position of the Caribbean states, which are physically close to North America and economically dependent upon that region. At the same time, Caribbean isolation fosters strong loyalties to locality and limited economic opportunity.

Jainism A religious group in South Asia that emerged as a protest against orthodox Hinduism in the 6th century BCE. Jains are noted for their practice of nonviolence, which prohibits them from taking the life of any animal.

kanakas Melanesian workers imported to Australia, historically concentrated along Queensland's "sugar coast."

Khmer Rouge Literally, "Red (or communist) Cambodians." The left-wing insurgent group led by French-educated Marxists that ruled Cambodia from 1975 to 1979, during which time it engaged in genocidal acts against the Cambodian people.

kibbutzim Collective farms in Israel.

kleptocracy A state where corruption is so institutionalized that politicians and bureaucrats siphon off a large percentage of a country's wealth for personal gain.

laissez-faire An economic system in which the state has minimal involvement and in which market forces largely guide economic activity.

latifundia A large estate or landholding in Latin America.

Lesser Antilles The arc of small Caribbean islands from St. Maarten to Trinidad.

Levant The eastern Mediterranean region.

lingua franca An agreed-upon common language to facilitate communication on specific topics such as international business, politics, sports, or entertainment.

linguistic nationalism The promotion of one language over others that is, in turn, linked to shared notions of political identity. In India, some nationalists promote Hindi as the unifying language of the country, yet this is resisted by many non-Hindi-speaking peoples.

location factors The various influences that explain why an economic activity takes place where it does.

loess A fine, wind-deposited sediment that makes fertile soil but is very vulnerable to water erosion.

Maghreb A region in northwestern Africa, including portions of Morocco, Algeria, and Tunisia.

maharaja Historical term for Hindu royalty, usually a king or prince, who ruled specific areas of South Asia before independence, but who was usually subject to overrule by British colonial advisers.

mallee A tough and scrubby eucalyptus woodland of limited economic value that is common across portions of interior Australia.

mandarins A member of the high-level bureaucracy of Imperial China (before 1911). Mandarin Chinese is the official spoken language of the country and is the native tongue of the vast majority of people living in north, central, and southwestern China.

Maori Indigenous Polynesian people of New Zealand.

maquiladoras Assembly plants on the Mexican border built and owned by foreign companies. Most of their products are exported to the United States.

marine west-coast climate Moderate climate with cool summers and mild winters that is heavily influenced by maritime conditions. Such climates are usually found on the west coasts of continents between latitudes of 45 to 50 degrees.

maritime climate Climate moderated by proximity to oceans or large seas. It is usually cool, cloudy, and wet, and lacks the temperature extremes of continental climates.

maroons Runaway slaves who established communities rich in African traditions throughout the Caribbean and Brazil.

Marxism A term referring to the political philosophy developed by Karl Marx in the 1800s and based on the ideas of communism.

medieval landscape Urban landscapes from 900 to 1500 CE characterized by narrow, winding streets, three- or four-story structures (usually in stone, but sometimes wooden), with little open space except for the market square. These landscapes are still found in the centers of many European cities.

medina The original urban core of a traditional Islamic city.

Mediterranean climate A unique climate, found in only five locations in the world, that is characterized by hot, dry summers with very little rainfall. These climates are located on the west side of continents, between 30 and 40 degrees latitude.

megacities Urban conglomerations of more than 10 million people.

megalopolis A large urban region formed as multiple cities grow and merge with one another. The term is often applied to the string of cities in eastern North America that includes Washington, DC; Baltimore; Philadelphia; New York City; and Boston.

Melanesia Pacific Ocean region that includes the culturally complex, generally darker-skinned peoples of New Guinea, the Solomon Islands, Vanuatu, New Caledonia, and Fiji.

Mercosur The Southern Common Market established in 1991 that calls for free trade among member states and common external tariffs for nonmember states. Argentina, Paraguay, Brazil, and Uruguay are full members and Venezuela's full membership is pending; the Andean countries of Colombia, Ecuador, Peru, Bolivia and Chile are associate members.

mestizo A person of mixed European and Indian ancestry.

Micronesia Pacific Ocean region that includes the culturally diverse, generally small islands north of Melanesia. Includes the Mariana Islands, Marshall Islands, and Federated States of Micronesia.

microstates Usually independent states that are small in both area and population.

mikrorayons Large, state-constructed urban housing projects built during the Soviet period in the 1970s and 1980s.

Millennium Development Goals Part of a group of programs implemented since 2000 to foster development in the world's poorest countries. The Millennium Development Goals are part of a global United Nations effort to reduce extreme poverty by 2015.

minifundia A small landholding farmed by peasants or tenants who produce food for subsistence and the market.

monocrop production Agriculture based upon a single crop, often for export.

Monroe Doctrine A proclamation issued by U.S. President James Monroe in 1823 that the United States would not tolerate European military action in the Western Hemisphere. Focused on the Caribbean as a strategic area, the doctrine was repeatedly invoked to justify U.S. political and military intervention in the region.

monotheism A religious belief in a single God.

monsoon The seasonal pattern of changes in winds, heat, and moisture in South Asia and other regions of the world that is a product of larger meteorological forces of land and water heating, the resultant pressure gradients, and jet-stream dynamics. The monsoon produces distinct wet and dry seasons.

Mughal Empire (also spelled Mogul) The Muslim-dominated state that covered most of South Asia from the early 16th to late 17th centuries. The last vestiges of the Mughal dynasty were dissolved by the British following the rebellion of 1857.

nation-state A relatively homogeneous cultural group (a nation) with its own political territory (the state). While useful conceptually, the reality of today's globalized world is that there are very few countries that fit this simplistic definition because of the influx of migrants and/or the presence of minority ethnic groups.

Native Title Bill Australian legislation signed in 1993 that provides Aborigines with enhanced legal rights over land and resources within the country.

neocolonialism Economic and political strategies by which powerful states indirectly (and sometimes directly) extend their influence over other, weaker states.

neoliberal policies Economic policies widely adopted in the 1990s that stress privatization of services, export production, and few restrictions on imports.

net migration rate A statistic that assesses whether more people are entering or leaving a country by measuring the amount of immigration (in-migration) and emigration (out-migration). A positive figure means the population is growing because of in-migration, whereas a negative number means a population is shrinking because of out-migration.

new urbanism An urban design movement stressing higher density, mixed-use, pedestrian-scaled neighborhoods where residents might be able to walk to work, school, and local entertainment.

nonmetropolitan growth A pattern of migration in which people leave large cities and suburbs and move to smaller towns and rural areas.

North American Free Trade Agreement (NAFTA) An agreement made in 1994 among Canada, the United States, and Mexico that established a 15-year plan for reducing all barriers to trade among the three countries.

Oceania A major world subregion that includes New Zealand and the major islands of Melanesia, Micronesia, and Polynesia.

offshore banking Islands or microstates that offer financial services that are typically confidential and tax-exempt. As part of a global financial system, offshore banks have developed a unique niche, offering their services to individual and corporate clients for set fees. The Bahamas and Cayman Islands are leaders in this sector.

Organization of American States (OAS) Founded in 1948 and headquartered in Washington, DC, the organization advocates hemispheric cooperation and dialog. Most states in the Americas belong except Cuba.

Organization of the Petroleum Exporting Countries (OPEC) An international organization of 12 oil-producing nations (formed in 1960) that attempts to influence global prices and supplies of oil. Algeria, Gabon, Indonesia, Iran, Iraq, Kuwait, Libya, Nigeria, Qatar, Saudi Arabia, UAE, and Venezuela are members.

orographic rainfall Enhanced precipitation over uplands that results from lifting (and cooling) of air masses as they are forced over mountains.

Ottoman Empire A large, Turkish-based empire (named for Osman, one of its founders) that dominated large portions of southeastern Europe, North Africa, and Southwest Asia between the 16th and 19th centuries.

Outback Australia's large, generally dry, and thinly settled interior.

outsourcing A business practice that transfers portions of a company's production and service activities to lower-cost settings, often located overseas.

over-urbanization A process in which the rapid growth of a city, most often because of in-migration, exceeds the city's ability to provide jobs, housing, water, sewers, and transportation.

Palestinian Authority (PA) A quasi-governmental body that represents Palestinian interests in the West Bank and Gaza.

Pan-African Movement Founded in 1900 by U.S. intellectuals W. E. B. Du Bois and Marcus Garvey, this movement's slogan was "Africa for Africans," and its influence extended across the Atlantic.

pastoralists Nomadic and sedentary peoples who rely upon livestock (especially cattle, camels, sheep, and goats) for their sustenance and livelihood.

pastoral nomadism A traditional subsistence agricultural system in which practitioners depend on the seasonal movements of livestock within marginal natural environments.

perestroika A program of partially implemented, planned economic reforms (or restructuring) undertaken during the Gorbachev years in the Soviet Union designed to make the Soviet economy more efficient and responsive to consumer needs.

permafrost A cold-climate condition in which the ground remains permanently frozen.

physiological density A population statistic that relates the number of people in a country to the amount of arable land.

Pidgin English (Pijin) A version of English that also incorporates elements of other local languages, often utilized to foster trade and basic communication between different culture groups.

plantation America A cultural region that extends from midway up the coast of Brazil, through the Guianas and the Caribbean, and into the southeastern United States. In this coastal zone, European-owned plantations, worked by African laborers, produced agricultural products for export.

plate tectonics The theory that explains the gradual movement of large geological platforms (or plates) along Earth's surface.

podzol soils A Russian term for an acidic soil of limited fertility, typically found in northern forest environments.

pollution exporting The process of exporting industrial pollution and other waste material to other countries. Pollution exporting can be direct, as when waste is simply shipped abroad for disposal, or indirect, as when highly polluting factories are constructed abroad.

Polynesia Pacific Ocean region, broadly unified by language and cultural traditions, that includes the Hawaiian Islands, Marquesas Islands, Society Islands, Tuamotu Archipelago, Cook Islands, American Samoa, Samoa, Tonga, and Kiribati.

population density The number of people per areal unit, usually measured in people per square kilometer or per square mile.

population pyramid A graph representing the structure of a population, including the percentage of young and old. The percentages of all different age groups are plotted along a vertical axis that divides the population into male and female. In a fast growing population with a large percentage of young people and a small percentage of elderly, the graph will have a wide base and a narrow tip, giving it a pyramidal shape.

postindustrial economy An economy in which the tertiary and quaternary sectors dominate employment and expansion.

prairie An extensive area of grassland in North America. In the more humid eastern portions, grasses are usually longer than in the drier western areas, which are in the rain shadow of the Rocky Mountain range.

primate cities Massive urban settlements that dominate all other cities in a given country. Often—yet not always—the primate city is also the country's capital.

privatization The process of moving formerly state-owned firms into the contemporary capitalist private sector.

protectorates During the period of global Western imperialism, a state or other political entity that remained autonomous, yet sacrificed its foreign affairs to an imperial power in exchange for "protection" from other imperial powers.

purchasing power parity (PPP) A method of reducing the influence of inflated currency rates by adjusting a local currency to a composite baseline of one U.S. dollar based upon its ability to purchase a standardized "market basket" of goods.

qanat system A traditional system of gravity-fed irrigation that uses gently sloping tunnels to capture groundwater and direct it to needed fields.

Quran (also spelled Koran) A book of divine revelations received by the prophet Muhammad that serves as a holy text in the religion of Islam.

Ramayana One of the two main epic poems of the Hindu religion, the Ramayana is also commonly performed in the shadow puppet theaters of the predominately Muslim island of Java.

rate of natural increase (RNI) The standard statistic used to express natural population growth per year for a country, region, or the world based upon the difference between birth and death rates. RNI does not consider population change from migration. Though most often a positive figure (such as 1.7 percent), RNI can also be expressed either as zero or even as a negative number for no-growth countries.

refugee A person who flees his or her country because of a well-founded fear of persecution based on race, ethnicity, religion, ideology, or political affiliation.

regulatory lakes A term applied to a series of lakes in the middle Yangtze Valley of China. Regulatory lakes take excess water from the river during flood periods, and supply water to the river during dry periods.

remittances Money sent by immigrants to their country of origin to support family members left behind. For many countries, remittances are a principal source of foreign exchange.

Renaissance-Baroque landscape An urban landscape generally constructed during the period from 1500 to 1800 characterized by wide ceremonial boulevards, large monumental structures, and ostentatious houses for the urban elite.

renewable energy sources Energy sources such as hydroelectric, solar, wind, and geothermal that are known for their enduring availability and their potentially lower environmental costs

rift valleys A surface landscape feature formed where two tectonic plates are diverging or moving apart. Usually, this forms a depression or large valley.

rimland The mainland coastal zone of the Caribbean, beginning with Belize and extending along the coast of Central America to northern South America.

rural-to-urban migration The flow of internal migrants from rural areas to cities that began in the 1950s and intensified in the 1960s and 1970s.

Russification A policy of the Soviet Union designed to spread Russian settlers and influences to non-Russian areas of the country.

rust belt Regions of heavy industry that experience marked economic decline after their factories cease to be competitive.

Sahel The semidesert region at the southern fringe of the Sahara, and the countries that fall within this region, which extends from Senegal to Sudan. Droughts in the 1970s and early 1980s caused widespread famine and dislocation of population.

salinization The accumulation of salts in the upper layers of soil, often causing a reduction in crop yields, resulting from irrigation with water of high natural salt content and/or irrigation of soils that contain a high level of mineral salts.

samurai The warrior class of traditional Japan. After 1600, the military role of the samurai declined as they assumed administrative positions, but their military ethos remained alive until the class was abolished in 1868.

Schengen Agreement The 1985 agreement between some—but not all—European Union member countries to reduce border formalities in order to facilitate free movement of citizens between member countries of this new "Schengenland." For example, today there are no border controls between France and Germany, or between France and Italy.

sectoral transformation The evolution of a labor force from being highly dependent on the primary sector to being oriented around more employment in the secondary, tertiary, and quaternary sectors.

secularization The widespread movement in western Europe away from regular participation and engagement with traditional organized religions such as Protestantism or Catholicism.

sediment load The amount of sand, silt, and clay carried by a river.

Shanghai Cooperation Organization (SCO) An international organization composed of China, Russia, Kazakhstan, Kyrgyzstan, Tajikistan, and Uzbekistan that aims to enhance security and economic cooperation in Central Asia.

shields Large upland areas of very old exposed rocks that range in elevation from 600 to 5,000 feet (200 to 1,500 meters). The three major shields in South America are the Guiana, Brazilian, and Patagonian.

shifted cultivators Migrants farmers who are either transplanted by government relocation schemes or forced to move on their own when their lands are expropriated.

Shiites Muslims who practice one of the two main branches of Islam; especially dominant in Iran and nearby southern Iraq.

shogunate The political order of Japan before 1868, in which power was held by the military leader known as the shogun, rather than by the emperor, whose authority was merely symbolic.

Sikhism An Indian religion combining Islamic and Hindu elements, founded in the Punjab region in the late 15th century.

Slavic peoples A group of peoples in eastern Europe and Russia who speak Slavic languages, a distinctive branch of the Indo-European language family.

social and regional differentiation "Social differentiation" refers to a process by which certain classes of people grow richer when others grow poorer; "regional differentiation" refers to a process by which certain places grow more prosperous while others become less prosperous.

socialist realism An artistic style once popular in the Soviet Union that was associated with realistic depictions of workers in their patriotic struggles against capitalism.

Spanglish A hybrid combination of English and Spanish spoken by Hispanic Americans.

Special Economic Zones (SEZs) Relatively small districts in China were fully opened to global capitalism after China began to reform its economy in the 1980s.

spheres of influence In countries not formally colonized in the 19th and early 20th centuries (particularly China and Iran), limited areas called "spheres of influence" were gained by particular European countries for trade purposes and more generally for economic exploitation and political manipulation.

squatter settlements Makeshift housing on land not legally owned or rented by urban migrants, usually in unoccupied open spaces within or on the outskirts of a rapidly growing city.

steppe Semiarid grasslands found in many parts of the world. Grasses are usually shorter and less dense than in prairies.

structural adjustment programs Controversial yet widely implemented programs used to reduce government spending, encourage the private sector, and refinance foreign debt. Typically, these IMF and World Bank policies trigger drastic cutbacks in government-supported services and food subsidies, which disproportionately affect the poor.

subcontinent A large segment of land separated from the main land mass on which it sits by lofty mountains or other geographical barriers. South Asia, separated from the rest of Eurasia by the Himalayas, is often called the "Indian subcontinent."

subduction zone Areas where two tectonic plates are converging or colliding. In these areas, one plate usually sinks below another. They are characterized by earthquakes, volcanoes, and deep oceanic trenches.

subnational organizations Groups that form along ethnic, ideological, or regional lines that can induce serious internal divisions within a state.

Suez Canal Pivotal waterway connecting the Red Sea and the Mediterranean opened by the French in 1869.

Sunda Shelf An extension of the continental shelf from the Southeast Asia mainland to the large islands of Indonesia. Because of the shelf, the overlying sea is generally shallow (less than 200 feet [61 meters] deep).

Sunnis Muslims who practice the dominant branch of Islam.

superconurbation A massive urban agglomeration that results from the coalescing of two or more formerly separate metropolitan areas.

supranational organizations Governing bodies that include several states, such as trade organizations, and often involve a loss of some state powers to achieve the organization's goals.

sustainable agriculture A system of agriculture where organic farming principles, a limited use of chemicals, and an integrated plan of crop and livestock management combine to offer both producers and consumers environmentally friendly alternatives.

sweatshops Small manufacturing units in developing countries where menial tasks are performed by largely unskilled and poorly paid workers.

swidden A form of tropical cultivation in which forested or brushy plots are cleared of vegetation, burned, and then planted in crops, only to be abandoned a few years later as soil fertility declines. Also called slash-and-burn agriculture or shifting cultivation.

syncretic religions The blending of different belief systems. In Latin America, many animist practices were folded into Christian worship.

taiga The vast coniferous forest of Russia that stretches from the Urals to the Pacific Ocean. The main forest species are fir, spruce, and larch.

Taliban A harsh, Islamic fundamentalist political group that ruled most of Afghanistan in the late 1990s. In 2001, the Taliban lost power, but it later regrouped in Pakistan and continues to fight against U.S.-led forces in southern and eastern Afghanistan.

Tamil Tigers The common name of the rebel forces in Sri Lanka (officially known as the Liberation Tigers of Tamil Eelam, or LTTE) that fought the Sri Lankan army from 1983 until their defeat in 2009.

tectonic plates The basic building blocks of Earth's crust; large blocks of solid rock that move very slowly over the underlying semimolten material.

theocracy A government run by religious leaders.

theocratic state A political state led by religious authorities.

tonal language A language in which the meaning of a syllable varies in accordance with the tone in which it is uttered.

total fertility rate (TFR) The average number of children who will be borne by women of a hypothetical, yet statistically valid, population, such as that of a specific cultural group or within a particular country. Demographers consider TFR a more reliable indicator of population change than the crude birthrate.

townships Racially segregated neighborhoods created for nonwhite groups under apartheid in South Africa. They are usually found on the outskirts of cities and classified as black, coloured, or South Asian.

Trans-Siberian Railroad Key southern Siberian railroad connection completed during the Russian empire (1904) that links European Russia with the Russian Far East terminus of Vladivostok.

transhumance A form of pastoralism in which animals are taken to high-altitude pastures during the summer months and returned to low-altitude pastures during the winter.

transmigration The planned, government-sponsored relocation of people from one area to another within a state territory.

transnational firms A firm or corporation that does international business through an array of global subsidiaries.

transnational migration Complex social and economic linkages that form between home and host countries through international migration. Unlike earlier generations of migrants, 21st century immigrants can maintain more enduring and complex ties to their home countries as a result of technological advances.

Treaty of Tordesillas A treaty signed in 1494 between Spain and Portugal that drew a north–south line some 300 leagues west of the Azores and Cape Verde islands. Spain received the land to the west of the line and Portugal the land to the east.

tribalism Allegiance to a particular tribe or ethnic group rather than to the nation-state. Tribalism is often blamed for internal conflict within Sub-Saharan states.

tribes A group of families or clans with a common kinship, language, and definable territory but not an organized state.

tsars A Russian term (also spelled czar) for "Caesar," or ruler; the authoritarian rulers of the Russian empire before its collapse in the 1917 revolution.

tsetse flies A fly that is a vector for a parasite that causes sleeping sickness (typanosomiasis), a disease that especially affects humans and livestock. Livestock is rarely found in those areas of Sub-Saharan Africa where the tsetse fly is common.

tsunamis Very large sea waves induced by earthquakes.

tundra Arctic region with a short growing season in which vegetation is limited to low shrubs, grasses, and flowering herbs.

typhoons Large tropical storms, synonymous to hurricanes, that form in the western Pacific Ocean in tropical latitudes and cause widespread damage to the Philippines and coastal Southeast and East Asia.

uncontacted peoples Cultures that have yet to be contacted and influenced by the Western world.

unitary states A political system in which power is centralized at the national level.

universalizing religions A religion, usually with an active missionary program, that appeals to a large group of people regardless of local culture and conditions. Christianity and Islam both have strong universalizing components.

urban decentralization The process in which cities spread out over a larger geographical area.

urban form The physical arrangement or landscape of the city, made up of building architecture and style, street patterns, open spaces, housing types, and so on.

urbanized population That percentage of a country's population living in settlements characterized as cities. Usually, high rates of urbanization are associated with higher levels of industrialization and economic development because these activities are usually found in and around cities. Conversely, lower urbanized populations (less than 50 percent) are characteristic of developing countries.

urban primacy The situation found in a country in which a disproportionately large city, such as London, New York, or Bangkok, dominates the urban system and is the center of economic, political, and cultural life.

urban realms model A simplified description of urban land use, especially descriptive of the modern North American city. It features a number of dispersed, peripheral centers of dynamic commercial and industrial activity linked by sophisticated urban transportation networks.

urban structure The distribution and pattern of land use, such as commercial, residential, or manufacturing, within the city. Often, commonalities give rise to models of urban structure characteristic of the cities of a certain region or of a shared history, such as cities shaped by European colonialism.

viticulture Grape cultivation.

water stress An environmental planning tool used to predict areas that have—or will have—serious water problems based upon the per capita demand and supply of freshwater.

White Australia Policy Before 1975, a set of stringent Australian limitations on nonwhite immigration to the country. Largely replaced by a more flexible policy today.

World Trade Organization (WTO) Formed as an outgrowth of the General Agreement on Tariffs and Trade (GATT) in 1995, the WTO is a large collection of member states dedicated to reducing global barriers to trade.

Photo Credits

Chapter 1 opening photo Image Source/Photolibrary 1.1 Rob Crandall 1.2 Sherwin Crasto/Reuters/Corbis 1.3 Sean Sprague/ The Image Works 1.4 Rob Crandall 1.5 Stephanie Kuykendal/ Corbis 1.7 Rob Crandall 1.8 Tim Boyle/Getty Images 1.9 AP Images 1.11 Bobby Yip/Reuters/Landov 1.12 Thorvaldur Kristmundsson/AP Images 1.13 Caroline Penn/Panos Pictures 1.14 Ramzi Haidar/Newscom 1.1.1 Les Rowntree 1.15 Brynjar Gauti/ AP Images 1.16 Photo Researchers, Inc. 1.18 Maurice Joseph/ Robert Harding 1.2.2 Bill Bachmann/Photo Edit 1.19 Philippe Michel/Robert Harding 1.22 Chris Stowers/Panos Pictures 1.3.1 Desire Martin/AFP/Getty Images 1.23 Trygve Bolstad/Panos Pictures 1.26 Liz Gilbert/India Government Tourist Office 1.27a Craig Aurness/Corbis 1.27b Tony Waltham/Robert Harding 1.29 Rob Crandall 1.30 Jay Directo/AFP/Getty Images 1.4.1 Leonid Serebrennikov/AGE Fotostock 1.31 Ajit Solanki/AP Images 1.32a Rob Crandall 1.32b Rob Crandall 1.32c Rob Crandall 1.32d Rob Crandall 1.5.1 Alfredo Estrella/AFP/Getty Images 1.33 Arko Datta/Reuters/Corbis 1.35 Rob Crandall 1.37 Rob Crandall 1.38 Photodisc/Getty Images 1.39 GAIZKA IROZ/AFP/Getty Images 1.42 Catherine Karnow/Woodfin Camp& Associates, Inc. 1.43 Hubert Boesl/dpa/Corbis 1.45 Ajay Verma/Reuters/Corbis 1.6.1 Rafael Ramirez Lee/Shutterstock 1.47 Rob Crandall 1.50 SUPRI/ Reuters/Corbis 1.51 Ron Giling/Panos Pictures

Chapter 2 opening photo James Kay/DanitaDelimont.com 2.1 Chris James/Peter Arnold, Inc./Photolibrary 2.4 aerialarchives.com/ Alamy 2.5 Paul A. Souders/Corbis 2.6 Jorge Silva/Reuters 2.8 Alberto Garcia/Corbis 2.9 iStockphoto 2.11 Jim Edds/Corbis 2.15 Steven J. Kazlowski/Alamy 2.16 Reuters/Corbis 2.1.1 imagebroker/ Alamy 2.17 Liu Liqun/Corbis 2.19 Ajay Verma/Reuters 2.21 Gary Braasch/Woodfin Camp & Associates, Inc. 2.22 James P. Blair/Getty Images 2.2.1 Nathalie van Vliet/Center for International Forestry Research/Handout/Reuters 2.23 Wofgang Kaehler/Alamy 2.24 Calvin Larsen/Photo Researchers, Inc. 2.25 EPA/Chun Lei/Corbis 2.26 Mark Edwards/Photolibrary/Peter Arnold, Inc. 2.27 Martin Wendler/Photolibrary/Peter Arnold, Inc.

Chapter 3 opening photo Martin Thomas Photography/Alamy 3.2 Bill Wyckoff 3.1.1 Kevin Schafer/CORBIS 3.5 Danny E. Hooks/ Shutterstock 3.6 Bill Wyckoff 3.8 Earth Satellite Corporation/ Photo Researchers, Inc. 3.9 Joe Sohm/The Image Works 3.2.1 Gabriel Bouys/AFP/Getty Images 3.11 Courtesy of GNP Archives and Karen Holzer, USGS 3.15 Jeremy Woodhouse/Getty Images 3.17 Rob Crandall/The Image Works 3.18 Soffer Organization 3.19 Bill Wyckoff 3.3.1 Mansur Real Estate Services 3.20 Craig Aurness/Corbis 3.26 Jim Noelker/The Image Works 3.4.2 Rob Crandall 3.4.3 Rob Crandall 3.28 Bill Wyckoff 3.30 Worldsat International Inc./Photo Researchers, Inc. 3.32 Alison Wright/Corbis 3.33 Bill Wyckoff 3.35 Rob Crandall 3.5.2 Richard Hamilton Smith/CORBIS 3.36 Getty Images 3.37 David R. Frazier/DanitaDelimont/Newscom 3.38 George Hall/Woodfin Camp & Associates, Inc. 3.39 Dennis MacDonald/Photo Edit 3.41 Bill Wyckoff 3.42 Comstock/Photolibrary 3.6.1 Michael Newman/PhotoEdit

Chapter 4 opening photo Pablo Caridad/Alamy 4.2 Rob Crandall 4.4 Rob Crandall 4.5a Biological Resources Division, U.S. Geological Survey 4.5b Biological Resources Division, U.S. Geological Survey 4.1.1 Rob Crandall 4.6 Rob Crandall 4.7 Jorge Uzon/ AFP/Getty Images 4.8 Hubert Stadler/Corbis 4.9 Stephaine Maze/ National Geographic Image Collection 4.10 Rob Crandall 4.12 Sue Cunningham/Worldwide Picture Library/Alamy 4.15 Rob

Crandall 4.17a Rob Crandall 4.17b Rob Crandall 4.17c Rob Crandall 4.17d Rob Crandall 4.18 Rob Crandall 4.2.1 Bruno Domingos/ Reuters 4.2.2 VANDERLEI ALMEIDA/AFP/Getty Images 4.20 Holger Leue/age fotostock 4.21 ORLANDO KISSNER/AFP/Getty Images 4.22 Eric Gay/AP Images 4.23 Rob Crandall 4.24 Rob Crandall 4.25 Rob Crandall 4.27 Rob Crandall 4.28 Fernando Soutello/Reuters/Corbis 4.3.1 Bruno Domingos/Reuters 4.29a Rob Crandall 4.29b Christian Hebb/Aurora Photos, Inc. 4.31 Rob Crandall 4.4.1 Susana Gonzalez/Bloomberg/Getty Images 4.34 Eltana Aponte/Reuters/Bettmann/Corbis 4.35 Bob Daemmrich/ Corbis 4.36 Rob Crandall 4.37 Paulo Fridman/Corbis 4.38 Rob Crandall 4.6.1 Rob Crandall 4.6.2 Rob Crandall 4.41 Alejandro Pagni/AFP/Getty Images

Chapter 5 opening photo Cameron Davidson/Corbis 5.2 Rob Crandall 5.3 Gideon Mendel/Corbis 5.5 Rob Crandall 5.6 Rob Crandall 5.7 European Space Agency 5.1.2 Hal Pierce/Laboratory of Atmospheres/NASA/Goddard Space Flight Center 5.9 Lucas Oleniuk/Zuma Press 5.11 Steve Bly/Alamy 5.13 Rob Crandall 5.14 Rob Crandall 5.2.1 AGE Fotostock/Robert Harding 5.15 Rob Crandall 5.2.2 Philip Wolmuth/Alamy 5.16 Michael Holford/ Michael Holford Photographs 5.17 Steve Raymer/Corbis 5.19 Robert Caputo/Getty Images 5.20b AFP/Getty Images 5.3.1 Rob Crandall 5.3.2 Paivi Varisanen/Association of Samba Schools Finland 5.22 Rob Crandall 5.23 Rob Crandall 5.4.2 Stock Connection Blue/Alamy 5.26 David Frazier/The Image Works 5.5.1 David Mercado/Reuters/Newscom 5.27 AP Images 5.29 Frank Heuer/ Redux Pictures 5.31 Duane StevensAlamy 5.32 Rob Crandall 5.6.1 Angel Valentin/The Guardian

Chapter 6 opening photo Eric Nathan/Alamy 6.2 Dung Vo Trung/ Sygma/Corbis 6.3 Rob Crandall 6.4 Buddy Mays/Corbis 6.5 Images of Africa Photobank/Alamy 6.7 Rob Crandall 6.8 Louis Gubb/ The Image Works 6.10 Daniel Berehulak/Getty Images 6.1.1a USGS Center for Earth Resources Observation and Science 6.1.1b USGS Center for Earth Resources Observation and Science 6.11 Louise Gubb/SABA/Corbis 6.12 Roberto Schmidt/AFP/Getty Images 6.13 Rob Crandall 6.15 Nomi Baumgart/Photolibrary/Peter Arnold, Inc. 6.17 Jorgen Schytte/Photolibrary 6.19 Hereward Holland/Reuters 6.20 Ton Koene/Picture Contact BV/Alamy 6.21 Jeremy Horner/ Corbis 6.22 James Marshall/Corbis 6.24 Rob Crandall 6.2.2 Alexander Joe/AFP/Getty Images 6.2.3 Hoberman Collection/Photolibrary 6.27 Rob Crandall 6.28 Ed Kashi/Corbis 6.30 Greenshoots Communication/Alamy 6.3.1 Rob Crandall 6.32 Frans Lemmens/Alamy 6.33 David Eulitt/Newscom 6.37 Englebert Photography Inc. 6.40 David Wall/Alamy 6.4.1 Des Willie/Alamy 6.42 David Lewis/Reuters 6.43 Marc & Evelyn Bernheim/Woodfin Camp & Associates 6.44 Tom Kirkwood/Reuters 6.5.1 Shao Jie/AP Images 6.46 PRNewsFoto/Marathon Oil Corporation/Newscom 6.6.1 John Hrusa/epa/Corbis 6.6.2 Anup Shah/Nature Picture Library 6.47 Washington Post Writers Group

Chapter 7 opening photo Motty Levy/Photolibrary 7.2 Rob Crandall 7.3 Minosa/Scorpio/Sygma Collection 7.4 Chris Hellier/ Corbis 7.7 NASA 7.8 Ccharleson/Dreamstime.com 7.9 NASA 7.10 Alan Carey/Corbis 7.1.1 Patrick Baz/Pool/Getty Images 7.12 Buiten-Beeld/Alamy 7.13 Dott Giorgio Gualco/Photo Shot 7.14 Patrick Ben Luke/Lonely Planet Images 7.16 imagebroker/Alamy 7.18 Glen Allison/Getty Images 7.19 NASA 7.2.1 Imagestate Media Partners Limited-Impact Photos/Alamy 7.20 Monique Jacot/ Woodfin Camp & Associates, Inc. 7.21 Stuart Franklin/Magnum

Index

Page numbers in italics indicate figures and tables.